# U.S. ARMY WEAPONS SYSTEMS 2013–2014

## DEPARTMENT OF THE ARMY



SKYHORSE PUBLISHING

10 9 8 7 6 5 4 3 2 1

ISBN 978-1-62087-374-8

Printed in China

# U.S. ARMY WEAPONS SYSTEMS 2013–2014

DESIGN, DEVELOP, DELIVER, DOMINATE
SOLDIERS AS THE DECISIVE EDGE

# Dear Reader:

In the Army Acquisition community, it is our solemn responsibility to enable Soldiers to dominate the battlespace safely and securely by achieving the first look, first strike advantage with unprecedented speed, accuracy, and lethality.

Soldiers are our most important customers. They are the focus of all our plans and are central to all that we accomplish. We are a workforce that is dedicated to meeting the needs of Soldiers around the clock and around the world. We are an organization comprised of 10 Program Executive Offices, two Joint Program Executive Offices, eight Deputy Assistant Secretaries, one Deputy for Acquisition and Systems Management, and several major subordinate commands of the U.S. Army Materiel Command.

The Army Acquisition, Logistics, and Technology community joins with our key stakeholders to develop and field a versatile and affordable mix of weapon systems and equipment to allow Soldiers and units to succeed in full-spectrum operations and maintain our decisive advantage over any enemy we face. We make Soldiers strong by providing them with leading-edge technologies and advanced capabilities to dominate in our current operations across the battlespace, while simultaneously preparing them to respond decisively to future threats.

In providing our Soldiers with world-class capabilities, we remain aware that our most important asset is our people. Our skilled and dedicated professionals execute diverse responsibilities on a daily basis to enable the disciplined management of an extensive acquisition portfolio of programs that include tactical wheeled vehicles; Soldier systems; air and missile defense; network; simulation; aviation; ground combat systems; intelligence, surveillance, and reconnaissance; and precision fires. These responsibilities include science and technology as well as research and development, program management, contracting, systems engineering, procurement policy, logistics policy, chemical weapons destruction and demilitarization, defense exports and international cooperation, and other areas.

As we move forward, I will continue to emphasize sound business practices, program management, and effective execution of major weapons systems while we help the Army to prioritize capabilities and modify existing programs to achieve long-term success. With this in mind, I think all of you realize the future resource environment will be challenging. We can expect that budgets are going to be tighter, which means we have to become a lot more efficient in the way we do business.

Every day America's Soldiers put mission, unit, and country first. They serve with distinction in nearly 135 countries worldwide: Afghanistan, Iraq, Bosnia, Kuwait, the Sinai, South Korea, the Philippines, and on every continent. They face threats that constantly evolve, and their skill and courage in meeting these challenges is second to none. As you read this publication and learn more about the Acquisition, Logistics, and Technology community and our major acquisition programs, you will understand that our highest priority is to continually improve force protection and Soldier survivability. Soldiers are our most important customers. We will not let them down.

**Heidi Shyu**
Acting Assistant Secretary of the Army
(Acquisition, Logistics, and Technology)
and Army Acquisition Executive

# Table of Contents

# Table of Contents

# How to Use this Book

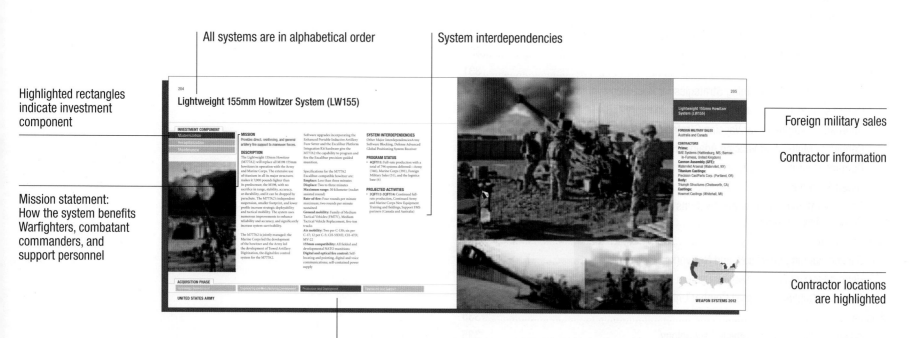

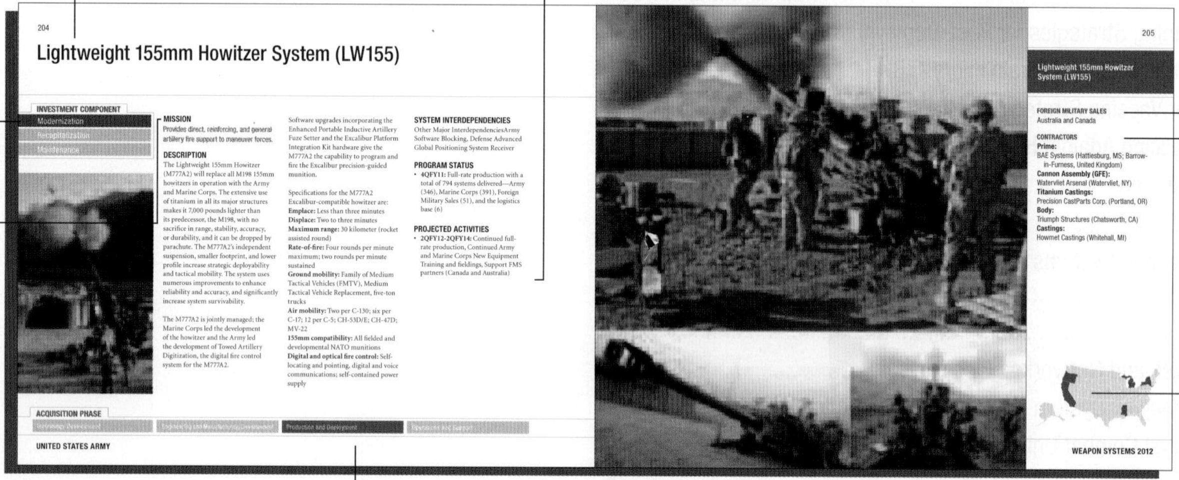
All systems are in alphabetical order
System interdependencies
Highlighted rectangles indicate investment component
Mission statement: How the system benefits Warfighters, combatant commanders, and support personnel
Foreign military sales
Contractor information
Contractor locations are highlighted
Highlighted rectangles indicate acquisition phase
204
Lightweight 155mm Howitzer System (LW155)
INVESTMENT COMPONENT
MISSION
DESCRIPTION
SYSTEM INTERDEPENDENCIES
PROGRAM STATUS
PROJECTED ACTIVITIES
ACQUISITION PHASE
UNITED STATES ARMY
205
Lightweight 155mm Howitzer System (LW155)
FOREIGN MILITARY SALES
CONTRACTORS
WEAPON SYSTEMS 2012

## WHAT ARE SYSTEM INTERDEPENDENCIES?

The purpose of the **System Interdependencies** section is to identify which other weapon systems or components (if any) the main system works in concert with or relies upon for its operation. We categorize the interdependencies in two ways: 1) under the heading "In this Publication," which is a listing of systems in this 2012 edition and 2) "Other Major Interdependencies," which is a listing of systems that are not included in this publication.

## WHAT ARE INVESTMENT COMPONENTS?

**Modernization** programs develop and/or procure new systems with improved warfighting capabilities.

**Recapitalization** programs rebuild or provide selected upgrades to currently fielded systems to ensure operational readiness and a zero-time, zero-mile system.

**Maintenance** programs include the repair or replacement of end items, parts, assemblies, and subassemblies that wear out or break.

## WHAT ARE ACQUISITION PHASES?

**Technology Development** refers to the development of a materiel solution to an identified, validated need. During this phase, the Mission Needs Statement is approved, technology issues are considered, and possible alternatives are identified. This phase includes:

- Concept exploration
- Decision review
- Component advanced development

**Engineering and Manufacturing Development** is the phase in which a system is developed, program risk is reduced, operational supportability and design feasibility are ensured, and feasibility and affordability are demonstrated. This is also the phase in which system integration, interoperability, and utility are demonstrated. It includes:

- System integration
- System demonstration
- Interim progress review

**Production and Deployment** achieves an operational capability that satisfies mission needs. Components of this phase are:

- Low-rate initial production
- Full-rate production criteria
- Full-rate production and deployment
- Military equipment valuation

**Operations and Support** ensures that operational support performance requirements and life cycle sustainment of systems are met in the most cost-effective manner. Support varies but generally includes:

- Supply
- Maintenance
- Transportation
- Sustaining engineering
- Data management
- Configuration management
- Human factors engineering
- Personnel
- Manpower
- Training
- Habitability
- Survivability
- Safety and occupational health
- Information technology supportability
- Environmental management functions
- Anti-tamper provisions
- Interoperability
- Disposal/demilitarization

Because the Army is spiraling technology to the troops as soon as it is feasible, some programs and systems may be in all four phases at the same time. Mature programs are often only in one phase, such as operations and support, while newer systems are only in technology development.

For additional information and definitions of these categories and terms, please see the Glossary.

THE AMERICAN SOLDIER IS
OUR HIGHEST PRIORITY AND MOST PRECIOUS ASSET
UNITED STATES ARMY

UNITED STATES ARMY

# ASA(ALT)

## MISSION

Provide our Soldiers a decisive advantage in any mission by developing, acquiring, fielding, and sustaining the world's best equipment and services and leveraging technologies and capabilities to meet current and future Army needs

## VISION

Highly efficient, effective, agile organization responsible for acquiring, developing, delivering, supporting, and sustaining the most capable affordable systems and services for our Soldiers:

- Enabling our Soldiers to dominate the battlespace, safely and securely
- Enabling our Soldiers to achieve first look, first strike advantage with unprecedented speed and accuracy

# STRATEGIC CONTEXT

The U.S. Army is involved in combat operations around the world against adaptive enemies able to take advantage of the ever-increasing pace of technological change. Concurrently, we are facing an increasingly constrained fiscal environment. In this challenging environment, our goal in the Acquisition, Logistics, and Technology community is to do everything we can to provide the best equipment and services to our Soldiers, to enable them to be successful across the full range of military operations today and into the future. Our Soldiers need the fire and maneuver capabilities that allow them to communicate, engage, and disengage. Our troops must continue to operate with confidence in their equipment, operational capabilities, communication, enhanced situational awareness, and force protection. We must provide our Soldiers a decisive advantage in every fight so they return safely from every operation and engagement.

Modernizing the Army enables us to counter rapidly emerging threats that change the nature of battlefield operations. This is accomplished by capturing lessons learned from the range of combat to include close combat and improved explosive devices. The Army must develop and field new capabilities or sustain, improve, or divest current systems based on operational value, capabilities shortfalls, and available resources. These decisions are based on the principles identified in the Army's Modernization and Equipping Strategies and are influenced by the results of detailed deliberations within the Army's maturing Capability Portfolio Reviews.

Decentralized operations are required within the context of Mission Command. The complex and uncertain strategic environment dictates the need for capabilities and weapon systems that provide the essential qualities of adaptability and versatility to operate in current and future environments across the full spectrum of military operations.

Lessons learned from the current operating environment and a capability-based assessment revealed that some current capabilities do not adequately counter the current threats and lack the capability needed to adequately meet the operational requirements of future warfighting concepts and threats. We are working with key stakeholders to build a versatile mix of tailorable and networked organizations, operating on a rotational cycle, to provide a sustained flow of trained, equipped, and ready forces for full-spectrum operations and to hedge against unexpected contingencies—at a tempo that is predictable and sustainable for our all-volunteer force.

# SOLDIERS AS THE DECISIVE EDGE

The Assistant Secretary of the Army for Acquisition, Logistics, and Technology (ASA(ALT)) is deeply invested in developing, delivering, and sustaining the best weapons technology available to assist Soldiers in executing the myriad of operational requirements in a fluid and volatile strategic environment. With the Soldier as the key focus, ASA(ALT) seeks to equip Soldiers with the best in cutting-edge technology and effectively manage up to 600+ programs that are vital to success in combat.

ASA(ALT)'s focus is closely aligned with the Army Modernization Strategy, which outlines a series of key goals—such as the continued development of new technologies engineered to provide Soldiers with the decisive edge in battle. These technologies in development span a range of new capability to include robots, sensors, Unmanned Aircraft Systems, missiles and missile guidance systems, emerging combat platforms such as the Ground Combat Vehicle, and key technologies such as the Army's maturing network, designed to connect Soldiers, sensors, and multiple nodes to one another in real-time to improve operational effectiveness across the full spectrum of combat operations.

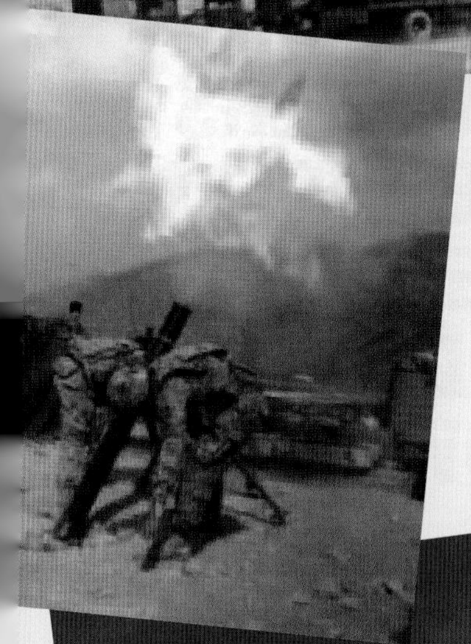

At the same time, the modernization strategy places a premium on finding affordable solutions, identifying and applying efficiencies designed to maximize the value of dollars spent on development, and more rapidly delivering greater technological capability within an increasingly constrained fiscal environment. To this end, the Army has developed an Affordable Modernization Strategy that seeks to develop needed systems while ever mindful of budgetary responsibility. Part of this involves synchronizing and integrating programs, platforms, and systems in relation to one another from a system-of-systems point of view in order to maximize interoperability, reduce redundancy, and prioritize an acquisition strategy that correctly organizes and develops technologies as interconnected systems.

- ASA(ALT) is working vigorously to implement guidance from the office of the Secretary of Defense, which calls upon the Services to sustain Current Force structure and needed modernization by achieving two to three percent real growth. The current and planned base defense budget has steady but modest growth of one percent per year, necessitating innovative processes and doing more without more.
- To make up the difference and preclude reductions in needed military capability, the difference of one to two percent per year will be made up elsewhere across the Department of Defense and the Services. The goal is to significantly reduce excess overhead costs and apply savings to force structure and modernization.
- The structural approach to achieve these savings includes the application of Lean Six Sigma methodologies and Continuous Process Improvement guidelines.

This modernization process success—emphasizing this system-of-systems engineering and validation of core-required capabilities—hinges upon the results of the Army's Capability Portfolio Reviews (CPRs). These CPRs are designed to conduct a detailed examination of groups of technologies and systems from a portfolio perspective—with a focus on perceiving how they relate to one another and the full capability perspective of the operating force. A key emphasis of the CPRs is to identify areas where efficiencies can be increased and redundancies can be eliminated. The reviews are grounded in the reality that the defense budget will not increase nor be sustained at the levels it has in recent years, therefore creating an uncertain fiscal and geo-political environment that demands strict discipline in developing and preserving battlefield dominance in a time of reduced resources.

The CPRs include Aviation; Network; Radios; Precision Fires; Air and Missile Defense; Tactical Wheeled Vehicles; Combat Vehicle Modernization; Soldier Systems; Engineer Mobility/Countermobility; Intelligence, Surveillance, and Reconnaissance (ISR); Training Ammunition; Software/Hardware; and Watercraft.

The CPRs are also aimed at informing the Army's overarching investment strategy that seeks to effectively manage taxpayer dollars, and provide the best technologies to our Soldiers while maintaining affordability. For instance, the Precision Fires CPR determined that the Army no longer needed to develop the Non-Line-of-Sight Launch System (NLOS-LS) because it already has similar capabilities in its arsenal. As a result of the CPR, the requirement for the NLOS-LS was cancelled in an effort to remove redundancy while still developing the best capabilities for Soldiers in combat.

# LEADING ARMY MODERNIZATION SO OUR SOLDIERS DOMINATE THE BATTLEFIELD TODAY AND TOMORROW

ASA(ALT) is developing technologies that will successfully counter the ever-changing contingencies in today's combat environment. Soldiers are the decisive edge in a wide range of potential conflict scenarios ranging from peacekeeping and nation-building to fighting conventional, irregular, or hybrid enemies. Army doctrine calls upon the force to be prepared for what is called full-spectrum operations, meaning they must be equipped for all potential scenarios to include high-, medium-, and low-intensity conflict. The Army's acquisition strategy and weapons platforms must accommodate this operational reality and prepare Soldiers to be adaptive to an entire range of potential operations. We must make sure that the equipment we provide Soldiers is the best hedge against the wide range of threats that will be a central feature of an uncertain strategic environment in the coming decades, particularly existential threats to our Nation or allies that only a ground force can counter.

For this reason, acquisition processes need to be synchronized with the requirements process to best identify needs and capability gaps experienced by Soldiers in battle today; ASA(ALT) will continue to work closely with the Army's Training and Doctrine Command to ensure that the requirements development process is deeply interwoven with weapon systems modernization. There are times when systems in development need to change, adjust, and tailor their requirements to meet with current capabilities and urgent needs coming from combatant commanders in theater. This process is one that requires continuous evaluation and reassessment throughout the weapon systems development process.

Also for this reason, the Army's acquisition strategy is designed to counter changing threats and addresses the emergence of hybrid threats—the dynamic combination of conventional, irregular, terrorist, and criminal capabilities. The Army seeks to train, develop, and equip Soldiers who are able to stay in front of an adaptive, fast-changing adversary. By emphasizing the best design, delivery, and sustainment of Army equipment, ASA(ALT) will remain focused on harnessing scientific innovations in order to identify and develop the most promising new technologies.

## THE ARMY MODERNIZATION STRATEGY

The primary goal of ASA(ALT) is to ensure that America's Army remains the world's most capable and decisive force by equipping and sustaining Soldiers in a timely and responsible manner with the best technologies available. The Army's Modernization Strategy is squarely aimed at supporting this goal; ASA(ALT) is constantly working to identify and develop emerging technologies that have the potential to strengthen Soldiers. As a result, continued scientific and technological innovation is a constant Army focus; the Army works to preserve and build upon its relationships with its partners in academia and industry to enhance the learning curve and advance technology for the benefit of Soldiers. A key focus of the modernization effort is the need to prepare Soldiers for the fast pace of change on today's battlefield by keeping abreast of the latest in scientific discovery.

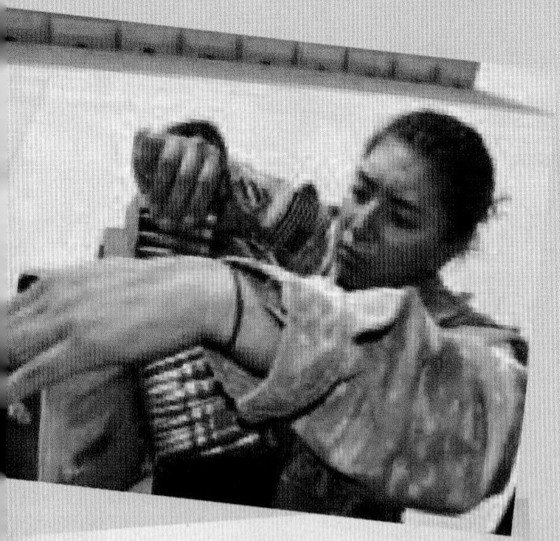

A centerpiece of this strategy is the recognition that many of the systems in this handbook are interdependent, meaning they rely upon and reinforce one another. For this reason, ASA(ALT) approaches acquisition from a system-of-systems point of view that places a premium upon looking at how technologies work in tandem as part of a larger system. Modernization and development of new capability must accommodate this system-of-systems approach.

For instance, the Army is changing the way it supplies network systems and capabilities to operational units by incrementally aligning the delivery of new technology with the Army Force Generation process. This effort will drive networked and non-networked capabilities to the Small Unit and Soldier level—those that need these critical capabilities the most.

As the Army aligns network programs and developmental efforts, it will rely on a series of coordinated, Soldier-driven Network Integration Evaluations (NIEs) that will help solidify the integrated network baseline and help to validate the Capability Sets.

In July 2011 the Army concluded the first NIE. The NIE is the first in a series of semi-annual evaluations designed to integrate and mature the Army's tactical network and is a key element of the Army's emerging Network Strategy. The evaluation was a six week effort conducted at White Sands Missile Range, NM, involving the 2nd Brigade Combat Team, 1st Armored Division. Its primary purpose was to conduct formal tests of acquisition programs of record, with a secondary purpose to less formally evaluate developmental and emerging network and non-networked capabilities. The 2011 exercise was the first of this type of combined test and evaluation, which brought together the doctrine, acquisition, and test communities as part of a new process to demonstrate the Army's holistic focus to integrate network components simultaneously in one operational venue.

The June-July 2011 NIE at White Sands Missile Range put a large number of emerging systems in combat-like scenarios for the purpose of assessing their utility to Soldiers. The NIE placed six systems under test and as many as 29 systems under evaluation. This was the first in a series of semi-annual exercises aimed at assessing and integrating emerging and developmental technologies before they are deployed in theater. At the heart of the exercise is an overarching effort to develop a single battlefield network able to push key information to the Soldier, linking them to command posts, vehicles on-the-move, and higher headquarters. The idea is to use the best available technologies to move information, voice, video, data, and images faster, further, and more efficiently across the force, and develop systems within a Common Operating Environment (COE), meaning they are built on software foundations that enable the maximum amount of interoperability.

By utilizing an "open architecture" and building systems to operate within the aforementioned COE, we intend to not only improve interoperability but increase efficiency. A COE means that there will no longer be as many independent, stove-piped software systems separately developed in isolation; rather, new systems will be built to work within a common foundation or common computing environment. New applications can be built to operate within an existing framework, using common Internet Protocol standards, thus speeding up development and maximizing interoperability, while also driving down costs and increasing efficiency.

During 2012 the Army will continue to conduct NIEs. A triad—the Brigade Modernization Command, Army Test and Evaluation Command, and ASA(ALT)—will assess network and non-network capabilities and determine their implications across the force. The evaluations will also begin to establish the Objective Integrated Network Baseline and common connectivity across the Brigade Combat Team structure, and introduce industry participation in the NIE evaluation cycle.

Central to the network baseline is the continued evaluation of non-proprietary high-bandwidth waveforms such as Soldier Radio Waveform and Wideband Networking Waveform. These use a larger portion of the available spectrum than legacy waveforms to move voice, video, images, and data in real-time across multiple nodes in the force.

The NIE provided Army testers and program managers the advantage of assessing how new and emerging technologies work in relation to one another from a system-of-systems perspective. The NIE is aimed at refining the acquisition of new technologies and blending programs of record with commercial-off-the-shelf solutions as part of a process designed to keep pace with rapid technological change. Some of the promising technologies demonstrated at the NIE include: Joint Tactical Radio Systems, software-programmable radios; Connecting Soldiers to Digital Apps, smartphones placed in the hands of Soldiers to pass combat-relevant information in real-time; and Joint Capabilities Release, software with digital mapping technology designed to provide forces with position-location information.

UNITED STATES ARMY

# THE NETWORK AND ARMY MODERNIZATION

The idea of the Army network is to connect multiple echelons and move information from the dismounted Soldier on the tactical edge, up to the platoon and company level, and all the way up to higher headquarters. The Army's network will make it possible for Soldiers in a vehicle on-the-move to view and share real-time feeds from a nearby robot, ground sensor, or Unmanned Aircraft System (UAS)—instantaneously providing them combat-relevant information and enabling them to share that information with other units on-the-move, dismounted Soldiers, and higher echelons of the force.

The technologies and systems are being developed in tandem with one another; a sensor feed needs a network to travel through for Soldiers to gain the benefit of accessing real-time, battle-relevant information across the force at the battalion level, above and below. The network uses high-bandwidth waveforms to move more information faster and more efficiently across the force in real-time—marking a substantial technological leap beyond the capabilities on today's battlefields.

The information travels through a terrestrial network able to send voice, video, data, and imagery through Joint Tactical Radio Systems (JTRS), software-programmable radios, using high-bandwidth waveforms such as Soldier Radio Waveform and Wideband Networking Waveform. Information sent and received by the terrestrial layer is connected to Warfighter Information Network-Tactical (WIN-T), a satellite network able to send information over long distances using fixed nodes as well as vehicles on-the-move.

The Army's "network" can use the terrestrial layer in addition to beyond-line-of-sight satellite connections; the line-of-sight radio connections can be extended through use of an "aerial layer" that places JTRS Rifleman Radios on aircraft such as Aerostat blimps, UH-60 Black Hawks, AH-64 Apaches, and Shadow UAS. With the aerial layer, units do not have to place a relay team on the top of a mountain ridge or reposition a command post to ensure communication between ground units over extended distances.

The "aerial layer" connects multiple nodes in a mobile-ad hoc network able to move voice, video, data, and images across the force in real-time. The aerial layer is an example of extending a terrestrial line-of-sight network for Soldiers who might be operating in an austere environment and not be able to rely on satellites. As demonstrated during the June-July 2011 NIE, there is tremendous value in being able to move combat-relevant information across the force in real-time. JTRS uses encryption so that information can be safeguarded.

## COMBAT VEHICLE MODERNIZATION

The Combat Vehicle Modernization Capability Portfolio Review functions to provide a holistic view of the combat vehicles in the Heavy Brigade Combat Team and Stryker Brigade Combat Team formations in order to maintain portfolio health, set vehicle priorities for modernization, and ensure portfolio affordability.

Within the portfolio, the Armored Multi-Purpose Vehicle represents the Army's ongoing effort to find a suitable replacement for the aging M113 inventory of vehicles, which are slated to be divested from the fleet. The Army is currently exploring a range of vehicles that might be capable of performing the mission sets required for the M113s.

Other areas of the modernization strategy include modifications to the existing Stryker fleet of vehicles, such as the addition of the Double V-Hull (DVH), engineered to improve Soldier protection by building in a blast-debris-deflecting V-shaped hull. The first Stryker DVH vehicles, which were delivered in 2011, have performed well in combat. The vehicles have been built with a stronger suspension designed to accommodate the extra weight of the DVH.

The Army has also initiated elements of the Combat Vehicle Modernization strategy to upgrade and sustain its fleet through at least 2050. Efforts include improving the protection, space utilization, weight capacity, and power generation capabilities resident in existing vehicles in the fleet, specifically the Abrams and Bradley, to more closely match emerging development of the Ground Combat Vehicle. The idea is to engineer, upgrade, and modernize the formations to meet a range of capability gaps identified for the force to include such areas as force protection, mobility, and networking.

The Ground Combat Vehicle represents a leap forward in the area of protected mobility, networking, and space, weight, and power capabilities, and is engineered as a single vehicle able to deliver a full nine-man squad under armor into the full spectrum of potential combat scenarios. It is being designed with growth potential so as to have the ability to accept technological innovations as they emerge in such areas as networking and lighter weight armor composites, among others.

## MRAP FORCE PROTECTION SAVING LIVES

As further force protection, ASA(ALT) has continued investment in proven technologies such as Mine Resistant Ambush Protected (MRAP) vehicles. MRAPs are engineered with a blast-debris deflecting V-shaped hull and an armored capsule to protect Soldiers from roadside bombs and improvised explosive devices (IEDs). The MRAPs, and the lighter weight more mobile MRAP All Terrain Vehicles, have proven their ability to save Soldiers' lives in combat. As a result of their performance in battle and proven value to Soldiers, MRAPs will remain a vital part of the Army's Tactical Wheeled Vehicle fleet for years to come. MRAPs will be assigned to specific Brigade Combat Teams so that they are available to perform key functions such as route clearance and Soldier transportation when needed.

Also, some MRAPs have been outfitted with the latest in Army networking technology. Using a software-programmable radio such as JTRS and satellite technology such as WIN-T, the networked MRAPs are able to share real-time information, such as sensor feeds from nearby robots and UAS across the force, while on-the-move. This new capability—validated in technical field tests and network exercises such as the NIE—connects units at the battalion and company levels and below to one another and to higher headquarters in real-time using Force XXI Battle Command Brigade and Below display screens.

MRAPs and other vehicles in the Army fleet will take advantage of lighter weight armor composites as they become available. The Army Research Laboratory is testing combinations of lighter weight materials that can out-perform traditional steel; these technologies will spin out into the force as they become available.

A prime example of the search for efficiencies within major programs, the Department of Defense, Army, and Marine Corps have succeeded in achieving a $2 billion cost avoidance on the MRAP program by applying systems engineering techniques and Lean Six Sigma practices to the program. The thrust of the cost avoidance was achieved through several key methodologies; MRAP program managers streamlined and coordinated the requirements process to better determine which vehicles to upgrade and developed a database portal aimed at sharing key information across the 25,000-strong fleet of vehicles.

## PAVING THE WAY FOR THE GROUND COMBAT VEHICLE (GCV)

The Army is developing a GCV Infantry Fighting Vehicle (IFV) as a centerpiece of its combat vehicle modernization strategy. The Army requires an IFV that can deliver a squad to the battlefield in a full-spectrum operation under armor. Plans for the vehicle include development of a system that has abilities equivalent to or surpassing the mobility of the Stryker and the protection of an MRAP.

Based on lessons learned in over ten years of war, the Army has confirmed that the existing fleets, including the Bradley IFV, cannot provide the needed combination of space, weight, and power, advanced force protection, and mobility needed to prevail in 21st century full-spectrum operations.

The Ground Combat Vehicle will be able to maneuver in urban environments, withstand IED attacks, and house the state of-the-art in vehicle computing technology—all while delivering a squad to the battlefield under the best armor protection available. Further, it will be engineered in an incremental fashion with built-in growth potential so that it can accommodate new technologies as they emerge, such as advances in networking and lighter-weight armor composites.

The Army's GCV acquisition strategy, which emphasizes affordability and a seven-year schedule, calls for aggressive exploration of GCV IFV capabilities trade-space via continued requirements and affordability analysis during a 24-month Technology Development Phase. These efforts will help the Army realize program schedule and affordability objectives as GCV requirements are finalized prior to the next major program milestone. The Army remains committed to a seven-year schedule as the appropriate amount of time necessary to design, develop, build, and test the next-generation IFV.

To support well-informed decision points prior to Milestone B, the Army has undertaken a three-pronged approach. First, contractors will work collaboratively with the Army to develop competitive, best-value engineering designs to meet critical Army needs. At the same time, the Army has initiated an update to its GCV IFV analysis of alternatives and is conducting a separate technical and operational assessment of existing non-developmental vehicles. Results from this assessment, along with contractors design efforts, will inform final GCV requirements and facilitate a full and open competition for the next phase of the GCV program.

## GRAY EAGLE UAS QUICK REACTION CAPABILITY

The Army has deployed two "Quick Reaction Capabilities" (QRC) of its MC-1Q Gray Eagle UAS, a 28-foot-long surveillance aircraft with a 56-foot wingspan that is capable of beaming images from up to 29,000 feet for more than 24 consecutive hours.

The QRCs are designed to bring valuable emerging technologies to theater while simultaneously developing a formal program of record; they consist of four aircraft and two ground stations each. The QRC concept is intended to sharpen requirements for the program and get desired capability in the hands of Soldiers sooner for the benefit of the war effort.

One QRC is deployed with Army Soldiers in Iraq and another is with U.S. Special Operations Forces in Afghanistan.

The Gray Eagle aircraft are equipped with a laser designator, signals intelligence capability, and an electro-optical/infrared camera designed to survey the ground below, track enemy movements, and hone in on targets. They are also equipped to carry HELLFIRE missiles.

The Gray Eagle addresses an ever-increasing demand for greater range, altitude, endurance, and payload flexibility. At 3,200 pounds, this UAS has improved take-off and landing performance, coupled with the flexibility to operate with or without satellite communications data links.

# TRANSFORMING ARMY ACQUISITION AND BUSINESS PRACTICES

The Army remains sharply focused on finding ways to continually examine and improve the acquisition process while increasing efficiency and serving as a full partner in the Department of Defense's Better Buying Power Initiatives. For instance, at the request of the Secretary of the Army, an independent panel of experts has completed a 120-day study—an Army Acquisition Review—aimed at assessing the strengths and weaknesses implicitly woven into the acquisition processes with the intent to further transformation; the idea of the study was to take a holistic look at the many nuances of acquisition management to include policy, funding, requirements, major programs, and synchronization with the Army Force Generation process.

As a result of this Army Acquisition Review, the Secretary of the Army and ASA(ALT) are implementing 63 specific recommendations aimed at improving the acquisition process. Among the many reforms being implemented are: streamlining the requirements process to focus on more collaboration in order to properly align requirements and ensure greater affordability, technological maturity, and realistic "achievability" of program goals; more widespread Army purchasing of Technical Data Packages in order to encourage competition and drive down prices; better codifying of rapid acquisition procedures; and increasing testing and prototyping earlier in the developmental cycle as a way to reduce costs and risks.

A major challenge to acquisition continues to be the need to properly prioritize, streamline, and collaborate on requirements at the front end of the process in order to emphasize technological maturity, affordability, and productivity. The revised Request for Proposal for the Ground Combat Vehicle is an excellent demonstration of how we approached reform in this area; requirements were properly "tiered" and industry was given "trade space" designed to encourage innovation.

Also, the Army continues to build upon the challenge area of codifying rapid acquisition procedures with more traditional approaches, with Quick Reaction Capabilities (QRC) such as the Army's Gray Eagle Unmanned Aircraft Systems program. QRCs place emerging technologies in the hands of Soldiers to address requirements while simultaneously developing a longer-term program of record complete with milestones and various check and balances.

The ultimate goal of acquisition reform is for ASA(ALT) to work with our industry and academic partners to more efficiently develop and deliver capabilities needed by the Soldier. A key aspect of this is an effort to identify and address inefficiencies discovered in the acquisition process. The rationale for this effort is based on the idea of accomplishing more acquisition objectives without necessarily receiving more financial resources. ASA(ALT) continuously seeks to improve its capacity to Design, Develop, Deliver, Dominate—and Sustain. We must do more without more.

In addition, the Army is emphasizing Lean Six Sigma business practices in many of its programs. These are specific, business-proven methods aimed at identifying ways to streamline productivity and reduce overhead costs. Applying these methods recently resulted in a $2 billion cost-avoidance on the MRAP program because program managers found ways to consolidate and streamline vehicle upgrade requirements.

A system-of-systems approach is vital to these ongoing efforts to transform business practices. The Army must look at developing, managing, and acquiring technologies in the most efficient way possible, an approach which includes the need to understand the interdependencies among systems. There must be an emphasis upon maturing the capability to synchronize programs and integrate schedules, deliveries, and other developments across the acquisition process.

As a result of these and other practices, the acquisition community remains acutely aware of its need to further the transformation of its business efforts. These initiatives help the Army transform as an institution and ensure that the best value possible is provided to the taxpayer and the Soldier—who is at the very center of these efforts.

## COMMUNICATING AND COLLABORATING WITH INDUSTRY

The Army must continue to foster, develop, and enhance its relationships with vital industry partners as a way to ensure the best possible development of new and emerging systems. With this as an organizing principle, ASA(ALT) has created an industry outreach engagement program squarely focused on furthering partnerships with industry and facilitating constructive dialogue designed to achieve the best results for Soldiers in combat. Recognizing the importance of revitalizing industry engagement, the Army continues to nurture this outreach program, fostering and preserving strong relationships between the Army and its key industry partners.

Often there are circumstances where procurement sensitivities and ongoing competition may preclude the occasion to dialogue with industry. There are, nonetheless, ample opportunities for positive, proactive, and constructive engagement with industry partners. While placing a premium upon the importance of properly defining the parameters for discussion with industry partners, ASA(ALT) seeks to foster an environment of open dialogue.

The ASA(ALT) industry engagement program brings leaders of industry together with key Army decision makers in an effort to facilitate dialogue and collaboration; both the Army and its industry partners benefit from this forum. The rationale behind such an approach is based on the effort to minimize misunderstandings and "eleventh hour" reactions. This industry program is designed to anticipate future developments, recognize and communicate industry trends, and identify the evolution of key technologies that will support and protect our Soldiers in combat.

## ELIMINATING CHEMICAL WEAPONS

Achieving excellence in acquisition involves continuous stewardship and superb management of highly sensitive and visible programs for which ASA(ALT) has executive agent authority, such as the Nation's chemical weapons disposal program.

The U.S. Army Chemical Materials Agency (CMA), using acquisition processes as its baseline, works with private industry, academia, and other interested policy and environmental stakeholders to eliminate America's obsolete chemical weapons.

Overall, CMA has destroyed 88 percent of the Nation's obsolete chemical weapons stockpile and anticipates that it will reach at least 90 percent destruction by 2012.

So far, four sites have completed operations: Johnston Atoll Chemical Agent Disposal System, Newport Chemical Agent Disposal Facility in Indiana, Aberdeen Chemical Agent Disposal Facility in Maryland, and Pine Bluff Chemical Agent Disposal Facility in Arkansas.

Operations continue at Tooele Chemical Agent Disposal Facility in Utah, Anniston Chemical Agent Disposal Facility in Alabama, and Umatilla Chemical Agent Disposal Facility in Oregon.

CMA also responds to discoveries of non-stockpile chemical weapons and safely stores those weapons until their disposal. Moreover, CMA partners with the Federal Emergency Management Agency to prepare local communities to deal with potential emergencies involving those weapons.

# PATH FORWARD

We will provide whatever it takes to achieve the Nation's objectives in the current fight. At the same time, we will develop a shared vision to build the Army of 2020—designing and preparing units, developing Soldiers, and growing leaders to win in an increasingly competitive learning environment. We will continue to maintain battlefield dominance but remain versatile and adaptable to any task our Nation may call upon us to perform. Continuous modernization is key to transforming Army capabilities and maintaining a technological advantage over our adversaries across the full spectrum of operations. ASA(ALT) looks forward to continued support from members of Congress to achieve its broad modernization goals while supporting a cost-conscious culture.

The systems listed in this book are not isolated, individual products. Rather, they are part of an integrated system-of-systems investment approach designed to make the Army of the future able to deal successfully with the challenges it will face. Each system and capability is important. We have an obligation to provide our Soldiers with the most effective, high-quality equipment in the most sustainable, cost-effective manner. Our goal is to develop and field a versatile and affordable mix of equipment that will enable Soldiers to succeed in full-spectrum operations today and tomorrow, ensuring that we maintain our decisive advantage over any enemy we face.

# WEAPON SYSTEMS

## LISTED IN ALPHABETICAL ORDER

# 2.75 Inch Rocket Systems (Hydra-70)

**INVESTMENT COMPONENT**

Modernization

Recapitalization

Maintenance

## MISSION

Provides air-to-ground suppression, smoke screening, illumination, and direct and indirect fires to defeat area materiel and personnel targets at close and extended ranges.

## DESCRIPTION

The Hydra-70 Rocket System of 2.75 inch air-launched rockets is employed by tri-service and special operating forces on both fixed- and rotary-wing aircraft and is inherently immune to countermeasures. This highly modular rocket family incorporates several different mission-oriented warheads for the Hydra-70 variant, including high-explosive, anti-personnel, multipurpose submunition, red phosphorus smoke, flechette, training, visible-light illumination flare, and infrared illumination flare.

**Diameter:** 2.75 inches
**Weight:** 23-27 pounds (depending on warhead)
**Length:** 55-70 inches (depending on warhead)
**Range:** 300-8,000 meters
**Velocity:** 700+ meters per second
**Area suppression:** No precision

## SYSTEM INTERDEPENDENCIES

None

## PROGRAM STATUS

- **Current:** Producing annual replenishment for training, theater combat expenditures, and war reserve requirements

## PROJECTED ACTIVITIES

- **FY11:** Continue Hydra-70 production and safety, reliability, and producibility program activities

**ACQUISITION PHASE**

Technology Development | Engineering and Manufacturing Development | Production and Deployment | Operations and Support

## 2.75 Inch Rocket Systems (Hydra-70)

**FOREIGN MILITARY SALES**

**Hydra-70:** Colombia, Japan, Kuwait, the Netherlands, Singapore, Thailand, and United Arab Emirates

**CONTRACTORS**

**Prime System:**
General Dynamics (Burlington, VT)
**Grain:**
Alliant Techsystems (Radford, VA)
**Warhead Fuzes:**
Action Manufacturing (Philadelphia, PA)
**Shipping Container (Fastpack):**
CONCO (Louisville, KY)
**Fin and Nozzle:**
General Dynamics Ordnance and Tactical Systems (Anniston, AL)

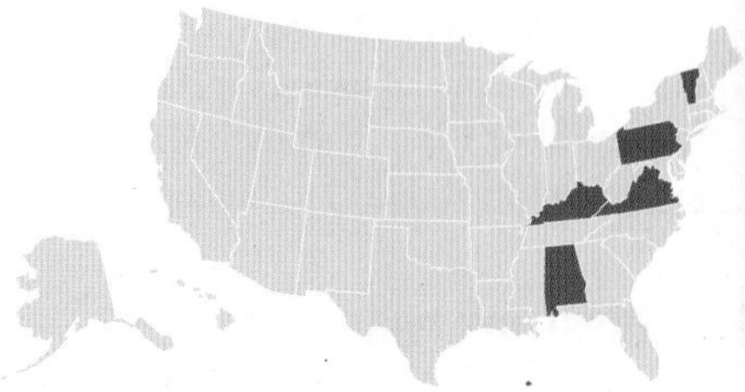

# Abrams Tank Upgrade

## INVESTMENT COMPONENT

Modernization

Recapitalization

Maintenance

## MISSION

Closes with and destroys enemy forces on the integrated battlefield using mobility, firepower, and shock effect with lethality, survivability, and fightability necessary to defeat advanced threats.

## DESCRIPTION

The Abrams tank upgrade includes two powerful variants, the M1A1 SA (Situational Awareness) and the M1A2 SEP (System Enhancement Program) version 2. The 1,500-horsepower AGT turbine engine, the 120mm main gun, and special armor make the Abrams tank particularly lethal against heavy armor forces.

**M1A1 SA:** Improvements include the Gunners Primary Sight (GPS) with improved thermal imaging capabilities of the new Block I 2nd generation forward-looking infrared (FLIR) technology. Lethality improvements include the Stabilized Commander's Weapon Station (SCWS) and ballistic solution upgrades for the M829A3 kinetic and the M1028 canister rounds. Common Abrams modifications include Blue Force Tracking (BFT), which is a digital command and control system that gives Army commanders across the battlefield current information about their location relative to friendly forces; and the Power Train Improvement and Integration Optimization Program (TIGER engine and improved transmission), which provides more reliability, durability, and a single standard for the vehicle's power train. Survivability improvements include frontal armor and turret side armor upgrades.

**M1A2 SEP v2:** Upgrades include improved survivability, automotive power pack, computer systems, and night vision capabilities. Lethality improvements include Common Remotely Operated Weapon Station (CROWS) and ballistic solution upgrades for the M829A3 kinetic and the M1028 canister rounds. The M1A2 SEP v2 has improved microprocessors, color flat panel displays, improved memory capacity, better Soldier-machine interface, and a new open operating system designed to run the Common Operating Environment (COE) software. Both the GPS and the Commander's Independent Thermal Viewer (CITV) on the M1A2 SEP tank include the improved thermal imaging capabilities of the new Block I second-generation FLIR technology. The M1A2 SEP has improved frontal and side armor for enhanced crew survivability. The M1A2 SEP is also equipped with battery-based auxiliary power, Total InteGrated Engine Revitalization (TIGER), and an upgraded transmission for improved automotive reliability and durability.

## SYSTEM INTERDEPENDENCIES

None

## PROGRAM STATUS

- **Current:** The 1st Brigade, 2nd Infantry Division; 2nd Brigade, 1st Armored Division; 3rd Infantry Division; and the Training and Doctrine Command, Ft. Benning, GA, are equipped with the Abrams M1A2 SEP v2
- **Current:** Abrams production of the M1A2 SEP v2 tank continues for both the Active Army and the Army National Guard (ARNG) to meet the Army's modularity goals by 2013

## PROJECTED ACTIVITIES

- **FY12-14:** Army Prepositioned Stock 4 (Korea); 1st and 2nd Brigades, 1st Infantry Division; 116th Heavy Brigade Combat Team, Idaho ARNG; 170th Heavy Brigade Combat Team or 172nd Heavy Brigade Combat Team; and Forces Command will be fielded with the Abrams M1A2 SEP v2 tank. M1A1 SA fielding continues to the 30th North Carolina ARNG, 81st Washington ARNG, 155th Mississippi ARNG, 1-145th Ohio Combined Arms Army Battalion (CAB), 2-137th Kansas CAB, and the 11th ACR
- **FY12-13:** Continue M1A2 SEP v2 multiyear contract production with final delivery in June 2013
- **FY12:** Continue TIGER production

## ACQUISITION PHASE

Technology Development | Engineering and Manufacturing Development | Production and Deployment | Operations and Support

## Abrams Tank Upgrade

**FOREIGN MILITARY SALES**

**M1A1:** Australia (59), Egypt (1,005), Iraq (140)
**M1A2:** Kuwait (218), Saudi Arabia (329)

**CONTRACTORS**

**Prime:**
General Dynamics Land Systems (Sterling Heights, MI)
**Engine:**
Honeywell (Phoenix, AZ)
**Transmission:**
Allison Transmission (Indianapolis, IN)
Anniston Army Depot (Anniston, AL)

**Combat weight (tons):** M1A1 - 68.59; M1A2 SEP v1 - 68.57; M1A2 SEP v2 - 69.29
**Speed:** 42 mph, 30 mph x-country
**Main gun/rounds (basic load):** M1 - 105mm/55 rounds; M1A1 - 120mm/40 rounds; M1A2 - 120mm/42 rounds
**Machine guns:** .50 caliber 900 rounds, 7.62mm 11,400 rounds

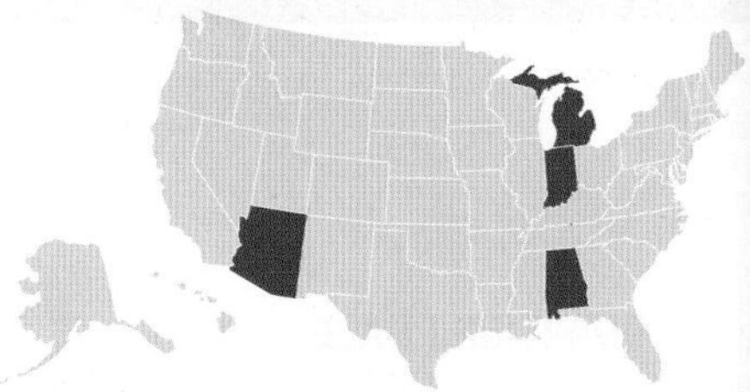

# Advanced Field Artillery Tactical Data System (AFATDS)

**INVESTMENT COMPONENT**

- **Modernization**
- Recapitalization
- Maintenance

## MISSION

Provides the Army, Navy, and Marine Corps automated fire support command, control, and communications.

## DESCRIPTION

The Advanced Field Artillery Tactical Data System (AFATDS) pairs targets to weapons to provide optimum use of fire support assets and timely execution of fire missions. AFATDS automates the planning, coordinating, and controlling of all fire support assets (field artillery, mortars, close air support, naval gunfire, attack helicopters, offensive electronic warfare, fire support meteorological systems, forward observers, and fire support radars).

AFATDS will automatically implement detailed commander's guidance in the automation of operational planning, movement control, targeting, target value analysis, and fire support planning. AFATDS is designed to interoperate with the other Army battle command systems; current and future Navy and Air Force command and control weapon systems; and the German, French, British, and Italian fire support systems. The system has been used in operations in Iraq and Afghanistan.

## SYSTEM INTERDEPENDENCIES

**In this Publication**

Tactical Mission Command (TMC)/ Maneuver Control System (MCS); Battle Command Sustainment Support System (BCS3); Distributed Common Ground System-Army (DCGS-A); Global Command and Control System-Army (GCCS-A)

**Other Major Interdependencies**

Lightweight Forward Entry Device (LFED), Pocket-Sized Forward Entry Device (PFED), Joint Automated Deep Operations Coordination System (JADOCS), Theater Battle Management Core System (TBMCS), Gun Display Unit-Replacement (GDU-R)

## PROGRAM STATUS

- **2QFY11:** Full Materiel Release (FMR) of AFATDS 6.7.0 (BC11)

## PROJECTED ACTIVITIES

- **1QFY13:** FMR of AFATDS 6.8.0 (BC13)

**ACQUISITION PHASE**

- Technology Development
- Engineering and Manufacturing Development
- **Production and Deployment**
- Operations and Support

## Advanced Field Artillery Tactical Data System (AFATDS)

**FOREIGN MILITARY SALES**
Australia, Bahrain, Egypt, Jordan, Portugal, Taiwan, Turkey

**CONTRACTORS**
**Software:**
Raytheon (Ft. Wayne, IN)
**Hardware:**
General Dynamics (Taunton, MA)
Raytheon (Ft. Wayne, IN)
**NET:**
VIATECH (Lawton, OK)
**Technical:**
Computer Sciences Corp. (CSC) (Eatontown, NJ)
**Fielding:**
CACI (Eatontown, NJ)
**IV&V:**
L-3 (Lawton, OK)

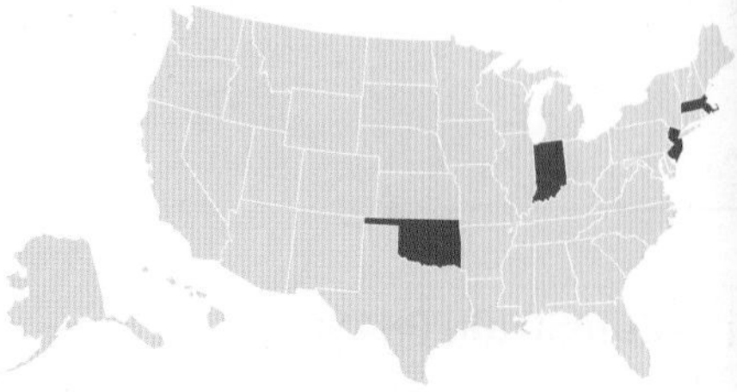

# Advanced Threat Infrared Countermeasure/Common Missile Warning System (ATIRCM/CMWS)

**INVESTMENT COMPONENT**

Modernization

Recapitalization

Maintenance

## MISSION

Detects missile launches/flights, protects aircraft from Tier 1 infrared (IR)-guided missiles, and provides threat awareness and IR countermeasures using an airborne self-protection system.

## DESCRIPTION

The Advanced Threat Infrared Countermeasure/Common Missile Warning System (ATIRCM/CMWS) integrates defensive infrared countermeasures capabilities into existing current-generation aircraft to engage and defeat multiple IR-guided missile threats simultaneously.

The U.S. Army operational requirements concept for IR countermeasure systems is the Suite of Integrated Infrared Countermeasures (SIIRCM). It mandates an integrated warning and countermeasure system to enhance aircraft survivability against IR-guided threat missile systems. The ATIRCM/CMWS program forms the core element of the SIIRCM concept. ATIRCM/CMWS has a modular configuration consisting of an integrated ultraviolet missile warning system, an Infrared Laser Jammer, and Improved Countermeasure Dispensers (ICMDs). This configuration can vary with aircraft and type.

CMWS can function as a stand-alone system with the capability to detect missiles and provide audible and visual warnings to pilots. When installed with the Advanced IRCM Munitions and ICMDs, it activates expendables to decoy/defeat IR-guided missiles. ATIRCM adds the Directed Energy Laser Countermeasure Technology to CMWS and is a key for Future Force Army aircraft.

## SYSTEM INTERDEPENDENCIES

**Other Major Interdependencies**

AH-64A, AH-64D, C-12R/T/U, C-23, C-26, Constant Hawk-A, Constant Hawk-I, DHC-7, HH-60L, HH-60M, MH-47E/G, MH-60K/L/M, RC-12/C-12, RC-12K/N/P/Q, UC-35

## PROGRAM STATUS

- **Current:** All aircraft deployed to Operation Iraqi Freedom/Operation Enduring Freedom equipped with CMWS prior to deployment; OH-58D, Kiowa Warrior is latest platform to integrate CMWS
- **Current:** In process, next-generation Electronic Control Unit (ECU) and Missile Warning Algorithms for all aircraft

## PROJECTED ACTIVITIES

- **Continue:** ATIRCM Quick Reaction Capability (QRC), the Army's latest Aircraft Survivability Equipment (ASE) initiative to protect crews and aircraft from advanced threat Man-Portable Air Defense Systems (MANPADS)
- **Ongoing:** Fielding to CH-47D/F models
- **3QFY12:** Start of fielding next-generation ECU (for CMWS)

**ACQUISITION PHASE**

Technology Development | Engineering and Manufacturing Development | Production and Deployment | Operations and Support

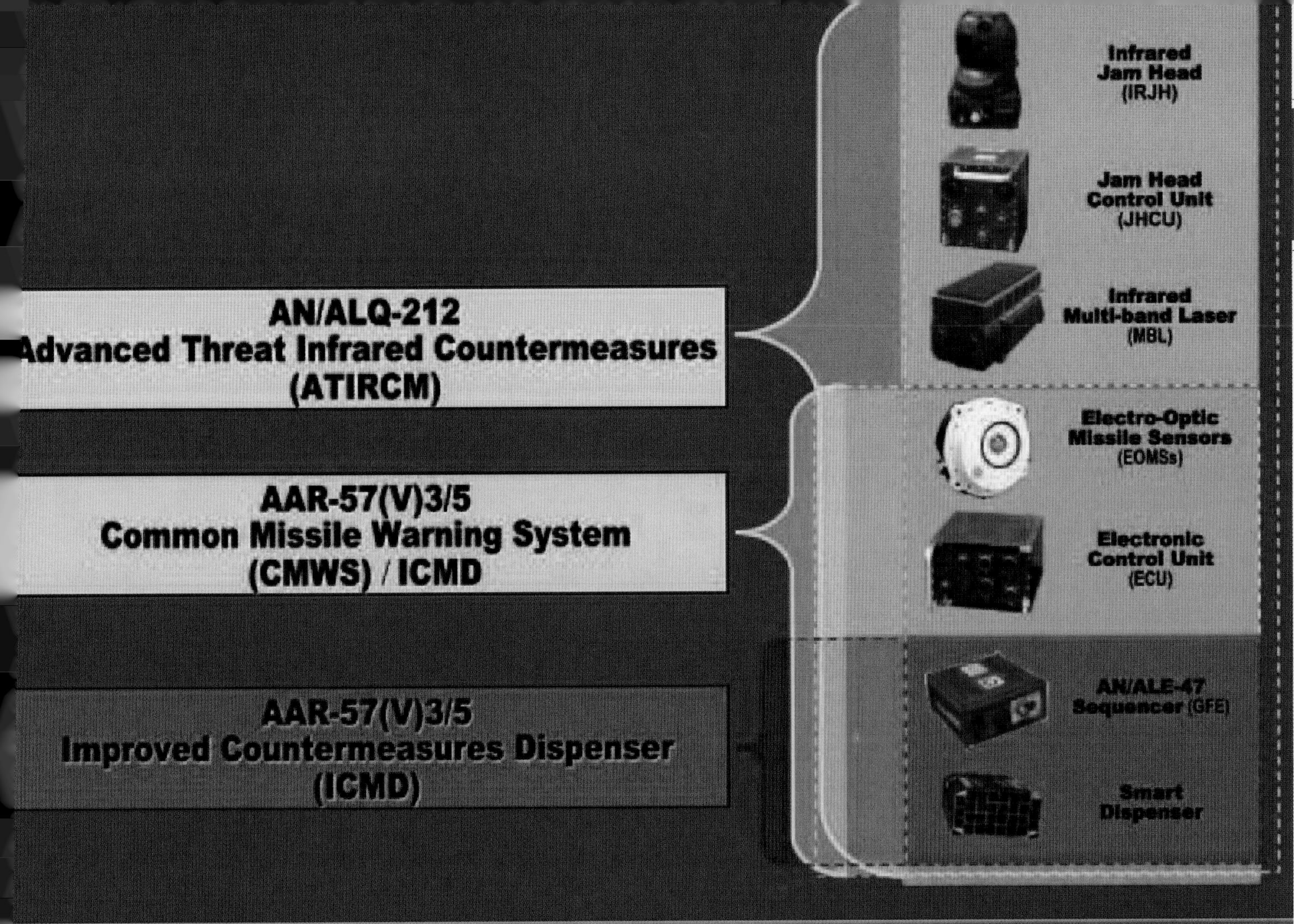

## Advanced Threat Infrared Countermeasure/Common Missile Warning System (ATIRCM/CMWS)

**FOREIGN MILITARY SALES**

United Kingdom

**CONTRACTORS**

**ATIRCM/CMWS (Prime):**
BAE Systems (Nashua, NH)
**Logistics Support:**
AEPCO (Huntsville, AL)
**Software Configuration Management Support:**
Science Applications International Corp. (SAIC) (Huntsville, AL)
**CMWS-GTRI E2E Data Analysis/SIL Development:**
Georgia Tech Applied Research Corp. (Atlanta, GA)
**OH-58D Product Documentation Update:**
Bell Helicopter Textron (Ft. Worth, TX)
**Test Support Data Analysis:**
MacAulay-Brown Inc. (Dayton, OH)
**UH-60A/L P31 Upgrade:**
Rockwell Collins (Cedar Rapids, IA)
**Engineering/Tech Production Support:**
Computer Sciences Corp. (CSC) (Huntsville, AL)
**OATS Phase 3:**
David H. Pollock Consultants (Eatontown, NJ)

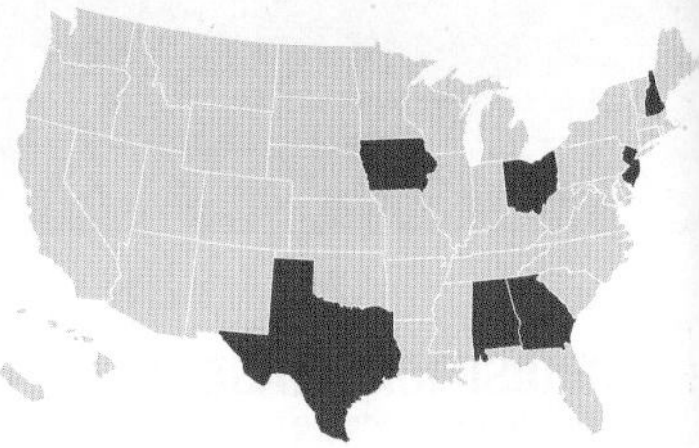

# Air Warrior (AW)

**INVESTMENT COMPONENT**

Modernization

Recapitalization

Maintenance

## MISSION

Provides enhanced mission effectiveness, leveraging clothing and equipment to maximize aircrew member survivability.

## DESCRIPTION

Air Warrior (AW) is a modular, integrated, rapidly reconfigurable combat aircrew ensemble that saves lives and maximizes Army aircrew mission performance. Previous aviation life support equipment consisted of a non-integrated assemblage of protective and survival gear. AW uses a systems approach to equipping the aircrew and closes the capability gap between human and machine. Fielded incrementally in blocks to rapidly provide enhanced capabilities to the Warfighter, AW leverages and integrates clothing and equipment, such as the Army Aircrew Combat Uniform and ballistic protection, from other Product Managers.

**AW Block I provides:**

- Survival Equipment Subsystem, which integrates first aid, survival, signaling, and communications equipment with body armor and over-water survival subsystems
- Microclimate Cooling System, which increases effective mission duration in heat-stress environments by more than 350 percent
- Aircrew Integrated Helmet System, a lighter helmet with increased head and hearing protection

**AW Increment III:**

- Electronic Data Manager (EDM), a portable digital-mission planning device for over-the-horizon messaging and enhanced situational awareness capabilities through connectivity to Blue Force Tracking, Aviation
- Aircraft Wireless Intercom System (AWIS) for secure cordless, hands-free aircrew communications
- Survival Kit, Ready Access, Modular (SKRAM) Go-Bag with integrated hydration
- Portable Helicopter Oxygen Delivery System, a Soldier-worn supplemental breathing oxygen system for high-altitude operations
- Communication Enhancement and Protection System (CEPS) provides helmet hear-through capability

## SYSTEM INTERDEPENDENCIES

**In this Publication**

Fixed Wing

## PROGRAM STATUS

- **FY09:** Fielded Air Warrior Increment III systems
- **FY10:** Fielding of the CEPS and SKRAM

## PROJECTED ACTIVITIES

- **FY11:** Continue fielding and reset of Air Warrior to units prior to deployment
- **FY12-14:** Field Encrypted AWIS

**ACQUISITION PHASE**

Technology Development | Engineering and Manufacturing Development | Production and Deployment | Operations and Support

## Air Warrior (AW)

**FOREIGN MILITARY SALES**
Australia, Bahrain, Canada, United Arab Emirates

**CONTRACTORS**
Telephonics Corp. (Farmingdale, NY)
General Dynamics C4 Systems Inc. (Scottsdale, AZ)
BAE Systems (Phoenix, AZ)
Aerial Machine and Tool Corp. (Vesta, VA)
Westwind Technologies Inc. (Huntsville, AL)
Carleton Technologies Inc. (Orchard Park, NY)
Med-Eng Systems Inc. (Ogdensburg, NY)
Raytheon Technical Services (Indianapolis, IN)
Secure Communication Systems Inc. (Santa Ana, CA)
US Divers (Vista, CA)
CEP Inc. (Enterprise, AL)
Science and Engineering Services Inc. (SESI) (Huntsville, AL)
Gibson and Barnes (Santa Clara, CA)
Oxygen Generating Systems International (Buffalo, NY)
Gentex Corp. (Rancho Cucamonga, CA)
Mountain High Equipment and Supply Co. (Redmond, OR)
Taylor-Wharton (Huntsville, AL)

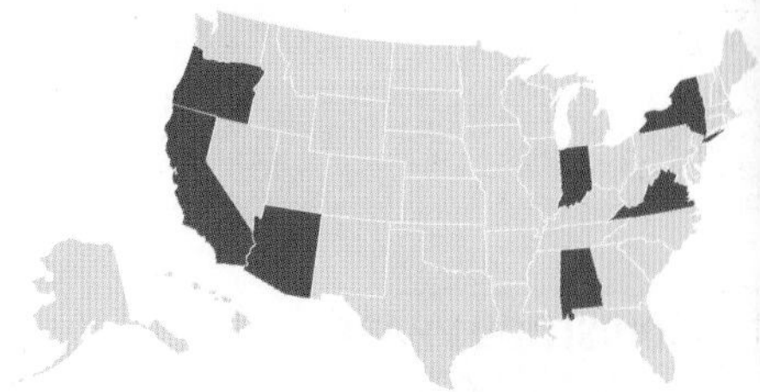

# Air/Missile Defense Planning and Control System (AMDPCS)

**INVESTMENT COMPONENT**

Modernization

Recapitalization

Maintenance

## MISSION

Provides an automated command and control (C2) system that integrates Air and Missile Defense (AMD) planning and operations for Air Defense Airspace Management (ADAM) systems in Brigade Combat Teams (BCTs) and at every Air Defense Artillery (ADA) echelon, battery through theater.

## DESCRIPTION

The AMDPCS is an Army Objective Force system that provides integration of AMD operations at all echelons. AMDPCS systems are deployed with ADAM systems, ADA brigades, and Army Air and Missile Defense Commands (AAMDCs).

ADAM provides the commanders at BCTs, fires brigades, combat aviation brigades, and division and corps tactical operations systems with situational awareness (SA) of the airspace. ADAM provides collaboration and staff planning capabilities through the Army Battle Command System and operational links for airspace coordination with Joint, interagency, multinational, and coalition forces.

AMDPCS in ADA brigades and AAMDCs provides expanded staff planning and coordination capabilities for integrating defense of the air battlespace. AMDPCS includes shelters, automated data processing equipment, tactical communications, standard vehicles, tactical power, and the following two software systems for force operations/engagement operations: Air and Missile Defense Workstation (AMDWS) and Air Defense System Integrator (ADSI).

AMDWS is a staff planning and battlespace SA tool that provides commanders with a common tactical and operational air picture. It is the ADA component of Army mission command. ADSI is a joint multicommunications processor that provides external joint messaging for operations by subordinate or attached units.

## SYSTEM INTERDEPENDENCIES

None

## PROGRAM STATUS

- **1QFY11:** Complete fielding of 10 ADAMs procured in FY10
- **1QFY11:** Complete FY10 reset of 32 ADAMs
- **3QFY11:** Fielded AMDPCS to the 164th ADA Brigade (FL ARNG)
- **4QFY11:** Fielded AMDPCS to the 11th ADA Brigade (Ft. Bliss)

## PROJECTED ACTIVITIES

- **1QFY12:** Complete FY11 reset of 15 ADAMs
- **2QFY12:** Fielding AMDWS version 6.5.1 with 3D display
- **2QFY12:** Fielding AMDPCS to 174th ADA Brigade (OH ARNG)
- **4QFY12:** Fielding AMDPCS to 357th AAMDC
- **4QFY13:** Fielding AMDPCS to 94th AAMDC

**ACQUISITION PHASE**

Technology Development | Engineering and Manufacturing Development | Production and Deployment | Operations and Support

## Air/Missile Defense Planning and Control System (AMDPCS)

**FOREIGN MILITARY SALES**
Netherlands (AMDWS)

**CONTRACTORS**
Northrop Grumman (Huntsville, AL)
Ultra Inc. (Austin, TX)

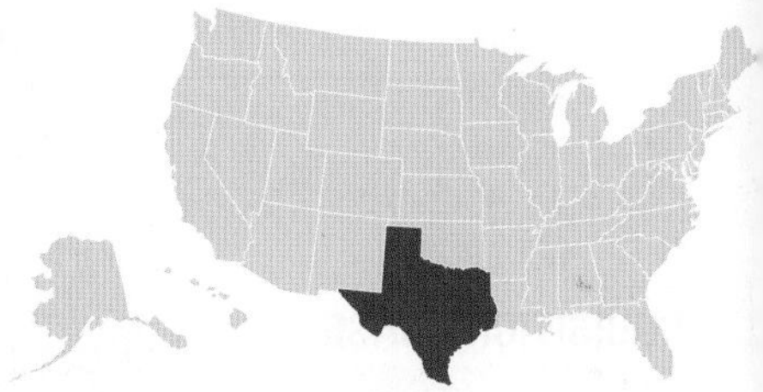

# Airborne Reconnaissance Low (ARL)

**INVESTMENT COMPONENT**

- Modernization
- Recapitalization
- Maintenance

## MISSION

Provides tactical commanders with a day/night, near all-weather, real-time airborne communications intelligence/imagery intelligence (COMINT/IMINT) collection and designated area surveillance system. It consists of a modified DeHavilland DHC-7 fixed-wing aircraft equipped with COMINT, IMINT, Ground Moving Target Indicator/Synthetic Aperture Radar (GMTI/SAR), and electro-optical (EO)/infrared (IR) full-motion video capability. Four onboard operators control the payloads via onboard open-architecture, multifunction workstations and can communicate directly with ground units.

## DESCRIPTION

Airborne Reconnaissance Low (ARL) is a self-deploying, multisensor, day/night, all-weather reconnaissance, intelligence system. It consists of a modified DeHavilland DHC-7 fixed-wing aircraft equipped with COMINT/IMINT and Ground Moving Target Indicator/Synthetic Aperture Radar (GMTI/SAR) and electro-optical (EO)/infrared (IR) full-motion video capability. The payloads are controlled and operated via onboard open-architecture, multifunction workstations. Intelligence collected on the ARL can be analyzed, recorded, and disseminated on the aircraft workstations in real-time and stored on-board for post-mission processing. During multi-aircraft missions, data can be shared between cooperating aircraft via ultra high-frequency air-to-air data links, allowing multiplatform COMINT geolocation operations. The ARL system includes a variety of communications subsystems to support near-real-time dissemination of intelligence and dynamic retasking of the aircraft. ARL provides real-time down-link of MTI data to the Common Ground Station (CGS) at the Brigade Combat Team through echelon-above-corps level. Eight aircraft are configured as ARL-Multifunction (ARL-M), equipped with a combination of IMINT, COMINT, and SAR/MTI payload and demonstrated hyperspectral imager applications and multi-intelligence (multi-INT) data fusion capabilities. Four mission workstations are on-board the aircraft and are remote-operator capable. The Intelligence and Security Command (INSCOM) operates all ARL systems and currently supports Southern Command (SOUTHCOM) with one to four ARL-M aircraft, United States Forces Korea (USFK) with three ARL-M aircraft, and U.S. Central Command (CENTCOM) with one aircraft. Future sensor enhancements are focused on upgrades to the COMINT, IMINT, and radar payloads to support emerging threats.

**Capabilities include:**

- **Endurance/ceiling:** 8 hours/20,000 feet
- **Speed/gross weight:** 231 knots/ 47,000 pounds
- **Range with max payload:** Greater than 1,400 nautical miles
- **Mission completion rate:** Greater than 90 percent

## SYSTEM INTERDEPENDENCIES

None

## PROGRAM STATUS

- **4QFY11:** Field ARL-M8
- **4QFY11:** Completed workstation upgrade

## PROJECTED ACTIVITIES

- **FY12-14:** Continue imagery, radar, COMINT, system interoperability, and workstation architecture upgrades

**ACQUISITION PHASE**

Technology Development | Engineering and Manufacturing Development | Production and Deployment | Operations and Support

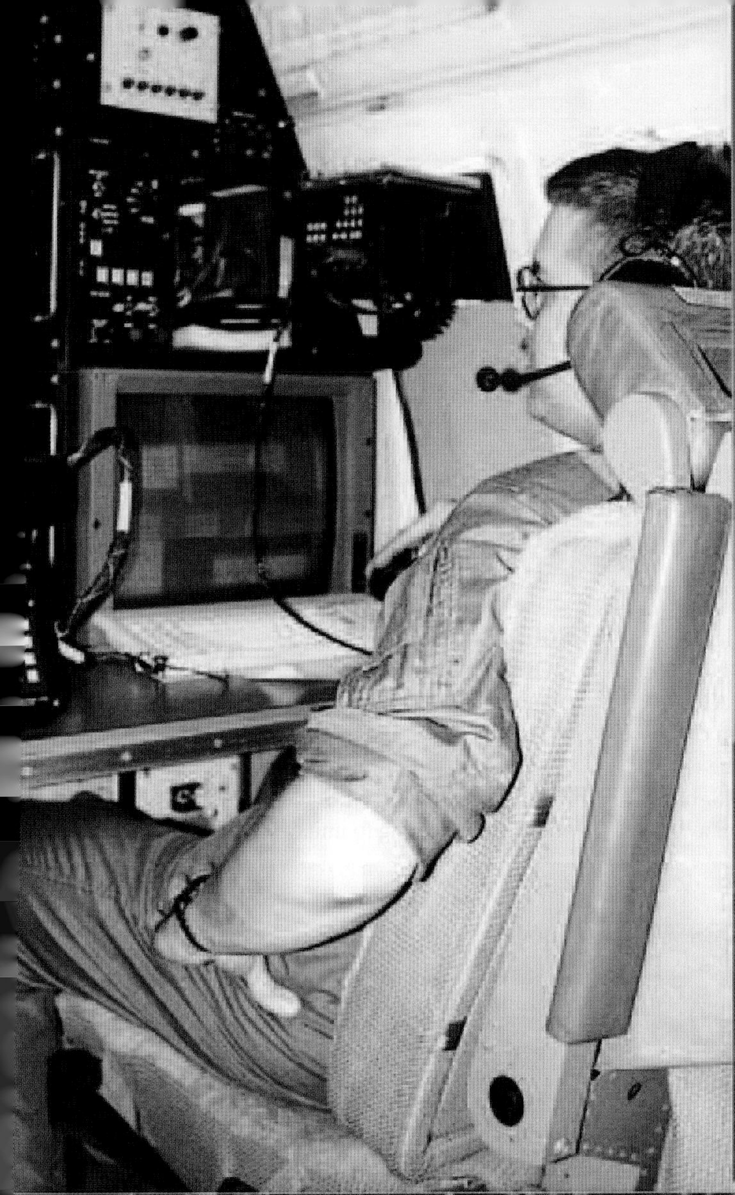

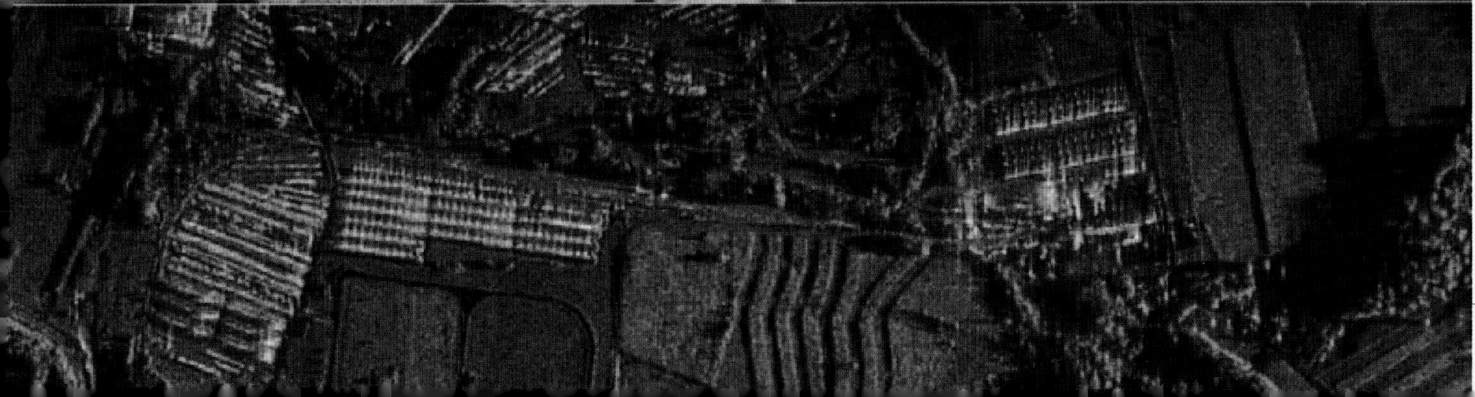

## Airborne Reconnaissance Low (ARL)

**FOREIGN MILITARY SALES**
None

**CONTRACTORS**
Sierra Nevada Corp. (Hagerstown, MD)
**Aircraft Survivability:**
Litton Advanced Systems (Gaithersburg, MD)
**COMINT Subsystem:**
BAE Systems (Manchester, NH)
**EO/IR Subsystem:**
WESCAM (Hamilton, Ontario, Canada)
**Engineering Support:**
CACI (Berryville, VA)
**Radar Subsystem:**
Lockheed Martin (Phoenix, AZ)

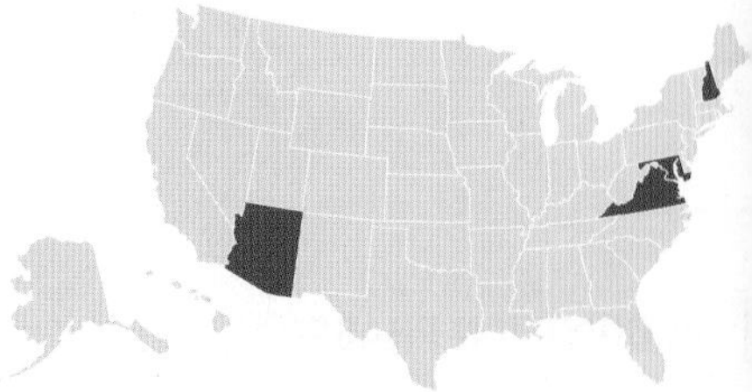

# All Terrain Lifter Army System (ATLAS)

**INVESTMENT COMPONENT**

Modernization

Recapitalization

Maintenance

## MISSION

Provides a mobile, variable reach, rough terrain forklift (RTFL) capable of handling all classes of supplies.

## DESCRIPTION

The All Terrain Lifter Army System (ATLAS) is a C-130 air-transportable, 10,000 pound-capacity, variable-reach RTFL. ATLAS supports transportation, quartermaster, ordnance, missiles and munitions, engineer, aviation, and medical Army units. ATLAS' cross-country mobility allows it to support the Brigade Combat Teams, and it is a critical asset supporting an expeditionary Army.

ATLAS is a military-unique vehicle: commercial forklifts cannot meet military requirements. It is capable of lifting 4,000 pounds at a 21.5 feet reach, 6,000 pounds at 15 feet, and 10,000 pounds at four feet. ATLAS is equipped with two interchangeable fork carriages: a 6,000-pound carriage for stuffing and unstuffing standard Army pallets with 24-inch load centers from 20-foot containers weighing up to 6,000 pounds; and a 10,000-pound carriage for handling loads weighing up to 10,000 pounds at 48-inch load center (Air Force 463L pallets).

ATLAS is a key component of the Army's Container Oriented Distribution System. The ATLAS II is an Environmental Protection Agency Tier III-compliant ATLAS with improved reliability, performance, survivability, and transportability. ATLAS I and ATLAS II systems are used to handle all classes of supply and are essential to the deployment of a continental U.S.-based Army and to the sustainment of a deployed force.

Crew survivability is being addressed in accordance with the Army's Long Term Armor Strategy.

**ATLAS Features:**
**Length:** 27.02 feet
**Width:** 8.35 feet (ATLAS II is four inches narrower)
**Height:** 8.92 feet
**Weight:** 33,500 pounds
**Power train:** 165-horsepower Cummins diesel engine; Funk 1723 PowerShift (three-speed forward and reverse) mechanical transmission
**Cruising range:** 10 hours of operation before refueling
**Road speed:** 23 miles per hour
**Force protection:** Integrated armor

## SYSTEM INTERDEPENDENCIES

None

## PROGRAM STATUS

- **2QFY07:** ATLAS II contract award; ongoing production and fielding of ATLAS I

## PROJECTED ACTIVITIES

- **Continue:** Fielding to units

**ACQUISITION PHASE**

Technology Development | Engineering and Manufacturing Development | **Production and Deployment** | Operations and Support

## All Terrain Lifter Army System (ATLAS)

**FOREIGN MILITARY SALES**
None

**CONTRACTORS**
JLG Industries Inc. (McConnellsburg, PA)

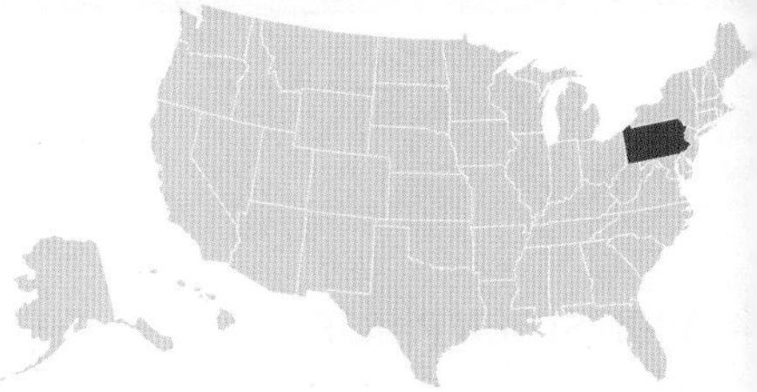

# Armored Knight

INVESTMENT COMPONENT

Modernization

Recapitalization

Maintenance

## MISSION

Assists Heavy and Infantry Brigade Combat Teams (HBCTs and IBCTs) in performing terrain surveillance, target acquisition and location, and fire support for combat observation lasing team missions.

## DESCRIPTION

The M1200 Armored Knight provides precision strike capability by locating and designating targets for both ground- and air-delivered laser-guided ordnance and conventional munitions. It replaces the M707 Knight High Mobility Multipurpose Wheeled Vehicle (HMMWV) base and M981 fire support team vehicles used by combat observation lasing teams (COLTs) in both HBCTs and IBCTs. It operates as an integral part of the brigade reconnaissance element, providing COLT and fire support mission planning and execution.

The Armored Knight is a M117 Armored Security Vehicle (ASV) chassis/hull with add-on armor fragmentation kits installed, providing enhanced survivability and maneuverability over the unarmored M707. The system includes a full 360-degree armored cupola and integrated Knight mission equipment package.

The mission equipment package includes: Fire Support Sensor System (FS3) mounted sensor, Targeting Station Control Panel, Mission Processor Unit, Inertial Navigation Unit, Defense Advanced Global Positioning System Receiver (DAGR), Power Distribution Unit, and Rugged Handheld Computer Unit (RHC) Forward Observer Software (FOS).

**Other Armored Knight specifications:**
**Crew:** Three COLT members
**Combat loaded weight:** Approximately 15 tons
**Maximum speed:** 63 miles per hour
**Cruising range:** 440 miles
**Target location accuracy:** Less than 20 meters circular error probable

## SYSTEM INTERDEPENDENCIES

**In this Publication**

Advanced Field Artillery Tactical Data System (AFATDS), Force XXI Battle Command Brigade and Below (FBCB2)

**Other Major Interdependencies**

FS3, FOS

## PROGRAM STATUS

- **FY11:** Cumulative total of 370 M1200 Armored Knight vehicle systems produced out of 465 vehicle systems procured, with FY11 being the last procurement FY, meeting Army Acquisition Objective of 465s

## PROJECTED ACTIVITIES

- **FY12:** Complete Validation of Targeting Under Armor (TUA), increased force protection/survivability capability for M1200 Armored Knight
- **1QFY13:** Procure TUA retrofit kits for M1200 AK fleet retrofit and field M1200 TUAs to next deploying units in HBCTs/IBCTs/BfSBs in Active Component and Army National Guard
- **3QFY13:** Complete M1200 Armored Knight Production

ACQUISITION PHASE

Technology Development | Engineering and Manufacturing Development | Production and Deployment | Operations and Support

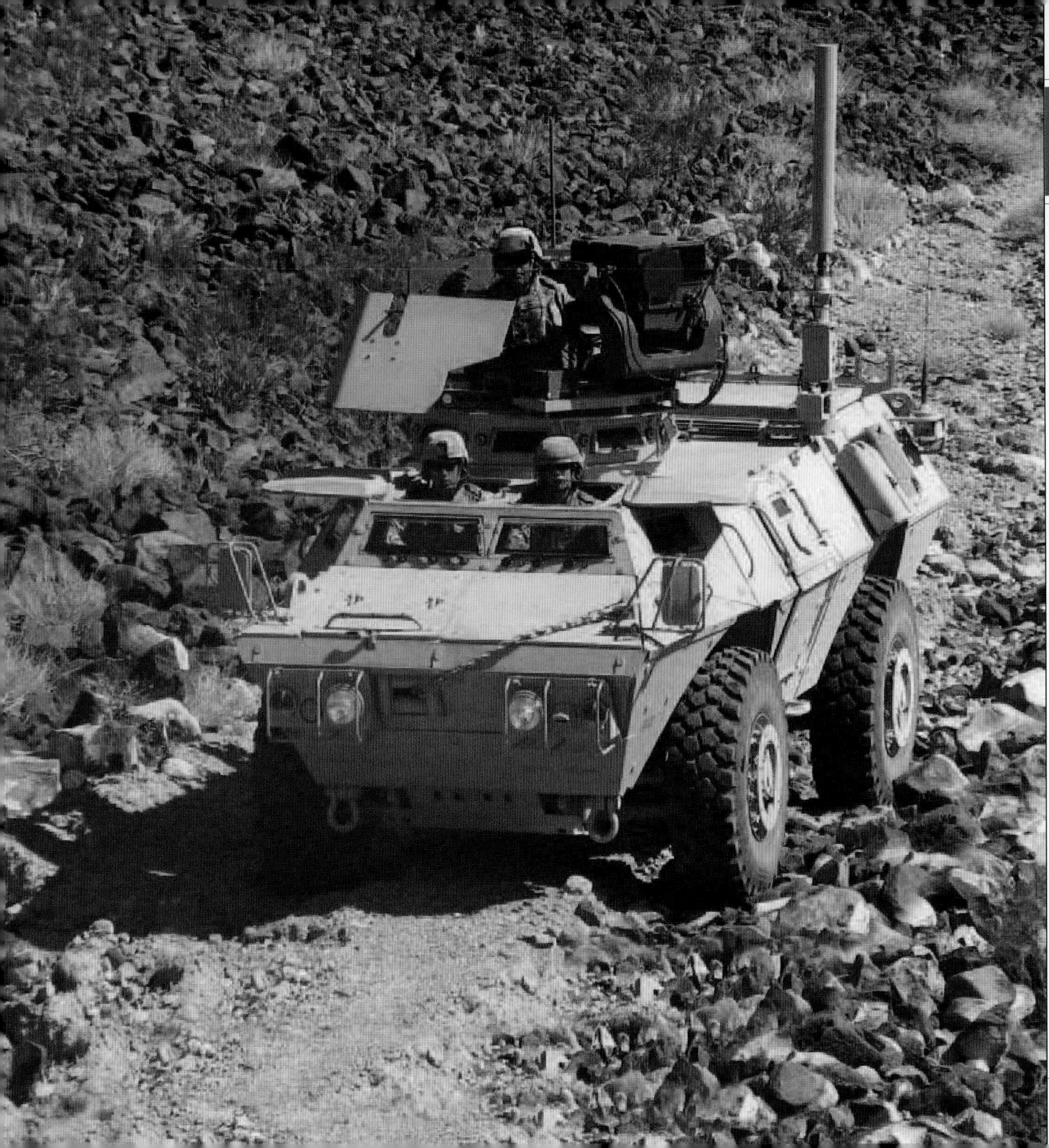



## Armored Knight

**FOREIGN MILITARY SALES**
None

**CONTRACTORS**
**M1117 ASV Hull:**
Textron Marine & Land Systems (New Orleans, LA)
**Precision Targeting Systems Production/Vehicle Integration:**
DRS Sustainment Systems Inc. (St. Louis, MO; West Plains, MO)
**FS3 Sensor:**
Raytheon (McKinney, TX)
**Inertial Navigation Unit:**
Honeywell (Clearwater, FL)
**Common Display Unit:**
DRS Tactical Systems (Melbourne, FL)

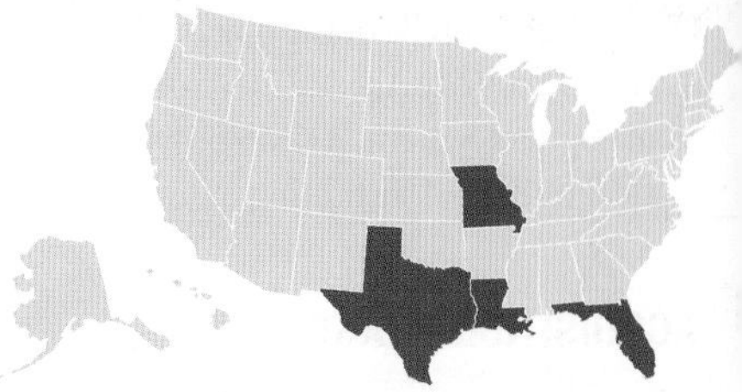

# Army Key Management System (AKMS)

## INVESTMENT COMPONENT

Modernization
Recapitalization
Maintenance

## MISSION

Automates the functions of communication securities (COMSEC) key management, control, and distribution; electronic protection generation and distribution; and signal operating instruction management to provide planners and operators with automated, secure communications at theater/tactical and strategic/sustaining base levels.

## DESCRIPTION

The Army Key Management System (AKMS) is a fielded system composed of three subsystems: Local COMSEC Management Software (LCMS), Automated Communications Engineering Software (ACES), and the Data Transfer Device/Simple Key Loader (SKL). Under the umbrella of the objective National Security Agency Electronic Key Management System, AKMS provides tactical units and sustaining bases with an organic key generation capability and an efficient secure electronic key distribution means. AKMS provides a system for distribution of COMSEC, electronic protection, and signal operating instructions (SOI) information from the planning level to the point of use in support of current, interim, and objective forces at division and brigade levels.

The LCMS (AN/GYK-49) workstation provides automated key generation, distribution, and COMSEC accounting. The ACES (AN/GYK-33), which is the frequency management portion of AKMS, has been designated by the Military Communications Electronics Board as the Joint standard for use by all Services in development of frequency management and cryptographic net planning and SOI generation. The SKL (AN/PYQ-10) is the associated support item of equipment that provides the interface between the ACES workstation, the LCMS workstation, the Warfighters' End Crypto Unit, and the Soldier. It is a small, ruggedized handheld key loading device.

AKMS supports the Army transition to NSA's Key Management Infrastructure (KMI), which will replace the current AKMS infrastructure to provide increased security. PD COMSEC has been involved in the transition planning and will procure and field the KMI Management Client (MGC) workstations and provide New Equipment Training (NET) and total life-cycle management support for the system.

## SYSTEM INTERDEPENDENCIES

### Other Major Interdependencies

AKMS systems are considered enabling systems for equipment/systems to receive key and frequency allotments

## PROGRAM STATUS

- **FY11:** AACES software upgrade version 3.0; SKL software upgrade version 7.0
- **FY11:** Initiate ACES hardware Refresh
- **FY11:** Initiate LCMS software upgrade version v5.1.0.5, Common User Application Software v5.1 and the Card Loader User Application Software v5.1
- **3QFY11:** Fielding of the Common User Application Software Training Simulator

## PROJECTED ACTIVITIES

- **FY12-FY14:** Continue to procure and field SKLs for Air Force, Navy, Foreign Military Sales, and other government organizations
- **2QFY12:** Complete refresh of ACES hardware
- **2QFY12:** Complete LCMS software upgrade version v5.1.0.5
- **FY12:** ACES software upgrade version 3.1; SKL software upgrade version 8.0
- **3QFY12:** KMI IOC
- **FY13:** ACES software upgrade version 3.2; SKL software upgrade version 9.0
- **FY13:** SKL upgrade to Common Load Device (CLD)
- **FY14:** ACES software upgrade version 3.3; SKL software upgrade version 10.0

## ACQUISITION PHASE

Technology Development | Engineering and Manufacturing Development | Production and Deployment | Operations and Support

## Army Key Management System (AKMS)

**FOREIGN MILITARY SALES**
Australia, Belgium, Bulgaria, Canada, Czech Republic, Estonia, Germany, Greece, Hungary, Latvia, Lithuania, Luxembourg, NATO, Netherlands, New Zealand, Norway, Poland, Portugal, Slovenia, Spain, Turkey, United Kingdom

**CONTRACTORS**
Sierra Nevada Corp. (SNC) (Sparks, NV)
Mantech Sensors Technology Inc. (MSTI) (Red Bank, NJ)
Science Applications International Corp. (SAIC) (San Diego, CA)
CACI (Eatontown, NJ)
Sypris (Tampa, FL)
CSS (Augusta, GA)

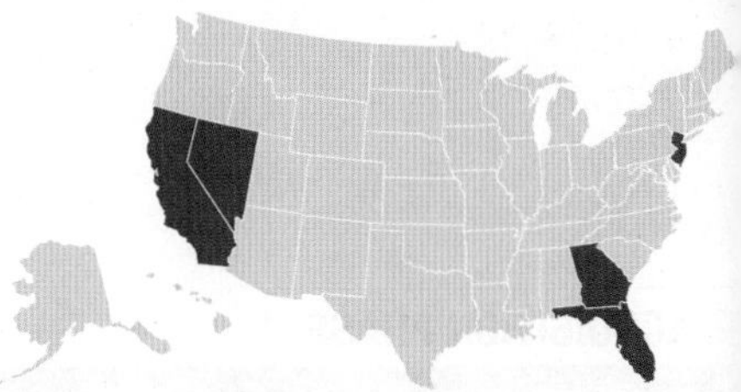

# Artillery Ammunition

INVESTMENT COMPONENT

Modernization

Recapitalization

Maintenance

## MISSION

Provides field artillery forces with modernized munitions to destroy, neutralize, or suppress the enemy by cannon fire.

## DESCRIPTION

The Army's artillery ammunition program includes 75mm (used for ceremonies and simulated firing), 105mm, and 155mm projectiles and their associated fuzes and propelling charges.

Semi-fixed ammunition for short and intermediate ranges, used in 105mm howitzers, is characterized by adjusting the number of multiple propelling charges. Semi-fixed ammunition for long ranges contains a single bag of propellant optimized for obtaining high velocity and is not adjustable. The primer is an integral part of the cartridge case and is located in the base. All 105mm cartridges are issued in a fuzed or unfuzed configuration. Both cartridge configurations are packaged with propellant.

Separate-loading ammunition, used in 155mm howizters, has separately issued projectiles, fuzes, propellant charges, and primers. After installing the appropriate fuze on the projectile, the fuzed projectile is loaded into the cannon along with the appropriate amount of propellant charges and a primer.

The artillery ammunition program includes fuzes for cargo-carrying projectiles, such as smoke and illumination, and bursting projectiles, such as high-explosives. This program also includes bag propellant for the 105mm semi-fixed cartridges and modular artillery charge system for 155mm howitzers.

## SYSTEM INTERDEPENDENCIES

None

## PROGRAM STATUS

- **4QFY11:** Type Classification of the 105mm M1130 high-explosive

## PROJECTED ACTIVITIES

- **2QFY12:** Full Materiel Release of the M1122 high-explosive projectile

ACQUISITION PHASE

Technology Development | Engineering and Manufacturing Development | Production and Deployment | Operations and Support

## Artillery Ammunition

**FOREIGN MILITARY SALES**
Australia, Canada, Israel, Lebanon

**CONTRACTORS**
General Dynamics Ordnance and Tactical Systems (Le Gardeur, Canada)
General Dynamics Ordnance and Tactical Systems (Valleyfield, Canada)
General Dynamics Ordnance and Tactical Systems-Scranton Operations (Scranton, PA)
American Ordnance (Middletown, IA)
McAlester Army Ammunition Plant (McAlester, OK)

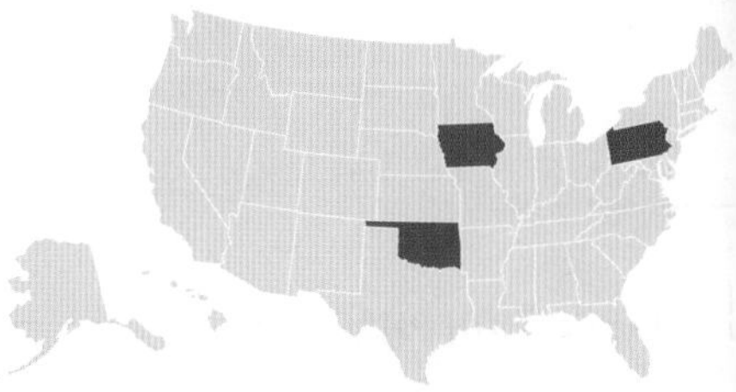

# Aviation Combined Arms Tactical Trainer (AVCATT)

INVESTMENT COMPONENT

Modernization

Recapitalization

Maintenance

## MISSION

Provides a collective training system to meet aviation training requirements and to support institutional, organizational, and sustainment training for Active and Reserve Army aviation units worldwide in combined arms training and mission rehearsal in support of full-spectrum operations.

## DESCRIPTION

The Aviation Combined Arms Tactical Trainer (AVCATT) is a mobile, transportable, multistation virtual simulation device designed to support unit collective and combined arms training. AVCATT provides six manned modules reconfigurable to any combination of attack, reconnaissance, lift, and/or cargo helicopters. There are four role player stations for battalion/squadron staff, combined arms elements, integrated threat, or friendly semi-automated forces (SAF). Exercise record/playback with simultaneous AAR capability is provided. The Non-Rated Crew Member Manned Module (NCM3, a sub-system of AVCATT) will be a mobile, transportable, multistation virtual simulation device designed to support training of non-rated crew members in crew coordination, flight, aerial gunnery, hoist, and slingload-related tasks.

The AVCATT single suite of equipment consists of two mobile trailers that house six reconfigurable networked simulators to support the Apache, Apache Longbow, Kiowa Warrior, Chinook, and Black Hawk. An after-action review theater and a battle master control station are also provided as part of each suite.

AVCATT builds and sustains training proficiency on mission-essential tasks through crew and individual training by supporting aviation collective tasks, including armed reconnaissance (area, zone, route); deliberate attack; covering force operations; downed aircrew recovery operations; Joint air attack team; hasty attack; and air assault operations. The system also has multiple correlated visual databases to include Iraq and Afghanistan.

AVCATT is fully mobile, capable of using commercial and generator power, and is transportable worldwide. The system is interoperable via local area network/wide area network with other AVCATT suites and the Close Combat Tactical Trainer (CCTT).

## SYSTEM INTERDEPENDENCIES

**Other Major Interdependencies**

AVCATT requires Synthetic Environment Core (SE Core) to provide terrain databases and virtual models; AVCATT requires the OneSAF program to provide the common SAF available to multiple virtual training simulators

## PROGRAM STATUS

- **1QFY11:** Block II Kiowa Warrior upgrade complete
- **4QFY11:** Fielding of the first Non-Rated Crew Member Manned Module (NCM3) to Ft. Campbell, KY

## PROJECTED ACTIVITIES

- **1QFY12:** SE Core and OneSAF integration complete; begin fielding new software baseline with new model/database/SAF capabilities
- **1QFY12:** Production and fielding of the 2nd NCM3 to Ft. Campbell, KY
- **2QFY12:** UH-60M and CH-47F upgrade contract awarded
- **2QFY12:** Production and fielding of 3rd, 4th, and 5th NCM3s

ACQUISITION PHASE

Technology Development | Engineering and Manufacturing Development | Production and Deployment | Operations and Support

## Aviation Combined Arms Tactical Trainer (AVCATT)

**AVCATT-A**
2 Trailer Suite

**NCM3 Trailer Diagram**

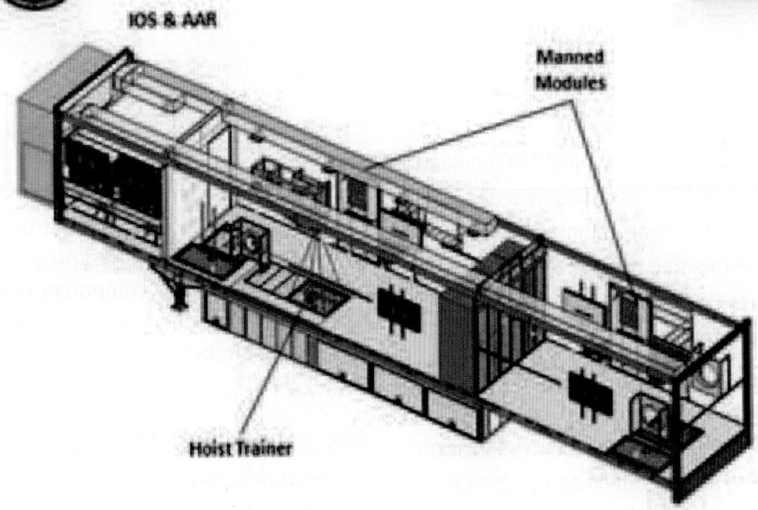


**Manned Simulator**

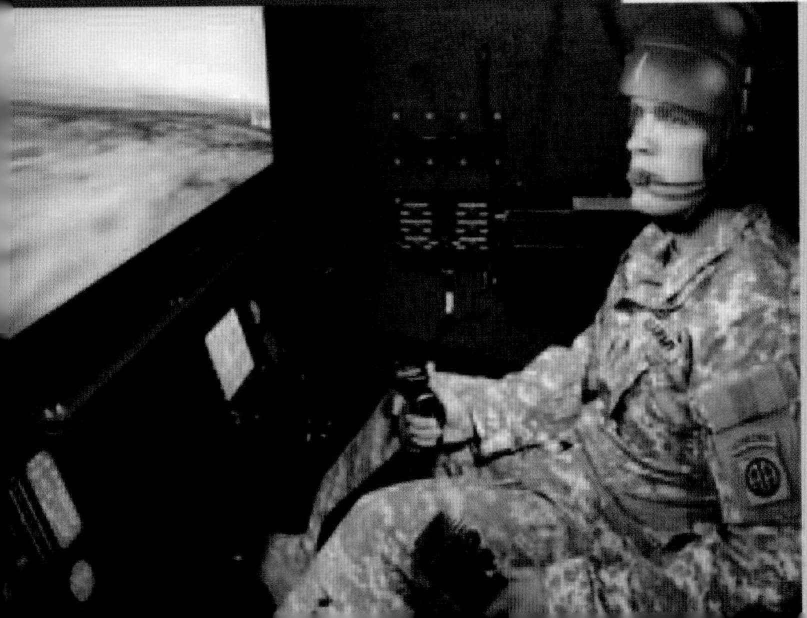

**Manned Simulators**

**Apache** AH-64A

**Kiowa Warrior** OH-58D

**Chinook** Ch-47D

**Black Hawk** UH-60A/L

**Apache Longbow** AH-64D

**FOREIGN MILITARY SALES**
None

**CONTRACTORS**
**AVCATT:**
L-3 Communications (Arlington, TX)
**NCM3:**
SAIC (Orlando, FL)
**Technology Refresh:**
AVT (Orlando, FL)

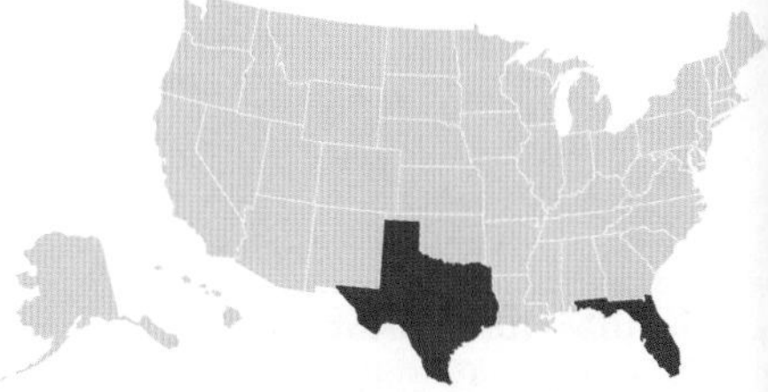

# Battle Command Sustainment Support System (BCS3)

**INVESTMENT COMPONENT**

- **Modernization**
- Recapitalization
- Maintenance

## MISSION

To provide integrated logistics command and control (C2) functionality onto a common mission command (MC) architecture and provide critical logistics C2 to Joint, interagency, intergovernmental, and multinational (JIIM) users in order to enhance the commander's and staff's ability to effectively conduct collaborative mission planning and execution across the full spectrum of military operations.

## DESCRIPTION

Battle Command Sustainment Support System (BCS3) enables commanders and their staffs to effectively conduct collaborative mission planning, coordination, control, and execution across the full spectrum of military operations. It is an automated sustainment support system that provides integrated functionality within a common Battle mission command architecture.

BCS3 supports sustainment operations by providing a COP with map-centric functionalities that enable end users to access, scale, and tailor critical sustainment information in near-real-time. Specifically, BCS3 offers its users access to a Logistics Reporting Tool (LRT) that provides a standardized format for submission of sustainment status reports, in-transit visibility (ITV) of supplies and equipment in the distribution pipeline, and asset visibility (AV) of resources with the units and supply points.

## SYSTEM INTERDEPENDENCIES

**In this Publication**

Movement Tracking System (MTS), Global Transportation Network (GTN)

**Other Major Interdependencies**

LIW/LOGSA, ILAP, SARSS, SASS-MOD, PBUSE, EMILPO, RFID, Joint-Automatic Identification Technology (JAIT), Radio Frequency (RF), Satellite Transponders and Enhanced ITV data feeds (Orbit One, Global Track, and SUPREME (Hawkeye) Class I shipments), Container Intrusion and Detection Devices (CIDD) Radio Frequency Tag capability, Integrated Data Environment/Asset Visibility and Global Transportation Network Convergence (IGC), Global Air Transportation and Execution Management System/Worldwide Port system (GATES/WPS), In-Transit Visibility (ITV) for Surface Deployment and Distribution Cargo (ISDDC), United States Marine Corps Last Tactical Mile System (LTM), Sustain Business System Modernization-Energy (BSM-E)

## PROGRAM STATUS

- **2QFY11:** SW Delivery BCS3-NM P16.1
- **3QFY11:** SW Delivery BCS3-NM P16.2

## PROJECTED ACTIVITIES

- **1QFY12:** SW Delivery BC10.02
- **1QFY14:** BC 13.0.0

**ACQUISITION PHASE**

- Technology Development
- Engineering and Manufacturing Development
- **Production and Deployment**
- Operations and Support

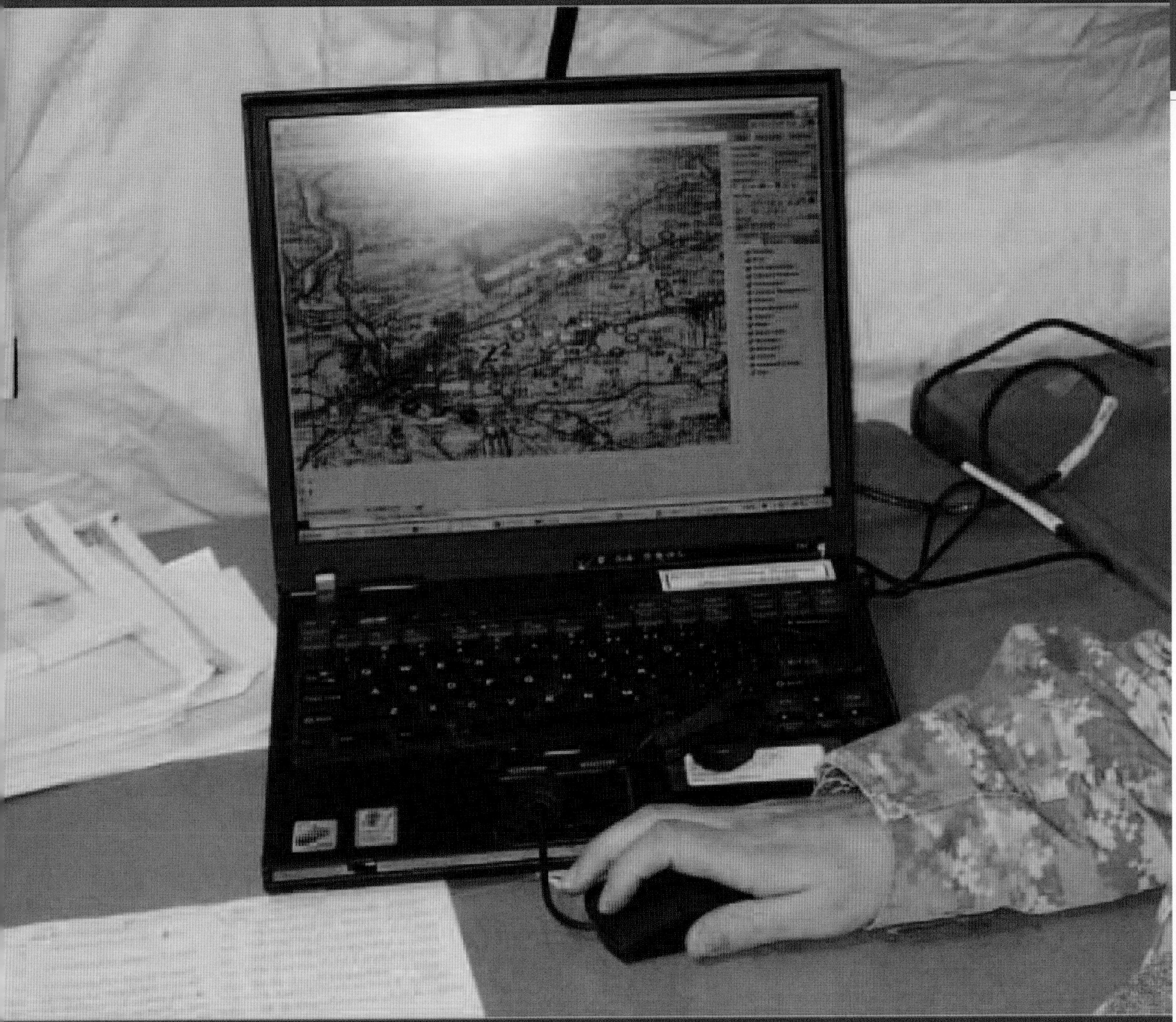



## Battle Command Sustainment Support System (BCS3)

**FOREIGN MILITARY SALES**
None

**CONTRACTORS**
**Software Development/Engineering Services:**
IBM (San Diego, CA)
**Program Support:**
CACI (Chantilly, VA)
Tapestry (Yorktown, VA)
LMI (McLean, VA)
**Hardware:**
Dell Computer Corporation (Round Rock, TX)
**New Equipment Training:**
Raytheon (Ft. Wayne, IN)

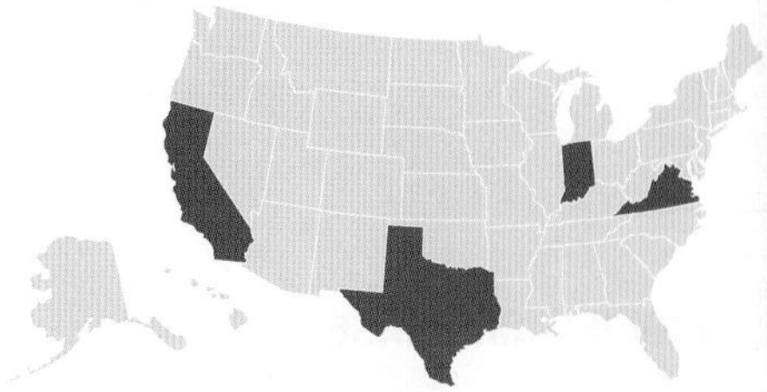

# Biometric Enabling Capability (BEC)

**INVESTMENT COMPONENT**

Modernization

Recapitalization

Maintenance

## MISSION

Serves as the Department of Defense authoritative biometric repository enabling identity superiority.

## DESCRIPTION

Biometric Enabling Capability (BEC), using an Enterprise System-of-Systems architecture, will serve as DoD's biometric repository, enabling multimodal matching, storing, and sharing in support of identity superiority across the Department.

## SYSTEM INTERDEPENDENCIES

**In this Publication**

Joint Personnel Identification Version 2 (JPIv2)

**Other Major Interdependencies**

Automated Identity Management System (AIMS), Department of Homeland Security IDENT, FBI Integrated Automated Fingerprint Identification System (IAFIS), U.S. Navy Personnel Identification Version 1 Program (PIv1), Special Operations Identity Dominance (SOID)

## PROGRAM STATUS

- **4QFY08:** DoD Biometrics Acquisition Decision Memorandum (ADM) directs Milestone B no later than FY10
- **1QFY09:** Biometrics in support of Identity Management Initial Capabilities Document approved by Joint Requirements Oversight Council
- **4QFY09:** DoD Biometrics ADM directs Analysis of Alternatives (AoA) to be completed 2QFY10
- **3QFY10:** DoD Biometrics ADM approved name change from Biometric Enterprise Core Capability (BECC) to Biometric Enabling Capability (BEC)
- **2QFY11:** DoD Biometrics ADM approved Biometric AoA final report; ADM also directed the current operational Next Generation-Automated Biometric Identification System to a full deployment decision (BEC Increment 0) in FY11; DoD Biometrics ADM directed Milestone B for BEC Increment 1 in FY12 and delegated Milestone Decision Authority to Army Acquisition Executive
- **3QFY11:** Milestone Decision Authority for BEC Increment 0 delegated to Program Executive Officer Enterprise Information Systems (PEO EIS)
- **4QFY11:** NG-ABIS Capability Production Document approved
- **4QFY11:** Full deployment decision for BEC Increment 0

## PROJECTED ACTIVITIES

- **2QFY12:** Biometrics BEC Increment 1 Capability Development Document approved
- **3QFY12:** Milestone B for BEC Increment 1, i.e., permission to enter system development and demonstration

**ACQUISITION PHASE**

Technology Development | Engineering and Manufacturing Development | **Production and Deployment** | Operations and Support

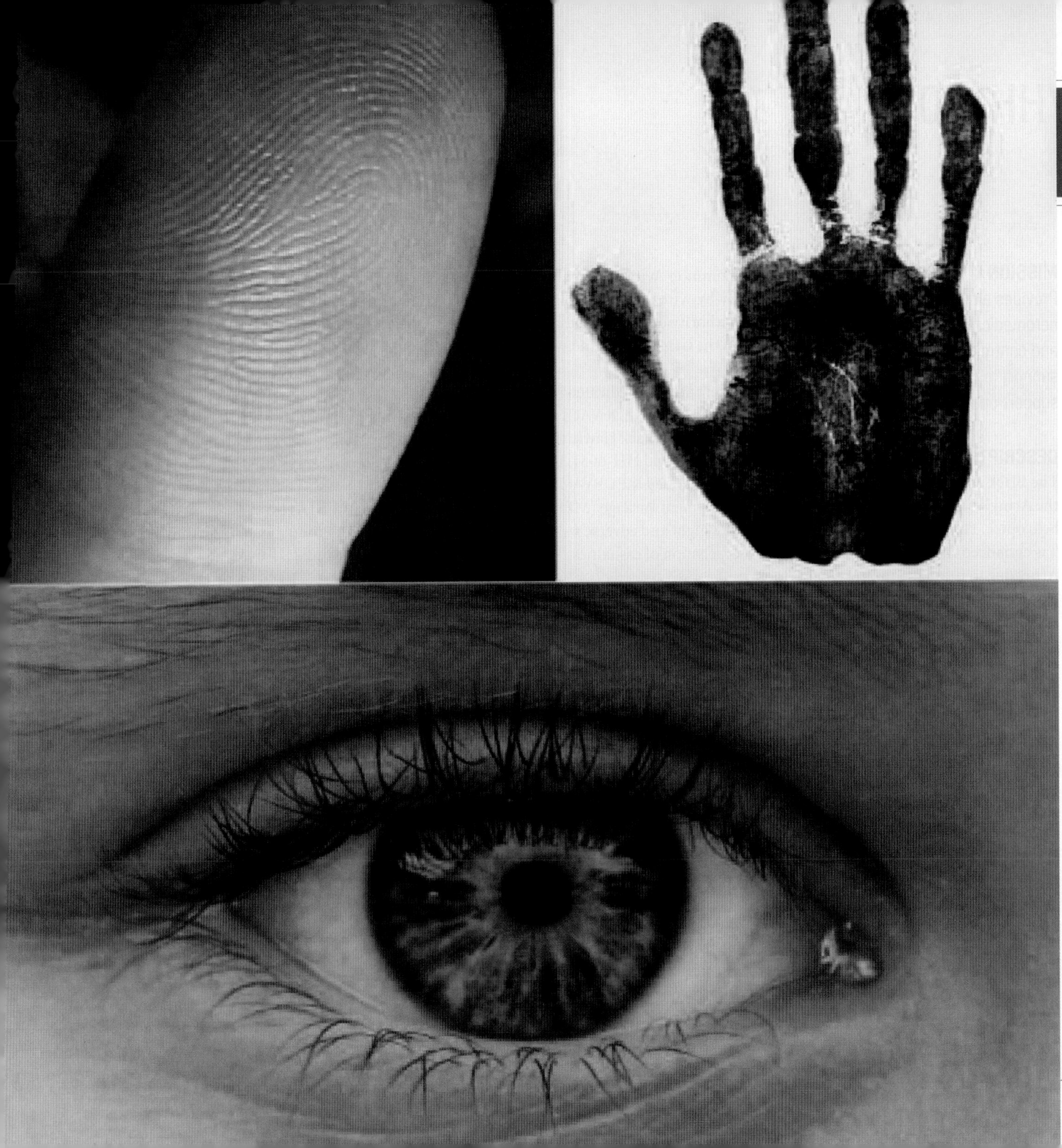



## Biometric Enabling Capability (BEC)

**FOREIGN MILITARY SALES**
None

**CONTRACTORS**
**Program Management Support Services:**
CACI (Arlington, VA)
The Research Associates (New York, NY)
**System Development and Integration:**
BEC Increment 0-System Integrator: Northrop Grumman
BEC Increment 1-System Integrator: To be determined

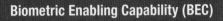

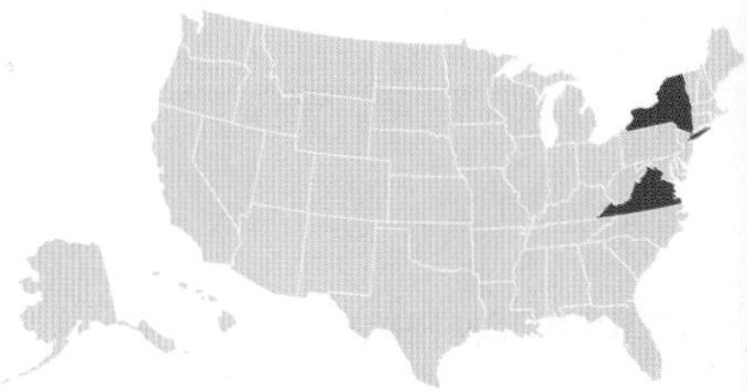

# Black Hawk/UH/HH-60

**INVESTMENT COMPONENT**

Modernization

Recapitalization

Maintenance

## MISSION

Provides air assault, general support, aeromedical evacuation, command and control, and special operations support to combat, stability, and support operations.

## DESCRIPTION

The Black Hawk (UH/HH-60) is the Army's utility tactical transport helicopter. The versatile Black Hawk has enhanced the overall mobility of the Army due to dramatic improvements in troop capacity and cargo lift capability. It will serve as the Army's utility helicopter in the Future Force.

There are multiple versions of the UH-60 Black Hawk: the original UH-60A; the UH-60L, which has greater gross weight capability, higher cruise speed, rate of climb, and external load; and the UH-60M, which includes the improved GE-701D engine and provides greater cruising speed, rate of climb, and internal load than the UH-60A and UH-60L versions. During FY10, the Army decided to continue only with developmental testing of the UH-60M P3I Upgrade components, including Common Avionics Architecture System, fly-by-wire flight controls, and full authority digital engine control upgrade to the GE-701D Engine.

There are also dedicated Medical Evacuation (MEDEVAC) versions of the UH-60 Black Hawk: the HH-60A, HH-60L, and HH-60M. Each includes an integrated MEDEVAC Mission Equipment Package (MEP) kit, providing day/night and adverse weather emergency evacuation of casualties.

On the asymmetric battlefield, the Black Hawk enables the commander to get to the fight quicker and to mass effects throughout the battlespace across the full spectrum of conflict. A single Black Hawk can transport an entire 11-person, fully equipped infantry squad faster than predecessor systems and in most weather conditions. The aircraft's critical components and systems are armored or redundant, and its airframe is designed to crush progressively on impact, thus protecting crew and passengers. The UH-60M is a digital networked platform with greater range and lift to support maneuver commanders through air assault, general support command and control, and aeromedical evacuation. Full rate production for the new-build UH-60M began in 2007, and the UH-60M and HH-60M MEDEVAC aircraft continue to be deployed in combat rotations.

## SYSTEM INTERDEPENDENCIES

**Other Major Interdependencies**

Blue Force Tracker (BFT)

## PROGRAM STATUS

- **Current:** Production and fielding of UH-60M and HH-60M aircraft

## PROJECTED ACTIVITIES

- **Continue:** Production and fielding of UH-60M and HH-60M aircraft
- **FY12:** Multiyear/Multiservice VIII contract award
- **FY12:** Materiel Development Decision for Improved Turbine Engine Program (ITEP)
- **FY13:** Milestone A for ITEP

**ACQUISITION PHASE**

Technology Development | Engineering and Manufacturing Development | Production and Deployment | Operations and Support

## Black Hawk/UH/HH-60

| | UH-60A | UH60L | UH60M |
|---|---|---|---|
| **MAX GROSS WEIGHT** (pounds): | 20,250 | 22,000 | 22,000 |
| **CRUISE SPEED** (knots): | 149 | 150 | 152 |
| **RATE CLIMB** (feet per minute): | 814 | 1,315 | 1,646 |
| **ENGINES** (2 each): | GE-700 | GE-701C | GE-701D |
| **EXTERNAL LOAD** (pounds): | 8,000 | 9,000 | 9,000 |
| **INTERNAL LOAD** (troops/pounds): | 11/2,640 | 11/2,640 | 11/3,190 |
| **CREW:** | two pilots, two crew chiefs | | |
| **ARMAMENT:** | two 7.62mm machine guns | | |

FOREIGN MILITARY SALES

**UH-60M:**
Bahrain, Jordan, Mexico, United Arab Emirates, Taiwan, Thailand, Sweden

**UH-60L:**
Brazil, Colombia, Egypt, Saudi Arabia, Thailand

CONTRACTORS

**UH-60M:**
Sikorsky (Stratford, CT)

**701D Engine:**
General Electric (Lynn, MA)

**Multifunction Displays:**
Rockwell Collins (Cedar Rapids, IA)

**Flight Controls:**
Hamilton Sundstrand (Windsor Locks, CT)

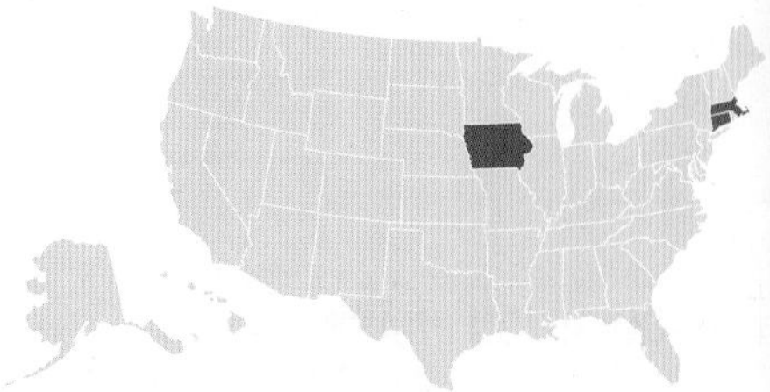

# Bradley Fighting Vehicle Systems Upgrade

**INVESTMENT COMPONENT**

Modernization

Recapitalization

Maintenance

## MISSION

Provides infantry and cavalry fighting vehicles with digital command and control capabilities, significantly increased situational awareness, enhanced lethality and survivability, and improved sustainability and supportability.

## DESCRIPTION

The Bradley M2A3 Infantry/M3A3 Cavalry Fighting Vehicle (IFV/CFV) features two second-generation, forward-looking infrared (FLIR) sensors—one in the Improved Bradley Acquisition Subsystem (IBAS), the other in the Commander's Independent Viewer (CIV). These systems provide "hunter-killer target handoff" capability with ballistic fire control. The Bradley A3 also has embedded diagnostics and an Integrated Combat Command and Control (IC3) digital communications suite hosting a Force XXI Battle Command Brigade and Below (FBCB2) package with digital maps, messages, and friend/foe information. These systems provide the vehicle with increased shared battlefield situational awareness (SA). The Bradley's position navigation with GPS, inertial navigation, and enhanced squad SA includes a squad leader display integrated into vehicle digital images and IC3.

## SYSTEM INTERDEPENDENCIES

**Other Major Interdependencies**

Army Battle Command System (ABCS), Blue Force Tracker (BFT), FM Voice-Advanced SINCGARS Improvement Program (ASIP) Radio, Forward Observer Systems (BFIST Only), Ground Mobile Radio System (GMRS), System of Systems Common Operating Environment (SOSCOE)

## PROGRAM STATUS

- **2QFY11:** Field Bradley A3 2nd Brigade, 1st Armor Division and 3rd Brigade, 3rd Infantry Division; Field ODS SA 30th Heavy Brigade Combat Team North Carolina Army National Guard
- **3QFY11:** Field Bradley A3 2nd Brigade, 3rd Infantry Division
- **4QFY11:** Field Bradley A3 1st Brigade, 2nd Infantry Division and 3rd Brigade, 4th Infantry Division; ODS fielded to TSS, Korea
- **4QFY11:** Field Bradley A3 1st Brigade, 3rd Infantry Division

## PROJECTED ACTIVITIES

- **1QFY12:** Army Prepositioned Stocks-4 (Korea) Field Bradley A3
- **2QFY12:** 4th Brigade, 1st Cavalry Division

**ACQUISITION PHASE**

Technology Development | Engineering and Manufacturing Development | Production and Deployment | Operations and Support

**SPEED:** 40 mph
**RANGE:** 250 miles
**PAYLOAD:** 6,000 pounds
**VEHICLE WEAPONS:** 25mm, TOW II, 7.62mm
**M2/M3A3 MMBF REQUIRED/ACTUAL:** 400/681
**DEPLOYABLE AIRCRAFT:** C17, C5

## Bradley Fighting Vehicle Systems Upgrade

**FOREIGN MILITARY SALES**
None

**CONTRACTORS**

**Prime:**
BAE Systems (York, PA; Santa Clara, CA)
DRS Technologies (Palm Bay, FL)
Raytheon (McKinney, TX)
L-3 Communications (Muskegon, MI)
Curtiss-Wright (Littleton, MA)
Elbit Systems of America (Ft. Worth, TX)

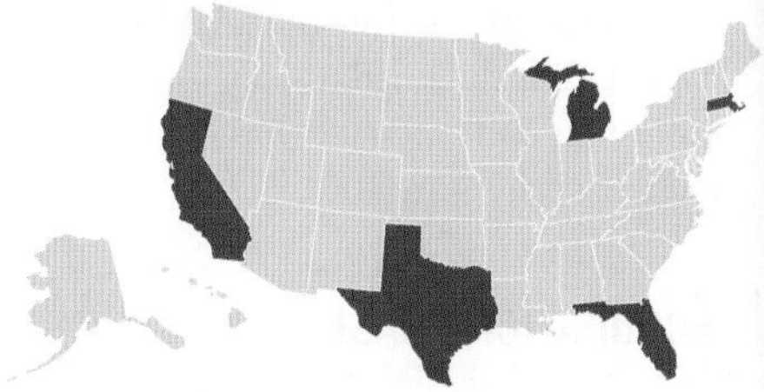

# Calibration Sets Equipment (CALSETS)

## INVESTMENT COMPONENT

Modernization

Recapitalization

Maintenance

## MISSION

Provides the capability to test, adjust, synchronize, repair, and verify the accuracy of Army test, measurement, and diagnostic equipment across all measurement parameters.

## DESCRIPTION

Calibration Sets Equipment (CALSETS) consists of calibration instrumentation housed in fixed facilities or contained within tactical shelters with accompanying power generation equipment. CALSETS provides support to maintenance units and area support organizations from brigade to multitheater sustainment operations and ensures a cascading transfer of precision accuracy originating from the U.S. National Institute of Standards. CALSETS is designed to plug into Army enterprise and battle networks. CALSETS tactical shelters are 100 percent mobile and transportable by surface mode or aircraft (C-130, C-5, and C-17). CALSETS is designed to calibrate 90 percent of the Army's test, measurement, and diagnostic equipment workload with an objective of 98 percent. CALSETS is configured in several set configurations.

**Secondary Transfer Standards Basic, AN/GSM-286:** This set consists of baseline instruments and components capable of supporting precision maintenance equipment in the physical, dimensional, electrical, and electronic parameters.

**Secondary Transfer Standards Augmented, AN/GSM-287:** This set consists of baseline instruments and augmented components with expanded capability to support a wider variety of precision maintenance equipment. It is capable of supporting precision maintenance equipment in the physical, dimensional, electrical, electronic, radiological, electro-optical, and microwave frequency parameters.

**Secondary Transfer Standards, AN/GSM-705:** This set configuration contains baseline instruments and augmented components designed for a tactical support mission. The platform applies a network-centric approach to precision maintenance support operations and data handling via an integrated data network, capable of sending calibration management system data to higher Army headquarters and obtaining calibration software updates. The set of instruments is contained in a 37-foot semi-trailer with a M1088A1 Medium Tactical Vehicle Tractor with an integrated 15-kilowatt power generator.

**Secondary Transfer Standards, AN/GSM-421:** This set is a subset of the baseline instruments designed to support up to 70 percent of the Army's high-density precision measurement equipment in forward areas. The system is modular and configurable to meet mission requirements and can operate in a true split-based mission posture. Designed for rapid deployment by surface or air, AN/GSM-421 will not radiate or be disrupted by electromagnetic interference. This set is contained in a shelter mounted on an M1152 High Mobility Multipurpose Wheeled Vehicle with an integrated 10-kilowatt power generator.

## SYSTEM INTERDEPENDENCIES

None

## PROGRAM STATUS

- **1Q-4QFY11:** Total-package fielding to National Guard TASMG units of CALSETS Secondary Transfer Standards, AN/GSM-705
- **Current:** Sustainment of CALSETS Secondary Transfer Standards Basic, AN/GSM-286; Secondary Transfer Standards Augmented, AN/GSM-287; Secondary Transfer Standards, AN/GSM-421 and AN/GSM-705
- **Current:** Fielding of CALSETS Secondary Transfer Standards, AN/GSM-705 (National Guard, TASMG)
- **Current:** System demonstration of an up-armor capable CALSETS Secondary Transfer Standards, AN/GSM-421(v2)

## PROJECTED ACTIVITIES

- **2QFY12:** AN/GSM-421(v2) limited user assessment
- **4QFY12:** AN/GSM-421(v2) first unit equipped

## ACQUISITION PHASE

Technology Development | Engineering and Manufacturing Development | Production and Deployment | Operations and Support

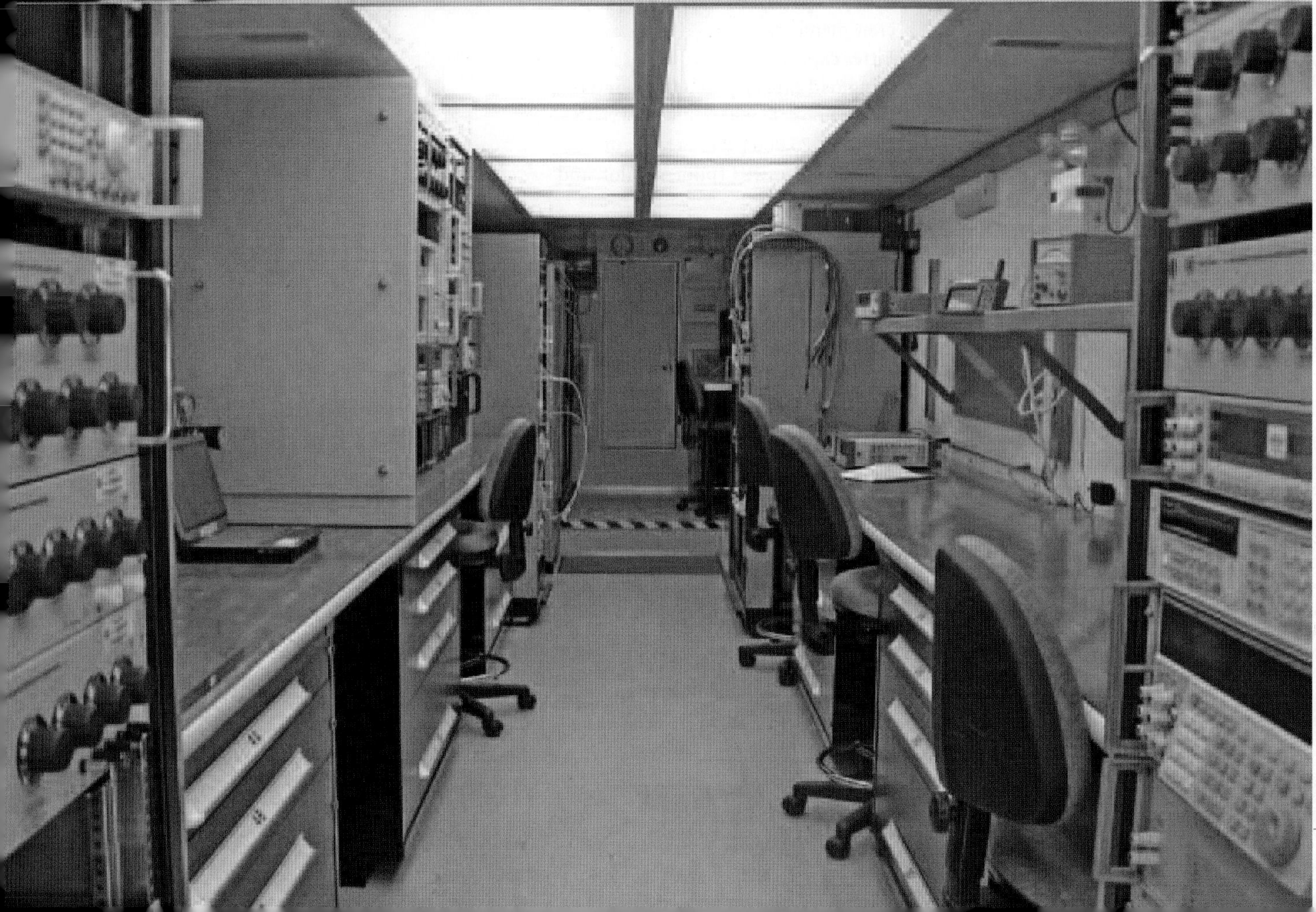

## Calibration Sets Equipment (CALSETS)

**FOREIGN MILITARY SALES**
Afghanistan, Egypt, Japan, Lithuania, Saudi Arabia, Taiwan, United Arab Emirates

**CONTRACTORS**
Dynetics Inc. (Huntsville, AL)
Agilent Technologies Inc. (Santa Clara, CA)
Fluke Corp. (Everett, WA)

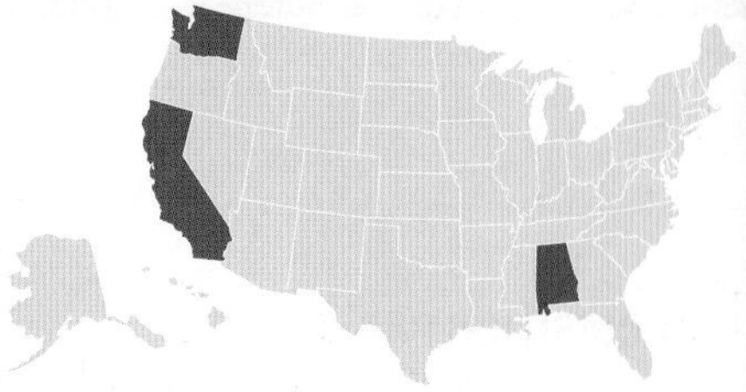

# CH-47F Chinook

## INVESTMENT COMPONENT

Modernization

Recapitalization

Maintenance

## MISSION

Supports a full spectrum of operations including disaster relief, homeland defense and security, and current overseas contingency operations with a Future Force system design.

## DESCRIPTION

The CH-47F Chinook is the Army's only heavy-lift cargo helicopter, supporting combat operations and many other critical operations other than war. The CH-47F aircraft has a suite of improved features such as an upgraded digital cockpit featuring the Common Avionics Architecture System (CAAS), a new monolithic airframe with vibration reduction, and the Digital Automatic Flight Control System (DAFCS), which provides coupled controllability for operations in adverse environments (reduced visibility, brown out, high winds). The CH-47F's common cockpit enables multiservice digital compatibility and interoperability for improved situational awareness, mission performance, and survivability, as well as future growth potential. The CH-47F has an empty weight of 24,578 pounds and a maximum gross weight of 50,000 pounds. The CH-47F can lift intra-theater payloads up to 16,000 pounds in high/hot environments.

- **Max gross weight:** 50,000 pounds
- **Max cruise speed:** 160 knots
- **Troop capacity:** 36 (33 troops plus 3 crew members)
- **Litter capacity:** 24
- **Slingload capacity:** 26,000 pounds center hook, 17,000 pounds forward/aft hook, 25,000 pounds tandem
- **Minimum crew:** 3 (pilot, copilot, and flight engineer)

## SYSTEM INTERDEPENDENCIES

**Other Major Interdependencies**

ARC-231, BFT, CXP (APX-118), CXP (APX-123), IDM, AMPS

## PROGRAM STATUS

- **2QFY07:** Complete Initial Operational Testing
- **4QFY07:** First unit equipped
- **1QFY08:** Multiyear procurement contract award
- **3QFY10:** Six units equipped

## PROJECTED ACTIVITIES

- **FY13:** Multiyear II contract award
- **1QFY18:** CH-47F fielding complete

## ACQUISITION PHASE

Technology Development | Engineering and Manufacturing Development | Production and Deployment | Operations and Support

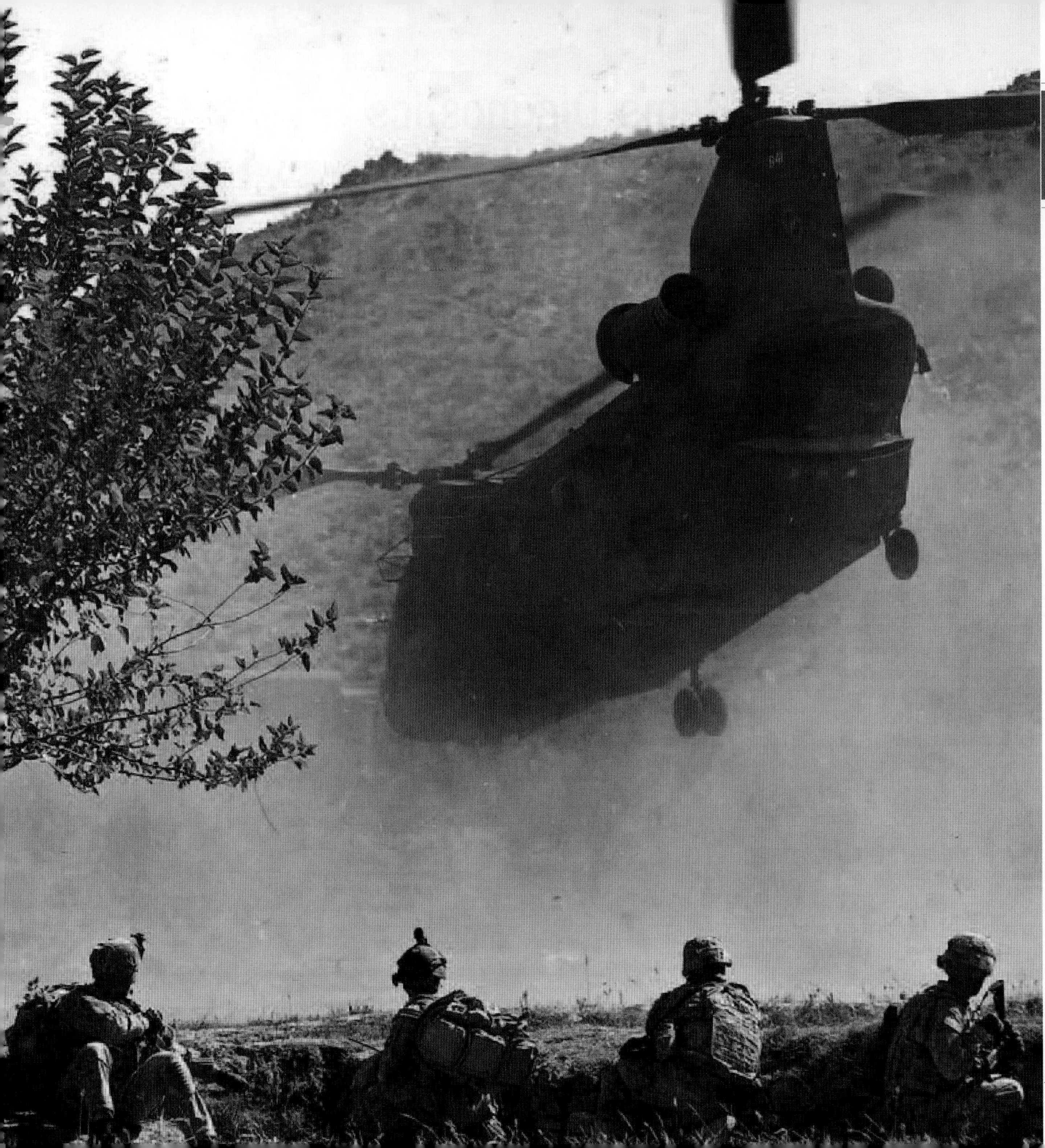



## CH-47F Chinook

**FOREIGN MILITARY SALES**
Australia

**CONTRACTORS**
**Aircraft and Recap:**
Boeing (Philadelphia, PA)
**Engine:**
Honeywell (Phoenix, AZ)
**Software:**
Rockwell Collins (Cedar Rapids, IA)
**Engine Controls:**
Goodrich (Danbury, CT)

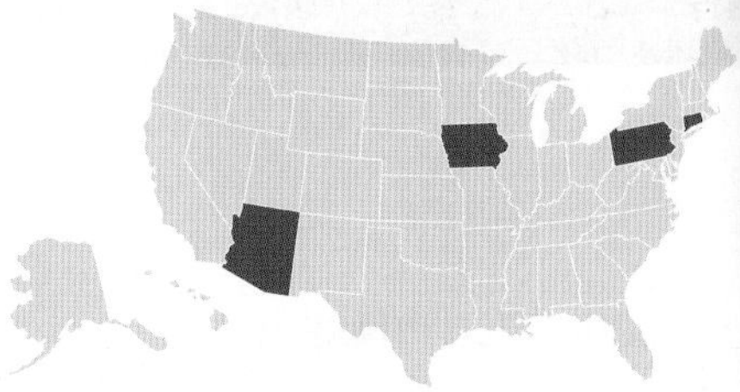

# Chemical Biological Medical Systems-Diagnostics

**INVESTMENT COMPONENT**

**Modernization**
Recapitalization
Maintenance

## MISSION

Delivers safe, effective, and robust medical products that protect U.S. forces against validated CBRN threats. CBMS applies government and industry best practices to develop or acquire Food and Drug Administration (FDA)-approved products within rigorously managed cost, schedule, and performance constraints.

## DESCRIPTION

The Joint Biological Agent Identification and Diagnostic System (JBAIDS) is a reusable, portable, modifiable biological agent identification and diagnostic system capable of rapid, reliable, and simultaneous identification of multiple biological agents and other pathogens of operational concern. The ruggedized and hardened system is configured to support deployed medical personnel with the ability to identify specific biological organisms from clinical and environmental sources and samples. The JBAIDS anthrax, tularemia, plague, H5N1, and Q-fever detection systems are FDA-cleared for diagnostic use. JBAIDS is operated throughout the combat zone by medical laboratory personnel.

## SYSTEM INTERDEPENDENCIES

None

## PROGRAM STATUS

- **1QFY10:** FDA clearance for Avian Flu (H5N1) in vitro diagnostic (IVD) kit
- **3QFY11:** FDA clearance for Q-Fever IVD Kit
- **4QFY11:** Complete Navy fielding (31 systems)

## PROJECTED ACTIVITIES

- **FY12-14:** Procurement of Next Generation Diagnostic System (NGDS)

**ACQUISITION PHASE**

Technology Development | Engineering and Manufacturing Development | **Production and Deployment** | Operations and Support

## Chemical Biological Medical Systems-Diagnostics

**FOREIGN MILITARY SALES**
None

**CONTRACTORS**
Idaho Technologies (Salt Lake City, UT)

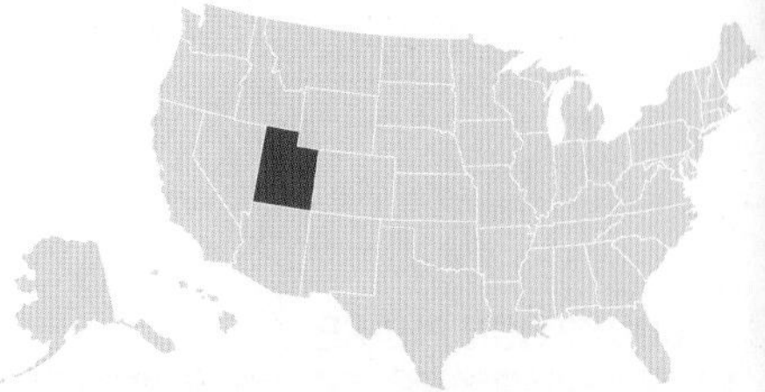

# Chemical Biological Medical Systems-Prophylaxis

INVESTMENT COMPONENT

Modernization

Recapitalization

Maintenance

## MISSION

Delivers safe, effective, and robust medical products that protect U.S. forces against validated CBRN threats. CBMS applies government and industry best practices to develop or acquire Food and Drug Administration (FDA)-approved products within rigorously managed cost, schedule and performance constraints.

## DESCRIPTION

Chemical Biological Medical Systems-Prophylaxis consists of the following components:

**Anthrax Vaccine Absorbed (AVA):**
The Anthrax Vaccine Absorbed is the only FDA-licensed anthrax vaccine in the United States that provides cutaneous, gastrointestinal, and aerosol infection by battlefield exposure to Bacillus anthracis.

**Recombinant Plague Vaccine (rF1V):**
The Recombinant Plague Vaccine is a highly purified polypeptide produced from non-sporeforming bacterial cells transfected with a recombinant vector from Yersinia pestis to prevent pneumonic plague.

**Recombinant Botulinum Toxin Vaccine A/B (rBV A/B):**
The Recombinant Botulinum Bivalent Vaccine is comprised of nontoxic botulinum toxin heavy chain (Hc) fragments of serotypes A and B formulated with an aluminum hydroxide adjuvant and delivered intramuscularly prior to potential exposure to botulinum toxins.

**Bioscavenger (BSCAV):**
The Bioscavenger program fills an urgent capability gap in Warfighter's defense against nerve agents by development of a nerve agent prophylactic that significantly reduces or eliminates the need for post-exposure antidotal therapy.

**Smallpox Vaccine System (SVS):**
The Smallpox Vaccine System Program provides both the ACAM2000™ smallpox vaccine and the Vaccinia Immune Globulin, Intravenous (VIGIV) to vaccinate and protect the Warfighter from potential exposure to smallpox. Both products are FDA-approved.

## SYSTEM INTERDEPENDENCIES

None

## PROGRAM STATUS

- **1QFY11:** rF1V manufacture scale-up and validation ongoing
- **1QFY11:** BSCAV In Process Review
- **3QFY11:** Plague Vaccine completes Phase 2b clinical trial volunteer vaccinations
- **4QFY11:** rF1V large-scale manufacturing validation
- **4QFY11:** rBV A/B large-scale manufacturing process validation complete
- **Current:** Smallpox and AVA in sustainment

## PROJECTED ACTIVITIES

- **1QFY12:** rBV A/B consistency lot manufacturing begins
- **1QFY12:** BSCAV Milestone Decision
- **2QFY12:** rBV A/B Milestone C Decision
- **3QFY12:** rF1V manufacturing process validation complete
- **4QFY12:** rF1V Phase 3 clinical trial begins

ACQUISITION PHASE

Technology Development | Engineering and Manufacturing Development | Production and Deployment | Operations and Support

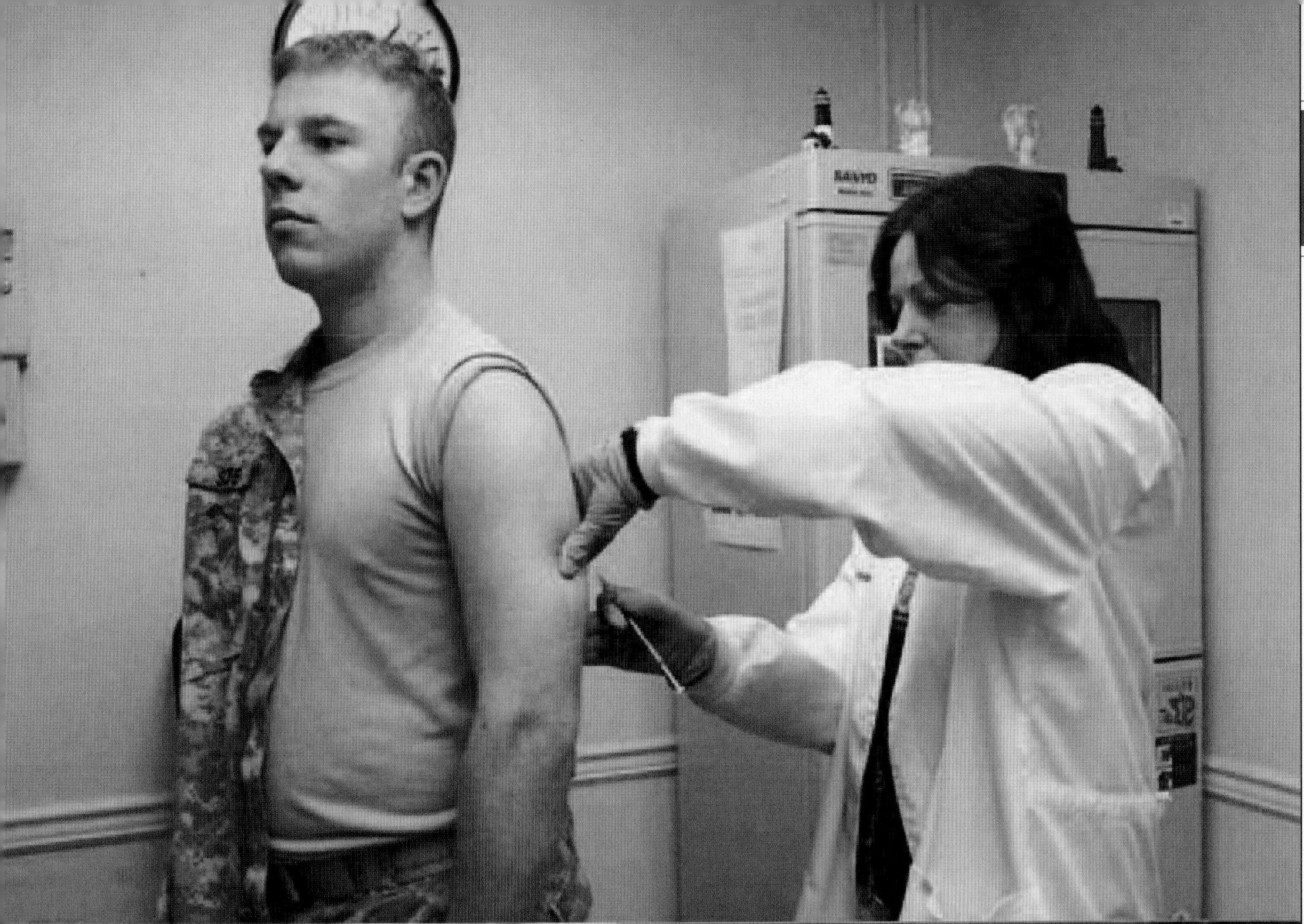

## Chemical Biological Medical Systems-Prophylaxis

**FOREIGN MILITARY SALES**
None

**CONTRACTORS**

**AVA:**
Emergent BioSolutions (Bioport) (Lansing, MI)

**rF1V:**
DynPort Vaccine (Frederick, MD)

**rBV A/B:**
DynPort Vaccine (Frederick, MD)

**BSCAV:**
To be determined

**SVS:**
Acambis plc. (Cambridge, MA)
Cangene Corp. (Winnipeg, Manitoba, Canada)

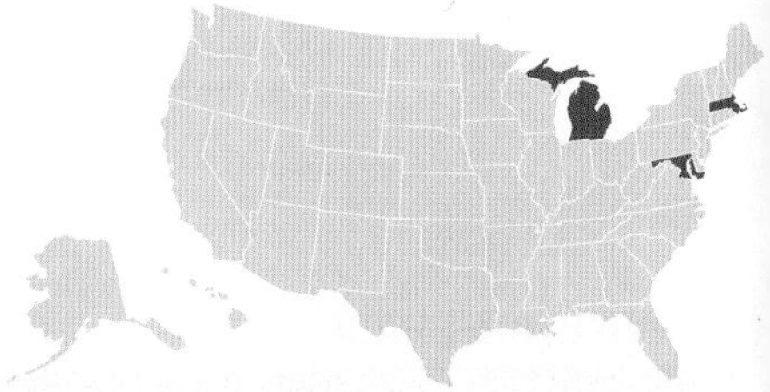

# Chemical Biological Medical Systems-Therapeutics

**INVESTMENT COMPONENT**

- Modernization
- Recapitalization
- Maintenance

## MISSION

Delivers safe, effective, and robust medical products that protect U.S. forces against validated CBRN threats. CBMS applies government and industry best practices to develop or acquire Food and Drug Administration (FDA)-approved products within rigorously managed cost, schedule, and performance constraints.

## DESCRIPTION

Chemical Biological Medical Systems-Therapeutics consists of the following components:

**Advanced Anticonvulsant System (AAS)** will consist of the drug midazolam in an autoinjector. The midazolam-filled autoinjector will replace the fielded Convulsant Antidote for Nerve Agents (CANA) that contains diazepam. Midazolam, injected intramuscularly, will treat seizures and prevent subsequent neurological damage caused by exposure to nerve agents. AAS will not eliminate the need for other protective and therapeutic systems.

**Improved Nerve Agent Treatment System (INATS)** is an enhanced treatment regimen against the effects of nerve agent poisoning. The new oxime component of INATS will replace 2-PAM in the Antidote Treatment Nerve Agent Autoinjector (ATNAA).

**Medical Radiation Countermeasure (MRADC)** Acute Radiation Syndrome (ARS) manifests primarily as hematopoietic (bone marrow), gastrointestinal, and cerebrovascular subsyndromes, depending on the dose of radiation received. The lead MRADC is Protectan CBLB502, a recombinant protein under investigation to reduce the risk of death following whole body irradiation. The portfolio of MRADC will, when used as a system, provide a robust capability to the Warfighter.

**Intracellular Bacterial Pathogens (IBP)** will mitigate the threat of illness or death, as well as lessen issues with performance degradation resulting from exposure.

**Hemorrhagic Fever Viruses (HFV)** medical countermeasures will mitigate the threat of illness or death, as well as lessen issues with performance degradation resulting from exposure. Due to the general severity of these diseases, HFV therapeutics will be administered to infected Warfighters while under direct medical observation.

## SYSTEM INTERDEPENDENCIES

None

## PROGRAM STATUS

- **1QFY11:** HFV Phase 1 trials begin
- **2QFY11:** In-life portion of RAMPART study (DoD autoinjectors complete)
- **1QFY11:** HFV Milestone B Decision
- **3QFY11:** IBP Phase 1 trials begin
- **4QFY11:** HFV Phase II Pivitol Animal Studies

## PROJECTED ACTIVITIES

- **1QFY12:** INATS Phase 1 Clinical Trial begins
- **1QFY13:** INATS Milestone B
- **1QFY13:** AAS Milestone C
- **1QFY13:** MRADC Milestone B

**ACQUISITION PHASE**

- Technology Development
- Engineering and Manufacturing Development
- Production and Deployment
- Operations and Support

## Chemical Biological Medical Systems-Therapeutics

**FOREIGN MILITARY SALES**
None

**CONTRACTORS**

**AAS:**
Meridian Medical Technologies (Columbia, MD)
Battelle Biomedical Research Center (Columbus, OH)

**INATS:**
Southwest Research Institute (San Antonio, TX)
Battelle Memorial Institute (Columbus, OH)

**MRADC:**
Osiris Therapeutics (Columbia, MD)

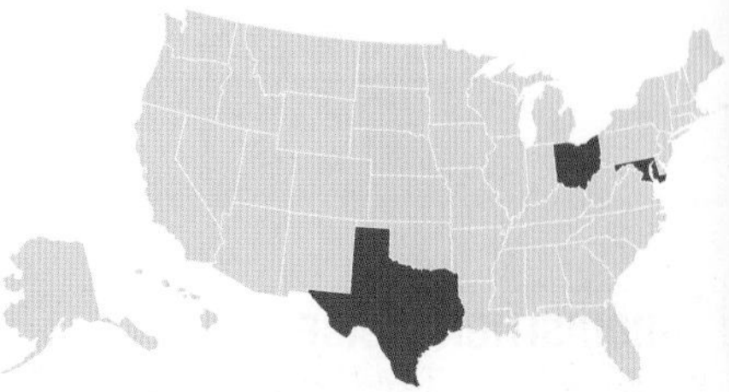

# Chemical Biological Protective Shelter (CBPS) M8E1

**INVESTMENT COMPONENT**

Modernization

Recapitalization

Maintenance

## MISSION

Provides medical personnel with a collective protection capability to perform their mission in a toxic-free area without the encumbrance of individual protective equipment in the forward battle area.

## DESCRIPTION

The Chemical and Biological Protective Shelter (CBPS) is a mobile, self-contained, rapidly deployable, chemically and biologically protected shelter that provides a contamination-free, environmentally controlled medical treatment area for U.S. Army medical units. CBPS provides the operating crew with a chemical, biological, and radiological (CBR)-protected toxic-free area (TFA) to execute their mission without the encumbrance of individual protective clothing/equipment. Key components include: 400-square-feet CBR protected, decontaminable, air beam-supported fabric shelter that allows for rapid deployable and strike; maintained internal temperature of 60° F to 90° F in environments from 40° F to +125° F; and onboard primary and fully redundant auxiliary power for uninterrupted power during CBR medical operations. Armor-equipped M1085A1R2 prime-mover provides crew protection during mobile/convoy operations. Provides 400 cubic feet per minute of CBR filtered air to maintain the TFA. CBPS will be assigned to trauma treatment teams/squads of maneuver battalions, medical companies of forward and division support battalions, nondivisional medical treatment teams, squads, division and corps medical companies, and forward surgical teams, and can provide a dual-use medical capability for homeland defense.

## SYSTEM INTERDEPENDENCIES

**In this Publication**

Family of Medium Tactical Vehicles (FMTV), Single Channel Ground and Airborne Radio System (SINCGARS)

**Other Major Interdependencies**

The shelter system is integrated onto an armored MTV

## PROGRAM STATUS

- **1-2QFY11:** First Article Testing (FAT)
- **2QFY11:** Follow-on Operational Testing (FOT)

## PROJECTED ACTIVITIES

- **1QFY12:** Production
- **2QFY12:** Type classification/ Materiel Release (TC/MR)

**ACQUISITION PHASE**

Technology Development | Engineering and Manufacturing Development | Production and Deployment | Operations and Support

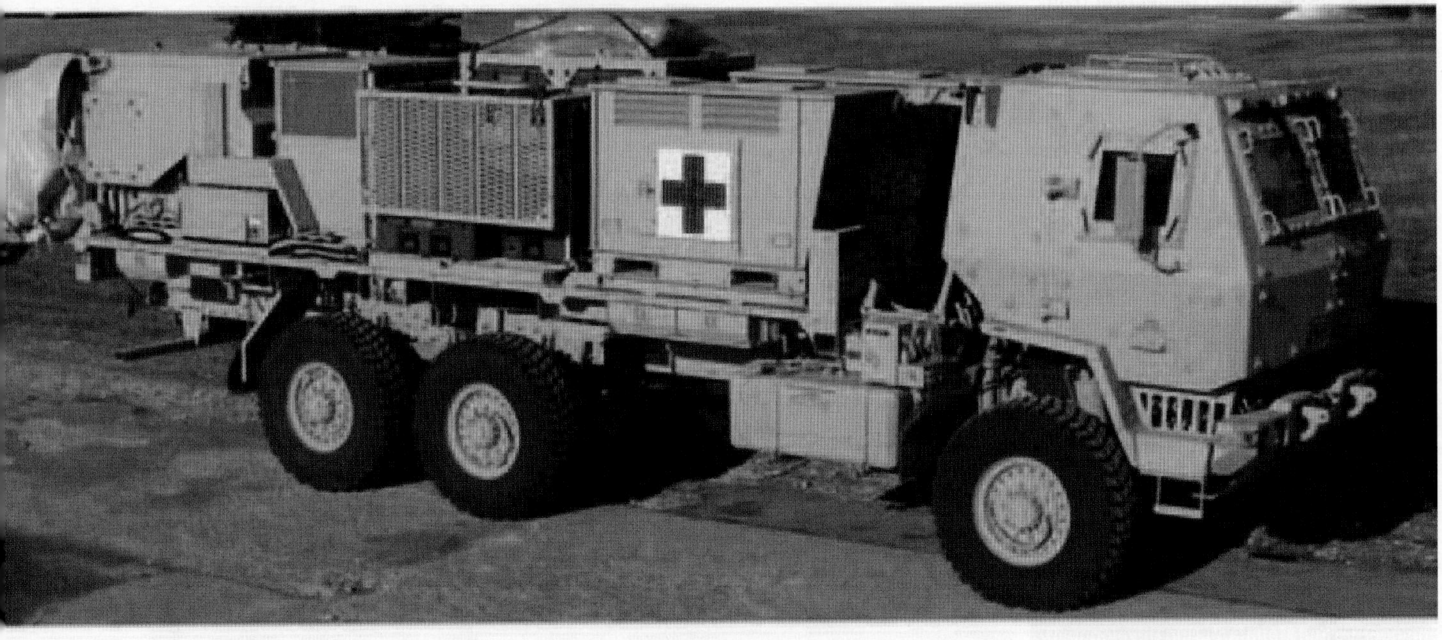

## Chemical Biological Protective Shelter (CBPS) M8E1

**FOREIGN MILITARY SALES**
None

**CONTRACTORS**
Smiths Detection Inc. (Edgewood, MD)

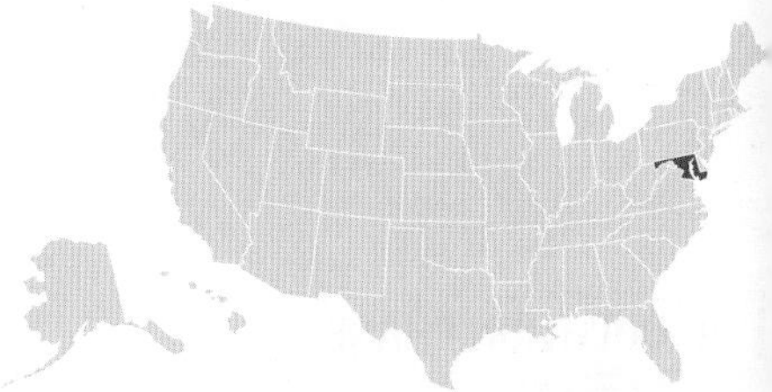

# Chemical, Biological, Radiological, Nuclear Dismounted Reconnaissance Sets, Kits, and Outfits (CBRN DR SKO)

**INVESTMENT COMPONENT**

- Modernization
- Recapitalization
- Maintenance

## MISSION

Provides chemical, biological, radiological, and nuclear (CBRN) reconnaissance in confined spaces and terrain inaccessible by traditional CBRN reconnaissance-mounted platforms/vehicles.

## DESCRIPTION

The Chemical, Biological, Radiological, Nuclear Dismounted Reconnaissance Sets, Kits, and Outfits (CBRN DR SKO) system consists of commercial- and government-off-the-shelf equipment that provides personnel protection from CBRN hazards, as well as detection, identification, sample collection, decontamination, marking, and hazard reporting of CBRN threats. The system is composed of handheld, man-portable detectors that detect and identify potential Weapons of Mass Destruction (WMD) and/or WMD precursors and determine levels of protection required to assess a sensitive site. The system supports dismounted reconnaissance, surveillance, and CBRN site-assessment missions to enable more detailed CBRN information reports for commanders. These site locations may be enclosed or confined, and are therefore inaccessible by traditional CBRN reconnaissance-mounted platforms. CBRN site assessments help planners determine if more thorough analysis is required to mitigate risks or gather intelligence on adversaries' chemical warfare agents, biological warfare agents, or toxic industrial material capabilities.

From 2008 to 2010, 27 DR SKO-like systems were fielded in support of Joint Urgent Operational Needs Statements (JUONS) to Central Command and the Services.

## SYSTEM INTERDEPENDENCIES

None

## PROGRAM STATUS

- **2QFY11:** Critical Design Review
- **2QFY11:** Milestone B Decision

## PROJECTED ACTIVITIES

- **2QFY11:** Operational Assessment
- **4QFY13:** Milestone C, Low-Rate Initial Production Decision
- **1-2QFY13:** Multiservice Operational Testing
- **4QFY13:** Full-Rate Production Decision

**ACQUISITION PHASE**

- Technology Development
- Engineering and Manufacturing Development
- Production and Deployment
- Operations and Support

## Chemical, Biological, Radiological, Nuclear Dismounted Reconnaissance Sets, Kits, and Outfits (CBRN DR SKO)

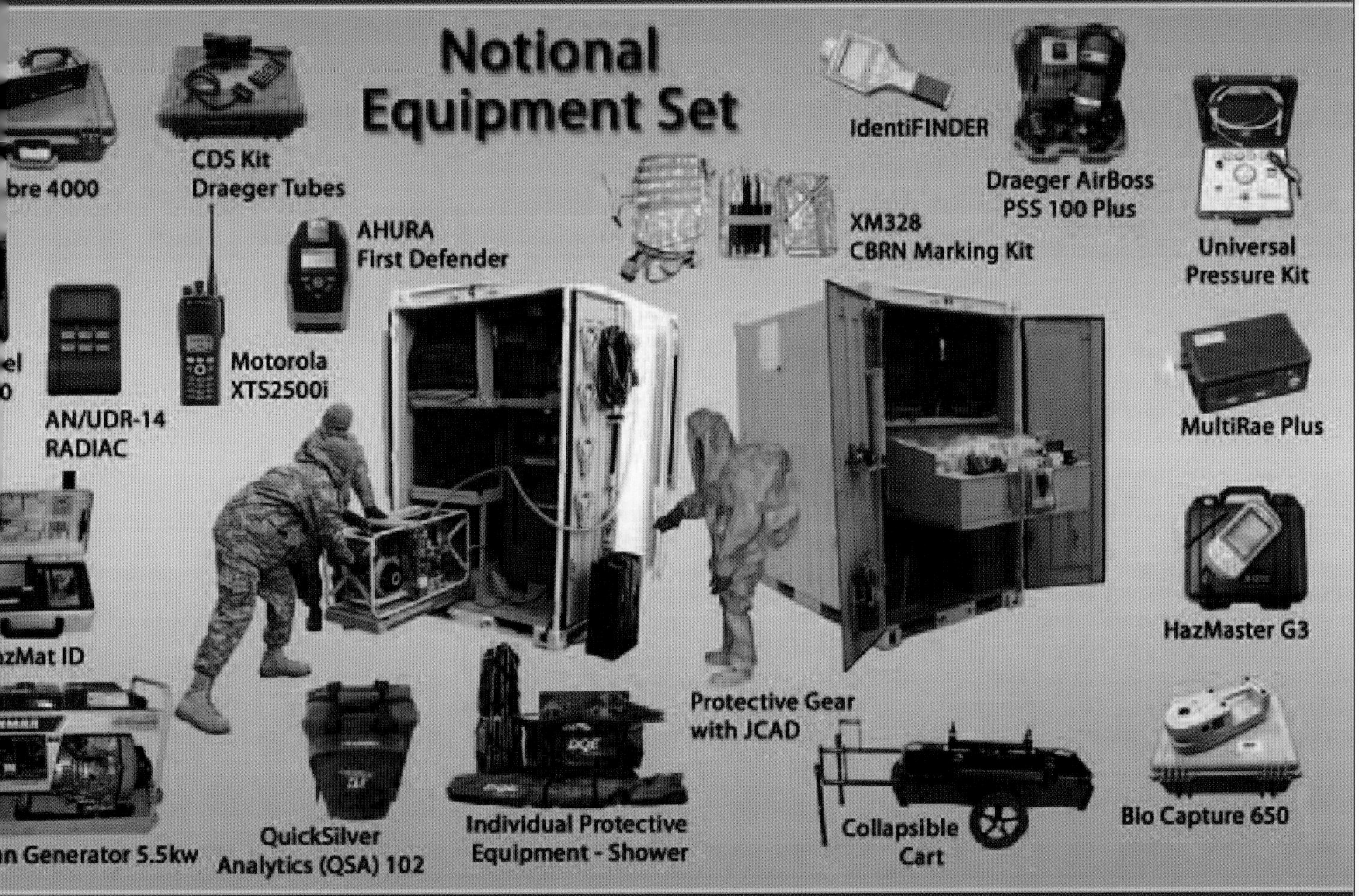


**FOREIGN MILITARY SALES**
None

**CONTRACTORS**
ICx Technologies (Pittsburgh, PA)

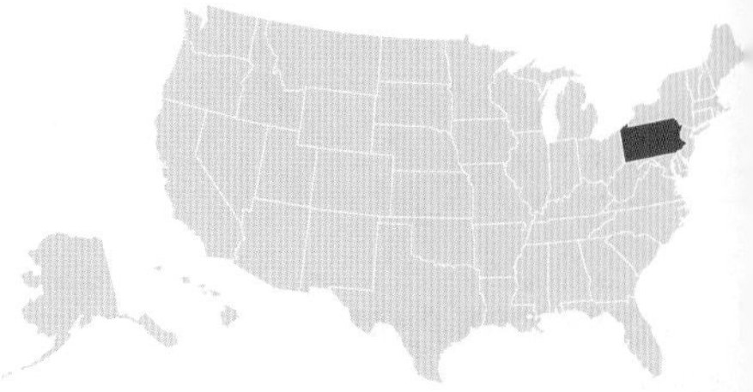

# Chemical Demilitarization

**INVESTMENT COMPONENT**

- Modernization
- Recapitalization
- Maintenance

## MISSION

Enhances national security by eliminating U.S. chemical warfare materiel (CWM) and supporting CWM responses, while ensuring maximum protection for the public, workers, and the environment.

## DESCRIPTION

The Chemical Materials Agency (CMA) mission is mandated by public law and includes the design, construction, systemization, operations, and closure of chemical agent disposal facilities in Alabama, Arkansas, Indiana, Maryland, Oregon, Utah, and Johnston Atoll in the South Pacific. Demilitarization operations have been completed in Indiana, Maryland, Arkansas, and Johnston Atoll. Stockpile disposal at locations in Colorado and Kentucky is the responsibility of the Assembled Chemical Weapons Alternatives Program, which reports directly to the Office of the Secretary of Defense.

CMA is also responsible for emergency preparedness activities at the chemical weapons storage depots and assessment and destruction of non-stockpile and recovered chemical warfare materiel.

## SYSTEM INTERDEPENDENCIES

None

## PROGRAM STA PROGRAM STATUS

- **1QFY11:** Completed final agent disposal campaign at Pine Bluff, AR
- **2QFY11:** CMA destroyed 85 percent of the chemical agent stockpile since entry into force of the Chemical Weapons Convention
- **3QFY11:** Tooele, UT completes scheduled plant operations, destroying last mustard ton container
- **3QFY11:** Anniston, AL completes final HD ton container campaign
- **4QFY11:** CMA exceeded the destruction of 88 percent of the chemical agent stockpile since entry into force of the Chemical Weapons Convention

## PROJECTED ACTIVITIES

- **4QFY12:** Complete final agent disposal campaign at Anniston, AL
- **2QFY12:** Complete final agent disposal campaign at Tooele, UT and Umatilla, OR
- **2QFY12:** CMA achieves 90 percent destruction of the chemical agent stockpile since entry into force of the Chemical Weapons Convention
- **2QFY12:** Complete closure of Pine Bluff, AR facility
- **2QFY12:** Complete closure of Anniston, AL facility

**ACQUISITION PHASE**

Technology Development | Engineering and Manufacturing Development | Production and Deployment | Operations and Support

## Chemical Demilitarization

**FOREIGN MILITARY SALES**
None

**CONTRACTORS**
URS Corp. (Anniston, AL; Pine Bluff, AR; Umatilla, OR; Tooele, UT)

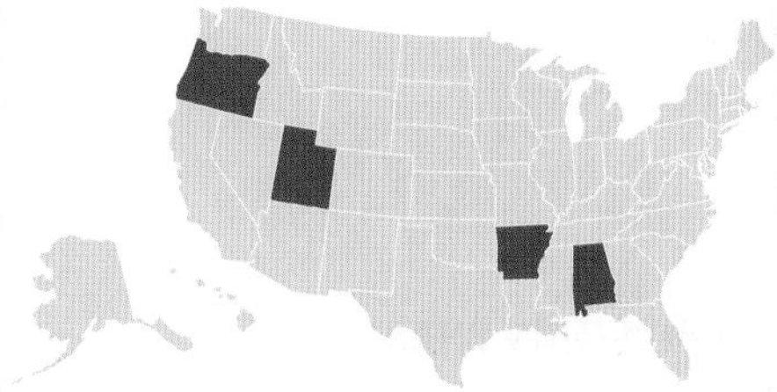

# Clip-on Sniper Night Sight (SNS)

**INVESTMENT COMPONENT**

- Modernization
- Recapitalization
- Maintenance

## MISSION

Enables the sniper to acquire and engage targets using the M110 Semi-Automatic Sniper System (SASS) during periods of limited visibility and at low-light levels.

## DESCRIPTION

The AN/PVS-29 Sniper Night Sight (SNS) is a lightweight, in-line weapon-mounted sight used in conjunction with the day optic sight on the M110 SASS. It employs a variable gain image intensification tube that can be adjusted by the sniper depending on ambient light levels. When used in conjunction with the M110 day optical sight, it provides for personnel-sized target recognition at quarter moon illumination in clear air to a range of 600 meters. The SNS has an integrated rail adapter that interfaces directly to the MIL-STD-1913 rail for quick and easy mounting to or dismounting from the weapon.

The SNS allows a sniper to maintain the current level of accuracy with the M110 and to deliver precise fire within 1 minute of angle. Use of the SNS does not affect the zero of the day optical sight and allows the M110 SASS to maintain bore sight throughout the focus range of the SNS and the M110 day optical sight.

**Weight:** < 3.5 pounds
**Focus range:** 25 meters to infinity
**Power:** One AA battery

## SYSTEM INTERDEPENDENCIES

None

## PROGRAM STATUS

- **FY11:** Competitive procurement; fielded to snipers supporting Operation Enduring Freedom and Operation New Dawn

## PROJECTED ACTIVITIES

- **FY12:** Continue to field in accordance with Headquarters Department of the Army guidance
- **FY13:** Continue to field in accordance with Headquarters Department of the Army guidance

**ACQUISITION PHASE**

- Technology Development
- Engineering and Manufacturing Development
- Production and Deployment
- Operations and Support

## Clip-on Sniper Night Sight (SNS)

**FOREIGN MILITARY SALES**
None

**CONTRACTORS**
Knight's Armament Co. (Titusville, FL)

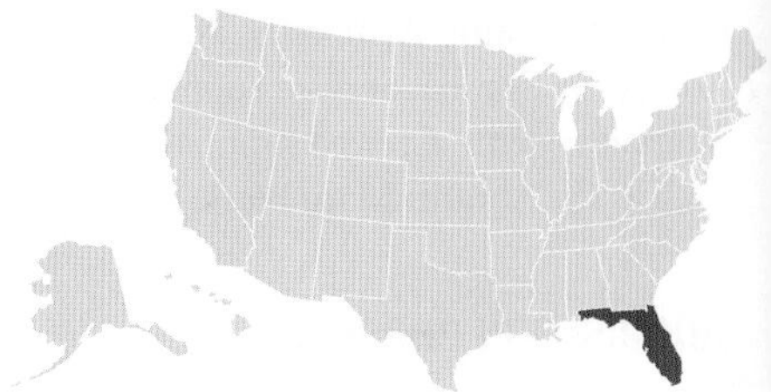

# Close Combat Tactical Trainer (CCTT)

**INVESTMENT COMPONENT**

Modernization

Recapitalization

Maintenance

## MISSION

Provides collective training for infantry, armor, mechanized infantry, cavalry units, and their associated staffs using manned module simulators within a virtual, synthetic environment, to improve readiness, provide more realistic collective training, and support urgent full-spectrum operations training requirements.

## DESCRIPTION

The Close Combat Tactical Trainer (CCTT) is a virtual, collective training simulator that is fully interoperable with the Aviation Combined Arms Tactical Trainer (AVCATT). Soldiers operate from simulators representing Dismounted Infantry, Mechanized Infantry/Tank, Company Teams, Armored Cavalry Troops, or Combat Service Support weapon systems. Crewed simulators, such as the Abrams Main Battle Tank, the Bradley Fighting Vehicle, the High Mobility Multipurpose Wheeled Vehicle (HMMWV), the Heavy Expanded Mobility Tactical Truck (HEMTT), and the M113A3 Armored Personnel Carrier offer sufficient fidelity for collective mission training. Modular components include the Reconfigurable Vehicle Simulator/Reconfigurable Vehicle Tactical Trainer (RVS/RVTT), which simulates the HMMWV, the Armored Security Vehicle (ASV), and the HEMTT. An additional capability for CCTT instructors/operators and training units is the Mobile Theater After-Action Review (MTAAR). The newest addition to the CCTT family of simulators is Dismounted Soldier (DS), which will provide individual Soldiers, fire teams, and squad leaders a capability to train infantry and Improvised Explosive Device-Defeat (IED-D) tasks in a fully immersive, virtual environment.

Soldiers use command and control equipment to simulate the battle direction of artillery, mortar, combat engineers, and logistics units to support their training mission. A semi-automated forces (SAF) workstation provides supporting units (such as aviation and air defense artillery) and all opposing forces. All battlefield operating systems are represented, ensuring an effective simulation of a combat environment that encompasses daylight, night, and fog conditions. CCTT's virtual terrain databases cover 100 by 150 kilometers, 3.5 kilometers of active visual terrain, and eight kilometers of extended range for the M1A2 System Enhancement Program Abrams tank and the M2A3 Bradley Fighting Vehicle. CCTT supports training of both Active Army and Army National Guard units at installations and posts in the U.S., Europe, and South Korea.

## SYSTEM INTERDEPENDENCIES

**Other Major Interdependencies**

CCTT requires Synthetic Environment Core (SE Core) to provide terrain databases and virtual models; the One Semi-Automated Force (OneSAF) will provide a common SAF through SE Core in the future

## PROGRAM STATUS

- **1QFY11:** Production and fielding of the RVTT to Ft. Sill, OK; Ft. Dix, NJ; Ft. Lee, VA; Ft. Hood, TX; and Ft. Campbell, KY
- **2QFY11:** Award of the Dismounted Soldier (DS) contract
- **2-4QFY11:** Production and fielding of the RVS/RVTT to Camp Shelby, MS; Ft. Jackson, SC; Camp Atterbury, IN; Camp Casey, South Korea; Camp Roberts, CA; and Ft. McCoy, WI

## PROJECTED ACTIVITIES

- **2QFY12:** Production and fielding of the fixed and mobile RVTT to Camp Bullis, TX; Ft. Bragg, NC; and Gowen Field, ID
- **2QFY12:** User Acceptance Testing for DS, fielding of DS test suites at Ft. Benning, GA; Ft. Bragg, NC; and Ft. Leonard Wood, MO
- **3QFY12-4QFY12:** Production and fielding of Low-Rate Initial Production DS suites to Ft. Bliss, TX; Ft. Hood, TX; and Ft. Campbell, KY
- **4QFY12-2QFY14:** Production and fielding of CCTT Concurrency Upgrades for 8th U.S. Army, CCTT Mobiles, Ft. Hood, TX; Ft. Bliss, TX; Ft. Stewart, GA; Ft. Benning, GA; Ft. Riley, KS; and Ft. Carson, CO

**ACQUISITION PHASE**

Technology Development | Engineering and Manufacturing Development | Production and Deployment | Operations and Support

## Close Combat Tactical Trainer (CCTT)

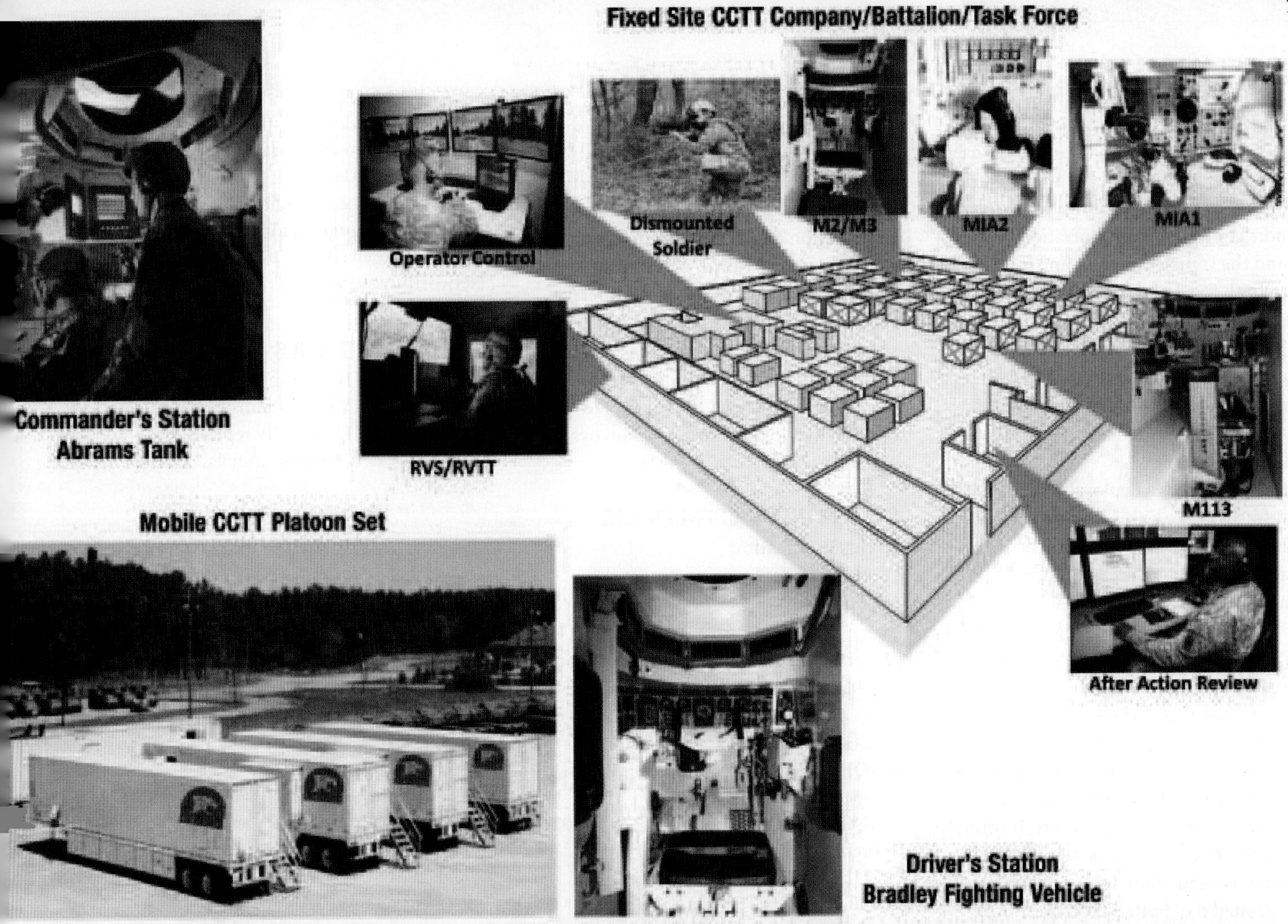


**FOREIGN MILITARY SALES**

None

**CONTRACTORS**

**Prime - RVS/RVTT:**
Lockheed Martin (Orlando, FL)
**Prime - Dismounted Soldier:**
Intelligent Decisions (Ashburn, VA)
**Prime - Post Deployment Software Support (PDSS):**
Kaegan Corporation (Orlando, FL)
**Prime - Visual System:**
Rockwell Collins (Salt Lake City, UT)
**Prime - Man-Year Equivalents:**
Electronic Consulting Services Inc. (Fairfax, VA)
**Sub - RVTT:**
DRS Mobile Environmental (Cincinnati, OH)
Meggitt Training (Suwanee, GA)
**Sub - Visual System:**
Dedicated Computing (Waukesha, WI)

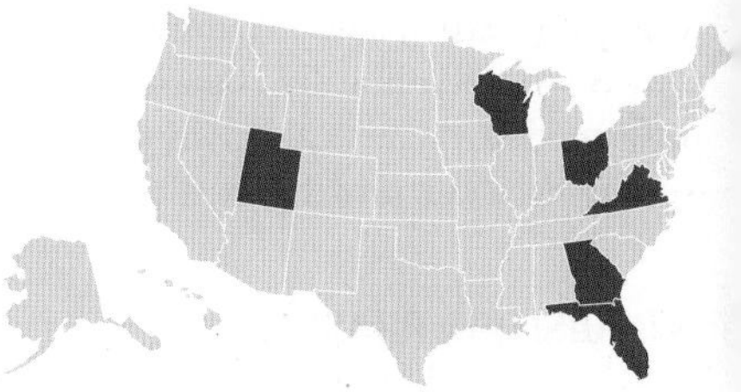

# Combat Service Support Communications (CSS Comms)

## INVESTMENT COMPONENT

- **Modernization**
- Recapitalization
- Maintenance

## MISSION

Provides a worldwide commercial satellite communications network, engineering services, Integrated Logistics Support, infrastructure, and portable remote terminal units in support of Army Combat Service Support (CSS) Logistics Management Information Systems operating from garrison or while deployed.

## DESCRIPTION

Combat Service Support Communications (CSS Comms) includes the Combat Service Support Automated Information Systems Interface (CAISI) and the Combat Service Support Satellite Communications (CSS SATCOM) system. CAISI allows current and emerging battlefield CSS automation devices to electronically exchange information via tactical networks. CAISI also interfaces with other battlefield and sustaining base automated systems. CAISI provides unit commanders and logistics managers an interface device to support CSS doctrine for full-spectrum operations. This capability supports a non-contiguous concentration of users and the transfer of real-time information in both fixed and mobile operating environments. CAISI allows deployed Soldiers to connect CSS automation devices to a secure wireless network and electronically exchange information via tactical or commercial communications.

CAISI employs a deployable wireless LAN infrastructure linking Army Logistics Information System computers in a seven square-kilometer area. It is certified in accordance with Federal Information Processing Standards (FIPS) 140-2 Level 2-approved encryption for use with sensitive information.

CSS SATCOM includes commercial off-the-shelf Ku-band auto-acquire satellite terminals, called Combat Service Support Very Small Aperture Terminals (CSS VSATs), repackaged in fly-away transit cases, along with a contractor-operated fixed infrastructure of four primary and three COOP teleports and high-speed terrestrial links that provide a highly effective, easy-to-use, transportable, SATCOM-based solution to CSS nodes. CSS SATCOM supports information exchange up to the Sensitive Information level, is rapidly deployable anywhere in the world, and is fully integrated into the Non-secure Internet Protocol Router Network (NIPRNET) segment of the Global Information Grid (GIG). CSS SATCOM eliminates the often dangerous need for Soldiers to hand-deliver requisitions via convoys in combat areas.

## SYSTEM INTERDEPENDENCIES

**In this Publication**

Global Combat Support System-Army (GCSS-Army)

**Other Major Interdependencies**

CAISI, CSS SATCOM

## PROGRAM STATUS

- **1QFY11:** Received Authority to Operate for CAISI
- **1QFY11:** Participated in GCSS-A test events
- **2QFY11:** Completed CSS VSAT TM and distributed to users
- **2QFY11:** Completed extended SATCOM COOP failover testing and performance evaluation
- **2QFY11:** Initiated major software upgrade for CAISI
- **3QFY11:** Initiated Condition Based Replacement program for CSS VSAT
- **3QFY11:** Received Certificate of Networthiness for CAISI

## PROJECTED ACTIVITIES

- **2QFY12-4QFY12:** Complete fielding of CAISI and CSS VSAT systems
- **2QFY12-4QFY12:** Identify replace modem for CSS VSAT terminals

## ACQUISITION PHASE

- Technology Development
- Engineering and Manufacturing Development
- **Production and Deployment**
- Operations and Support

## Combat Service Support Communications (CSS Comms)

**FOREIGN MILITARY SALES**
None

**CONTRACTORS**

**Equipment:**

Telos Corp. (Ashburn, VA)
LTI DataComm Inc. (Reston, VA)
Juniper Networks (Herndon, VA)
L-3 Global Communications Solutions Inc. (Victor, NY)
Segovia Global IP Services (Herndon, VA)

**Project support/training:**

Systems Technologies (Systek) Inc. (West Long Branch, NJ)
Tobyhanna Army Depot (Tobyhanna, PA)
Software Engineering Center-Belvoir (SEC-B) (Ft. Belvoir, VA)
U.S. Army Information Systems Engineering Command (USAISEC) (Ft. Huachuca, AZ)
CACI (Eatontown, NJ; Arlington, VA)
DISA Satellite Transmission Services-Global NETCOM (Ft. Huachuca, AZ)

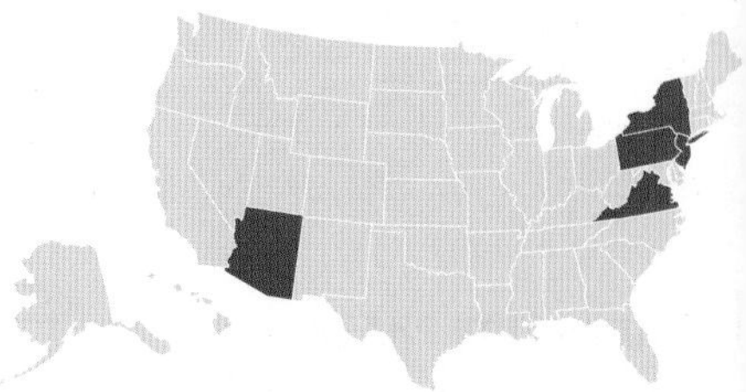

# Command Post Systems and Integration (CPS&I) Standardized Integrated Command Post Systems (SICPS)

**INVESTMENT COMPONENT**

- **Modernization**
- Recapitalization
- Maintenance

## MISSION

Provides commanders standardized and mobile command posts with a tactical, fully integrated, and digitized physical infrastructure to execute Networked-enabled Mission Command (NeMC) and achieve information dominance.

## DESCRIPTION

The Command Post Systems and Integration (CPS&I) product office provides commanders with standardized, mobile, and fully integrated command posts for the modular expeditionary force, including support for Future Force capabilities and Joint and coalition forces. The Standardized Integrated Command Post System (SICPS)-based command post is where commanders and their staffs collaborate, plan, and execute NeMC, maintain situational awareness using the Common Operational Picture (COP), and make decisions based on available information. Per the SICPS Capabilities Production Document (CPD), a family of Command Post Platforms (CPP) with standardized shelters, Command Center Systems (CCS), Command Post Communications Systems (CPCS), and Trailer Mounted Support Systems (TMSS) is currently being fielded to the Army's Active component, Army National Guard, and Army Reserve units.

SICPS provides the integrated NeMC platform and infrastructure to allow shared situational understanding of the COP based on the various Army and Joint command and control, communications, and network systems in the command post. Scalable and modular, SICPS supports echelons from battalion through Army Services Component Command by providing tactical flexibility to support all phases of operations. By integrating the tactical internet with current and future mission command capabilities, command post operations are revolutionized through a combination of state-of-the-art data processing, communications, and information transport methods to achieve information dominance.

## SYSTEM INTERDEPENDENCIES

**Other Major Interdependencies**

Warfighter Information Network-Tactical (WIN-T) Battle Command Common Services (BCCS) Server, Distributed Common Ground Systems (DCGS), Mobile Electric Power (MEP), Command Post of the Future (CPOF)

## PROGRAM STATUS

- **1QFY11-4QFY11:** Fielded SICPS to 45 brigade level or higher units, seven separate battalions, and several Battle Command Training Centers

## PROJECTED ACTIVITIES

- **QFY12-2QFY14:** Continue SICPS fielding and NET to 101 units and organizations in accordance with the Unit Set Fielding schedule

**ACQUISITION PHASE**

- Technology Development
- Engineering and Manufacturing Development
- **Production and Deployment**
- **Operations and Support**

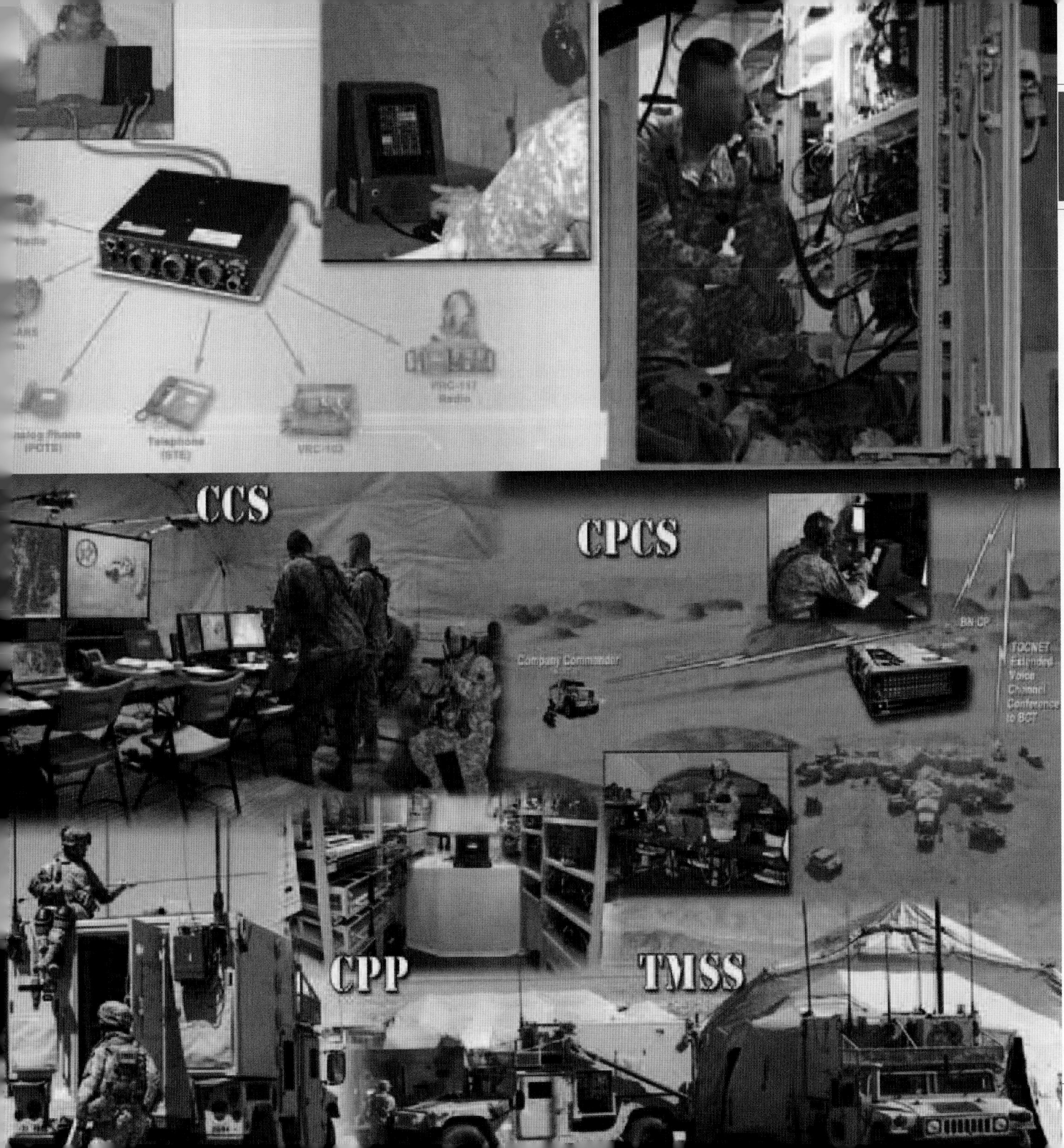


## Command Post Systems and Integration (CPS&I) Standardized Integrated Command Post Systems (SICPS)

**FOREIGN MILITARY SALES**
None

**CONTRACTORS**
**Command Post Platform/NET:**
Northrop Grumman (Huntsville, AL)
**Trailer Mounted Support System:**
Northrop Grumman (Huntsville, AL)
**SICPS AMCOM EXPRESS (SETA):**
Sigmatech Inc. (Huntsville, AL)
**Materiel Fielding:**
Tobyhanna Army Deport (Tobyhanna, PA)
**SICPS (TOCNET Intercommunications Systems):**
SCI Technology Inc. (Huntsville, AL)
**Common Hardware Systems:**
General Dynamics C4 Systems Inc. (Tauton, MA)

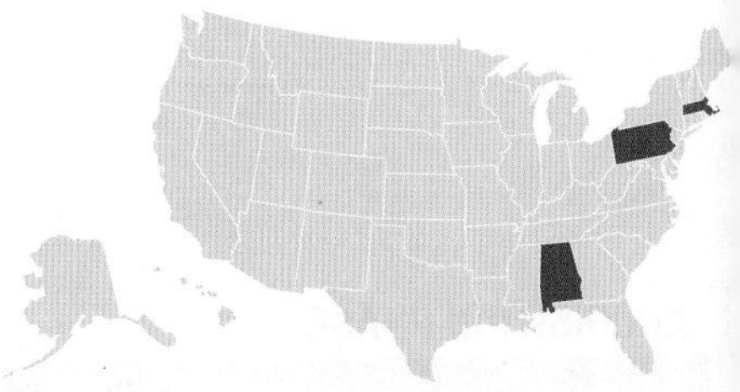

# Common Hardware Systems (CHS)

INVESTMENT COMPONENT

Modernization

Recapitalization

Maintenance

## MISSION

Provides state-of-the-art, fully qualified, interoperable, compatible, deployable, and survivable hardware for command, control, and communications at all echelons of command for the Army and other DoD Services with worldwide repair, maintenance, and logistics support through contractor-operated CHS Regional Support Centers and management of a comprehensive warranty program.

## DESCRIPTION

The Common Hardware Systems (CHS) program is the command and control enabler for Army Transformation, providing modularity, interoperability, and compatibility to support implementation of net-centricity. The CHS contract includes a technology insertion capability to continuously refresh the network-centric architectural building blocks, add new technology, and prevent hardware obsolescence. CHS products can be procured in four versions: version 1 (non ruggedized), version 1+ (moderate ruggedization of version 1), version 2 (ruggedized), and version 3 (fully rugged, MIL-SPEC Rugged Handheld Unit).

CHS also provides worldwide repair, maintenance, logistics, and technical support through strategically located contractor-operated regional support centers (RSC) for tactical military units and management of a comprehensive five-year warranty.

## SYSTEM INTERDEPENDENCIES

**Other Major Interdependencies**

Army Battle Command Systems (ABCS)

## PROGRAM STATUS

- **4QFY11:** CHS-4 contract award award with $3.7 billion ceiling
- **4QFY11:** Total Asset Visibility (TAV) contract award

## PROJECTED ACTIVITIES

- **FY12:** HEMP and NBC testing
- **FY12-FY14:** Continuing data collection for TAV database
- **FY12-FY14:** Manage the acquisition and delivery of CHS equipment in support of customer requirements

ACQUISITION PHASE

Technology Development | Engineering and Manufacturing Development | Production and Deployment | Operations and Support

## Common Hardware Systems (CHS)

**FOREIGN MILITARY SALES**
Australia, Colombia, Philippines

**CONTRACTORS**

**CHS-3 Production Contract:**
General Dynamics (Taunton, MA)

**CHS-4 Production Contract:**
To be determined

**Engineering:**
Engineering Solutions and Products (ESP) (Oceanport, NJ)
CACI (Eatontown, NJ)
Sensor Technologies (Red Bank, NJ)

**Logistics, Ordering:**
Engineering Solutions and Products (ESP) (Oceanport, NJ)

**Lab/Tech Support:**
Northrop Grumman (Eatontown, NJ)

**Consultant:**
Sensor Technologies (Red Bank, NJ)

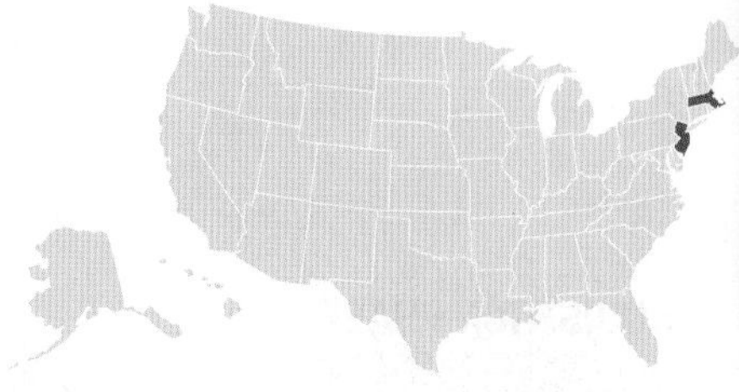

# Common Remotely Operated Weapon Station (CROWS)

**INVESTMENT COMPONENT**

- **Modernization**
- Recapitalization
- Maintenance

## MISSION

Enables Soldiers to acquire and engage targets with precision effects while protected inside an armored vehicle.

## DESCRIPTION

The Common Remotely Operated Weapon Station (CROWS) is a stabilized mount that contains a sensor suite and fire control software, allowing on-the-move target acquisition and first-burst target engagement. Capable of target engagement under day and night conditions, the CROWS sensor suite includes a daytime video camera, thermal camera, and laser rangefinder. CROWS is designed to mount on any tactical vehicle and supports the MK19 Grenade Machine Gun, M2 .50 Caliber Machine Gun, M240B Machine Gun, and M249 Squad Automatic Weapon.

CROWS also features programmable target reference points for multiple locations, programmable sector surveillance scanning, automatic target ballistic lead, automatic target tracking, and programmable no-fire zones.

Potential enhancements include integration of other weapons, escalation-of-force systems, sniper detection, integrated 360-degree situational awareness, increased weapon elevation, Javelin integration, and commander's display.

## SYSTEM INTERDEPENDENCIES

**Other Major Interdependencies**

CROWS mounts the MK19, M2, M240B, or M249 machine guns

## PROGRAM STATUS

- **Current:** Fielded over 5,000 CROWS under urgent materiel release in support of Operation New Dawn (OND) and Operation Enduring Freedom (OEF)
- **Current:** Integrated on multiple types of platforms
- **3QFY11:** Type Classified

## PROJECTED ACTIVITIES

- **Continue:** Field and sustain CROWS in support of OND and OEF
- **4QFY12:** Full Materiel Release

**ACQUISITION PHASE**

- Technology Development
- Engineering and Manufacturing Development
- **Production and Deployment**
- Operations and Support

## Common Remotely Operated Weapon Station (CROWS)

**FOREIGN MILITARY SALES**
None

**CONTRACTORS**
Kongsberg Defense & Aerospace
(Johnstown, PA)

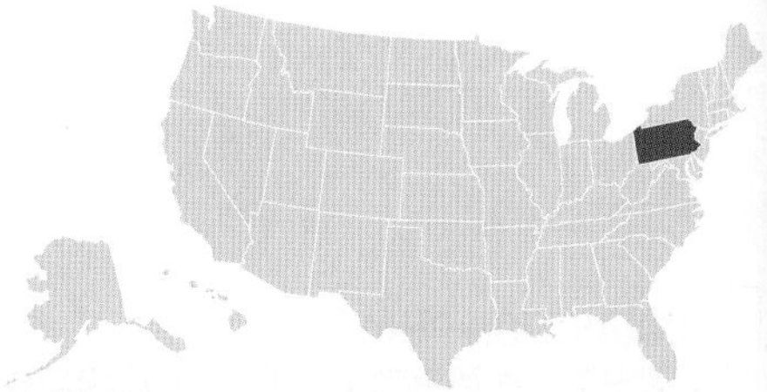

# Countermine

**INVESTMENT COMPONENT**

- Modernization
- Recapitalization
- Maintenance

## MISSION

Provides Soldiers and maneuver commanders with a full range of countermine capabilities, plus immediate solutions to counter improvised explosive devices (IEDs) and other explosive hazards, allowing the maneuver commander to achieve assured mobility on the battlefield.

## DESCRIPTION

The Countermine product line comprises several different systems:

- The **AN/VSS-6 Husky Mounted Detection System (HMDS)** is a ground-penetrating radar that upgrades the Vehicle Mounted Mine Detection (Husky) platform with the capability to detect and mark buried, low metal, and metallic-cased IEDs and anti-tank landmines.
- The **Vehicle Optics Sensor System (VOSS)** is a multisensor camera system that allows route-clearance and explosive ordnance disposal (EOD) Medium Mine Protected Vehicles (MMPV) the capability for on-the-move detection of IEDs.
- The **Interrogation Arm** provides route-clearance MMPVs the capability for mechanical standoff interrogation of suspected IEDs.
- The **AN/PSS-14 Mine Detecting Set** is a handheld multisensor mine detector.
- The **Area Mine Clearance System (AMCS)** is a flail system that destroys all types of landmines.
- The **Autonomous Mine Detection System (AMDS)** will detect, mark, and neutralize hazards from a small, robotic platform.

## SYSTEM INTERDEPENDENCIES

**Other Major Interdependencies**

AMDS, HMDS

## PROGRAM STATUS

- **Current:** AN/VSS-6 HMDS, VOSS, and IED Interrogation Army Joint Urgent Operational Needs (JOUNS) production and fielding continues in support of overseas contingency operations
- **Current:** AN/PSS-14 and MTRS full-rate production and Army-wide fielding continues through FY14

## PROJECTED ACTIVITIES

- **4QFY11:** AMCS Production Decision
- **4QFY12:** VOSS Milestone C
- **2QFY13:** AMDS Milestone B
- **2QFY13:** HMDS Milestone B
- **2QFY14:** HMDS Milestone C
- **2QFY14:** VOSS Full-Rate Production

**ACQUISITION PHASE**

- Technology Development
- Engineering and Manufacturing Development
- Production and Deployment
- Operations and Support

## Countermine

**FOREIGN MILITARY SALES**

**IED Interrogation Arm:**
Netherlands
**VOSS:**
Canada
**AN/VSS-6 HMDS:**
Canada

**CONTRACTORS**

**AN/PSS-14:**
L-3 CyTerra Corp. (Waltham, MA; Orlando, Fl)
**VOSS:**
Lockheed Martin Gyrocam Systems LLC (Sarasota, FL)
**IED Interrogation Arm:**
FASCAN International (Baltimore, MD)
**HMDS:**
NITEK (Sterling, VA)
**AMCS:**
A/S Hydrenna (Denmark)

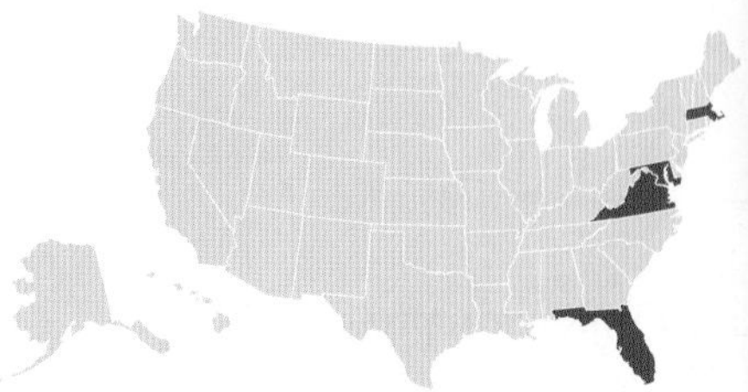

# Counter-Rocket, Artillery, Mortar (C-RAM)/ Indirect Fire Protection Capability (IFPC)

**INVESTMENT COMPONENT**

Modernization

Recapitalization

Maintenance

## MISSION

Integrates multiple Army- and DoD-managed systems and commercial-off-the-shelf systems with a command and control (C2) system to provide protection of fixed and semi-fixed sites from rockets and mortar rounds.

## DESCRIPTION

The Counter-Rocket, Artillery, Mortar (C-RAM) System-of-Systems (SoS) was developed in response to a Multi-National Force-Iraq Operational Needs Statement (ONS) that was validated in September 2004. An innovative SoS approach was implemented in which multiple DoD Program of Record systems were integrated with commercial-off-the-shelf items to provide seven C-RAM functions: sense, warn, respond, intercept, C2, shape, and protect.

C-RAM component systems are: Forward Area Air Defense Command and Control (FAAD C2) system and Air and Missile Defense Workstation for "C2"; Lightweight Counter Mortar Radar and Firefinder Radars for "sense"; Land-based Phalanx Weapon System (LPWS) for "intercept"; and Wireless Audio/Visual Emergency System and a wireless LAN for "warn." "Response" is provided thru C-RAM integration with Army/Joint mission command systems.

Using this SoS approach, C-RAM completed development, integration, and testing in April 2005, meeting the requirements of the ONS. The C-RAM system was fielded five months after initial funding and just eight months after ONS validation. C-RAM SoS is currently deployed in two theaters of operation.

In transition to the IFPC acquisition program, IFPC Increment 1 will field the C-RAM warn capability to all Army Brigade Combat Teams.

## SYSTEM INTERDEPENDENCIES

**Other Major Interdependencies**

Army and Marine Corps Battle Command Systems, Sentinel Radar

## PROGRAM STATUS

- **1QFY11:** LPWS theater upgrades complete
- **1QFY11-4QFY11:** C-RAM sense and warn fielding to Operation Enduring Freedom (OEF)
- **1QFY11:** Near-term C-RAM initiatives approved as a result of 2010 Air and Missile Defense (AMD) Capability Portfolio Review (CPR)
- **3QFY11:** C-RAM Program Directorate transition to PEO Missiles and Space
- **3QFY11:** C-RAM SoS demonstration
- **Current:** Sustainment of fielded C-RAM SoS capability

## PROJECTED ACTIVITIES

- **1QFY12:** Complete C-RAM sense and warn fielding to OEF
- **2QFY12:** Initiate C-RAM support to Department of State/Office of Security Cooperation-Iraq efforts
- **2QFY12:** Initiate development/test/integration for near-term C-RAM initiatives
- **2QFY12:** Conduct IFPC Increment 1 Operational Assessment
- **3QFY12:** IFPC Increment 1 Milestone C
- **4QFY13:** Field C-RAM intercept capability to 5-5 ADA Battalion
- **2QFY14:** Begin fielding C-RAM initiatives

**ACQUISITION PHASE**

Technology Development | Engineering and Manufacturing Development | Production and Deployment | Operations and Support

## Counter-Rocket, Artillery, Mortar (C-RAM)/Indirect Fire Protection Capability (IFPC)

**FOREIGN MILITARY SALES**
Australia, United Kingdom

**CONTRACTORS**

**Hardware/Integration/Fielding/ Contractor Logistics Support:**
Northrop Grumman (Huntsville, AL)

**LPWS:**
Raytheon Missile Systems (Tucson, AZ)

**Software Development/Maintenance:**
Northrop Grumman (Redondo Beach, CA)

**Common Hardware, Software:**
General Dynamics (Taunton, MA)

**Shelters and Training:**
Northrop Grumman (Huntsville, AL)

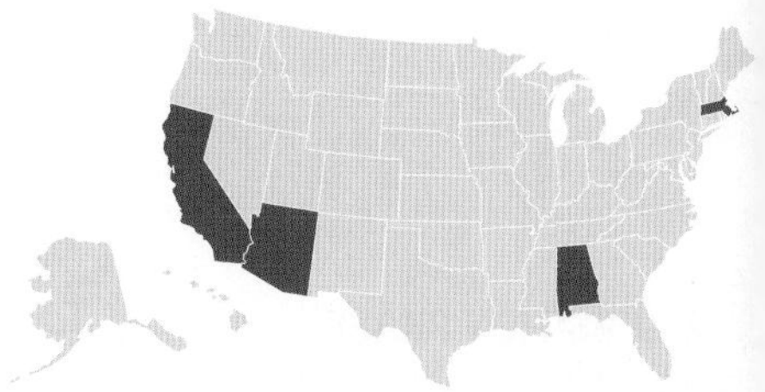

# Cryptographic Systems

**INVESTMENT COMPONENT**

- Modernization
- Recapitalization
- Maintenance

## MISSION

To provide Army users strategic and tactical advantages through Communication Security (COMSEC) superiority by modernizing and fielding cryptographic equipment and systems, which protect against cyber threats, increase battlefield survivability/lethality, and enable critical mission command activities.

## DESCRIPTION

Cryptographic Systems are composed of three fielded families of systems: In-Line Network Encryptors (INE), Link/Trunk Encryptor Family (LEF), and Secure Terminal/Enhanced Cryptographic Cards (ST/ECC). New and emerging network architectures are driving the need to replace the current inventory of stovepipe systems with technologically advanced devices that incorporate Chairman of the Joint Chiefs of Staff- and Joint Requirements Oversight Council-directed cryptographic modernization, advanced key management, and network-centric performance capabilities.

The INE family of network encryption devices provides network communications security on Internet Protocol (IP) and Asynchronous Transfer Mode (ATM) networks. These systems are used in both tactical and strategic networks. The family consists of systems such as the KG-250, Talon, and the KG-175 series. In addition, Cryptographic Systems continue to support four legacy devices that are crucial to the COMSEC capability of other fielded systems.

The LEF family is used to multiplex and encrypt numerous signals into wideband data streams to be transmitted over fiber, cable, or satellites. The wideband circuits require systems with extremely fast encryption capabilities. The backbone of the modernized LEF is the KIV-7 series and the KIV-19 series. There are nine legacy devices that also are supported and maintained.

Finally, the ST/ECC family uses security tokens and/or public key encryption to provide secure communication. This portfolio is rapidly changing as modernized systems, such as the Sectera IP viPer, KSV-21 Electronic Crypto Card (ECC), and Secure Mobile Equipment Portable Electronic Devices (SME PED), replace the twelve available legacy devices. This is driven by the substitution in preference from wide-bandwidth to narrow-bandwidth communication channels.

## SYSTEM INTERDEPENDENCIES

**Other Major Interdependencies**

Cryptographic Systems are considered enabling systems, which provide required COMSEC capabilities

## PROGRAM STATUS

- **3QFY11:** Cryptographic Systems assigned to chartered Project Director Communications Security
- **3QFY11:** Coordinate and validate existing and future requirements
- **4QFY11:** Complete evaluation of equipment obsolescence
- **4QFY11:** Solidify processes to minimize fielding wait time

## PROJECTED ACTIVITIES

- **FY12-13:** Continued modernization of KG-175 series
- **FY12-13:** Continued procurement of Sectera IP viper
- **3QFY12:** Develop operational plans for layered COMSEC
- **2QFY13:** Final replacement of STU-III

**ACQUISITION PHASE**

- Technology Development
- Engineering and Manufacturing Development
- Production and Deployment
- Operations and Support

## Cryptographic Systems

**FOREIGN MILITARY SALES**
None

**CONTRACTORS**
VIA SAT (Carlsbad, CA)
General Dynamics Communication Systems (Needham, MA)
L3 Communications (Camden, NJ)
Harris Corp (Palm Bay, FL)
Communications Security Logistics Activity (Sierra Vista, AZ)

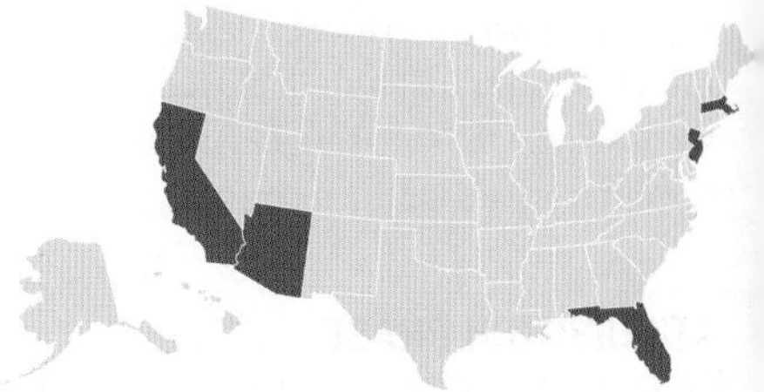

# Defense Enterprise Wideband SATCOM System (DEWSS)

## INVESTMENT COMPONENT

**Modernization**

Recapitalization

Maintenance

## MISSION

Provides combatant commanders, deployed Warfighters, and senior leadership with secure, high-capacity satellite connectivity, enabling reachback for voice, video, and data communications and transfer of intelligence information.

## DESCRIPTION

The Defense Enterprise Wideband SATCOM System (DEWSS) provides strategic Army and DoD satellite communications (SATCOM) infrastructure, enabling national and senior leader communications; JCS-validated command, control, communications, and intelligence (C3I) requirements; tactical reachback to sustaining base for deployed Warfighters; and transport for critical intelligence information transfer to deployed forces worldwide. DEWSS is modernizing the enterprise satellite terminals, baseband systems, and payload and network control systems required to support Warfighter use of the high-capacity Wideband Global SATCOM (WGS) satellite constellation, which DoD began launching in October 2007. DEWSS capabilities include super high-frequency (SHF), beyond-line-of-sight communications; tactical reachback via DoD Teleport and Standardized Tactical Entry Point (STEP) sites; survivable communications for critical nuclear command and control; and an anti-jam, High-Altitude Electromagnetic Pulse (HEMP) hardened, anti-scintillation capability for key strategic forces. Management capabilities include the Common Network Management System (CNPS), Wideband Global Spectrum Monitoring System (WGSMS), Wideband Remote Monitoring Sensor (WRMS), Remote Monitoring and Control Equipment (RMCE), Joint Management Operations System (JMOS), and the Replacement Frequency Management Orderwire (RFMOW).

## SYSTEM INTERDEPENDENCIES

None

## PROGRAM STATUS

- **1QFY11:** Complete installation and checkout of Wahiawa, HI starter kit
- **2QFY11:** Joint Management Operations System (JMOS) System Integration Test
- **3QFY11:** JMOS First Article Test
- **3QFY11:** Common Network Planning Software (CNPS) v3.1 Government Confidence Test
- **3QFY11:** Wideband Global Spectrum Monitoring System (WGSMS) v2.0 Authority to Operate
- **3QFY11:** Replacement Frequency Modulation Orderwire (RFMOW) v2.4 Government Confidence Test
- **4QFY11:** Wideband Remote Monitoring Sensor (WRMS) System Integration Test
- **4QFY11:** Begin MET First Article Terminal (HEMP) installation
- **4QFY11:** JMOS System Verification Test and Logistics Demonstration
- **4QFY11:** Remote Monitor and Control Equipment (RMCE) Delivery and In-House Acceptance Testing
- **4QFY11:** Global Satellite Configuration Control Element (GSCCE) v2.11 MR
- **1QFY12:** Begin MET First Article Test
- **1QFY12:** RMCE DIACAP Certification Test

## PROJECTED ACTIVITIES

- **2QFY12:** MET First Article Acceptance and Commissioning
- **2QFY12:** Begin Ft. Detrick Earth Terminal Relocation
- **2QFY12:** Begin DEWSS TRANSEC Modernization
- **2QFY12:** MET Large Fixed First Article Terminal (non-HEMP) installation
- **3QFY12:** RMCE Onsite Acceptance Test and On Orbit Test
- **1QFY13:** Ft. Detrick First MET installation Complete
- **3QFY13:** Ft. Detrick Second MET Installation Complete
- **3QFY13:** Ft. Detrick Earth Terminal Relocation Complete

## ACQUISITION PHASE

Technology Development

Engineering and Manufacturing Development

**Production and Deployment**

Operations and Support

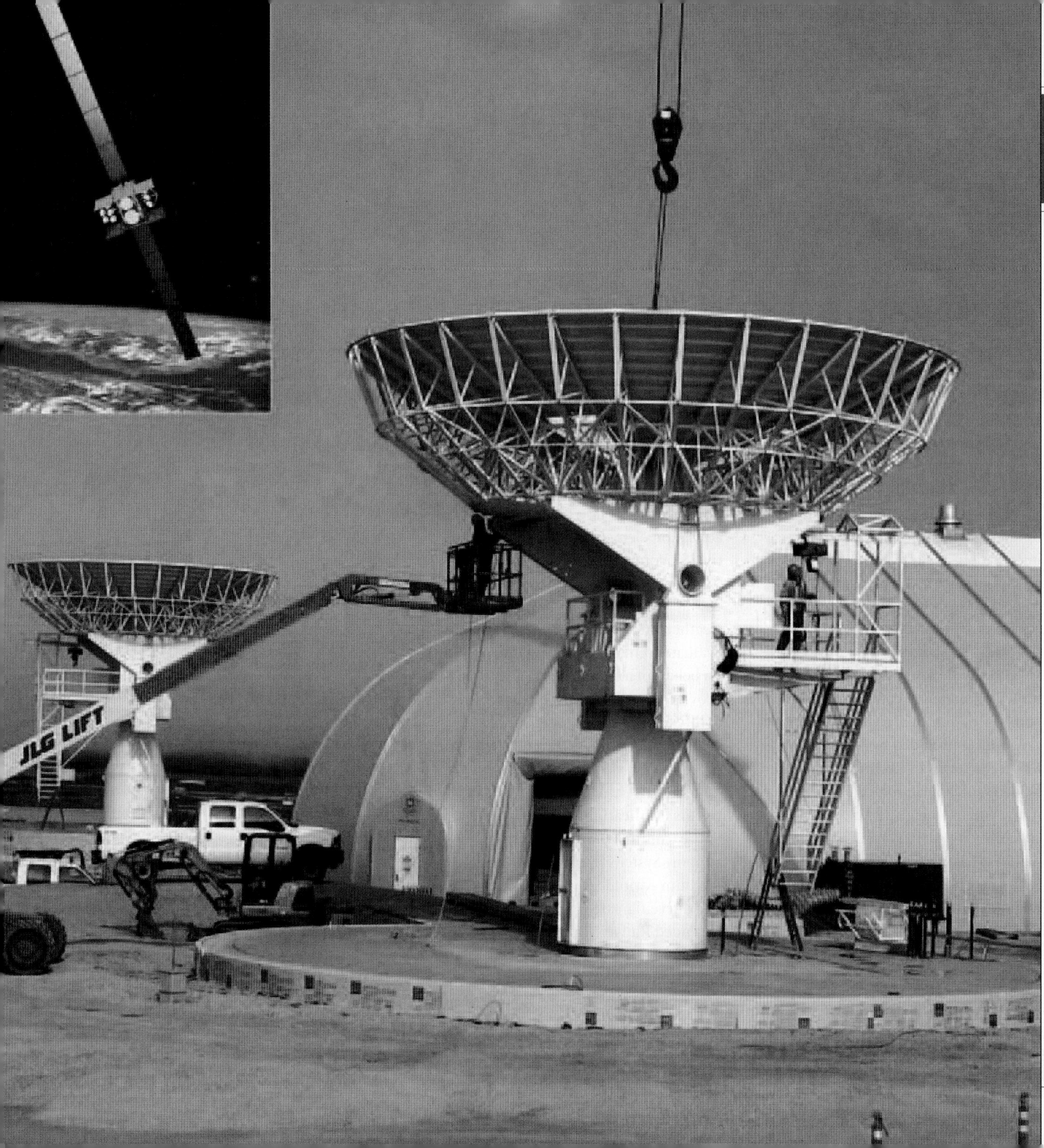


## Defense Enterprise Wideband SATCOM System (DEWSS)

**FOREIGN MILITARY SALES**
None

**CONTRACTORS**
Johns Hopkins University Applied Physics Laboratory (Laurel, MD)
Northrop Grumman (Winter Park, FL)
ITT (Colorado Springs, CO)
Harris Corp. (Melbourne, FL)
Computer Sciences Corp. (CSC) (Eatontown, NJ)

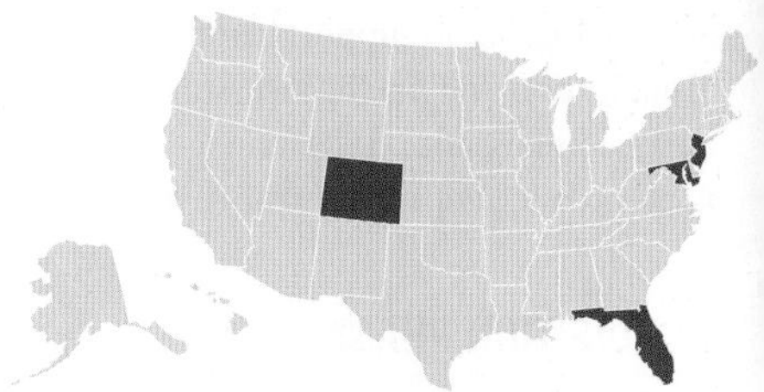

# Distributed Common Ground System-Army (DCGS-A)

## INVESTMENT COMPONENT

- Modernization
- Recapitalization
- Maintenance

## MISSION

Provides distributed ISR planning, management, control, and tasking; multi-intelligence fusion; and robust Joint, allied, and coalition forces interoperability.

## DESCRIPTION

The Distributed Common Ground System-Army (DCGS-A) is the Army's cornerstone system for Tasking of sensors, Processing of data, Exploitation of data, and Dissemination (TPED) of intelligence, geospatial, space, and weather information at all echelons. DCGS-A provides unprecedented timely, relevant, and accurate targetable data to the Warfighter. DCGS-A will be fully interoperable with the Army's Unified Mission Command System (UMCS) and will provide access to data, information, and intelligence to support battlefield visualization and intelligence, surveillance, and reconnaissance (ISR) management in accordance with (IAW) the Army Common Operating Environment. It provides a flattened network, enabling information discovery, collaboration, production, and dissemination to combat commanders and staffs along tactically useful timelines—seconds and minutes vice hours and days. DCGS-A provides unprecedented timely, relevant, and accurate targetable data to the Warfighter. This system enables the commander to achieve situational understanding by leveraging multiple sources of data, information, and intelligence, and to synchronize Joint and combined arms combat power to see first, understand first, act first, and finish decisively.

DCGS-A will incrementally assume life-cycle management responsibility and consolidate/replace the operational capabilities provided by several Post MS C Programs of Record (PORs) and fielded Quick Reaction Capabilities. The Army will produce and field DCGS-A capability on various Hardware (HW) platforms using a consolidated DCGS-A Software Baseline (DSB). HW platforms will range from single laptops to multiserver transportable configurations to large cloud-based computing nodes able to process and store the enormous volumes of data that DCGS-A must manage. DCGS-A's modular, open systems architecture and heavy emphasis on "design for change" allows rapid adaptation to changing circumstances.

DCGS-A will support three primary roles: as an analyst tool set, DCGS-A enables the user to collaborate, synchronize, and integrate organic and non-organic direct and general-support collection elements with operations; as the ISR component of the Army Battle Command, DCGS-A can discover and use all relevant threat, noncombatant, weather, and geospatial data and evaluate technical data and information on behalf of a commander; and DCGS-A provides organizational elements the ability to control select sensor platforms/payloads and process the collected data.

## SYSTEM INTERDEPENDENCIES

**In this Publication**

Battle Command Sustainment Support System (BCS3), Enhanced Medium Altitude Reconnaissance and Surveillance System (EMARSS), Extended Range/Multiple Purpose (ER/MP) Unmanned Aircraft System (UAS), Guardrail Common Sensor (GR/CS)

**Other Major Interdependencies**

DCGS Family of Systems (services), Global Information Grid (GIG), Long Endurance Multi-intelligence Vehicle (LEMV), Network Enabled Command Capability (NECC)

## PROGRAM STATUS

- **1QFY11:** DCGS-A DSB maintenance demonstration
- **1QFY11:** DCGS-A DSB logistics demonstration
- **1QFY11:** DCGS-A DSB FCA/PCA
- **3QFY11:** DCGS-A DSB DT/EUT
- **3QFY11:** JFCOM Lead Empire Challenge 2011, demonstration of Joint Interoperability and Netcentric Operations

## PROJECTED ACTIVITIES

- **1QFY12:** DCGS-A DSB 1.0 MS C
- **2QFY12:** DCGS-A DSB 1.0 IOT&E
- **4QFY12:** DCGS-A DSB 1.0 FDD
- **FY12:** DCGS-A DSB 1.1 Build Complete
- **FY13:** DCGS-A DSB 1.1 Fielding
- **FY13:** DCGS-A DSB 1.2 Build Complete
- **FY14:** DCGS-A DSB 1.2 Fielding
- **FY14:** DCGS-A DSB 1.3 Build Complete
- **FY15:** DCGS-A DSB 1.3 Fielding

## ACQUISITION PHASE

- Technology Development
- Engineering and Manufacturing Development
- Production and Deployment
- Operations and Support

## Distributed Common Ground System-Army (DCGS-A)

**FOREIGN MILITARY SALES**

None

**CONTRACTORS**

**Mobile Basic Prime Contractor for System Integration and Design:**
Northrop Grumman (Linthicum, MD)
**Software Engineering:**
Azimuth Inc. (Morgantown, WV)
**All Source Integration:**
Lockheed Martin (Denver, CO)
**GMTI Integration:**
General Dynamics (Scottsdale, AZ)
**Program Support:**
CACI (Tinton Falls, NJ)
**Engineering Support:**
MITRE (Eatontown, NJ)
**Battle Command Integration and Interoperability:**
OverWatch Systems (Austin, TX)
**Program Support, System Engineering, Architecture:**
Booz Allen Hamilton (Eatontown, NJ)
MITRE (Eatontown, NJ)
**DCGS Integrated Backbone (DIB):**
Raytheon (Garland, TX)
**Other Support:**
NetApp (CA), Cloudera (CA), Vmware (CA), Esri (CA), Tucson Embedded Systems (AZ), L3 Comm (AZ), Dell (TX), Potomac Fusion (TX), Overwatch (TX), Ringtail Design (TX), Redhat (NC), Digital Reasoning (TN)

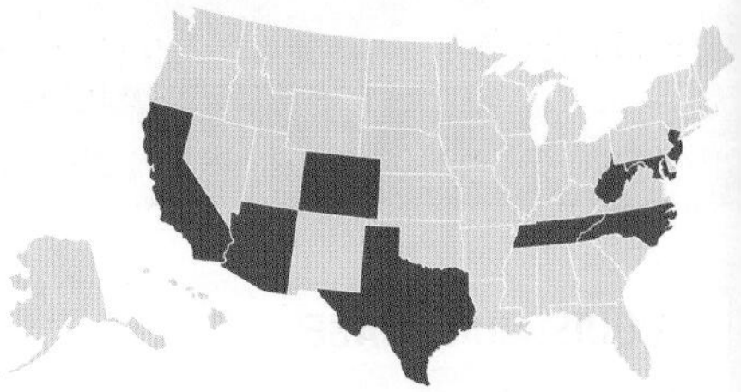

# Distributed Learning System (DLS)

**INVESTMENT COMPONENT**

Modernization

Recapitalization

Maintenance

## MISSION

Acquires, deploys, and maintains a worldwide, distributed learning system to ensure our nation's Soldiers receive critical training for mission success.

## DESCRIPTION

The Distributed Learning System (DLS) provides a worldwide information technology infrastructure that innovatively combines hardware, software, and telecommunications resources with training facilities and Web-based applications to electronically deliver course content for training of Soldiers and Department of the Army (DA) Civilians anytime, anywhere. DLS leverages technology to increase training efficiencies, increase individual and unit readiness, support Soldiers' career advancement, and improve their quality of life.

DLS provides users:

- Access to Army e-Learning, Web-based training, consisting of more than 5,400 commercial business, information technology, and 32 Rosetta Stone foreign language courses
- Globally located Digital Training Facilities (DTFs) capable of delivering multimedia courseware for individual or group training via computer or Video Tele-Training (VTT)
- Enterprise management of the DLS infrastructure, with customer support for training applications
- The Army Learning Management System (ALMS), for Web-based delivery of multimedia training and streamlined, automated training management functions
- Deployed Digital Training Campuses (DDTC) to deliver multimedia courseware to deployed Soldiers

## SYSTEM INTERDEPENDENCIES

**Other Major Interdependencies**

Army Knowledge Online is used for identification, authorization, and to gain access to the ALMS. Student training results are transmitted via the ALMS to the Army Training Requirements and Resources System (ATRRS) as the system of record for Army training.

## PROGRAM STATUS

- **2QFY04-4QFY10:** Sustained a centrally managed global training enterprise; electronically delivered training in military occupational specialties and self-development; supported migration of courseware to ALMS; began fielding DDTC; increased Army e-Learning and Rosetta Stone (foreign language training) enrollments

## PROJECTED ACTIVITIES

- **2QFY11:** Upgrade ALMS to ALMS 3.0 software
- **4QFY11:** Complete fielding of 14 DDTCs
- **4QFY13:** Full deployment of DDTCs
- **4QFY14:** Complete production of DDTCs
- **1QFY11-4QFY21:** Continue to sustain all fielded DLS training capabilities; continue to produce, deploy and maintain a total of 50 DDTCs

**ACQUISITION PHASE**

Technology Development | Engineering and Manufacturing Development | Production and Deployment | Operations and Support

## Distributed Learning System (DLS)

**FOREIGN MILITARY SALES**
Nonc

**CONTRACTORS**

**Army Learning Management System (ALMS):**
IBM (Fairfax, VA)

**DTF Management:**
N-Link Corp (Bremerton, WA)

**Language Training:**
Rosetta Stone (Harrisonburg, VA)

**Enterprise Management Services:**
IBM (Fairfax, VA)

**Army e-Learning:**
Skillsoft Corp. (Nashua, NH)

**Deployed Digital Training Campus:**
Lockheed Martin (Alexandria, VA)

**Program Management Support Services:**
MPRI, an L-3 Company (Alexandria, VA)

**VTT Communications Support:**
Sprint Communications Co. (Reston, VA)

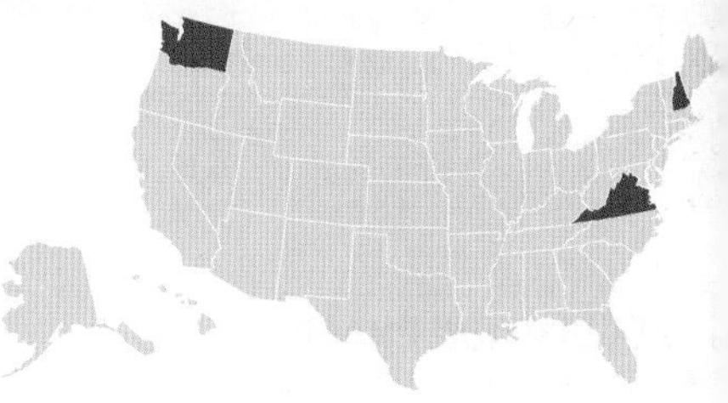

# Dry Support Bridge (DSB)

INVESTMENT COMPONENT

- Modernization
- Recapitalization
- Maintenance

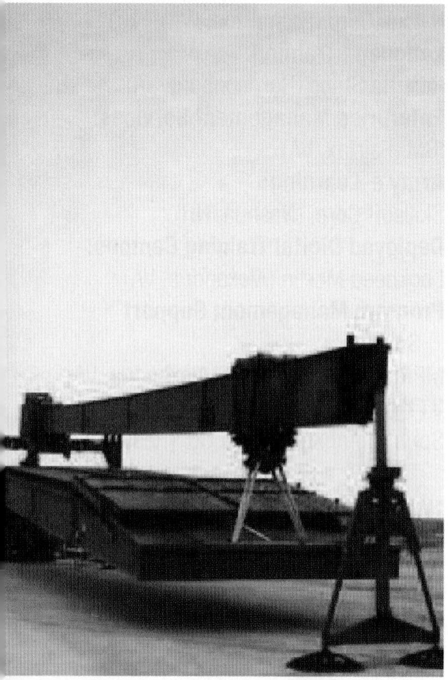

## MISSION

Supports military load classification 100 (wheeled)/80 (tracked) vehicles over 40-meter gaps via a modular military bridge.

## DESCRIPTION

The Dry Support Bridge (DSB) is a mobile, rapidly erected, modular military bridge system. DSB is fielded to Multi-Role Bridge Companies (MRBCs) and requires a crew of eight Soldiers to deploy a 40-meter bridge in fewer than 90 minutes (daytime). DSB sections have a 4.3-meter road width and can span a 40-meter gap or two 20-meter gaps at military load classification (MLC) 100 (wheeled)/80 (tracked) normal crossing and MLC 110 (W) caution crossing. The system includes a DSB bridge, a launcher mounted on a dedicated Palletized Load System (PLS) chassis that deploys the modular bridge sections, and seven M1077 Flatracks to transport the bridge sections. The bridge modules are palletized onto seven flat racks and transported by equipment organic to the MRBC. DSB is designed to replace the M3 Medium Girder Bridge.

DSB modular structure allows launch and retrieval from either end without a dedicated or special training area and can be placed directly over pavement to reinforce damaged sections, bridges, or spans. Air transport for the DSB system is accomplished by C-130 if divided (bridge: one flat-rack per a/c; launcher vehicle: split into 3 loads, five hours work), or by C-17 and C-5 intact.

## SYSTEM INTERDEPENDENCIES

**Other Major Interdependencies**

DSB operations rely and are interdependent upon fully mission-capable M1977 Common Bridge Transporters and M1076 PLS trailer assets within a fully Modified Table of Organization and Equipment-equipped MRBC

## PROGRAM STATUS

This system has been fielded since 2003.

- **1QFY11:** Fielding to 1041st MRBC
- **2QFY11:** Fielding to 50th MRBC
- **3QFY11:** Fielding to 189th MRBC
- **4QFY11:** Fielding to 502nd MRBC

## PROJECTED ACTIVITIES

- **2QFY12:** Fielding to 50th MRBC
- **2QFY12:** Fielding to 341st MRBC
- **3QFY12:** Fielding to 250th MRBC

ACQUISITION PHASE

- Technology Development
- Engineering and Manufacturing Development
- Production and Deployment
- Operations and Support

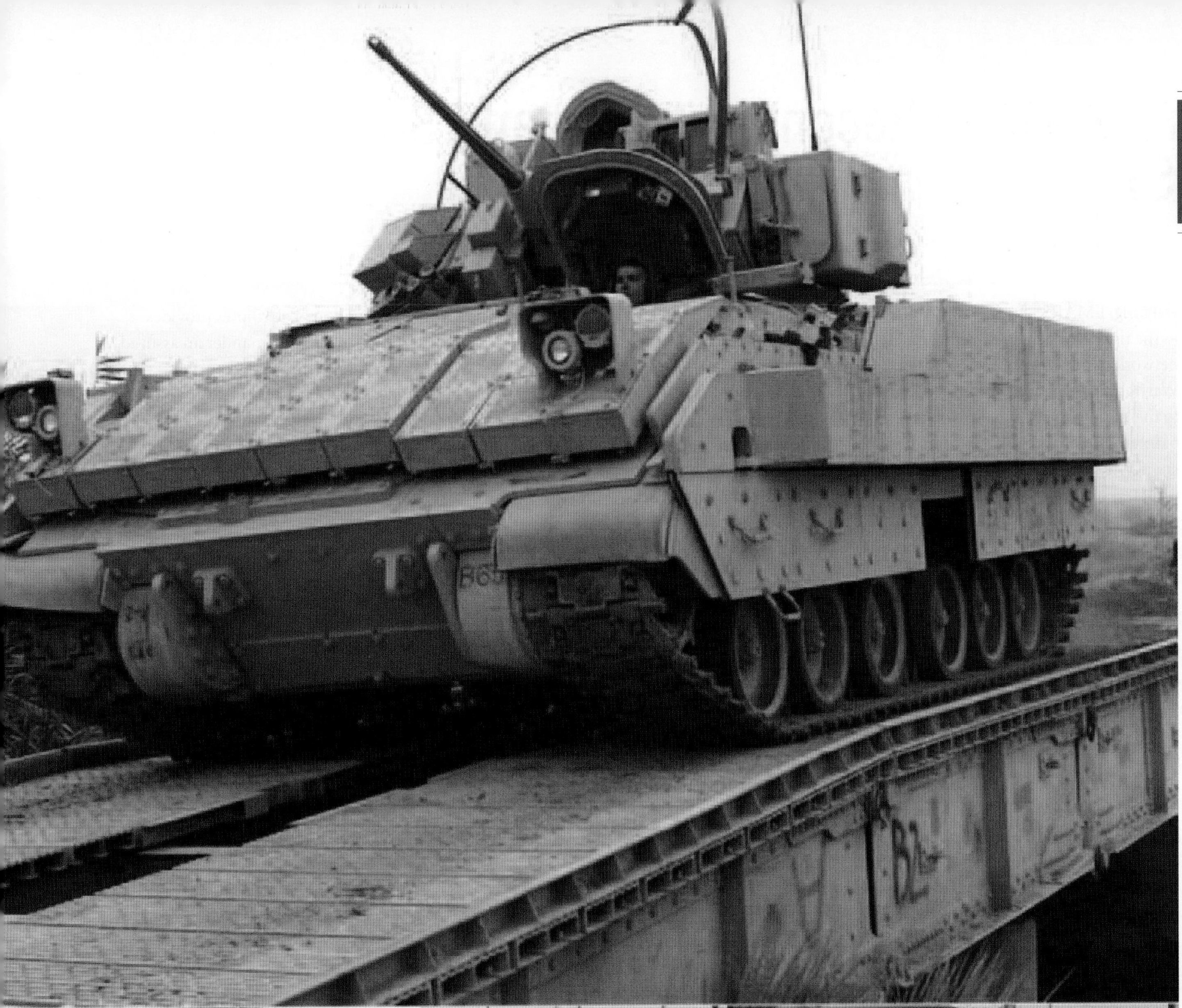

## Dry Support Bridge (DSB)

**FOREIGN MILITARY SALES**
None

**CONTRACTORS**
**Manufacturer:**
Williams Fairey Engineering Ltd.
(Stockport, United Kingdom)
**PLS Chassis:**
Oshkosh Corp. (Oshkosh, WI)
**Logistics:**
XMCO (Warren, MI)

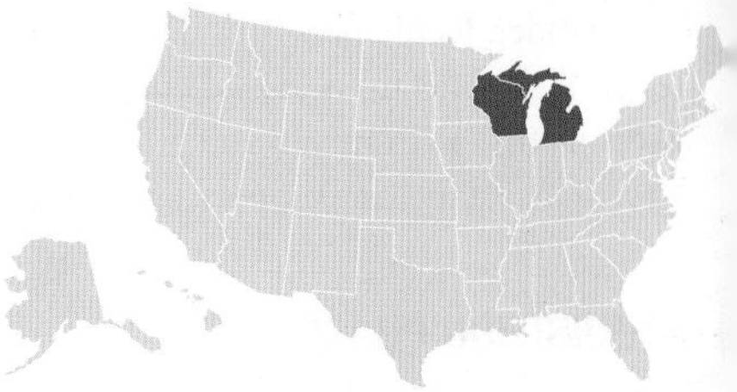

# Enhanced Medium Altitude Reconnaissance and Surveillance System (EMARSS)

**INVESTMENT COMPONENT**

- Modernization
- Recapitalization
- Maintenance

## MISSION

EMARSS is the Army's next generation C-12 based, direct support, manned airborne intelligence collection, processing, and targeting support system. EMARSS provides a persistent multi-intelligence capability to detect, locate, classify/identify, and track surface targets with a high degree of timeliness and accuracy. EMARSS aircraft will be assigned to the U.S. Army Intelligence and Security Command's (INSCOM's) Aerial Exploitation Battalions (AEB).

## DESCRIPTION

EMARSS is a multi-intelligence airborne intelligence, surveillance, and reconnaissance (AISR) system dedicated specifically to direct support of the tactical commander. It enhances Brigade Combat Team (BCT) effectiveness by defining and assessing the environment and providing surveillance, targeting support, and threat warning. EMARSS is a key contributor to the tightly woven, highly integrated network of intelligence and operations Warfighting functions that is necessary to maintain contact and develop targets of interest in an Irregular Warfare (IW) environment and across the range of military operations (ROMO).

EMARSS is a multi-INT AISR system that provides the capability to detect, locate, classify/identify, and track surface targets in day/night, near-all-weather conditions with a high degree of timeliness and accuracy. The EMARSS AISR capabilities include an electro-optical/infrared (EO/IR) with full motion video (FMV) sensor, a communications intelligence (COMINT) sensor, and an Aerial Precision Guidance (APG) sensor—all supported by line-of-sight (LOS) and beyond-line-of-sight (LOS/BLOS) communications and hosted on a manned, medium-altitude, derivative of the commercial Hawker-Beechcraft King Air 350ER aircraft. EMARSS operates as a single platform in support of tactical missions, but through connectivity to tactical and national networks also contributes to the Joint overall AISR constellation.

EMARSS contains a tailored set of Distributed Common Ground System-Army (DCGS-A)-enabled software and ISR processing software functionalities to process, exploit, and rapidly disseminate the intelligence derived from the imagery sensor. The APG operator brings onboard his processing and software tools to control the APG sensor and perform analysis and reporting. The imagery and APG operators release time-sensitive information directly to the supported BCT and subordinate units, and to the DCGS-A. The COMINT sensor is controlled through LOS and BLOS communications at the DCGS-A, where the processing, analysis, and timely reporting to the supported tactical force is accomplished. Selected EMARSS imagery is immediately processed on the aircraft and the collected imagery is also forwarded to the DCGS-A for further processing, analysis, and reporting. EMARSS complies with the DoD Information Technology Standards Registry and Defense Information Systems Network (DISN). This architecture permits interoperability with any multiservice or Joint system that complies with DoD-standard formats for data transfer and dissemination.

This combination of attributes provides the ground tactical commander an assured near-real-time operational view of the battlespace, enabling tactical ground forces to operate at their highest potential.

## SYSTEM INTERDEPENDENCIES

**In this Publication**

Distributed Common Ground System-Army (DCGS-A)

## PROGRAM STATUS

- **1QFY11:** Milestone B Completed, Engineering and Manufacturing Development (EMD) contract awarded
- **1QFY11:** Industry GAO Protests resulting in Stop Work Order
- **3QFY11:** Protests resolved, EMD contract efforts resume

## PROJECTED ACTIVITIES

- **4QFY12:** Joint Requirements Oversight Council consideration of the CPD
- **FY13:** Developmental Test and Limited User Testing
- **FY13:** Milestone C

**ACQUISITION PHASE**

Technology Development | Engineering and Manufacturing Development | Production and Deployment | Operations and Support

## Enhanced Medium Altitude Reconnaissance and Surveillance System (EMARSS)

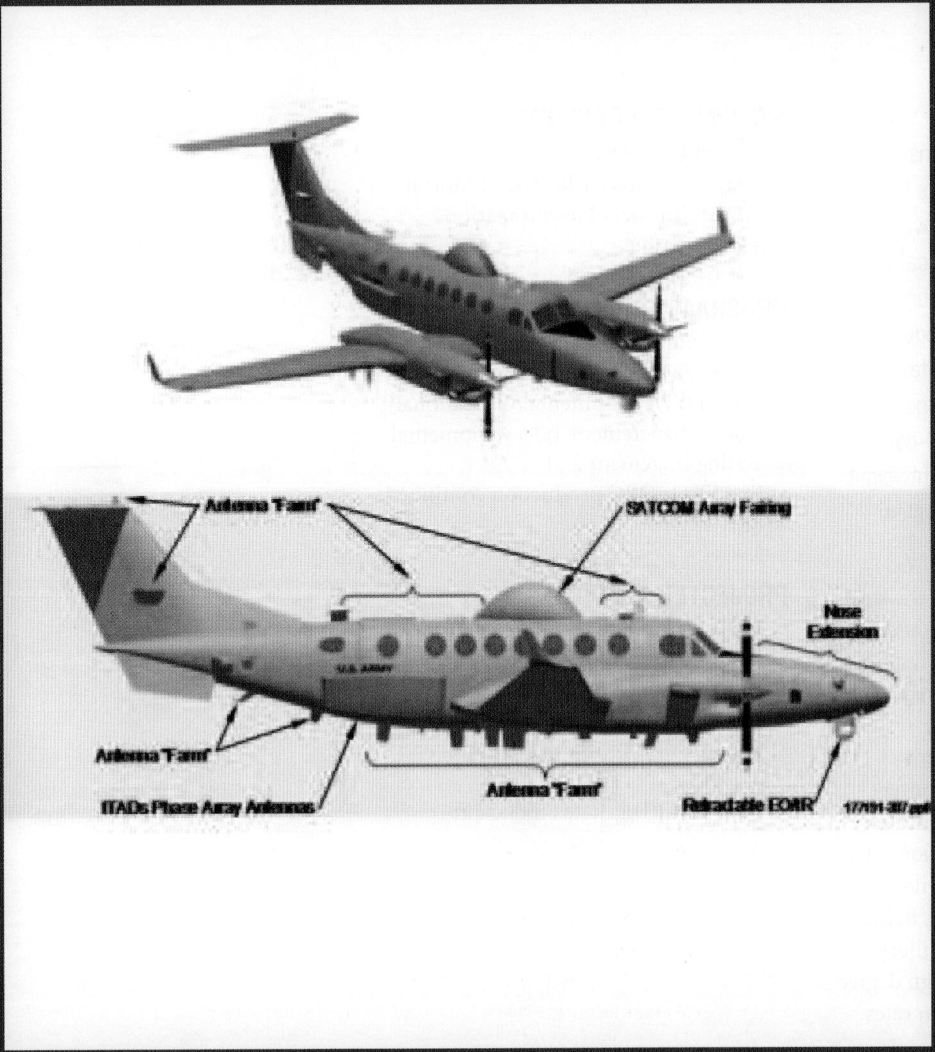


**FOREIGN MILITARY SALES**
None

**CONTRACTORS**

**EMD Contractor:** The Boeing Company (Prime) (Ridley Park, PA), Hawker-Beechcraft (Airframe) (Wichita, KS), L-3 Communications West (SATCOM) (Salt Lake City, UT), BAE Systems (COMINT Hardware/Software) (Nashua, NH), Avenge (Training and Operational Testing) (Dulles, VA), Rockwell Collins (Cockpit Avionics) (Cedar Rapids, IA)

**Systems Engineering/Technical Assistance (SETA) Support:** CACI (Tinton Falls, NJ), Booz Allen Hamilton (Eatontown, NJ)

**Engineering/Program Management:** MITRE (Eatontown, NJ)

**Aircraft Engineering:** CAS Inc. (Huntsville, AL), Science Applications International Corp. (SAIC) (Huntsville, AL)

**Information Assurance:** Sensor Technologies (Red Bank, NJ)

**Program Support:** CACI (Arlington, VA)

**Software Engineering Support:** Lockheed Martin (Tinton Falls, NJ)

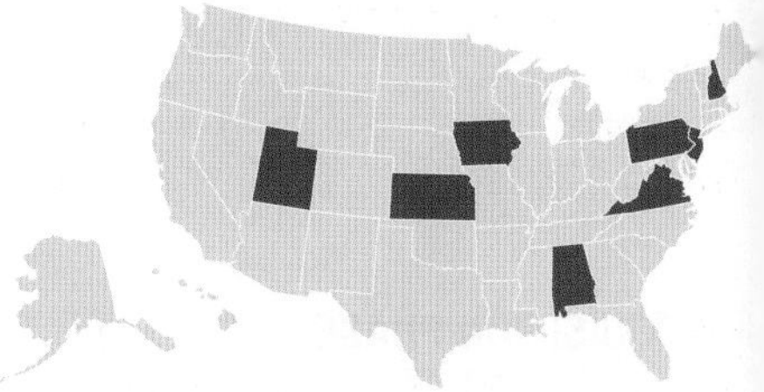

# Enhanced Q-36

**INVESTMENT COMPONENT**

Modernization

Recapitalization

Maintenance

## MISSION

To provide the next generation answer to the aging legacy Firefinder radars (the AN/TPQ-36 and AN/TPQ-37), by providing improved acquisition and identification of artillery, mortar, and rocket munitions in the 90-degree mode and introducing the additional capability to operate in the 360-degree mode at greater ranges and capabilities than the current 360-degree AN/TPQ-48 and AN/TPQ-49 Lightweight Counter Mortar Radar (LCMR) system.

## DESCRIPTION

The EQ-36 is a replacement of the legacy AN/TPQ-36 and AN/TPQ-37 target acquisition counter-fire radar systems. It provides improved operational capability over the legacy radar systems. The EQ-36 provides Warfighters continuous and responsive counter-battery target acquisition capabilities for all types of military operations. The EQ-36 detects in-flight projectiles and determines and communicates firing point locations of mortars, artillery, rockets, and missiles with a high degree of accuracy and low false alarm rates.

## SYSTEM INTERDEPENDENCIES

**In this Publication**

Counter-Rocket, Artillery, and Mortar (C-RAM)/Indirect Fire Protection Capability (IFPC)

## PROGRAM STATUS

- **FY11:** Non-Recurring Engineering Increment 2 for system integration
- **3QFY11:** Developmental/Operational Test LUT Increment 1; Developmental Testing Increment 2
- **End FY11:** QRC production continued; LRIP begins

## PROJECTED ACTIVITIES

- **3QFY12:** Limited Users Test #2 scheduled
- **4QFY12:** Quick Reaction Capability Production continued until 4QFY12
- **End of FY12:** LRIP ongoing until end of FY12
- **FY13-FY15:** Full-Rate Production

**ACQUISITION PHASE**

Technology Development | Engineering and Manufacturing Development | Production and Deployment | Operations and Support

## Enhanced Q-36

**FOREIGN MILITARY SALES**
None

**CONTRACTORS**
**Integration/ICS:**
Lockheed Martin (Syracuse, NY)
**Technical Support:**
(statewide, MD)
(statewide, NJ)
**FSRs:**
JB Management (Alexandria, VA)

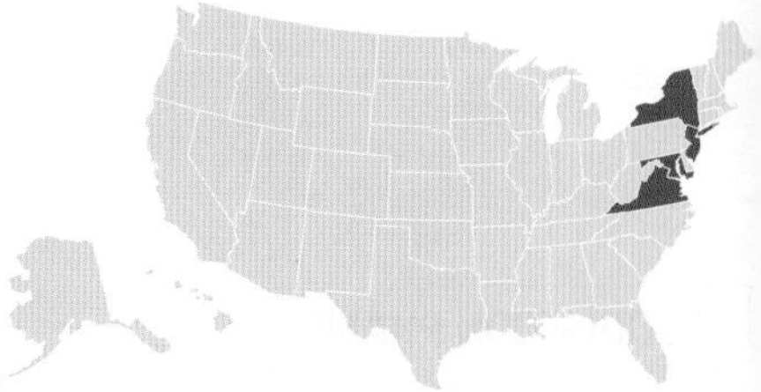

# Excalibur (M982)

**INVESTMENT COMPONENT**

Modernization

Recapitalization

Maintenance

## MISSION

Provides improved fire support to the maneuver force commander through a precision-guided, extended-range, artillery projectile that increases lethality and reduces collateral damage.

## DESCRIPTION

Excalibur (M982) is a 155mm, Global Positioning System (GPS)-guided, extended-range artillery projectile, in use as the Army's next-generation cannon artillery precision munition. The target, platform location, and GPS-specific data are entered into the projectile's mission computer through an Enhanced Portable Inductive Artillery Fuze Setter (EPIAFS).

Excalibur uses a jam-resistant internal GPS receiver to update the inertial navigation system, providing precision in-flight guidance and dramatically improving accuracy regardless of range. Excalibur has three fuze options: height-of-burst, point-detonating, and delay/penetration. It is employable in all weather conditions and terrain.

The program is using an incremental approach to provide a combat capability to the Soldier as quickly as possible, and to deliver advanced capabilities and lower costs as technology matures. The initial variant (Increment Ia-1) includes a unitary high-explosive warhead capable of penetrating urban structures and is also effective against personnel and light materiel targets. Increment Ia-2 will provide increased range (up to 37.5 kilometers) and reliability improvements. The third variant (Increment Ib) will maintain performance and capabilities while significantly reducing unit cost and increasing reliability.

Excalibur is designed for fielding to the Lightweight 155mm Howitzer (M777A2), the 155mm M109A6 self-propelled howitzer (Paladin), and the Swedish Archer howitzer. Excalibur is an international cooperative program with Sweden, which contributes resources toward the development in accordance with established Cooperative Development and Production agreements.

## SYSTEM INTERDEPENDENCIES

**In this Publication**

Advanced Field Artillery Tactical Data System (AFATDS)

**Other Major Interdependencies**

Enhanced Portable Inductive Artillery Fuze Setter (EPIAFS), Modular Artillery Charge System (MACS)

## PROGRAM STATUS

- **Current:** Army and Marine Corps units in Afghanistan and Iraq are Excalibur capable
- **2QFY11:** Approved Full-rate Production of Increment Ia-2

## PROJECTED ACTIVITIES

- **1QFY12:** Increment Ia-2 Initial Operational Capability
- **3QFY12:** Milestone C Low-Rate Initial Production Decision for Increment Ib
- **4QFY12-1QFY13:** Initial Operational Test & Evaluation for Increment Ib
- **2QFY14:** Increment Ib Initial Operational Capability

**ACQUISITION PHASE**

Technology Development | Engineering and Manufacturing Development | Production and Deployment | Operations and Support

## Excalibur (M982)

**FOREIGN MILITARY SALES**
Australia, Canada, Sweden, United Kingdom

**CONTRACTORS**
Raytheon (Tucson, AZ)
L3 Communications (Anaheim, CA)
General Dynamics Ordnance and Tactical Systems (Healdsburg, CA)
General Dynamics Ordnance and Tactical Systems (Niceville, FL)
Atlantic Inertial Units (Plymouth, England)

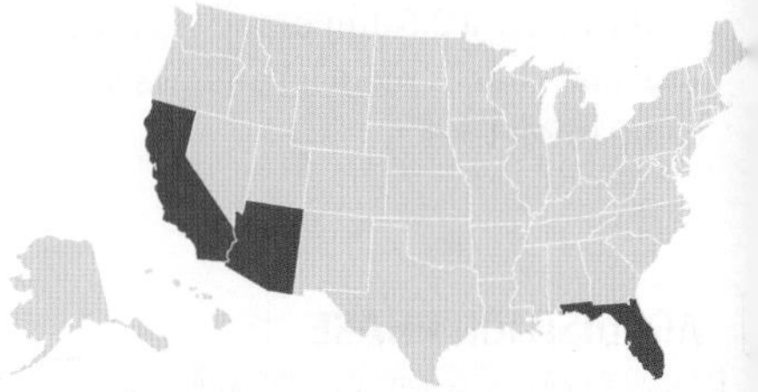

# Family of Medium Tactical Vehicles (FMTV)

**INVESTMENT COMPONENT**

- **Modernization**
- Recapitalization
- Maintenance

## MISSION

Provides unit mobility/resupply, equipment/personnel transportation, and key ammunition distribution, using a family of vehicles based on a common chassis.

## DESCRIPTION

The Family of Medium Tactical Vehicles (FMTV) is a system of strategically deployable vehicles that performs general resupply, ammunition resupply, maintenance and recovery, engineer support missions, and serves as weapon systems platforms for combat, combat support, and combat service support units in a tactical environment.

The Light Medium Tactical Vehicle (LMTV) has a 2.5-ton capacity (cargo, van, and chassis models) and has a companion trailer.

The Medium Tactical Vehicle (MTV) has a 5-ton capacity (cargo, long-wheelbase-cargo with and without materiel handling equipment, tractor, van, wrecker, 8.8-ton Load Handling System (LHS), 8.8-ton LHS trailer, and 10-ton dump truck models). Three truck variants and two companion trailers, with the same cube and payload capacity as their prime movers, provide air drop capability. MTV also serves as the platform for the High Mobility Artillery Rocket System (HIMARS) and resupply vehicle for PATRIOT and HIMARS. MTV operates worldwide in all weather and terrain conditions.

FMTV enhances crew survivability through the use of hard cabs, three-point seat belts, automatic braking system, and central tire inflation capability. FMTV enhances tactical mobility and is strategically deployable in C5, C17, and C130 aircraft. It reduces the Army's logistical footprint by providing commonality of parts and components, reduced maintenance downtime, high reliability, and high operational readiness rate (more than 90 percent). FMTV incorporates a vehicle data bus and class V interactive electronic technical manual, significantly lowering operating and support costs compared with older trucks.

Units are equipped with FMTVs at more than 68 locations worldwide; 54,835 trucks and 13,293 trailers are in field units as of June 2011. The Army developed, tested, and installed add-on-armor and enhanced add-on-armor kits, and a Low Signature Armored Cab (LSAC) for Southwest Asia. The newest armored version, the Long-term Armor Strategy (LTAS) A-Cabs are integral to new production and are being fielded. The LTAS B-kit is available. Approximately 6,000 FMTVs have been armored in Southwest Asia in support of Operation New Dawn and Operation Enduring Freedom.

## SYSTEM INTERDEPENDENCIES

**In this Publication**

Chemical Biological Protective Shelter (CBPS) M8E1, Enhanced Q-36, High Mobility Artillery Rocket System (HIMARS)

**Other Major Interdependencies**

AGSE, CBDP-CP, HMMWV Replacement Interchange, LMS-788 Ops Shelter and Sensor Pallet, Other Interchange, P/M CAP, Surface Launched Advanced Medium Range Air-To-Air Missile (SLAMRAAM), USAF AN/TPS-75 Radar

## PROGRAM STATUS

- **3QFY11:** Government PVT of select non-wrecker Oshkosh FMTV variants to include live fire tests completed
- **3QFY11:** Oshkosh FMTV trucks and companion trailers began shipping to the field

## PROJECTED ACTIVITIES

- **2QFY12:** Complete Government PVT of Oshkosh FMTV wrecker variant

**ACQUISITION PHASE**

Technology Development | Engineering and Manufacturing Development | **Production and Deployment** | Operations and Support

FMTV with Armor Kit

## Family of Medium Tactical Vehicles (FMTV)

**FOREIGN MILITARY SALES**

Afghanistan, Canada, Djibouti, Greece, Iraq, Jordan, Macedonia, Saudi Arabia, Singapore, Taiwan, Thailand, United Arab Emirates

**CONTRACTORS**

**Prime:**
Oshkosh Corp. (Oshkosh, WI)

**Axles:**
Meritor (Troy, MI)

**Transmission:**
Allison Transmission (Indianapolis, IN)

**Engine:**
Caterpillar (Greenville, SC)

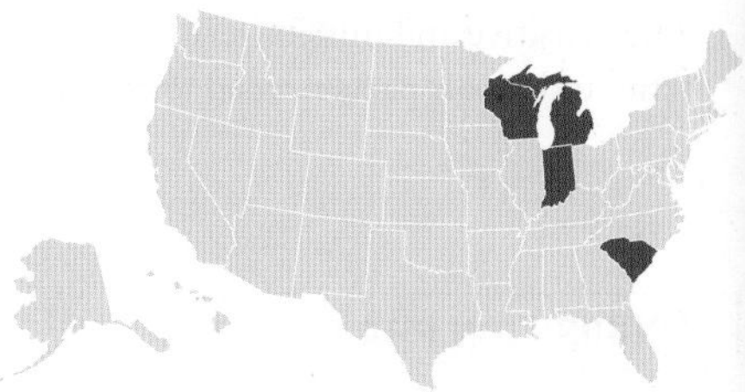

| | LMTV A1 Cargo | MTV A1 Cargo |
|---|---|---|
| **Payload:** | 5,000 pounds | 10,000 pounds |
| **Towed load:** | 12,000 pounds | 21,000 pounds |
| **Engine:** | Caterpillar 6-cylinder diesel | Caterpillar 6-cylinder diesel |
| **Transmission:** | Allison Transmission Automatic | Allison Transmission Automatic |
| **Horsepower:** | 275 | 330 |
| **Drive:** | 4 x 4 | 6 x 6 |

# Fixed Wing

## INVESTMENT COMPONENT

Modernization

Recapitalization

Maintenance

## MISSION

Provides operational support and focused logistics missions for U.S. Army, Joint Services, national agencies, and multinational users in support of intelligence and electronic warfare, transportation of key personnel, and movement of critical time-sensitive logistical support for battle missions and homeland security.

## DESCRIPTION

Army Fixed Wing aviation units support their customers by enhancing the lethality and survivability on the battlefield with intelligence and electronic warfare assets. The Fixed Wing fleet provides timely movement of key personnel to critical locations throughout the theater of operations, transports time-sensitive and mission-critical supply items and repair parts needed to continue the warfight, and worldwide peacetime contingencies and humanitarian relief (Homeland Defense) support.

The Fixed Wing fleet consists of 19 aircraft platforms and 319 aircraft that allow the Army to perform day-to-day operations in a more timely and cost-efficient manner without reliance on commercial transportation. Special electronic mission aircraft provide commanders with critical intelligence and targeting information, enhancing lethality and survivability on the battlefield. All Army aircraft are commercial-off-the-shelf products or are commercial derivative aircraft.

The fleet includes:

- C-12 Utility
- C-20 Long-range Executive Transport
- C-37 Long-range Executive Transport
- C-23 Cargo
- C-26 Utility
- EO-5 Airborne Reconnaissance Low (ARL)
- RC-12 Guardrail Common Sensor (GR/CS)
- UC-35 Utility
- O-2 Research, Development, Test & Evaluation
- C-208 Research, Development, Test & Evaluation
- TG-14 Research, Development, Test & Evaluation
- T-34 Research, Development, Test & Evaluation
- UV-18 Golden Knights
- C-31 Golden Knights
- U-21 Training
- B-300 Medium Altitude Reconnaissance Surveillance System (MARSS)
- CE-182 USMA-West Point

The EO-5, RC-12, and B-300 are classified as special electronic mission aircraft and provide the real-time intelligence collection in peace and wartime environments. The C-12, C-23, C-26, and UC-35 are classified as operational support aircraft and provide direct fixed wing support to warfighting combatants.

## SYSTEM INTERDEPENDENCIES

None

## PROGRAM STATUS

- **1QFY11-4QFY11:**
  - C-12, RC-12, and UC-35 aircraft are sustained using a Life Cycle Contractor Support (LCCS) maintenance contract (L-3 Vertex)
  - C-23 and C-26 aircraft are sustained using a Life Cycle Contractor Support (LCCS) maintenance contract (M-7 Aerospace)
  - C-20 and C-37 aircraft are sustained using Life Cycle Contractor Support (LCCS) maintenance contracts (NGST and Gulfstream)
  - EO-5 aircraft are sustained using a Life Cycle Contractor Support (LCCS) maintenance contract (King Aerospace)
- **2QFY11:** Procured and delivered two HBC King Air 350ER aircraft for Precision Light Detection and Ranging (LIDAR) capability supporting the U.S. Army's intelligence, reconnaissance, and surveillance (ISR) mission

## PROJECTED ACTIVITIES

- **FY12-13:** Delivery of three UV-18 (Twin Otter) Replacement Aircraft for the U.S. Army Parachute Team (Golden Knights)
- **FY12-13:** Acquire four T-34 Replacement Aircraft for the Army Test and Evaluation Command (ATEC)
- **FY15:** Acquire one Replacement Aircraft for the Air Traffic Services Command (ATSCOM)

## ACQUISITION PHASE

Technology Development | Engineering and Manufacturing Development | Production and Deployment | **Operations and Support**

C-20/37

C-26

RC-12

EO-5 (ARL)

C-12

C23

**FOREIGN MILITARY SALES**
None

**CONTRACTORS**
L-3 Vertex (Madison, MS)
M-7 Aerospace (San Antonio, TX)
King Aerospace (Addison, TX)
Gulfstream (Savannah, GA)
Hawker Beech Corporation (Wichita, KS)

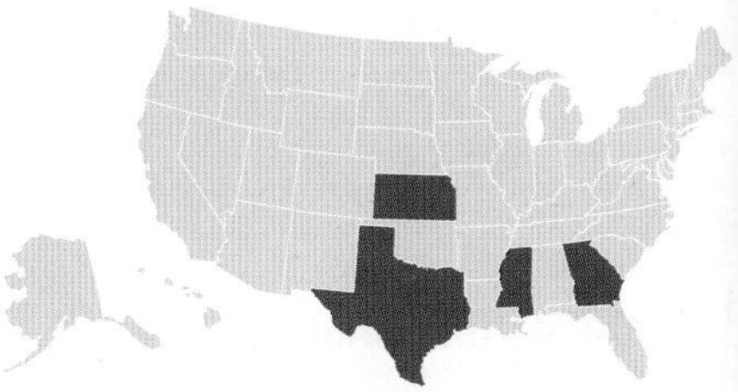

# Force Protection Systems

**INVESTMENT COMPONENT**

Modernization

Recapitalization

Maintenance

## MISSION

Detects, assesses, and responds to unauthorized entry or attempted intrusion into installations or facilities.

## DESCRIPTION

Force Protection Systems consist of the following components:

Automated Installation Entry (AIE) is a software and hardware system designed to read and compare vehicles and personnel identification media. The results of the comparison are used to permit or deny access to installation in accordance with installation commanders' criteria. AIE will use a database of personnel and vehicles that have been authorized entry onto an Army installation and appropriate entry lane hardware to permit/deny access to the installation. The system will validate the authenticity of credentials presented by a person with data available from defense personnel and vehicle registration databases. AIE will have the capability to process permanent personnel and enrolled visitors and to present a denial barrier to restrict unauthorized personnel. The system will also be capable of adapting to immediate changes in threat conditions and apply restrictive entrance criteria consistent with the force protection condition.

The Battlefield Anti-Intrusion System (BAIS) is a compact, modular, sensor-based warning system that can be used as a tactical stand-alone system. The system consists of a handheld monitor and three seismic/acoustic sensors and provides coverage across a platoon's defensive front (450 meters). It delivers early warning and situational awareness information, classifying detections as personnel, vehicle, wheeled, or tracked intrusions.

The Lighting Kit, Motion Detector (LKMD) is a simple, compact, modular, sensor-based, early-warning system providing programmable responses of illumination and sound. The LKMD enhances unit awareness during all types of operations and environments, including those in urban terrain.

## SYSTEM INTERDEPENDENCIES

None

## PROGRAM STATUS

**BAIS:**

- **2QFY11:** BAIS First Article Testing successfully completed
- **4QFY11:** BAIS production systems delivery and fielding

**LKMD:**

- **1QFY11-4QFY11:** LKMD production and fielding
- **4QFY11:** LKMD RFP release for follow-on procurement contract

## PROJECTED ACTIVITIES

**BAIS:**

- **2QFY12-4QFY13:** BAIS production and fielding
- **2QFY13:** BAIS RFP release for follow-on procurement

**LKMD:**

- **2QFY12:** Award LKMD follow-on procurement contract
- **2QFY12-2QFY14:** LKMD production and fielding

**ACQUISITION PHASE**

Technology Development | Engineering and Manufacturing Development | **Production and Deployment** | Operations and Support

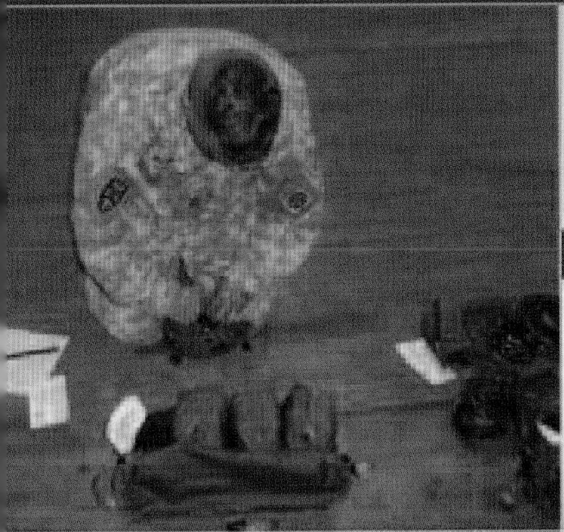

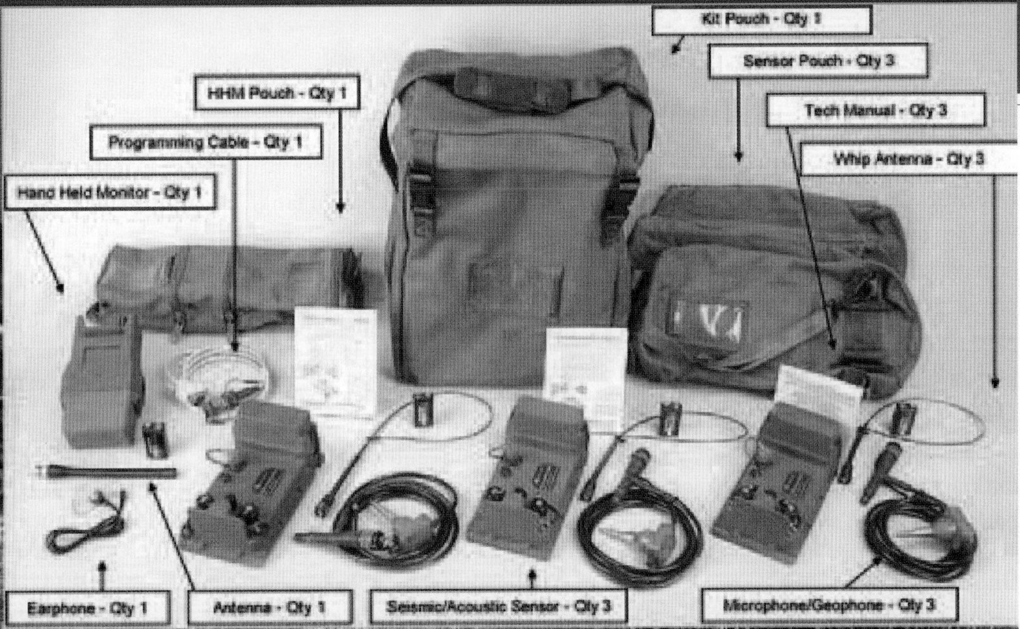

**FOREIGN MILITARY SALES**
None

**CONTRACTORS**
**BAIS:**
L-3 Communications-East (Camden, NJ)
**LKMD:**
EG&G Technical Services Inc.
(Albuquerque, NM)

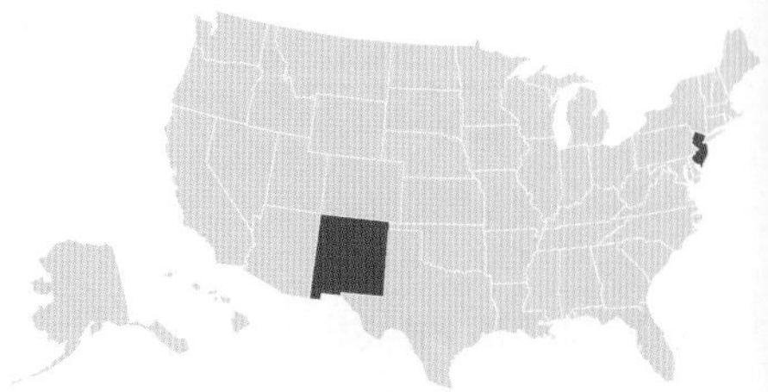

# Force Provider (FP)

## INVESTMENT COMPONENT

**Modernization**
Recapitalization
Maintenance

## MISSION

Provides the Army, Joint U.S. military, host nation, and coalition forces personnel with a high-quality deployable base camp to support the expeditionary missions; develops, integrates, acquires, fields, sustains, and modernizes base camp support systems to improve the Warfighter's fighting capabilities, performance, and quality of life.

## DESCRIPTION

Each Force Provider (FP) is a high-quality deployable base camp that provides billeting, laundry, shower, latrine, food service, shower water reuse, and morale, welfare, and recreation (MWR) kits to support 600 Soldier camps. Additionally, FP can be configured to support 150 base camps. FP includes 75 deployable triple container (TRICON) systems, with eight latrine systems, eight shower systems, four kitchen systems, containerized batch laundry systems, four TRICON refrigerated containers, 26 60-kilowatt tactical quiet generators, 26 modular personnel tents (air supported), four 400,000 BTU water heaters, four improved fuel distribution systems, two wastewater evacuation tank/trailers, 26 mobile electric power distribution replacement systems, and 56 environmental control units. FP is prepositioned in Army Prepositioned Stocks (APS) 1, 3, and 4 to support combatant commanders' requirements. All system components weigh less than 10,000 pounds and are prepacked for rapid transport via air (C-130, C-141, C-5, C-17), sea, road, or rail.

Additional operational add-on kits include: a cold-weather kit that allows operation to -15 degrees Fahrenheit, prime-power kit, large-scale electric kitchen, and resource efficiency add-ons to include a shower water reuse system and energy saving shelter shade and insulating liner systems. New modules use an Airbeam Shelter technology that reduces set-up time from days to hours.

## SYSTEM INTERDEPENDENCIES

**Other Major Interdependencies**

60-kilowatt Tactical Quiet Generator

## PROGRAM STATUS

- **2QFY10:** Production underway for 17 modules to replace deployed APS assets
- **3QFY10:** Deployment of two FP 600-man base camps configured in 150-man subsets to support an operational needs statement (ONS)
- **3QFY11:** Integration of the Shower Water Reuse System (SWRS) into FP 600-man base camps through urgent materiel release to support ONS

## PROJECTED ACTIVITIES

- **1QFY12:** Capabilities production document approval supporting improved capabilities
- **1QFY12:** Integration of additional resource efficiency upgrades into FP baseline
- **3QFY12:** Projected completion of delivery of FP production modules to APS

## ACQUISITION PHASE

Technology Development | Engineering and Manufacturing Development | **Production and Deployment** | Operations and Support

## Force Provider (FP)

**FOREIGN MILITARY SALES**
None

**CONTRACTORS**
**Force Provider Assembly:**
Global Defense Engineering (Easton, MD)
Letterkenny Army Depot (Chambersburg, PA)
**Expeditionary TRICON Kitchen System and FP Electric Kitchen:**
Tri-Tech USA Inc. (South Burlington, VT)
**Airbeam TEMPER Tent:**
Vertigo Inc. (Lake Elsinore, CA)
**Environmental Control:**
Hunter Mfg. (Solon, OH)
**TRICON Container:**
Charleston Marine Containers (Charleston, SC)
**Waste Water Evacuation Tank/Trailer:**
Marsh Industrial (Kalkaska, MI)
**Cold Weather Kit Assembly:**
Berg Companies Inc. (Spokane, WA)
**Mobile Electric Power Distribution System Replacement:**
Lex Products Corp. (Stamford, CT)
**Expeditionary TRICON Systems (shower, laundry, latrine):**
To be determined

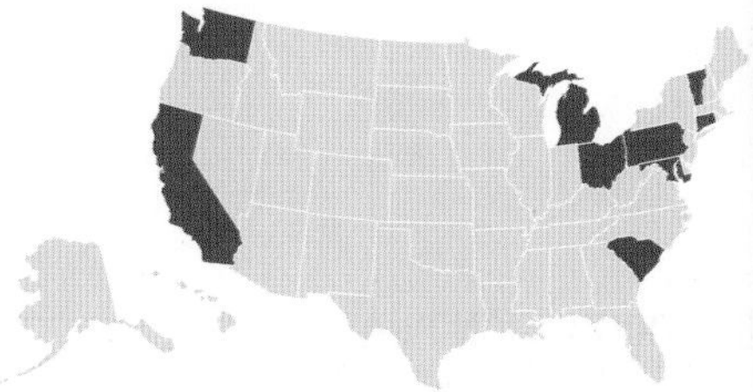

# Force XXI Battle Command Brigade and Below (FBCB2)

**INVESTMENT COMPONENT**

- **Modernization**
- Recapitalization
- Maintenance

## MISSION

Provides integrated, on-the-move, timely, relevant battle command information to tactical combat leaders and Soldiers from brigade to platform and across platforms within the brigade task force and other Joint forces.

## DESCRIPTION

The Force XXI Battle Command Brigade and Below (FBCB2) forms the principal digital command and control system for the Army at brigade levels and below. It provides increased situational awareness (SA) on the battlefield by automatically disseminating throughout the network timely friendly force locations, reported enemy locations, and graphics to visualize the commander's intent and scheme of maneuver.

FBCB2 is a key component of the Army Battle Command System (ABCS). Appliqué hardware and software are integrated into the various platforms at brigade-and-below, as well as at appropriate division and corps slices necessary to support brigade operations.

The system features platform interconnections through two communication systems: FBCB2-Enhanced Position Location Reporting System (EPLRS), supported by the tactical Internet; and FBCB2-Blue Force Tracking, supported by L-Band satellite. The Joint Capabilities Release (JCR) is the next software release and addresses Joint requirements, database simplification, Type 1 encryption, a product line software approach, and enables the transition to the Blue Force Tracking II (BFT II) transceiver, allowing a tenfold increase in data throughput. FBCB2 is the primary platform-level digital Battle Command (BC) for the Army and Marine Corps at brigade-and-below, consisting of computer hardware and software integrated into tactical vehicles and aircraft. The system distributes SA data and BC messages within/between platforms and command posts using the Lower Tactical Internet EPLRS or L-Band satellite as its means of communication.

## SYSTEM INTERDEPENDENCIES

**In this Publication**

Advanced Field Artillery Tactical Data System (AFATDS), Battle Command Sustainment Support System (BCS3), Distributed Common Ground System-Army (DCGS-A), Movement Tracking System (MTS), Nett Warrior (NW), Warfighter Information Network-Tactical (WIN-T) Increment 1, Warfighter Information Network-Tactical (WIN-T) Increment 2, Warfighter Information Network-Tactical (WIN-T) Increment 3

**Other Major Interdependencies**

AMDWS, ASAS, BFT-AVN, DTSS, CPOF, JTCW, JSTARS, MCS, JC2C

## PROGRAM STATUS

- **Current:** In production

## PROJECTED ACTIVITIES

- **Current:** Continue production

**ACQUISITION PHASE**

- Technology Development
- Engineering and Manufacturing Development
- **Production and Deployment**
- Operations and Support

## Force XXI Battle Command Brigade and Below (FBCB2)

**FOREIGN MILITARY SALES**
Australia

**CONTRACTORS**

**Software, Encryption, and Installation Kits Prime:**
Northrop Grumman (Carson, CA)

**Field Service Representatives, Trainers, Installers:**
Engineering Solutions and Products (ESP) (Eatontown, NJ)

**Hardware:**
DRS Technologies (Palm Bay, FL)
ViaSat Inc. (Carlsbad, CA)

**Program Management Support:**
CACI (Eatontown, NJ)

**Test Support:**
MANTECH (Killeen, TX)

**Aviation Hardware:**
Prototype Integration Facility (Huntsville, AL)

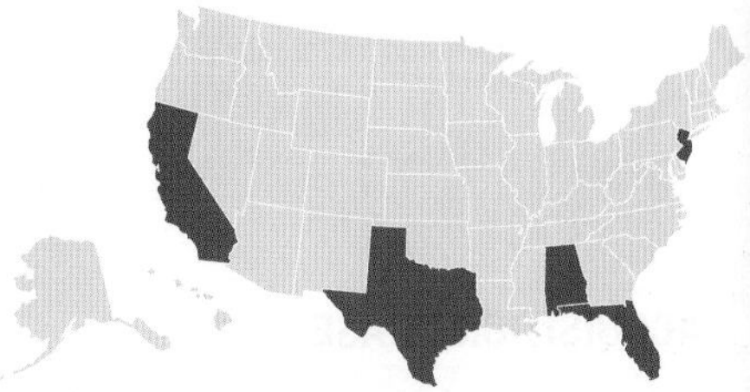

# Forward Area Air Defense Command and Control (FAAD C2)

INVESTMENT COMPONENT

**Modernization**

Recapitalization

Maintenance

## MISSION

Collects, processes, and disseminates real-time target tracking and cuing information to all short-range air defense weapons and provides command and control (C2) for the Counter-Rocket, Artillery, Mortar (C-RAM) System-of-Systems (SoS).

## DESCRIPTION

Forward Area Air Defense Command and Control (FAAD C2) software provides critical C2, situational awareness, and automated air track information by integrating engagement operations software for multiple systems, including:

- Avenger
- Sentinel
- Army Mission Command
- C-RAM SoS

FAAD C2 supports air defense and C-RAM weapon systems engagement operations by tracking friendly and enemy aircraft, cruise missiles, unmanned aerial systems, and mortar and rocket rounds as identified by radar systems and by performing C2 engagement operations for Short Range Air Defense (SHORAD) and C-RAM SoS. FAAD C2 uses the following communication systems:

- Enhanced Position Location Reporting System (EPLRS)
- Multifunctional Information Distribution System (MIDS)
- Single Channel Ground and Airborne Radio System (SINCGARS)

FAAD C2 provides Joint C2 interoperability and horizontal integration with all Army C2 and air defense artillery systems, including, but not limited to:

- PATRIOT
- Avenger
- Theater High-Altitude Area Defense (THAAD)
- Airborne Warning and Control System (AWACS)
- C-RAM
- Army Mission Command

## SYSTEM INTERDEPENDENCIES

**Other Major Interdependencies**

Radar systems providing input data such as Sentinel, Firefinder, Lightweight Counter-Mortar Radar (LCMR), and Joint external sensors (e.g., AWACS)

## PROGRAM STATUS

- **1QFY11:** Complete FY10 reset effort of 37 FAAD C2 shelter systems
- **2QFY11:** Field final Maneuver Air and Missile Defense Battalion (1-188 Air Defense Artillery)
- **4QFY11:** Field FAAD C2 software version 5.5A with 3D display
- **4QFY11:** Complete fielding of Sensor C2 nodes to all COMPO 1 divisions

## PROJECTED ACTIVITIES

- **1QFY12:** Complete FY11 reset effort of 23 FAAD C2 shelter systems
- **4QFY12:** Technology Refresh of FAAD C2 systems in three BNs
- **4QFY12:** Full Materiel Release of FAAD C2 version 5.5A
- **1QFY13:** Complete fielding of Sensor C2 nodes to all COMPO 2 divisions

ACQUISITION PHASE

Technology Development | Engineering and Manufacturing Development | **Production and Deployment** | Operations and Support

## Forward Area Air Defense Command and Control (FAAD C2)

**FOREIGN MILITARY SALES**
Australia, Egypt, United Kingdom

**CONTRACTORS**

**Software:**
Northrop Grumman Space and Mission Systems Corp. (Redondo Beach, CA)

**Hardware:**
Tobyhanna Army Depot (Scranton, PA)
PKMM (Las Vegas, NV)

**CHS 3:**
General Dynamics (Taunton, MA)

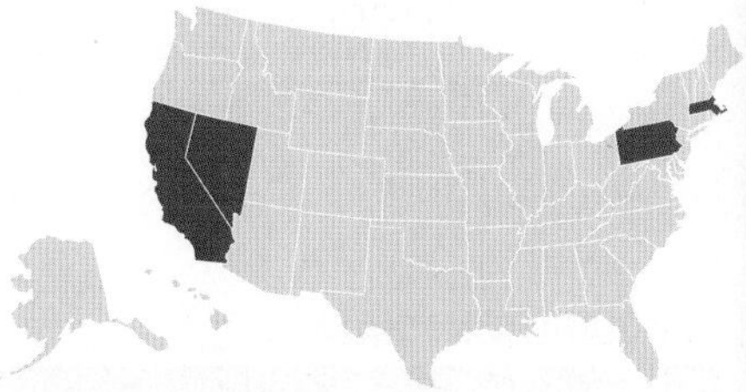

# Future Tank Main Gun Ammunition (FTMGA)

INVESTMENT COMPONENT

Modernization

Recapitalization

Maintenance

## MISSION

Provides overwhelming lethality overmatch to the heavy armor fleet.

## DESCRIPTION

The Future Tank Main Gun Ammunition (FTMGA) suite consists of two cartridges and will provide enhanced lethality and increased capability to the Heavy Brigade Combat Team.

The next-generation kinetic energy (KE) cartridge, designated M829E4, will use an advanced penetrator to defeat future heavy armor targets equipped with explosive reactive armor and active protection systems. This will increase survivability of the Abrams tank in the 0-4 kilometer range.

The Advanced Multi-Purpose (AMP) cartridge will combine the capabilities of a number of existing munitions into one cartridge. This cartridge will utilize air-bursting warhead and multimode fuze technology to combine those capabilities and provide new capability against dismounted infantry at longer ranges. This cartridge will employ high-explosive, anti-personnel, obstacle-reduction, and anti-helicopter capabilities into one munition, thus streamlining the logistical footprint associated with deploying heavy forces. This cartridge will further enhance survivability and lethality for Abrams tanks in the 0-4 kilometer range.

## SYSTEM INTERDEPENDENCIES

**In this Publication**

Abrams Tank Upgrade

**Other Major Interdependencies**

The FTMGA suite must be compatible with the Abrams tank fleet through the remainder of its service life

## PROGRAM STATUS

- **4QFY09:** Milestone B for M829E4
- **FY10:** M829E4 engineering and manufacturing development (EMD) initiation
- **FY11:** Award of two competing EMD contracts for M829E4
- **Current:** M829E4 TRL-6 demonstrated, AMP TRL-6 demonstrated

## PROJECTED ACTIVITIES

- **FY12:** Milestone B for AMP

ACQUISITION PHASE

Technology Development | Engineering and Manufacturing Development | Production and Deployment | Operations and Support

## Future Tank Main Gun Ammunition (FTMGA)

**FOREIGN MILITARY SALES**
None

**CONTRACTORS**
**M829E4:**
Alliant Techsystems (Plymouth, MN)

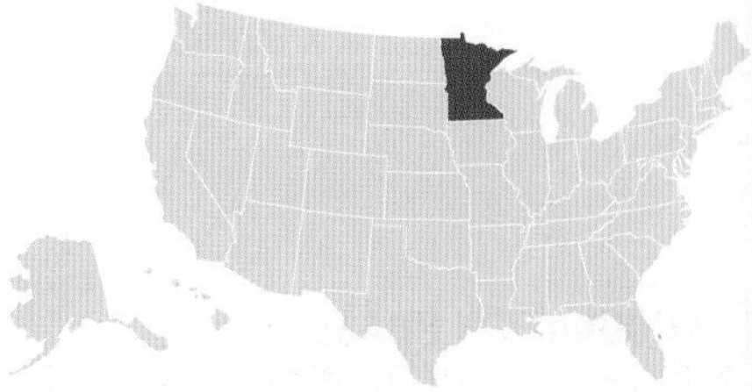

# General Fund Enterprise Business Systems (GFEBS)

**INVESTMENT COMPONENT**

- **Modernization**
- Recapitalization
- Maintenance

## MISSION

Provides a new core financial management capability that is compliant with congressional mandates, administers the Army's General Fund, and improves performance, standardizes processes, and meets future needs.

## DESCRIPTION

The Army will implement a commercial off-the-shelf Enterprise Resource Planning (ERP) system that meets the requirements of the *Chief Financial Officers Act* and the *Federal Financial Management Improvement Act of 1996* and that is capable of supporting the Department of Defense with accurate, reliable, and timely financial information. The General Fund Enterprise Business Systems (GFEBS) implementation involves standardizing financial management, accounting functions, real property inventory, and management across the Army. As a result, Army financial and real property professionals will have access to timely, reliable, and accurate information. GFEBS will also improve cost management and control, allow more time to perform financial analysis, and facilitate a more accurate understanding of the value, location, and characteristics of all property. GFEBS will provide a comprehensive system for many of the Army's financial and accounting functions including general ledger, accounts payable, revenue and accounts receivable, cost management, financial reporting, and real property inventory and management. Anticipated benefits to be realized are $960 million between FY10 and Life Cycle FY22.

## SYSTEM INTERDEPENDENCIES

None

## PROGRAM STATUS

- Current end users are approximately 33,000 at over 160 sites
- **FY11:** Deployed to Waves 3, 4, 5, and 6
- **1QFY11:** Deploy release 1.4.2
- **3QFY11:** Deploy release 1.4.3
- **3QFY11:** Received Full Deployment Decision

## PROJECTED ACTIVITIES

- **2QFY12:** Deploy release 1.4.4
- **4QFY12:** Complete deployment to remaining sites
- **4QFY12:** Move to full Army-wide deployment—Operations and Support phase

**ACQUISITION PHASE**

- Technology Development
- Engineering and Manufacturing Development
- **Production and Deployment**
- Operations and Support

## General Fund Enterprise Business Systems (GFEBS)

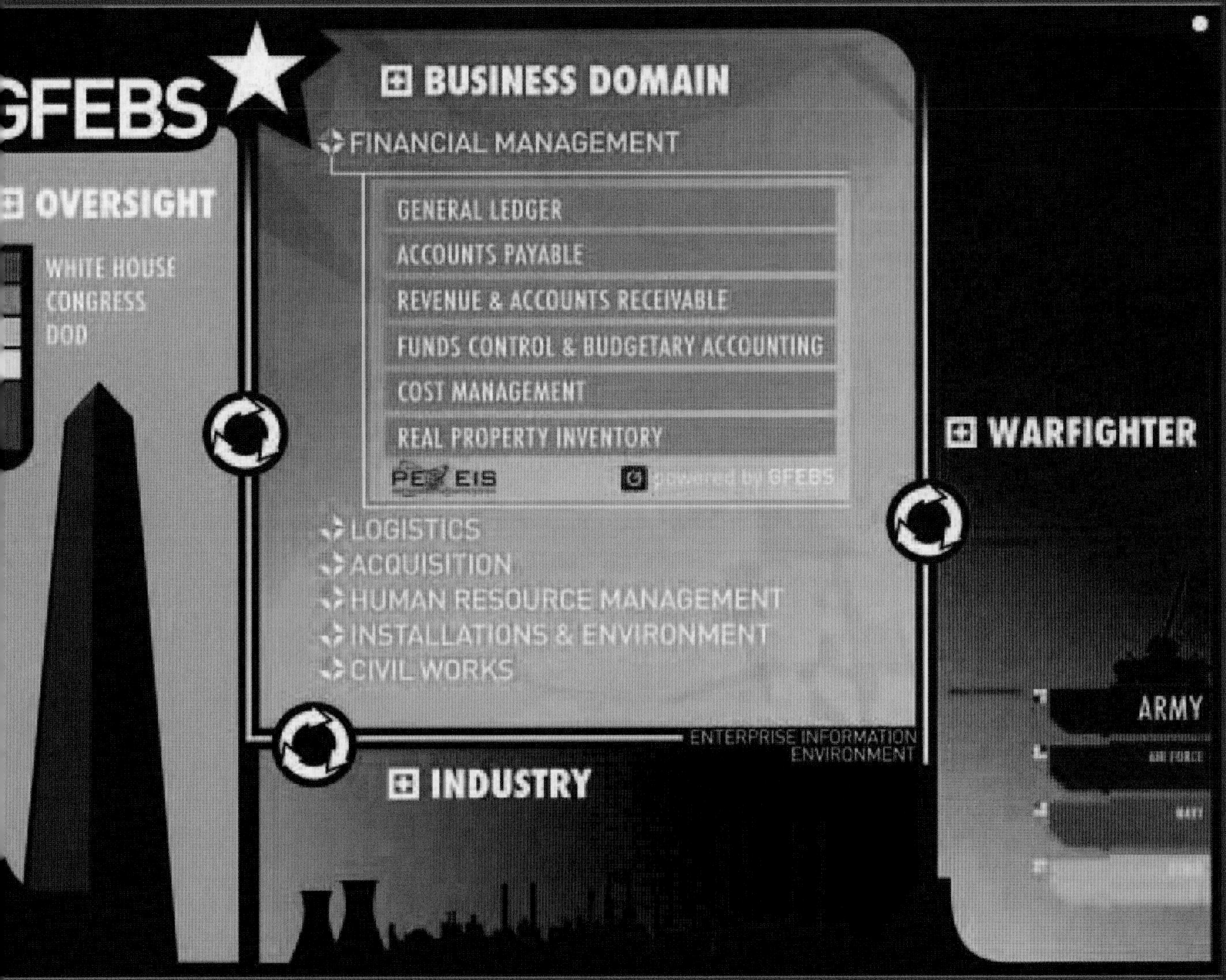


**FOREIGN MILITARY SALES**
None

**CONTRACTORS**
**System Integrator:**
Accenture (Reston, VA)
**Program Management Support-Acquisition:**
Binary Group (Bethesda, MD)
**Program Management Support Services-Engineering:**
iLuMinA Solutions (California, MD)

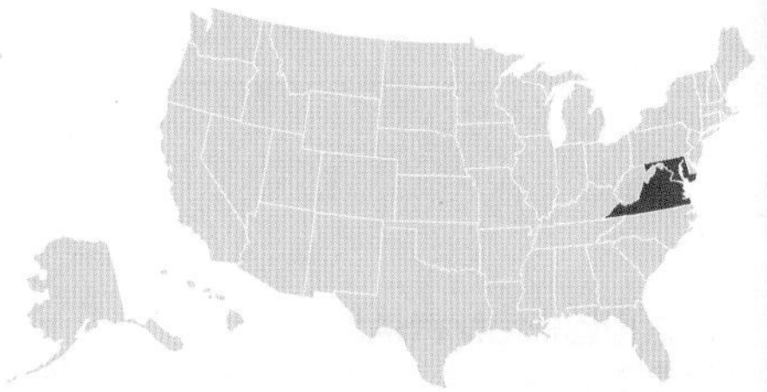

# Global Combat Support System-Army (GCSS-Army)

**INVESTMENT COMPONENT**

Modernization

Recapitalization

Maintenance

## MISSION

Provides commanders and staffs with a responsive and efficient automated system that provides one coherent source for accurate and timely logistics information to improve situational awareness and facilitate the decision-making cycle.

## DESCRIPTION

Global Combat Support System-Army (GCSS-Army) is one program with two components. GCSS-Army Enterprise Resource Planning (ERP) Solution is an automation information system that serves as the primary tactical logistics enabler to support Army and Joint Transformation for Sustainment using an ERP system. The program re-engineers current business processes to achieve end-to-end logistics and integration with applicable command and control (C2)/Joint systems. The second component, Army Enterprise Systems Integration Program (AESIP), formerly known as Product Lifecycle Management Plus (PLM+), integrates Army business functions by providing a single source for enterprise hub services, master data, and business intelligence.

GCSS-Army uses commercial-off-the-shelf (COTS) ERP software products to support rapid force projection in the battlefield functional areas of fixing, fueling, sustaining, and tactical logistics financial processes. The GCSS-Army solution replaces the logistics Standard Army Management Information Systems (STAMIS) in tactical and installation units and will establish an interface/integration with applicable C2 and Joint systems.

GCSS-Army (ERP Solution) is the primary enabler for the Army transformation vision of a technologically advanced ERP that manages the flow of logistics resources and information to satisfy the Army's modernization requirements. AESIP integrates Army business functions by providing a single source for enterprise hub services, business intelligence and analytics, and centralized master data management across the business domain. GCSS-Army will meet the Warfighter's need for responsive support at the right place and time and improve the commander's situational awareness with accurate and responsive information.

## SYSTEM INTERDEPENDENCIES

**In this Publication**

General Fund Enterprise Business Systems (GFEBS), Logistics Modernization Program

## PROGRAM STATUS

- **4QFY08:** Milestone B
- **1QFY09:** Acquisition program baseline signed
- **4QFY10:** Release 1.1 "Go-Live"
- **4QFY10:** Developmental test and evaluation, initial government test
- **4QFY11:** MS C Decision

## PROJECTED ACTIVITIES

- **1QFY12:** Initial Operational Test and Evaluation
- **3QFY12:** Full Deployment Decision

**ACQUISITION PHASE**

Technology Development | Engineering and Manufacturing Development | Production and Deployment | Operations and Support

## What GCSS-Army Provides

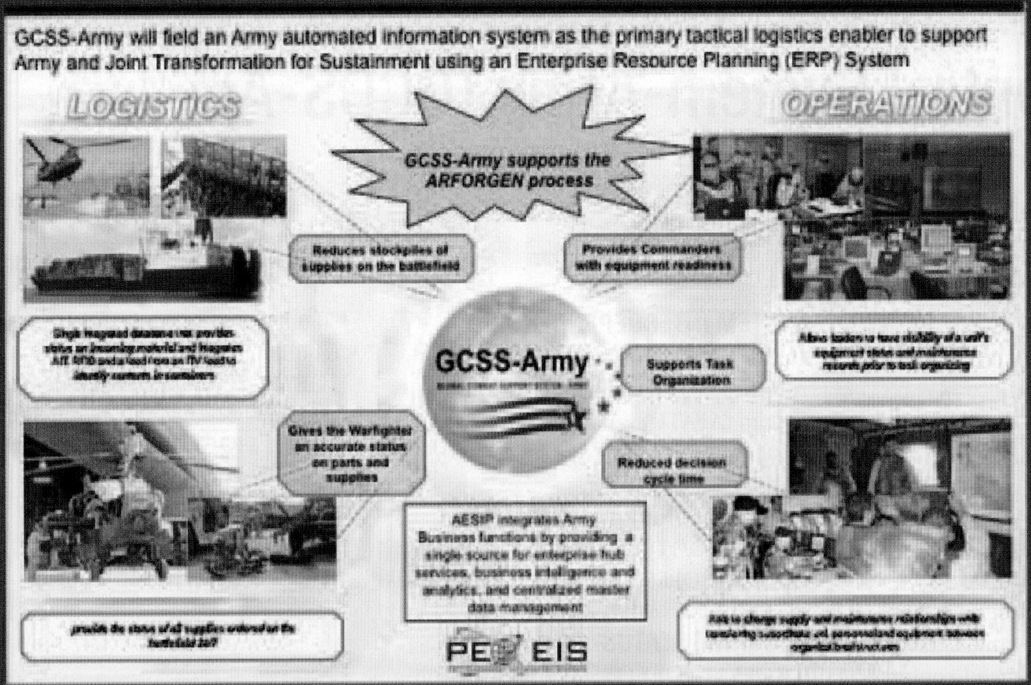


## System Architecture

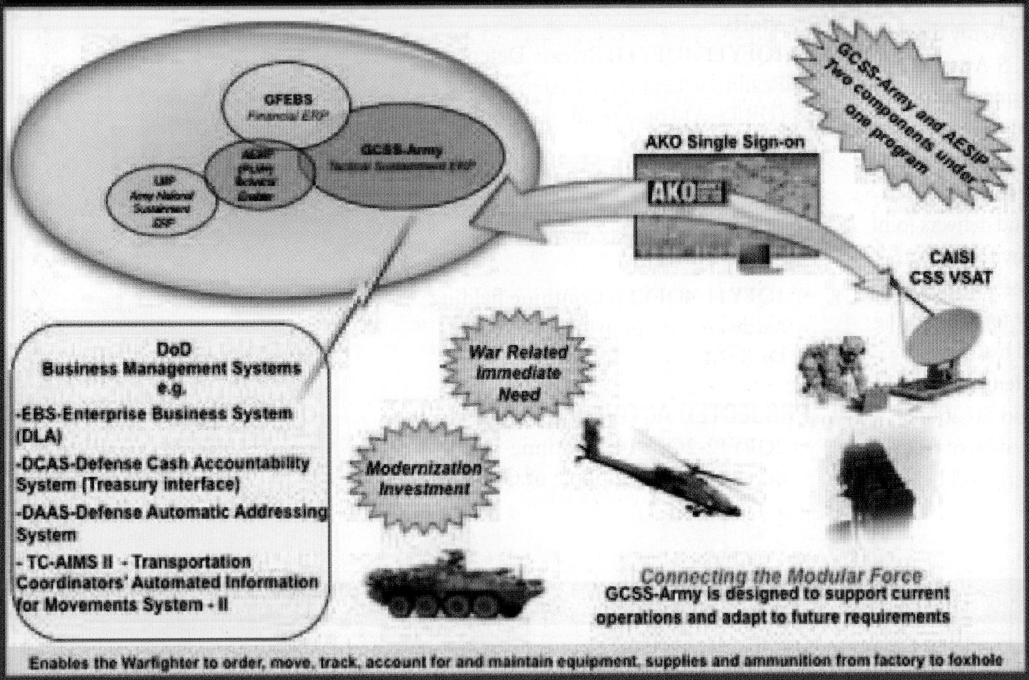


## Global Combat Support System-Army (GCSS-Army)

**FOREIGN MILITARY SALES**

None

**CONTRACTORS**

**Prime:**

Northrop Grumman Information Systems (Richmond, VA)

**PMO Support:**

LMI Consulting (McLean, VA)

MPRI, an L-3 Company (Alexandria, VA)

Capgemini (IV&V) (New York, NY)

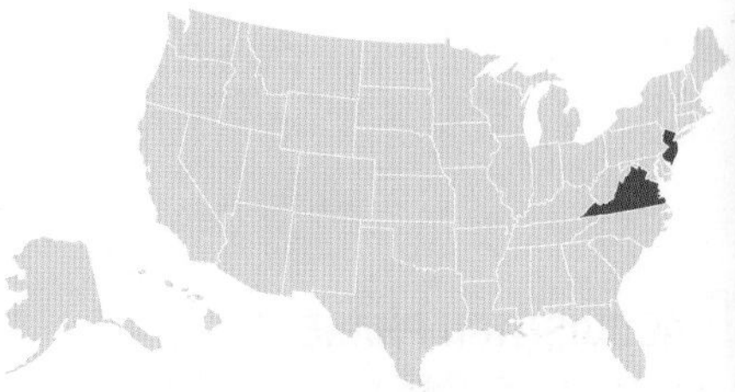

# Global Command and Control System-Army (GCCS-A)

**INVESTMENT COMPONENT**

Modernization

Recapitalization

Maintenance

## MISSION

Provides critical automated command and control (C2) tools for combatant commanders to enhance Warfighter capabilities throughout the spectrum of conflict during Joint and combined operations.

## DESCRIPTION

Global Command and Control System-Army (GCCS-A) is the Army's strategic, theater, and tactical command, control, communications (C3) system. It provides a seamless link of operational information and critical data from the strategic Global Command and Control System-Joint (GCCS-J) to Army theater elements and below. GCCS-A assists in mission planning, deployment support, operations in theater, and redeployment. It provides a common picture of Army tactical operations to the Joint and coalition communities and delivers Joint asset visibility to the Army to facilitate operations. GCCS-A is the commander's battle command asset for force planning and projection (provided by Defense Readiness Reporting System-Army (DRRS-A)), readiness, and situational awareness, and it is the system of record for theater Army headquarters worldwide.

## SYSTEM INTERDEPENDENCIES

**In this Publication**

Advanced Field Artillery Tactical Data System (AFATDS), Battle Command Sustainment Support System (BCS3)

**Other Major Interdependencies**

ABCS, CPOF, DRRS-A, DTSS, GCCS-J, GSORTS, JOPES

## PROGRAM STATUS

- **1QFY11-4QFY11:** Support Operation New Dawn and Operation Iraqi Freedom (OND/OIF)
- **1QFY11-4QFY11:** Development in support of GCCS-A modernization efforts
- **1QFY11-4QFY11:** Release Defense Readiness Reporting System-Army (DRRS-A) Force Readiness Tool (Phase 3) to the field
- **1QFY11-2QFY11:** Support to the Joint Command and Control (JC2) Capability Analysis of Alternatives (AoA)
- **1QFY11-4QFY11:** Continue fielding hardware to support GCCS-A and DRRS-A

## PROJECTED ACTIVITIES

- **2QFY12-2QFY14:** Continue development in support of GCCS-A "modernization" and DRRS-A Phase 4 requirements
- **2QFY12-2QFY14:** Development of assigned JC2 capability requirements
- **2QFY12-4QFY14:** Continue support for OND/OIF
- **2QFY12-4QFY14:** Continue fielding hardware to support GCCS-A and DRRS-A

**ACQUISITION PHASE**

Technology Development | Engineering and Manufacturing Development | Production and Deployment | Operations and Support

## Global Command and Control System-Army (GCCS-A)

**FOREIGN MILITARY SALES**

None

**CONTRACTORS**

**Develop and Field Software:**
Lockheed Martin (Springfield, VA; Tinton Falls, NJ)
**System Hardware:**
GTSI (Chantilly, VA)
**Systems Engineering and Support:**
Accenture (Reston, VA)
**Field Support Representatives (FSRs):**
Engineering Solutions and Products (ESP) (Eatontown, NJ)
General Dynamics (GDIT) (Fairfax, VA)
**Systems Engineering and Integration:**
Systems Technologies (Systek) Inc. (West Long Branch, NJ)
**Program Support:**
Booz Allen Hamilton (Eatontown, NJ)
**Systems Integration and Testing:**
General Dynamics (GDIT) (Fairfax, VA)

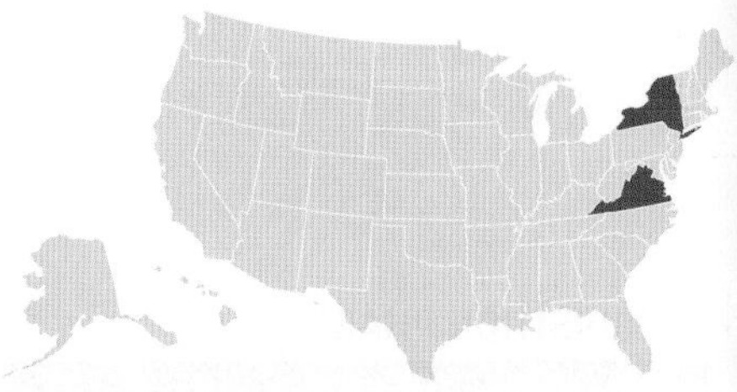

# Ground Combat Vehicle (GCV)

**INVESTMENT COMPONENT**

Modernization

Recapitalization

Maintenance

## MISSION

Provides the infantry squad with a highly mobile, protected transport to decisive locations on the battlefield.

## DESCRIPTION

The Ground Combat Vehicle (GCV) is a critical element of the Army's effort to transform, replace, and improve its Combat Vehicle fleet. The GCV Infantry Fighting Vehicle (IFV) will provide force protection to deliver a nine Soldier infantry squad in an improvised explosive device (IED) threat environment. It will protect occupants from IEDs, mines, and other ballistic threats with scalable armor that provides mission flexibility for the commander. GCV IFV will be designed with sufficient power and space to host the Army's advanced network. The IFV will feature an open architecture to facilitate the integration of current and future communications, computers, and surveillance and reconnaissance systems. The GCV IFV will have enhanced mobility to allow it to operate effectively in a variety of complex environments, including urban and cross county terrain. The GCV IFV's organic weapons will be capable of providing both destructive fires against armored vehicle threats and direct fire support for the squad during dismounted assaults. Flexible capabilities can shape the operating environment with effects that can vary from a "shove" to a lethal overmatch.

## SYSTEM INTERDEPENDENCIES

None

## PROGRAM STATUS

- **FY11:** Competitive Development prior to Engineering and Manufacturing Development Phase; issued Request for Proposals for Technology Development Phase of three phase program; DAE approved entry of GCV into the Technology Development Phase on 17 August 2011 in accordance with the Milestone A Acquisition Decision Memorandum
- **1QFY12:** Technology Development Phase began

## PROJECTED ACTIVITIES

- **3QFY13:** Technology Development Phase completed, Milestone B

**ACQUISITION PHASE**

Technology Development | Engineering and Manufacturing Development | Production and Deployment | Operations and Support

## Ground Combat Vehicle (GCV)

**FOREIGN MILITARY SALES**
None

**CONTRACTORS**
To be determined

## Concept of Operation: Squad Deployment

**GCV Platoon**

## Concept of Operation: Platoon Deployment

**GCV Infantry Company**

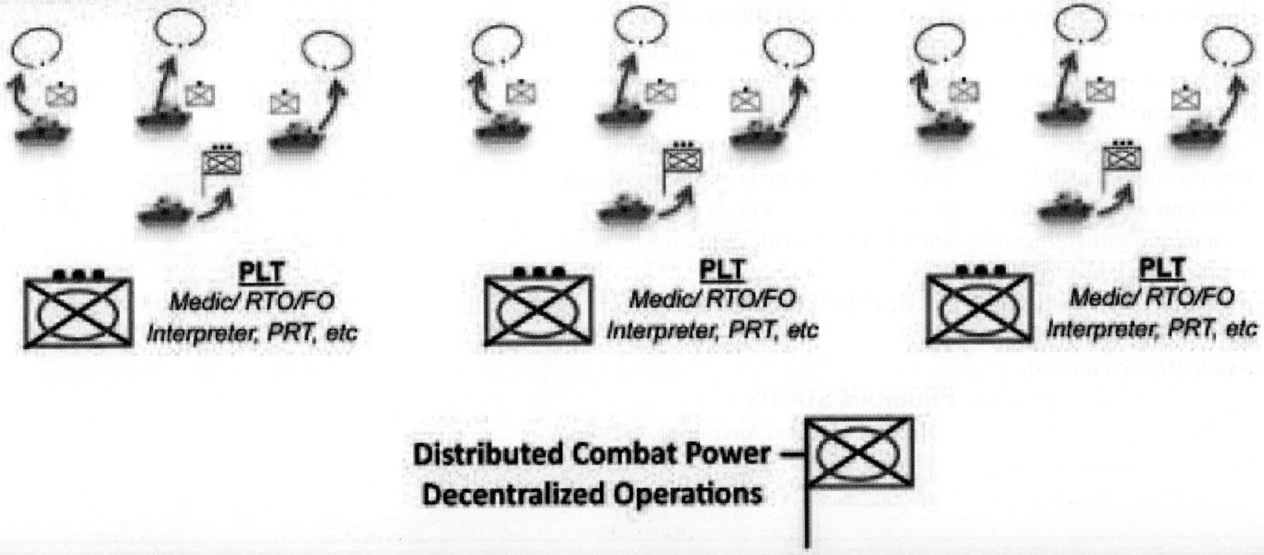


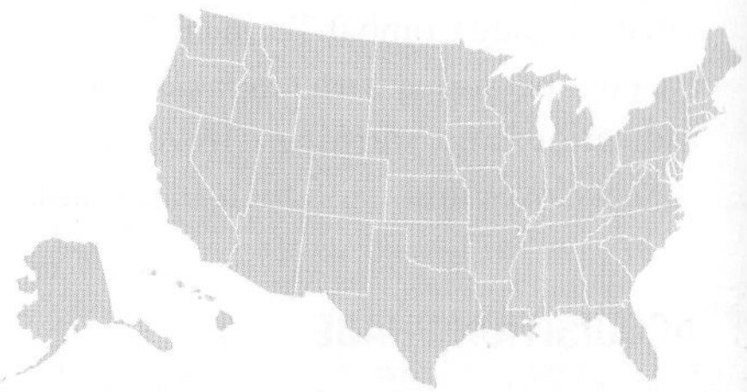

# Guardrail Common Sensor (GR/CS)

**INVESTMENT COMPONENT**

- **Modernization**
- Recapitalization
- Maintenance

## MISSION

Provides signals intelligence (SIGINT) collection and precision targeting that intercepts, collects, and precisely locates hostile communications intelligence radio frequency emitters and electronic intelligence threat radar emitters. Provides near-real-time info to tactical commanders in the Joint Task Force Area supporting full spectrum of operations (close in and deep look collections).

## DESCRIPTION

The Guardrail Common Sensor (GR/CS) is a fixed-wing, airborne, SIGINT collection and precision targeting location system. It provides near-real-time information to tactical commanders in the corps/Joint task force/Brigade Combat Team (BCT) area of operations with emphasis on Indications and Warnings (I&W). It collects low-, mid-, and high-band radio signals and ELINT signals; identifies and classifies them; determines source location; and provides near-real-time reporting, ensuring information dominance to commanders. GR/CS uses a Guardrail Mission Operations Facility (MOF) for the control, data processing, and message center for the system. GR/CS includes:

- Integrated COMINT and ELINT collection and reporting
- Enhanced signal classification and recognition and precision emitter geolocation
- Near-real-time direction finding
- Advanced integrated aircraft cockpit
- Tactical Satellite Remote Relay System

A standard system has RC-12 aircraft flying operational missions in single ship or multiship operations. Up to three aircraft/systems simultaneously collect communications and electronics emitter transmissions and gather lines of bearing and time-difference-of-arrival data, which is transmitted to the Mission Operations Facility (MOF), correlated, and supplied to supported commands via NSA net.

Planned improvements through Guardrail modernization efforts support a full spectrum of operations. Enhancements include precision geo-location subsystem, the Communications High-Accuracy Location Subsystem-Compact (CHALS-C), with increased frequency coverage and a higher probability to collect targets; a modern COMINT infrastructure and core COMINT subsystem, providing a frequency extension, Enhanced Situational Awareness (ESA); a capability to process special high-priority signals through the high-end COMINT subsystems High Band COMINT (HBC) and X-Midas; and elimination of non-supportable hardware and software. Ground processing software and hardware are being upgraded for interoperability with the Distributed Common Ground System-Army (DCGS-A) architecture and Distributed Information Backbone.

## SYSTEM INTERDEPENDENCIES

None

## PROGRAM STATUS

- **2QFY11:** Fielded Aircraft #1, #2, to 1st MI
- **3QFY11:** Fielded Aircraft #3, #4 to 1st MI
- **4QFY11:** Fielded Aircraft #5 to 224th MI

## PROJECTED ACTIVITIES

- **FY12-14:** Field the remaining 9 aircraft, retrofit aircraft 1 thru 9 with enhancement and begin de-fielding systems from Korea

**ACQUISITION PHASE**

- Technology Development
- Engineering and Manufacturing Development
- Production and Deployment
- **Operations and Support**

## Guardrail Common Sensor (GR/CS)

**FOREIGN MILITARY SALES**

None

**CONTRACTORS**

**System Integrator, ESA Subsystem, and MOF Software/System Support:**

Northrop Grumman (Sacramento, CA)

**Data Links:**

L-3 Communications (Salt Lake City, UT)

**CHALS-C:**

Lockheed Martin (Owego, NY)

**X-MIDAS Subsystem:**

ZETA (Fairfax, VA)

**HBC Subsystem:**

ArgonST Radix (Mountain View, CA)

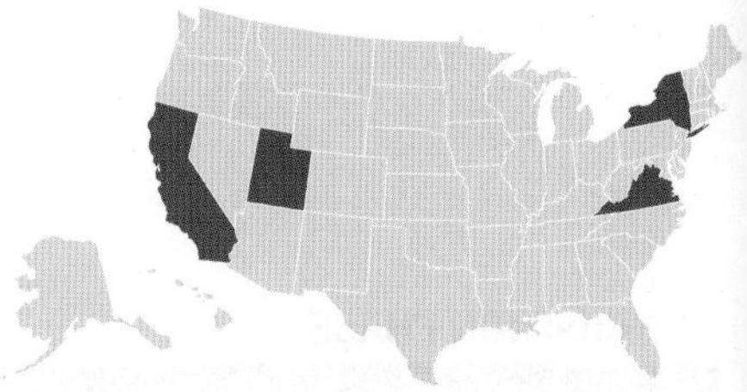

# Guided Multiple Launch Rocket System (GMLRS) DPICM/ Unitary/Alternative Warhead (Tactical Rockets)

**INVESTMENT COMPONENT**

- Modernization
- Recapitalization
- Maintenance

## MISSION

Provides a persistent, responsive, all-weather, rapidly deployed, long-range, surface-to-surface, area-and-point precision strike capability.

## DESCRIPTION

The Guided Multiple Launch Rocket System (GMLRS) is a major upgrade to the M26 rocket, producing precise destructive and shaping fires against a variety of target sets. GMLRS is employed with the M270A1 upgraded MLRS tracked launcher and the M142 High Mobility Artillery Rocket System (HIMARS) wheeled launchers. GMLRS munitions have greater accuracy with a resulting higher probability of kill, smaller logistics footprint, and minimized collateral damage.

There are two fielded variants of the GMLRS: the previously produced dual-purpose improved conventional munitions (DPICM) variant designed to service area targets; and the unitary variant with a single 200-pound class high-explosive charge to provide precision strike blast and fragmentation effects with low collateral damage. The development of a third variant incorporating an alternative warhead (AW) has been initiated. The AW will be compliant with the 2008 DoD Policy on Cluster Munitions & Unintended Harm to Civilians. The AW rocket will service area target sets without producing unexploded ordnance and will begin fielding in FY16.

The original GMLRS development was an international cooperative program with the United Kingdom, Germany, France, and Italy. An urgent materiel release version of the GMLRS unitary variant has been produced and fielded in support of U.S. Central Command (CENTCOM) forces with over 2,000 rockets used in operations through July 2010.

**Rocket Length:** 3,937mm
**Rocket Diameter:** 227mm
**Rocket Reliability:** Threshold 92 percent; objective 95 percent
**Ballistic Range(s):** 15 to 70+ kilometers

## SYSTEM INTERDEPENDENCIES

**In this Publication**

Advanced Field Artillery Tactical Data System (AFATDS), High Mobility Artillery Rocket System (HIMARS), Multiple Launch Rocket System (MLRS) M270A1

**Other Major Interdependencies**

GPS, Joint Systems, National Systems

## PROGRAM STATUS

- **2-3QFY08:** GMLRS Unitary initial operational test
- **1QFY09:** GMLRS AW Configuration Steering Board (CSB) Acquisition Decision Memorandum (ADM) halts new DPICM procurements
- **1QFY09:** GMLRS Unitary Full-Rate Production Decision
- **4QFY09:** GMLRS AW Milestone A
- **4QFY10:** GMLRS AW Warhead Prototype Technical Demonstrations
- **4QFY11:** Selection of GMLRS AW warhead vendor for further development in Engineering and Manufacturing Development (EMD) Phase

## PROJECTED ACTIVITIES

- **1QFY12:** GMLRS AW Milestone B
- **1QFY17:** GMLRS AW Initial Operational Capability

**ACQUISITION PHASE**

- Technology Development
- Engineering and Manufacturing Development
- Production and Deployment
- Operations and Support

## Guided Multiple Launch Rocket System (GMLRS) DPICM/ Unitary/Alternative Warhead (Tactical Rockets)

**FOREIGN MILITARY SALES**

United Kingdom, United Arab Emirates, Singapore, Bahrain, Japan, Canada, Jordan, Thailand, Finland, Germany, and France

**CONTRACTORS**

Lockheed Martin (Camden, AR; Grand Prairie, TX)

Lockheed Martin Missiles and Fire Control (Las Cruces, NM)

**Guidance Set:**

Honeywell (Clearwater, FL)

**Rocket Motors:**

Aerojet (Camden, AR)

**Technical System Support:**

Systems, Studies, and Simulation (Huntsville, AL)

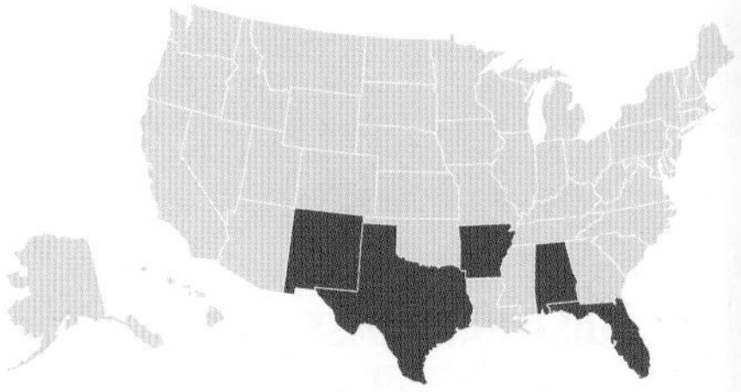

# Harbormaster Command and Control Center (HCCC)

**INVESTMENT COMPONENT**

Modernization

Recapitalization

Maintenance

## MISSION

Serves as a deployable and tactically mobile system to provide the Army logistician conducting distributed logistics the sensors and knowledge management tools to establish and maintain battle awareness (BA) and command and control (C2) of the harbor and littoral environment for all worldwide Overseas Contingency Operations (OCOs).

## DESCRIPTION

The Command Post Systems and Integration (CPS&I) product office provides a Harbormaster Command and Control Center (HCCC) System that provides the ability to facilitate safe navigation of watercraft in the harbor and littorals. The HCCC System is capable of Command, Control, and Communications operations that incorporate Local Area Network (LAN) equipment and Satellite Communications (SATCOM). The system provides sensors and management tools to collect and process environmental and asset tracking data relevant to supporting distribution in the littorals. The HCCC System possess Non-Secure Internet Protocol (IP) Network (NIPRNET) and Secret IP Router Network (SIPRNET) technical connectivity to populate the Common Operating Picture (COP).

The system provides the technical command and control (C2) connectivity to shift time and point of delivery of forces, equipment, sustainment, and support. The HCCC System is composed of a main and remote command center. Each system consists of two Command Post Platforms (CPPs), two Trailer Mounted Support Systems-Medium (TMSS-M), two Harbormaster Trailer Sensor Platforms (HTSPs), two Dual 18kw Generator Set, and two Family of Medium Tactical Vehicles (FMTVs).

## SYSTEM INTERDEPENDENCIES

**Other Major Interdependencies**

Global Command and Control System (GCCS), Movement Tracking System (MTS), SIPR/NIPR Access Point (SNAP), Battle Command Sustainment Support System (BCS3)

## PROGRAM STATUS

- **1QFY11:** System-of-Systems Demonstration at Redstone Arsenal, Huntsville, AL
- **3QFY11:** Reliability, Availability, and Maintainability (RAM) event at Redstone Test Center, Huntsville, AL
- **3QFY11:** Technical Manuals (TM) Verification at Tobyhanna Army Depot (TYAD), PA
- **4QFY11:** 492nd New Equipment Training (NET) and fielding at Ft. Eustis, VA
- **4QFY11:** New Equipment Material In-Brief (NMIB) 653rd at Tacoma, WA
- **4QFY11:** NMIB with 201st Mare Island, CA
- **4QFY11:** Logistics Maintainability Demonstration (LMD) at TYAD, PA
- **4QFY11:** Battle Command System-of-Systems Integration Training (BCSoSIT) at Ft. Eustis, VA
- **4QFY11:** Operational Test (OT) at Ft. Eustis, VA

## PROJECTED ACTIVITIES

- **1QFY12:** TM Final
- **1QFY12:** Type Classification/Materiel Release (TC/MR)
- **2QFY12:** 653rd and 201st NET and fielding
- **3QFY12:** 338th NET and fielding
- **4QFY12:** 393rd and 545th NET and fielding
- **2QFY13:** 651st NET and fielding

**ACQUISITION PHASE**

Technology Development | Engineering and Manufacturing Development | Production and Deployment | Operations and Support

## Harbormaster Command and Control Center (HCCC)

**FOREIGN MILITARY SALES**
None

**CONTRACTORS**
**Command Post Platform:**
Northrop Grumman (Huntsville, AL)
**Trailer Mounted Support System:**
Northrop Grumman (Huntsville, AL)
**AMCOM EXPRESS (SETA):**
Sigmatech Inc. (Huntsville, AL)
**Materiel Fielding:**
Tobyhanna Army Deport (Tobyhanna, PA)
**TOCNET Intercommunications Systems:**
SCI Technology Inc. (Huntsville, AL)
**Common Hardware Systems:**
General Dynamics C4 Systems Inc. (Tauton, MA)
**Harbormaster Trailer Sensor Package (HTSP):**
SPAWAR Pacific (San Diego, CA)
**HP-6G 18KW Generator:**
DHS Systems (Huntsville, AL)

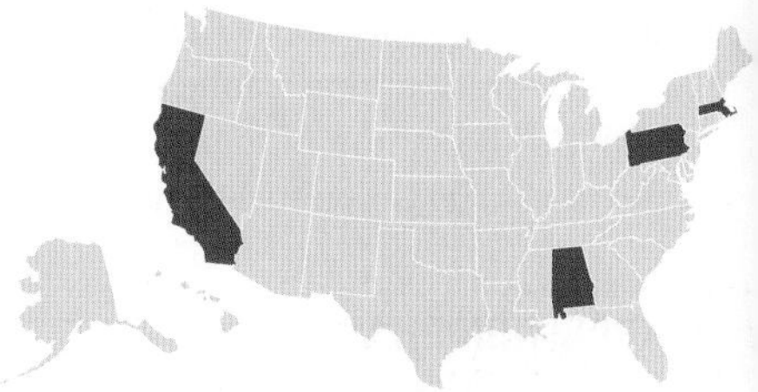

# Heavy Expanded Mobility Tactical Truck (HEMTT)/ HEMTT Extended Service Program (ESP)

**INVESTMENT COMPONENT**

Modernization

Recapitalization

Maintenance

## MISSION

Supports combat units by performing line and local haul, unit resupply, aviation refueling, tactical vehicle refueling, and related missions in a tactical environment.

## DESCRIPTION

The Heavy Expanded Mobility Tactical Truck (HEMTT) 10-ton, 8-wheel drive is designed for cross-country military missions up to 11 tons to transport ammunition, petroleum, oils, and lubricants. Variants include: M977, M985, M978, M983, M984 and M1120.

The M977 is utilized for delivery of general supplies, equipment, and ammunition with an onboard crane with 4,500 pounds load capacity. The M985 cargo has an onboard crane with 5,400 pounds load capacity and is the primary transporter for Multiple Launch Rocket System (MLRS) ammunition. The M978 tanker is a 2,500 gallon fuel transporter for field refueling of ground vehicles and aircraft. The M984 wrecker includes a crane and winch retrieval system and serves the primary role of recovery and evacuation of heavy wheel vehicles and combat systems. The M983 Tractor is the prime mover for the PATRIOT missile. The M983 Light Equipment Transporter (LET) Tractor serves as the prime mover for tactical semitrailers in engineering units to include the M870 series, Intermediate Stryker Recovery System (ISRS), and Mine Resistant Ambush Protected (MRAP) vehicles. The HEMTT Load Handling System (LHS) provides NATO interoperability with standard flatrack and mission modules for delivery of general supplies, equipment, and ammunition with Palletized Load System (PLS) style load handling systems. The system is compatible with the PLS Trailer, capable of a 26,000 pound payload.

The HEMTT A4 began fielding in December 2008. Enhancements include a modern power train consisting of a Caterpillar C-15/500 horsepower Engine and Allison Transmission (4500 SP/5-speed automatic), anti-lock braking system and traction control, air-ride suspension, a J-1939 data-bus providing an updated electrical system, climate control, and a larger common cab.

HEMTT ESP, known as HEMTT RECAP, is a recapitalization program that converts high-mileage, older version HEMTT trucks into the current A4 production configuration. Modernizing the fleet to one model reduces logistic footprint and operational and sustainment (O&S) cost of maintaining old vehicles.

HEMTT has several configurations:

- M977: Cargo truck with light materiel handling crane
- M985: Cargo truck with heavy materiel handling crane
- M978: 2,500-gallon fuel tanker
- M984: Wrecker
- M983: Tractor
- M983 LET: LET fifth wheel vertical loading has 45K winch with gross towing weight of 45.4 kilograms
- M1120: LHS transports palletized materiel and International Standards Organization (ISO) containers

## SYSTEM INTERDEPENDENCIES

**Other Major Interdependencies**

The M983 HEMTT LET Tractor paired with the Fifth Wheel Towing Device and High Mobility Recovery Trailer are together designated as the Interim Stryker Recovery System (ISRS) for Stryker and MRAP recovery. Other vehicles that utilize the HEMTT chassis are: M1142 Tactical Fire Fighting Trucks, M1158 Heavy Mobility Water Tender Truck, M1977 HEMTT Common Bridge Transporter (CBT), Theatre High Altitude Area Defense Missile System (THAAD), and the M985 GMT Guided Missile Transport used in PATRIOT Battalions.

## PROGRAM STATUS

- **1QFY09:** HEMTT A4 Family of Vehicles was type classified standard and full materiel released (TC/MR)

## PROJECTED ACTIVITIES

- **FY12:** Distribute HEMTT A4s in accordance with Headquarters Department of the Army G8 distribution plan to next deployers to Theater, Army National Guard, Army Reserve, Homeland Defense, and Army Prepositioned Stock

**ACQUISITION PHASE**

Technology Development | Engineering and Manufacturing Development | Production and Deployment | Operations and Support

## Heavy Expanded Mobility Tactical Truck (HEMTT)/HEMTT Extended Service Program (ESP)

**FOREIGN MILITARY SALES**
Egypt

**CONTRACTORS**
**Prime:**
Oshkosh Corp. (Oshkosh, WI; Killeen, TX)
**Engine:**
Caterpillar (Peoria, IL)
**Transmission:**
Allison Transmission (Indianapolis, IN)
**Tires:**
Michelin (Greenville, SC)

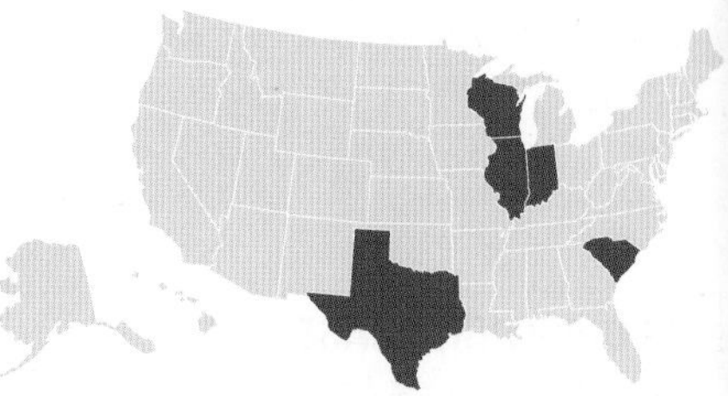

# Heavy Loader

**INVESTMENT COMPONENT**

- **Modernization**
- Recapitalization
- Maintenance

## MISSION

Provides engineering units the capability to perform lifting, loading, hauling, digging, and trenching operations in support of Combat Support Brigades and Brigade Combat Teams.

## DESCRIPTION

The Heavy Loader is a commercial vehicle modified for military use. The military version of the loader will be armored with an A-kit (armored floor plate) on all loaders and a C-kit (armored cab) on select loaders. There are two types of loaders: the Type I-Quarry Teams, with a capacity of 4.5 cubic yards, and Type II-General Use, with a capacity of 5 cubic yards. The Heavy Loader currently has state-of-the-art operator displays, onboard diagnostics and prognostics, and blackout lighting. For operator comfort, each loader is equipped with heating and air conditioning as well as an air suspension seat. Modifications include chemical-resistant coating paint, rifle rack, military standard (MIL-STD-209) lift and tie-down, and hydraulic quick coupler systems for attachments.

Heavy Loaders provide the capability to lift, move, and load a variety of materials. They are also used to perform horizontal and vertical construction tasks supporting military construction operations including construction of roads, bridges, airfields, medical facilities, and demolition of structures, as well as loading in quarry operations.

## SYSTEM INTERDEPENDENCIES

**Other Major Interdependencies**

M916/M870 truck trailer for highway transportability

## PROGRAM STATUS

- **Current:** Completing fielding

## PROJECTED ACTIVITIES

- **Future:** Continue fielding to units

**ACQUISITION PHASE**

- Technology Development
- Engineering and Manufacturing Development
- **Production and Deployment**
- Operations and Support

## Heavy Loader

**FOREIGN MILITARY SALES**
Afghanistan

**CONTRACTORS**

**OEM:**
Caterpillar Defense and Federal Products (Peoria, IL)

**Armor:**
BAE Systems (Rockville, MD)

**Logistics:**
XMCO (Warren, MI)

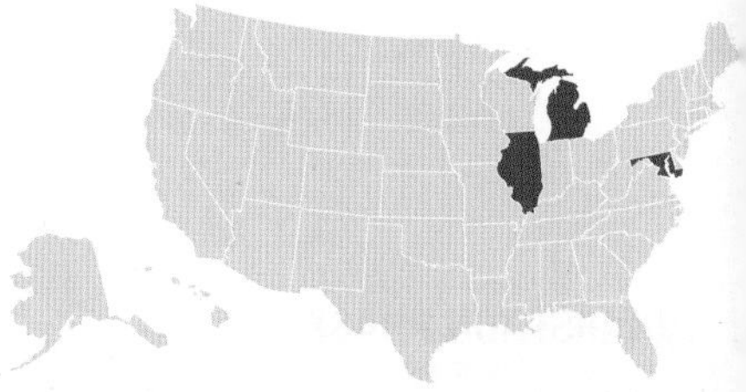

# HELLFIRE Family of Missiles

**INVESTMENT COMPONENT**

Modernization

Recapitalization

Maintenance

## MISSION

Engages and defeats individual moving or stationary advanced armor, mechanized or vehicular targets, patrol craft, buildings, or bunkers while increasing aircraft survivability.

## DESCRIPTION

The AGM-114 HELLFIRE Family of Missiles includes the HELLFIRE II and Longbow HELLFIRE missiles. HELLFIRE II is a precision strike, Semi-Active Laser (SAL) guided missile and is the principal air-to-ground weapon for the Army AH-64 Apache, OH-58 Kiowa Warrior, Gray Eagle Extended Range Multipurpose (ERMP) Unmanned Aircraft System (UAS), Special Operations aircraft, Marine Corps AH-1W Super Cobra, and Air Force's Predator/Reaper UAS.

The SAL HELLFIRE II missile is guided by laser energy reflected off the target. It has three warhead variants: a dual warhead, shaped charge high-explosive anti-tank (HEAT) capability for armored targets (AGM-114K); a blast fragmentation warhead (BFWH) for urban, patrol boat and other "soft" targets (AGM-114M); and a metal augmented charge (MAC) warhead (AGM-114N) for urban structures, bunkers, radar sites, communications installations, and bridges. Beginning in 2012, a HELLFIRE multipurpose warhead variant (AGM-114R) will be available to the Warfighter that allows selection of warhead effects corresponding to a specific target type. The AGM-114R is capable of being launched from Army rotary-wing and UAS platforms and provides the pilot increased operational flexibility.

The Longbow HELLFIRE (AGM-114L) is also a precision strike missile using millimeter wave (MMW) radar guidance instead of the HELLFIRE II's semi-active laser. It is the principal anti-tank system for the AH-64D Apache Longbow helicopter and uses the same anti-armor warhead as the HELLFIRE II. The MMW seeker provides beyond line-of-sight fire and forget capability, as well as the ability to operate in adverse weather and battlefield obscurants.

**Diameter:** 7 inches
**Weight:** 99.8-107 pounds
**Length:** 64-69 inches

**Maximum range:**
**Direct fire:** 7 kilometers
**Indirect fire:** 8 kilometers
**Minimum range:** .5-1.5 kilometers

## SYSTEM INTERDEPENDENCIES

None

## PROGRAM STATUS

- **Current:** Laser HELLFIRE II missiles are procured annually to replace combat expenditures and war reserve requirements

## PROJECTED ACTIVITIES

**Laser HELLFIRE**
- **Continue:** In production

**Longbow HELLFIRE**
- **Continue:** Sustainment activities

**ACQUISITION PHASE**

Technology Development | Engineering and Manufacturing Development | Production and Deployment | Operations and Support

| System Description | Production | Characteristics | Performance |
|---|---|---|---|
| M-114A, B, C, F, FA – HELLFIRE<br>Weight = 45 kg Length = 163 cm<br> | 1982 – 1992 | A, B, C have a Single Shaped-Charge Warhead; Analog Autopilot | • Not Capable Against Reactive Armor<br>• Non-Programmable |
| | | F has Tandem Warheads; Analog Autopilot | • Reactive Armor Capable<br>• Non-Programmable |
| GM-114K/K2/K2A – HELLFIRE II<br>Weight = 45 kg Length = 163 cm<br> | 1993 – Until Complete | • Tandem Warheads<br>• Electronic Safe & Arm Device<br>• Digital Autopilot & Electronics<br>• Improved Performance Software | • Capable Against 21st Century Armor<br>• Hardened Against Countermeasures<br>• K-2 adds Insensitive Munitions (IM)<br>• K-2A adds Blast-Frag Sleeve |
| GM-114L – HELLFIRE LONGBOW<br>Weight = 49 kg Length = 180 cm<br> | 1995 – 2005 | • Tandem Warheads<br>• Digital Autopilot & Electronics<br>• Millimeter-Wave (MMW) Seeker<br>• IM Warheads | • Initiate on Contact<br>• Hardened Against Countermeasures<br>• Programmable Software<br>• All-Weather |
| M-114M – HELLFIRE II (Blast Frag)<br>Weight = 49 kg Length = 180 cm<br> | 1998 – 2010 | • Blast-Frag Warhead<br>• 4 Operating Modes<br>• Digital Autopilot & Electronics<br>• Delayed-Fuse Capability | • For Buildings, Soft-Skin Vehicles<br>• Optimized for Low Cloud Ceilings<br>• Hardened Against Countermeasures<br>• WH Penetrates Target Before Detonation |
| AGM-114N – HELLFIRE II (MAC)<br>Weight = 49 kg Length = 180 cm<br> | 2003 – Until Complete | • Metal-Augmented Charge<br>– Sustained Pressure Wave<br>• 4 Operating Modes<br>• Delayed-Fuse Capability | • For Buildings, Soft-Skin Vehicles<br>• Optimized for Low Cloud Ceilings<br>• Hardened Against Countermeasures<br>• WH Penetrates Target Before Detonation |
| AGM-114R – HELLFIRE II<br>(Bridge to JAGM – RW/UAS)<br>Weight = 49 kg Length = 180 cm<br> | 2010 – Until Complete | • Integratef Blast Frag Sleeve Warhead<br>• Designed for all platforms<br>• Health Monitoring | • For all Target Sets<br>• Increased Lethality and Engagement Envelope |

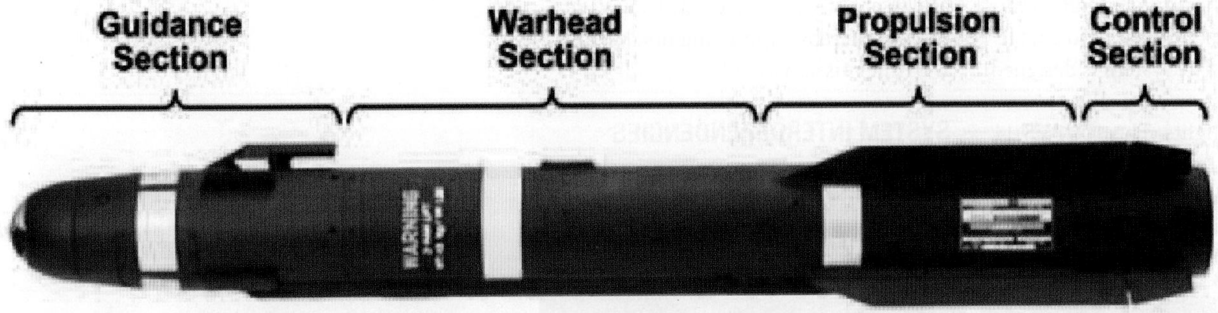


## HELLFIRE Family of Missiles

**FOREIGN MILITARY SALES**

**Laser Hellfire:**
Australia, Egypt, France, Greece, Israel, Japan, Kuwait, Netherlands, Saudi Arabia, Singapore, Spain, Taiwan, Sweden, United Arab Emirates, and United Kingdom

**Direct commercial sale:**
United Kingdom, Norway, Netherlands, Saudi Arabia and Turkey

**Longbow Hellfire:**
Israel, Japan, Kuwait, Singapore, Taiwan, and United Arab Emirates

**Direct commercial sale:**
United Kingdom

**CONTRACTORS**

**Prime Contractor:**
Lockheed Martin (Orlando, FL)

**Seeker:**
Lockheed Martin (Ocala, FL)

**Rocket Motor/Warhead:**
Alliant Techsystems (Rocket City, WV)

**Control Section:**
Moog Inc. (Salt Lake, UT)

**Firing Component (ESAF):**
L-3 Communications (Chicago, IL)

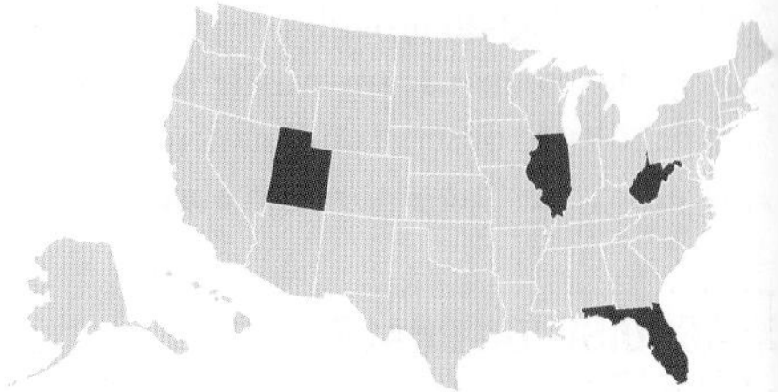

# Helmet Mounted Night Vision Devices (HMNVD)

**INVESTMENT COMPONENT**

- Modernization
- Recapitalization
- Maintenance

## MISSION

Enhances the Warfighter's visual ability and situational awareness while successfully engaging and executing operations day or night, whether in adverse weather or visually obscured battlefield conditions.

## DESCRIPTION

Helmet Mounted Night Vision Devices (HMNVD) support the tactical level of war, enabling the individual Soldier to see, understand, and act first and permitting superior tactical mobility and decisive engagement during limited visibility conditions. These devices include:

**The AN/PSQ-20 Enhanced Night Vision Goggle (ENVG)**
The AN/PSQ-20 provides dismounted Brigade Combat Team Warfighters the capability to observe and maneuver in all weather conditions through obscurants during limited visibility, and under all lighting conditions while enabling rapid detection and engagement with rifle-mounted aiming lasers. The ENVG combines the visual detail in low light conditions that is provided by image intensification with the thermal sensor's ability to see through fog, dust, and smoke that obscure vision. This thermal capability makes the ENVG, unlike earlier night vision devices, useful during the day as well as at night. The ENVG allows Soldiers to rapidly detect and engage targets because it permits use of existing rifle-mounted aiming lights.

**AN/PVS-14 Monocular Night Vision Device (MNVD)**
The AN/PVS-14 provides the Warfighter with the ability to perform night time operations, while driving, walking, performing first aid, reading maps, and conducting maintenance. The AN/PVS-14 MNVD is a helmet-mounted passive device that amplifies ambient light and very near infrared (IR) energy to enable night operations. The system is designed for use in conjunction with rifle-mounted aiming lights. The AN/PVS-14 has a helmet mount assembly compatible with the Advanced Combat Helmet for hands-free operation. The AN/PVS-14 can also be mounted to the M16 Rifle/M4 Carbine receiver rail.

**AN/AVS-6 Aviator's Night Vision Imaging System (ANVIS)**
The AN/AVS-6 provides Army aircraft the capability to support missions of target acquisition, target engagement, troop lift, and logistical support during periods of reduced visibility at night, by enhancing the tactical advantage and capability of the aircrew. The AN/AVS-6 provides the capability for Army aircraft to conduct missions at night and during periods of reduced visibility, by amplifying ambient light from sources such as the moon, stars, and sky glow, making the viewed scene clearly visible to the operator. Additionally, the ANVIS enables the aircrew to maneuver the aircraft during low-level, nap-of-the-earth (NOE) flights, providing the capability to gather combat intelligence and to acquire and successfully engage targets, thereby supporting normal and wartime missions.

## SYSTEM INTERDEPENDENCIES

None

## PROGRAM STATUS

- **FY11:** Fielded to units supporting Operation Enduring Freedom and Operation New Dawn
- **FY11:** Production and fielding
- **FY11:** Awarded two 3-year Indefinite Delivery/Indefinite Quantity contracts for AN/PVS-14 and related spares for sustainment, other Services, and Foreign Military Sales
- **FY11:** Performed Production Qualification Testing of new AN/PSQ-20 systems from multiple vendors

## PROGRAM STATUS

- **FY12:** Production and fielding in accordance with Headquarters Department of the Army G8 priorities
- **FY12:** Complete AN/PSQ-20 qualification testing, reach a Full-Rate Production Decision, and issue a production award(s)
- **FY12:** Award new production contract(s) for AN/AVS-6(v)3
- **4QFY12:** Final Army AN/PVS-14 delivery

**ACQUISITION PHASE**

- Technology Development
- Engineering and Manufacturing Development
- Production and Deployment
- Operations and Support

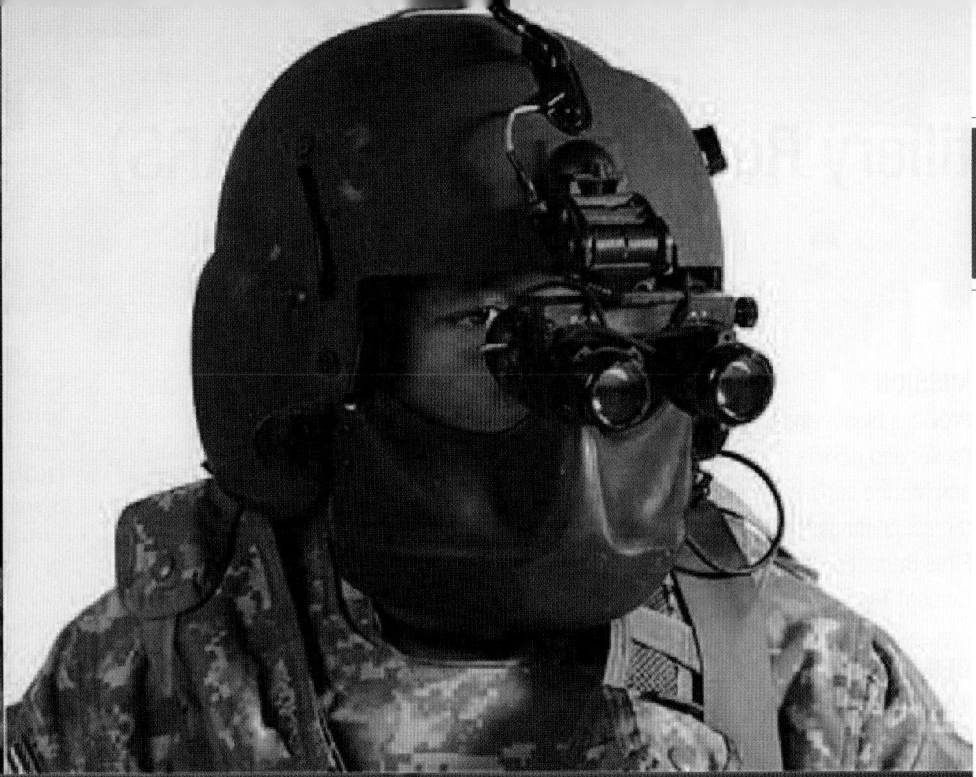

## Helmet Mounted Night Vision Devices (HMNVD)

**FOREIGN MILITARY SALES**

Support approved cases for AN/PVS-7, AN/PVS-14, and AN/AVS-6

**CONTRACTORS**

**AN/PVS-14:**

ITT (Roanoke, VA)

L-3 Communications Electro-Optic Systems (Tempe, AZ; Garland, TX; Londonderry, NH)

**AN/AVS-6(V)3:**

ITT (Roanoke, VA)

**AN/PSQ-20:**

ITT Geospatial Systems (Roanoke, VA), L-3 Insight (Londonderry, NH), DRS (Parsippany, NJ), Raytheon (Dallas, TX)

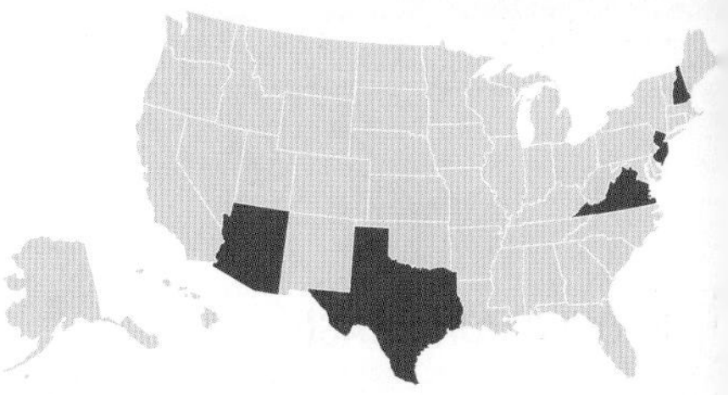

# High Mobility Artillery Rocket System (HIMARS)

**INVESTMENT COMPONENT**

- **Modernization**
- Recapitalization
- Maintenance

## MISSION

Provides close- and long-range precision rocket and missile fire support for Army and Marine early-entry expeditionary forces, contingency forces, and Modular Fires Brigades supporting Brigade Combat Teams.

## DESCRIPTION

The M142 High Mobility Artillery Rocket System (HIMARS) is a combat-proven, wheeled artillery system, rapidly deployable via C-130 and operable in all weather and visibility conditions. HIMARS is mounted on a five-ton modified Family of Medium Tactical Vehicles chassis. The wheeled chassis allows for faster road movement and lower operating costs, and requires far fewer strategic airlifts (via C-5 or C-17) to transport a firing battery than the tracked M270 Multiple Launch Rocket System (MLRS) that it replaces. The M142 provides responsive, highly accurate, and extremely lethal surface-to-surface rocket and missile fires from 15 to 300 kilometers. HIMARS can fire all munitions in the current and planned suite of the MLRS Family of Munitions (MFOM), including Army Tactical Missile System (ATACMS) missiles and Guided MLRS (GMLRS) rockets. HIMARS carries either six rockets or one missile, is self-loading and self-locating, and is operated by a three-man crew protected from launch exhaust/debris and ballistic threats by an armored man-rated cab. It operates within the MLRS command, control, and communications structure.

**Ordnance options:** All current and future MLRS rockets and ATACMS missiles, to include GMLRS DPICM and Unitary
**Empty weight:** 29,800 pounds
**Max speed:** 100 kilometers per hour
**Max cruising range:** 480 kilometers

## SYSTEM INTERDEPENDENCIES

**Other Major Interdependencies**
C130/C-17, CNR (Combat Net Radio), GPS, JSTARS, MLRS MODS, PEO Integration, Q36/Q37 FIREFINDER, Sensor Suite, TBMCS (Air Space Clearance)

## PROGRAM STATUS

- **1QFY11:** Last Full-Rate Production VI contract award
- **2QFY11:** Hot panel quick strike successfully demonstrated and fielded
- Fielded two Army National Guard (ARNG) battalions for total of 13 battalions fielded
- Continued Increased Crew Protection (ICP) and Universal Fire Control System (UFCS) fleet upgrades
- Provide support to fielded units/units in combat
- Field and provide sustainment and support activities for foreign military sales customers

## PROJECTED ACTIVITIES

- Continue fielding to active and reserve components, with the last of 17 battalions fielded in FY13
- Continue ICP and UFCS fleet retrofit
- Field Long Range Communication, Blue Force Tracker, and Drivers Vision Enhancement (DVE) mods

**ACQUISITION PHASE**

- Technology Development
- Engineering and Manufacturing Development
- **Production and Deployment**
- Operations and Support

## High Mobility Artillery Rocket System (HIMARS)

**FOREIGN MILITARY SALES**
Jordan, Singapore, United Arab Emirates

**CONTRACTORS**
**Prime:** Lockheed Martin (Grand Prairie, TX; Camden, AR)
**Increased Crew Protection (ICP) Cab:** BAE Systems (Sealy, TX)
**LIU, WIU, PSU:** Harris Corp. (Melbourne, FL)
**Chassis:** BAE Systems (Sealy, TX)
**PNU:** L-3 Communications Space & Navigation (Budd Lake, NJ)
**Universal Gun Display Unit:** EFW (Ft. Worth, TX)
**Controller Assembly, Ball Screw:** R&D Electronics (Brownsboro, AL)
**Pump, Reservoir, Motor:** Eaton-Vickers (Jackson, MS)
**ADU, Boom/Hydraulic Gear Box:** Smiths Industries (Whippany, NJ)
**Metal Parts:** Beacon Industries (Dallas, TX)
**Hydraulic Lines:** Eaton Aeroquip (Jackson, MI)
**Reloader Hoist:** Breeze (Union, NJ)
**Manifolds:** Real Time Labs (Boca Raton, FL)
**Geared Bearing:** Kaydon (Muskegon, MI)
**Fire Control System:** Various vendors

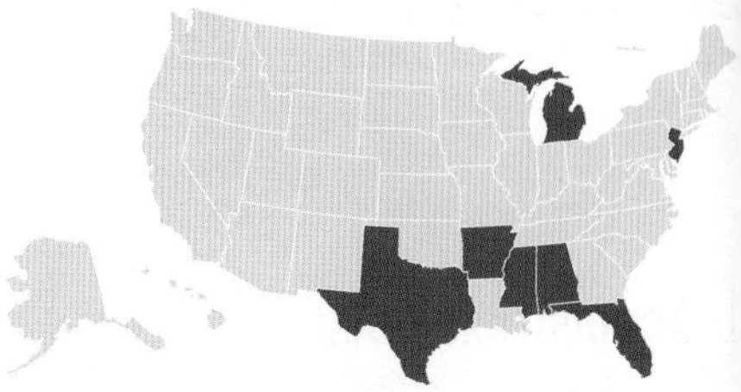

# High Mobility Engineer Excavator (HMEE) I and III

**INVESTMENT COMPONENT**

Modernization

Recapitalization

Maintenance

## MISSION

Provides the Army with earthmoving vehicles that support self-deployability, mobility, and speed to keep pace with the Brigade Combat Teams (BCTs). The HMEE-III Backhoe Loader (BHL) provides the Army with general excavation and earthmoving capabilities for general engineer construction units.

## DESCRIPTION

The High Mobility Engineer Excavator Type I (HMEE-I) is a non-developmental, military-unique vehicle fielded to the Army's BCTs and other selected engineer units. The HMEE-I can travel up to 60 miles per hour on primary roads and up to 25 miles per hour on secondary roads. The high mobility of the HMEE-I provides earthmoving machines capable of maintaining pace with the Army's current combat systems. All HMEE-Is will be capable of accepting armor in the form of an armor cab (Crew Protection Kit), are C-130 transportable without armor, and diesel driven. HMEE-I replaces Small Emplacement Excavators (SEEs) in BCTs and IHMEEs in Stryker BCTs. The HMEE-I is employed in IBCTs, HBCTs, SBCTs, Multi-Role Bridge Companies, and Engineer Support Companies.

The HMEE-III Backhoe Loader (BHL) is a commercial-off-the-shelf backhoe loader with minor military modifications intended for units that are relatively stationary and do not require the speed and rapid deployability of an HMEE-I. Its maximum speed is 23 miles per hour on improved roads, and 7 miles per hour off-road. The HMEE-III Backhoe Loader is used by Combat Support Brigades in general construction tasks. It is employed by Horizontal and Vertical Construction Units and other non-engineer units. such as Military Police and Quarter Master Units. Tasks performed by the HMEE-I/III include repair and improvement of roads, trails, bridges, and airfields.

## SYSTEM INTERDEPENDENCIES

None

## PROGRAM STATUS

- Currently in fielding

## PROJECTED ACTIVITIES

- Fielding is ongoing for both HMEE-I and III

**ACQUISITION PHASE**

Technology Development | Engineering and Manufacturing Development | Production and Deployment | Operations and Support

## High Mobility Engineer Excavator (HMEE) I and III

**FOREIGN MILITARY SALES**
**HMEE-I:**
Australia, Germany, New Zealand

**CONTRACTORS**
**HMEE-I OEM:**
JCB Inc. (Pooler, GA)
**Armor:**
ADSI (Hicksville, NY)
**Logistics:**
XMCO (Warren, MI)
**HMEE-III Backhoe Loader OEM:**
Case New Holland (Racine, WI)
**Armor:**
BAE (Columbus, OH)
**Logistics:**
XMCO (Warren, MI)

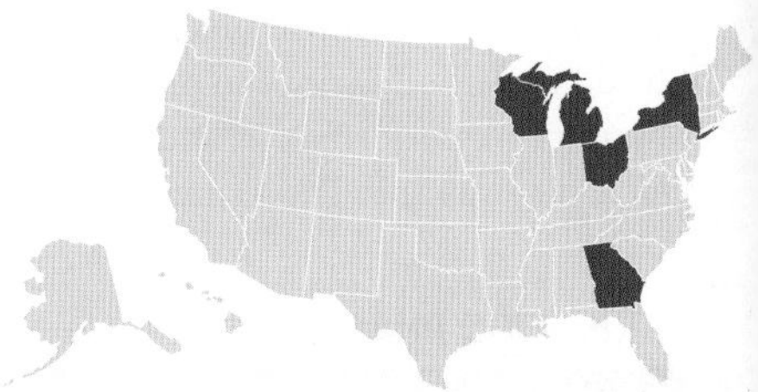

# High Mobility Multipurpose Wheeled Vehicle (HMMWV) Recapitalization (RECAP) Program

**INVESTMENT COMPONENT**

Modernization

Recapitalization

Maintenance

## MISSION

Supports combat and combat service support units with a versatile, light, mission-configurable, tactical wheeled vehicle.

## DESCRIPTION

The High Mobility Multipurpose Wheeled Vehicle (HMMWV) Recapitalization (RECAP) program supports the recapitalization of Up-Armored HMMWVs (UAH) returning from theater and Non-Armored HMMWVs (NAH) for National Guard homeland security and disaster relief missions. The RECAP of UAHs will incorporate the latest HMMWV technical insertions common to the fleet. The Army initiated a Modernized Expanded Capacity Vehicle (MECV) UAH RECAP Modernization effort that will add underbody armor to protect the crew, improve performance, and increase vehicle survivability. The Army plans to commence production upon successful completion of the integration and testing of these efforts in FY13. The RECAP of UAHs will migrate exclusively to the MECV.

The HMMWV is a lightweight, highly mobile, high-performance, diesel-powered, four-wheel drive, air-transportable, and air-droppable family of tactical vehicles that satisfy Army, Marine Corps, Navy, and Air Force requirements. The HMMWV uses common components to enable its reconfiguration as a troop carrier, armament carrier, shelter carrier, ambulance, TOW missile carrier, and scout vehicle. Since its inception, the HMMWV has undergone continuous evolution, including: improved survivability; technological upgrades; higher payload capacity; radial tires; Environmental Protection Agency emissions updates; commercial bucket seats; three-point seat belts and other safety enhancements; four-speed transmissions; and, in some cases, turbocharged engines and air conditioning.

There are numerous HMMWV variants. During RECAP, the non-armored configurations are converted to the M1097R1 configuration. The HMMWV M1097R1 configuration incorporates a four-speed, electronic transmission; a 6.5-liter diesel engine; and improvements in transportability. It has a payload of 4,400 pounds.

The M1114 UAH may be converted to the M1151 during RECAP, and the M1151, M1152, and M1165 remain in their current configuration after RECAP. The M1114, M1151, M1152, and M1165 UAH configurations are based on the expanded capacity vehicle (ECV) chassis. The UAH was developed to provide increased ballistic and blast protection, primarily for military police, special operations, and contingency force use.

## SYSTEM INTERDEPENDENCIES

**Other Major Interdependencies**

The HMMWV supports numerous data interchange customers, who mount various shelters and other systems on it; the M1101/1102 Light Tactical Trailer is the designed trailer for this vehicle

## PROGRAM STATUS

- Initiated the UAH Depot RECAP Program
- Initiated the Modernized Expanded Capacity Vehicle (MECV) Competitive HMMWV RECAP Program

## PROJECTED ACTIVITIES

- Evaluate responses to the Request for Proposals
- Award contract for prototypes for test and evaluation HMMWV RECAP Program
- Conduct Technical Development Testing
- Award Production contract
- Conduct production qualification testing and operational testing
- Procure Low-Rate Initial Production vehicles

**ACQUISITION PHASE**

Technology Development | Engineering and Manufacturing Development | Production and Deployment | Operations and Support

## High Mobility Multipurpose Wheeled Vehicle (HMMWV) Recapitalization (RECAP) Program

**FOREIGN MILITARY SALES**
None

**CONTRACTORS**
Red River Army Depot (Texarkana, TX)
Letterkenny Army Depot (Chambersburg, PA)
AM General (South Bend, IN)
GEP (Franklin, OH)
General Transmissions Products (South Bend, IN)

**MECV:**
To be determined

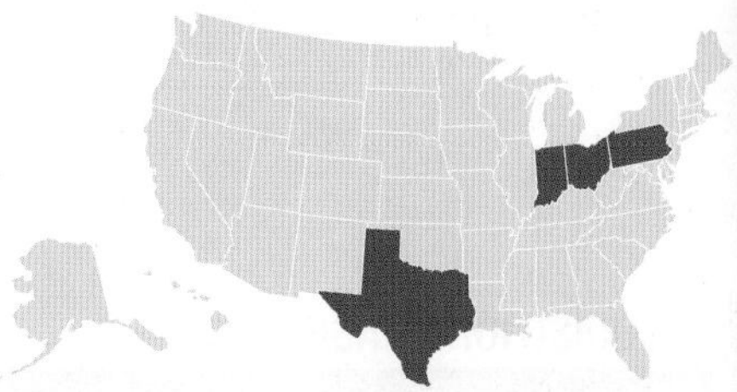

# Improved Environmental Control Units (IECU)

**INVESTMENT COMPONENT**

Modernization

Recapitalization

Maintenance

## MISSION

Provides standardized environmental control capabilities to the Department of Defense (DoD) in support of national security.

## DESCRIPTION

The Improved Environmental Control Units (IECU) program consists of four standard sizes: 9,000 BTUH (British thermal units per hour), 18,000 BTUH, 36,000 BTUH, and 60,000 BTUH — all in five configurations. Once fielded, these systems will provide critical cooling to vital command, control, communications, computers, and intelligence (C4I), and other military electronic and support systems equipment for the U.S. Army and the wider DoD. The IECUs:

- Use R-410A refrigerant, a commercial industry standard that is compliant with all current environmental legislative requirements
- Increase reliability and decrease weight and power consumption compared to current military standard systems
- Leverage current industry standards while being ruggedized for military environments
- Are organically supportable
- Are fully operable up to more than 125 degrees Fahrenheit
- Provide quality cooling, heating, and dehumidification for command posts; command, control, communications, computers, intelligence, surveillance, and reconnaissance (C4ISR) systems; weapon systems; and other battlefield support equipment while using a non-ozone-depleting refrigerant

Additional improvements to the Warfighter in theatre are the IECU's soft start and limited inrush current; nuclear, biological, and chemical compatible and electromagnetic interference protected interface; fully embedded diagnostics; automatic safety controls; and remote control capability for operations that require users to be out of the direct area.

## SYSTEM INTERDEPENDENCIES

None

## PROGRAM STATUS

- **1QFY11-4QFY11:** 60k IECU Full-Rate Production (FRP)
- **1QFY11-4QFY11:** 9/18/36k IECU Engineering and Manufacturing Development (EMD) Phase II

## PROJECTED ACTIVITIES

- **1QFY12-3QFY15:** 60k IECU Full-Rate Production (FRP)
- **1QFY12-2QFY13:** 9k/18k/36k IECU Engineering and Manufacturing Development (EMD) Phase II
- **2QFY13:** 9k/18k/36k IECU Milestone C—Enter Production and Deployment
- **3QFY13-4QFY14:** 9k/18k/36k IECU Low-Rate Initial Production (LRIP)
- **4QFY13:** 120k IECU Milestone B—Enter Engineering and Manufacturing Development (EMD)
- **1QFY14-4QFY16:** 120k IECU Engineering and Manufacturing Development (EMD)

**ACQUISITION PHASE**

Technology Development | Engineering and Manufacturing Development | Production and Deployment | Operations and Support

## Improved Environmental Control Units (IECU)

**FOREIGN MILITARY SALES**
None

**CONTRACTORS**
**9,000, 18,000, and 36,000 BTUH IECU (EMD Phase II):**
Mainstream Engineering (Rockledge, FL)
**60,000 BTUH IECU:**
DRS-ES (Environmental Systems) (Florence, KY)

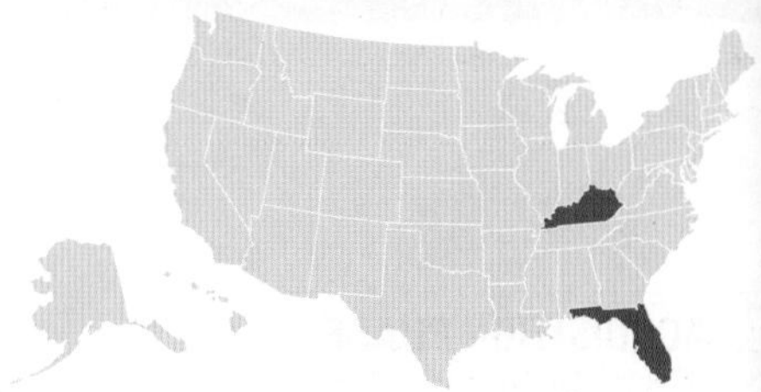

# Improved Ribbon Bridge (IRB)

**INVESTMENT COMPONENT**

Modernization

Recapitalization

Maintenance

## MISSION

Improves mobility by providing continuous roadway or raft capable of crossing military load classification 96 (wheeled)/80 (tracked) vehicles over non-fordable wet gaps.

## DESCRIPTION

The Improved Ribbon Bridge (IRB) Float Ribbon Bridge System is issued to the Multi-Role Bridge Company (MRBC). The U.S. Army Modified Table of Organization and Equipment (MTOE) authorizes MRBCs to consist of: 42 IRB bridge bays (30 interior bays and 12 ramp bays), 42 Bridge Adapter Pallets (BAP), 14 Bridge Erection Boats (BEB), 14 Improved Boat Cradles (IBC), and 56 Common Bridge Transporters (CBT). These assets collectively address Tactical Float Ribbon Bridge "wet gap" bridging. All components are required to transport, launch, erect, and retrieve up to 210 meters of floating bridge per MRBC. The IRB can be configured as either a continuous "full closure" bridge or assembled and used for rafting operations. The IRB has a Military Load Capacity (MLC) of 105 wheeled/85 tracked (normal) and 110 wheeled/90 tracked (caution crossing). This MLC will support the Joint force commander's ability to employ and sustain forces worldwide. The IRB is used to transport weapon systems, troops, and supplies over water when permanent bridges are not available. Bridge capabilities are provided in water currents moving at up to 10 feet per second.

The bridge system allows two-way traffic for HMMWV-width vehicles and increased MLC at all water current speeds over those of the Standard Ribbon Bridge. It is usable on increased bank heights over 2.2 meters (7.2 feet) and the improved folding/unfolding mechanism avoids cable breakage. Partially disassembled bays are C-130 transportable and externally transportable by CH-47 and CH-53 aircraft.

## SYSTEM INTERDEPENDENCIES

**Other Major Interdependencies**

IRB operations rely and are interdependent upon fully mission-capable CBTs, BAPs, IBCs, and BEB assets within a fully MTOE equipped MRBC

## PROGRAM STATUS

This system has been fielded since 2002.

- **1QFY11:** 189th and 401st MRBCs
- **2QFY11:** 132nd and 551st MRBCs
- **3QFY11:** 35th EN TNB BDE

## PROJECTED ACTIVITIES

Fieldings are ongoing based on the Army Requirements Prioritization List.

- **2QFY12:** Fielding 361st and 892nd MRBCs
- **3QFY12:** Fielding 125th and 502nd MRBCs
- **4QFY12:** Fielding 250th MRBC

**ACQUISITION PHASE**

Technology Development | Engineering and Manufacturing Development | Production and Deployment | Operations and Support

## Improved Ribbon Bridge (IRB)

**FOREIGN MILITARY SALES**

None

**CONTRACTORS**

General Dynamics European Land Systems-Germany (GDELS-G) (Kaiserslautern, Germany)

**Logistic support:**

AM General (AMG) (Livonia, MI)

**CBT manufacturer:**

Oshkosh Corp. (Oshkosh, WI)

**BEB manufacturer:**

FBM Babcock Marine (Isle of Wight, United Kingdom)

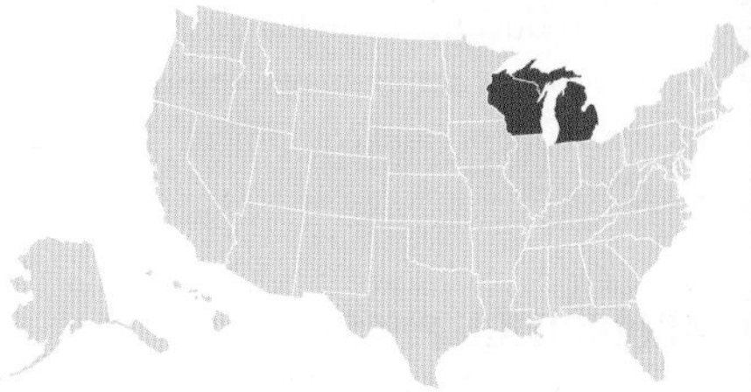

# Improved Target Acquisition System (ITAS)

**INVESTMENT COMPONENT**

Modernization

Recapitalization

Maintenance

## MISSION

Provides long-range sensor and anti-armor/precision assault fire capabilities, enabling the Soldier to shape the battlefield by detecting and engaging targets at long range with tube-launched, optically-tracked, wire-guided (TOW) missiles or directing the employment of other weapon systems to destroy those targets.

## DESCRIPTION

The Improved Target Acquisition System (ITAS) is a multipurpose weapon system, used as a reconnaissance, surveillance, and target acquisition sensor. ITAS provides long-range anti-armor/precision assault fire capabilities to the Army's Infantry and Stryker Brigade Combat Teams (BCTs) as well as to the Marine Corps. ITAS is a major product upgrade that greatly reduces the number of components, minimizing logistics support and equipment requirements. Built-in diagnostics and improved interfaces enhance target engagement performance.

ITAS' second-generation forward-looking infrared sensors double the long-range surveillance of its predecessor, the M220 TOW system. It offers improved hit probability with aided target tracking, improved missile flight software algorithms, and an elevation brake to minimize launch transients. The ITAS includes an integrated far target location capability (day/night sight with laser rangefinder), a position attitude determination subsystem, a fire-control subsystem, a lithium-ion battery power source, and a modified traversing unit. Soldiers can also detect and engage long-range targets with TOW missiles or, using the ITAS far-target location (FTL) enhancement, direct other fires to destroy them. The FTL enhancement consists of a position attitude determination subsystem (PADS) that provides the gunner with his own Global Positioning System (GPS) location and a 10-digit grid location to his target through the use of differential GPS. With the PAQ-4/PEQ-2 Laser Pointer, ITAS can designate .50 caliber or MK-19 grenade engagements. The ITAS can fire all versions of the TOW family of missiles.

The TOW 2B Aero and the TOW Bunker Buster have an extended maximum range to 4,500 meters. The TOW 2B Aero flies over the target (off-set above the gunner's aim point) and uses a laser profilometer and magnetic sensor to detect and fire two downward-directed, explosively formed penetrator warheads into the target. TOW Bunker Buster, with its high-explosive blast-fragmentation warhead, is optimized for performance against urban structures, earthen bunkers, field fortifications, and light-skinned armor threats. ITAS operates from the High Mobility Multipurpose Wheeled Vehicle (HMMWV), the dismount tripod platform, and Stryker anti-tank guided missile (ATGM) vehicles.

## SYSTEM INTERDEPENDENCIES

**Other Major Interdependencies**

The ITAS system is integrated on the M1121/1167 HMMWV and the Stryker ATGM; the ITAS system is the guidance for the TOW missile

## PROGRAM STATUS

- **Current:** ITAS has been fielded to 20 active and 16 reserve component Infantry BCTs and ten Stryker BCTs
- **Current:** The Marine Corps has begun fielding the ITAS to infantry and tank battalions to replace all Marine Corps M220A4 TOW 2 systems by 2012

## PROJECTED ACTIVITIES

- **Continue:** ITAS total package fielding
- **FY12:** Complete fielding

**ACQUISITION PHASE**

Technology Development | Engineering and Manufacturing Development | Production and Deployment | Operations and Support

## Improved Target Acquisition System (ITAS)

**FOREIGN MILITARY SALES**
NATO Maintenance and Supply Agency, Canada

**CONTRACTORS**
Raytheon (McKinney, TX)
**Training Devices:**
Intercoastal Electronics (Mesa, AZ)

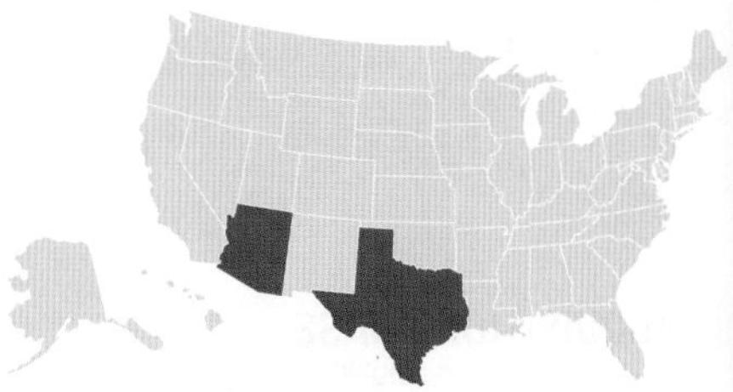

# Improvised Explosive Device (IEDD)

**INVESTMENT COMPONENT**

Modernization

Recapitalization

Maintenance

## MISSION

Provides both mounted and dismounted Soldiers with rapid and enduring capabilities to detect, defeat, and neutralized explosive hazards.

## DESCRIPTION

The Improvised Explosive Device (IEDD) Defeat product is comprised of several highlighted systems:

- The **Self Protection Adaptive Roller Kit (SPARK)** provides a pre-detonation capability mounted on the family of MRAP vehicles; the latest version, SPARK II has key improvements: variable stand-off, quick disconnect, and improved articulation from inside the cab, increased down pressure, and power generation.
- **Entry Control Point (ECP) in a box** is a suite of systems that provide the Soldier the ability to detect and protect against personal borne and vehicle borne IEDs. The suite is comprised of explosive detection systems, non-lethal systems, and blast mitigation systems. This effort is a coordinated effort with PdM FPS.
- **Jackal** is an IR defeat system integrated with MRAP platforms. While the PIR is a low-density threat, it is a very lethal threat.
- **Rhino** is a high-density, low-cost system integrated on MRAP platforms used to defeat the PIR threat.

## SYSTEM INTERDEPENDENCIES

**In this Publication**

Mine Resistant Ambush Protected Vehicles (MRAPs)

## PROGRAM STATUS

SPARK II is currently in OEF, with over 2000 rollers procured and delivered; the program is transitioning to a program of record in FY12 under the Explosive Hazard Pre-Detonation (EHP) CPD

## PROJECTED ACTIVITIES

SPARK II is a New Start in FY12

**ACQUISITION PHASE**

Technology Development | Engineering and Manufacturing Development | Production and Deployment | Operations and Support

## Improvised Explosive Device (IEDD)

**FOREIGN MILITARY SALES**

**SPARK:**
ANA

**CONTRACTORS**

**SPARK:**
Pearson Engineering (Newcastle upon Tyne, England)

**ECP:**
Aardvark Technical (Azusa, CA)

**Jackal:**
Raytheon Technical Services (Indianapolis, IN)

**Rhino:**
Letterkenny Army Depot (Chambersburg, PA)

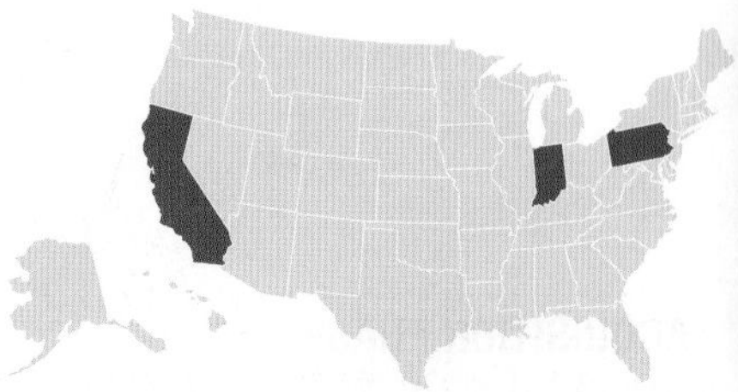

# Individual Semi-Automatic Airburst System (ISAAS)-XM25

INVESTMENT COMPONENT

- **Modernization**
- Recapitalization
- Maintenance

## MISSION

Provides the Soldier with a "smart" revolutionary weapon system that breaks the current small arms direct fire parity and dramatically increases our forces' lethality and range with a family of 25mm programmable ammunition.

## DESCRIPTION

The XM25 Individual Semi-Automatic Airburst System (ISAAS) enables the small unit and individual Soldier to engage defilade targets by providing a 25mm air-bursting capability that can be used in all operational environments. The ISAAS is an individually fired, semi-automatic, man-portable weapon system. An individual Soldier employing basic rifle marksmanship skills can effectively engage exposed or defilade targets in just seconds out to 700 meters.

The system allows the individual Soldier to quickly and accurately engage targets by producing an adjusted aimpoint based on range, environmental factors, and user inputs. The target acquisition/fire control integrates thermal capability with direct-view optics, laser rangefinder, compass, fuze setter, ballistic computer, and an internal display.

The ISAAS reduces the reliance of small units on non-organic assets (mortars, artillery, and air support) and the need to compete for priority of fires when time is critical. In addition to air bursting ammunition, a family of ammunition is being developed to support other missions, which could include armor-piercing and nonlethal scenarios.

## SYSTEM INTERDEPENDENCIES

None

## PROGRAM STATUS

- **2QFY11:** Capabilities Development Document approved
- **1QFY11:** Milestone B Decision
- **1QFY-4QFY11:** Prototype units engaged in OEF Forward Operational Assessment (FOA)
- **2QFY11:** Engineering & Manufacturing Development (EMD) contract awarded
- **3QFY11:** Integrated Baseline Review
- **3QFY11:** System Requirements Review

## PROJECTED ACTIVITIES

- **2QFY11-2QFY14:** Conduct EMD phase
- **1QFY12:** FOA continuation
- **1QFY13:** Conduct Government Development Testing
- **2-4QFY13:** Milestone C decision

ACQUISITION PHASE

- Technology Development
- **Engineering and Manufacturing Development**
- Production and Deployment
- Operations and Support

## Individual Semi-Automatic Airburst System (ISAAS)-XM25

**FOREIGN MILITARY SALES**
None

**CONTRACTORS**
**Prime:**
Alliant Techsystems (Plymouth, MN)
**25mm Airburst Weapon:**
H&K Gmbh (Oberdorf, Germany)
**Target Acquisition/Fire Control:**
L-3 Communications/Brashear (Pittsburgh, PA)
**25mm Ammunition:**
Alliant Techsystems (Plymouth, MN)

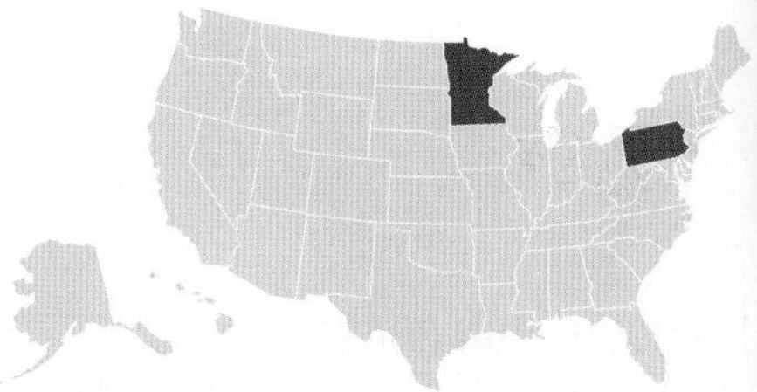

# Installation Protection Program (IPP)

INVESTMENT COMPONENT

Modernization

Recapitalization

Maintenance

## MISSION

Provides an effective chemical, biological, radiological, and nuclear (CBRN) protection, detection, identification, and warning system for military installations.

## DESCRIPTION

The Installation Protection Program (IPP) will allow Department of Defense installations to effectively protect personnel and critical operations against a CBRN event, to effectively respond with trained and equipped emergency personnel, and to ensure installations can continue critical operations during and after an attack.

IPP uses a tiered approach of government and commercial off-the-shelf capabilities optimized for an installation. The Baseline Tier provides a foundation for installations to maintain a standard level of preparedness for a CBRN incident. This tier consists of non-materiel solutions that address military-civilian interoperability, system architecture, policy, doctrine, training, and administration. It includes Joint training products, planning templates, Mutual Aid Agreement templates, and exercise templates and scenarios. The IPP Portal (IP3) makes these solutions available through Joint Knowledge Online (JKO) and Army Knowledge Online (AKO) at https://www.us.army.mil/suite/page/449823 or through a link on the Joint Acquisition CBRN Knowledge System (JACKS) website at https://jacks.jpeocbd.osd.mil.

Tier 1 focuses on enhancing an installation's existing emergency responder capabilities and enables an installation to prepare, respond, and transfer the mission after a CBRN attack. Tier 1 installations are critical to the overall accomplishment of the national military strategy or installations that provide combat service support. Tier 1 includes all Baseline Tier capabilities and adds individual protective equipment for emergency responders and first receivers, portable radiological and chemical detection equipment, portable biological collectors with analysis and identification laboratory support, personal dosimeters, hazard marking and controlling equipment, medical countermeasures for first responders/receivers, mass casualty decontamination showers and tents, mass casualty litters and support equipment, mass notification systems, an incident management system, and new equipment training and field exercise support.

Tier 2 applies to installations hosting one-of-a-kind, critical strategic missions or capabilities. The objective of Tier 2 is to provide installations with the capability to prepare, react, and continue critical missions or capabilities without significant interruption. The Tier 2 capability package includes Baseline and Tier 1 capabilities plus fixed chemical detectors for warfare agents and toxic industrial materials/chemicals, fixed biological collectors with analysis and identification laboratory support, radiological monitoring equipment for entry controllers, collective protection for one of a kind strategic assets (up to 3,000 square feet), and a decision support system of software tools and networked sensors.

## SYSTEM INTERDEPENDENCIES

None

## PROGRAM STATUS

- **4QFY11:** Complete 16 additional installations

ACQUISITION PHASE

Technology Development | Engineering and Manufacturing Development | Production and Deployment | Operations and Support

## Installation Protection Program (IPP)

**FOREIGN MILITARY SALES**
None

**CONTRACTORS**
Science Applications International Corp. (SAIC) (Falls Church, VA)
**AIE:**
Computer Sciences Corp. (CSC) (Falls Church, VA)

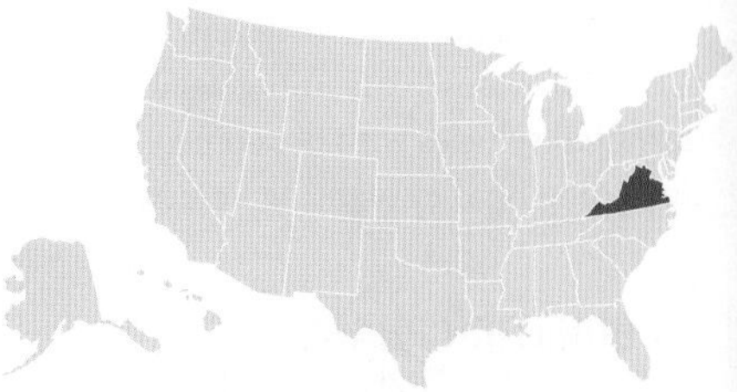

# Instrumentable-Multiple Integrated Laser Engagement System (I-MILES)

**INVESTMENT COMPONENT**

Modernization

Recapitalization

Maintenance

## MISSION

Provides force-on-force and force-on-target collective training at home stations and Combat Training Centers (CTCs).

## DESCRIPTION

The Instrumentable-Multiple Integrated Laser Engagement System (I-MILES) is the Army's primary live simulation system and is composed of several component systems. I-MILES products include man-worn systems, combat vehicle systems, target systems, shoulder-launched systems, and controller devices. The system operates within a live, virtual, and constructive integrated architecture that supports Army and Joint exercises.

The I-MILES Combat Vehicle Tactical Engagement Simulation System (CV TESS) provides live training devices for armored vehicles with fire control systems including Bradley Fighting Vehicles and Abrams Tanks. It interfaces and communicates with CTCs and home station instrumentation, providing casualty and battlefield damage assessments for after-action reporting. I-MILES CV TESS provides real-time casualty effects necessary for tactical engagement training in direct fire force-on-force and instrumented training scenarios.

The I-MILES Individual Weapons System (IWS) is a man-worn dismounted system, providing event data that can be downloaded for use in an after-action review and training assessment. The IWS replaces Basic MILES IWS at home stations and Maneuver CTCs Army-wide.

The Tactical Vehicle Systems (TVS) encompasses the Wireless Independent Target System (WITS) and replaces the previously fielded Independent Target System (ITS) and other Basic MILES currently fielded on non-turret military vehicles. TVS/WITS designs include Stryker variants, tactical wheeled vehicle configurations, and a separate configuration for tracked/oversized vehicles such as the M113 and Mine Resistant Ambush Protected Vehicles.

The Shoulder Launched Munitions (SLM) replaces Basic MILES and provides better training fidelity for blue forces' AT4 weapons and threat weapons using opposing force RPG7 visual modifications.

The Universal/Micro Controller Devices (UCD/MCD) are low-cost, lightweight devices used by observer controllers and maintenance personnel to initialize, set up, troubleshoot, reload, reset, resurrect, and manage participants during live force-on-force training exercises. These modular, self-contained devices interact and provide administrative control of all other MILES devices.

## SYSTEM INTERDEPENDENCIES

None

## PROGRAM STATUS

**IWS:**

- **Current:** Fielded approximately 14,000 IWS kits to the National Training Center (NTC) and over 64,000 kits Army-wide

**MXXI CVS:**

- **Current:** Fielded over 400 systems to the NTC and Joint Readiness Training Center

**SLM:**

- **Current:** Fielded over 1,000 SLM kits to NTC and over 6,000 kits Army-wide

**UCD/MCD:**

- **Current:** Fielded over 14,000 UCD/MCD kits Army-wide

**TVS/WITS:**

- **Current:** Fielded approximately 11,000 WITS kits to various home stations

## PROJECTED ACTIVITIES

**IWS:**

- **FY12:** IWS testing completed and begin fielding

**UCD/MCD:**

- **FY12:** Complete basis of issue

**CV TESS:**

- **FY12:** CV TESS will complete testing

**TVS:**

- **FY12:** TVS will begin fielding

**ACQUISITION PHASE**

Technology Development | Engineering and Manufacturing Development | Production and Deployment | Operations and Support

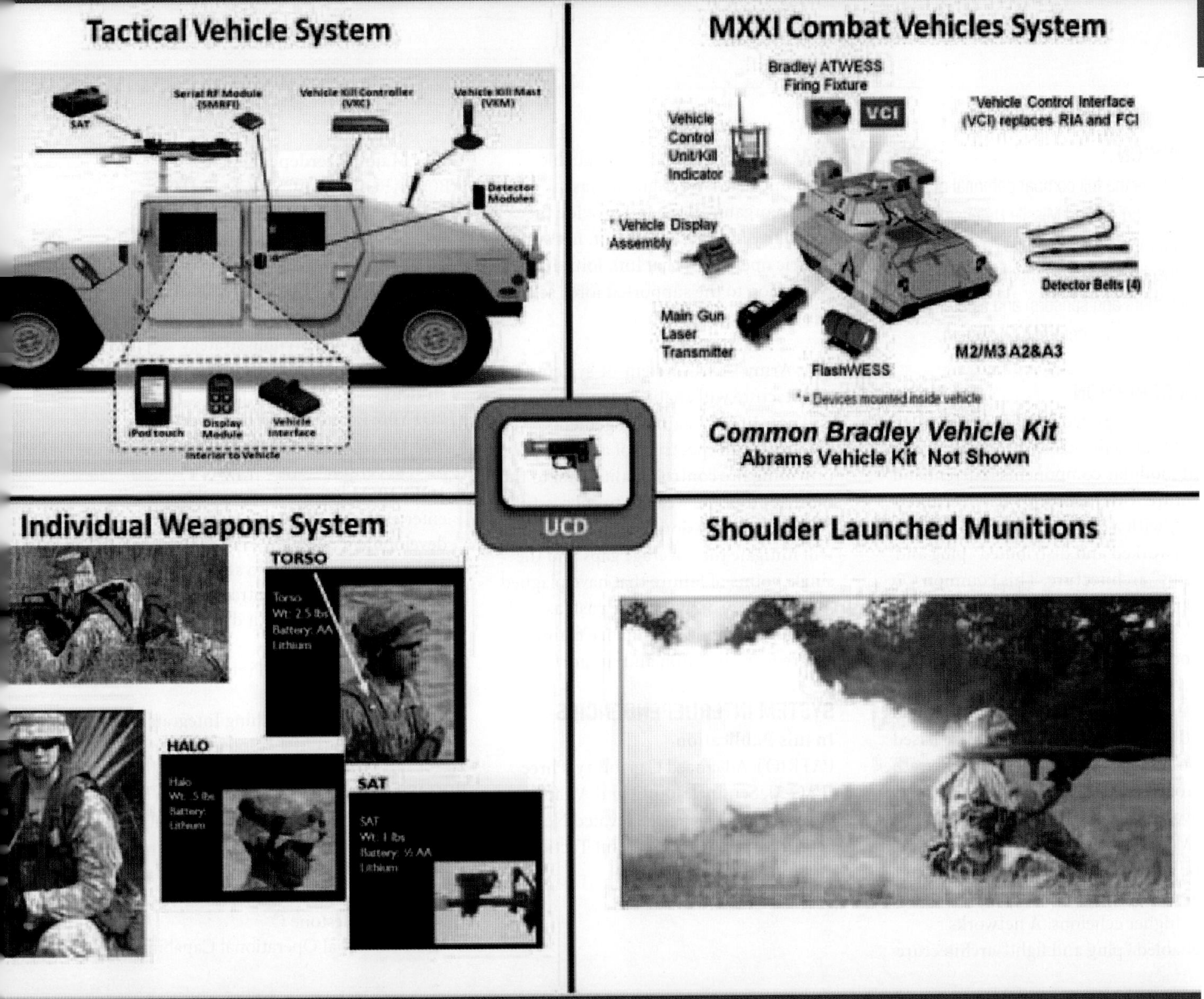


## Instrumentable-Multiple Integrated Laser Engagement System (I-MILES)

**FOREIGN MILITARY SALES**
None

**CONTRACTORS**
**IWS:**
CUBIC Defense Sys. (San Diego, CA)
**WITS:**
Lockheed Martin (Orlando, FL)
**TVS:**
CUBIC Defense Systems (San Diego, CA)
**MXXI CVS:**
Lockheed Martin (Orlando, FL)
**SLM:**
Lockheed Martin (Orlando, FL)
**CV TESS:**
To be determined

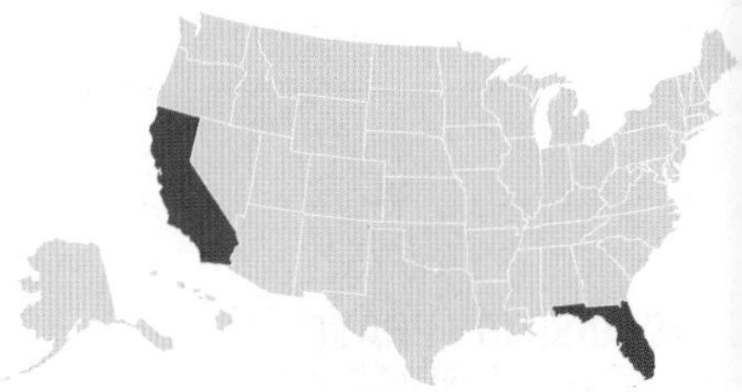

# Integrated Air and Missile Defense (IAMD)

**INVESTMENT COMPONENT**

- Modernization
- Recapitalization
- Maintenance

## MISSION

Provides the full combat potential of an Integrated Air and Missile Defense capability through a network-centric "plug and fight" architecture at the component level (e.g., launchers and sensors) and a common command and control (C2) system.

## DESCRIPTION

Army Integrated Air and Missile Defense (IAMD) will enable the integration of modular components (current and future AMD sensors, weapons, and C2) with a common C2 capability in a networked and distributed "plug and fight" architecture. This common C2, called the IAMD Battle Command System (IBCS), will provide standard configurations and capabilities at each echelon. This allows Joint, interagency, intergovernmental, and multinational (JIIM) AMD forces to organize based on mission, enemy, terrain and weather, troops and support available, time available, and civil considerations (METT-TC). Shelters and vehicles may be added to enable broader missions and a wider span of control executed at higher echelons. A network-enabled "plug and fight" architecture and common C2 system will enable dynamic defense design and task force reorganization, and provide the capability for interdependent, network-centric operations that link Joint IAMD protection to the supported force scheme of operations and maneuver.

This Army IAMD system-of-systems architecture will enable extended range and non-line-of-sight engagements across the full spectrum of aerial threats, providing fire control quality data to the most appropriate weapon to successfully complete the mission. Furthermore, it will mitigate the coverage gaps and the single points of failure that have plagued AMD defense design in the past, as well as reduce manpower, enhance training, and reduce operation and support costs.

## SYSTEM INTERDEPENDENCIES

**In this Publication**

PATRIOT Advanced Capability-Three (PAC-3), Sentinel, Joint Land Attack Cruise Missile Defense Elevated Netted Sensor System (JLENS), Joint Tactical Ground Stations (JTAGS)

**Other Major Interdependencies**

ABCS, AEGIS, AWACS, BCS, BMDS, CAC2S, C2BMC Planner, DD(X), E-2C, THAAD

## PROGRAM STATUS

- **4QFY07:** Approval of two-contractor competitive prototyping strategy
- **1QFY08:** Approval of acquisition strategy
- **2QFY08:** Request for proposal released
- **4QFY08:** IAMD Battle Command System contract award
- **1QFY10:** Milestone B approval to enter engineering and manufacturing development
- **1QFY10:** Down-select to single IBCS development prime contractor
- **2QFY10:** Award of A-Kit design and development contract
- **1QFY11:** IAMD Delta Preliminary Design Review (PDR)
- **3QFY11:** OSD Overarching Integrated Product Team (OIPT) Update

## PROJECTED ACTIVITIES

- **3QFY12:** IAMD Increment 2 Critical Design Review
- **4QFY12:** Defense Acquisition Board in process review
- **3QFY15:** Milestone C
- **4QFY16:** Initial Operational Capability

**ACQUISITION PHASE**

Technology Development | Engineering and Manufacturing Development | Production and Deployment | Operations and Support

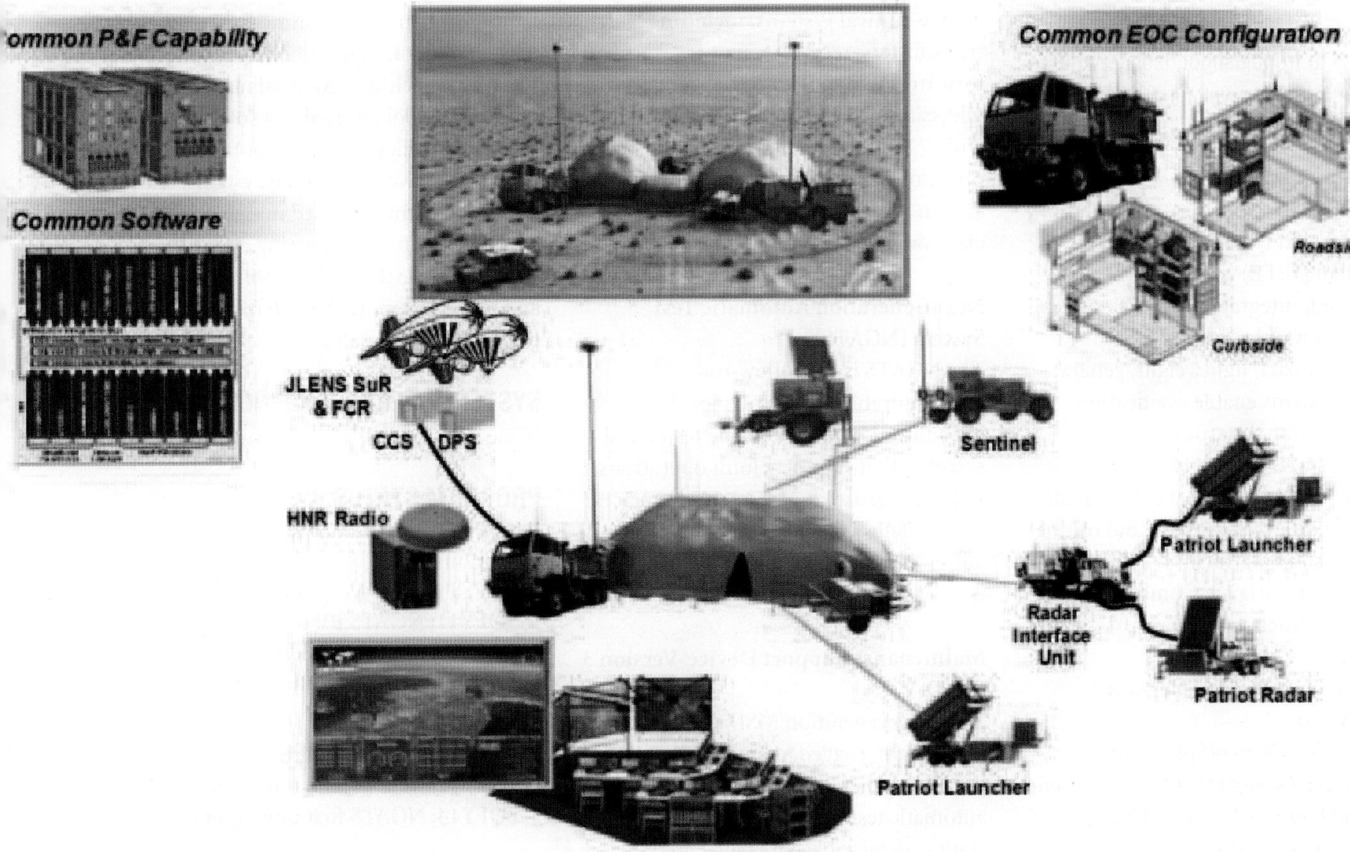


## Integrated Air and Missile Defense (IAMD)

**FOREIGN MILITARY SALES**
None

**CONTRACTORS**
**IBCS Development:**
Northrop Grumman (Huntsville, AL)
**A-Kit Design and Development:**
Raytheon (Andover, MA; Tewksbury, MA)
**SETA Support:**
DMD (Huntsville, AL)

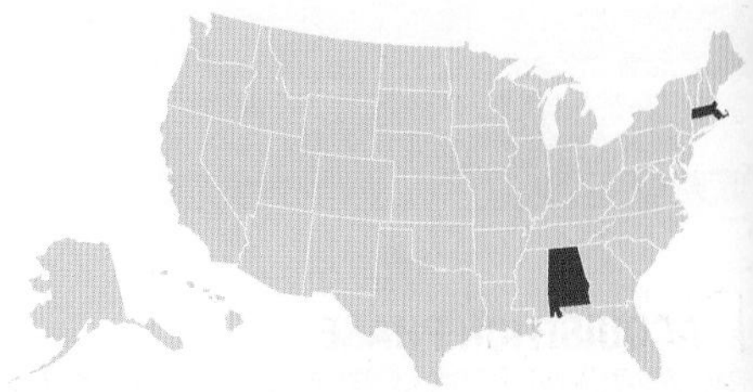

# Integrated Family of Test Equipment (IFTE)

**INVESTMENT COMPONENT**

- Modernization
- Recapitalization
- Maintenance

## MISSION

Develops, acquires, fields, and sustains automatic test equipment with the capability to troubleshoot, isolate, and diagnose faults, as well as verify the operational status of the weapon system.

## DESCRIPTION

The Integrated Family of Test Equipment (IFTE) consists of interrelated, integrated, mobile, tactical, and man-portable systems. These rugged, compact, lightweight, general-purpose systems enable verification of the operational status of weapon systems, as well as fault isolation to the Line-Replaceable Unit (LRU) at all maintenance levels, both on and off the weapon system platform. IFTE is an Early Infantry Brigade Combat Team (E-IBCT) Associate Program.

**Base Shop Test Facility-Version 3 (BSTF(V)3):**
The BSTF(V)3 is an off platform automatic test system that tests electronic LRUs and Shop-Replaceable Units (SRU) of ground and aviation systems.

**Electro-Optics Test Facility (EOTF):**
The EOTF tests the full range of Army electro-optical systems, including laser transmitters, receivers, spot trackers, forward-looking infrared systems, and television systems. It is fully mobile with VXI instrumentation, touch-screen operator interface, and an optical disk system for test program software and electronic technical manuals.

**Next Generation Automatic Test System (NGATS):**
The NGATS is the follow-on reconfigurable, rapidly deployable, expeditionary interoperable tester and screener that supports Joint operations, reduces logistics footprint, and replaces/consolidates obsolete, unsupportable automatic test equipment in the Army's inventory.

**Maintenance Support Device-Version 3 (MSD-V3):**
The latest generation MSD is a lightweight, rugged, compact, man-portable, general-purpose, at platform automatic tester that has a docking station, detachable core tablet, and swivel and touch screen capabilities. It is used to verify the operational status of aviation, automotive, electronic, and missile weapon systems and to isolate faulty components for immediate repair or replacement. MSD-V3 hosts Interactive Electronic Technical Manuals and the Digital Logbook, is used as a software uploader/verifier to provide or restore mission software to weapon systems, and supports condition-based maintenance data collection and reporting. MSD-V3 supports more than 50 weapon systems and is used by more than 30 military occupational specialties.

## SYSTEM INTERDEPENDENCIES

None

## PROGRAM STATUS

- **1QFY11:** NGATS Logistics Demonstration
- **2QFY11:** MSD-V3 production
- **3QFY11:** NGATS PVT
- **Current:** MSD-V2 fielding
- **Current:** EOTF operations and support

## PROJECTED ACTIVITIES

- **1QFY12:** MSD-V3 first unit equipped
- **2QFY14:** NGATS first unit equipped

**ACQUISITION PHASE**

Technology Development | Engineering and Manufacturing Development | Production and Deployment | Operations and Support

## Integrated Family of Test Equipment (IFTE)

At-Platform Automatic Test Systems (APATS)

**FOREIGN MILITARY SALES**

**MSD:**
Afghanistan, Australia, Bahrain, Chile, Djibouti, Egypt, Ethiopia, Germany, Israel, Iraq, Jordan, Korea, Kuwait, Lithuania, Macedonia, Morocco, Netherlands, Oman, Poland, Portugal, Saudi Arabia, Taiwan, Turkey, United Arab Emirates, Uzbekistan, Yemen

**CONTRACTORS**

**MSD-V3:**
Vision Technology Miltope Corp. (Hope Hull, AL)

**BSTF(V)3:**
Northrop Grumman (Rolling Meadows, IL)

**EOTF:**
Northrop Grumman (Rolling Meadows, IL)

**NGATS:**
Northrop Grumman (Rolling Meadows, IL)
DRS-TEM (Huntsville, AL)

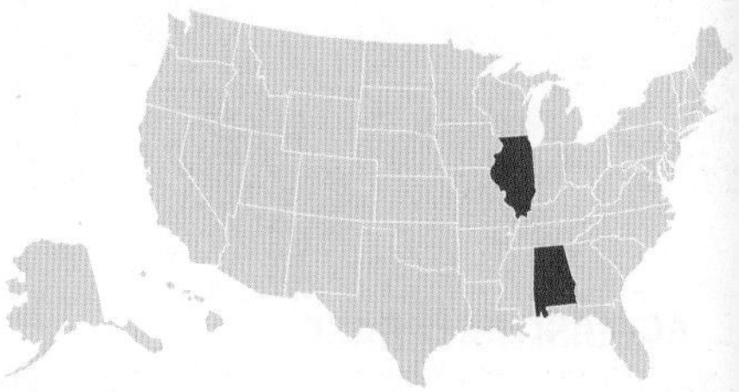

# Interceptor Body Armor

**INVESTMENT COMPONENT**

- Modernization
- Recapitalization
- Maintenance

## MISSION

Increases Warfighter lethality and mobility by optimizing Soldier protection while effectively managing all life-cycle aspects of personal protective equipment.

## DESCRIPTION

The U.S. Army's body armor and components offer highly effective ballistic protection for our Soldiers. The system includes two types of "soft armor": the Improved Outer Tactical Vest (IOTV) with mission-tailored protective attachments that protect the neck, shoulders, groin, and lower back; and the Soldier Plate Carrier System (SPCS), which offers decreased area of coverage in order to increase Soldier mobility in various terrain conditions. Two types of hard armor plate systems are available for use with the IOTV and SPCS: the Enhanced Small Arms Protective Inserts (ESAPI) and Enhanced Side Ballistic Inserts (ESBI); and the X Small Arms Protective Inserts (XSPI) and X Side Ballistic Inserts (XSBI). Both systems provide classified multihit protection against numerous stressing threats. The IOTV base vest (size medium) weighs 9.86 lbs. The IOTV with yoke and collar ensemble, groin, and lower back components weighs 15.09 lbs. All components provide robust fragmentation and 9mm protection. The ESAPI (10.9 lbs per set) and ESBI (5.1 lbs per set) provide classified multihit small arms protection. The total system with all components weighs 31.09 lbs (size medium). The IOTV is produced in eleven sizes to accommodate every Soldier on the battlefield. ESAPI and XSAPI are produced in five sizes. ESBI and XSBI are produced in one-size. Attachable throat, groin, shoulder, and lower back protectors increase fragmentation and 9mm protection. Webbing attachment loops on the vest accommodate Modular Lightweight Load-Carrying Equipment (MOLLE). A medical access panel on the IOTV allows for treatment to vital areas while a quick-release mechanism on both systems allows for rapid doffing of the system during emergency situations. The complete IOTV system provides 1,085 square inches of fragmentation and 9mm handgun protection and 456 square inches of ballistic protection for the SPCS (size medium).

## SYSTEM INTERDEPENDENCIES

None

## PROGRAM STATUS

- **Current:** In production and being fielded
- **FY11:** Fielded 172,000 IOTV; 31,000 SPCS; 71,000 XSPI; 14,000 XSBI

## PROJECTED ACTIVITIES

- **Continue:** Fielding

**ACQUISITION PHASE**

- Technology Development
- Engineering and Manufacturing Development
- Production and Deployment
- Operations and Support

## Interceptor Body Armor

**FOREIGN MILITARY SALES**
None

**CONTRACTORS**
Ceradyne Inc. (Costa Mesa, CA)
Protective Products (Sunrise, FL)
KDH Defense Systems (Johnstown, PA)

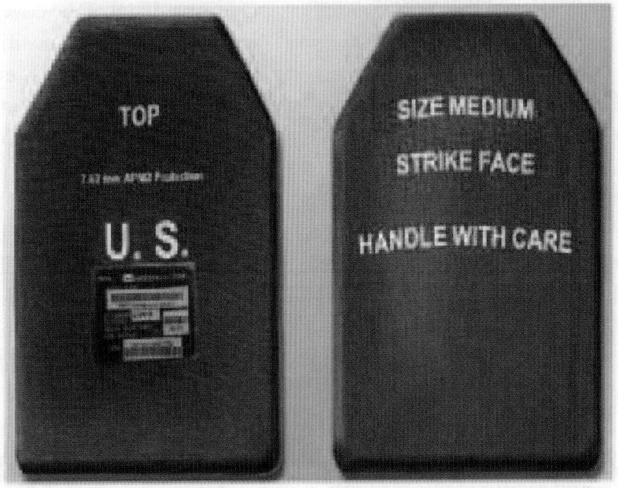


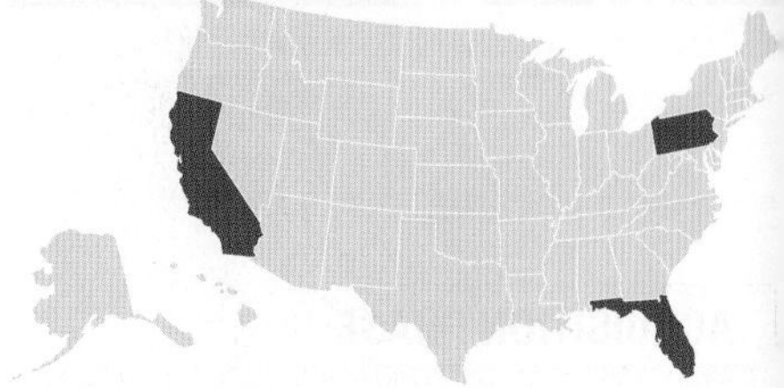

# Javelin

## INVESTMENT COMPONENT

Modernization

Recapitalization

Maintenance

## MISSION

Provides the dismounted Soldier a man-portable, fire-and-forget system that is highly lethal against targets ranging from main battle tanks to fleeting targets of opportunity found in current threat environments facing the Army.

## DESCRIPTION

The Close Combat Missile System-Medium (CCMS-M) Javelin is highly effective against a variety of targets at extended ranges under day/night, battlefield obscurants, adverse weather, and multiple counter-measure conditions. The system's soft-launch feature permits firing from enclosures commonly found in complex urban terrain. Javelin's modular design allows the system to evolve to meet changing threats and requirements via both software and hardware upgrades. The system consists of a reusable command launch unit (CLU) with a built-in-test (BIT), and a modular missile encased in a disposable launch tube assembly. The CLU provides stand-alone all-weather and day/night surveillance capability ideally suited for infantry operations in Afghanistan. The Javelin missile and CLU together weigh 48.8 pounds. The system also includes training devices for tactical training and classroom training.

Javelin's fire-and-forget technology allows the gunner to fire and immediately take cover, to move to another fighting position, or to reload. The Javelin provides enhanced lethality through the use of a tandem warhead that will defeat all known armor threats. It is effective against both stationary and moving targets. This system also provides defensive capability against attacking/hovering helicopters. The performance improvements in current production Javelin Block I CLUs are increased target identification range, increased surveillance time with new battery and software management of the "on" time, and external RS-170 interface for video output. The performance improvements in current production Javelin Block I missiles are increased probability of hit/kill at 2,500 meters, improved warhead lethality, and reduced time of flight. In current conflicts the CLU is being used as a stand-alone surveillance and target acquisition asset. The Army is the lead for this Joint program with the Marine Corps.

Javelin is a complementary system as the lethality solution for the Armed Robotic Vehicle-Assault (Light).

## SYSTEM INTERDEPENDENCIES

None

## PROGRAM STATUS

- **3QFY07:** Received Full Materiel Release on Block I CLU
- **4QFY08:** Received Full Materiel Release on Block I missile
- **Current:** Missile and CLU production
- **Current:** CLU total package fielding and CLU Retrofit
- **Current:** Javelin has been fielded to more than 95 percent of active duty units; fielding is underway to the National Guard

## PROJECTED ACTIVITIES

- **Continue:** Multipurpose Warhead is planned to improve lethality against irregular/soft targets
- **Complete:** CLU production
- **Continue:** CLU total package fielding and CLU Retrofit
- **Continue:** Missile production

## ACQUISITION PHASE

Technology Development | Engineering and Manufacturing Development | Production and Deployment | Operations and Support

## Javelin

**FOREIGN MILITARY SALES**

Australia, Czech Republic, France, Ireland, Jordan, Lithuania, New Zealand, Norway, Oman, Taiwan, United Arab Emirates, United Kingdom

**CONTRACTORS**

**CLU:** Raytheon Missile Systems (Tucson, AZ)
DRS Technologies (Dallas, TX)
Raytheon (McKinney, TX; Dallas, TX; Garland, TX)
**GEU:** Raytheon Missile Systems (Tucson, AZ)
Raytheon (McKinney, TX; Dallas TX; Garland, TX)
**ESAF/Seeker:** Lockheed Martin (Orlando, FL; Ocala, FL)
**FPA:** DRS Technologies (Dallas, TX)
**Propulsion Unit:** Aerojet (Camden, AR)
**Missile Final Assembly:** Lockheed Martin (Troy, AL)
**FTT, EPBST:** ECC International (Orlando, FL)
**Batteries:** Acme Electric (Tempe, AZ)
**Precursor Whd:** General Dynamics Ordnance and Tactical Systems (Camden, AR)
**Containers:** Independent Pipe Products (Grand Prairie, TX)
**Test Support:** Javelin Joint Venture (Huntsville, AL)

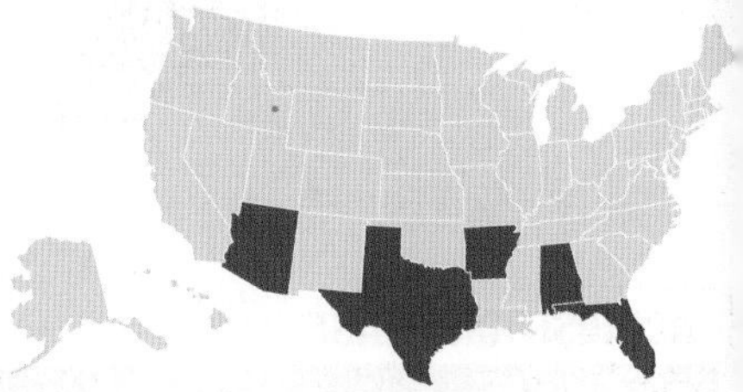

# Joint Air-to-Ground Missile (JAGM)

**INVESTMENT COMPONENT**

- **Modernization**
- Recapitalization
- Maintenance

## MISSION

Provides a single variant, precision-guided, air-to-ground weapon for use by Joint service manned and unmanned aircraft to destroy stationary and moving high-value land and naval targets.

## DESCRIPTION

The Joint Air-to-Ground Missile (JAGM) System is a precision-guided munition (PGM) for use on Joint rotary and fixed-wing platforms and unmanned aerial systems (UAS) to destroy high-value stationary, moving, and relocatable land and naval targets. JAGM is the intended replacement for HELLFIRE, air-launched TOW, and Maverick families of missiles.

JAGM will increase the Warfighter's operational flexibility by effectively engaging a variety of stationary and mobile targets on the battlefield from longer ranges, including advanced heavy/light armored vehicles, bunkers, buildings, patrol craft, command and control vehicles, transporter/erector (e.g., SCUD) launchers, artillery systems, and radar/air defense systems. The JAGM System is a Joint program with the Army, Navy, and Marine Corps and includes missiles, trainers, containers, support equipment, and launchers. Its multimode seeker will provide robust capability in adverse weather, day or night, and in an obscured/counter-measured environment. The warhead is designed for high performance against both armored and non-armored targets, and the firing platform is interoperable with the command, control, communications, computer, intelligence, surveillance, and reconnaissance (C4ISR) network. JAGM will be fielded to the Super Hornet (F/A-18E/F), Apache (AH-64D), and the Super Cobra (AH-1Z) in 2016. Follow-on fieldings of JAGM on the OH-58D Cockpit and Sensor Upgrade Program (CASUP), Seahawk (MH-60R), and the MQ-1C UAS are planned for 2017.

- **Diameter:** 7 inches
- **Weight:** 108 pounds
- **Length:** 70 inches
- **Range:** 500-16,000 meters for rotary wing; 2,000-28,000 meters for fixed-wing

## SYSTEM INTERDEPENDENCIES

**Other Major Interdependencies**

Rotary-wing Launcher/Rack: M299; Fixed-wing Launcher Rack: Design to be determined

## PROGRAM STATUS

- **4QFY08:** Competitive technology development contracts awarded
- **1QFY09:** Integrated baseline review
- **4QFY09:** System requirements review
- **3QFY10:** Preliminary design review
- **1QFY11:** Technology Development Phase completed

## PROJECTED ACTIVITIES

- **1QFY12:** Milestone B

**ACQUISITION PHASE**

- **Technology Development**
- Engineering and Manufacturing Development
- Production and Deployment
- Operations and Support

## Joint Air-to-Ground Missile (JAGM)

**FOREIGN MILITARY SALES**
None

**CONTRACTORS**
**Prime:** Raytheon (Tucson, AZ)
Lockheed Martin (Orlando, FL)
**Launcher Integration:** Boeing (St. Louis, MO)
**Rocket Motor:** Aerojet (Gainesville, VA)
Alliant Techsystems (Rocket Center, WV)
**Ordnance & Tactical Systems:** General Dynamics (St. Petersburg, FL)
**Warhead:** GD-OTS (Niceville, FL)
**Seeker:** Lockheed Martin (Ocala, FL)
**CAS:** Moog Inc. (East Aurora, NY)
**Optical Assembly:** Perkin Elmer (Ohio, OH)
**CCAs Distribution:** Avnet (Chandler, AZ)
TJM Electronic (Tempe, AZ)
**F/W Plat Int:** ATK (Woodland Hills, CA)
**FPA:** CMC Electronics (Mason, OH)
**Comp Midbody:** GD-ATP (Lincoln, NE)
**Final Assembly:** Lockheed Martin (Troy, AL)
**R/W Launcher:** Marvin Engineering (Inglewood, CA)
**FM:** Perkin Elmer (Ohio, OH)
**Rocket Motor:** Aerojet (Camden, AR)

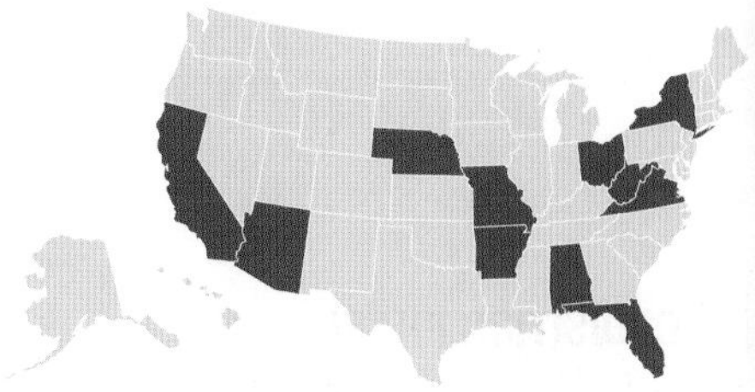

# Joint Battle Command-Platform (JBC-P)

**INVESTMENT COMPONENT**

- Modernization
- Recapitalization
- Maintenance

## MISSION

Provides accurate, on-the-move, digital command and control and situational awareness to tactical leaders at all echelons to the platform and dismounted domains.

## DESCRIPTION

Joint Battle Command-Platform (JBC-P) is a foundation for achieving information interoperability between Joint warfighting elements on current and future battlefields. As the next generation of Force XXI Battle Command Brigade and Below (FBCB2) technology, it will be the principal command and control system for the Army and Marine Corps at the brigade-and-below level, providing users access to the tactical information necessary to achieve information dominance over the enemy. It consists of computer hardware and software integrated into tactical vehicles, aircraft, and provided to dismounted forces. JBC-P uses a product line approach to software development to save costs and promote a common architecture. Components include a core software module that provides common functionality required of all platforms and tailored software modules with unique capabilities for dismounted, vehicle, logistic, aviation, and command post elements. JBC-P software is designed for use over the Blue Force Tracking II transceiver and associated satellite networks, as well as ground-based networks. Other key enhancements include a redesigned, intuitive user interface and faster mapping software to quickly process and display critical graphics. It will be the primary provider and user of digital battle command and situational awareness across the spectrum of operations and will allow Warfighters to more effectively and consistently communicate critical information over networks that connect the most distant and remote locations.

## SYSTEM INTERDEPENDENCIES

**In this Publication**

Advanced Field Artillery Tactical Data System (AFATDS), Battle Command Sustainment Support System (BCS3), Distributed Common Ground System-Army (DCGS-A), Force XXI Battle Command Brigade and Below (FBCB2), Movement Tracking System (MTS), Nett Warrior (NW), Warfighter Information Network-Tactical (WIN-T) Increment 1, Warfighter Information Network-Tactical (WIN-T) Increment 2, Warfighter Information Network-Tactical (WIN-T) Increment 3

**Other Major Interdependencies**

AMDWS, ASAS, BFT-Avn, DTSS, CPOF, JTCW, JSTARS MCS, JTRS HMS, JC2C

## PROGRAM STATUS

- **4QFY09:** Milestone B
- **4QFY10:** Battlefield automation appraisal

## PROJECTED ACTIVITIES

- **2QFY11:** Awarded two Broad Area Announcement (BAA) contracts for Handheld prototyping and evaluation
- **3QFY12:** JBC-P Milestone C Decision review
- **Continuing:** JBC-P development and testing for Capability Set (CS) 13-14; evaluate and select hardware candidates; conduct integration with legacy hardware; conduct developmental and operational testing; continue software development for CS15-16 and CS17-18

**ACQUISITION PHASE**

Technology Development | Engineering and Manufacturing Development | Production and Deployment | Operations and Support

## Joint Battle Command-Platform (JBC-P)

**FOREIGN MILITARY SALES**
None

**CONTRACTORS**

**Software Development (Government performing):**
Software Engineering Directorate (SED), AMRDEC (Huntsville, AL)

**Program Support:**
CACI (Eatontown, NJ)

**Subject Matter Expert:**
MITRE (Eatontown, NJ)

**Handheld Prototyping:**
General Dynamics C4 Systems (Scottsdale, AZ)

**Handheld Prototyping:**
DRS (Palm Bay, FL)

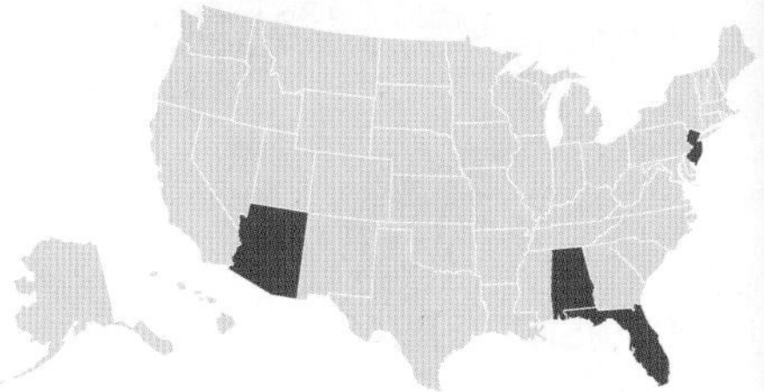

# Joint Biological Point Detection System (JBPDS)

INVESTMENT COMPONENT

Modernization

Recapitalization

Maintenance

## MISSION

Protects the Soldier by providing rapid and fully automated detection, identification, warning, and sample isolation of high-threat biological warfare agents.

## DESCRIPTION

The Joint Biological Point Detection System (JBPDS) is the first Joint biological warfare agent (BWA) detection system designed to meet the broad spectrum of operational requirements encountered by the Services, across the entire spectrum of conflict.

It consists of a common biosuite that can be integrated onto a service platform, shipboard, or trailer-mounted to provide biological detection and identification to all service personnel. The JBPDS is portable and can support bare-base or semi-fixed sites. JBPDS will presumptively identify 10 BWAs simultaneously. It will also collect a liquid sample for confirmatory analysis and identification. Technology refresh efforts will focus on reducing life-cycle costs and obsolescence.

JBPDS can operate from a local controller on the front of each system, remotely, or as part of a network of up to 26 systems. JBPDS meets all environmental, vibration, and shock requirements of its intended platforms, as well as requirements for reliability, availability, and maintainability.

The JBPDS includes both military and commercial global positioning, meteorological, and network modem capabilities. The system will interface with the Joint Warning and Reporting Network (JWARN).

The JBPDS is currently fielded on the Stryker Nuclear, Biological, Chemical, Reconnaissance Vehicle (NBCRV), the M31A2 Biological Integrated Detection System, and Navy Ships.

## SYSTEM INTERDEPENDENCIES

**In this Publication**

Nuclear Biological Chemical Reconnaissance Vehicle (NBCRV)-Stryker Sensor Suites

## PROGRAM STATUS

- **1QFY11-4QFY11:** Continued unit fieldings
- **2QFY11:** Engineering change proposal (ECP)decision review

## PROJECTED ACTIVITIES

- **1QFY12-4QFY12:** Developmental testing
- **1QFY13-4QFY13:** First article testing
- **3QFY14:** Engineering Change Proposal production decision review

ACQUISITION PHASE

Technology Development | Engineering and Manufacturing Development | Production and Deployment | Operations and Support

## Joint Biological Point Detection System (JBPDS)

**FOREIGN MILITARY SALES**
None

**CONTRACTORS**
General Dynamics Armament and Technical Products (Charlotte, NC)

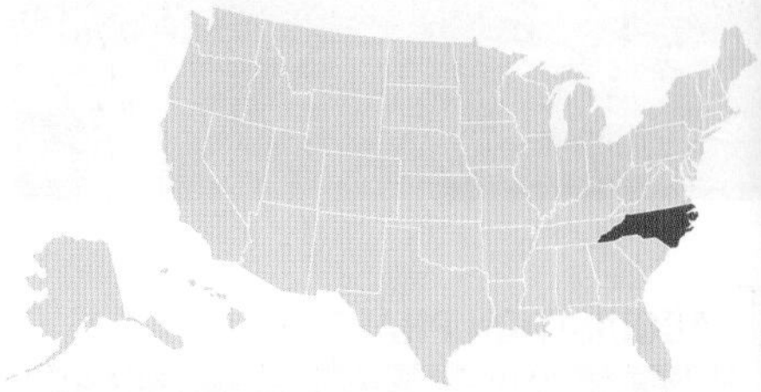

# Joint Biological Standoff Detection System (JBSDS)

**INVESTMENT COMPONENT**

Modernization
Recapitalization
Maintenance

## MISSION

Provides advanced, early-warning (Detect to Warn), standoff detection of biological warfare agents (BWA) on a stationary platform or fixed site, used in conjunction with other biological point detectors for advanced warning, reporting, and protection.

## DESCRIPTION

The Joint Biological Standoff Detection System (JBSDS) will be the first biological defense Detect to Warn capability to protect individual Warfighters.

The JBSDS Increment 1 provides initial early warning capability against biological warfare agent attack by detecting aerosol clouds out to five kilometers with infrared (IR) light detection and ranging (LIDAR). JBSDS Increment 1 operates at fixed sites or in a stationary mode on mobile platforms. JBSDS Increment 1 system will be used for training to support Increment 2 concept of operations development.

JBSDS Increment 2 will provide 24/7 near-real-time biological warfare agent (BWA) detection and will network with existing biological detection systems to provide early warning (Detect to Warn) theater-wide to limit the effects of biological agent hazards against U.S. forces at the tactical and operational levels of war. JBSDS Increment 2 can be employed in support of various areas (e.g., fixed sites, air ports of debarkation/sea ports of debarkation, forward operating bases, amphibious landing sites), on platforms, or stationary vehicles. JBSDS Increment 2 will pass detection information and warnings through existing and planned communications networks (e.g., Joint Warning and Reporting Network). Commanders may integrate JBSDS Increment 2 outputs with information from intelligence, meteorological, radar, medical surveillance, local area operations, and other available assets to increase force protection, mitigate the consequences of biological hazards, and maximize combat effectiveness.

## SYSTEM INTERDEPENDENCIES

**In this Publication**

Joint Warning and Reporting Network (JWARN)

**Other Major Interdependencies**

Combat Service Support Automated Information Systems Interface (CAISI)-Inc 1, JWARN-Inc 2

## PROGRAM STATUS

- **2QFY11:** JBSDS Increment 2 Milestone A decision

## PROJECTED ACTIVITIES

- **1QFY12-3QFY13:** Prototypes testing
- **3QFY14:** Preliminary design review

**ACQUISITION PHASE**

Technology Development | Engineering and Manufacturing Development | Production and Deployment | Operations and Support

## Joint Biological Standoff Detection System (JBSDS)

**FOREIGN MILITARY SALES**
None

**CONTRACTORS**
**Increment 1:**
Science and Engineering Services Inc. (SESI) (Columbia, MD)
**Increment 2:**
To be determined

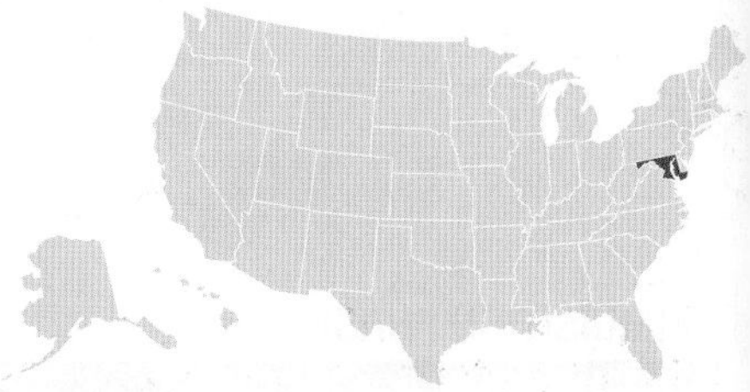

# Joint Biological Tactical Detection System (JBTDS)

INVESTMENT COMPONENT

Modernization

Recapitalization

Maintenance

## MISSION

Provides a tactical, lightweight, battery-operated, biological warfare agent (BWA) system capable of detecting, warning, and presumptively identifying and collecting samples for follow-on confirmatory analysis.

## DESCRIPTION

The Joint Biological Tactical Detection Systems (JBTDS) will be a lightweight, man-portable, battery-operated system that detects, warns, and provides presumptive identification and sample collection of BWA to provide near-real-time detection of biological attacks and hazards in the area of operation. It will have a local alarm and be networked to provide cooperative capability with reduced probability of false alarms.

JBTDS will be employed organically at the battalion and lower levels by non-chemical, biological, radiological, and nuclear personnel in tactical environments across multiple operational locations (e.g. forward operating bases, operationally engaged units, amphibious landing sites, air base operations, etc.)

JBTDS will ultimately support force protection and maximize combat effectiveness by enhancing medical response decision making. When networked, JBTDS will augment existing biological detection systems to provide a theater-wide, seamless array capable of detection and warning.

## SYSTEM INTERDEPENDENCIES

None

## PROGRAM STATUS

- **2QFY11:** Milestone A decision
- **3QFY11-4QFY11:** Competitive prototyping

## PROJECTED ACTIVITIES

- **1QFY12-3QFY12:** Continue competitive prototyping
- **2QFY12:** Preliminary Design Review
- **3QFY13:** Milestone B Decision
- **1QFY14-2QFY14:** Operational assessment
- **2QFY14:** Critical Design Review
- **3QFY14-4QFY14:** Developmental testing

ACQUISITION PHASE

Technology Development | Engineering and Manufacturing Development | Production and Deployment | Operations and Support

## Joint Biological Tactical Detection System (JBTDS)

**Notional Equipment Set**

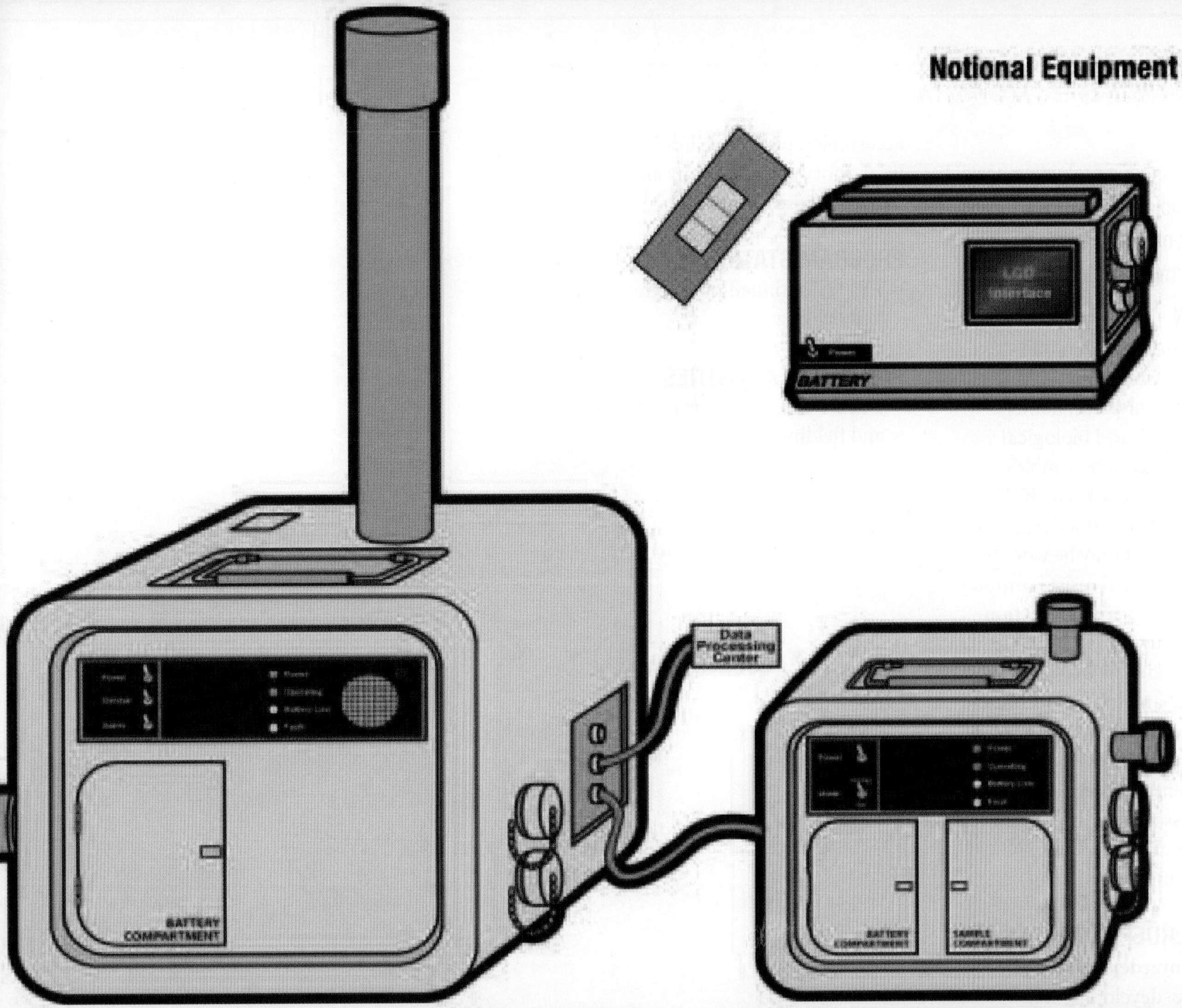


**FOREIGN MILITARY SALES**
None

**CONTRACTORS**
To be determined

# Joint Chem/Bio Coverall for Combat Vehicle Crewman (JC3)

**INVESTMENT COMPONENT**

Modernization

Recapitalization

Maintenance

## MISSION

Provides percutaneous protection against chemical and biological (CB) warfare agents to personnel who serve as crew members on armored vehicles.

## DESCRIPTION

The Joint Chem/Bio Coverall for Combat Vehicle Crewman (JC3) is a lightweight, one-piece, flame-resistant, chemical, and biological protective coverall that resembles a standard CVC coverall. The JC3 is intended to be worn as a duty uniform; however, it may be worn as an overgarment. It will resist ignition and will provide thermal protection to allow emergency egress. The JC3 will not be degraded by exposure to petroleum, oils, and lubricants present in the operational environment. The JC3 will be compatible with current and developmental protective masks and mask accessories, headgear, gloves/mittens, footwear, and other CVC ancillary equipment (e.g., Spall vest).

## SYSTEM INTERDEPENDENCIES

**Other Major Interdependencies**

Existing and co-developmental protective masks, appropriate mask accessories, protective headwear, hand-wear, footwear, and Army and Marine Corps armored vehicles

## PROGRAM STATUS

- **FY11:** Continued production and fielding

## PROJECTED ACTIVITIES

- **FY12-FY14:** Continue production and fielding

**ACQUISITION PHASE**

Technology Development | Engineering and Manufacturing Development | Production and Deployment | Operations and Support

## Joint Chem/Bio Coverall for Combat Vehicle Crewman (JC3)

**FOREIGN MILITARY SALES**
None

**CONTRACTORS**
Group Home Foundation Inc. (Belfast, ME)
ReadyOne Industries (El Paso, TX)

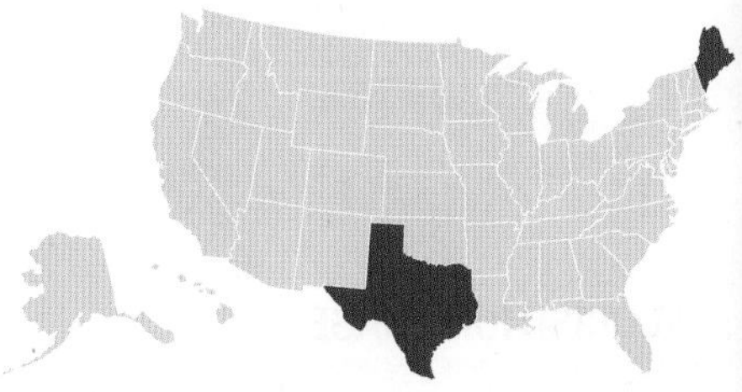

# Joint Chemical Agent Detector (JCAD) M4E1

**INVESTMENT COMPONENT**

- Modernization
- Recapitalization
- Maintenance

## MISSION

Protects U.S. forces by detecting, identifying, alerting, and reporting the presence of chemical warfare agents and toxic industrial chemical vapors.

## DESCRIPTION

The Joint Chemical Agent Detector (JCAD) is a pocket-size, rugged, handheld detector that automatically detects, identifies, and alarms to chemical warfare agents and toxic industrial chemical vapors.

The Services can use the system on mobile platforms, at fixed sites, and on individuals designated to operate in a chemical threat area. The system can operate in a general chemical warfare environment and can undergo conventional decontamination procedures by the Warfighter.

The Enhanced JCAD (M4E1 JCAD) goes into production in FY11. The M4E1 JCAD will reduce operation and sustainment costs, has an improved user interface, and is net-ready.

The JCAD replaces the Automatic Chemical Agent Detector and Alarm (ACADA or M22), M90, and M8A1 systems. The JCAD may replace the Chemical Agent Monitor (CAM) and Improved Chemical Agent Monitor (ICAM).

Specific capabilities include:

- Instant feedback of hazard (mask only or full Mission-Oriented Protective Posture)
- Real-time detection of nerve, blister, and blood agents
- Stores up to 72 hours of detection data
- The M4E1 will be net-ready through implementation of the common chemical, biological, radiological, and nuclear standard interface

## SYSTEM INTERDEPENDENCIES

**In this Publication**

Abrams Tank Upgrade, Bradley Fighting Vehicle Systems Upgrade, Family of Medium Tactical Vehicles (FMTV)

**Other Major Interdependencies**

Modular Lightweight Load-carrying Equipment (MOLLE)

## PROGRAM STATUS

- **FY11:** Continued fielding M4 variant to the Services
- **2QFY11:** Production cut-in decision review for M4E1

## PROJECTED ACTIVITIES

- **FY12-FY14:** Production and deployment

**ACQUISITION PHASE**

- Technology Development
- Engineering and Manufacturing Development
- Production and Deployment
- Operations and Support

## Joint Chemical Agent Detector (JCAD) M4E1

**FOREIGN MILITARY SALES**
None

**CONTRACTORS**
Smiths Detection Inc. (Edgewood, MD)

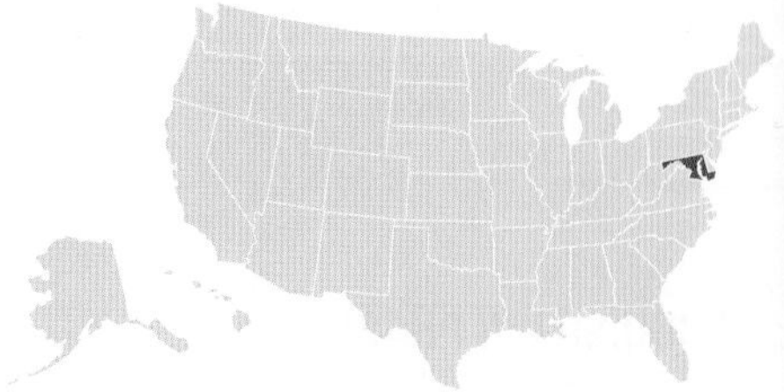

# Joint Chemical, Biological, Radiological Agent Water Monitor (JCBRAWM)

**INVESTMENT COMPONENT**

- Modernization
- Recapitalization
- Maintenance

## MISSION

Protects U.S. forces by detecting and identifying the presence of biological warfare agents and radiological contaminants in water supplies.

## DESCRIPTION

The Joint Chemical, Biological, Radiological Agent Water Monitor (JCBRAWM) is a kit that provides a waterborne biological and radiological agent detection capability. The JCBRAWM kit is one-man portable and detects two biological toxins and radiation (alpha and beta particles) in drinking water. JCBRAWM provides the ability to detect and identify biological and radiological contamination during three water-monitoring missions: source site selection/reconnaissance, treatment verification, and quality assurance of stored and distributed product water. The system performs biological detection and identification functions with an immunoassay ticket and radiological detection using the fielded AN/PDR-77 Radiac Set system and accessory package.

JCBRAWM leverages commercial technologies and fielded systems. JCBRAWM supplements the currently fielded M272 water-testing kit.

The system is being fielded to the Army and Navy.

## SYSTEM INTERDEPENDENCIES

**Other Major Interdependencies**

AN/PDR-77 Radiac Set

## PROGRAM STATUS

- **FY11:** Complete fielding

**ACQUISITION PHASE**

- Technology Development
- Engineering and Manufacturing Development
- Production and Deployment
- Operations and Support

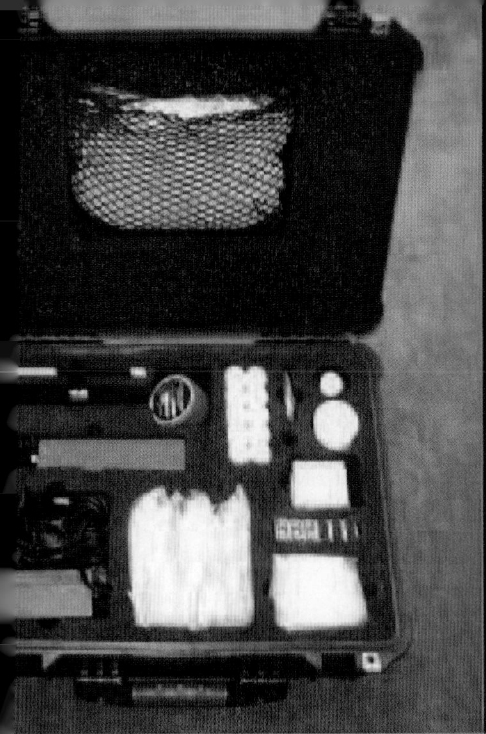

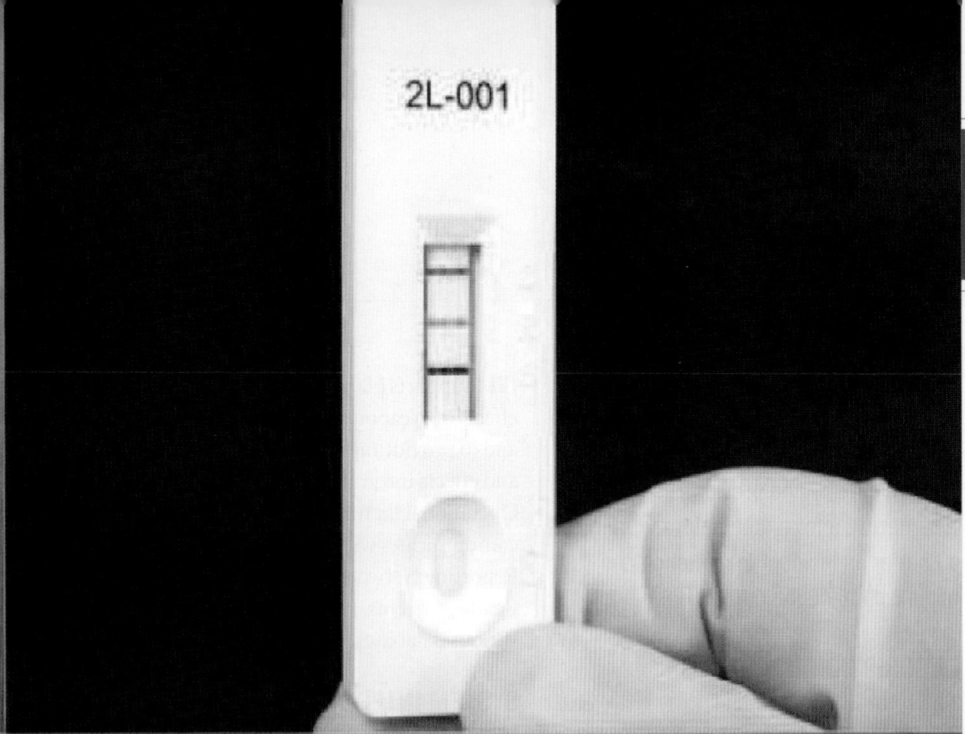


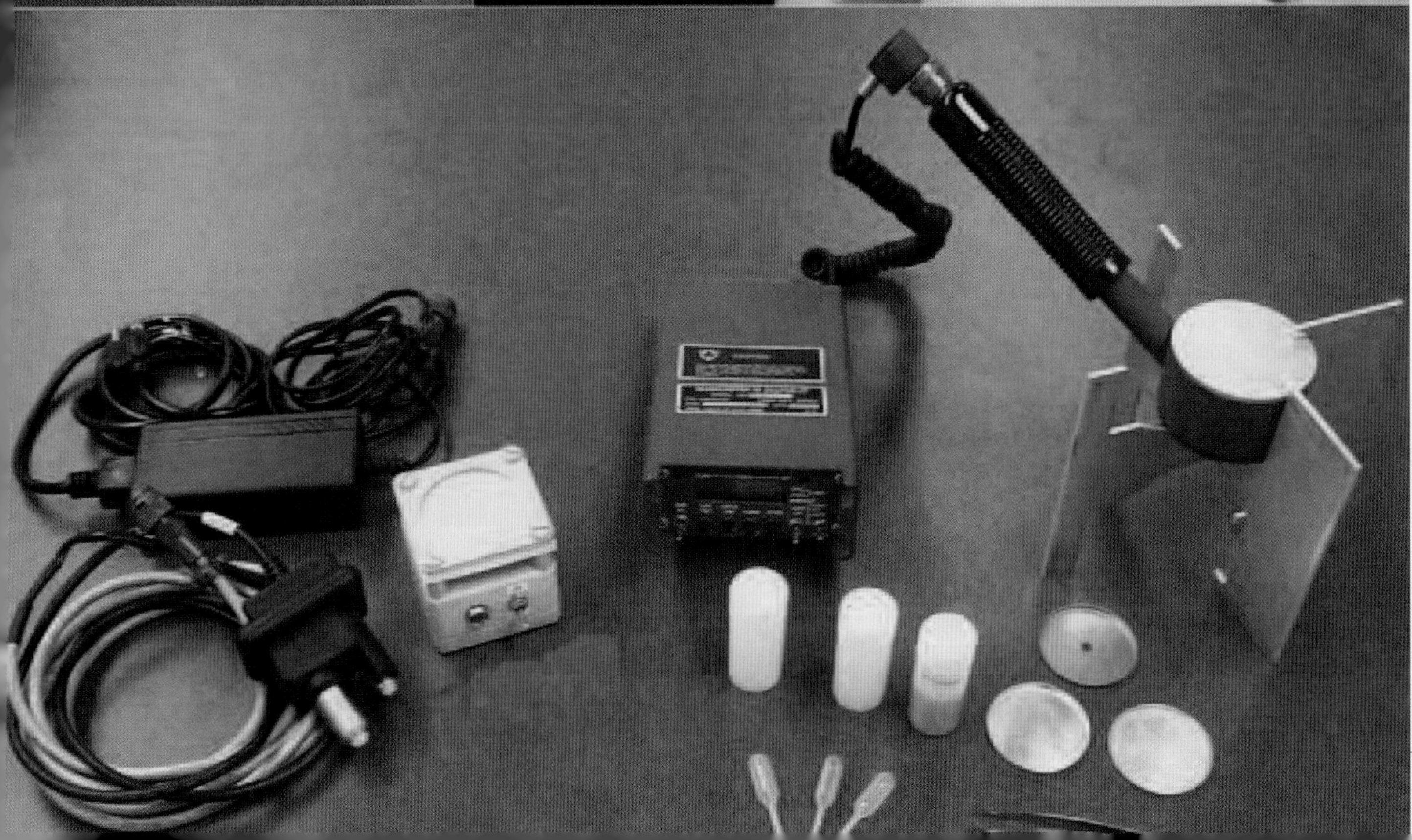

## Joint Chemical, Biological, Radiological Agent Water Monitor (JCBRAWM)

**FOREIGN MILITARY SALES**
None

**CONTRACTORS**
ANP Technologies (Newark, DE)

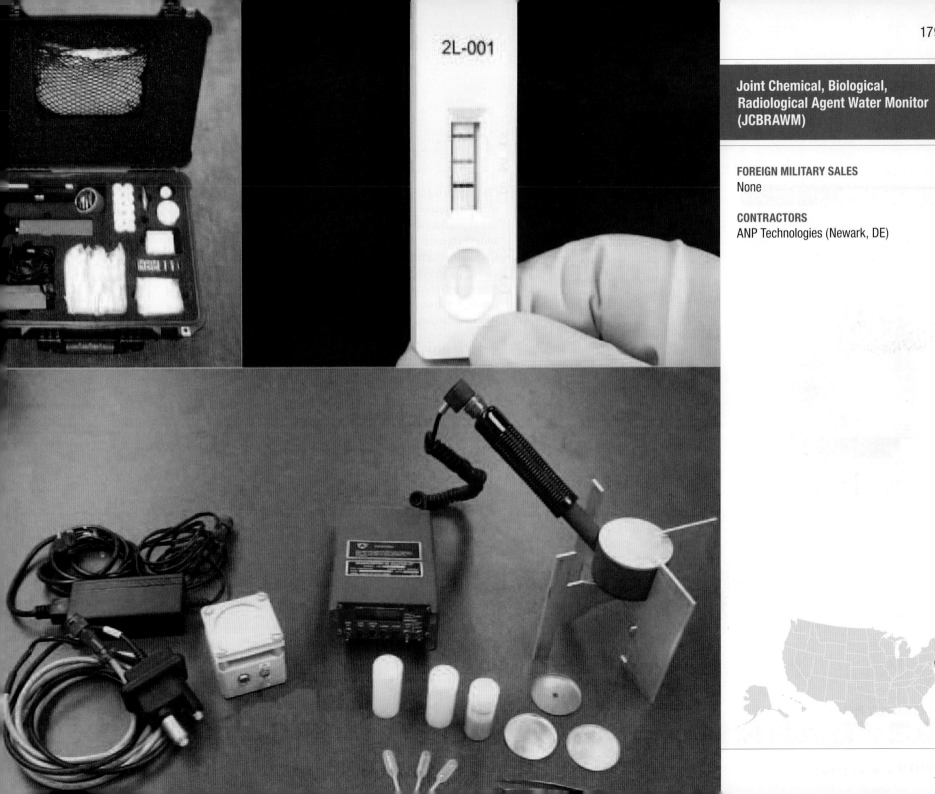

# Joint Effects Model (JEM)

**INVESTMENT COMPONENT**

Modernization

Recapitalization

Maintenance

## MISSION

Provides enhanced operational and tactical-level situational awareness of the battlespace and provides near real-time hazard information before, during, and after an incident to influence and minimize effects on current operations.

## DESCRIPTION

The Joint Effects Model (JEM) is a Web-based software program. It is the only accredited DoD computer-based tactical and operational hazard prediction model capable of providing common representation of chemical, biological, radiological, nuclear (CBRN), and toxic industrial chemicals/toxic industrial material hazard areas and effects. It may be used in two variants: as either a standalone system, or as a resident application on host command, control, communications, computers, and intelligence systems. It is capable of modeling hazards in various scenarios, including counterforce, passive defense, accidents, incidents, high-altitude releases, urban environments, building interiors, and human performance degradation.

JEM supports planning to mitigate the effects of Weapons of Mass Destruction and to provide rapid estimates of hazards and effects integrated into the Common Operational Picture. JEM interfaces and communicates with the Joint Warning and Reporting Network (JWARN), associated weather systems, intelligence systems, and various databases.

## SYSTEM INTERDEPENDENCIES

**In this Publication**

Global Command and Control System-Army (GCCS-A), Joint Warning and Reporting Network (JWARN)

**Other Major Interdependencies**

Global Command and Control System-Joint, Joint Tactical Common Operational Picture Workstation (JTCW)/Command and Control Personal Computer (C2PC), Meteorological Data Server

## PROGRAM STATUS

- **FY11:** Continued Increment 1 deployment
- **2QFY11:** Increment 2 Milestone A

## PROJECTED ACTIVITIES

- **FY12-FY14:** Continue Increment 1 production and deployment
- **4QFY13:** Increment 2 Milestone B
- **4QFY14:** Increment 2 Milestone C

**ACQUISITION PHASE**

Technology Development | Engineering and Manufacturing Development | Production and Deployment | Operations and Support

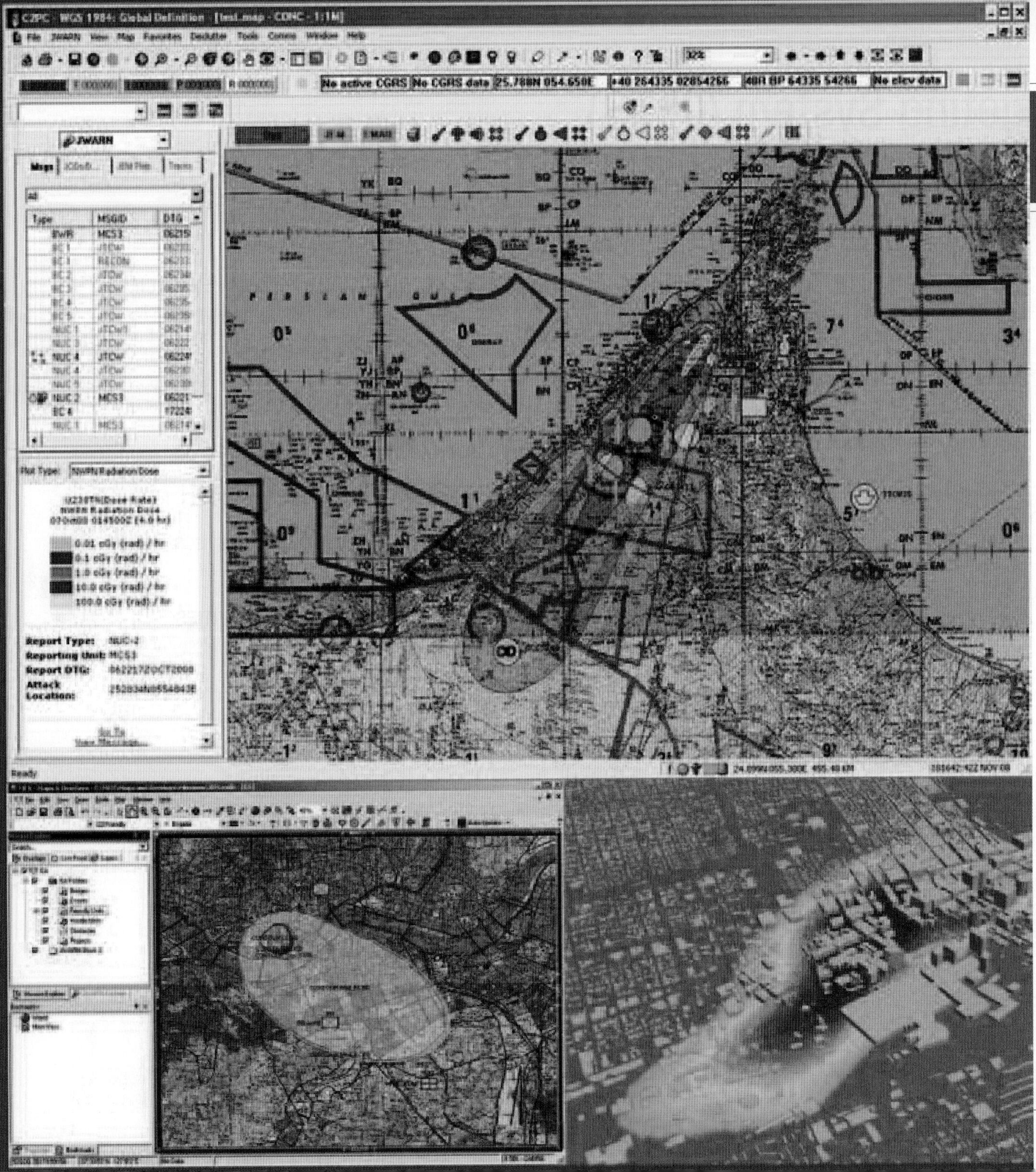


## Joint Effects Model (JEM)

**FOREIGN MILITARY SALES**
Pending

**CONTRACTORS**
Northrop Grumman Mission Systems (San Diego, CA)

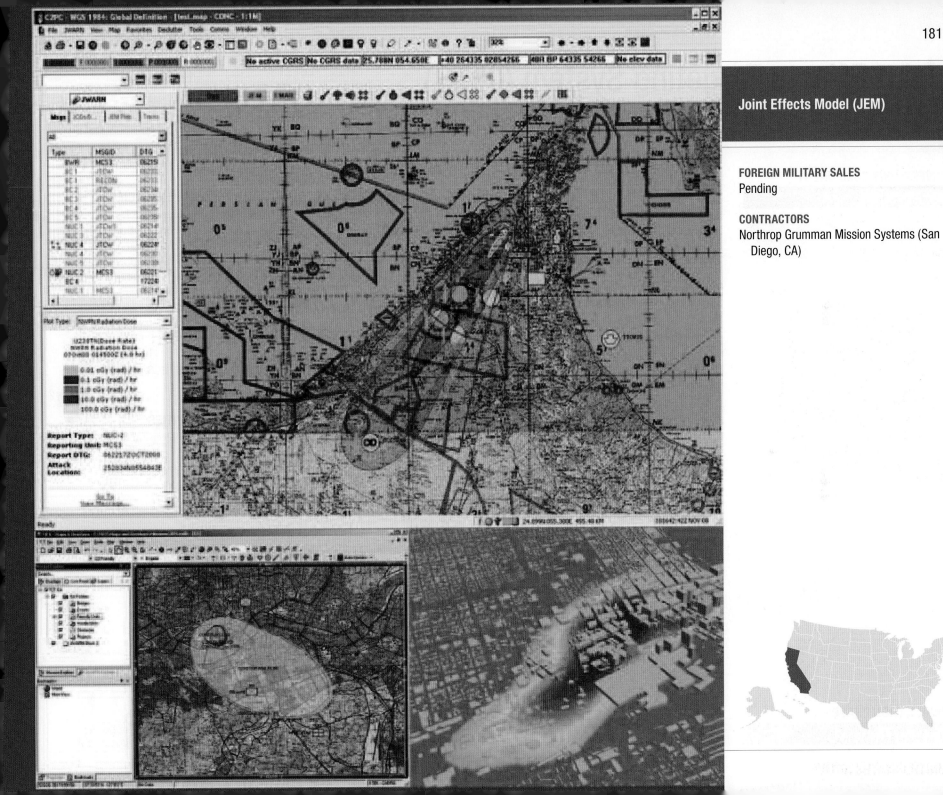

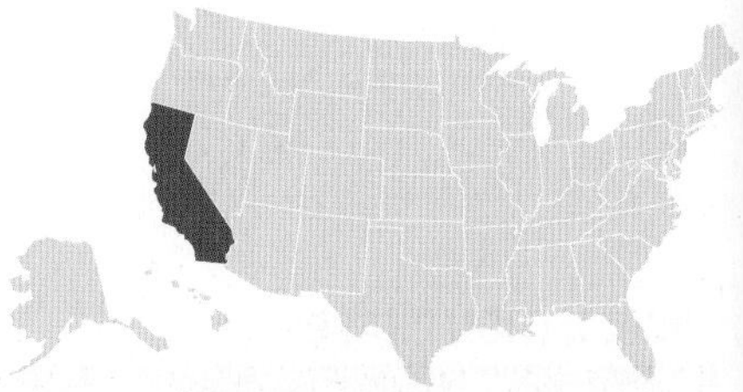

# Joint Effects Targeting System (JETS) Target Location Designation System (TLDS)

**INVESTMENT COMPONENT**

- **Modernization**
- Recapitalization
- Maintenance

## MISSION

Provides the dismounted Forward Observer and Joint Terminal Attack Controller the ability to acquire, locate, mark, and designate for precision GPS-guided and laser-guided munitions, and provides connectivity to the Joint forces through fire and close air support digital planning/messaging devices.

## DESCRIPTION

The Joint Effects Targeting System (JETS) is an Army-led, Joint interest program with the Air Force (USAF) and Marine Corps to develop and field a one-man portable targeting system for forward observers and Joint Terminal Attack Controllers (JTACS).

This future system will answer the need for a very lightweight, highly accurate targeting system that will allow target engagements with precision munitions (e.g., JDAM, Excalibur, and laser-guided weapons) and provide crucial digital connectivity to request and control indirect fires and close air support from all joint assets. The JETS' light weight will allow small units supported by Army forward observers or JTACs to have access to precision targeting in all operational environments.

The JETS consists of two major subsystems: the Target Location Designation System (TLDS) and the Target Effects Coordination System (TECS).

The TLDS will provide the dismounted observer and JTAC with a common enhanced lightweight handheld capability to rapidly acquire, accurately locate, positively identify, and precisely designate targets. The TECS will interface with the TLDS and will provide a networked, automated communications capability to plan, coordinate, and deliver fire support, as well as provide terminal close air support guidance. Based on a strategy approved in FY11 by the Army Acquisition Executive and endorsed by the Joint Fire Support Executive Steering Committee (JFS ESC), the TECS requirement will be satisfied by continued development of existing service-specific forward entry systems, which will comply with a Joint common minimum messaging set.

## SYSTEM INTERDEPENDENCIES

**Other Major Interdependencies**

U.S. Army Portable Forward Entry Device, U.S. Air Force Tactical Air Control Party-Close Air Support System, and U.S. Marine Corps StrikeLink

## PROGRAM STATUS

- **FY11:** Technology Development Activities for JETS TLDS for Milestone B
- **FY11:** Approval of TECS development strategy

## PROJECTED ACTIVITIES

- **FY13:** Milestone B Decision for JETS TLDS
- **FY16:** Initial operational capability for JETS TLDS

**ACQUISITION PHASE**

- **Technology Development**
- Engineering and Manufacturing Development
- Production and Deployment
- Operations and Support

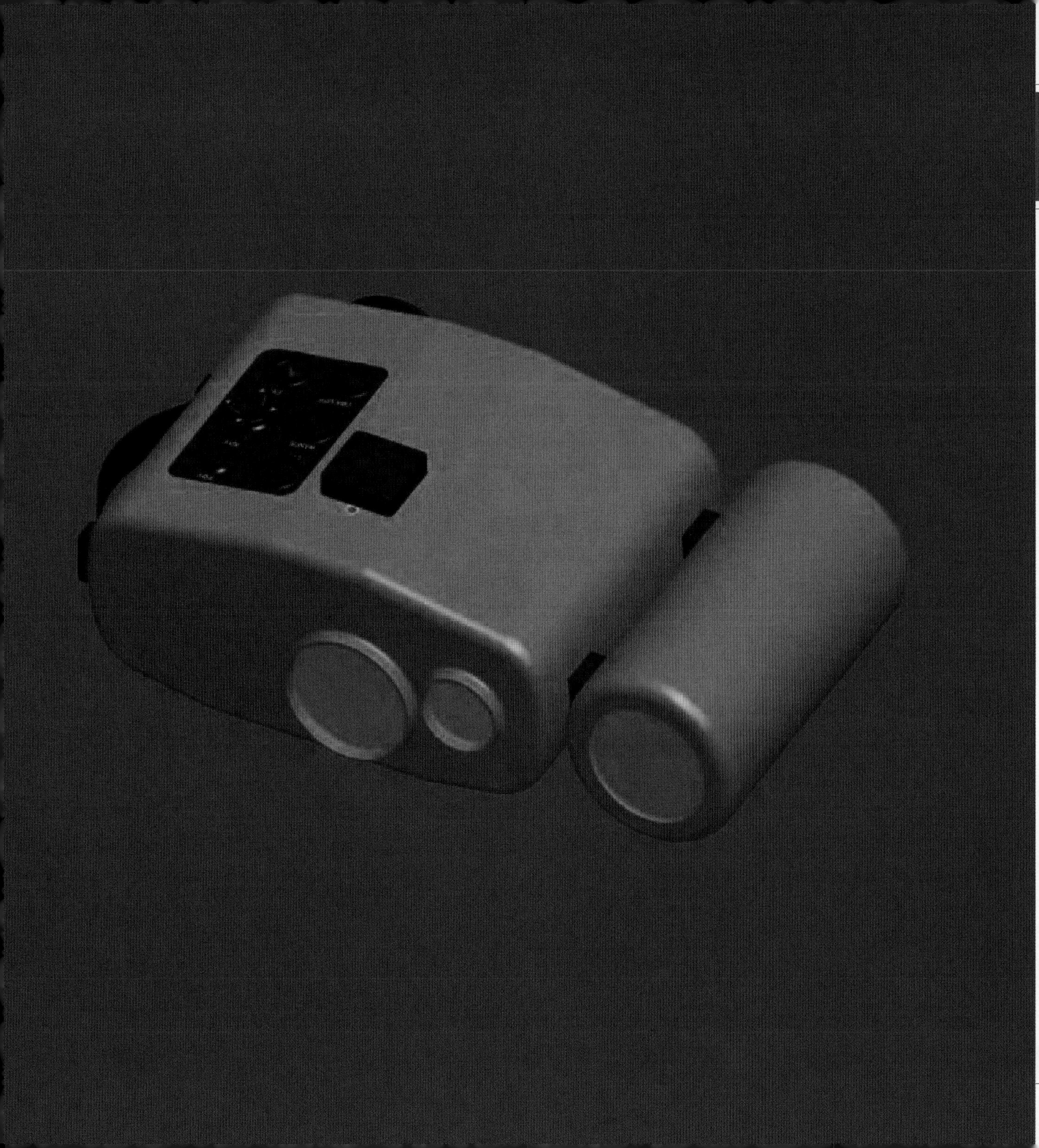



## Joint Effects Targeting System (JETS) Target Location Designation System (TLDS)

**FOREIGN MILITARY SALES**
None

**CONTRACTORS**
BAE Systems (Nashua, NH)
Northrop Grumman Guidance and Electronics, Laser Systems (Apopka, FL)

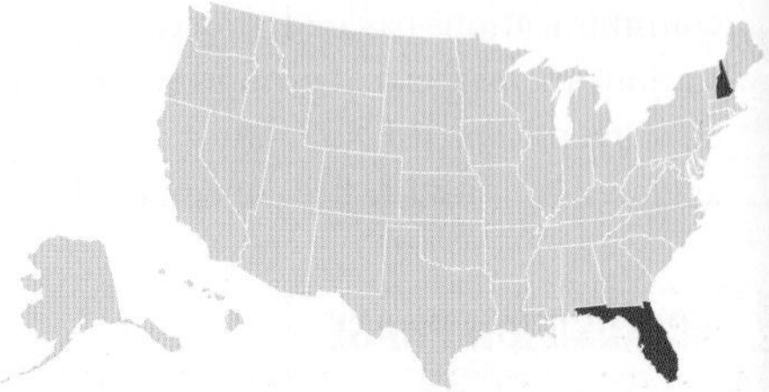

# Joint Land Attack Cruise Missile Defense Elevated Netted Sensor System (JLENS)

**INVESTMENT COMPONENT**

**Modernization**
Recapitalization
Maintenance

## MISSION

Provides elevated, persistent, over-the-horizon detection, tracking, classification, and engagement data of cruise missiles, aircraft, unmanned aerial vehicles, tactical ballistic missiles, large caliber rockets, and surface-moving targets, enabling rapid defensive engagement by air-directed, surface-to-air, or air-to-air missile systems.

## DESCRIPTION

The Joint Land Attack Cruise Missile Defense Elevated Netted Sensor System (JLENS) orbit comprises two systems: a fire control radar system and a wide-area surveillance radar system. Each system has a 74-meter tethered aerostat, a mobile mooring station, radar, communications payload, processing station, and associated ground support equipment. The JLENS mission is achieved by both the fire control radar and the surveillance radar systems operating as an "orbit;" however, each system can operate autonomously and contribute to the JLENS mission.

JLENS uses its advanced sensor and networking technologies to provide 360-degree wide-area surveillance and tracking of cruise missiles and other aircraft. Operating as an orbit, the surveillance radar generates information that enables the fire control radar to readily search for, detect, and track low-altitude cruise missiles and other airborne threats. Once the fire control radar develops tracks, this information is provided to tactical data networks so other network participants can assess threat significance and assign systems to counter the threat. The fire control data supports extended engagement ranges by other network participants by providing high-quality track data on targets that may be terrain-masked from surface-based radar systems. JLENS information is distributed via the Joint service networks and contributes to the development of a single, integrated air picture.

JLENS also performs as a multirole platform, enabling extended range communication and control linkages, communications relay, and battlefield situational awareness, and can be configured to detect and track surface moving targets. JLENS can stay aloft up to 30 days, providing 24-hour radar coverage of the assigned areas. The radar systems can be transported by aircraft, railway, ship, or roadway.

## SYSTEM INTERDEPENDENCIES

**Other Major Interdependencies**

The JLENS System is dependent on capabilities provided by Cooperative Engagement Capability (CEC), Multifunctional Information Distribution System (MIDS), and the Integrated Broadcast System (IBS); the JLENS program is interdependent with PAC-3, MEADS, and Navy Integrated Fire Control-Counter Air (NIFC-CA)

## PROGRAM STATUS

- **2QFY08:** Orbit preliminary design review
- **1QFY09:** Orbit critical design review
- **4QFY09:** Platform first flight
- **4QFY10:** Orbit 1 system integration begins

## PROJECTED ACTIVITIES

- **3QFY12:** Limited User Test
- **4QFY12:** Milestone C Decision
- **1QFY13:** LRIP 1
- **4QFY13:** First Unit Equipped
- **2QFY14:** Initial Operational Capability

**ACQUISITION PHASE**

Technology Development | **Engineering and Manufacturing Development** | Production and Deployment | Operations and Support

## Joint Land Attack Cruise Missile Defense Elevated Netted Sensor System (JLENS)

| JLENS KPPs: | Objective | Threshold |
|---|---|---|
| Combat ID: | Yes | Yes |
| SIAP: | 360° | 100° |
| IFC: | SLAMRAAM / PAC 3 / SM | SLAMRAAM / PAC 3 |
| Net-Ready: | Meet all top-level IERs | Meet critical top-level IERs |

**FOREIGN MILITARY SALES**
None

**CONTRACTORS**
**Radar and Systems Engineering:**
Raytheon (Andover, MA)
**Surv. Radar:**
Raytheon (El Segundo, CA)
**Platform:**
TCOM (Columbia, MD; Elizabeth City, NC)
**SETA Support:**
SETA (Huntsville, AL)
**Engineering and Technical Support:**
E&TS Ktrs (Huntsville, AL)
**Software:**
Raytheon Solipsys (Fulton, MD)
**Software Engineering:**
Northrop Grumman (Huntsville, AL)

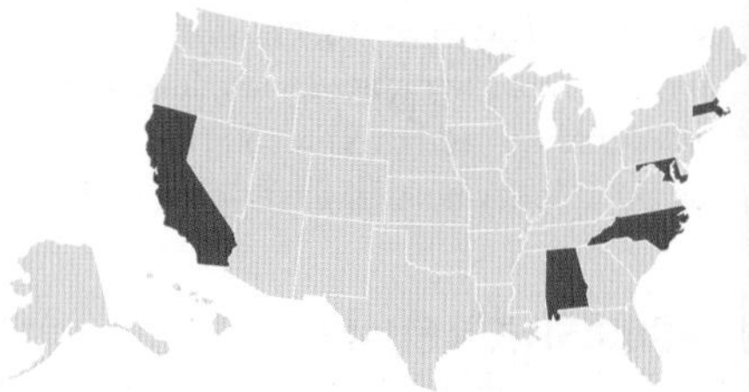

# Joint Land Component Constructive Training Capability (JLCCTC)

**INVESTMENT COMPONENT**

Modernization
Recapitalization
Maintenance

## MISSION

Provides unit commanders and their battle staffs the capability to train in a constructive environment from battalion to echelons above corps to support Army and Joint training requirements through a federation of legacy and developing objective systems including Warfighters' Simulation, One Semi-Automated Forces (OneSAF), Corps Battle Simulation, Tactical Simulation, and the Entity Resolution Federation (ERF).

## DESCRIPTION

The Joint Land Component Constructive Training Capability (JLCCTC) is a modeling and simulation software capability that contributes to the Joint training functional concept and the Army training mission area by providing the appropriate levels of model and simulation resolution as well as the fidelity needed to support both Army and Joint training requirements. JLCCTC is comprised of two separate federations, JLCCTC-Multi-Resolution Federation (MRF) and JLCCTC-ERF.

The JLCCTC-MRF is a Command Post Exercise driver designed to train Army commanders and their staffs at division through echelons above corps. JLCCTC provides the simulated operational environment in which computer-generated forces stimulate and respond to the mission command (MC) processes of the commanders and staffs. JLCCTC models will provide full training functionality for leader and battle staff for the Army and the Joint, intergovernmental, interagency, and multinational spectrum. JLCCTC provides an interface to MC Systems, allowing commanders and their staffs to train with their organizational real-world MC equipment.

JLCCTC-ERF is a federation of simulations, data collection, and after-action review tools. It simulates the mission command networks and systems to facilitate battle staff collective training by requiring staff reaction to incoming digital information while executing the commander's tactical plan. The targeted training audience is comprised of brigade and battalion battle staffs, functional Command Post (CP) training, and full CP training. Battle staffs of higher echelons may also employ JLCCTC-ERF to achieve specific training objectives.

## SYSTEM INTERDEPENDENCIES

None

## PROGRAM STATUS

- **4QFY11:** JLCCTC MRF-W V6.0.1 Tech Control forward/distributed site fielding to JBLM, Ft. Hood, and Schofield Barracks
- **4QFY11:** JLCCTC-ERF v5.3 fielding to Ft. Stewart, Ft. Drum, Ft. Campbell, Ft. Carson, Ft. Bliss, and Ft. Dix

## PROJECTED ACTIVITES

- **1QFY12:** The JLCCTC MRF-W system will be utilized by the KBSC to support the U.S. Army 2nd Infantry Division's (2ID) WARPATH II exercise in South Korea
- **1QFY12:** The JLCCTC MRF-W system will be utilized by the MCTP to support the 2ID Full Spectrum Exercise (FSX)
- **1QFY12:** JLCCTC ERF V6.0 VE with the NSC, this version includes OneSAF as the ground maneuver model and the upper enclave (TS/SCI) WIM capability
- **2QFY12:** JLCCTC MRF-W V6.1 (Corps capability) VE with the NSC
- **3QFY12:** The JLCCTC MRF-W system will be utilized by the MCTP to support a Corps Level Exercise at Ft. Hood, TX
- **1QFY13-2QFY13:** JLCCTC MRF-W First Use in Japan (Corps level-Yama Sakura 63)
- **4QFY13:** JLCCTC MRF-W First Use Exercise at the Echelons Above Corps level during the KBSC supported UFG
- **1QFY14-2QFY14:** The JLCCTC MRF-W system will be utilized by the KBSC to support the Yama Sakura 65 Exercise
- **2QFY14:** The JLCCTC MRF-W system will be utilized by the KBSC to support the Key Resolve Exercise

**ACQUISITION PHASE**

Technology Development | Engineering and Manufacturing Development | Production and Deployment | Operations and Support

## Joint Land Component Constructive Training Capability (JLCCTC)

**FOREIGN MILITARY SALES**
None

**CONTRACTORS**
Lockheed Martin Global Training and Logistics (Orlando, FL)
Tapestry Solutions Inc. (San Diego, CA)
Booz/Allen/Hamilton (Orlando, FL)

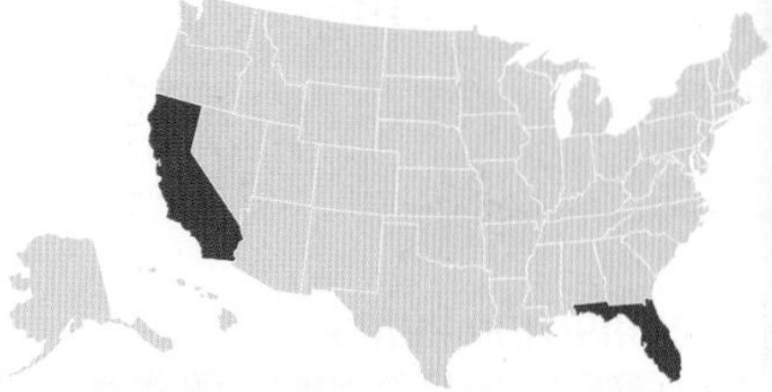

# Joint Light Tactical Vehicle (JLTV)

**INVESTMENT COMPONENT**

Modernization

Recapitalization

Maintenance

## MISSION

Provides a family of vehicles, with companion trailers, capable of performing multiple mission roles that will be designed to provide protected, sustained, networked mobility for personnel and payloads across the full range of military operations.

## DESCRIPTION

The Joint Light Tactical Vehicle (JLTV) Family of Vehicles (FoV) is a Joint service and international program that will be capable of operating across a broad spectrum of terrain and weather conditions. The Joint Services require enhanced performance, exceeding the existing High Mobility Multipurpose Wheeled Vehicle, supporting the Joint Functional Concepts of Battlespace Awareness, Force Application, and Focused Logistics. The JLTV FoVs consist of two variants: Combat Tactical Vehicle and Combat Support Vehicle. The JLTV is transportable by a range of lift assets, including rotary-wing aircraft, to support operations across the range of military operations. Its maneuverability enables operations across the spectrum of terrain, including urban areas, while providing inherent and supplemental armor against direct fire and improvised explosive device threats.

**Payloads:** CTV-3,500 pounds, CSV-5,100 pounds

**Transportability:** Internal-C-130, External-CH-47@ Curb Weight plus 2000 lbs and CH-53, Sea-Height-restricted decks

**Protection:** Scalable armor to provide mission flexibility while protecting the force

**Mobility:** Maneuverability to enable operations across the spectrum of terrain, including urban areas

**Networking:** Connectivity for improved battlespace awareness and responsive, well-integrated command and control for embarked forces

**Sustainability:** Reliable, maintainable, maximum commonality across mission role variants, onboard and exportable power, and reduced fuel consumption

The JLTV FoV balances the "Iron Triangle" of payload, protection, and performance.

## SYSTEM INTERDEPENDENCIES

None

## PROGRAM STATUS

- **4QFY11:** Capability Development Document approved

## PROJECTED ACTIVITIES

- **2QFY12:** Milestone B, enter engineering and manufacturing development (EMD)
- **2QFY12:** Award two full and open competition EMD contracts

**ACQUISITION PHASE**

Technology Development | Engineering and Manufacturing Development | Production and Deployment | Operations and Support

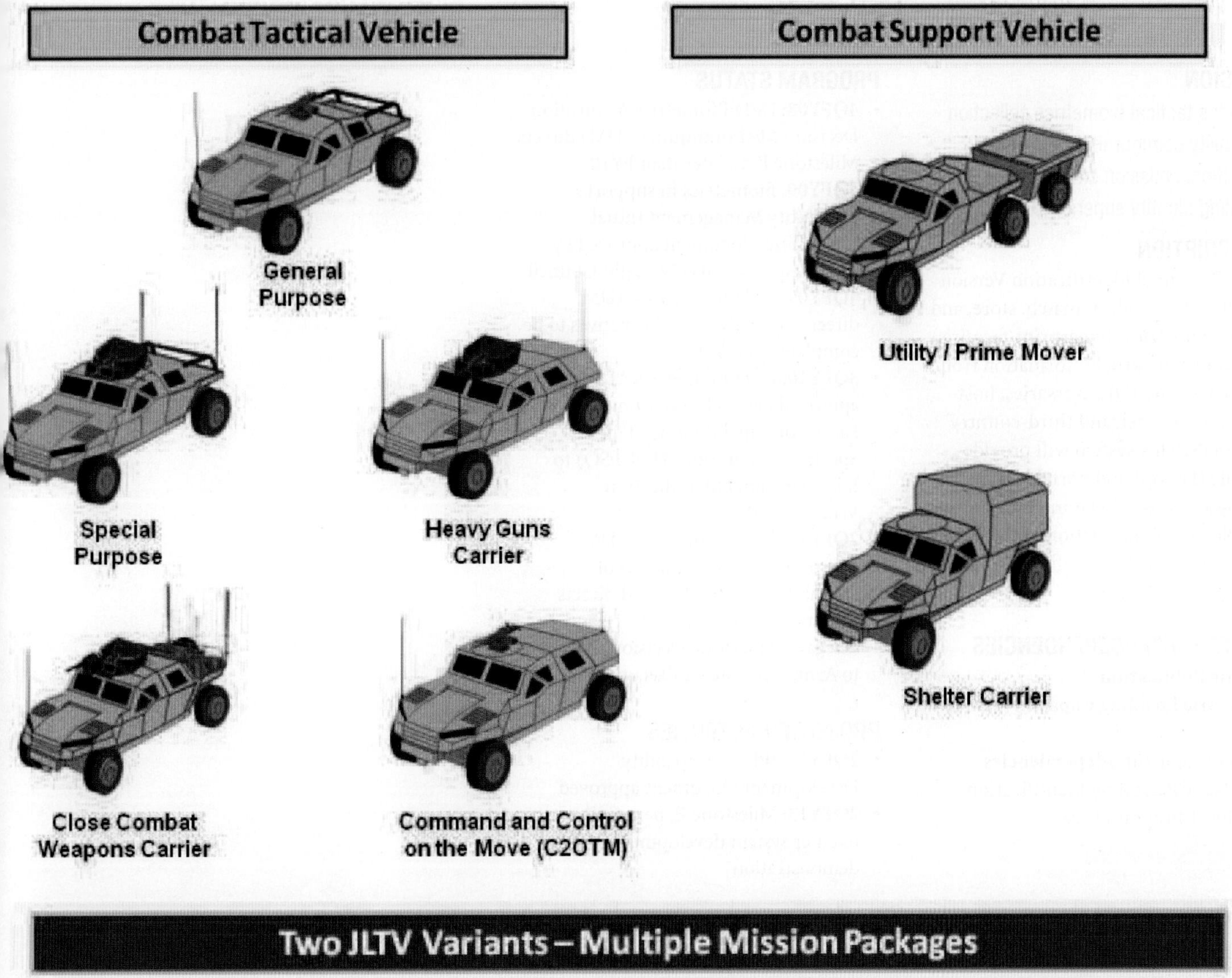


## Joint Light Tactical Vehicle (JLTV)

**FOREIGN MILITARY SALES**
None

**CONTRACTORS**
To be determined for EMD

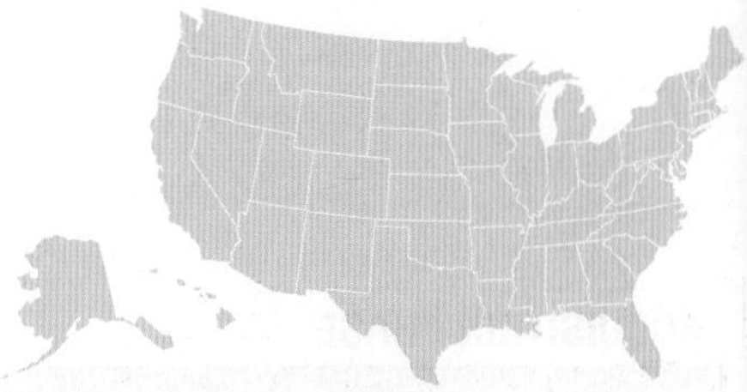

# Joint Personnel Identification Version 2 (JPIv2)

INVESTMENT COMPONENT

- **Modernization**
- Recapitalization
- Maintenance

## MISSION

Provides tactical biometrics collection capability configurable for multiple operational mission environments, enabling identity superiority.

## DESCRIPTION

Joint Personnel Identification Version 2 (JPIv2) will collect, match, store, and share biometrics (fingerprint/face/iris) data and contextual information from actual or potential adversaries, host-nation personnel, and third-country nationals. This system will provide mobile (laptop) and portable (handheld) configurations. This Joint and common solution is a continuation of the U.S. Navy's Personnel Identification Version 1 Program (PIv1).

## SYSTEM INTERDEPENDENCIES

**In this Publication**

Biometric Enabling Capability (BEC)

**Other Major Interdependencies**

U.S. Navy Personnel Identification Version 1 Program (PIv1).

## PROGRAM STATUS

- **4QFY08:** DoD Biometrics Acquisition Decision Memorandum (ADM) directs Milestone B no later than FY10
- **1QFY09:** Biometrics in support of Identity Management Initial Capabilities document approved by Joint Requirements Oversight Council
- **4QFY09:** DoD Biometrics ADM directs the analysis of alternatives to be completed 2QFY10
- **3QFY10:** DoD Biometrics ADM approved name change from Biometric Family of Capabilities for Full Spectrum Operations (BFCFSO) to Joint Personnel Identification Version 2 (JPIv2)
- **2QFY11:** DoD Biometrics ADM approves Biometric analysis of alternatives final report and directs Milestone B for JPIv2 in FY12 and delegates Milestone Decision Authority to Army Acquisition Executive

## PROJECTED ACTIVITIES

- **2QFY12:** JPIv2 1 Capability Development Document approved
- **2QFY13:** Milestone B, permission to enter system development and demonstration

ACQUISITION PHASE

**Technology Development** | Engineering and Manufacturing Development | Production and Deployment | Operations and Support

## Joint Personnel Identification Version 2 (JPIv2)

**FOREIGN MILITARY SALES**
None

**CONTRACTORS**
**Program Management Support Services:**
CACI (Arlington, VA)
The Research Associates (New York, NY)
**System Development and Integration:**
To be determined pending Milestone B

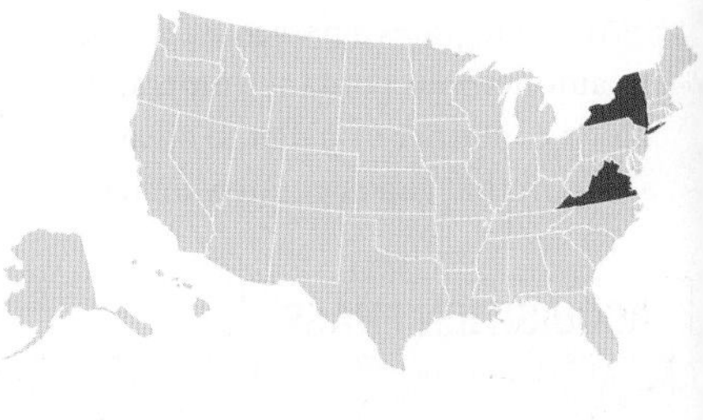

# Joint Precision Airdrop System (JPADS)

## INVESTMENT COMPONENT

**Modernization**

Recapitalization

Maintenance

## MISSION

Provides the Warfighter with precision airdrop capability, ensuring an accurate delivery of supplies to forward-operating forces, reducing vehicular convoys, and allowing aircraft to drop cargo at safer altitudes and offset distances.

## DESCRIPTION

The Joint Precision Airdrop System (JPADS) is a precision-guided airdrop system that provides rapid, precise, high-altitude delivery capabilities that do not rely on ground transportation. The system ensures accurate and timely delivery in support of operational missions, while providing aircraft with increased survivability.

JPADS integrates a parachute decelerator, an autonomous guidance unit, and a load container or pallet to create a system that can accurately deliver critical supplies with great precision along a predetermined glide and flight path. The system is being developed in two weight classes: 2,000 pounds and 10,000 pounds. The guidance system uses military global positioning satellite data for precise navigation and interfaces with a wirelessly updatable mission-planning module on board the aircraft to receive real-time weather data and compute multiple aerial release points.

JPADS is being designed for aircraft to drop cargo from altitudes of up to 24,500 feet mean sea level. It will release cargo from a minimum offset of eight kilometers from the intended point of impact, with an objective capability of 25 kilometers offset. This offset allows aircraft to stay out of range of many anti-aircraft systems. It also enables aircraft to drop systems from a single aerial release point and deliver them to multiple or single locations, thus reducing aircraft exposure time. Once on the ground, the precise placement of the loads greatly reduces the time needed to recover the load as well as minimizing exposure to ground forces.

## SYSTEM INTERDEPENDENCIES

None

## PROGRAM STATUS

- **3QFY07-4QFY08:** Testing for 2,000-pound variant completed
- **1QFY08:** Milestone B (permission to enter system development and demonstration phase) received for 10,000-pound variant
- **2QFY08:** Testing began for 10,000-pound variant and currently in developmental testing
- **3QFY09:** Milestone C, Type Classification-Standard, and Full Materiel Release approved for the 2,000-pound variant, with production contract
- **4QFY09:** Fielding began for 2,000-pound variant and will continue through FY12
- **4QFY11:** Complete product improvements to provide increased capabilities for the 2,000-pound variant in accordance with joint urgent operations statement to include: accuracy improvements, adding terrain avoidance capability, and reducing the retrograde burden

## PROJECTED ACTIVITIES

- **1QFY12:** Complete testing of the 10,000-pound variant
- **3QFY12:** Milestone C (Full-Rate Production and fielding decision) for 10,000-pound variant with subsequent award production contract
- **1QFY13:** Fielding begins for 10,000-pound variant

## ACQUISITION PHASE

Technology Development | **Engineering and Manufacturing Development** | **Production and Deployment** | Operations and Support

Airborne Guidance Unit (AGU)

## Joint Precision Airdrop System (JPADS)

**FOREIGN MILITARY SALES**
None

**CONTRACTORS**
Airborne Systems North America (Pennsauken, NJ)
Draper Laboratories (Cambridge, MA)

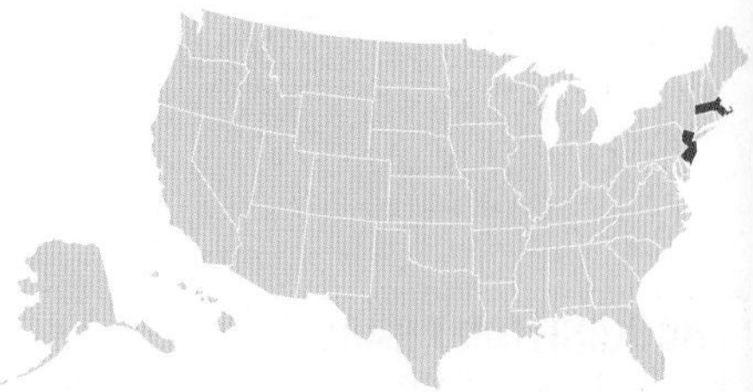

# Joint Service General Purpose Mask (JSGPM) M-50/M-51

**INVESTMENT COMPONENT**

- **Modernization**
- Recapitalization
- Maintenance

## MISSION

Provides face, eye, and respiratory protection from battlefield concentrations of chemical and biological (CB) agents, toxins, toxic industrial materials, and radiological particulate matter.

## DESCRIPTION

The Joint Service General Purpose Mask (JSGPM) is a lightweight, protective mask system incorporating state-of-the-art technology to protect U.S. Joint forces from actual or anticipated threats. The JSGPM provides above-the-neck, head-eye-respiratory protection against CBRN threats, including toxic industrial chemicals. The M-50/M-51 provides improved CB protection, enhanced field of view, lower breathing resistance, reduced weight/bulk, improved drinking system design, and improved compatibility over fielded systems. The JSGPM is interoperable with existing legacy and commercial radio systems, while ensuring future operation with the next generation of communications equipment. The M-50/M-51 mask system replaces the M40/M42 series of field protective masks for the Army and Marine Corps ground and combat vehicle operations, as well as the MCU-2/P series of protective masks for Air Force and Navy shore-based and shipboard applications. This mask is currently being fielded to all four Services—a first in the history of development and fielding.

## SYSTEM INTERDEPENDENCIES

**Other Major Interdependencies**

The JSGPM will interface with Joint service vehicles, weapons, communication systems, individual clothing, protective equipment, and CBRN personal protective equipment

## PROGRAM STATUS

- **FY11:** Production and fielding

## PROJECTED ACTIVITIES

- **FY12-FY13:** Continued production and fielding

**ACQUISITION PHASE**

Technology Development | Engineering and Manufacturing Development | **Production and Deployment** | **Operations and Support**

## Joint Service General Purpose Mask (JSGPM) M-50/M-51

**FOREIGN MILITARY SALES**
None

**CONTRACTORS**
Avon Protection Systems (Cadillac, MI)

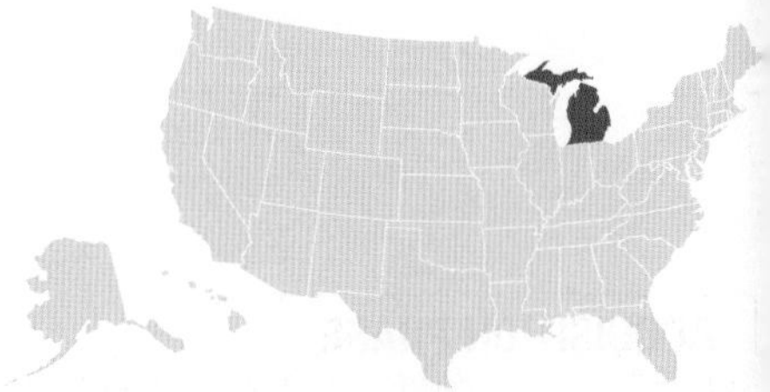

# Joint Service Transportable Small Scale Decontaminating Apparatus (JSTSS DA) M26

**INVESTMENT COMPONENT**

- Modernization
- Recapitalization
- Maintenance

## MISSION

Provides the capability to conduct operational and support thorough decontamination operations.

## DESCRIPTION

The Joint Service Transportable Small Scale Decontaminating Apparatus (JSTSS DA) will enable Warfighters to conduct operational and support thorough decontamination of non-sensitive military materiel and limited facility decontamination at logistics bases, airfields (and critical airfield assets), naval ships, ports, key command and control centers, and fixed facilities that have been exposed to chemical, biological, radiological, and nuclear (CBRN) warfare agents/contamination and toxic industrial materials. The system may also support other hazard abatement missions as necessary. The M26 is supported with one accessory kit and one water blivet per system.

The M26 is transportable by a non-dedicated platform (i.e., High Mobility Multipurpose Wheeled Vehicle (HMMWV)/Trailer, Family of Medium Tactical Vehicles (FMTV)/Trailer) off-road over any terrain.

The M26 will decontaminate Chemical Warfare Agents (Nerve-G, Nerve V, Blister H) on tactical vehicles and crew served weapons below detection levels of M8 detector paper within 5 minutes contact time after an attack. The M26 will have a reliability of greater than or equal to 0.89.

## SYSTEM INTERDEPENDENCIES

**In this Publication**

Family of Medium Tactical Vehicles (FMTV)

**Other Major Interdependencies**

High Mobility Multipurpose Wheeled Vehicle (HMMWV) Family of Vehicles; all individual protective equipment, decontaminants, and detectors

## PROGRAM STATUS

- **2QFY11:** Achieved IOC Milestone
- **3QFY11:** Procured the Total Service Requirement (TSR) for the U.S. Army, Navy, and Marine Corps

## PROJECTED ACTIVITIES

- **4QFY13:** Complete fielding to achieve Full Operational Capability (FOC) for all Services

**ACQUISITION PHASE**

Technology Development | Engineering and Manufacturing Development | Production and Deployment | Operations and Support

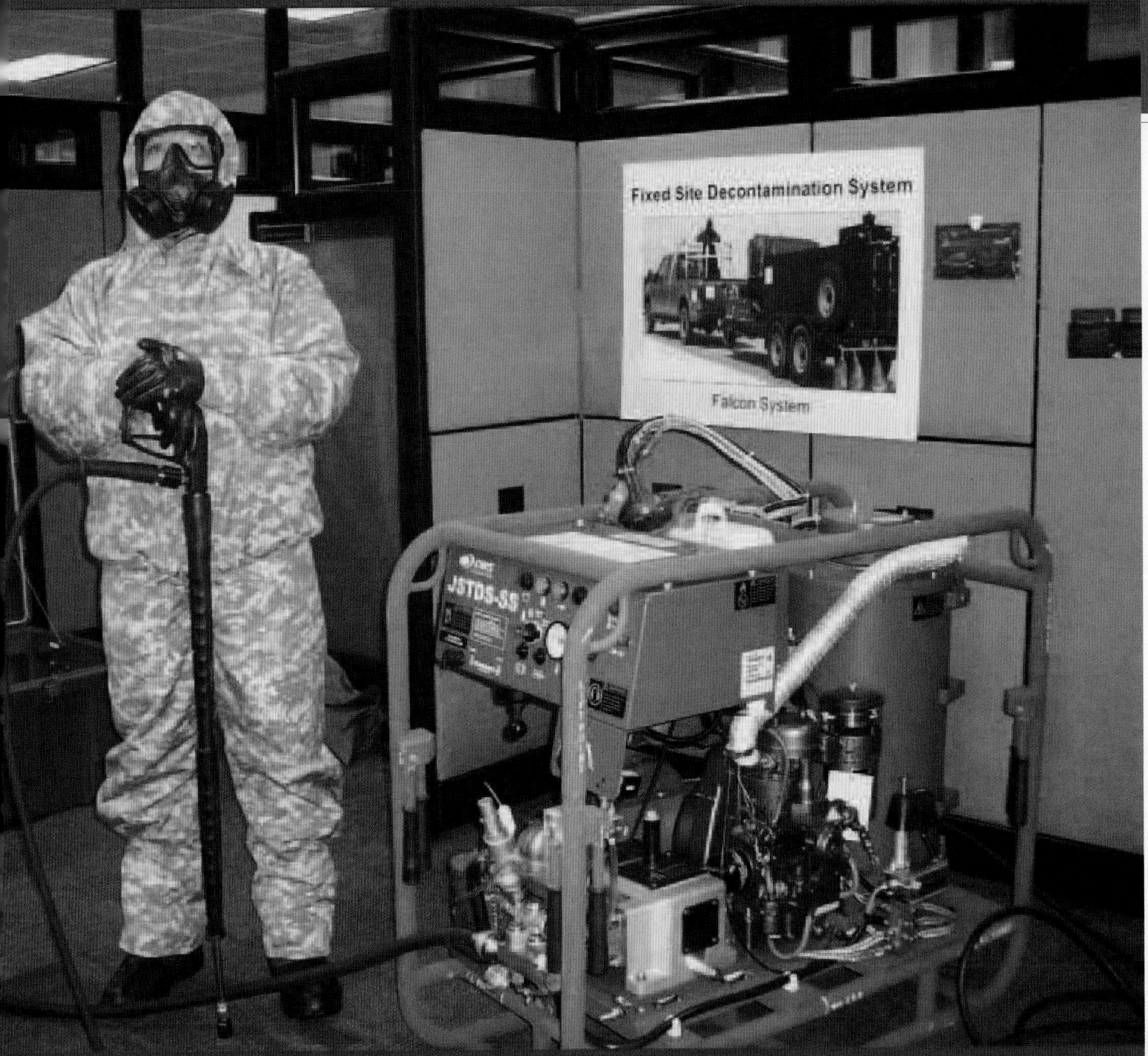


## Joint Service Transportable Small Scale Decontaminating Apparatus (JSTSS DA) M26

**FOREIGN MILITARY SALES**
None

**CONTRACTORS**
DRS Technologies (Florence, KY)

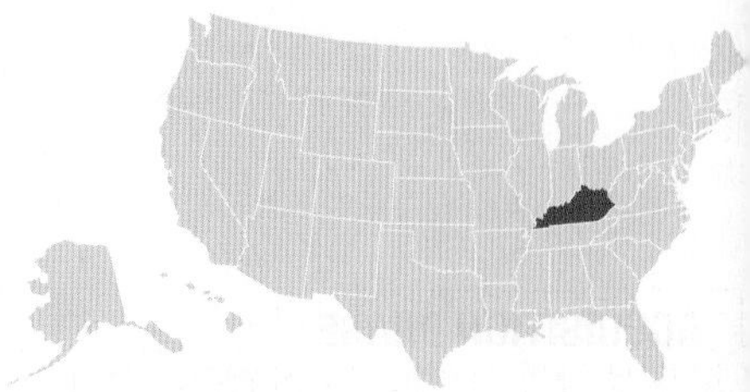

# Joint Tactical Ground Station (JTAGS)

**INVESTMENT COMPONENT**

Modernization

Recapitalization

Maintenance

## MISSION

Disseminates early-warning, alerting, and cueing information of ballistic missile attack and other infrared events to theater combatant commanders by using real-time, direct downlinked satellite data.

## DESCRIPTION

Joint Tactical Ground Stations (JTAGS) are forward-deployed, echelon-above-corps, transportable systems designed to receive, process, and disseminate direct downlinked infrared data from space-based sensors. Ongoing product improvement efforts will integrate JTAGS with the next-generation Space-Based Infrared System (SBIRS) satellites. SBIRS sensors will significantly improve in-theater missile-warning parameters. Expected improvements include higher quality cueing of active defense systems, decreased missile launch search area, faster initial report times, and improved impact ellipse prediction.

JTAGS processes satellite data and disseminates ballistic missile warning or special event messages to Warfighters in support of regional combatant commanders over multiple theater communication systems. Five JTAGS are deployed worldwide as part of the U.S. Strategic Command's Tactical Event System. Army Space and Missile Defense Command Soldiers operate JTAGS, providing 24/7/365 support to theater operations.

## SYSTEM INTERDEPENDENCIES

**Other Major Interdependencies**

U.S. Air Force's ACAT I, SBIRS satellite program

## PROGRAM STATUS

- **1QFY09-4QFY09:** Worldwide fielding of JTAGS upgrades: Common Data Link Interface, Joint Tactical Terminal, Multifunctional Information Distribution System, and information assurance improvements; upgrades to all five JTAGS units and the JTAGS development lab

## PROJECTED ACTIVITIES

- **1QFY12-3QFY12:** Complete fielding of JTAGS block upgrades including commercial antenna systems and information assurance
- **2QFY12-4QFY12:** Fielding of the Initial SBIRS Geosynchronous Orbit (GEO) satellite capability
- **4QFY12:** Initial SBIRS GEO certification for operational use
- **1QFY12-4QFY13:** Software support, contractor logistics support, and depot operations continue.
- **3QFY12:** Begin new contract for support of Pre-Planned Product Improvement program, includes full GEO satellite integration and de-shelter

**ACQUISITION PHASE**

Technology Development | Engineering and Manufacturing Development | Production and Deployment | Operations and Support

## Joint Tactical Ground Station (JTAGS)

**FOREIGN MILITARY SALES**
None

**CONTRACTORS**
**Develop, Deploy, Sustain (CLS):**
Northrop Grumman Electronic Systems (Colorado Springs, CO)
**SETA support:**
BAE Systems (Huntsville, AL)

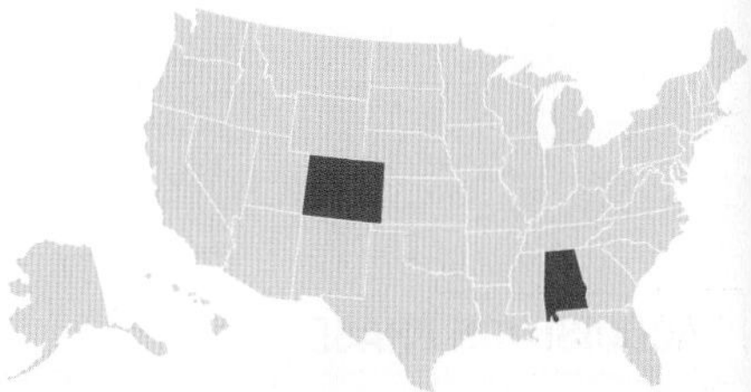

# Joint Tactical Radio System Airborne and Maritime/Fixed Station (JTRS AMF)

INVESTMENT COMPONENT

Modernization

Recapitalization

Maintenance

## MISSION

Provides scalable and modular networked radio frequency-installed communication capability to meet Joint service requirements through two Joint tactical radio sets with common ancillary equipment for both radio form factors and aircraft, as well as maritime and shore sites.

## DESCRIPTION

The Joint Tactical Radio System Airborne and Maritime/Fixed Station (JTRS AMF) will provide a four-channel, full duplex, software-defined radio integrated into airborne, shipboard, and fixed-station platforms, enabling maritime and airborne forces to communicate seamlessly and with greater efficiency through implementation of five initial waveforms (i.e., Ultra-High Frequency Satellite Communications, Mobile User Objective System, Wideband Network Waveform, Soldier Radio Waveform, and Link 16) providing data, voice, and networking capabilities. JTRS AMF is software-reprogrammable, multiband/multimode capable, mobile ad-hoc network capable, and it provides simultaneous voice, data, and video communications. The system is flexible enough to provide point-to-point and netted voice and data, whether it is between Service Command Centers, Shipboard Command Centers, Joint Operations Centers or other functional centers (e.g., intelligence, logistics).

AMF will assist U.S. Armed Forces in the conduct of prompt, sustained, and synchronized operations, allowing Warfighters the freedom to achieve information dominance in all domains — land, sea, air, and space.

## SYSTEM INTERDEPENDENCIES

**Other Major Interdependencies**

Multiple aircraft, maritime, and fixed site platforms

## PROGRAM STATUS

- **2QFY11:** Delivery of AMF Small Airborne (SA) Engineering Development Models (EDM) for Apache Integration

## PROJECTED ACTIVITIES

- **2QFY12:** Link-16 Waveform (WF) available for platform integration
- **1QFY13:** Milestone C
- **2QFY13:** SA Limited Rate Initial Production (LRIP) delivery
- **4QFY13:** SRW/WNW WF available for platform integration

ACQUISITION PHASE

Technology Development | Engineering and Manufacturing Development | Production and Deployment | Operations and Support

## Joint Tactical Radio System Airborne and Maritime/Fixed Station (JTRS AMF)

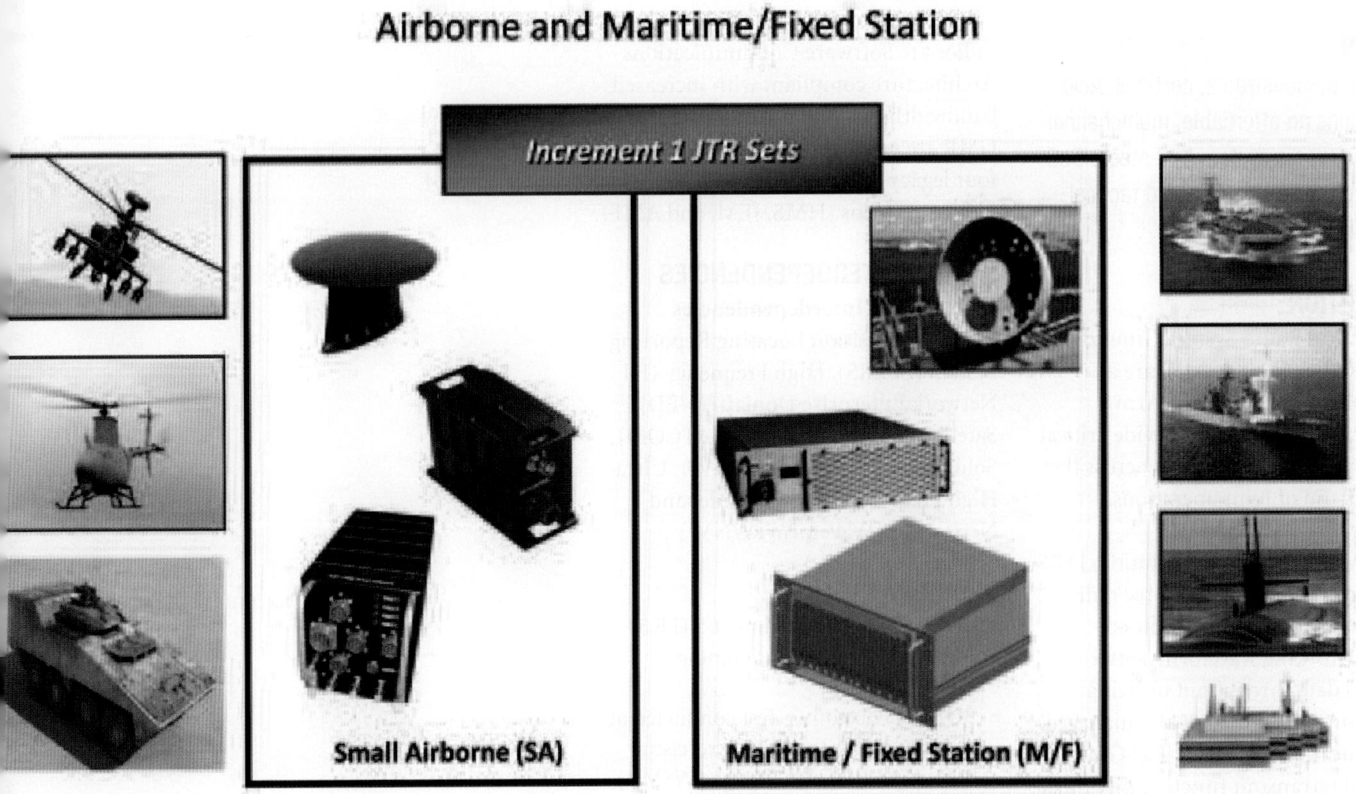


**FOREIGN MILITARY SALES**
None

**CONTRACTORS**
**Prime:**
Lockheed Martin (San Diego, CA; Alexandria, VA)
**Subcontractors:**
BAE Systems (Wayne, NJ)
Northrop Grumman (San Diego, CA)
General Dynamics C4 Systems, Inc. (Scottsdale, AZ)
Raytheon (Ft. Wayne, IN)

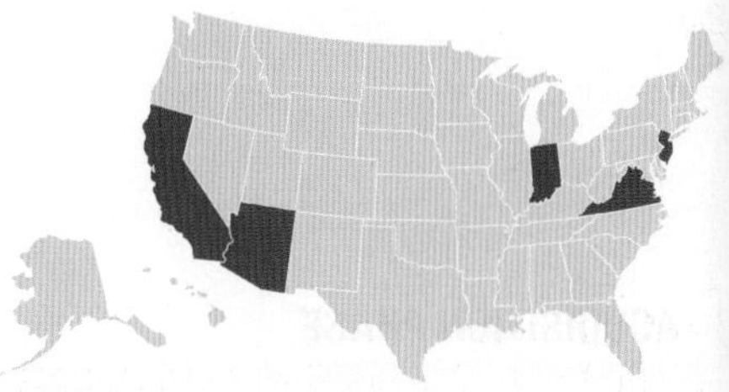

# Joint Tactical Radio System Ground Mobile Radios (JTRS GMR)

**INVESTMENT COMPONENT**

- **Modernization**
- Recapitalization
- Maintenance

## MISSION

Develops, demonstrates, certifies, fields, and sustains an affordable, multichannel networking radio system that meets DoD ground vehicle digitization and tactical communication requirements.

## DESCRIPTION

Joint Tactical Radio System Ground Mobile Radios (JTRS GMR) are a key enabler of the DoD and Army Transformation and will provide critical communications capabilities across the full spectrum of Joint operations.

Through software reconfiguration, JTRS GMR can emulate current force radios and operate new Internet protocol-based networking waveforms, offering increased data throughput utilizing self-forming, self-healing, and managed communication networks. The GMR route and retransmit functionality links various waveforms in different frequency bands to form one internetwork. GMR can scale from one to four channels supporting multiple security levels and effectively use the frequency spectrum within the two megahertz to two gigahertz frequency range. The radios are Software Communications Architecture compliant with increased bandwidth through future waveforms. GMR are interoperable with more than four legacy radio systems and the JTRS family of radios (HMS, JEM, and AMF).

## SYSTEM INTERDEPENDENCIES

**Other Major Interdependencies**

Enhanced Position Locating Reporting System (EPLRS), High Frequency (HF), Network Enterprise Domain (NED), Satellite Communications (SATCOM), Soldier Radio Waveform (SRW), Ultra-High Frequency (UHF), Wideband Networking Waveform (WNW)

## PROGRAM STATUS

- **2QFY11:** Field Experiment 5 (FE 5)
- **3QFY11:** Program undergoing Nunn-McCurdy
- **3QFY11:** Customer Test conducted at the Network Integration Exercise at White Sands Missile Range (WSMR)

## PROJECTED ACTIVITIES

- **2QFY13:** Initial Operational Capability (IOC)
- **2QFY13:** Full Rate Production (FRP)

**ACQUISITION PHASE**

- Technology Development
- **Engineering and Manufacturing Development**
- Production and Deployment
- Operations and Support

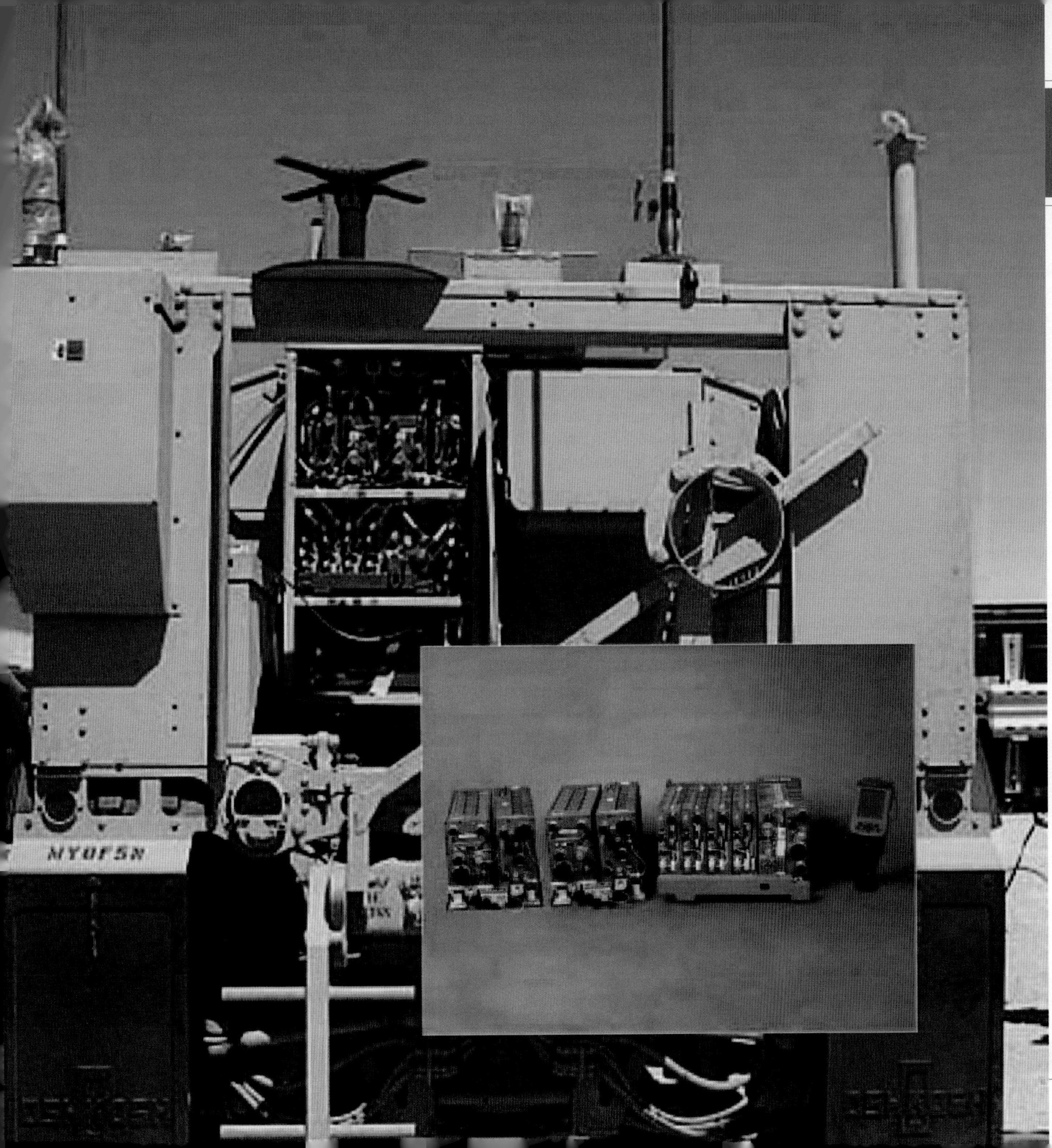

## Joint Tactical Radio System Ground Mobile Radios (JTRS GMR)

**FOREIGN MILITARY SALES**
None

**CONTRACTORS**
**Prime:**
Boeing (Huntington Beach, CA)
**Hardware:**
BAE Systems (Wayne, NJ)
Rockwell Collins (Cedar Rapids, IA)
Northrop Grumman (Carson, CA)

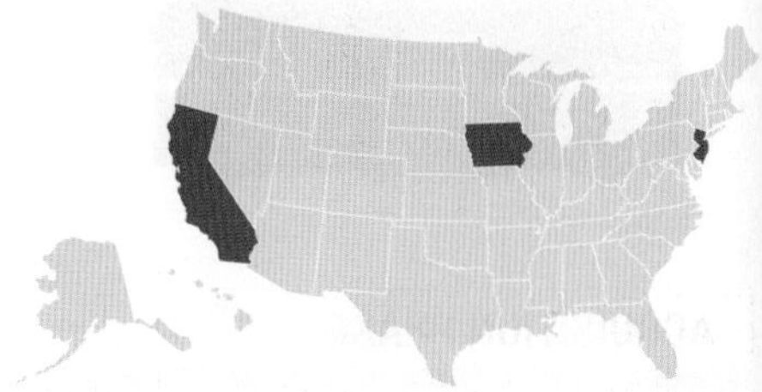

# Joint Tactical Radio System Handheld, Manpack, Small Form Fit (JTRS HMS)

**INVESTMENT COMPONENT**

- **Modernization**
- Recapitalization
- Maintenance

## MISSION

Provides the Warfighter with a software reprogrammable, networkable multimode system-of-systems capable of simultaneous voice, data, and video communications that meets the radio requirements for Soldiers and small platforms, such as missiles and ground sensors.

## DESCRIPTION

The Joint Tactical Radio System (JTRS) Handheld, Manpack, and Small Form Fit (HMS) is a materiel solution meeting the requirements of the Office of the Assistant Secretary of Defense for Networks and Information Integration/ DoD Chief Information Officer for a Software Communications Architecture (SCA) compliant hardware system hosting SCA-compliant software waveforms (applications). HMS is an Acquisition Category ID program that encompasses specific requirements to support Special Operations Command, Army, Marine Corps, Air Force, and Navy communication needs.

The Embedded Small Form Fit versions of HMS will be used for Joint Service Ground Sensor Networks, intelligent munitions deployment and usage, unmanned vehicles, and other platform applications, including support for the Early Infantry Brigade Combat Team and Ground Soldier System technical performance and integration.

## SYSTEM INTERDEPENDENCIES

**Other Major Interdependencies**

SRW, HF, UHF SATCOM, MUOS, IMS, UGS using SRW and various legacy WF mixes

## PROGRAM STATUS

- **2QFY11:** Rifleman Radio (RR) Verification of Deficiencies (VCD)
- **3QFY11:** Milestone C (MS C)
- **3QFY11:** Manpack (MP) Limited User Test (LUT)

## PROJECTED ACTIVITIES

- **1QFY12:** RR Initial Operational Test & Evaluation (IOT&E)
- **2QFY12:** RR Initial Operational Capability (IOC)
- **3QFY12:** MP IOT&E

**ACQUISITION PHASE**

| Technology Development | **Engineering and Manufacturing Development** | Production and Deployment | Operations and Support |
|---|---|---|---|

## Joint Tactical Radio System Handheld, Manpack, Small Form Fit (JTRS HMS)

**FOREIGN MILITARY SALES**
None

**CONTRACTORS**

**MP, 2 CH HH, SFFs -A, -B, -K, AN/PRC-154 (Rifleman Radio):**
General Dynamics (Scottsdale, AZ)

**2 CH HH, SFF-B, AN/PRC-154 (Rifleman Radio):**
Thales (Clarksburg, MD)

**SFF-A, -D, -K:**
BAE Systems (Wayne, NJ)

**MP, SFF-D:**
Rockwell Collins (Cedar Rapids, IA)

**PM Support:**
Science Applications International Corp. (SAIC) (San Diego, CA)

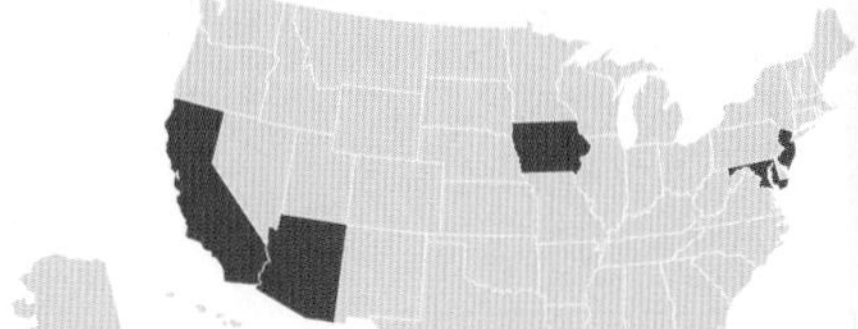

# Joint Tactical Radio System Multifunctional Information Distribution System (MIDS)

**INVESTMENT COMPONENT**

- Modernization
- Recapitalization
- Maintenance

## MISSION

Provides real-time information and situational awareness to the Joint and coalition Warfighter in the airborne, ground, and maritime domains through secure, scalable, modular, wireless, and jam-resistant digital data and voice communications.

## DESCRIPTION

The Joint Tactical Radio System Multifunctional Information Distribution System (JTRS MIDS) is a secure, scalable, modular, wireless, and jam-resistant digital information system currently providing Tactical Air Navigation (TACAN), Link-16, and J-Voice to airborne, ground, and maritime Joint and coalition warfighting platforms. MIDS provides real-time and low-cost information and situational awareness. The MIDS Program includes the MIDS-Low Volume Terminal (MIDS-LVT) and the MIDS JTRS Terminal.

MIDS-LVT is the foundation of the MIDS international cooperative program with Joint service participation. MIDS-LVT provides interoperability with NATO users, significantly increasing force effectiveness and minimizing hostile actions and friend-on-friend engagements. Three principle configurations of the terminal are in production and use an open-system, modular architecture. MIDS-LVT(1) provides a Link-16 capability to Navy and Air Force platforms, which were previously unable to use the Joint Tactical Information Distribution System (JTIDS) due to space and weight limitations. MIDS-LVT(2) is an Army variant of MIDS that is a functional replacement for the JTIDS Class 2M terminal. MIDS-LVT(3), also referred to as MIDS Fighter Data Link (FDL), is a reduced-function terminal for the Air Force.

MIDS JTRS is a Software Defined Radio (SDR) that is compliant with the JTRS Software Communications Architecture (SCA). MIDS JTRS maintains the Link-16, J-Voice, and TACAN functionality of MIDS-LVT, but it also accommodates future technologies and capabilities. MIDS JTRS improvements over MIDS-LVT include Link-16 enhanced throughput (ET), Link-16 frequency remapping (FR), and programmable crypto. MIDS JTRS accommodates incremental delivery of the advanced JTRS waveforms through MIDS JTRS platform capability packages, such as the Joint Airborne Networking-Tactical Edge (JAN-TE) capability.

## SYSTEM INTERDEPENDENCIES

**Other Major Interdependencies**

Link-16, TACAN, JAN-TE Waveforms, multiple Joint and coalition airborne, ground, and maritime platforms

## PROGRAM STATUS

- **1QFY11:** MIDS JTRS IOT&E report issued by commander, operational test and evaluation force
- **2QFY11:** MIDS JTRS IOT&E report issued by director, operational test and evaluation

## PROJECTED ACTIVITIES

- **2QFY12:** MIDS JTRS initial operational capability with the USN F/A-18E/F Super Hornet
- **2QFY12:** MIDS JTRS full production and fielding decision

**ACQUISITION PHASE**

Technology Development | Engineering and Manufacturing Development | Production and Deployment | Operations and Support

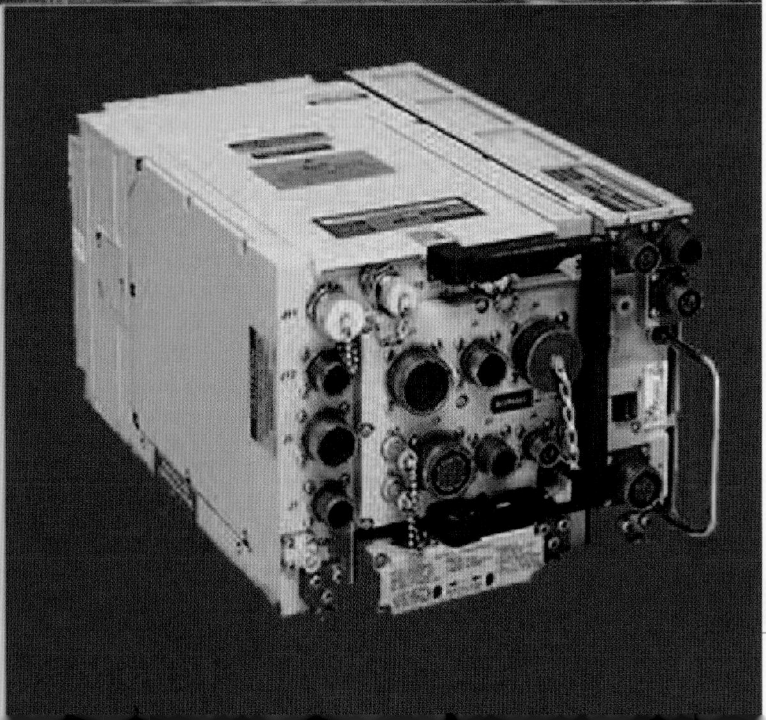

## Joint Tactical Radio System Multifunctional Information Distribution System (MIDS)

FOREIGN MILITARY SALES
**MIDS-LVT:**
1,881 terminals (internationally)
**JTRS MIDS:**
None

CONTRACTORS
ViaSat Inc. (Carlsbad, CA)
**Data Link Solutions:**
Rockwell Collins (Cedar Rapids, IA)
BAE Systems (Wayne, NJ)
EuroMIDS (Paris, France)
Thales (France)
Selex (Italy)
EADS (Germany)
Indra (Spain)

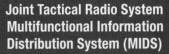

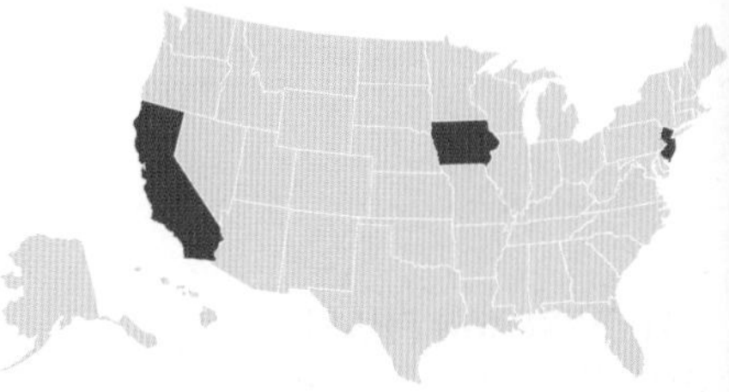

# Joint Tactical Radio System, Network Enterprise Domain (JTRS NED)

**INVESTMENT COMPONENT**

- **Modernization**
- Recapitalization
- Maintenance

## MISSION

Develops portable, interoperable, mobile, ad-hoc networking waveforms/ applications, providing combatant commanders with the ability to command, control, and communicate with their forces via secure voice, video, and data media forms during military operations.

## DESCRIPTION

The Joint Tactical Radio System, Network Enterprise Domain (JTRS NED) is responsible for the development, sustainment, and enhancement of interoperable networking and legacy software waveforms. NED's product line consists of: 14 legacy waveforms (Bowman VHF, COBRA, EPLRS, Have Quick II, HF SSB/ ALE, HF 5066, Link 16, SINCGARS, UHF DAMA SATCOM 181/182/183/184, UHF LOS, VHF LOS); three mobile ad-hoc networking waveforms (Wideband Networking Waveform (WNW), Soldier Radio Waveform (SRW), and Mobile User Objective System (MUOS)-Red Side Processing); Network Enterprise Services (NES) including the JTRS WNW Network Manager (JWNM), Soldier Radio Waveform Network Manager (SRWNM), JTRS Enterprise Network Manager (JENM), and Enterprise Network Services (ENS).

JTRS NED manages the development of Software Waveforms targeted to operate on platforms such as the Ground Mobile Radio (GMR), the Handheld, Manpack, and Small Form Fit (HMS) radios, the Airborne and Maritime/Fixed Site (AMF) radios, and the Multifunctional Information Distribution System (MIDS) radios. The JTRS NED software development and sustainment efforts leverage commercial technology and employ open-system architecture to better ensure interoperability and portability of each waveform. JTRS NED develops networking waveforms to support wireless networking with Global Information Grid connectivity for deployed Warfighters at the tactical edge. In addition, NED provides network management and network services software for the planning, execution, configuration, and monitoring of the JTRS radios and networks, including route and retransmit services between networking and legacy waveforms.

## SYSTEM INTERDEPENDENCIES

**Other Major Interdependencies**

Enhanced Position Location and Reporting System (EPLRS), MUOS, Link 16

## PROGRAM STATUS

- **1QFY11:** Complete ENS Phase 1 (SoftINC) FQT
- **1QFY11:** Complete SRWNM FQT
- **2QFY11:** Complete MUOS FQT
- **3QFY11:** Complete ENS Phase 1 (TDC) FQT
- **4QFY11:** Complete JENM Phase 2 FQT

## PROJECTED ACTIVITIES

- **4QFY12:** Complete JENM Phase 3 FQT

**ACQUISITION PHASE**

- Technology Development
- **Engineering and Manufacturing Development**
- Production and Deployment
- Operations and Support

## Joint Tactical Radio System, Network Enterprise Domain (JTRS NED)

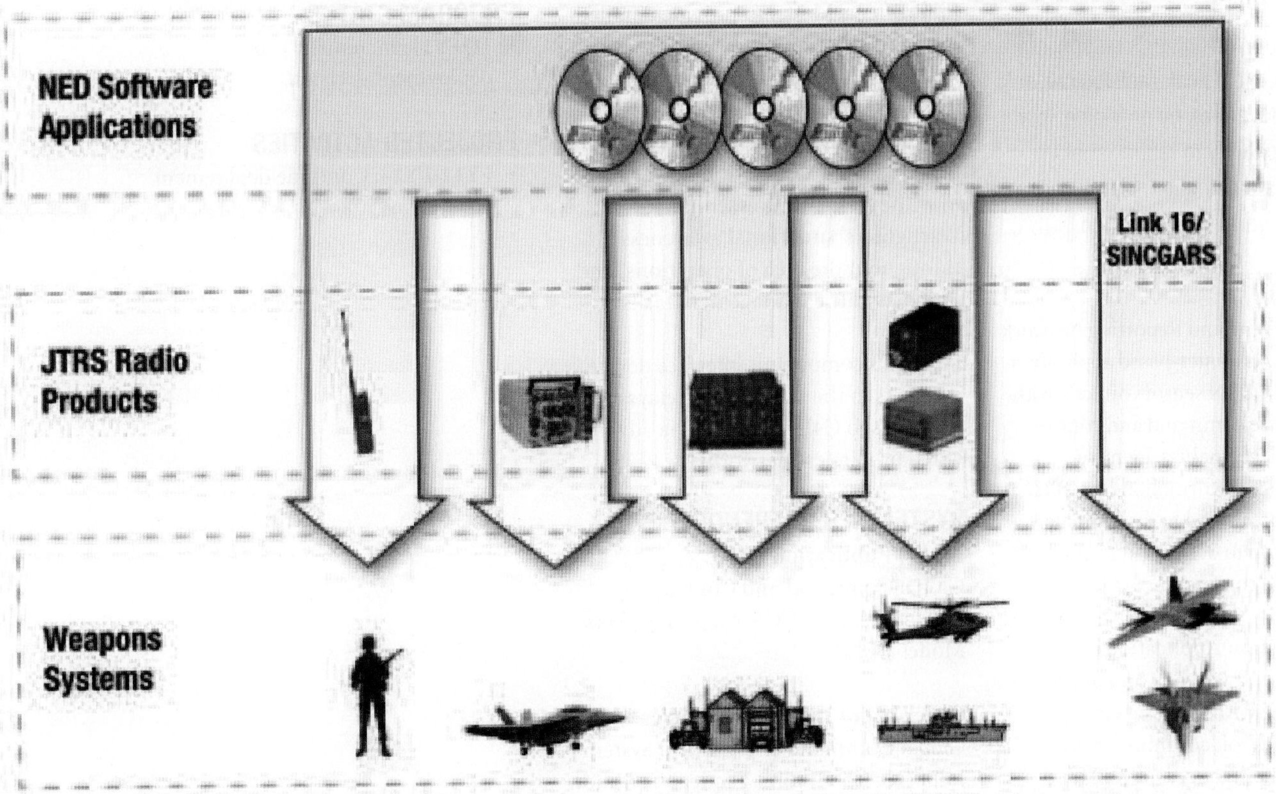


**FOREIGN MILITARY SALES**
None

**CONTRACTORS**
**MUOS:**
Lockheed Martin (Sunnyvale, CA)
**SRW, SRWNM, ENS Phase 1 (SoftINC):**
ITT (Ft. Wayne, IN)
**PM Support:**
SRA (Fairfax, VA)
**JWNM, WNW, JENM:**
Boeing (Huntington Beach, CA)
**ENS Phase 1 (TDC):**
Rockwell Collins (Cedar Rapids, IA)

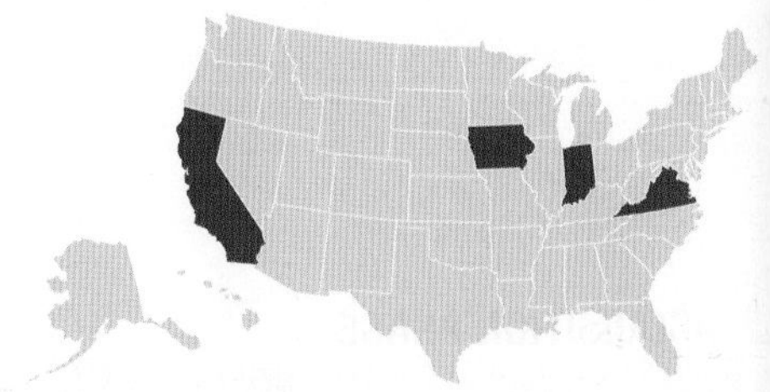

# Joint Warning and Reporting Network (JWARN)

INVESTMENT COMPONENT

Modernization

Recapitalization

Maintenance

## MISSION

Accelerates the Warfighter's response to a chemical, biological, radiological, or nuclear (CBRN) attack by providing Joint forces the capability to report, analyze, and disseminate detection, identification, location, and warning information.

## DESCRIPTION

The Joint Warning and Reporting Network (JWARN) is a computer-based application that networks CBRN sensors directly with Joint and service command and control systems to collect, analyze, identify, locate, and report information on CBRN activity and threats and to disseminate that information to decision-makers throughout the command.

JWARN's Mission Application Software (JMAS) will be compatible and integrated with Joint service command, control, communications, computers, intelligence, surveillance, and reconnaissance (C4ISR) systems. It will generate warning and dewarning information to affected forces via nuclear, biological, and chemical reports, Allied Tactical Publication-45 hazard plots, and integrates with the Joint Effects Model to provide detailed hazard prediction plume overlays. JWARN automates the recording and archiving of exposure data for effective force protection. It reduces the time from incident observation to warning to within two minutes, enhances Warfighters' situational awareness throughout the area of operations, and supports battle management tasks.

JWARN's component interface device connects to the sensors and relays warnings to C4ISR systems via advanced wired or wireless networks.

## SYSTEM INTERDEPENDENCIES

**In this Publication**

Global Command and Control System-Army (GCCS-A), Joint Effects Model (JEM)

**Other Major Interdependencies**

Global Command and Control System-Joint (GCCS-J), Joint Tactical Common Operational Picture (COP) Workstation (JTCW)/Command and Control Personal Computer (C2PC)

## PROGRAM STATUS

- **1QFY11:** Increment 1 full deployment decision

## PROJECTED ACTIVITIES

- **FY12-FY14:** Continue deployment

ACQUISITION PHASE

Technology Development | Engineering and Manufacturing Development | Production and Deployment | Operations and Support

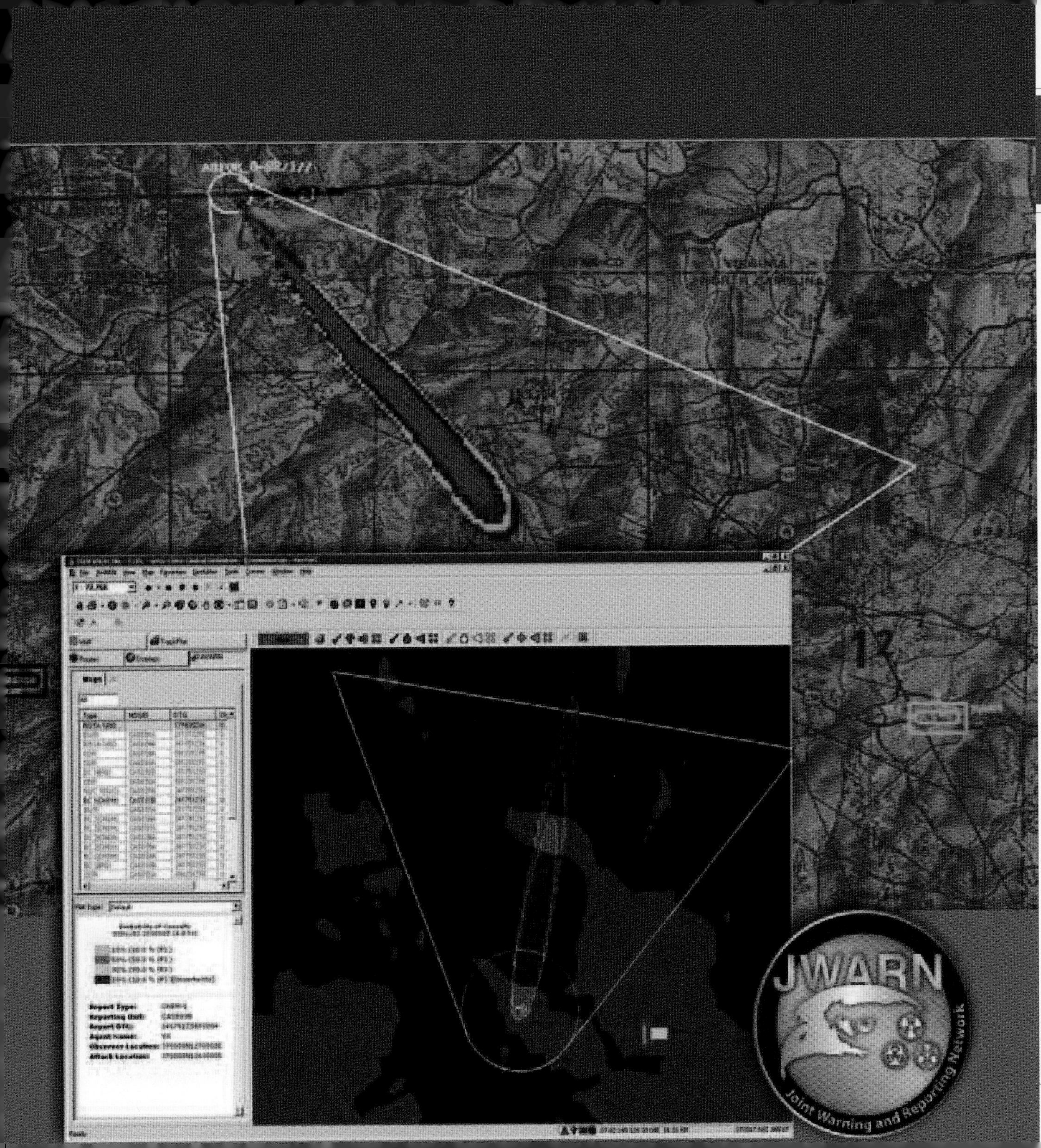


## Joint Warning and Reporting Network (JWARN)

**FOREIGN MILITARY SALES**
None

**CONTRACTORS**
Northrop Grumman Information Systems (Orlando, FL)

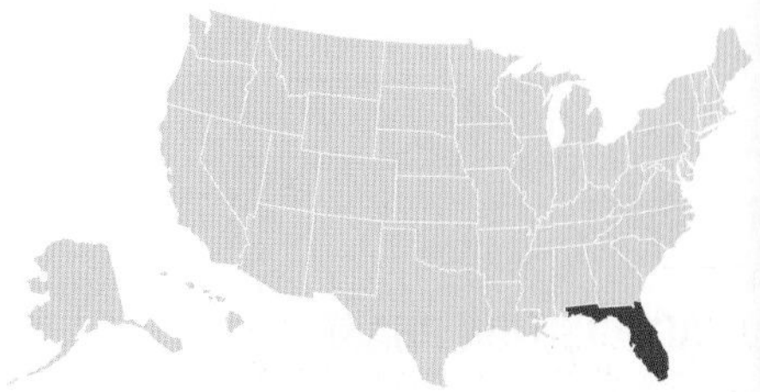

# Joint-Automatic Identification Technology (J-AIT)

**INVESTMENT COMPONENT**

- **Modernization**
- Recapitalization
- Maintenance

## MISSION

Manages the Radio Frequency-In Transit Visibility (RF-ITV) system, which provides automated, accurate, near-real-time data collection, aggregation, and retrieval of ITV data that allows the Warfighter to see and manage cargo and equipment shipments worldwide.

## DESCRIPTION

The Joint-Automatic Identification Technology (J-AIT) enables automatic data capture for logistics information systems and in-transit visibility (ITV) of cargo and equipment for commanders at all levels across the Department of Defense (DoD). J-AIT supports the Defense Reform Initiative Directive #54-Logistics Transformation Plans, Objective #3, which calls for achieving total asset visibility and accessibility through the use of AIT.

The focused logistics transformation path in Joint Vision 2020 requires the implementation of AIT and like-information-systems that provide accurate, actionable total asset visibility. AIT is also a critical component of DoD-mandated Item Unique Identification (IUID). J-AIT provides ITV to DoD through Web portals (Non-Secure Internet Protocol Router Network (NIPRNET) and Secure Internet Protocol Router Network (SIPRNET)) and feeds ITV data to 26 other systems across the DoD as depicted in the attached RF-ITV OV1 chart. J-AIT's RF-ITV system is the DoD's system of record for all active Radio Frequency Identification (RFID) data. J-AIT also provides procurement and technical services to DoD for AIT and RFID technology. The RF-ITV system consists of production server site in Continental United States (CONUS)—the site in Germany is being shut down—and a worldwide infrastructure of read sites covering key DoD transportation nodes. J-AIT provides product and technical services across the suite of AIT technologies by establishing and maintaining AIT and RFID contracts that are available to all users across DoD.

## SYSTEM INTERDEPENDENCIES

None

## PROGRAM STATUS

- RF-ITV system added satellite data feeds and other system upgrades to support the Warfighters in Southwest Asia; J-AIT established RF-ITV sites along the Northern Distribution Network in Europe

## PROJECTED ACTIVITIES

- **2QFY11:** Recompeted the RF-ITV II contract, which is in Agency Level Protest with Army Contracting Command, National Capital Region (ACC-NCR)
- **4QFY11:** Recompete the PM J-AIT Program Support Services 2 (PMSS 2) contract
- **2QFY13:** Transition to International Organization for Standardization based RFID tags

**ACQUISITION PHASE**

- Technology Development
- Engineering and Manufacturing Development
- **Production and Deployment**
- Operations and Support

## Joint-Automatic Identification Technology (J-AIT)

### RF-ITV Data Sources and Interfaces

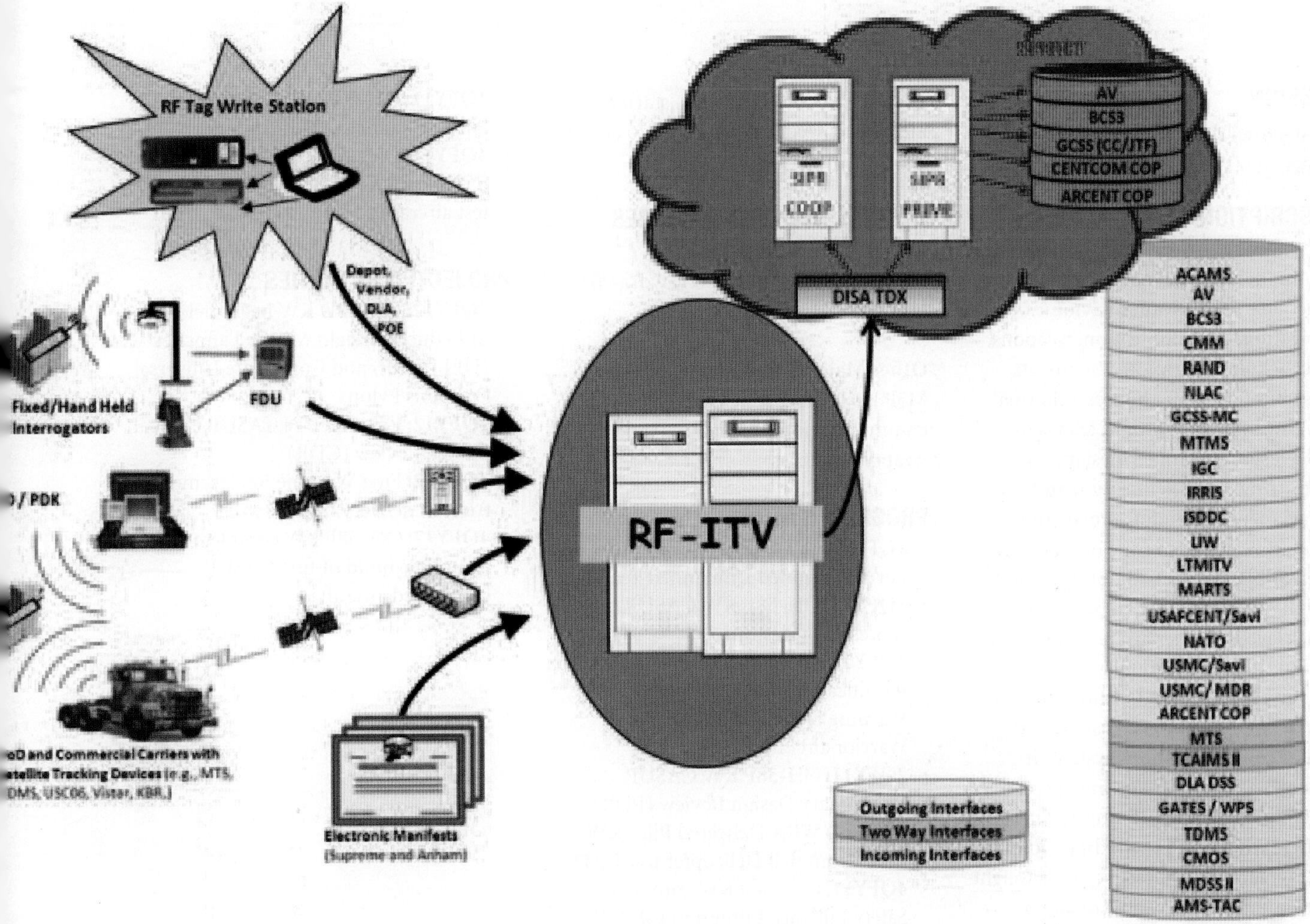


**FOREIGN MILITARY SALES**
None

**CONTRACTORS**
**Prime:**
Unisys Corporation (Reston, VA)
**Subcontractor:**
Kratos (San Diego, CA)
NextPoint Group (Warrenton, VA)

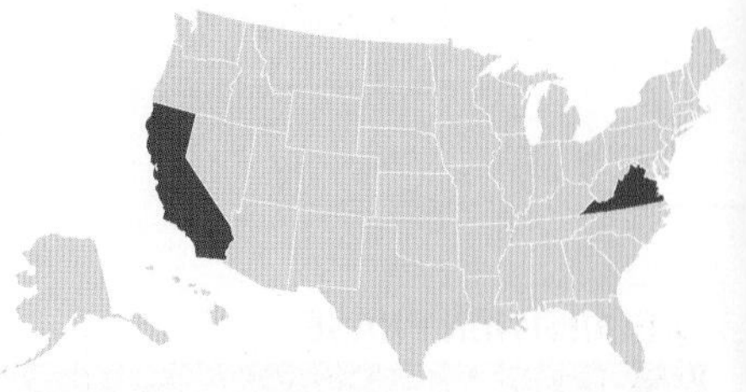

# Kiowa Warrior

**INVESTMENT COMPONENT**

Modernization

Recapitalization

Maintenance

## MISSION

Performs aerial reconnaissance and security in support of ground maneuver forces.

## DESCRIPTION

The Kiowa Warrior is a single-engine, two-man, lightly armed reconnaissance helicopter with advanced avionics, navigation, communication, weapons, and cockpit integration systems. Its mast-mounted sight houses a thermal imaging system, low-light television, and a laser rangefinder/designator permitting target acquisition and engagement at standoff ranges and in adverse weather. Sensor imagery from compatible Unmanned Aerial Systems and manned aircraft can be received and relayed to other aircraft or ground stations. The navigation system can convey precise target locations to other aircraft or artillery via its advanced digital communications system. It provides anti-armor and anti-personnel capabilities at standoff ranges. The Army is currently installing modifications to address safety, obsolescence, and weight to keep the aircraft viable through its projected retirement date of FY25. Additionally, the Army has started an aircraft replacement program to address Kiowa Warrior losses.

## SYSTEM INTERDEPENDENCIES

**In this Publication**

2.75 Inch Rocket Systems (Hydra-70), HELLFIRE Family of Missiles

**Other Major Interdependencies**

M3P .50 Caliber Machine Gun, various communications, navigation, and weapons systems

## PROGRAM STATUS

- **1QFY11:** OH-58D KW begin fielding Level II Manned Unmanned Teaming
- **1QFY11:** OH-58F KW CASUP successful Milestone B
- **2QFY11:** OH-58D KW first production modifications of Common Missile Warning System-equipped Kiowa Warrior aircraft
- **2QFY11:** OH-58F KW CASUP Preliminary Design Review (PDR)
- **3QFY11:** WRA Delivered Pilot KW cabin from Bell Helicopter to CCAD
- **4QFY11:** OH-58D KW complete Safety Enhanced Program (SEP) lot 13; program completion
- **4QFY11:** OH-58D KW begin Fielding Single Channel FADEC improvements
- **4QFY11:** OH-58F KW began structural modifications on first KW CASUP test aircraft

## PROJECTED ACTIVITIES

- **2QFY12:** OH-58D KW begin fielding of Reduced Weight Missile Launcher (HELLFIRE) and Composite Universal Weapons Pylon
- **2QFY12:** OH-58F KW CASUP Critical Design Review (CDR)
- **4QFY12:** First Wartime Replacement Aircraft delivery from CCAD
- **4QFY12:** OH-58F KW complete prototype build of first CASUP configured aircraft

**ACQUISITION PHASE**

Technology Development | Engineering and Manufacturing Development | Production and Deployment | Operations and Support

## Kiowa Warrior

**FOREIGN MILITARY SALES**
Taiwan

**CONTRACTORS**
**Airframe:**
Bell Helicopter Textron (Ft. Worth, TX)
**Sensor:**
DRS Optronics Inc. (Palm Bay, FL)
**Engine:**
Rolls Royce Corp. (Indianapolis, IN)
**Mission Computer:**
Honeywell (Albuquerque, NM)
**Cockpit Displays:**
Elbit Systems of America (Ft. Worth, TX)

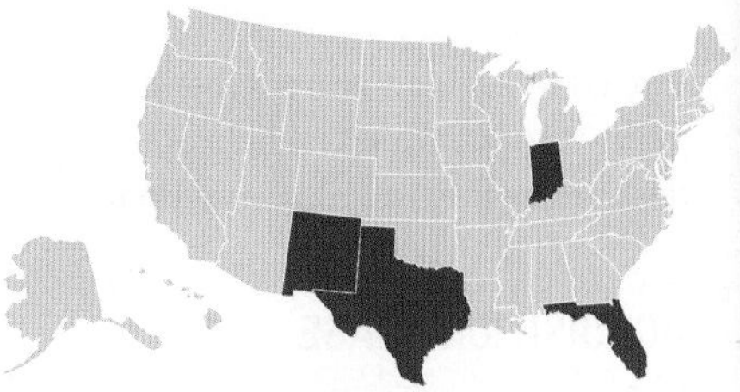

# Light Utility Helicopter (LUH)/UH-72A Lakota

## INVESTMENT COMPONENT

Modernization

Recapitalization

Maintenance

## MISSION

Provides a flexible response to homeland security requirements such as search and rescue operations, reconnaissance and surveillance, and medical evacuation (MEDEVAC) missions.

## DESCRIPTION

The UH-72A Lakota Light Utility Helicopter (LUH) will conduct general support utility helicopter missions and execute tasks as part of an integrated effort with other Joint Services, government agencies, and non-governmental organizations. The LUH is to be deployed only to noncombat, non-hostile environments. The UH-72A is a variant of the American Eurocopter U.S.-produced EC-145.

The UH-72A is a twin-engine, single-main-rotor commercial helicopter. It has seating for two pilots and up to six passengers or two NATO standard litters. Two Turbomeca Arriel 1E2 engines, combined with an advanced four-blade rotor system, provide lift and speed in a wide range of operating conditions. When equipped for medical evacuation (MEDEVAC) operations with two NATO standard litters, there is passenger seating for a medical attendant and a crew chief.

The UH-72A is equipped with modern communication and navigation avionics, which facilitate operation in civilian airspace systems. It includes a 3-axis autopilot and single pilot Instrument Flight Rules (IFR) capability. The cockpit is compatible with night vision devices. In addition to the MEDEVAC configuration, the UH-72A is also being fielded in a VIP, ARNG Security & Support (S&S), and Combined Training Center (CTC) configurations.

The United States Navy Test Pilot School (TPS) ordered five UH-72A aircraft in 2008. These were fielded in early FY10 and support experimental pilot training at the school.

In 2011 the Security and Support (S&S) Battalion MEP and the CTC MEP were added to the UH-72A fleet. The S&S MEP provides the National Guard to conduct Homeland Security, patrol, and counter drug missions. 100 UH-72A will be equipped with the MEP and fielded across the CONUS to include Puerto Rico and Hawaii. The CTC MEP provides the ability to conduct Opposing Force and Observor/Controller missions to support training at the National Training Center (NTC), Joint Readiness Training Center (JRTC), and the Joint Multinational Readiness Center (JMRC). 40 aircraft will be retrofitted with the MEP.

## SYSTEM INTERDEPENDENCIES

**Other Major Interdependencies**

ARC-231, C-5 (RERP), C-17, Civil Comms, GATM, OH-58A/C, UH-1, Sealift, USCG Comms, VHF/UHF Comms

## PROGRAM STATUS

- **1QFY11:** Completed first CTC MEP retrofit
- **2QFY11:** 232 aircraft are on contract with 59 to be delivered
- **3QFY11:** Placed S&S MEP production and retrofits on contract
- **4QFY11:** Completed first S&S MEP retrofit

## PROJECTED ACTIVITIES

- **1QFY12:** 271 aircraft are on contract with 49 to be delivered
- **2QFY12:** First production delivery of S&S MEP aircraft
- **4QFY12:** Complete production of 235 aircraft
- **4QFY13:** Complete CTC MEP retrofits
- **2QFY14:** 331 aircraft placed on contract

## ACQUISITION PHASE

Technology Development | Engineering and Manufacturing Development | Production and Deployment | Operations and Support

## Light Utility Helicopter (LUH)/ UH-72A Lakota

**FOREIGN MILITARY SALES**
None

**CONTRACTORS**

**Airframe:**
American Eurocopter (Columbus, MS; Grand Prairie, TX)

**CLS:**
Helicopter Support Inc. (Trumbull, CT)
American Eurocopter (Grand Prairie, TX)

**Training:**
American Eurocopter (Grand Prairie, TX)

**CFSR:**
American Eurocopter (Grand Prairie, TX)

**Program Management:**
EADS North America (Huntsville, AL; Arlington, VA)
Helicopter Support Inc. (Huntsville, AL; Grand Prairie, TX)

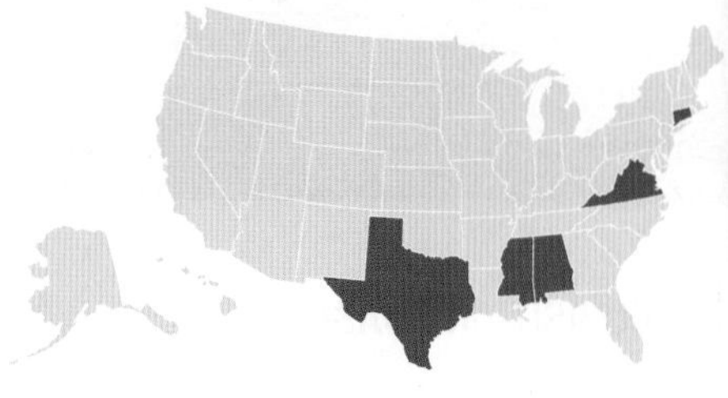

# Lightweight 155mm Howitzer System (LW155)

INVESTMENT COMPONENT

Modernization

Recapitalization

Maintenance

## MISSION

Provides direct, reinforcing, and general artillery fire support to maneuver forces.

## DESCRIPTION

The Lightweight 155mm Howitzer (M777A2) will replace all M198 155mm howitzers in operation with the Army and Marine Corps. The extensive use of titanium in all its major structures makes it 7,000 pounds lighter than its predecessor, the M198, with no sacrifice in range, stability, accuracy, or durability, and it can be dropped by parachute. The M777A2's independent suspension, smaller footprint, and lower profile increase strategic deployability and tactical mobility. The system uses numerous improvements to enhance reliability and accuracy, and significantly increase system survivability.

The M777A2 is jointly managed; the Marine Corps led the development of the howitzer and the Army led the development of Towed Artillery Digitization, the digital fire control system for the M777A2.

Software upgrades incorporating the Enhanced Portable Inductive Artillery Fuze Setter and the Excalibur Platform Integration Kit hardware give the M777A2 the capability to program and fire the Excalibur precision-guided munition.

Specifications for the M777A2 Excalibur-compatible howitzer are:
**Emplace:** Less than three minutes
**Displace:** Two to three minutes
**Maximum range:** 30 kilometer (rocket assisted round)
**Rate-of-fire:** Four rounds per minute maximum; two rounds per minute sustained
**Ground mobility:** Family of Medium Tactical Vehicles (FMTV), Medium Tactical Vehicle Replacement, five-ton trucks
**Air mobility:** Two per C-130; six per C-17; 12 per C-5; CH-53D/E; CH-47D; MV-22
**155mm compatibility:** All fielded and developmental NATO munitions
**Digital and optical fire control:** Self-locating and pointing, digital and voice communications; self-contained power supply

## SYSTEM INTERDEPENDENCIES

**Other Major Interdependencies**
Army Software Blocking, Defense Advanced Global Positioning System Receiver

## PROGRAM STATUS

- **4QFY11:** Full-Rate Production with a total of 794 systems delivered—Army (346), Marine Corps (391), Foreign Military Sales (51), and the logistics base (6)

## PROJECTED ACTIVITIES

- **2QFY12-2QFY14:** Continued full-rate production, Continued Army and Marine Corps New Equipment Training and fieldings, Support FMS partners (Canada and Australia)

ACQUISITION PHASE

Technology Development | Engineering and Manufacturing Development | Production and Deployment | Operations and Support

## Lightweight 155mm Howitzer System (LW155)

**FOREIGN MILITARY SALES**
Australia and Canada

**CONTRACTORS**

**Prime:**
BAE Systems (Hattiesburg, MS; Barrow-in-Furness, United Kingdom)

**Cannon Assembly (GFE):**
Watervliet Arsenal (Watervliet, NY)

**Titanium Castings:**
Precision CastParts Corp. (Portland, OR)

**Body:**
Triumph Structures (Chatsworth, CA)

**Castings:**
Howmet Castings (Whitehall, MI)

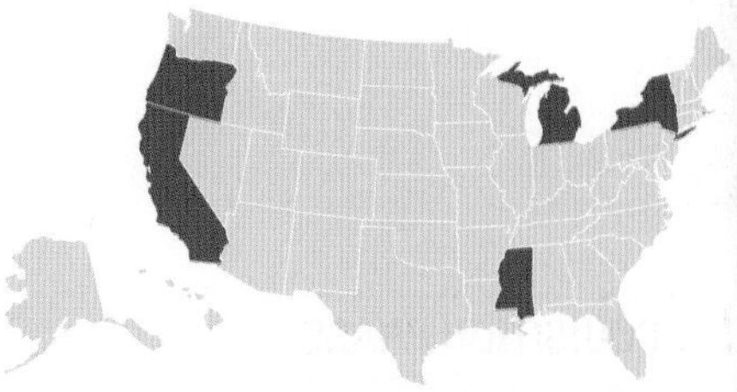

# Lightweight Counter Mortar Radar (LCMR)

**INVESTMENT COMPONENT**

- **Modernization**
- Recapitalization
- Maintenance

## MISSION

Identifies indirect fire threats by providing the ability to rapidly locate rockets, artillery, and mortar firing positions automatically by detecting and tracking the shell and backtracking to the weapon position. It provides observed fires (for friendly fires), will provide accurate "did hit" data of friendly fires, and will detect and template hostile locations.

## DESCRIPTION

The AN/TPQ-50 Lightweight Counter Mortar Radar (LCMR) is a man-portable and HMMWV 1152A-mountable lightweight radar system used to locate rocket, artillery, and mortar Points of Origin (POO) and Points of Impact (POI) out to a range of 10Km. The radar accomplishes this by detecting and tracking the projectile then extrapolating the POI and POO to with-in 50 meters Circular Error Probability (CEP). The AN/TPQ-50 has a continuous 360-degree surveillance using an electronically scanned antenna. The radar can be rapidly deployed by two Soldiers. The AN/TPQ-50 sends a warning message to indicate an incoming round and is a critical sensor to the Counter Rocket Artillery and Mortar (C-RAM) system of systems construct. The radar also is digitally interoperable with AFATDS and FAADC2.

## SYSTEM INTERDEPENDENCIES

**In this Publication**

Counter-Rocket, Artillery, and Mortar (C-RAM)/Indirect Fire Protection Capability (IFPC)

## PROGRAM STATUS

- **December 2011:** Milestone C Review; on track for mid-December review
- **September 2011:** First Unit Equipped
- Authority to Operate (ATO) received by PM on 10 May
- Army Interoperability Certificate (AIC) received by PM on 10 June
- Urgent Material Release (UMR) due to PM by 30 August

## PROJECTED ACTIVITIES

- **June 2012:** Initial Operational Test & Evaluation (IOT&E)
- **Jan 2013:** On track to meet all requirements, Full-Rate Production Decision
- On track to meet all requirements *One Year slip in the schedule for First Unit Equipped and Full-Rate Production Decision due to environmental testing improvements

**ACQUISITION PHASE**

- Technology Development
- Engineering and Manufacturing Development
- **Production and Deployment**
- Operations and Support

## Lightweight Counter Mortar Radar (LCMR)

**FOREIGN MILITARY SALES**
None

**CONTRACTORS**
SRCTec (North Syracuse, NY)
Syracuse Research Corporation (SRC)
(Syracuse, NY)
(statewide, MD)
Yuma Proving Ground (Yuma, AZ)
Tobyhanna Army Depot (Tobyhanna, PA)

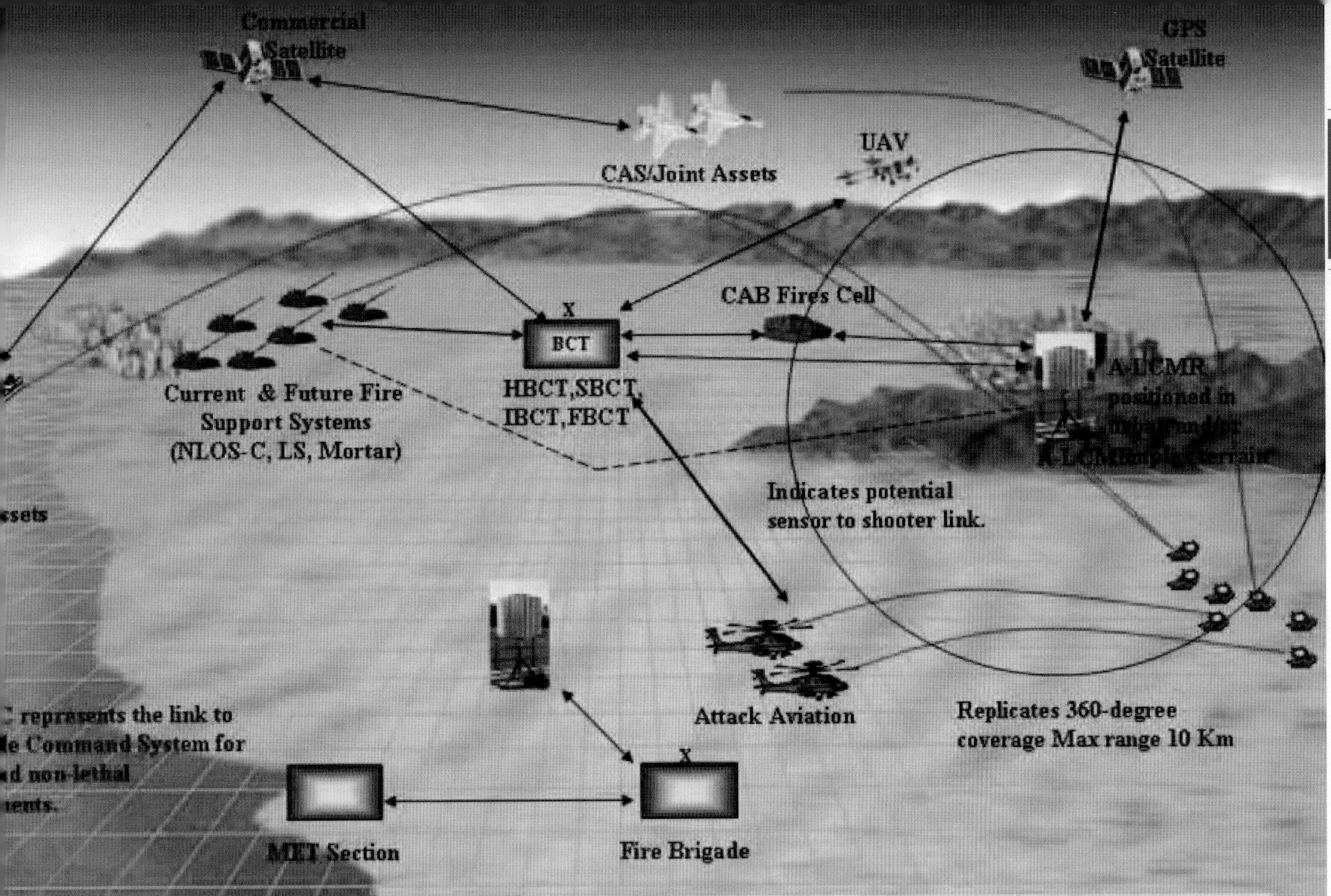


The A-LCMR is a lightweight, 360-degree, rapidly man-transportable, digitally connected, day/night mortar, cannon and rocket locating radar that uses computer-controlled signal processing of the radar signal data to perform target detection, verification, and tracking of enemy and friendly mortars. POO and POI are determined and provided to C2 nodes for engagement of Threat firing platform and early warning for force protection.

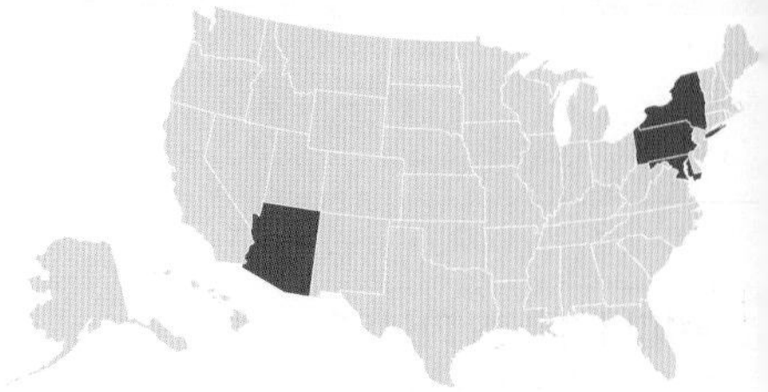

# Lightweight Laser Designator/Rangefinder (LLDR) AN/PED-1

**INVESTMENT COMPONENT**

- **Modernization**
- Recapitalization
- Maintenance

## MISSION

Provides the dismounted Fire Support Teams, Combat Observation and Lasing Teams, and Scouts with a precision target location and laser designation system that allows them to call for fire using precision, near-precision, and area munitions.

## DESCRIPTION

The AN/PED-1 Lightweight Laser Designator/Rangefinder (LLDR) is a crew-served man-portable, modular target locator and laser designation system. The primary components are the Target Locator Module (TLM) and the Laser Designator Module (LDM).

The TLM incorporates a thermal imager, day camera, laser designator spot imaging electronic display, eye-safe laser rangefinder, digital magnetic compass, Selective Availability/Anti-Spoofing Module Global Positioning System (SAASM GPS), and digital export capability. The original LLDR 1 operates on one BA-5699 battery, but it can also use a Single Channel Ground and Airborne Radio System (SINCGARS) battery when laser designation is not required. A new compact laser designator is being fielded with the LLDR2, which requires less power and operates on one common SINCGARS battery (BA-5390 or BA-5590).

To provide a precision targeting capability to the dismounted Soldier, PM SPTD has developed the LLDR 2H, which integrates a celestial navigation system with the digital magnetic compass in the TLM to provide highly accurate target coordinates to allow the Soldier to call for fire with precision GPS-guided munitions.

The TLM can be used as a stand-alone device or in conjunction with the LDM. At night and in obscured battlefield conditions, the operator can recognize vehicle-sized targets at more than 3 kilometers. During day operations, targets can be recognized at more than 7 kilometers. The LDM emits coded laser pulses compatible with DoD and NATO laser-guided munitions. Targets can be designated at ranges greater than 5 kilometers.

Weight (total system): 35 pounds (LLDR 1), less than 30 pounds (LLDR 2), and less than 32 pounds (LLDR 2H) for a 24-hour mission

## SYSTEM INTERDEPENDENCIES

None

## PROGRAM STATUS

- **FY11:** Completed fielding of LLDR 1
- **FY11:** Began fielding reduced weight LLDR 2 units supporting Operation Enduring Freedom (OEF)
- **FY11:** Awarded a delivery order for high-accuracy LLDR 2H production

## PROJECTED ACTIVITIES

- **FY12:** Continue fielding LLDR 2 in accordance with Headquarters, Department of the Army guidance
- **FY12:** Award a new contract to retrofit existing LLDRs (1 & 2) to the high-accuracy LLDR 2H configuration
- **FY12:** Accept first deliveries of the LLDR 2H and begin fielding

**ACQUISITION PHASE**

Technology Development | **Engineering and Manufacturing Development** | **Production and Deployment** | Operations and Support

## Lightweight Laser Designator/ Rangefinder (LLDR) AN/PED-1

**FOREIGN MILITARY SALES**
None

**CONTRACTORS**
Northrop Grumman Guidance and Electronics, Laser Systems (Apopka, FL)

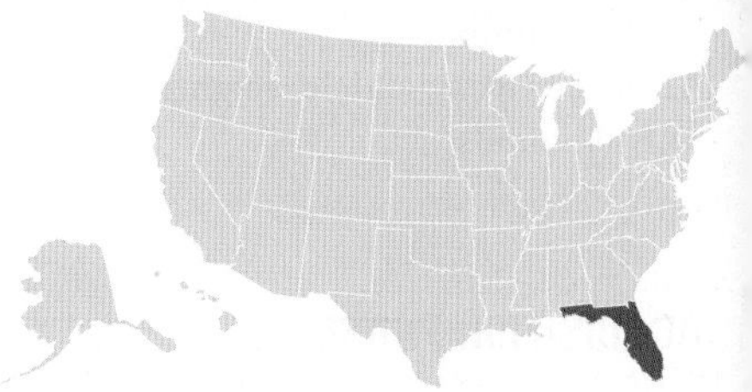

# Line Haul Tractor

## INVESTMENT COMPONENT

**Modernization**

Recapitalization

Maintenance

## MISSION

Supports combat service and support units with transportation of bulk petroleum products, containerized cargo, general cargo, and bulk water.

## DESCRIPTION

The M915A5 Truck Tractor is a 6x4 semi-tractor used to perform the Line Haul mission. The M915A5 is a block upgrade of the M915A3 system, incorporating enhanced suspension and power train components. This block upgrade allows the M915A5 to readily accept armor packages without reducing mission capability.

**Gross vehicle weight rating:**
120,000 pounds
**Unarmored Gross vehicle weight:**
26,500 pounds
**Armored Gross vehicle weight:**
33,500 pounds
**Fifth-wheel capacity:**
six-inch, 30,000 pounds
**Diagnosis:** Electronic
**Brake system:**
Anti-lock brake system (ABS)
**Towing speed:**
65 miles per hour with full payload
**Engine:** Detroit Diesel S60 (500 horse power, 1650 pound-foot torque, DDEC IV engine controller)
**Transmission:** Allison HD4500SP (six-speed automatic)

The M915A5 truck is equipped with a two-passenger cab and has an updated power distribution module, upgraded wiring harnesses, and a Roll Stability Control system. Auxiliary power connections have been added to supply emerging systems and added command, control, communications, computers, and intelligence communication systems. A pair of 60-gallon fuel tanks increases fuel capacity by 20 gallons to extend driving range. The cab is ten inches wider and extends 34 inches behind the driver and passenger seats. The vehicle has an improved ABS and an updated collision warning system.

The M915A3 Line Haul Tractor is the Army's key line haul distribution platform. It is a 6x4 tractor with a two-inch kingpin and 105,000-pound gross combination weight capacity.

**Gross vehicle weight:** 52,000 pounds
**Fifth-wheel capacity:**
two-inch, 30,000 pounds
**Diagnosis:** Electronic
**Brake system:** ABS
**Towing speed:**
65 miles per hour with full payload
**Engine:** Detroit Diesel S60 (430 horse power, 1,450 pound-foot torque, DDEC IV engine controller)
**Transmission:** Allison HD5460P (six-speed automatic) with power take-off

The M916A3 Light Equipment Transport (LET) is a 6x6 tractor with 68,000-pound gross vehicle weight tractor with 3-1/2-inch, 40,000-pound capacity, 45,000-pound winch for recovery and transport and compensator fifth wheel. It has an electronic diesel engine, automatic electronic transmission, ABS, and is capable of operating at speeds up to 60 miles per hour on flat terrain. This Non-Developmental Item (NDI) vehicle is used primarily to transport the M870 40-ton low-bed semi-trailer.

The M917A2 and M917A2 Truck Chassis, 75,000 gross vehicle weight rating, 8x6 (for 20-ton dump truck), 12-cubic yard dump truck vehicles are authorized in Corps units, primarily the construction and combat support companies and the combat heavy battalions. It has an electronic diesel engine, automatic electronic transmission, ABS, and is capable of operating at speeds up to 55 miles per hour on flat terrain.

## SYSTEM INTERDEPENDENCIES

**Other Major Interdependencies**
M872, 34-ton flatbed semi-trailer; M1062A1, 7,500-gallon semi-trailer; M967/M969, 5,000-gallon semi-trailer

## PROGRAM STATUS

- **FY10:** Full production continues in support of Army operations in the United States and abroad

## PROJECTED ACTIVITIES

- **FY11:** Bridge Contract

## ACQUISITION PHASE

Technology Development | Engineering and Manufacturing Development | **Production and Deployment** | Operations and Support

## Line Haul Tractor

**FOREIGN MILITARY SALES**
Afghanistan

**CONTRACTORS**
**Prime:**
Daimler Trucks North America LLC/ Freightliner (Portland, OR; Cleveland, NC)
**Engine:**
Detroit Diesel (Detroit, MI)
**ABS Brakes:**
Meritor (Troy, MI)
**Dump body:**
Casteel Manufacturing (San Antonio, TX)

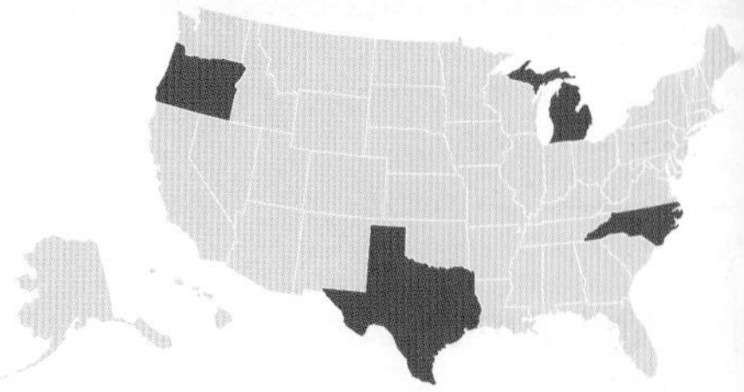

# Load Handling System Compatible Water Tank Rack (Hippo)

**INVESTMENT COMPONENT**

- **Modernization**
- Recapitalization
- Maintenance

## MISSION

Enhances and expedites the delivery of bulk potable water into the division and brigade areas, providing the Army with the capability to receive, store, and distribute potable water to units deployed throughout the battlefield.

## DESCRIPTION

The Load Handling System (LHS) Compatible Water Tank Rack (Hippo) represents the latest in bulk water distribution systems technology. It replaces the 3,000 and 5,000 Semi-trailer Mounted Fabric Tanks. The Hippo consists of a 2,000-gallon potable water tank in an International Organization for Standardization frame with an integrated pump, engine, alternator, filling stand, and 70-foot hose reel with bulk suction and discharge hoses. It has the capacity to pump 125 gallons of water per minute.

The Hippo is fully functional, mounted or dismounted, and is air transportable and ground transportable when full, partially full, or empty. It is Heavy Expanded Mobility Tactical Truck (HEMTT)-LHS, Palletized Load System (PLS), and PLS-Trailer-compatible, and it is designed to operate in cold weather environments and can prevent water from freezing at -25 degrees Fahrenheit. The Hippo can be moved, set up, and established rapidly using minimal assets and personnel. No site preparation by engineer assets is required, and its modular configuration supports Expeditionary Joint Forces Operations.

## SYSTEM INTERDEPENDENCIES

None

## PROGRAM STATUS

- **2QFY07:** Full Materiel Release
- **1QFY08:** Production and fielding
- **4QFY08:** Additional quantities placed on contract
- **FY09:** Updated integrated electronic technical manuals
- **FY10:** Continue production and fielding with 833 systems fielded as of July 20, 2011

## PROJECTED ACTIVITIES

- **FY11 and beyond:** Continue production and fielding
- **4QFY11:** Final draft submitted to Legal for Hippo Competitive Solicitation
- **4QFY11:** Request For Proposal Released and Post Synopsis

**ACQUISITION PHASE**

- Technology Development
- Engineering and Manufacturing Development
- **Production and Deployment**
- Operations and Support

## Load Handling System Compatible Water Tank Rack (Hippo)

**FOREIGN MILITARY SALES**
None

**CONTRACTORS**
Mil-Mar Century Inc. (Miamisburg, OH)

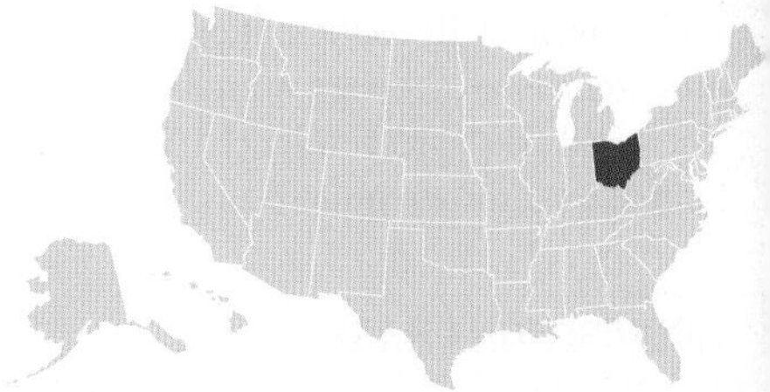

# Longbow Apache (AH-64D) (LBA)

**INVESTMENT COMPONENT**

Modernization

Recapitalization

Maintenance

## MISSION

Conducts armed reconnaissance, close combat, mobile strike, and vertical maneuver missions when required, in day, night, obscured battlefield, and adverse weather conditions.

## DESCRIPTION

The AH-64D Longbow Apache (LBA) is the Army's only heavy attack helicopter for both the Current and Future Force. It is capable of destroying armor, personnel, and materiel targets in obscured battlefield conditions. The Longbow Apache is a 2-engine, 4-bladed, tandem-seat attack helicopter with 30mm cannon, Hydra-70 2.75-inch rockets, laser, and Radio Frequency (RF) HELLFIRE missiles. It upgrades 634 Apaches into AH-64D Longbow Block III configuration with procurement of 259 Fire Control Radars. There will also be 56 new Block III aircraft built to meet force requirements. The Modernized-Target Acquisition Designation Sight/Pilot Night Vision Sensor (MTADS/PNVS) is a major combat multiplier on Longbow Apache.

The Apache fleet includes the A model Apache and D model Longbow. The A model fleet is being consumed by the Longbow remanufacturing program. There are fewer than 100 Apache A models remaining, with the last A model removed from the force structure in FY13. The Longbow remanufacturing effort uses the A model and incorporates a millimeter-wave FCR, radar frequency interferometer (RFI), fire-and-forget radar-guided HELLFIRE missiles, and other cockpit management and digitization enhancements. The Longbow is undergoing recapitalization modifications such as upgraded forward-looking infrared technology with the MTADS/PNVS, non-line-of-sight communications, video transmission/reception, and maintenance cost reductions. Longbow supports Brigade Combat Teams across the full spectrum of warfare. Apache is fielded to Active Army, National Guard and Army Reserve attack battalions, armed reconnaissance battalions, and cavalry units as defined in the Army Modernization Plan.
The Longbow Apache Block III (AB3) program is the next evolution of the Apache. Block III meets all the requirements for Army and Joint interoperability goals for the future and will add significant combat capability while addressing obsolescence issues, and the program will ensure the aircraft remains a viable combat multiplier beyond 2035.

The Block III modernized Longbows will be designed and equipped with an open systems architecture to incorporate the latest communications, navigation, sensor, and weapon systems.

- **Combat mission speed:** Longbow 145 knots (max speed); AB3 164 Knots (max speed)
- **Combat range:** 260 nautical miles
- **Combat endurance:** 2.5 hours
- **Maximum gross weight:** 20,260 pounds
- **Ordnance:** 16 HELLFIRE missiles, 76 2.75-inch rockets, and 1,200 30mm chain gun rounds
- **Crew:** Two (pilot and copilot gunner)

## SYSTEM INTERDEPENDENCIES

**In this Publication**

AVCATT; HELLFIRE Family of Missiles; 2.75 Inch Rocket Systems (Hydra-70); Air Warrior (AW); JTRS AMF; RQ-7B Shadow Tactical Aircraft System (TUAS); DCGS-A; GCCS-A; SINCGARS; Stryker Family of Vehicles; Black-Hawk/UH/HH-60; CH-47 Chinook

**Other Major Interdependencies**

TCDL; Link 16; JSTARS; AWACS; GPS; AMPS; BFT; Have Quick; SATCOM; Land Warrior; M-1 Tank; M-2 Bradley; Fire Support; A2C2S; OH-58D; ERMP UAS; Aircraft System (UAS); Laser Hellfire

## PROGRAM STATUS

- **1QFY09:** Block III system development and demonstration contract currently 83 percent complete
- **1QFY11:** Milestone C decision
- **Current:** Upgrade Block I and II Longbow to Block III configuration with eventual acquisition objective of 634 remanufacture airframes and 56 new build airframes for a total of 690 Block III Longbows

## PROJECTED ACTIVITIES

- **FY11:** Block I inductions into Block III remanufacturing assembly line
- **1QFY12:** Initial Block III deliveries
- **3QFY12:** Full-Rate Production Decision
- **3QFY13:** Initial operating capability
- **FY25:** End of production

**ACQUISITION PHASE**

Technology Development | Engineering and Manufacturing Development | Production and Deployment | Operations and Support

## Longbow Apache (AH-64D) (LBA)

**FOREIGN MILITARY SALES**
Egypt, Greece, Israel, Kuwait, Netherlands, Saudi Arabia, Singapore, United Arab Emirates

**DIRECT COMMERCIAL SALES**
Greece, Japan, United Kingdom

**CONTRACTORS**
**Airframe:** Boeing (Mesa, AZ)
**MTADS:** Lockheed Martin (Orlando, FL)
**REU:** Lockheed Martin (Orlando, FL)
Northrop Grumman (Linthicum, MD)
**APU:** Honeywell (Phoenix, AZ)
**Technical:** Aviation and Missile Solutions LLC (Huntsville, AL)
**FCR:** Longbow LLC (Orlando, FL)
**Radar:** Northrop Grumman (Linthicum, MD)
**Logistics:** AEPCO (Huntsville, AL)
**TADS/PNVS:** Lockheed Martin (Goodyear, AZ)
**Programmatics:** DynCorp (Ft. Worth, TX)
**EGI:** Honeywell (Clearwater, FL)
**LRUs:** Smiths (Clearwater, FL)
**IPAS:** Honeywell (Tempe, AZ)

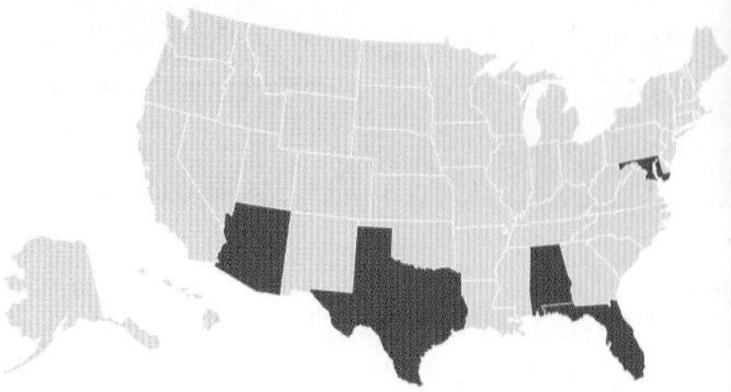

# M106 Screening Obscuration Device (SOD)-Visual Restricted Terrain (Vr)

**INVESTMENT COMPONENT**

Modernization

Recapitalization

Maintenance

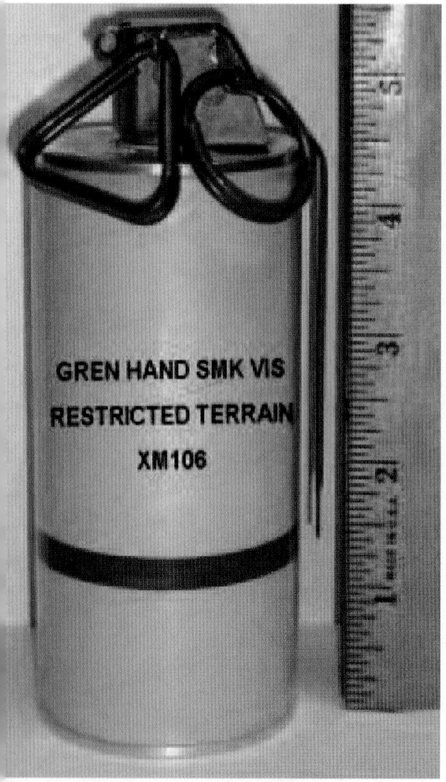


## MISSION

Provides the Warfighter with the ability to safely employ short-duration obscuration in the visual and near-infrared (IR) portions of the electromagnetic spectrum, screening dismounted maneuvers of the individual Soldier or team on restricted and complex terrain.

## DESCRIPTION

The M106 Screening Obscuration Device (SOD)-Visual Restricted (Vr) provides the Warfighter the capability to rapidly employ small-area, short-duration, screening obscuration effects in the visual through near-IR spectrum (0.4-1.2 micron range) during full-spectrum operations.

The SOD-Vr is designed for use in restrictive terrain (i.e., urban structures, subterranean locations, caves). The SOD-Vr degrades proper operation and performance of enemy battlefield weapon systems and enhances friendly capabilities.

The SOD-Vr provides a less hazardous alternative to current non-colored smoke and incendiary hand grenades because the fill is non-combustible and non-burning.

## SYSTEM INTERDEPENDENCIES

None

## PROGRAM STATUS

- **FY11:** Continued production and deployment

## PROJECTED ACTIVITIES

- **2QFY12:** Initial operating capability/ full operating capability

**ACQUISITION PHASE**

Technology Development | Engineering and Manufacturing Development | Production and Deployment | Operations and Support

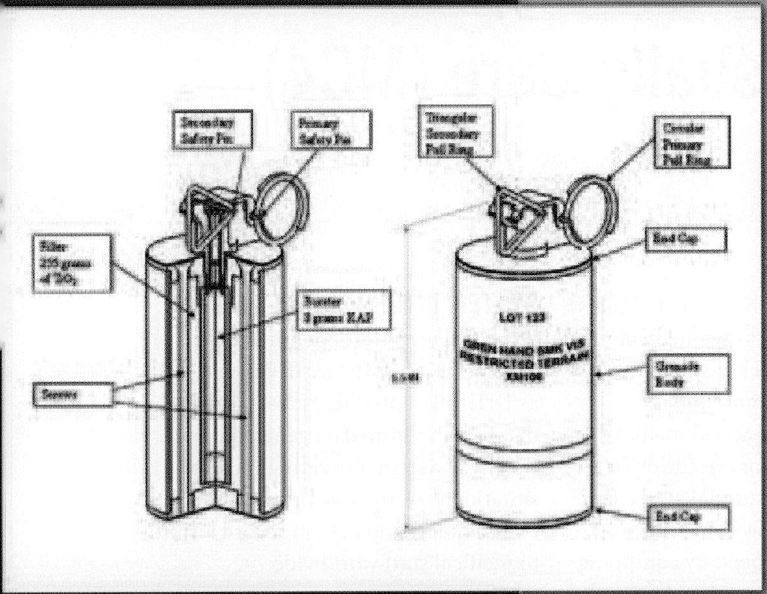

## M106 Screening Obscuration Device (SOD)-Visual Restricted Terrain (Vr)

**FOREIGN MILITARY SALES**
None

**CONTRACTORS**
Pine Bluff Arsenal (Pine Bluff, AR)

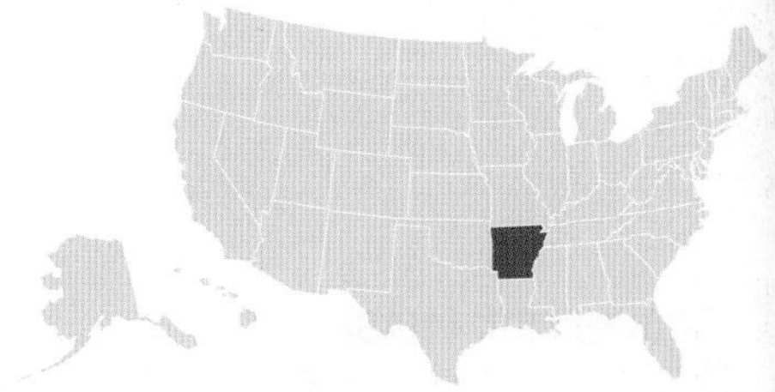

# Medical Communications for Combat Casualty Care (MC4)

INVESTMENT COMPONENT

Modernization

Recapitalization

Maintenance

## MISSION

Integrates, fields, and supports a comprehensive medical information system, enabling lifelong electronic medical records, streamlined medical logistics, and enhanced situational awareness for Army tactical forces.

## DESCRIPTION

Medical Communications for Casualty Care (MC4) is a ruggedized system-of-systems containing Joint software applications fielded to tactical medical forces throughout the combat zone, the U.S., and contingency operations worldwide. MC4 integrates Defense Health Information Management System (DHIMS) Theater Medical Information Program-Joint (TMIP-J) software, and other Army-unique applications, onto commercial- and government-off-the-shelf technology, providing the tools needed to digitally record and transfer critical medical data from the foxhole to medical treatment facilities worldwide.

Deployable medical forces use the MC4 system to gain quick, accurate access to patient histories and forward casualty resuscitation information. The system also provides units with automated tools facilitating patient tracking, medical reporting, and medical logistical support. Combatant commanders use the MC4 system to access medical surveillance information, resulting in enhanced medical situational awareness. Most importantly, MC4 is helping deployed service members. By equipping deployed medical units with automated resources, MC4 helps ensure service members have a secure, accessible, lifelong electronic medical record, which results in better-informed health care providers and easier access to Veterans Administration medical benefits.

The MC4 system comprises seven Army-approved line items that can be configured to support Army levels one through four and DoD roles one through three of the health care continuum. Future MC4 enhancements will be accomplished through minor system upgrades and major planned upgrades. With 10 years of experience managing DoD's first battlefield medical recording system, MC4 remains the most widely-used, comprehensive information management medical system on the battlefield.

## SYSTEM INTERDEPENDENCIES

**Other Major Interdependencies**

MC4 relies on software developers such as DHIMS to provide global software databases to store data generated by the MC4 system, providing medical situational awareness for operational commanders and patient record visibility to medical staff worldwide

## PROGRAM STATUS

- **1QFY11-4QFY1:** Fielding TMIP Block 2 Release 1 Service Pack 1 worldwide

## PROJECTED ACTIVITIES

- **1QFY13:** TMIP Increment 2 Release 2 (I2R2) software Full Deployment Decision Review
- **2QFY13:** Begin Fielding TMIP I2R2 software
- **4QFY17:** Full Operational Capability (objective)

ACQUISITION PHASE

Technology Development | Engineering and Manufacturing Development | Production and Deployment | Operations and Support

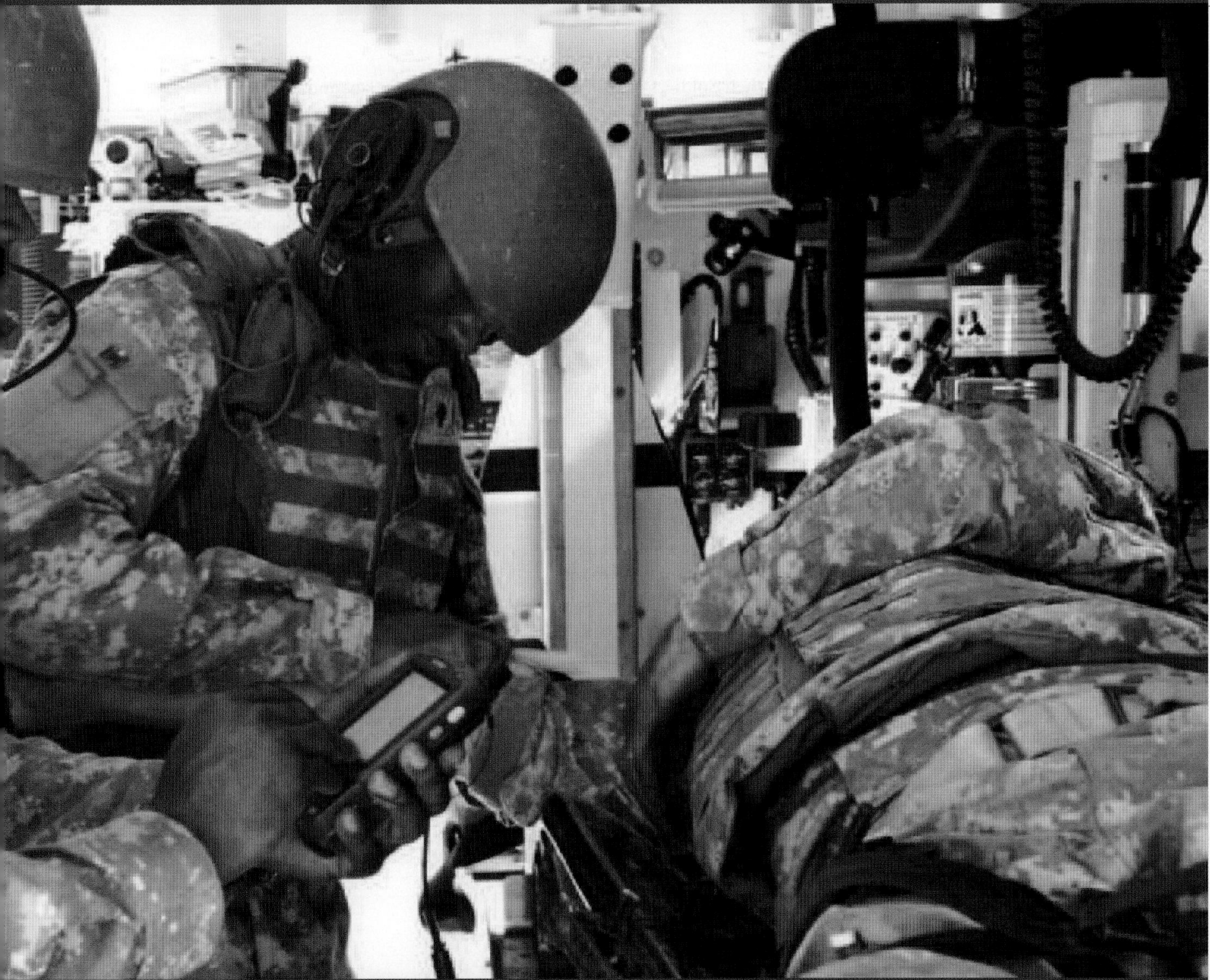

## Medical Communications for Combat Casualty Care (MC4)

**FOREIGN MILITARY SALES**
None

**CONTRACTORS**

**System Integration Support:**
L-3 Communications (Reston, VA)

**Fielding, Training, and System Administration Support:**
General Dynamics (Fairfax, VA)

**Program Management and Support Services (PMSS2):**
Booz Allen Hamilton (Herndon, VA)

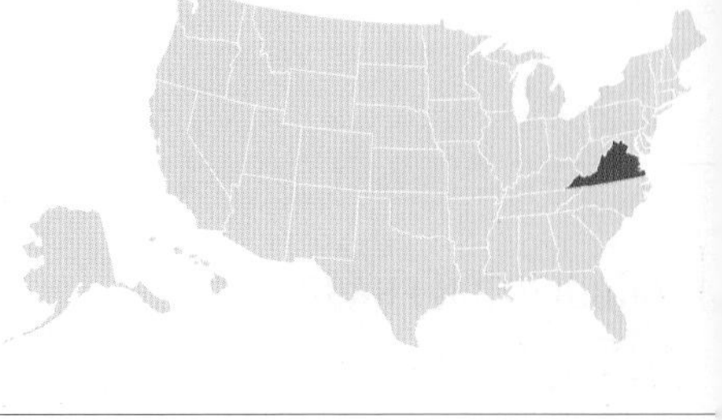

# Medical Simulation Training Center (MSTC)

**INVESTMENT COMPONENT**

Modernization

Recapitalization

Maintenance

## MISSION

Conducts standardized combat medical training for medical and nonmedical personnel in support of full-spectrum operations (FSO).

## DESCRIPTION

The Medical Simulation Training Center (MSTC) systems are an Army training asset, with a regional training requirement, located at installations, delivering effective medical training with a standardized training platform for both classroom and simulated battlefield conditions. The goal is to better prepare Soldiers for the application of medical interventions under combat conditions.

The MSTC offers a standardized platform for training Medical Education and Demonstration of Individual Competence (MEDIC), Tactical Combat Casualty Care (TC3), and Combat Life Saver (CLS) Programs of Instructions (POIs).

The MSTC is a medical skills training platform where Soldiers can obtain and sustain their medical skills in accordance with TC 8-800. The MSTC affords Commanders the flexibility to validate their Soldiers' medical skills prior to deployment and allows the greatest latitude in creating training relevant to the contemporary operating environment (COE) and the unit's mission essential task list (METL). The MSTCs are ideal locations where lessons learned from current military operations can be implemented and where Soldier medics can be educated on new battlefield procedures and equipment. The MSTC has the ability to provide comprehensive training in several formats: the classroom setting, practical hands-on training simulation, trauma lanes, and distance learning.

MSTC provides a standardized suite of supporting component systems including the Virtual Patient System (VPS), Instruction Support System (ISS), Medical Training Command and Control (MT-C2), and the Medical Training Evaluation System (MTES). MSTC maximizes the use of enabling technology and supporting training devices for both classroom and full tactical training capabilities. Computerized bleed-breathe mannequins that are weighted and airway equipped, part task trainers, audiovisual enhancements, camera surveillance, computer labs and instrumented control rooms with a remotely managed training platform are all components of a standardized MSTC suite. The MSTC training methodology maximizes a reconfigurable, modifiable, and sustainable training capability to fully meet COE and FSO training requirements.

## SYSTEM INTERDEPENDENCIES

None

## PROGRAM STATUS

- **1QFY11:** Fielded Camp Atterbury, IN, the last of the initial 18 MSTC sites

## PROJECTED ACTIVITIES

- Further development and procurement of tetherless mannequin training capability, the MTES System, and the MT-C2 System
- Production and fielding of additional MSTC suites toward meeting the full requirement of 34 sites

**ACQUISITION PHASE**

Technology Development | Engineering and Manufacturing Development | Production and Deployment | Operations and Support

## Medical Simulation Training Center (MSTC)

**FOREIGN MILITARY SALES**
None

**CONTRACTORS**
Medical Education Technologies (Sarasota, FL)
Computer Sciences Corp. (CSC) (Orlando, FL)
Kforce Government Solutions (KGS) (Fairfax, VA)

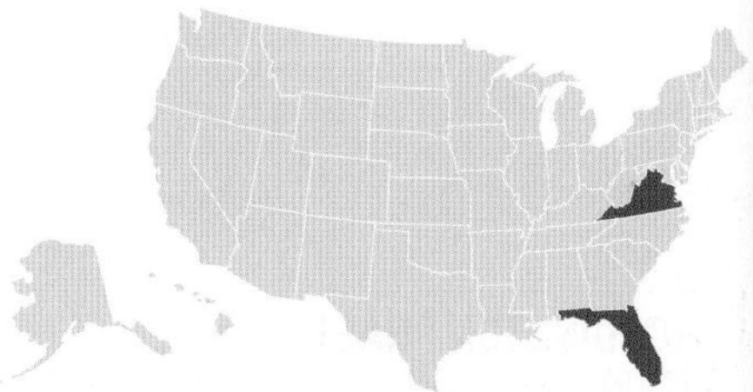

# Medium Caliber Ammunition (MCA)

**INVESTMENT COMPONENT**

- **Modernization**
- Recapitalization
- Maintenance

## MISSION

Provides overwhelming lethality in medium caliber ammunition and point- and area-target engagement via medium handheld and crew-served weapons.

## DESCRIPTION

Medium caliber ammunition (MCA) includes 20mm, 25mm, 30mm, and 40mm armor-piercing, high-explosive, smoke, illumination, training, and antipersonnel cartridges with the capability to defeat light armor, materiel, and personnel targets. The 20mm cartridge is a multipurpose tracer with self destruct, used in the Counter Rocket, Artillery, and Mortar (C-RAM) weapon system. The 25mm target practice (TP), high-explosive incendiary and armor-piercing cartridges are fired from the M242 Bushmaster Cannon for the Bradley Fighting Vehicle. The 30mm TP and high-explosive, dual-purpose (HEDP) cartridges are used in the Apache helicopter's M230 Chain Gun. A variety of 40mm TP, HEDP, and specialty cartridges are designed for use in the M203 Grenade Launcher, M320 Grenade Launcher, and the MK19 Grenade Machine Gun.

## SYSTEM INTERDEPENDENCIES

**Other Major Interdependencies**

Medium caliber ammunition is dependent upon the weapons platforms currently in use

## PROGRAM STATUS

- **Current:** In production

## PROJECTED ACTIVITIES

- **FY11:** Multiple year family buys for 25mm, 30mm, and 40mm ammunition

**ACQUISITION PHASE**

- Technology Development
- Engineering and Manufacturing Development
- **Production and Deployment**
- Operations and Support

## Medium Caliber Ammunition (MCA)

**FOREIGN MILITARY SALES**

**25mm:**
Israel, Philippines

**30mm:**
Egypt, Israel, Japan, Kuwait, Netherlands, Serbia, Taiwan, United Arab Emirates

**40mm:**
Afghanistan, Canada, Greece, Israel, Japan, Kenya, Philippines, Tunisia

**CONTRACTORS**

General Dynamics Ordnance and Tactical Systems (Marion, IL; Red Lion, PA)
Alliant Techsystems (Radford, VA; Rocket City, WV)
AMTEC Corp. (Janesville, WI; Camden, AR)
DSE (Balimoy) Corp. (Tampa, FL; Gaffney, SC)

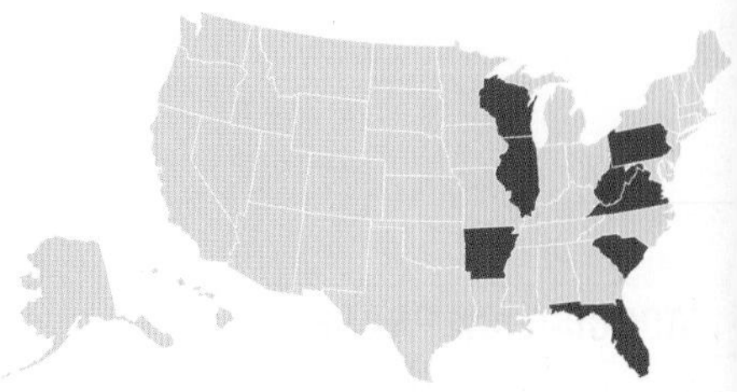

# Medium Extended Air Defense System (MEADS)

**INVESTMENT COMPONENT**

Modernization

Recapitalization

Maintenance

## MISSION

Defends maneuver forces and critical assets against the theater ballistic missile, cruise missile, and air-breathing threats in contingency and mature theaters.

## DESCRIPTION

The Medium Extended Air Defense System (MEADS) provides a robust, 360-degree defense using the PATRIOT PAC-3 hit-to-kill missile segment enhancement (MSE) against the full spectrum of theater ballistic missiles, anti-radiation missiles, cruise missiles, unmanned aerial vehicles, tactical air-to-surface missiles, and rotary- and fixed-wing threats. MEADS will also provide defense against multiple and simultaneous attacks by short-range ballistic missiles, cruise missiles, and other air-breathing threats. MEADS can be immediately deployed by air for early entry operations. MEADS also has the mobility to displace rapidly and protect maneuver force assets during offensive operations. Netted, distributed, open architecture, and modular components are utilized in the MEADS to increase survivability and flexibility of use in a number of operational configurations. The PAC-3 MSE improves upon the current missile configuration ranges/altitudes and improves performance against evolving threats.

The MEADS weapon system will use its netted and distributed architecture to ensure Joint and allied interoperability, and to enable a seamless interface to the next generation of battle management command, control, communications, computers, and intelligence (BMC4I). The system's improved sensor components and its ability to link other airborne and ground-based sensors facilitate the employment of its battle elements.

The MEADS weapon system's objective battle management tactical operations center (TOC) will provide the basis for the future common air and missile defense (AMD) TOC, leveraging modular battle elements and a distributed and open architecture to facilitate continuous exchange of information to support a more effective AMD system-of-systems.

## SYSTEM INTERDEPENDENCIES

None

## PROGRAM STATUS

- **1QFY11:** System program review
- **Feb. 11, 2011:** U.S. decision to continue development within funding limits set forth by the Design and Development (D&D) Memorandum of Understanding (MoU)

## PROJECTED ACTIVITIES

- Remaining activities to implement a "Demonstration of Capabilities" through 2013 with the remaining MoU funds to provide a meaningful capability for Germany and Italy and a possible future option for the U.S. Based on this decision, a new and detailed program/schedule for D&D is being developed by NAMEADSMA for the Board of Directors (BoD) review and National Armament Director (NAD) approval, with contract amendment signature expected October 2011
- **1QFY12:** Multifunction Fire Control Radar #1 delivery for integration/testing at Pratica di Mare, Italy
- **1QFY12:** Launcher-Missile Characterization Test (LMCT) at White Sands Missile Range (WSMR)

**ACQUISITION PHASE**

Technology Development | Engineering and Manufacturing Development | Production and Deployment | Operations and Support

## Medium Extended Air Defense System (MEADS)

**FOREIGN MILITARY SALES**

None

**CONTRACTORS**

**D&D Contract:**

MEADS, Intl. (Syracuse, NY; Orlando, FL; Huntsville, AL)

Lockheed Martin (Grand Prairie, TX)

**PM/SYS:**

government (statewide, AL)

**MSE:**

Lockheed Martin (Grand Prairie, TX)

**Security/Exciter:**

Lockheed Martin (Grand Prairie, TX)

**SETA:**

Intuitive Research and Technology (Huntsville, AL)

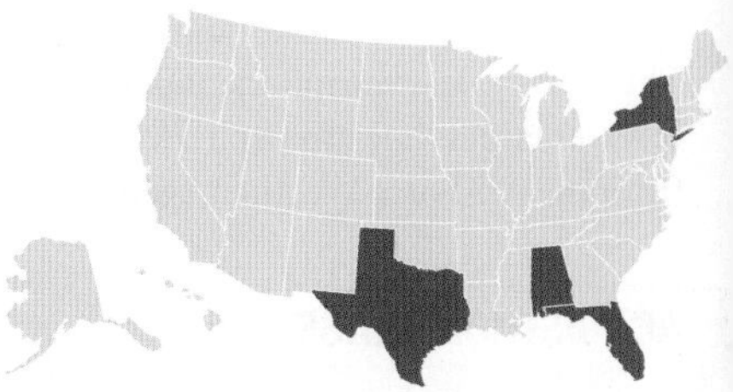

# Meteorological Measuring Set-Profiler (MMS-P)/Computer Meteorological Data-Profiler (CMD-P)

**INVESTMENT COMPONENT**

- **Modernization**
- Recapitalization
- Maintenance

## MISSION

Provides on-demand, real-time meteorological data over an extended battlespace.

## DESCRIPTION

The AN/TMQ-52 Meteorological Measuring Set-Profiler (MMS-P) uses a suite of meteorological sensors, meteorological data from satellites, and an advanced mesoscale atmospheric model to provide highly accurate meteorological data for indirect fire artillery forces. The system uses common hardware, software, and operating systems and is housed in a command post platform shelter and transported on an M1152A High Mobility Multipurpose Wheeled Vehicle (HMMWV).

The mesoscale atmospheric model receives large-scale atmospheric data from the Air Force Weather Agency and other meteorological sensors and produces a vertical profile of wind speed and direction, temperature, relative humidity, cloud base height, type precipitation, and horizontal visibility in the target area, all of which are necessary for precise targeting and terminal guidance of various munitions. Profiler transmits this data to indirect fire direction centers for use in developing the firing solution. The current Profiler provides meteorological coverage throughout a 60-kilometer radius.
For the first time, Army field artillery systems can apply meteorological data along the trajectory from the firing platform to the target area.

The Profiler Block III, or Computer Meteorological Data-Profiler (CMD-P) AN/GMK-2 System, is the next evolutionary block of the Profiler system and is designed to reduce the logistical footprint to a laptop configuration located in the Tactical Operations Center (TOC), thus eliminating the Standard Integrated Command Post Shelter (SICPS)/Command Post Platform (CPP), support vehicle, and crew. The CMD-P software on the laptop will port MMS-P software that presently runs on three operating systems (OS) and three separate computing processors onto one OS and processor.

Additionally, the local ground sensor will be removed to further reduce the logistical footprint. The system interface with the Advanced Field Artillery Tactical Data System (AFATDS) will change from the Single Channel and Airborne Radio Systems (SINCGARS) to a Local Area Network (LAN) connection in the TOC. The CMD-P will no longer require a dedicated Global Broadcast Service (GBS) receiver suite (AN/TSR-8) but instead will rely on the TOC GBS. The system software will be capable of providing Field Artillery Computer MET (METCM) and Gridded MET (METGM) messages on demand with or without an operator in-the-loop while extending coverage up to 500 kilometers. CMD-P will undergo Development Testing in FY11 and Operational Testing in FY12. Fielding is planned to begin in FY13. The CMD-P will reduce the system's footprint and result in a significant Operations and Support cost avoidance for the Army as it replaces the MMS-P.

## SYSTEM INTERDEPENDENCIES

**Other Major Interdependencies**

Navy Operational Global Atmospheric Prediction System, Global Broadcast System

## PROGRAM STATUS

- **1QFY11-4QFY11:** Completed production of the Army Authorization Objective of 108 systems
- **1QFY11-4QFY11:** With exception of two systems, completed all fieldings to Maneuver Brigade Combat Teams, Fire Brigades, Army Prepositioned Stock and the training base
- **1QFY11-4QFY11:** Began fielding of the Global Broadcast Service (GBS) Modification Work Order (MWO)

## PROJECTED ACTIVITIES

- **2QFY12-2QFY14:** Complete fielding of last systems and GBS MWO to Army units
- **2QFY12-2QFY14:** Complete development and testing of Profiler Block III during FY12 followed by procurement and fielding of the CMD-P starting in FY13

**ACQUISITION PHASE**

Technology Development | Engineering and Manufacturing Development | **Production and Deployment** | Operations and Support

## Meteorological Measuring Set-Profiler (MMS-P)/Computer Meteorological Data-Profiler (CMD-P)

**FOREIGN MILITARY SALES**
None

**CONTRACTORS**
**MMS-P - Block I:**
Smiths Detection Inc. (Edgewood, MD)
Pennsylvania State University (University Park, PA)
**CMD-P - Block III:**
**Prime:** Mantech Sensor Technologies Inc. (Red Bank, NJ)
**Sub:** CGI Federal (Lawton, OK)

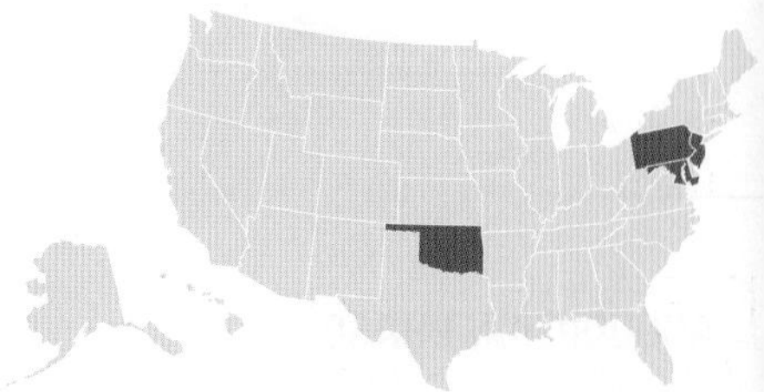

# Mine Protection Vehicle Family (MPVF)

**INVESTMENT COMPONENT**

- **Modernization**
- Recapitalization
- Maintenance

## MISSION

Provides blast-protected platforms capable of locating, interrogating, and classifying suspected explosive hazards, including improvised explosive devices (IEDs).

## DESCRIPTION

The Mine Protection Vehicle Family (MPVF) consists of the Medium Mine Protected Vehicle (MMPV), the Vehicle Mounted Mine Detection (VMMD) system, and the Mine Protected Clearance Vehicle (MPCV). Each of the systems in the MPVF has a blast-deflecting, V-shaped hull, and each conducts specific missions.

The MMPV system is a blast-protected command and control vehicle platform that operates in explosive hazardous environments and is adaptable to a wide range of security and force protection activities. The MMPV will support Engineer Units in route and area clearance operations and Explosive Ordnance Disposal (EOD) Companies as the rapid response vehicle for EOD. The MMPV will also support Chemical Biological Response Teams.

The VMMD is a blast-protected, vehicle-mounted mine-detection and lane-proofing system capable of finding and marking metallic explosive hazards, including metallic-encased IEDs and anti-tank mines on unimproved roads. It consists of two mine detection "Husky" vehicles, and a set of three mine detonation trailers used for proofing. The Husky detection platform detects, locates, and marks suspected metallic explosive hazards over a three-meters-wide path. The Husky provides protection against mine blasts under the wheels and under the centerline, in addition to ballistic protection of the operator cab. The system is designed to be quickly repairable in the field after a mine blast.

The MPCV provides deployed forces with an effective and reliable blast-protected vehicle capable of interrogating and classifying suspected explosive hazards, including IEDs. The MPCV has an articulating arm with a digging/lifting attachment and camera to remotely interrogate a suspected explosive hazard and allow the crew to confirm, deny, and/or classify the explosive hazard. It provides a blast-protected platform to transport Soldiers and allows them to dismount to mark and/or neutralize explosive hazards.

## SYSTEM INTERDEPENDENCIES

None

## PROGRAM STATUS

**MPCV:**

- **4QFY11:** Full Materiel Release/Type Classification Standard and Full-Rate Production Decision
- **1QFY12:** First Unit Equipped

**VMMD:**

- **4QFY11:** Full Materiel Release/Type Classification Standard and Full-Rate Production Decision
- **1QFY12:** First Unit Equipped

## PROJECTED ACTIVITIES

**MMPV:**

- **2QFY13:** Full Materiel Release/Type Classification Standard
- **3QFY13:** First Unit Equipped

**ACQUISITION PHASE**

Technology Development | Engineering and Manufacturing Development | **Production and Deployment** | Operations and Support

## Mine Protection Vehicle Family (MPVF)

**FOREIGN MILITARY SALES**

**MPCV:**
United Kingdom

**VMMD:**
Australia, Canada, Kenya, Saudi Arabia

**CONTRACTORS**

**MMPV:**
BAE Systems (York, PA)

**MPCV:**
Force Protection Industries Inc. (Ladson, SC)

**VMMD:**
Critical Solutions International Inc. (Dallas, TX)

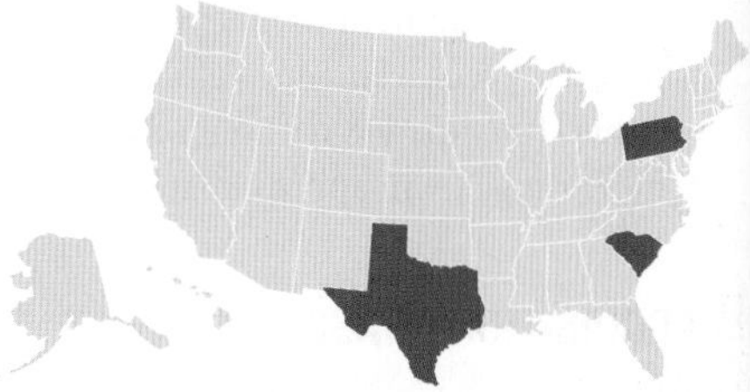

# Mine Resistant Ambush Protected Vehicles (MRAP)

**INVESTMENT COMPONENT**

- Modernization
- Recapitalization
- Maintenance

## MISSION

Provides tactical mobility for Warfighters with multimission platforms capable of mitigating the effects of improvised explosive devices (IEDs), underbody mines, and small arms fire threats.

## DESCRIPTION

The Joint Mine Resistant Ambush Protected (MRAP) Vehicle Program (JMVP) is a multiservice program currently supporting the Army, Navy, Marine Corps, Air Force, and the U.S. Special Operations Command. The program procures, tests, integrates, fields, and supports highly survivable vehicles that provide protection from IEDs and other threats. These four- to six-wheeled vehicles are configured with government furnished equipment to meet unique warfighting requirements. Vehicle combat weights (fully loaded without add-on armor) range from approximately 34,000 to 60,000 pounds, with payloads ranging from 1,000 to 18,000 pounds. Key components (e.g., transmissions, engines) vary between vehicles and manufacturers, but generally consist of common commercial and military parts.

Four categories of vehicles support the following missions:

- **Category (CAT) I:** Carries four to six passengers and designed to provide increased mobility and reliability in rough terrain
- **CAT II:** Multimission operations (such as convoy lead, troop transport, and ambulance), carries 10 passengers
- **CAT III:** Mine/IED clearance operations and explosive ordnance disposal (EOD); carries six passengers, plus specialized equipment to support EOD operations. The Force Protection Industries Buffalo is the only CAT III variant. This is the largest MRAP vehicle.
- **MRAP All Terrain Vehicle (M-ATV):** Carries four Soldiers plus a gunner. Supports small-unit combat operations in complex and highly restricted rural, mountainous, and urban terrains. The M-ATV provides better overall mobility characteristics than the original CAT I, II, and III MRAP vehicles yet retains the same survivability threshold.

## SYSTEM INTERDEPENDENCIES

**Other Major Interdependencies**

MRAP vehicles are equipped with multiple GFE items, including communications equipment and mine and IED countermeasure equipment, in addition to weapons and crew protection systems

## PROGRAM STATUS

- **1QFY11-4QFY11:** Produced and fielded MRAP vehicles to Army, Marine Corps, Air Force, Navy, U.S. Special Operations, and foreign military sales customers
- **2QFY11:** Began modernization of MRAP vehicles returning from theater in preparation for transition to enduring force requirements

## PROJECTED ACTIVITIES

- **2QFY12-2QFY14:** Continue support of MRAP vehicles fielded in response to urgent theater requirements
- **2QFY12-2QFY14:** Continue modernization of MRAP vehicles returning from theater in preparation for transition to enduring force requirements

**ACQUISITION PHASE**

- Technology Development
- Engineering and Manufacturing Development
- Production and Deployment
- Operations and Support

## Mine Resistant Ambush Protected Vehicles (MRAP)

**FOREIGN MILITARY SALES**

Canada, France, Italy, United Kingdom

**CONTRACTORS**

BAE Systems Land & Armaments, Ground Systems Division (York, PA)

BAE-TVS (Sealy, TX)

Force Protection Industries Inc. (Ladson, SC)

General Dynamics Land Systems, Canada (Ontario, Canada)

Navistar Defense (Warrenville, IL)

Oshkosh Corp. (Oshkosh, WI)

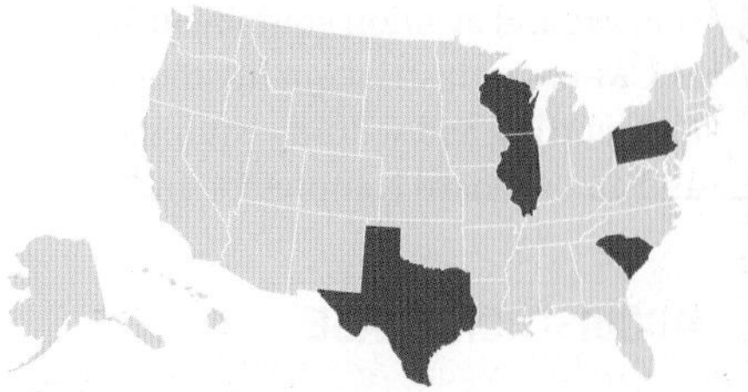

# Mobile Maintenance Equipment Systems (MMES)

**INVESTMENT COMPONENT**

Modernization

Recapitalization

Maintenance

## MISSION

Repairs battle-damaged combat systems on site and up through the direct support level in the forward battle area.

## DESCRIPTION

The Mobile Maintenance Equipment Systems (MMES) employ a system-of-systems approach to provide two-level maintenance capability to the Warfighter. Five interconnected maintenance systems distributed throughout the Army at multiple levels and echelons provide a holistic repair capability in all environments.

Shop Equipment Contact Maintenance (SECM) is a first responder providing immediate field-level maintenance and repair to battle-damaged ground support and aviation equipment. The SECM has industrial quality tools, light-duty cutting and welding equipment, and an on-board compressor and power inverter. The system consists of a fabricated enclosure mounted on an M113/M1152 High Mobility Multipurpose Wheeled Vehicle (HMMWV).

Forward Repair System (FRS) is a high-mobility, forward maintenance and repair system. The FRS places industrial-grade power tools, diagnostic test equipment, 35 kW generator, and heavy lift capability in one package. The FRS is configured with a 5.5-ton lift capacity with a 14-foot radius crane capable of removing and replacing major components on all models of military vehicles. Mounted to a flat rack, it is transported by Palletized Load System (PLS) trucks in Heavy Brigades, or by the Heavy Expanded Mobility Tactical Truck Load Handling System (HEMTT-LHS) in Stryker Brigade Combat Teams.

Standard Automotive Tool Set (SATS) provides the Warfighter a common tool set with the capability to perform field-level maintenance at all levels of materiel system repairs. The SATS includes a Base Tool Set and Field Maintenance Modules (FMMs) that allow the system to be tailored to support heavy, medium, and light combat units. SATS is transported by International Organization for Standardization 8x8x20 containers that can be mounted on a flat rack or a trailer. The system contains an electric power generator, Environmental Control Unit (ECU), Signal Entry Panel (SEP), ergonomic storage of a complete tool load of lifetime warranted industrial quality tools. SATS has communication capability that allows data and voice connections for Global Combat Support System-Army (GCSS-A). SATS is transported (towed) by a tactical cargo truck from the Family of Medium Tactical Trucks (FMTV).

Hydraulic System Test and Repair Unit (HSTRU) is designed to perform diagnostic testing and repair of hydraulic systems. HSTRU is capable of transporting and assembling hoses, tubes, and fitting components, and it is capable of fabricating industry standard hoses with crimping technology. HSTRU is trailer mounted, integrated, and transportable in a standardized enclosure that is capable of rapid deployment.

Shop Equipment Welding (SEW) provides a full spectrum of welding capabilities, and supports two-level maintenance utilizing the only qualified Welders (44B) in the Army. Repairs may be performed in all weather, climatic, and light conditions. The SEW integrates commercial off-the-shelf and NDI components in an enclosure mounted on an M103A3 Trailer.

## SYSTEM INTERDEPENDENCIES

None

## PROGRAM STATUS

- **FRS:** Production and fielding
- **SATS:** Production and fielding
- **SECM:** Production and fielding
- **HSTRU:** FUE (4QFY11)

## PROJECTED ACTIVITIES

- **SEW:** Establish reset program
- **HSTRU:** Production and fielding
- **Ongoing:** SECM
- **Ongoing:** SATS
- **Ongoing:** FRS

**ACQUISITION PHASE**

Technology Development | Engineering and Manufacturing Development | Production and Deployment | Operations and Support

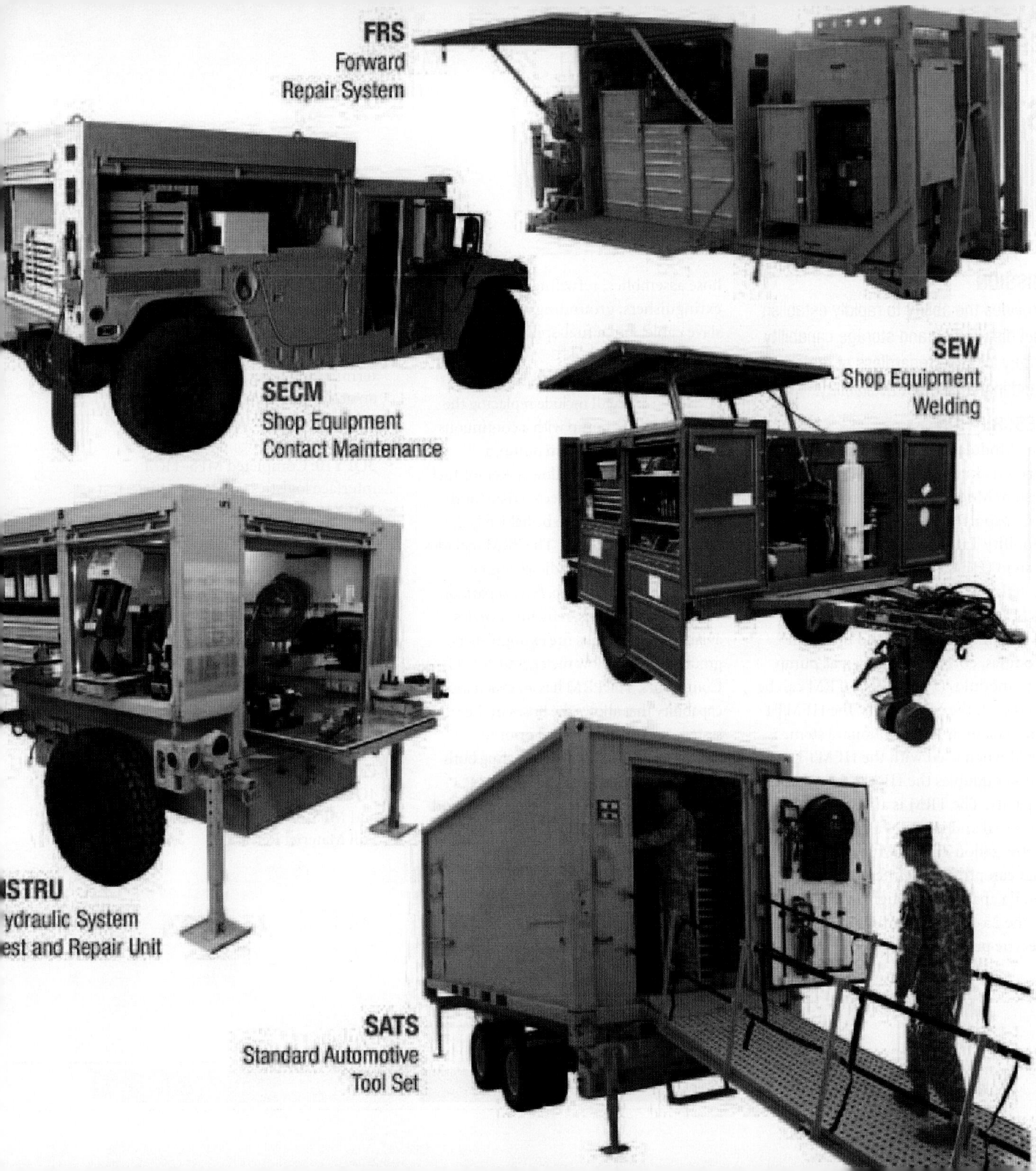


## Mobile Maintenance Equipment Systems (MMES)

**FOREIGN MILITARY SALES**
None

**CONTRACTORS**

**FRS and SECM:**
Rock Island Arsenal (Rock Island, IL)
Snap-on Industrial (Crystal Lake, IL)

**SATS:**
Kipper Tool Company (Gainesville, GA)
AAR Mobility Systems (Cadillac, MI)
MCT Industries Inc. (Albuquerque, NM)

**HSTRU:**
Mandus Group (Rock Island, IL)

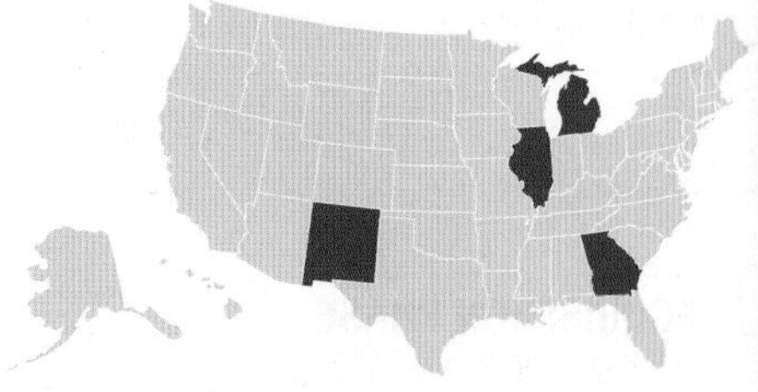

# Modular Fuel System (MFS)

INVESTMENT COMPONENT

Modernization

Recapitalization

Maintenance

## MISSION

Provides the ability to rapidly establish fuel distribution and storage capability at any location regardless of materiel handling equipment availability.

## DESCRIPTION

The Modular Fuel System (MFS), formerly known as the Load Handling System Modular Fuel Farm (LMFF), is transported by the Heavy Expanded Mobility Tactical Truck-Load Handling System (HEMTT-LHS) and the Palletized Load System. It is composed of 14 tank rack modules (TRM) and two each of the pump and filtration modules, commonly known as pump rack modules (PRMs). The TRM can be used with the MFS PRMs, the HEMTT Tankers, or as a stand-alone system. TRM when used with the HEMTT Tanker doubles the HEMTT Tanker's capacity. The TRM is air-transportable with fuel and includes a baffled, 2,500-gallon-capacity fuel storage tank that can provide unfiltered, limited retail capability through gravity feed or the 25-gallon per minute (gpm) electric pump. The TRM also includes hose assemblies, refueling nozzles, fire extinguishers, grounding rods, a NATO slave cable, and a fuel-spill control kit.

TRM full retail capability is being developed and will include replacing the existing electric pump with a continuous operating electric 20 gpm pump, a filtration system, and a flow meter for fuel accountability. The projected date for the TRM retail capability to be fielded is the fourth quarter of FY12. The PRM includes a self priming 600 gpm diesel engine-driven centrifugal pump, filter separator, valves, fittings, hoses, refueling nozzles, aviation fuel test kits, fire extinguishers, grounding rods, flow meter, and NATO Connectors. The PRM has an evacuation capability that allows the hoses in the system to be purged of fuel prior to recovery and is capable of refueling both ground vehicles and aircraft. MFS is capable of receiving, storing, filtering, and issuing all kerosene based fuels.

## SYSTEM INTERDEPENDENCIES

**Other Major Interdependencies**

MFS TRM is interdependent with HEMTT Palletized Load System (PLS) and LHS for transportation

## PROGRAM STATUS

- **3QFY08:** CS&CSS approved MFS HEMTT/TRM interface
- **1QFY09:** ASA(ALT) signed un-termination letter restoring the MFS as an active program.
- **2QFY09:** Completed MFS-TRM interface hardware
- **3QFY10:** Completed MFS-TRM interface logistics and First Article Test
- **1QFY10:** MFS-TRM initial operational test

## PROJECTED ACTIVITIES

- **2QFY11:** MFS-TRM type classification and Full Materiel Release
- **3QFY11:** MFS-TRM Retail Capability Operational Requirement Document Amendment Approved
- **1QFY12:** MFS-TRM Retail Capability and MFS PRM Full-Rate Production and MFS-TRM and MFS PRM Production Contract Award
- **4QFY12:** MFS TRM Retail Capability and MFS-PRM Type Classification and Full Materiel Release

ACQUISITION PHASE

Technology Development | Engineering and Manufacturing Development | Production and Deployment | Operations and Support

## Modular Fuel System (MFS)

**FOREIGN MILITARY SALES**
None

**CONTRACTORS**
DRS Sustainment Systems Inc. (St. Louis, MO)
E.D. Etnyre and Co. (Oregon, IL)

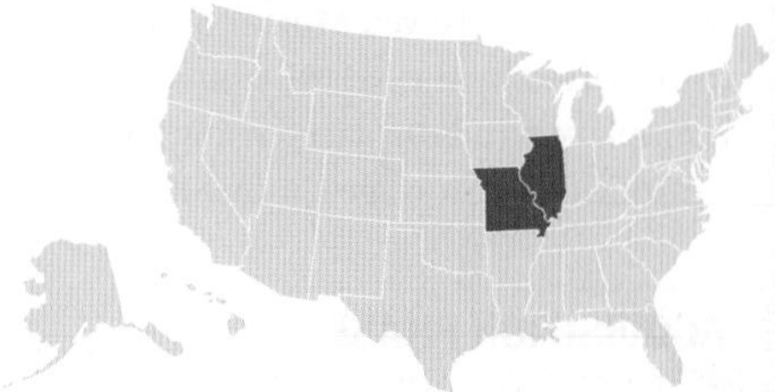

# Mortar Systems

## INVESTMENT COMPONENT

**Modernization**

Recapitalization

Maintenance

## MISSION

Provides enhanced lethality, accuracy, responsiveness, and crew survivability while reducing the logistics footprint.

## DESCRIPTION

Mortar Fire Control System (MFCS)-equipped mortar systems provide organic, indirect fire support to the maneuver unit commander. Mortars are employed in light and heavy forces, with towed- and tracked-carrier versions.

The Army uses three variants of 120mm mortar systems, and all have been qualified and are being equipped with MFCS. All of the mortar systems fire a full family of ammunition, including high-explosive, infrared and visible light illumination, smoke, and training. The M120 120mm Towed Mortar System is transported by the M1101 trailer and is emplaced and displaced using the M326 Mortar Stowage Kit (MSK). The mounted variants are the M121 120mm mortar, used on the M1064A3 Mortar Carrier (M113 variant), and the 120mm Recoiling Mortar System, used on the M1129 Stryker Mortar Carrier.

Lightweight variants of the M252 81mm Mortar System and M224 60mm Mortar System have been qualified and are in production/fielding. Both systems provide high-rate-of-fire capability and are man-portable.

The M95/M96 Mortar Fire Control System-Mounted (MFCS-M), used on the M1064A3 and M1129, and the M150/M151 Mortar Fire Control System-Dismounted (MFCS-D), used with the M120, combine a fire control computer with an inertial navigation and pointing system, allowing crews to fire in under a minute, greatly improving mortar lethality, accuracy, and crew survivability.

The M32 Lightweight Handheld Mortar Ballistic Computer (LHMBC) has a tactical modem and embedded global positioning system, allowing mortar crews to send and receive digital call-for-fire messages, calculate ballistic solutions, and navigate.

## SYSTEM INTERDEPENDENCIES

**In this Publication**

Advanced Field Artillery Tactical Data System (AFATDS)

**Other Major Interdependencies**

M95/M96 MFCS-M, M150/M151 MFCS-D

## PROGRAM STATUS

- **1QFY11-4QFY11:** MFCS-M fielded to one Heavy Brigade Combat Team (HBCT), one HBCT Reset, and two Stryker Brigade Combat Team (SBCT) Resets
- **1QFY11-4QFY11:** MFCS-D fielded to seven Infantry Combat Teams (IBCTs)
- **1QFY11-4QFY11:** LHMBC fielded to five IBCTs, one Special Forces Group (SFG), one HBCT Reset, and twelve IBCT Resets
- **1QFY11-4QFY11:** Mortar Weapon Systems (60mm, 81mm, 120mm) fielded to numerous IBCTs, HBCTs, SBCTs and Special Forces groups
- **1QFY11-4QFY11:** Mortar Stowage Kits (MSK) fielded to seven IBCTs.
- **3QFY11:** 60MM Lightweight Mortar (M224A1) fielded to one SFG, First Unit Equipped (FUE)
- **1QFY11-4QFY11:** Continue production and fielding of 60mm, 81mm, and 120mm mortar weapon systems
- **1QFY11-4QFY11:** Continue production and fielding of MSKs, MFCS-D and LHMBCs

## PROJECTED ACTIVITIES

- **1QFY12:** Initial Fielding of the 81mm Lightweight Mortar (M252A1)
- **1QFY12-4QFY12:** Continue production and fielding of 60mm and 81mm lightweight mortar systems
- **1QFY12-4QFY12:** Continue production and fielding of MSKs, MFCS-D, and LHMBCs
- **1QFY12-4QFY12:** Complete fielding of MFCS-M

## ACQUISITION PHASE

Technology Development | Engineering and Manufacturing Development | **Production and Deployment** | Operations and Support

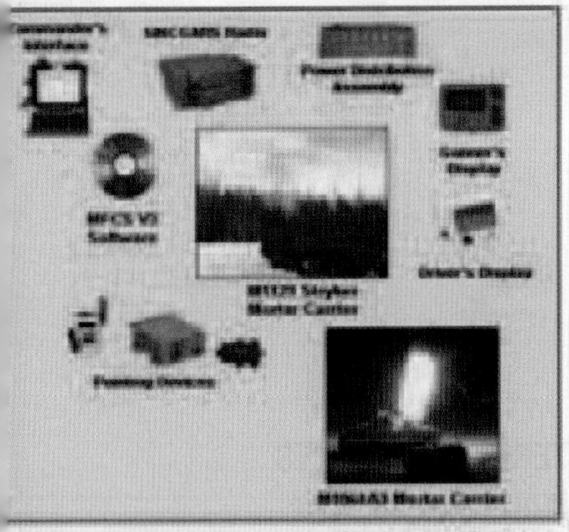

Mortar Fire Control System (MFCS-Mounted)

Mounted Weapon System Production

Motar Fire Control System (MFCS-Dismounted)

M1064A3 Motar Carrier

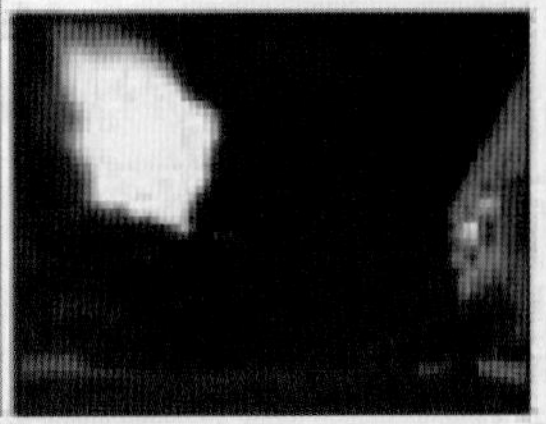

## Mortar Systems

**FOREIGN MILITARY SALES**
Afghanistan, Australia

**CONTRACTORS**

**60mm and 81mm Mortar Bipod Production:**
MaTech (Salisbury, MD)

**60mm and 81mm Baseplate Production:**
AMT (Fairfield, NJ)

**MFCS-D and MFCS-M Production, Fielding, and Installation:**
Elbit Systems of America (Ft. Worth, TX)

**M32 LHMBC (R-PDA):**
General Dynamics C4 Systems Inc. (Taunton, MA)

**120mm, 81mm, and 60mm Cannons and 120mm Baseplates:**
Watervliet Arsenal (Watervliet, NY)

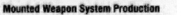

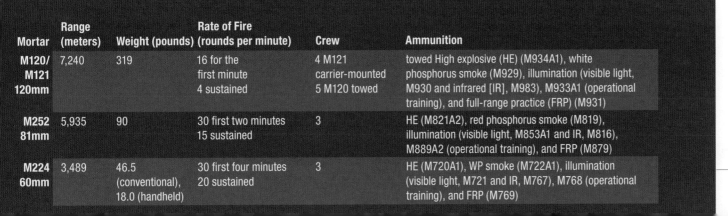

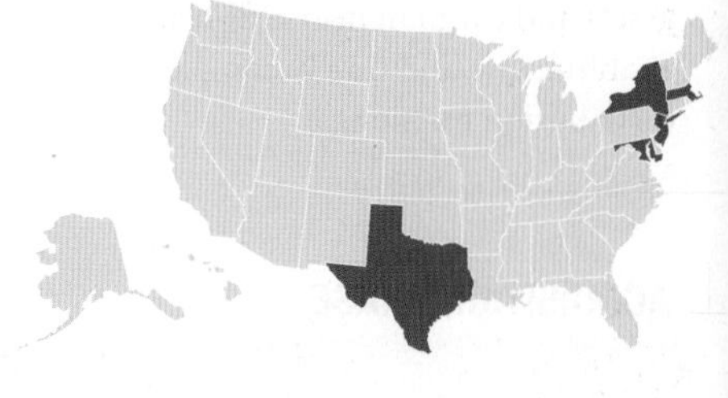

| Mortar | Range (meters) | Weight (pounds) | Rate of Fire (rounds per minute) | Crew | Ammunition |
|---|---|---|---|---|---|
| **M120/ M121 120mm** | 7,240 | 319 | 16 for the first minute 4 sustained | 4 M121 carrier-mounted 5 M120 towed | towed High explosive (HE) (M934A1), white phosphorus smoke (M929), illumination (visible light, M930 and infrared [IR], M983), M933A1 (operational training), and full-range practice (FRP) (M931) |
| **M252 81mm** | 5,935 | 90 | 30 first two minutes 15 sustained | 3 | HE (M821A2), red phosphorus smoke (M819), illumination (visible light, M853A1 and IR, M816), M889A2 (operational training), and FRP (M879) |
| **M224 60mm** | 3,489 | 46.5 (conventional), 18.0 (handheld) | 30 first four minutes 20 sustained | 3 | HE (M720A1), WP smoke (M722A1), illumination (visible light, M721 and IR, M767), M768 (operational training), and FRP (M769) |

# Movement Tracking System (MTS)

**INVESTMENT COMPONENT**

- Modernization
- Recapitalization
- Maintenance

## MISSION

Tracks the location of vehicles and logistics assets, communicates with vehicle operators, and redirects missions on a worldwide, near real-time basis during peacetime operations, operations other than war (natural disasters, homeland security, expeditionary missions), and war.

## DESCRIPTION

The Movement Tracking System (MTS) is the keystone to bringing logistics into the digitized battlefield of the 21st century. The system provides the technology necessary to communicate with and track tactical wheeled vehicles (TWV) and other select Combat Support (CS)/Combat Service Support (CSS) assets and cargo in near real-time, enabling safe and timely completion of distribution missions.

MTS is a non-developmental item (NDI) integrated system consisting of a vehicle mounted mobile unit and a control station. It is used to support missions through the full spectrum of military operations. Through the use of Global Positioning System (GPS), Radio Frequency Identification (RFID), and non-line-of-sight communications and mapping technologies, MTS provides the means for logistics commanders, transportation movement control, and CS/CSS operations sections to exercise assured positive control of assets anywhere in the world through the use of positioning and commercial satellites. Communications between MTS-equipped platforms and their control stations is conducted via text and pre-formatted messages and utilizes commercial satellites that enable units to send and receive traffic over the horizon, anytime, anywhere.

MTS plays a vital role in battlefield distribution operations. It helps to ensure that commanders and logisticians have the right information at the right time. It provides near-real-time data for In-Transit Visibility (ITV) and velocity management of logistics and other Army Combat Support assets, from the sustaining base to the theater of operations. MTS facilitates the rapid movement of supplies through a streamlined distribution system, bypassing routine warehouse/storage functions from the source to the combatant.

Common user logistic transport vehicles and CS/CSS units in the Active and Reserve Components and National Guard will be fitted with MTS systems according to the Army Acquisition Objective or "Good Enough" policy for system distribution. When employed within the distribution system, MTS improves the effectiveness and efficiency of limited distribution assets, provides the ability to identify and reroute supplies to higher priority needs, avoids identified hazards, and informs operators of unit location changes.

Planned enhancements for MTS include embedded equipment diagnostic and prognostic capabilities and two-way situational awareness with maneuver units (Blue Force Tracking).

## SYSTEM INTERDEPENDENCIES

**Other Major Interdependencies**

PM Joint-Automatic Identification Technology (PM J-AIT) In-Transit Visibility (ITV), PD Battle Command Sustainment Support System (BCS3)

## PROGRAM STATUS

- **2QFY10:** Began fielding v5.16 software
- **4QFY10:** Continued developing and testing MTS-ES (Enhanced Software)
- **4QFY10:** Began fielding ISO 18000-7 upgrade (RFID read capability)
- **2QFY11:** MTS follow-on procurement cancelled indefinitely
- **3QFY11:** Transitioned management of program from PEO EIS to PEO C3T

## PROJECTED ACTIVITIES

- **2QFY12:** Field Joint Capabilities Release-Logistics (JCR-Log) software (previously called MTS-ES)
- **1QFY14:** Transition to Joint Battle Command-Platform (Logistics) [JBC-P (Log)] software and BFT-2 transceiver

**ACQUISITION PHASE**

- Technology Development
- Engineering and Manufacturing Development
- Production and Deployment
- Operations and Support

## Movement Tracking System (MTS)

**FOREIGN MILITARY SALES**
None

**CONTRACTORS**
**System Hardware (Military Ruggedized Tablets):**
DRS Technologies (Melbourne, FL)
**System Hardware (transceivers):**
Comtech Mobile Datacom Corporation (CMDC) (Germantown, MD)
**Field Service Support:**
Engineering Solutions and Products Inc. (ESP) (Eatontown, NJ)
**Software v5.16:**
Comtech Mobile Datacom Corporation (CMDC) (Germantown, MD)
**Software JCR-Log:**
Northrop Grumman (Redondo Beach, CA)

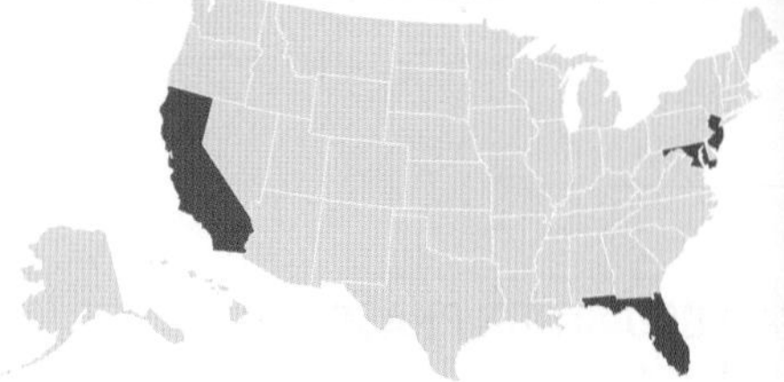

# MQ-1C Gray Eagle Unmanned Aircraft System (UAS)

**INVESTMENT COMPONENT**

- Modernization
- Recapitalization
- Maintenance

## MISSION

Provides combatant commanders a real-time responsive capability to conduct long-dwell, persistent stare, wide-area reconnaissance, surveillance, target acquisition, communications relay, and attack missions.

## DESCRIPTION

The MQ-1C Gray Eagle Unmanned Aircraft System (UAS) addresses the need for a long-endurance, armed (up to four HELLFIRE missiles), unmanned aircraft system that offers greater range, altitude, and payload flexibility.

The Gray Eagle UAS is powered by a heavy fuel engine (HFE) for higher performance, better fuel efficiency, common fuel on the battlefield, and a longer lifetime.

Its specifications include the following:

- **Length:** 28 feet
- **Wingspan:** 56 feet
- **Gross take-off weight:** 3,600 pounds
- **Maximum speed:** 150 knots
- **Ceiling:** 25,000 feet
- **Range:** 2,500 nautical miles via satellite communications (SATCOM)
- **Endurance:** 27+ hours

The Gray Eagle UAS is fielded in company sets, consisting of 12 unmanned aircraft, six One System Ground Control Stations (OGCS), six Ground Data Terminals (GDT), three Portable Ground Control Stations (PGCS), three Portable Ground Data Terminals (PGDT), three Satellite Ground Data Terminals (SGDT), an Automated Take-off and Landing System (ATLS), Light Medium Tactical Vehicles (LMTV), and other ground-support equipment, operated and maintained by a company of 128 Soldiers within the Combat Aviation Brigade.

## SYSTEM INTERDEPENDENCIES

**Other Major Interdependencies**

PM Robotic Unmanned Sensors (PM RUS) provides the electro-optical/infrared (EO/IR) and SAR/GMTI payloads, PM Joint Attack Munition Systems (PM JAMS) provides HELLFIRE missiles, PM Warfighter Information Network-Terrestrial (PM WIN-T) provides communications relay payload

## PROGRAM STATUS

- **Current:** Low-Rate Initial Production

## PROJECTED ACTIVITIES

- **4QFY12:** Initial Operational Test and Evaluation
- **2QFY13:** Full-Rate Production Decision

**ACQUISITION PHASE**

Technology Development | Engineering and Manufacturing Development | **Production and Deployment** | Operations and Support

## MQ-1C Gray Eagle Unmanned Aircraft System (UAS)

**FOREIGN MILITARY SALES**

None

**CONTRACTORS**

**Aircraft:**

General Atomics, Aeronautical Systems Inc. (San Diego, CA)

**Ground Control Station:**

AAI Corp. (Hunt Valley, MD)

**Tactical Common Data Link:**

L-3 Communications (Salt Lake City, UT)

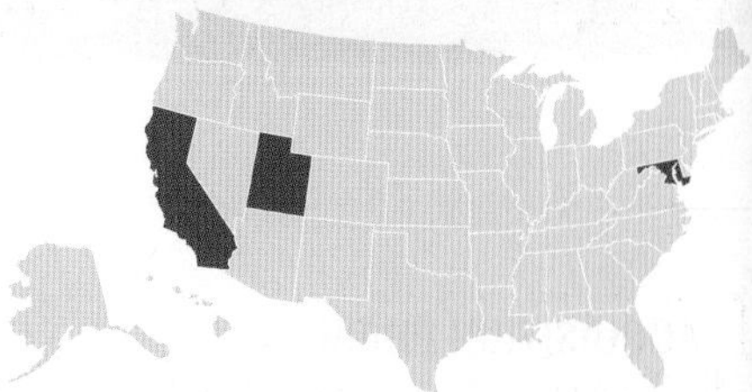

# Multiple Launch Rocket System (MLRS) M270A1

**INVESTMENT COMPONENT**

**Modernization**

Recapitalization

Maintenance

## MISSION

Provides coalition ground forces with highly lethal, responsive, and precise long-range rocket and missile fires that defeat point and area targets in both urban/complex and open terrain with minimal collateral damage, via a highly mobile, responsive multiple launch system.

## DESCRIPTION

The combat-proven Multiple Launch Rocket System (MLRS) M270A1 is a mechanized artillery weapon system that provides the combat commander with round-the-clock, all-weather, lethal, close- and long-range precision rocket and missile fire support for Joint forces, early-entry expeditionary forces, contingency forces, and modular fire brigades supporting Brigade Combat Teams.

The M270A1 is an upgraded version of the M270 launcher. The program entailed the concurrent incorporation of the Improved Fire Control System (IFCS) and the Improved Launcher Mechanical System (ILMS) on a rebuilt M993 Carrier (derivative of the Bradley Fighting Vehicle). With the IFCS, the M270A1 can fire future munitions and the ILMS reduces system load and reload times. The M270A1 provides responsive, highly accurate, and extremely lethal surface-to-surface, close- to long-range rocket and missile fires from 15 kilometers to a depth of 300 kilometers. It carries and fires either two launch pods containing six MLRS rockets each or two Army Tactical Missiles, and is capable of firing all current and future MLRS family of rockets and missiles. It operates with the same MLRS command, control, and communications structure and has the same size crew as the M142 High Mobility Artillery Rocket System (HIMARS).

## SYSTEM INTERDEPENDENCIES

**Other Major Interdependencies**

M993 Bradley derivative chassis

## PROGRAM STATUS

- **1QFY11:** Completed second M270A1 launcher overhaul
- **3QFY11:** Inducted third and fourth M270A1 launchers into overhaul program

## PROJECTED ACTIVITIES

- **Ramp up:** M270A1 launcher overhaul program
- **Continue:** Providing sustainment and support activities for MLRS strategic partners and foreign military sales customers
- **Continue:** Fielding Long-Range Communications, Driver-Vision Enhancement and Blue Force Tracker mods

**ACQUISITION PHASE**

Technology Development | Engineering and Manufacturing Development | Production and Deployment | **Operations and Support**

## Multiple Launch Rocket System (MLRS) M270A1

**FOREIGN MILITARY SALES**

**M270 and M270A1:**
Bahrain, Denmark, Egypt, Finland, France, Germany, Greece, Israel, Italy, Japan, Korea

**M270 and M270B1:**
Norway, Turkey, United Kingdom

**CONTRACTORS**

**Prime and Launcher:**
Lockheed Martin (Dallas, TX; Camden, AR)

**Chassis:**
BAE Systems (York, PA)

**Improved Weapons Interface Unit:**
Harris Corp. (Melbourne, FL)

**Position Navigation Unit:**
L-3 Communications Space & Navigation (Budd Lake, NJ)

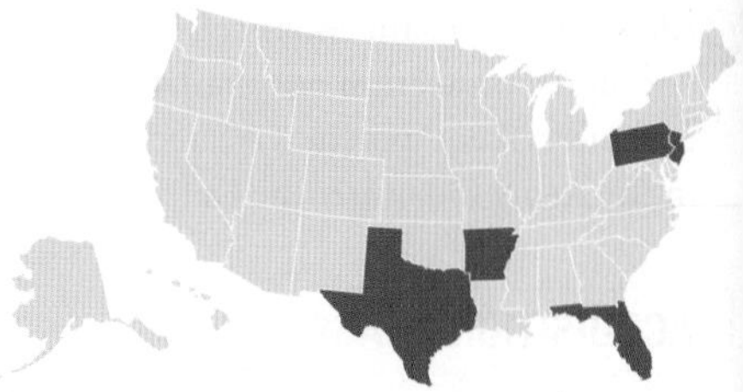

# NAVSTAR Global Positioning System (GPS)

**INVESTMENT COMPONENT**

- Modernization
- Recapitalization
- Maintenance

## MISSION

Provides real-time positioning, navigation, and timing data to tactical and strategic organizations.

## DESCRIPTION

The NAVSTAR Global Positioning System (GPS) is a space-based, Joint-service program led by the Air Force, which distributes positioning, navigation and timing (PNT) data to tactical and strategic organizations. The GPS has three segments: a space segment (nominally 24 satellites), a ground control segment, and a user equipment segment. User equipment consists of receivers configured for handheld, ground, aircraft, and watercraft applications. Military GPS receivers use the Precise Positioning Service (PPS) signal to gain enhanced accuracy and signal protection not available to commercial equipment. GPS receivers in the Army today are: the Defense Advanced GPS Receiver (DAGR), with more than 168,000 as handheld receivers and 128,000 distributed for platform installations for a total of nearly 300,000 DAGRs fielded; the Precision Lightweight GPS Receiver (PLGR), with more than 40,000 in handheld, installed, and integrated applications. In addition, GPS user equipment includes a Ground-Based GPS Receiver Applications Module (GB-GRAM). Over 95,000 GB-GRAMs have been procured and provide embedded PPS capability to a variety of weapon systems. The Army represents more than 80 percent of the requirement for user equipment.

**DAGR:**

- **Size:** 6.37 x 3.4 x 1.56 inches
- **Weight:** 1 pound; fits in a two-clip carrying case that attaches to load-bearing equipment
- **Frequency:** Dual (L1/L2)
- **Battery Life:** 19 hours (4 AA batteries)
- **Security:** Selective availability anti-spoofing module
- **Satellites:** All-in-view

**GB-GRAM:**

- **Size:** 0.6 x 2.45 x 3.4 inches
- **Weight:** 3.5 ounces
- **Frequency:** Dual (L1/L2)
- **Security:** Selective availability anti-spoofing module
- **Satellites:** All-in-view

## SYSTEM INTERDEPENDENCIES

**In this Publication**

PATRIOT PAC-3, Excalibur (M982), Paladin/Field Artillery Ammunition Support Vehicle (FAASV), Force XXI Battle Command Brigade and Below (FBCB2)

**Other Major Interdependencies**

Blue Force Tracking, mobile ballistic computers, laser rangefinders, movement tracking systems, and several unmanned aerial vehicle systems

## PROGRAM STATUS

- **1QFY11-4QFY11:** Continue DAGR fieldings and training for Army components
- **1QFY11-4QFY11:** DAGR designated as an ACAT II program

## PROJECTED ACTIVITIES

- **2QFY12-4QFY14:** Continue DAGR fieldings and training, including introduction of DAGR Selective Availability Anti-Spoofing Module (SAASM) version 3.7 and GB-GRAM SAASM version 3.7
- **2QFY12-4QFY14:** Continue Materiel Solution Analysis Phase for Tactical Assured Global Positioning System (GPS) Regional (TAGR) for GPS augmentation
- **2QFY12-4QFY14:** Military GPS User Equipment (MGUE) development

**ACQUISITION PHASE**

- Technology Development
- Engineering and Manufacturing Development
- Production and Deployment
- Operations and Support

## NAVSTAR Global Positioning System (GPS)

**FOREIGN MILITARY SALES**

PPS-capable GPS receivers have been sold to 41 authorized countries

**CONTRACTORS**

**DAGR/GB-GRAM Acquisition and PLGR Support:**

Rockwell Collins (Cedar Rapids, IA)

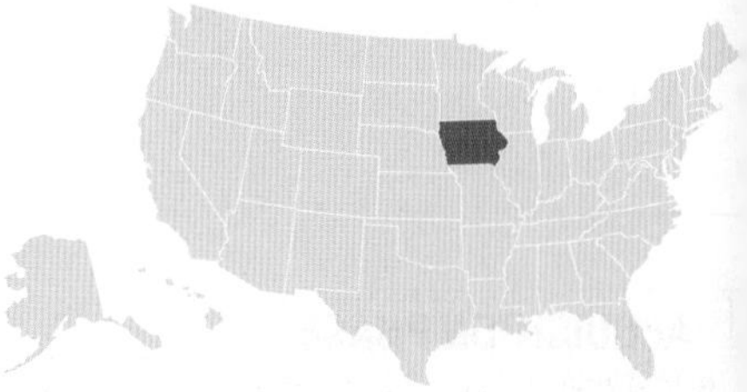

# Nett Warrior (NW)

**INVESTMENT COMPONENT**

- Modernization
- Recapitalization
- Maintenance

## MISSION

Provides overmatch operational capabilities to all ground combat Soldiers and small unit operations.

## DESCRIPTION

The Nett Warrior (NW) is an integrated dismounted leader situational awareness (SA) system for use during combat operations. The system provides unparalleled SA to the dismounted leader, allowing for faster and more accurate decisions in the tactical fight. With advanced navigation, SA, and information sharing capabilities, leaders are able to avoid fratricide and are more effective and more lethal in the execution of their combat missions.

The NW program focuses on the development of the SA system, which has the ability to graphically display the location of an individual leader's location on a digital geo-referenced map image. Additional Soldier and leader locations are also displayed on the hands-free digital display. NW is connected through a secure radio that will send and receive information from one NW to another, thus connecting the dismounted leader to the network. These radios will also connect the equipped leader to higher echelon data and information products to assist in decision making and situational understanding. Soldier position location information will be added to the network via interoperability with the Army's Rifleman Radio capability. All of this will allow the leader to easily see, understand, and interact in the method that best suits the user and the particular mission. NW will employ a system-of-systems approach, optimizing and integrating capabilities while reducing the Soldier's combat load and logistical footprint.

## SYSTEM INTERDEPENDENCIES

**Other Major Interdependencies**

Battle Command Product Line, Core Soldier System equipment, Joint Tactical Radio System Rifleman Radio

## PROGRAM STATUS

- **4QFY10-1QFY11:** Limited User Tests (three)

## PROJECTED ACTIVITIES

- **1QFY12:** Milestone C; RFP Release
- **2QFY12:** Low-Rate Initial Production Contract Award
- **3QFY12-4QFY13:** Low-Rate Initial Production

**ACQUISITION PHASE**

Technology Development | Engineering and Manufacturing Development | Production and Deployment | Operations and Support

## Nett Warrior (NW)

**FOREIGN MILITARY SALES**
To be determined

**CONTRACTORS**
General Dynamics (Scottsdale, AZ)
Raytheon (Plano, TX)
Rockwell Collins (Cedar Rapids, IA)

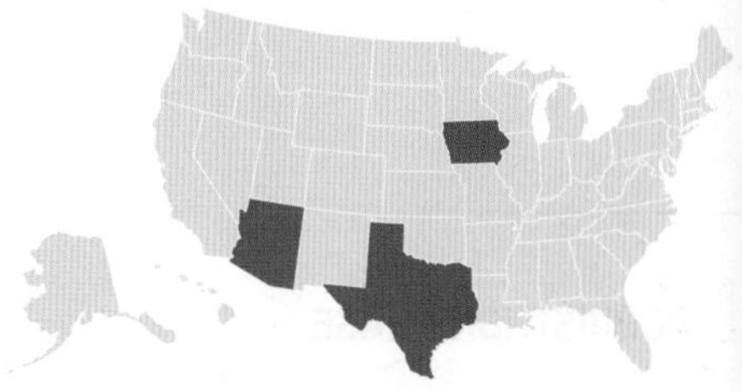

# Night Vision Thermal Systems-Thermal Weapon Sight (TWS)

**INVESTMENT COMPONENT**

Modernization

Recapitalization

Maintenance

## MISSION

Enables the Soldier to detect and engage targets, day or night, in all weather and visibility-obscured conditions.

## DESCRIPTION

The Night Vision Thermal Systems-Thermal Weapon Sight (TWS) family is a group of advanced infrared devices that can be both weapon mounted or used in an observation mode. The AN/PAS-13 TWS gives Soldiers with individual and crew served weapons the capability to see deep into the battlefield, increase surveillance and target acquisition range, and penetrate obscurants, day or night. The TWS systems use uncooled, forward-looking infrared technology and provide a standard video output for training, image transfer, or remote viewing. TWS systems are lightweight and mountable to a weapon rail. They operate to the maximum effective range of the weapon.

The TWS family comprises three variants, each of which is silent, lightweight, compact, durable, and battery-powered. They include:

- AN/PAS-13(V)1 Light Weapon Thermal Sight (LWTS) for the M16 and M4 series rifles and carbines, as well as the M136 Light Anti-Armor Weapon
  **Weight:** 1.9 pounds
  **Field of view:** 18 degrees
  **Operational time:** 7 hours
  **Power:** Four lithium AA batteries

- AN/PAS-13(V)2 Medium Weapon Thermal Sight (MWTS) for the M249 Squad Automatic Weapon and M240B series medium machine guns
  **Weight:** 2.8 pounds
  **Field of view:** 6 degrees/18 degrees (narrow/wide)
  **Operational time:** 7 hours
  **Power:** Six lithium AA batteries

- AN/PAS-13(V)3 Heavy Weapon Thermal Sight (HWTS) for the squad leader's weapon M16 and M4 series rifles and carbines, M24 and M107 sniper rifles, and M2 HB and MK19 machine guns
  **Weight:** 3.9 pounds
  **Field of view:** 3 degrees/9 degrees (narrow/wide)
  **Operational time:** 7 hours
  **Power:** Six lithium AA batteries

## SYSTEM INTERDEPENDENCIES

None

## PROGRAM STATUS

- **FY11:** Fielded to units supporting Operation Enduring Freedom and Operation New Dawn
- **FY11:** Completed 17 micron technology validation testing; 17 micron technology allows production of a LWTS clip-on and reduces power and weight in the MWTS and HWTS

## PROJECTED ACTIVITIES

- **FY12:** Continue to support and field in accordance with Headquarters Department of the Army G8 guidance; begin procurement of 17 micron TWS
- **FY13:** TWS III contract award (17 micron)

**ACQUISITION PHASE**

Technology Development | Engineering and Manufacturing Development | Production and Deployment | Operations and Support

## Night Vision Thermal Systems-Thermal Weapon Sight (TWS)

**FOREIGN MILITARY SALES**
Deputy Assistant Secretary of the Army Defense Exports and Cooperation (DASA DE&C)

**CONTRACTORS**
BAE Systems (Lexington, MA; Manchester, NH; Austin, TX; Manassas VA)
DRS Optronics (Dallas, TX; Melbourne, FL)
Raytheon (Dallas, TX; Goleta, CA; McKinney, TX)

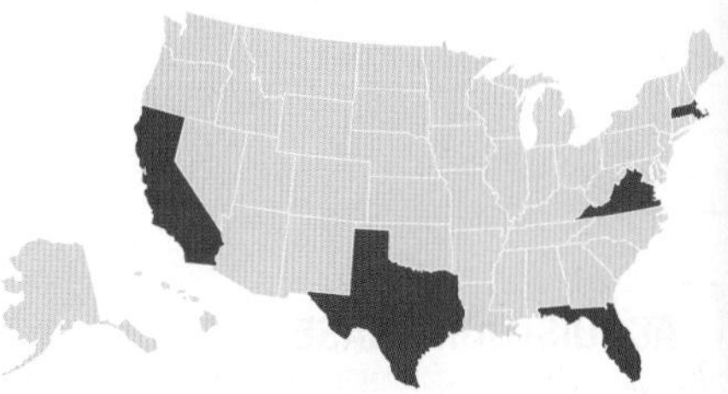

# Non-Intrusive Inspection Systems (NIIS)

INVESTMENT COMPONENT

Modernization

Recapitalization

Maintenance

## MISSION

Protects U.S. forces and critical warfighting materiel by inspecting cars, trucks, or cargo containers for the presence of explosives, weapons, drugs, or other contraband with nuclear (gamma) and X-ray technology.

## DESCRIPTION

The Non-Intrusive Inspection Systems (NIIS) program consists of commercial off-the-shelf (COTS) products that are employed within a layered force protection system that includes security personnel trained to maintain situational awareness aided by a range of other products including military working dogs, under-vehicle scanning mirrors, and handheld or desktop trace explosive detectors.

NIIS currently include a variety of products with differing characteristics that are added to the Army commander's "tool box." They include mobile, rail-mounted, but re-locatable, and fixed-site characteristics. The primary systems employed are as follows:

- The **Mobile Vehicle and Cargo Inspection System** (**MVACIS**) is a truck-mounted system that utilizes a nuclear source that can penetrate approximately 6.5 inches of steel.
- The **Re-locatable Vehicle and Cargo Inspection System** (**RVACIS**) is a rail-mounted system that utilizes the same nuclear source as the MVACIS. It operates on rails and is employed in static locations or moved within 24 hours to locations where prepared use of the rail system eliminates the requirement to maintain a truck platform.
- The **Militarized Mobile VACIS** (**MMVACIS**) uses the same gamma source as the other VACIS products but is mounted on a High Mobility Multipurpose Wheeled Vehicle.
- The **Z-Backscatter Van** (**ZBV**) is a van-mounted system that utilizes backscatter X-ray technology. It penetrates only approximately one-quarter inch of steel and can be employed in static locations where room is limited.
- The **BVMT** is a mobile inspection system for vehicles and cargo that uses the same backscatter X-ray technology as the ZBV. The BVMT trailer contains the X-Ray source and backscatter detectors while the Forward scatter trailer contains the forward scatter detectors.
- **Personnel Scanners** utilize Backscatter X-ray technology to non-intrusively scan people for the presence of explosives, weapons, or other contraband and are American National Standards Institute compliant. Depending on the model, these systems can scan between 140-240 people per hour.
- The **T-10 Trailer** is a high-energy gantry vehicle and cargo scanner and uses a 1 MeV Liner Accelerator that penetrates up to four inches of steel while scanning.

## SYSTEM INTERDEPENDENCIES

None

## PROGRAM STATUS

- Fielded 31 BVMT
- Fielded 154 Personnel Scanners
- Delivered One HE T-10 Trailer

## PROJECTED ACTIVITIES

- **2QFY12:** Program Management support; preparing documentation for a contract on replacement of 29 older systems that have reached their useful life and do not provide stand-off capabilities

ACQUISITION PHASE

Technology Development | Engineering and Manufacturing Development | Production and Deployment | Operations and Support

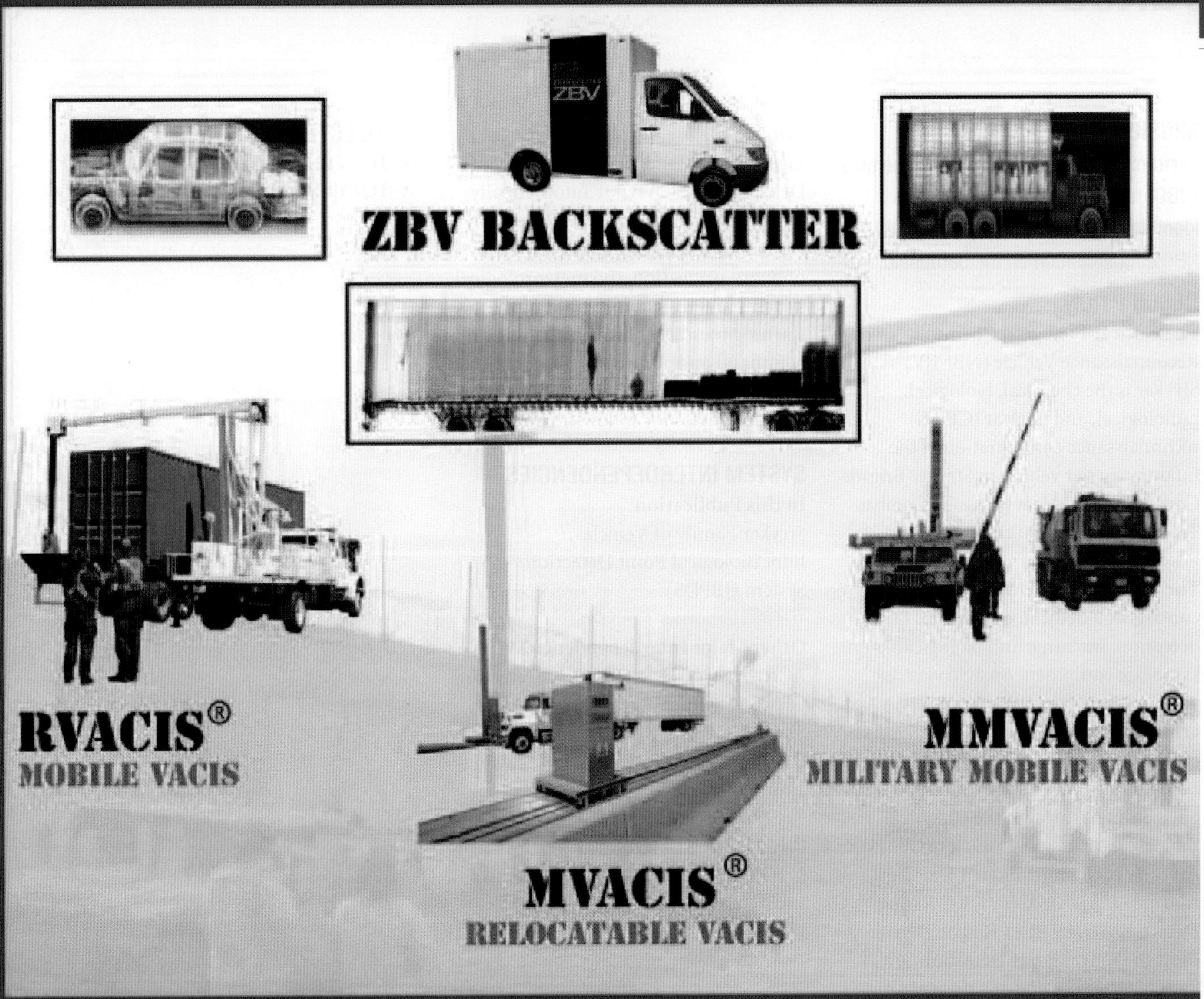


## Non-Intrusive Inspection Systems (NIIS)

**FOREIGN MILITARY SALES**
None

**CONTRACTORS**
American Science & Engineering Inc. (Billerica, MA)
Rapiscan Systems (Torrance, CA)
Science Applications International Corp. (SAIC) (San Diego, CA)

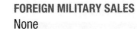

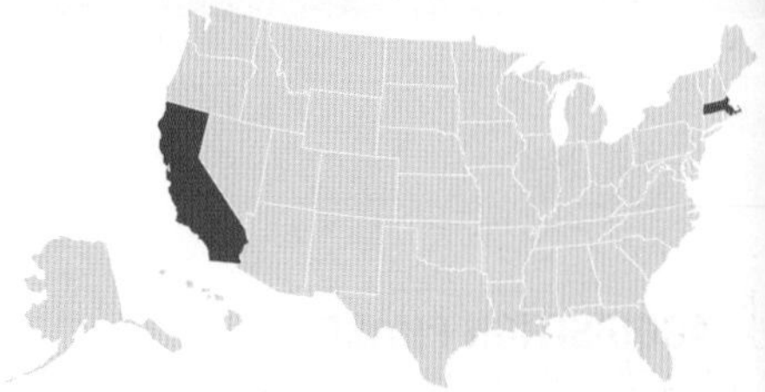

# Nuclear Biological Chemical Reconnaissance Vehicle (NBCRV)-Stryker Sensor Suites

INVESTMENT COMPONENT

Modernization

Recapitalization

Maintenance

## MISSION

Performs nuclear, biological, and chemical (NBC) reconnaissance and locates, identifies, marks, samples, and reports NBC contamination on the battlefield.

## DESCRIPTION

The Nuclear Biological Chemical Reconnaissance Vehicle (NBCRV)-Stryker is the chemical, biological, radiological, and nuclear (CBRN) reconnaissance configuration of the infantry carrier vehicle in Stryker Brigade Combat Teams, Heavy Brigade Combat Teams, and chemical companies.

The NBCRV-Stryker Sensor Suite consists of a dedicated system of CBRN detection, warning, and biological-sampling equipment on a Stryker vehicle (high speed, high mobility, armored carrier). The NBCRV detects chemical, radiological, and biological contamination in its immediate environment through the Chemical Biological Mass Spectrometer (CBMS), Automatic Chemical Agent Detector Alarm (ACADA), AN/VDR-2 Radiac Detector, AN/UDR-13 Radiac Detector, Joint Biological Point Detection System (JBPDS), and at a distance, through the use of the Joint Service Lightweight Standoff Chemical Agent Detector (JSLSCAD). It automatically integrates contamination information from detectors with input from onboard navigation and meteorological systems and transmits digital NBC warning messages through the vehicle's command and control equipment to warn follow-on forces. NBCRV can collect samples for follow-on analysis.

## SYSTEM INTERDEPENDENCIES

**In this Publication**

Stryker Family of Vehicles,
Joint Biological Point Detection System (JBPDS)

**Other Major Interdependencies**

ACADA, AN/UDR-13 Radiac Detector, CBMS, Chemical Vapor Sampler System (CVSS), JSLSCAD, Nuclear Biological Chemical Sensor Processing Group (NBCSPG)

## PROGRAM STATUS

- **1QFY11-2QFY11:** NBCRV Platform Operational Testing
- **3QFY11:** Platform Live Fire Testing

## PROJECTED ACTIVITIES

- **1QFY12:** Full-Rate Production
- **1QFY12:** Full Materiel Release

ACQUISITION PHASE

Technology Development | Engineering and Manufacturing Development | Production and Deployment | Operations and Support

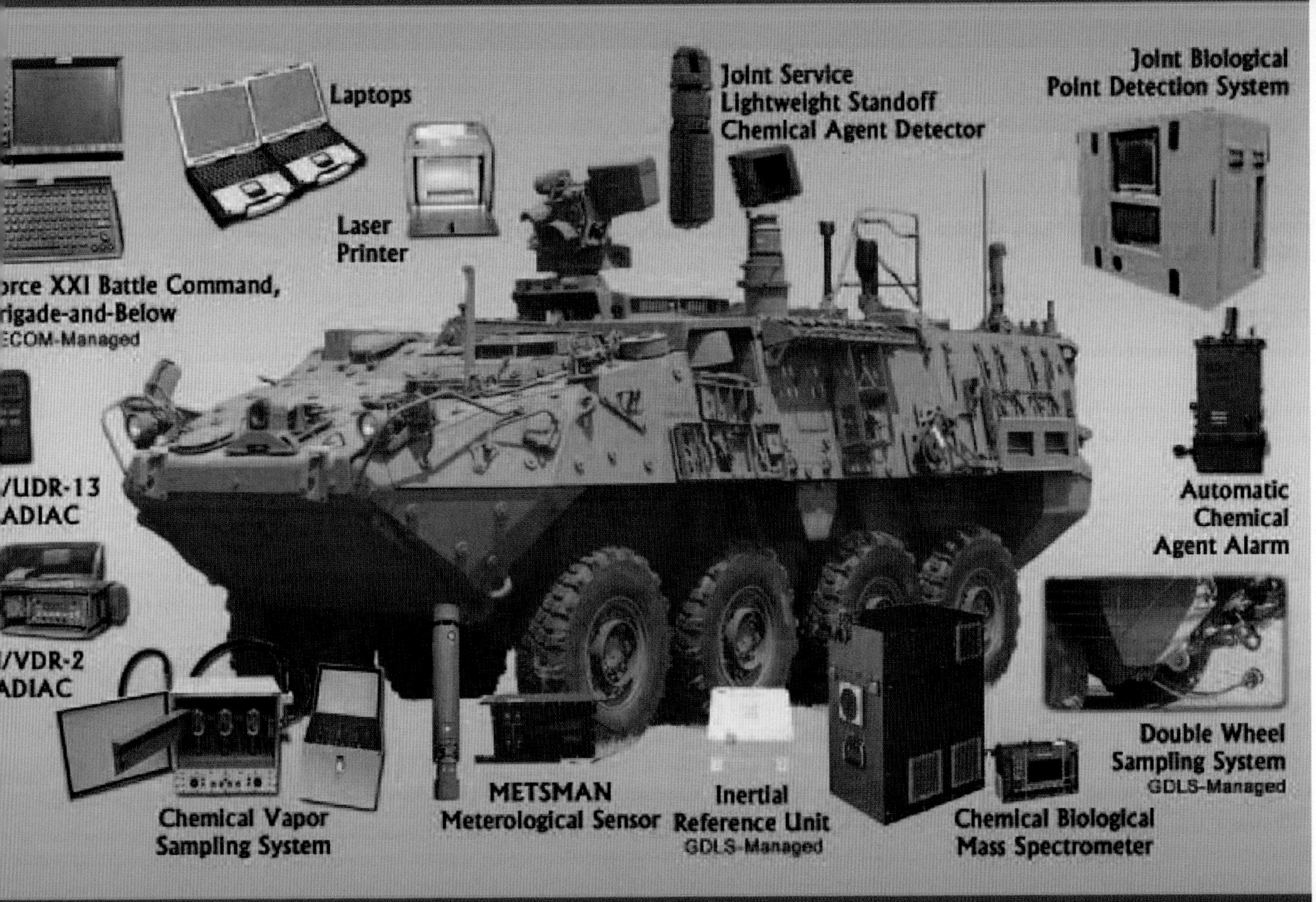


## Nuclear Biological Chemical Reconnaissance Vehicle (NBCRV)-Stryker Sensor Suites

**FOREIGN MILITARY SALES**
None

**CONTRACTORS**

**Prime Vehicle:**
General Dynamics Land Systems (Sterling Heights, MI)

**Sensor Software Integrator:**
CACI Technologies (Manassas, VA)

# One Semi-Automated Force (OneSAF)

## INVESTMENT COMPONENT

Modernization

Recapitalization

Maintenance

## MISSION

Provides simulation software that supports constructive and virtual training, computer-generated forces, and mission rehearsal designed for brigade-and-below, combat, and non-combat operations.

## DESCRIPTION

One Semi-Automated Forces (OneSAF) is a next generation, entity-level simulation that supports both computer-generated forces and Semi-Automated Forces applications. This enables it to support a wide range of Army brigade-and-below constructive simulations and virtual simulators.

OneSAF is currently being integrated by the Synthetic Environment Core program as the replacement SAF for virtual trainers such as the Aviation Combined Arms Tactical Trainer and the Close Combat Tactical Trainer. OneSAF will serve as the basis for subsequent modernization activities for simulators across the Army. OneSAF was designed to represent the modular and Future Force and provides entities, units, and behaviors across the spectrum of military operations in the contemporary operating environment. OneSAF has been crafted to be uniquely capable of simulating aspects of the contemporary operating environment and its effects on simulated activities and behaviors. OneSAF is unique in its ability to model unit behaviors from fire team to company level for all units — both combat and non-combat operations. Intelligent, doctrinally correct behaviors and improved graphical user interfaces are provided to increase the span of control for workstation operators.

OneSAF represents a full range of operations, systems, and control processes in support of simulation applications applied to advanced concepts and requirements; research, development, and acquisition; and training, exercise, and military operations. OneSAF is designed to meet the constructive training challenges presented by transformation. With a full range of Warfighter functional area representations, OneSAF displays a high fidelity environmental representation. OneSAF is a cross-domain simulation suitable for supporting training, analysis, research, experimentation, mission-planning, and rehearsal activities. It provides the latest physics-based modeling and data, enhanced data collection, and reporting capabilities.

Interoperability support is present for industry standards such as Distributed Interactive Simulation, High Level Architecture, Military Scenario Development Language, Joint Consultation Command and Control Information Exchange Data Model, and Army Battle Command System devices.

## SYSTEM INTERDEPENDENCIES

**Other Major Interdependencies**

OneSAF provides required capabilities for SE Core

## PROGRAM STATUS

- **2QFY11:** OneSAF version 5.1 released
- **4QFY11:** OneSAF version 5.0 (International) released

## PROJECTED ACTIVITIES

- **2QFY12:** Release OneSAF version 5.1.1

## ACQUISITION PHASE

Technology Development | Engineering and Manufacturing Development | Production and Deployment | Operations and Support

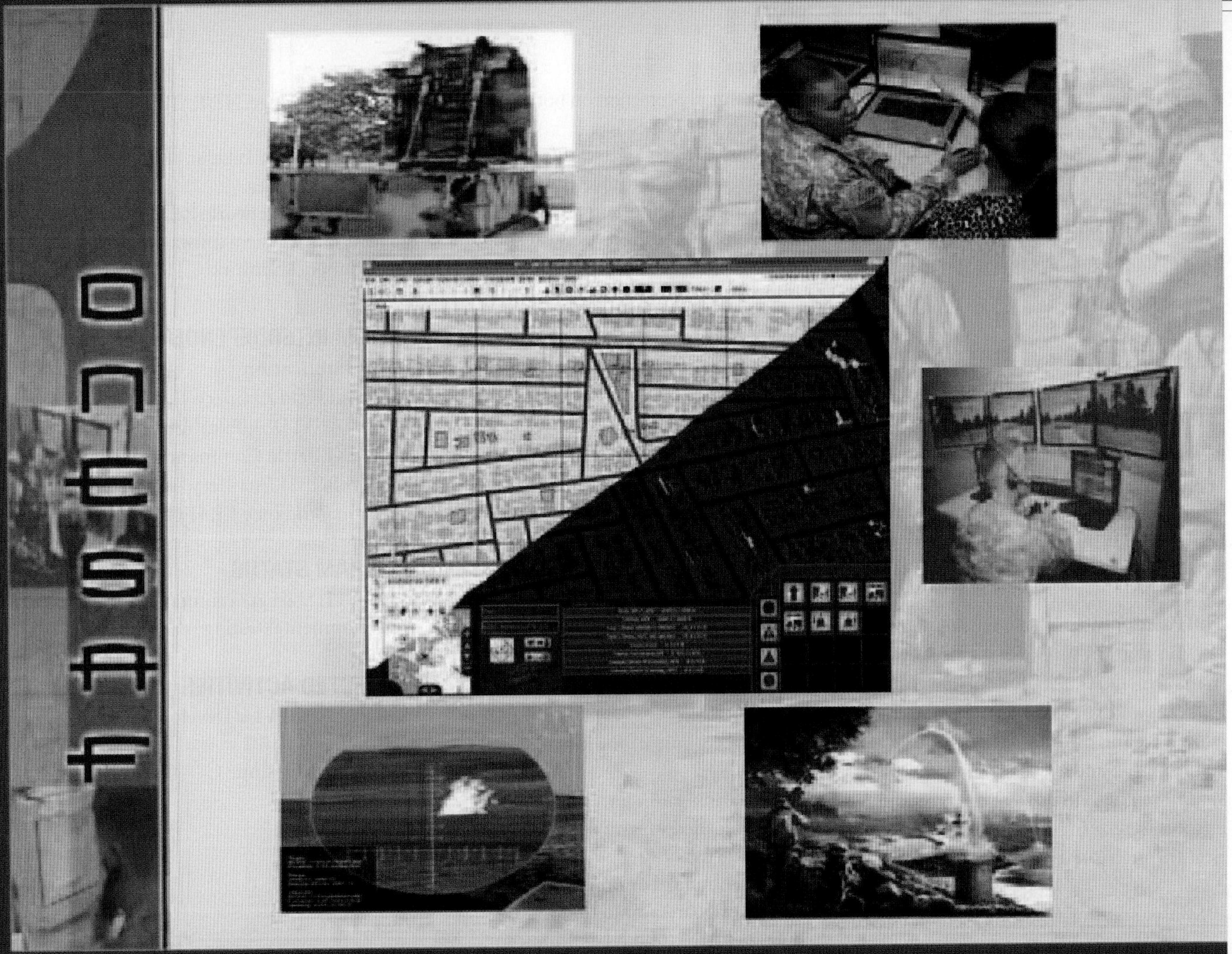


## One Semi-Automated Force (OneSAF)

**FOREIGN MILITARY SALES**
Australia, Bahrain, Canada, Czech Republic, Egypt, New Zealand, South Korea, United Kingdom

**CONTRACTORS**
To be determined

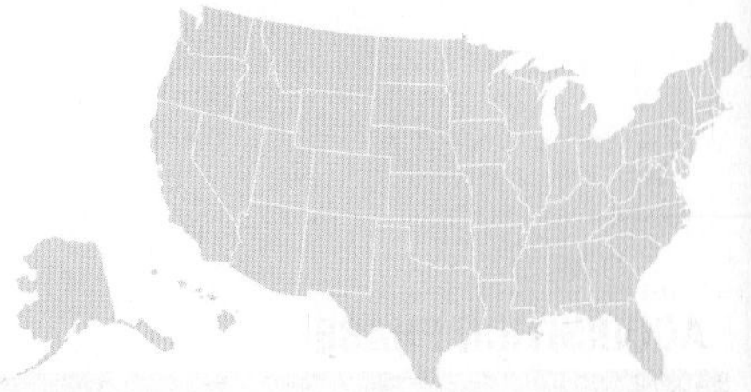

# Paladin/Field Artillery Ammunition Supply Vehicle (FAASV)

INVESTMENT COMPONENT

Modernization

Recapitalization

Maintenance

## MISSION

Provides the primary indirect fire support for modular Heavy Brigade Combat Teams and armored and mechanized infantry divisions, as well as an armored ammunition resupply vehicle in support of the Paladin.

## DESCRIPTION

The M109A6 (Paladin) 155mm Howitzer is the most technologically advanced self-propelled cannon system in the Army. The Field Artillery Ammunition Supply Vehicle (FAASV) provides an armored ammunition resupply vehicle in support of the Paladin.

The Paladin Integrated Management (PIM) program supports the fleet management strategy for current Paladins and FAASVs by providing a low-risk and affordable life-cycle solution that addresses obsolescence, space, weight, and power concerns and ensures long-term sustainment of the fleet through 2050.

PIM uses state-of-the art components to improve:

- **Survivability:** "Shoot and scoot" tactics; improved ballistic and nuclear, biological, and chemical protection on both the Howitzer and FAASV
- **Responsive fires:** Capable of firing within 45 seconds from a complete stop with onboard communications, remote travel lock, automated cannon slew capability, and pivot steer technology
- **Improved survivability:** New chassis structure and armoring provisions are built in.
- **Extended range:** 30 kilometers with high-explosive (HE), Rocket-Assisted Projectile (RAP) and Excalibur Projectiles using M203 or M232/M232A1 MACS propellant
- **Increased commonality and reliability:** Through Bradley common powertrain, track, and suspension components
- **Non-line-of-sight cannon technology:** Common electric elevation/traverse drives gun system and electric rammer are included

Other PIM specifications include the following:

- **Crew:** Paladin, four; FAASV, five
- **Combat loaded weight:** Paladin, 37 tons; FAASV, 28 tons
- **Paladin onboard ammo:** 39 rounds
- **FAASV onboard ammo:** 95 rounds
- **Rates of fire:** 4 rounds per minute for first 3 minutes maximum; 1 round per minute sustained
- **Maximum range:** HE/RAP, 22/30 kilometers
- **Cruising range:** Paladin, 180 miles; FAASV, 180 miles
- **Fire Support Network:** Paladin Digital Fire Control System software supports Fire Support Network

## SYSTEM INTERDEPENDENCIES

**In this Publication**

Advanced Field Artillery Tactical Data System (AFATDS), Excalibur (M982), Force XXI Battle Command Brigade and Below (FBCB2), Artillery Ammunition, Precision Guidance Kit (PGK)

## PROGRAM STATUS

- **3QFY11:** Start government developmental testing

## PROJECTED ACTIVITIES

- **3QFY11-3QFY14:** Developmental testing
- **3QFY13:** Milestone C

ACQUISITION PHASE

Technology Development | Engineering and Manufacturing Development | Production and Deployment | Operations and Support

## Paladin/Field Artillery Ammunition Supply Vehicle (FAASV)

**FOREIGN MILITARY SALES**
None

**CONTRACTORS**

**PIM Development:**
BAE Systems (York, PA)

**PIM SW Support/FATB/Matrix Support:**
Armaments R&D Center (Picatinny Arsenal, NJ)

**Program Management Support:**
Tank-Automotive and Armaments Command (TACOM) (Warren, MI)

**Testing:**
Yuma Proving Ground (Yuma, AZ)
Aberdeen Test Center (Aberdeen Proving Ground, MD)

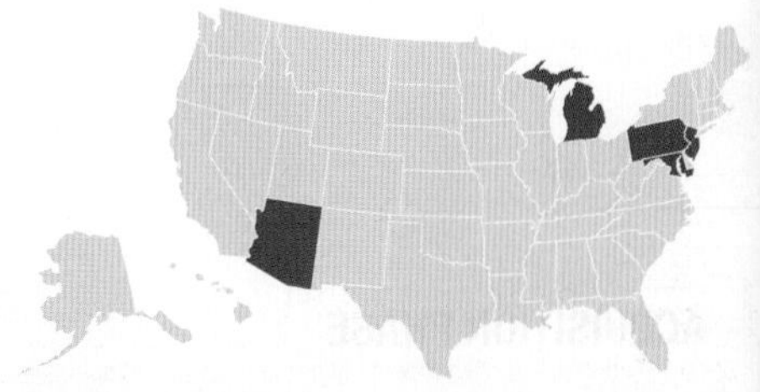

# Palletized Load System (PLS) and PLS Extended Service Program (ESP)

INVESTMENT COMPONENT

Modernization

Recapitalization

Maintenance

## MISSION

Supports combat units by performing cross-country movement of configured loads of ammunition and other classes of supply loaded on flat racks or in containers.

## DESCRIPTION

The Palletized Load System (PLS) is a 10-wheel-drive (10x10), multidrive truck with 16.5 ton capacity that provides the timely delivery of a high tonnage of ammunition, unit equipment, International Organization for Standardization (ISO) containers/shelters, and all classes of supply to using units and weapon systems as far forward in the maneuver battalion area as the tactical situation allows. The PLS consists of the PLS truck, PLS trailer (PLS-T), and demountable flat racks. The PLS truck is a 10x10 prime mover with an integral onboard load handling system that provides self-loading and unloading capability.

There are two PLS truck variants, the basic PLS truck (M1075) and the PLS truck with material handling crane (M1074). The system also includes the PLS trailer (M1076) container handling unit for transporting 20-foot ISO containers, the M3/M3A1 Container Roll-in/Out Platform, and the M1/M1077A1 flat racks. The PLS has the ability to operate with a degree of mobility commensurate with the supported weapon systems, to facilitate the fighting capabilities of the supported systems and units.

The PLSA1 model began fielding in 2011. It incorporates independent front suspension, a new C-15 engine, the Allison 4500 transmission, J-1939 data-bus, and a cab that will be common with the HEMTTA4, and it is long-term armor strategy compliant.

The PLS Extended Service Program (ESP) is a recapitalization program that converts high-mileage base PLS trucks to 0 miles/0 hours and to the current A1 production configurations. The trucks are disassembled and rebuilt with improved technology such as an electronically controlled engine, electronic transmission, air ride seats, four-point seatbelts, bolt-together wheels, increased corrosion protection, enhanced electrical package, and independent front suspension on the A1.

## SYSTEM INTERDEPENDENCIES

None

## PROGRAM STATUS

- **Current:** To date, fielded approximately 6,000 PLS trucks and 13,000 PLS trailers

## PROJECTED ACTIVITIES

- **FY10:** PLSA1 type classification/materiel release
- **FY11:** PLSA1 first unit equipped
- **FY12:** PLSA0 RECAP begins

ACQUISITION PHASE

Technology Development | Engineering and Manufacturing Development | Production and Deployment | Operations and Support

## Palletized Load System (PLS) and PLS Extended Service Program (ESP)

| | PLS | PLSA1 |
|---|---|---|
| **ENGINE** | DDC 8V92 - 500 horsepower | CAT C-15 - 600 hp @ 2100 RPM |
| **TRANSMISSION** | Allison CLT-755 - 5 Speed | Allison HD 4500 - 6 Speed |
| **TRANSFER CASE** | Oshkosh 55,000 - 2 Speed | New Oshkosh - 2 Speed |
| **AXLES FRONT: TANDEM** | Rockwell SVI 5MR | Oshkosh / Rockwell |
| **SUSPENSION: FRONT TANDEM** | Hendrickson RT-340 - Walking Beam | Oshkosh TAK-4TM Steel Spring |
| **AXLES: REAR TRIDEM** | Rockwell SVI 5MR | Rockwell SVI 5MR |
| **SUSPENSION - AXLE #3** | Hendrickson-Turner Air Ride | Hendrickson-Turner Air Ride |
| **SUSPENSION - AXLES #4 & #5** | Hendrickson RT-400 - Walking Beam | Hendrickson RT-400 - Walking Beam |
| **WHEEL ENDS** | Rockwell | Rockwell |
| **CONTROL ARMS** | N/A | Standard MTVR on Front Tandem |
| **STEERING GEARS - FRONT** | 492 Master / M110 Slave | M110 Master / M110 Slave |
| **STEERING GEARS - REAR** | 492 | M110 |
| **FRAME RAILS** | 14 inch | 14 inch |
| **CAB** | PLS | Common Cab |
| **RADIATOR** | PLS - Roof Mount | PLSA1 - Side Mount |
| **MUFFLER** | PLS | PLSA1 - New |
| **AIR CLEANER** | United Air | United Air |
| **LHS** | Multilift MK V | Multilift MK V |
| **CRANE** | Grove | Grove |
| **TIRES** | Michelin 16.00 R20 XZLT | Michelin 16.00 R20 XZLT |
| **SPARE TIRE** | 1 - Side Mounted | 1 - Roof Mounted |
| **CTI** | CM Automotive | Dana |
| **AIR COMPRESSOR** | 1400 Bendix | 922 Bendix |
| **STARTER** | Prestolite | Prestolite |
| **ALTERNATOR** | 12/24V | 24V - 260 Amp Niehoff |

**FOREIGN MILITARY SALES**
Israel, Jordan, Turkey

**CONTRACTORS**
**Prime:**
Oshkosh Corp. (Oshkosh, WI)
**Engine:**
Detroit Diesel (Emporia, KS; Redford, MI)
Caterpillar C-15 (Peoria, IL)
**Transmission:**
Allison Transmission (Indianapolis, IN)
**Tires:**
Michelin (Greenville, SC)

# PATRIOT Advanced Capability-Three (PAC-3)

**INVESTMENT COMPONENT**

- Modernization
- Recapitalization
- Maintenance

## MISSION

Protects ground forces and critical assets at all echelons from advanced aircraft, cruise missiles, and tactical ballistic missiles.

## DESCRIPTION

The PATRIOT Advanced Capability-Three (PAC-3) program is an air-defense, guided missile system with long-range, medium- to high-altitude, all-weather capabilities designed to counter tactical ballistic missiles (TBMs), cruise missiles, and advanced aircraft. The combat element of the PATRIOT missile system is the fire unit, which consists of a phased array radar set (RS), an engagement control station (ECS), a battery command post, an electric power plant, an antenna mast group, a communications relay group, and launching stations (LS) with missiles.

The RS provides the tactical functions of airspace surveillance, target detection, identification, classification, tracking, missile guidance, and engagement support. The ECS provides command and control. Depending upon configuration, the LS provides the platform for PAC-2 or PAC-3 missiles, which are sealed in canisters that serve as shipping containers and launch tubes.

The PAC-3 primary mission is to kill maneuvering TBMs and counter advanced cruise missile and aircraft threats. The PAC-3 missile uses hit-to-kill technology for greater lethality against TBMs armed with weapons of mass destruction. The PAC-3 system upgrades have provided improvements that increase performance against evolving threats, meet user requirements, and enhance Joint interoperability. PATRIOT's fast-reaction capability, high firepower, ability to track numerous targets simultaneously, and ability to operate in a severe electronic countermeasure environment make it the Army's premier air defense system. The PAC-3 Missile Segment Enhancement (MSE), currently in development, is planned to be used with the PAC-3 system and is the baseline interceptor for the Medium Extended Air Defense System.

## SYSTEM INTERDEPENDENCIES

**Other Major Interdependencies**

ABMOC, AEGIS, AMDTF, AOC, AWACS, CRC, HAWKEYE, PEO Integration, P/M CAP, RIVET-JOINT, SHORAD, TACC, TAOC, THAAD

## PROGRAM STATUS

- **1QFY09:** Post deployment build-6.5 (PDB-6.5) development, test, and evaluation

## PROJECTED ACTIVITIES

- **3QFY11-3QFY13:** Missile Segment Enhancement (MSE) Developmental and Operational Testing
- **3QFY12:** PDB-7
- **4QFY15:** MSE fielding begins

**ACQUISITION PHASE**

- Technology Development
- Engineering and Manufacturing Development
- Production and Deployment
- Operations and Support

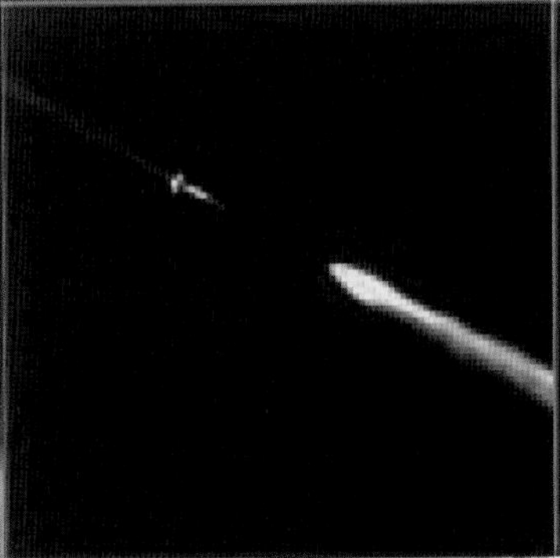
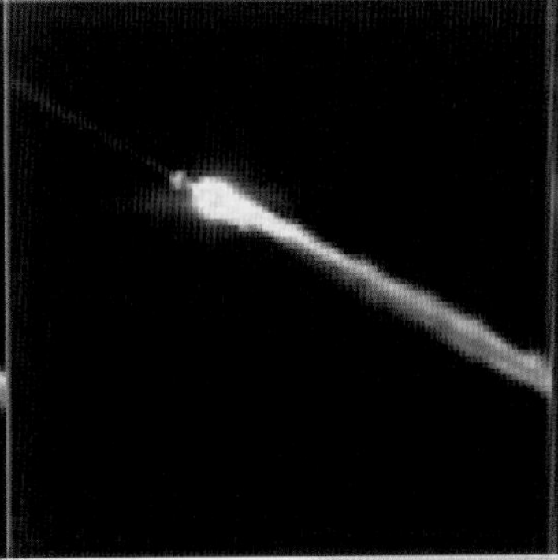
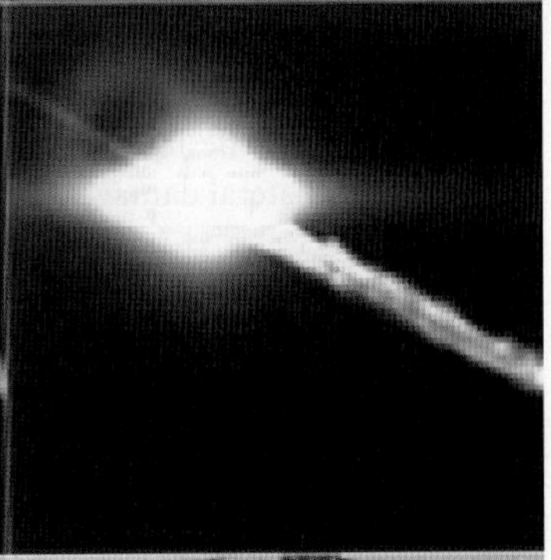

## PATRIOT Advanced Capability-Three (PAC-3)

**FOREIGN MILITARY SALES**
Germany, Japan, Netherlands, Taiwan, United Arab Emirates

**CONTRACTORS**
**Missile Program Management Team:** Lockheed Martin (Dallas, TX)
**Seeker Program Management Team:** Boeing (Anaheim, CA)
**Mods:** Raytheon (Tewksbury, MA; Long Beach, CA)
**Seeker Manufacturing/RFDL:** Lockheed Martin Missiles and Fire Control (Chelmsford, MA)
**ELES:** Lockheed Martin (Lufkin, TX)
**System Integration:** Raytheon-El Paso (El Paso, TX), Raytheon (Huntsville, AL)
Raytheon-Norfolk (Norfolk, VA)
Raytheon-Burlington (Burlington, MA)
**Missile Assembly:** Lockheed Martin (Camden, AR)
**Integration/GSE:** Raytheon (Andover, MA)
**Seeker:** Boeing (Huntsville, AL)
**Seeker Assembly:** Boeing (El Paso, TX)
**SRM/ACM:** Aerojet (Camden, AR)
**SETA:** Intuitive Research and Technology (Huntsville, AL)

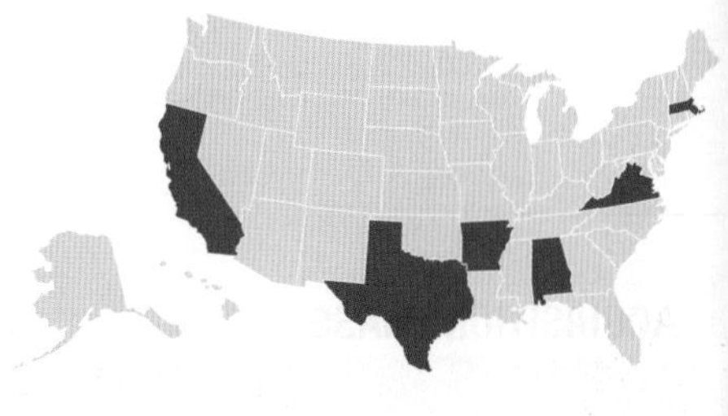

# Precision Guidance Kit (PGK)

## INVESTMENT COMPONENT

- Modernization
- Recapitalization
- Maintenance

## MISSION

Improve the accuracy of conventional 155mm high-explosive (HE) projectiles in the inventory.

## DESCRIPTION

Precision Guidance Kit (PGK) technology is state-of-the-art and provides a first-of-its-kind capability. PGK contains a Global Positioning System (GPS) guidance kit with fuzing functions and an integrated GPS receiver to correct the inherent errors associated with ballistic firing solutions, reducing the number of artillery projectiles required to attack targets. The increase in efficiency that PGK's "near-precision" capability provides allows operational commander's to engage assigned targets and rapidly achieve desired effects while minimizing collateral damage.

The PGK program is following an incremental program approach. Increment 1, the XM1156 PGK, will be compatible with the 155mm M795 and M549/A1 HE projectiles fired from the M109A6 Paladin and M777A2 Lightweight 155mm Howitzer. Future increments could expand this capability to projectiles containing an insensitive munition explosive fill and anti-jam capability.

## SYSTEM INTERDEPENDENCIES

None

## PROGRAM STATUS

- **Current:** Increment 1 program is in engineering and manufacturing development

## PROJECTED ACTIVITIES

- **1QFY13:** Increment 1 Milestone C

## ACQUISITION PHASE

Technology Development | **Engineering and Manufacturing Development** | Production and Deployment | Operations and Support

## Precision Guidance Kit (PGK)

**FOREIGN MILITARY SALES**
None

**CONTRACTORS**
**Increment 1**
**Prime:**
Alliant Techsystems (Plymouth, MN)
**Subcontractor:**
L-3 Interstate Electronics Corp. (Anaheim, CA)

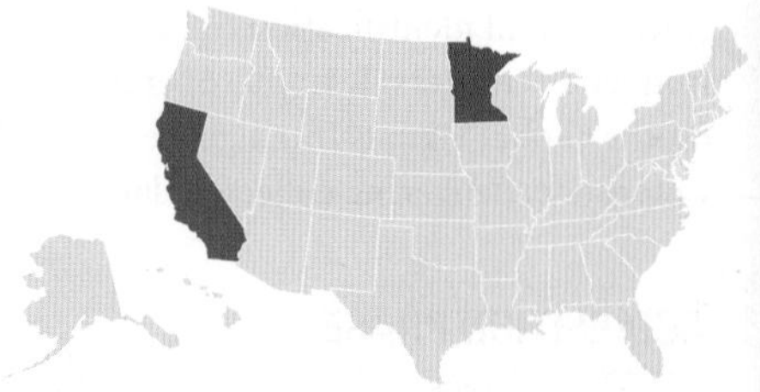

# Prophet

## INVESTMENT COMPONENT

- **Modernization**
- Recapitalization
- Maintenance

## MISSION

Provides a near-real-time picture of the battlespace through the use of signals intelligence sensors with the capability to detect, identify, and locate selected emitters.

## DESCRIPTION

Prophet is a 24-hour, all-weather, near-real-time, ground-based tactical signals intelligence/electronic warfare capability organic to the Brigade Combat Team (BCT), Stryker BCT, Armored Cavalry Regiment, and Battlefield Surveillance Brigade. Prophet contains two to four Electronic Support (ES) 1/Enhanced Systems and one to two Controls/ Prophet Analysis Cells (PACs). Prophet provides near-real-time force protection, situational awareness, and actionable intelligence by reporting the location, tracking, and identification of radio frequency emitters. It is interoperable on the Global Signals Intelligence Enterprise, delivering collected data to common databases for access by the intelligence community. Prophet's tactical mobility allows supported units to easily reposition its collection capability on the battlefield to support evolving situations.

The Prophet Enhanced System is a non-platform dependent modular system that will allow easy integration onto a vehicle. The Sensor supports both Stationary and On-The-Move (Mobile) Operations simultaneously. The Mobile configuration also has the capability to support Manpack Operations. The Prophet Enhanced System provides increased capability over existing Prophet ES 1 Systems. The Prophet Enhanced System was accelerated to provide upgraded capability integrated on an XM1229 Medium Mine Protected Vehicle to provide better crew protection and was fielded to units in preparation for deployment in support of Operation Enduring Freedom.

Prophet ES System is integrated on an armored M1165 High Mobility Multipurpose Wheeled Vehicle (HMMWV). The Prophet ES 1 System was fielded to active and reserve units in support of Operation Enduring Freedom/Operation New Dawn. Some Prophet ES 1 Systems were provided Wideband Beyond-Line-of-Site (WBLOS) capabilities, which is based on the present PM Warfighter Information Network-Tactical (WIN-T) architecture. This capability allows operation without the constraints of line-of-sight communication, increasing the system's capability to operate at extended distance and perform distributed operations. All Prophet Enhanced Systems have this capability.

Prophet Control (PC) is integrated on an armored M1165 HMMWV. PC/ PAC is the analytical node that tasks the Prophet ES 1 and Enhanced Systems for data collection and reporting. Each PC/PAC contains Satellite Communications (SATCOM). The PC has TROJAN-Lightweight Integrated Telecommunications Equipment (T-Lite) and PAC has a SATCOM Capability Set.

## SYSTEM INTERDEPENDENCIES

**Other Major Interdependencies**

Global Positioning System, Trojan-Lightweight Integrated Telecommunications Equipment, Tactical Radio Communications Systems, Light Tactical Vehicles, and Assured Mobility Systems

## PROGRAM STATUS

- **1QFY11-4QFY11:** Fielded Prophet ES 1 and Prophet Enhanced Systems
- **1QFY11-4QFY11:** Defield Prophet Block I systems as Prophet ES 1 and Prophet Enhanced Systems are fielded
- **3QFY11:** Prophet Enhanced Systems fielded to 504th Battlefield Surveillance Brigade (BfSB)

## PROJECTED ACTIVITIES

- **1QFY12-4QFY12:** Continue Prophet ES 1 and Prophet Enhanced Systems fieldings
- **1QFY12-4QFY12:** Continue to defield Prophet Block I systems as Prophet ES 1 and Prophet Enhanced Systems are fielded
- **2QFY12:** Prophet Analysis Cell (PAC)

## ACQUISITION PHASE

- Technology Development
- Engineering and Manufacturing Development
- **Production and Deployment**
- **Operations and Support**

**Prophet Enhanced**

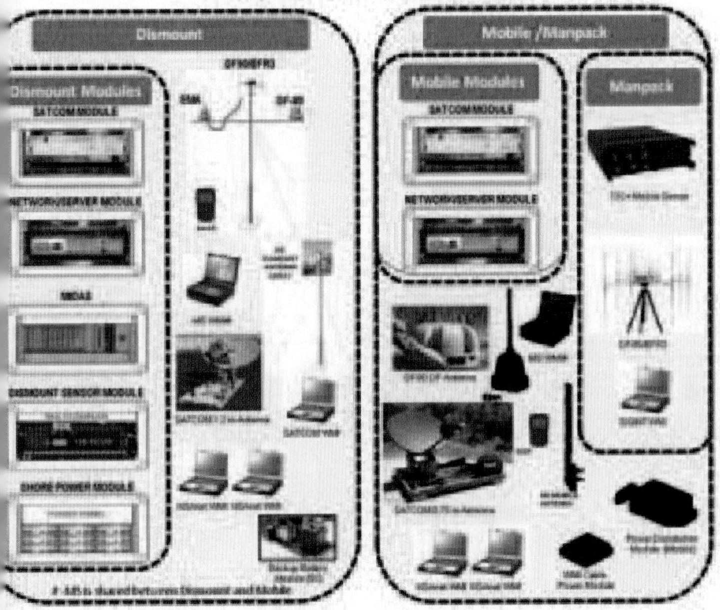


**Prophet Analysis Cell**

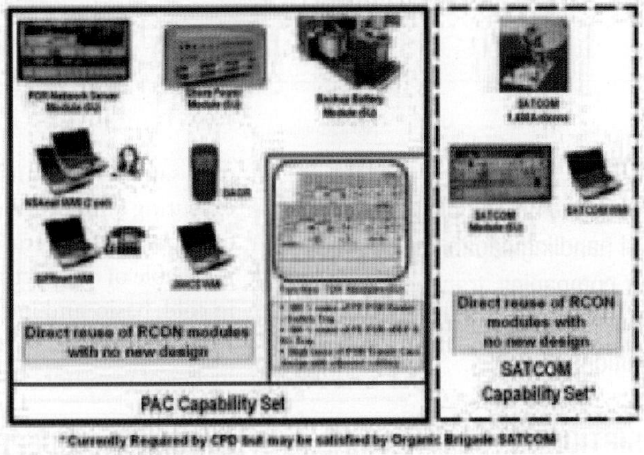

## Prophet

**FOREIGN MILITARY SALES**
None

**CONTRACTORS**
**Prophet Enhanced Sensor/Analysis Cell Production:**
General Dynamics (Scottsdale, AZ)

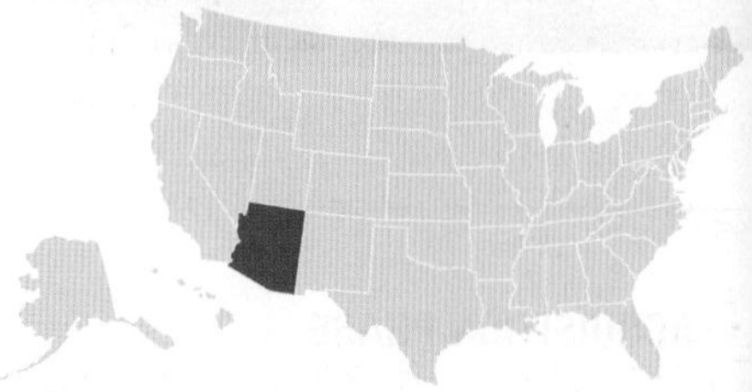

# Rough Terrain Container Handler (RTCH)

**INVESTMENT COMPONENT**

- Modernization
- Recapitalization
- Maintenance

## MISSION

Provides container handling and materiel handling capability in cargo transfer companies, transportation companies, quartermaster units, and ammunitions platoons.

## DESCRIPTION

The Rough Terrain Container Handler (RTCH) is a commercial, non-developmental item acquired for cargo-handling missions worldwide. The vehicle lifts, moves, and stacks both 20- and 40-foot American National Standards Institute/International Organization for Standardization containers and shelters weighing up to 53,000 pounds.

Improvements to RTCH include the capability to transport by rail, highway, or water in less than 2½ hours, reducing preparation time for air transport (C5A and C17) from 16 hours to less than one hour, stacking nine-foot, six-inch containers three high, achieving a forward speed of 23 miles per hour, and adding a full-range extendable boom and flexible top handler. RTCH will operate worldwide, on hard-stand, over-sand terrain, and cross-country, executing ammunition handling and transportation operations. The system is capable of conducting operations in cold, basic, and hot climates. Additionally, RTCH can ford up to 60 inches of seawater.

## SYSTEM INTERDEPENDENCIES

None

## PROGRAM STATUS

- **FY09:** Contractor completed the transfer to continental United States production

## PROJECTED ACTIVITIES

- **Continue:** Production and fielding

**ACQUISITION PHASE**

Technology Development | Engineering and Manufacturing Development | Production and Deployment | Operations and Support

## Rough Terrain Container Handler (RTCH)

**FOREIGN MILITARY SALES**
Australia, United Kingdom

**CONTRACTORS**
Kalmar Rough Terrain Center (KRTC) LLC (Cibolo, TX)

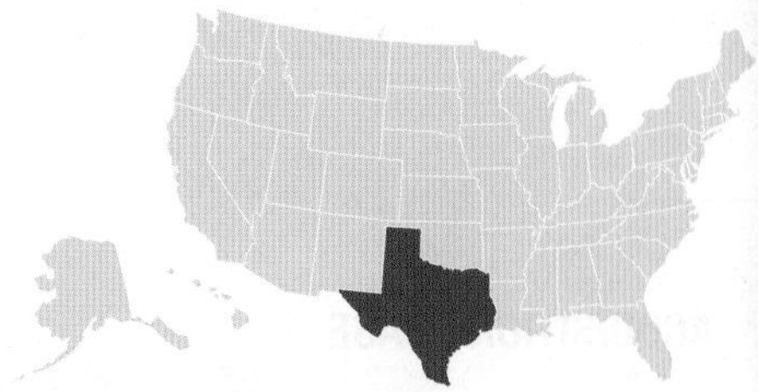

# RQ-7B Shadow Tactical Unmanned Aircraft System (TUAS)

**INVESTMENT COMPONENT**

- Modernization
- Recapitalization
- Maintenance

## MISSION

Provides reconnaissance, surveillance, target acquisition, and force protection for the Brigade Combat Team (BCT) in near-real-time during day/night and limited adverse weather conditions

## DESCRIPTION

The RQ-7B Shadow Tactical Unmanned Aircraft System (TUAS) has a wingspan of 20 feet and a payload capacity of approximately 60 pounds. Gross takeoff weight exceeds 440 pounds and endurance is more than eight hours on-station at a distance of 50 kilometers. The system is compatible with the All Source Analysis System, Advanced Field Artillery Tactical Data System, Joint Surveillance Target Attack Radar System Common Ground Station, Joint Technical Architecture-Army, Defense Information Infrastructure Common Operating Environment, and the One System Ground Control Station (OSGCS). The RQ-7B Shadow can be transported by six Air Force C-130 aircraft. It is currently operational in both the Army and Marine Corps.

The RQ-7B Shadow configuration, fielded in platoon sets, consistes of:

- Four air vehicles with day/night electro-optical/infrared (IR) with laser designator and IR illuminator payloads
- Two OSGCS on High Mobility Multipurpose Wheeled Vehicles (HMMWV)
- Four One System Remote Video Transceivers
- One hydraulic launcher
- Two ground data terminals
- Associated trucks, trailers, and support equipment

Shadow platoons are organic to the BCT. The Soldier platoon consists of a platoon leader, platoon sergeant, unmanned aerial vehicle (UAV) warrant officer, 12 Air Vehicle Operators/Mission Payload Operators, four electronic warfare repair personnel, and three engine mechanics supporting launch and recovery. The Maintenance Section Multifunctional is manned by Soldiers who also transport spares and provide maintenance support. The Mobile Maintenance Facility is manned by contractor personnel located with the Shadow platoon to provide logistics support to include "off system support" and "maintenance by repair."

The Shadow also has an early entry configuration of 15 Soldiers, one GCS, the air vehicle transport HMMWV, and the launcher trailer, which can be transported in three C-130s. All components can be slung under a CH 47 or CH-53 helicopter for transport.

## SYSTEM INTERDEPENDENCIES

None

## PROGRAM STATUS

- **Current:** In production and deployment; flown more than 480,000 hours in support of combat operations in Operation Enduring Freedom and Operation Iraqi Freedom since achieving initial operating capability. Total system flight hours are more than 650,000 hours

## PROJECTED ACTIVITIES

- **FY11-12:** Field remaining production systems; procure and field laser designator, Tactical Common Data Link, and Universal Ground Control Station retrofits; develop and field reliability and product improvements

**ACQUISITION PHASE**

Technology Development | Engineering and Manufacturing Development | **Production and Deployment** | Operations and Support

## RQ-7B Shadow Tactical Unmanned Aircraft System (TUAS)

**FOREIGN MILITARY SALES**

Australia

**CONTRACTORS**

**Shadow System:**
AAI Corp. (Textron Systems) (Hunt Valley, MD)

**TCDL:**
L-3 Communications (Salt Lake City, UT)

**Shelter Integration:**
CMI (Huntsville, AL)

**GDT:**
Tecom (Chatsworth, CA)

**Shelters:**
General Dynamics (Marion, VA)

**ACE II/II+/III Flight:**
Rockwell Collins (Warrenton, VA)

**Mode IV IFF:**
Raytheon (Baltimore, MD)

**Amplifiers:**
CTT (Santa Clara, CA)

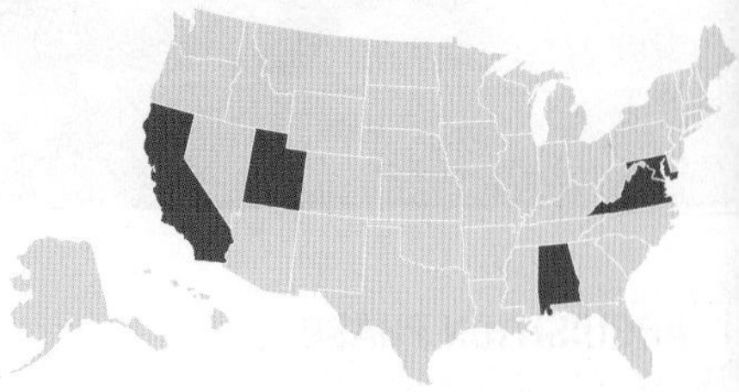

# RQ-11B Raven Small Unmanned Aircraft System (SUAS)

**INVESTMENT COMPONENT**

- Modernization
- Recapitalization
- Maintenance

## MISSION

Provides reconnaissance, surveillance, target acquisition (RSTA), and force protection for the battalion commander and below during day/night operations.

## DESCRIPTION

The RQ-11B Raven is a Small Unmanned Aircraft System (SUAS). It is a hand-launched, unmanned aircraft system capable of 90 minutes of flight time with an operational range of approximately 10 kilometers. The Raven system is comprised of three air vehicles, a ground control station (GCS), a remote video terminal (identical to GCS), EO/IR payloads, aircraft and GCS batteries, a field repair kit, and a spares package. Normal operational altitude is 500 feet or lower. The system, aircraft, and ground control station are assembled by operators in approximately five minutes. The aircraft has a wingspan of 4.5 feet and weighs 4.2 pounds. Both color electro-optical (EO) sensors and infrared (IR) sensors are fielded for day and night capabilities with each system. A hand controller displays live video and aircraft status. Mission planning is performed on the hand controller or ruggedized laptop running PFPS/Falcon View flight planning software. Aircraft flight modes include fully autonomous navigation, altitude hold, loiter, and return home. In-flight re-tasking and auto-loiter at sensor payload point of interest are also available. Raven incorporates secure global positioning system navigation. The digital data link incorporates encryption, improves spectrum management allowing more air vehicles to be flown in an operational area, and provides range extension via data relay between two Raven aircraft.

The Raven is operated by two Soldiers and has a rucksack-portable design. No specific military occupational specialty is required. Operator training is 10 days.

## SYSTEM INTERDEPENDENCIES

None

## PROGRAM STATUS

- **Current:** In production and deployment
- **Current:** Operational in both Operation New Dawn and Operation Enduring Freedom

## PROJECTED ACTIVITIES

- **FY11-12:** Continue Full-Rate Production and product improvements; integrate and field gimbaled payload (combined EO/IR/Laser Illuminator)

**ACQUISITION PHASE**

- Technology Development
- Engineering and Manufacturing Development
- Production and Deployment
- Operations and Support

## RQ-11B Raven Small Unmanned Aircraft System (SUAS)

**FOREIGN MILITARY SALES**
Denmark, Estonia, Lebanon, Uganda

**CONTRACTORS**
Aerovironment Inc. (Simi Valley, CA)
Indigo System Corp. (Goleta, CA)
All American Racers Inc. (Santa Ana, CA)
L-3 Communications (San Diego, CA)
Bren-Tronics (Commack, NY)

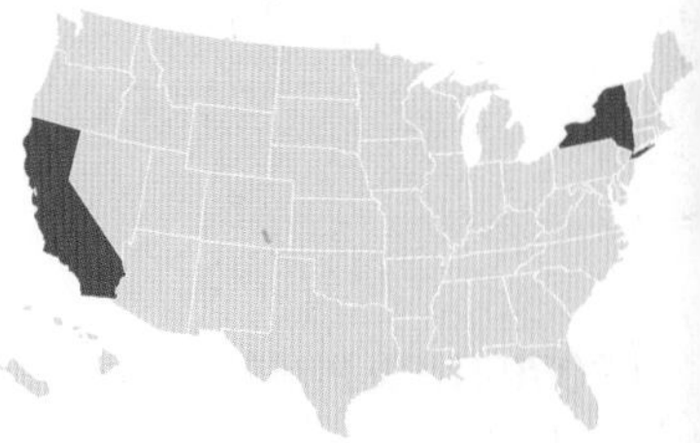

# Secure Mobile Anti-Jam Reliable Tactical Terminal (SMART-T)

**INVESTMENT COMPONENT**

- **Modernization**
- Recapitalization
- Maintenance

## MISSION

Provides range extension to the Army's current and future tactical communications networks.

## DESCRIPTION

The Secure Mobile Anti-Jam Reliable Tactical Terminal (SMART-T) is a mobile military satellite communication terminal that provides worldwide, anti-jam, low probability of intercept and detection, and secure voice and data capabilities for the Joint Warfighter. The SMART-T provides range extension to the Army's current and future tactical communications networks through DoD Milstar and Advanced Extremely High Frequency (AEHF) communication satellites. SMART-T's are being upgraded to interoperate with AEHF satellites and it now provides data rates up to 8.192 million bits per second (Mbps). An FY12 production contract is planned to procure 46 additional AEHF-capable SMART-Ts, which will bring the total Army procurement to 324. The AEHF satellite system will dramatically increase the Army's end-to-end anti-jam communications throughput capability.

The Army's 324 SMART-Ts will be fielded at the brigade, division, and corps echelons in the Active, National Guard, and Reserve components.

## SYSTEM INTERDEPENDENCIES

**Other Major Interdependencies**

The SMART-T communicates with Milstar military communication satellites and is being upgraded to communicate with AEHF communication satellites

## PROGRAM STATUS

- **1QFY11-4QFY11:** Upgrades to legacy EHF (Milstar-capable) SMART-Ts, giving them AEHF capability continues
- **1QFY11:** Began fielding of upgraded AEHF SMART-Ts
- **2QFY11:** Began development of acquisition package for the procurement of 46 AEHF SMART-Ts

## PROJECTED ACTIVITIES

- **2QFY12-2QFY14:** Continued upgrade and fielding of AEHF SMART-Ts
- **2QFY12-3QFY12:** Continued review and approval of acquisition package for procurement of 46 AEHF SMART-Ts
- **4QFY12:** Award contract for 46 AEHF SMART-T
- **2QFY13:** SMART-T will participate in Air Force AEHF multiservice operational test and evaluation

**ACQUISITION PHASE**

- Technology Development
- Engineering and Manufacturing Development
- **Production and Deployment**
- Operations and Support

## Secure Mobile Anti-Jam Reliable Tactical Terminal (SMART-T)

**FOREIGN MILITARY SALES**
19 SMART-Ts for Canada, 7 SMART-Ts for Netherlands

**CONTRACTORS**
**Production and Spares:**
Raytheon (Largo, FL)
**Engineering Support, Management:**
Raytheon (Marlborough, MA)
**Circuit Cards:**
Teledyne (Lewisburg, TN)
**Filters:**
Transtector (Hayden, ID)
**Amplifier Assemblies:**
Spectrum Microwave (Marlborough, MA)
**COMSEC:**
L-3 Communications (Camden, NJ )
**New Equipment Training/Fielding:**
EPS Corp. (Martinez, GA)
**Satellite Simulator:**
Lincoln Labs (Lexington, MA)
**Technical/Fielding Support:**
Linquest Corp. (Colorado Springs, CO)
**Admin/Tech:**
JANUS Research (Bellcamp, MD)
**Technical:**
Booz Allen Hamilton (Bellcamp, MD)

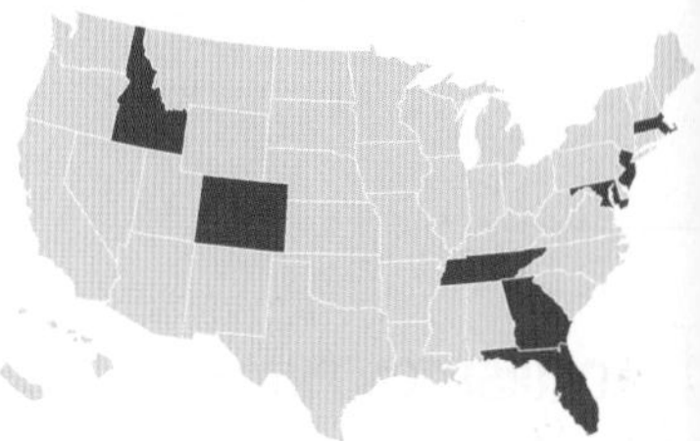

# Sentinel

INVESTMENT COMPONENT

**Modernization**

Recapitalization

Maintenance

## MISSION

Provides persistent surveillance and fire control quality data through external command and control platforms, enabling protection against cruise missiles, aircraft, unmanned aerial vehicles, and rocket, artillery, and mortar threats.

## DESCRIPTION

Sentinel is used with the Army's Forward Area Air Defense Command and Control (FAAD C2) system and provides key target data to Stinger-based weapon systems and battlefield commanders via FAAD C2 or directly, using an Enhanced Position Location Reporting System or the Single Channel Ground and Airborne Radio System.

Sentinel consists of the M1097A1 High Mobility Multipurpose Wheeled Vehicle, the antenna transceiver group mounted on a high-mobility trailer, the identification friend-or-foe system (IFF), and the FAAD C2 interface. The sensor is an advanced three-dimensional battlefield X-band air defense phased-array radar with a 75-kilometer range instrumented range.

Sentinel can operate day and night, in adverse weather conditions, and in battlefield environments of dust, smoke, aerosols, and enemy countermeasures. It provides 360-degree azimuth coverage for acquisition and tracking of targets (cruise missiles, unmanned aerial vehicles, rotary and fixed-wing aircraft) moving at supersonic to hovering speeds and at positions from the map of the earth to the maximum engagement altitude of short-range air defense weapons. Sentinel detects targets before they can engage, thus improving air defense weapon reaction time and allowing engagement at optimum ranges. Sentinel's integrated IFF system reduces the potential for engagement of friendly aircraft.

Sentinel modernization efforts include enhanced target range and classification upgrades to engage non-line-of-sight targets; increased detection and acquisition range of targets; enhanced situational awareness; and classification of cruise missiles. The system provides integrated air tracks with classification and recognition of platforms that give an integrated air and cruise missile defense solution for the Air and Missile Defense System of Systems Increment 1 architecture and subsequent increments. Sentinel provides critical air surveillance of the National Capital Region and other areas as part of ongoing homeland defense efforts, and is a component of the counter rocket, artillery, and mortar batteries in the area of responsibility.

## SYSTEM INTERDEPENDENCIES

None

## PROGRAM STATUS

- **4QFY10:** Delivery and installation of 14 Improved Sentinel Kits on radars

## PROJECTED ACTIVITIES

- **4QFY11:** Contract award for 56 Improved Sentinels
- **2QFY12:** Contract award for 143 AN/TPX-57 IFFs
- **FY11-12:** Procurement of 31 Improved Sentinel Kits
- **FY13-14:** Fielding/Installation of Improved Sentinel Kits
- **4QFY12:** Delivery of Finland and Netherlands F1 Software

ACQUISITION PHASE

Technology Development | Engineering and Manufacturing Development | **Production and Deployment** | Operations and Support

## Sentinel

**FOREIGN MILITARY SALES**
Egypt, Lithuania, Turkey

**CONTRACTORS**
Thales Raytheon Systems (Fullerton, CA; El Paso, TX; Forest, MS; Largo, FL)
CAS Inc. (Huntsville, AL)

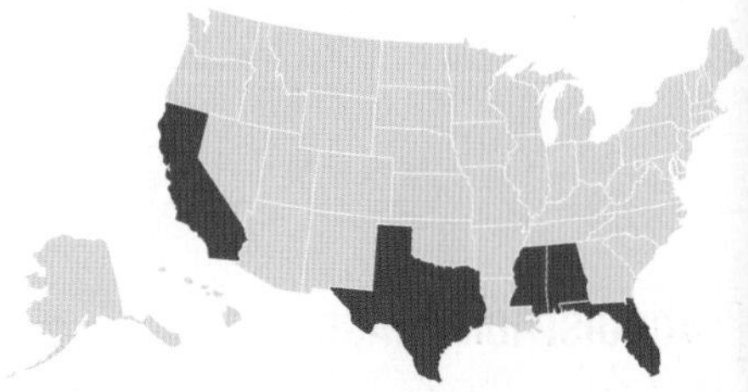

# Single Channel Ground and Airborne Radio System (SINCGARS)

**INVESTMENT COMPONENT**

- **Modernization**
- Recapitalization
- Maintenance

## MISSION

Provides Joint commanders with a highly reliable, low-cost, secure, and easily maintained Combat NET Radio (CNR) that has both voice and data handling capability in support of tactical command and control operations.

## DESCRIPTION

The Single Channel Ground and Airborne Radio System (SINCGARS) Advanced SINCGARS System Improvement Program (ASIP) radio is the DoD/Army multiservice fielded solution for voice communication for platoon level and above, operating over the 30.000 to 87.975MHz frequency range. This radio provides the capability of establishing two-way communications (including jam-resistance) using the SINCGARS waveform and provides multimode voice and data communications supporting ground, air-to-ground, and ground-to-air line-of-sight communications links. The ASIP radio is the newer version of the SINCGARS radio. It is smaller than the SIP and weighs significantly less, while still maintaining all the functionalities of the SIP for backward compatibility.

Enhancements include the Embedded Global Positioning System (GPS) Receiver (EGR) and the radio-based combat identification/radio-based situational awareness (RBCI/RBSA) capability, which provides Warfighters with enhanced situational awareness and identification of friendly forces in targeted areas. RBCI serves as a gap filler for combat identification, providing an interrogation/responder capability to satisfy the air-to-ground positive identification of platforms prior to release of weapons to prevent fratricide. RBSA adds a radio beaconing capability for every ASIP-equipped platform to enhance the Blue Force situational awareness picture. The Internet controller enhancements add improved addressing capabilities in support of tactical Internet enhancements being provided by Joint Battle Command-Platform for Joint interoperability. Crypto modernization is a programmable communications security capability for SINCGARS that will allow the radios to continue to provide secure communications to the secret and top-secret level of security.

## SYSTEM INTERDEPENDENCIES

None

## PROGRAM STATUS

- **1QFY11-4QFY11:** Continue to field in accordance with Headquarters Department of the Army guidance to support the Army Campaign Plan; National Guard, Army Reserve, and Active Army, Operation Enduring Freedom requirements and urgent Operational Needs Statement

## PROJECTED ACTIVITIES

- **2QFY12-2QFY14:** Continued fielding of SINCGARS

**ACQUISITION PHASE**

- Technology Development
- Engineering and Manufacturing Development
- **Production and Deployment**
- **Operations and Support**

## Single Channel Ground and Airborne Radio System (SINCGARS)

**FOREIGN MILITARY SALES**
Australia, Bahrain, Croatia, Egypt, Estonia, Finland, Georgia, Greece, Hungary, Ireland, Italy, Korea, Kuwait, Morocco, New Zealand, Portugal, Saudi Arabia, SHAPE Tech Center, Slovakia, Taiwan, Thailand, Ukraine, Uzbekistan, Zimbabwe

**CONTRACTORS**
**Radio design/production:**
ITT (Ft. Wayne, IN)
**Hardware Installation Kits:**
UNICOR (Washington, DC)
**Engineering Support and Testing:**
ITT (Clifton, NJ)
**Total Package Fielding:**
USFalcon/EPS Corp. (Morrisville, NC; Tinton Falls, NJ)

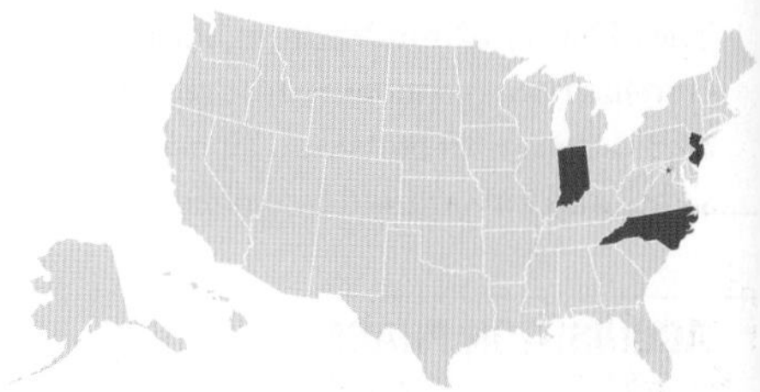

# Small Arms-Crew Served Weapons

**INVESTMENT COMPONENT**

- **Modernization**
- Recapitalization
- Maintenance

## MISSION

Enables Warfighters and small units to engage targets with lethal fire to defeat or deter adversaries.

## DESCRIPTION

The M249 Squad Automatic Weapon (SAW) replaced the M16A1 Automatic Rifle at the squad level, as well as some M60 multipurpose machine guns in non-infantry units. The M249 delivers greater range and rates of fire than the M16 or M4. A collapsible buttstock, and new short barrel improves weapons control in confined spaces and allows for improved egress and maneuver in close quarter combat. An improved bipod provides Soldiers with increased reliability and weapon accuracy.

The M240B 7.62mm Medium Machine Gun has been reconfigured for ground applications with buttstock, bipod, iron sights, and forward-rail assemblies. The M240B has a maximum effective range of 1,800 meters, a cyclic rate of fire of 650 rounds per minute, and a muzzle velocity of 2,800 feet per second.

The M240L 7.62mm Medium Machine Gun (Light) incorporates titanium construction and alternative manufacturing methods to achieve significant weight savings. At 22.3 pounds, the M240L is approximately five pounds lighter than the M240B.

The M2 .50 Caliber Machine Gun is belt-fed, recoil-operated, and air-cooled. It mounts on the M3 tripod and on most vehicles. Employed as an anti-personnel and anti-aircraft weapon, it is highly effective against light armored vehicles, low flying aircraft, and small boats. It is capable of single-shot and automatic fire.

The M2A1 is an enhancement to the standard M2 .50 Caliber Machine Gun offering Soldiers increased performance and design improvements that make it easier and safer to use. The M2A1 provides a Quick Change Barrel (QCB) with fixed headspace and timing, flash hider, and a removable carrying handle.

The MK19 Grenade Machine Gun supports the Soldier by delivering heavy, accurate, and continuous firepower against enemy personnel and lightly armored vehicles. The MK19 can be mounted on a tripod or on multiple vehicle platforms and is the primary suppression weapon for combat support and combat service support units.

## SYSTEM INTERDEPENDENCIES

**In this Publication**

Common Remotely Operated Weapon Station (CROWS)

## PROGRAM STATUS

**M249:**
- Production and fielding

**M240B:**
- Production and fielding
- Product Qualification/Verification activities on-going for the Colt M240B

**M240L:**
- Production and fielding
- **1QFY11:** First Unit Equipped
- **3QFY11:** Award bridge quantity of weapons
- **3QFY11:** Release competitive RFP

**M2/M2A1:**
- **1QFY11:** M2A1 Type Classification-Standard
- **2QFY11:** Anniston Army Depot began conversions of M2s into M2A1s using QCB conversion kits
- **4QFY11:** M2A1 First Unit Equipped
- U.S. Ordnance successfully completed M2 first article testing

**MK19:**
- Production and fielding
- Actions to address Foreign Military Sales (FMS) requirements are ongoing

## PROJECTED ACTIVITIES

**M249:**
- Continue production deliveries and Anniston Army Depot overhaul program
- Continue fielding in support of current operations

**M240B:**
- Continue fielding in support of current operations

**M240L:**
- **1QFY12:** Award new competitive contract

**M2/M2A1:**
- Continue M2A1 production (GDATP) deliveries and Anniston Army Depot overhaul/conversion program

**MK19:**
- Continue fielding in support of current operations
- Contract modifications to address near term FMS buys

**ACQUISITION PHASE**

- Technology Development
- Engineering and Manufacturing Development
- **Production and Deployment**
- **Operations and Support**

## Small Arms-Crew Served Weapons

**FOREIGN MILITARY SALES**

**M249 SAW:**
Afghanistan, Bangladesh, Colombia, Croatia, Philippines, Tunisia

**M240B:**
Azerbaijan, Bangladesh, Barbados, Jordan

**M2:**
Afghanistan, Lebanon, Oman

**MK19 Grenade Machine Gun:**
Afghanistan, Bahrain, Chili, Colombia, Croatia, Czech Republic, Kenya, Saudi Arabia

**CONTRACTORS**

**M249 SAW:**
Fabrique National Manufacturing LLC (Columbia, SC)

**M240B Machine Gun:**
Fabrique National Manufacturing LLC (Columbia, SC)
Colt Manufacturing Company LLC (West Hartford, CT)

**M2:** General Dynamics Armament and Technical Products (GDATP) (Williston, VT)
GDATP manufacturing facility (Saco, ME)
U.S. Ordnance (McCarran, NV)

**MK19 Grenade Machine Gun:**
General Dynamics Armament and Technical Products (Saco, ME)
Alliant Techsystems (Mesa, AZ)

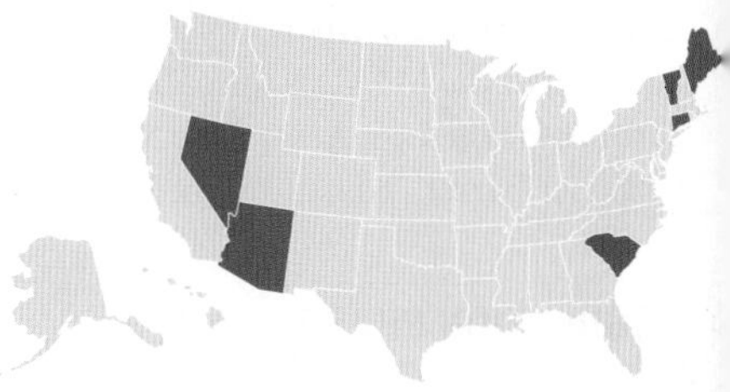

# Small Arms-Individual Weapons

**INVESTMENT COMPONENT**

Modernization

Recapitalization

Maintenance

## MISSION

Enables Warfighters and small units to engage targets with lethal fire to defeat or deter adversaries.

## DESCRIPTION

The M4 Carbine is designed for lightness, speed, mobility, and firepower and is standard issue for Brigade Combat Teams in theater. The M4 series of carbines can also be mounted with the M203A2 Grenade Launcher, M320 Grenade Launcher, or M26 Modular Accessory Shotgun System (MASS). The weapon incorporates 62 refinements since its inception. In post-combat surveys, 94 percent of Soldiers rate the M4 as an effective weapons system.

In September 2010, Headquarters Department of the Army G3/5/7 authorized the M4A1 as the standard carbine for the U.S. Army. The M4A1 has a heavier barrel and is fully automatic, improvements that deliver greater sustained rates of fire. The Army is upgrading both M4 configurations with an ambidextrous fire control assembly.

The M14 Enhanced Battle Rifle (EBR) has a new adjustable buttstock, cheek rest, and M4-style pistol grip, making the rifle effective in both close quarters combat and in the Squad Designated Marksman role. The upgraded weapons are currently in service with select Army units.

The M320 Grenade Launcher is the replacement to all M203 series grenade launchers on M16 Rifles and M4 Carbines. A modular system, it attaches under the barrel of the rifle or carbine and can convert to a stand-alone weapon. The M320 improves on current grenade launchers with an available integral day/night sighting system and improved safety features. It also has a side-loading unrestricted breech that allows the system to fire longer 40mm low-velocity projectiles (NATO standard and non-standard).

The lightweight M26 12-Gauge MASS attaches to the M4 Carbine and zeroes to the host weapon. It is also designed to operate as a stand-alone system and comes with a recoil-absorbing, collapsible buttstock. The MASS enables Soldiers to transition between lethal and less-than-lethal fires and adds the capability of a separate shotgun without carrying a second weapon. Additional features include a box magazine, flip-up sights, ambidextrous configurations, and an extendable stand-off device for door breaching.

## SYSTEM INTERDEPENDENCIES

None

## PROGRAM STATUS

**M4 Carbine:**
- Delivery and fielding complete

**M4A1:**
- Deliveries ongoing

**M14 EBR:**
- **3QFY09:** Army Requirements and Resourcing Board approved 5,000 systems
- **1QFY10:** 1,200 additional systems authorized
- **3QFY10:** First 5,000 complete

**M320 Grenade Launcher Module:**
- Production and fielding

**M26 Modular Accessory Shotgun System:**
- **4QFY09:** Limited user test and evaluation with MP units
- **2QFY10:** Low-Rate Initial Production approved
- **4QFY10:** First article testing complete

## PROJECTED ACTIVITIES

**M4 Carbine:**
- In sustainment

**M4A1:**
- New competitive M4A1 solicitation pending for 24,000 M4A1 systems
- Continue M4A1 production, deliveries, and fielding

**M14 EBR:**
- In sustainment

**M320 Grenade Launcher Module:**
- Competitive solicitation planned to select improved day/night sighting system
- Competitive solicitation planned to provide additional M320 GLs

**M26 Modular Accessory Shotgun System:**
- **1QFY12:** Materiel Release
- **2QFY12:** First Unit Equipped

**ACQUISITION PHASE**

Technology Development | Engineering and Manufacturing Development | Production and Deployment | Operations and Support

## Small Arms-Individual Weapons

**FOREIGN MILITARY SALES**

**M4 Carbine:**
Afghanistan, Colombia, Jamaica, Philippines, Thailand

**M4A1:**
Azerbaijan, Bahrain, Djibouti, Thailand, Pakistan

**CONTRACTORS**

**M4 Carbine:**
Colt's Manufacturing Co. (Hartford, CT)

**M320 Grenade Launcher Module:**
Heckler and Koch Defense Inc. (Ashburn, VA)

**M26 Modular Accessory Shotgun System:**
Vertu Corp. (Warrenton, VA)

# Small Caliber Ammunition

## INVESTMENT COMPONENT

Modernization

Recapitalization

Maintenance

## MISSION

Provides Warfighters with the highest quality, most capable small caliber ammunition for training and combat.

## DESCRIPTION

Small Caliber Ammunition consists of 5.56mm, 7.62mm, 9mm, 10- and 12-gauge, .22 Cal., .30 Cal., .50 Cal., and Grenade Rifle Entry Munition (GREM). The 5.56mm cartridge is used by the M16 Rifle, M249 Squad Automatic Weapon (SAW), and the M4 Carbine. The 7.62mm cartridge is used by the M240 Machine Gun and M60 Machine Gun, as well as the M24, M110, and M14 EBR Sniper Rifles. The 9mm cartridge is fired by the M9 Pistol. The M2 Machine Gun and the M107 Sniper Rifle use .50 Cal. cartridges. The remaining Small Caliber Ammunition is used in a variety of pistols, rifles, and shotguns.

Three categories of Small Caliber Ammunition are currently in use. War Reserve Ammo is modern ammunition that supports individual and crew served weapons during combat operations. Training Standard Ammunition is dual-purpose, and it is used to support training or operational requirements. Training Unique Ammunition is designed specifically for use in training and is not for combat use, i.e., blank, dummy, inert, and short-range training ammunition.

## SYSTEM INTERDEPENDENCIES

None

## PROGRAM STATUS

- **Current:** M855A1 Enhanced Performance Round (M855 replacement program) in full production

## PROJECTED ACTIVITIES

- **FY11:** Produce and deliver one billion rounds (5.56mm, 7.62mm, and 0.50 Cal.)
- **FY12:** Complete Lake City Army Ammunition Plant modernization program

## ACQUISITION PHASE

Technology Development | Engineering and Manufacturing Development | Production and Deployment | Operations and Support

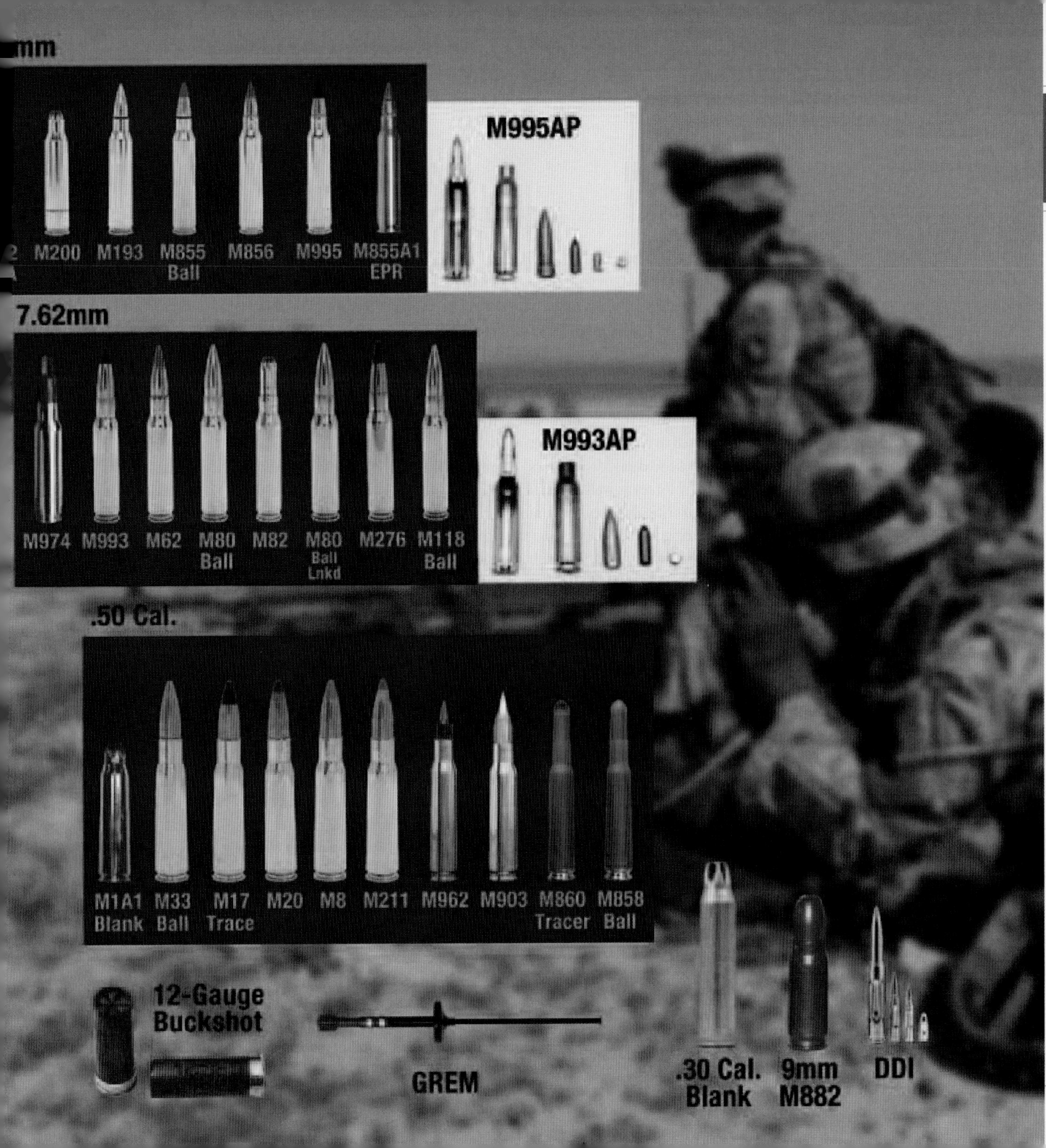




## Small Caliber Ammunition

**FOREIGN MILITARY SALES**

**5.56mm, 7.62mm, .50 Caliber:** Afghanistan, Colombia, Czech Republic, El Salvador, France, Hungary, India, Iraq, Israel, Japan, Jordan, Kenya, Lebanon, Philippines, Singapore, Thailand, Tunisia, Yemen

**CONTRACTORS**

Alliant Techsystems (Independence, MO)
General Dynamics Ordnance and Tactical Systems (St. Petersburg, FL)
Olin Corp. (East Alton, IL)
General Dynamics (Saint Marks, FL)
SNC Technologies (LeGardeur, Québec, Canada)

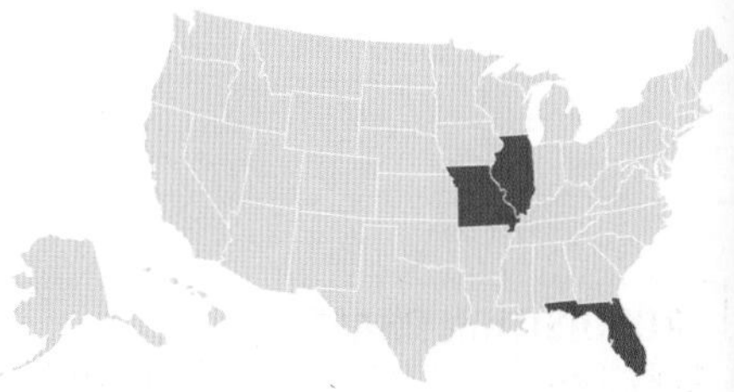

# Spider

INVESTMENT COMPONENT

Modernization

Recapitalization

Maintenance

## MISSION

Provides the commander with a new capability to shape the battlefield, protect the force, and respond to changing battlefield environments in a graduated manner while minimizing risk to friendly troops and non-combatants.

## DESCRIPTION

Anti-Personnel Landmine Alternatives (APL/A) Track I (Spider) is a hand-emplaced, remotely controlled, Man-in-the-Loop (MITL), anti-personnel munition system. Spider provides munition field effectiveness, but it does so without residual life-threatening risks after hostilities end. The fielding of this system with its sensors, communications, and munitions changes the way Soldiers operate in an otherwise unpredictable battlefield.

Each munition is controlled by a remotely stationed Soldier who monitors its sensors, allowing for more precise (non-lethal to lethal) responses—a significant advancement and advantage. The Spider Networked Munitions System enables the MITL to detect, track, classify, count, and destroy the enemy.

The Spider system contains three main components: the remote control unit, residing within a computer interface; the repeater, extending the remote control range; and a munition control unit for sending and receiving commands as well as activating the munitions. Spider can be used as a force-protection-reinforcing obstacle to delay, disrupt, and channel enemy forces as well as restrict their use of critical routes of terrain, thereby reducing civil casualties and the exposure of personnel to hostile fire. It can also be integrated into a base defense system, providing protection to Soldiers in forward operating bases and combat outposts.

The system's design allows for safe, flexible, and rapid deployment, reinforcement, and recovery as well as safe passage of friendly forces. Spider eliminates the possibility of an unintended detonation through early warning and selective engagement of enemy forces, and it has a self-destruct capability. Spider is designed for storage, transport, rough handling, and use in worldwide military environments.

## SYSTEM INTERDEPENDENCIES

**Other Major Interdependencies**

Interface with Tactical Internet through Force XXI Battle Command Brigade and Below and obstacle positioning through Global Positioning System

## PROGRAM STATUS

- **2QFY11:** Award of LRIP 4 contract
- **2QFY11:** Conditional Material Release
- **3QFY11:** Limited User Test
- **3QFY11:** Network Integration Evaluation participation

## PROJECTED ACTIVITIES

- **3QFY12:** Follow-on Operational Test #3
- **1QFY13:** Materiel Release/Type Classification Std.
- **1QFY13:** Full-Rate Production Decision
- **3QFY13:** Full-Rate Production Contract Award

ACQUISITION PHASE

Technology Development | Engineering and Manufacturing Development | Production and Deployment | Operations and Support

## Spider

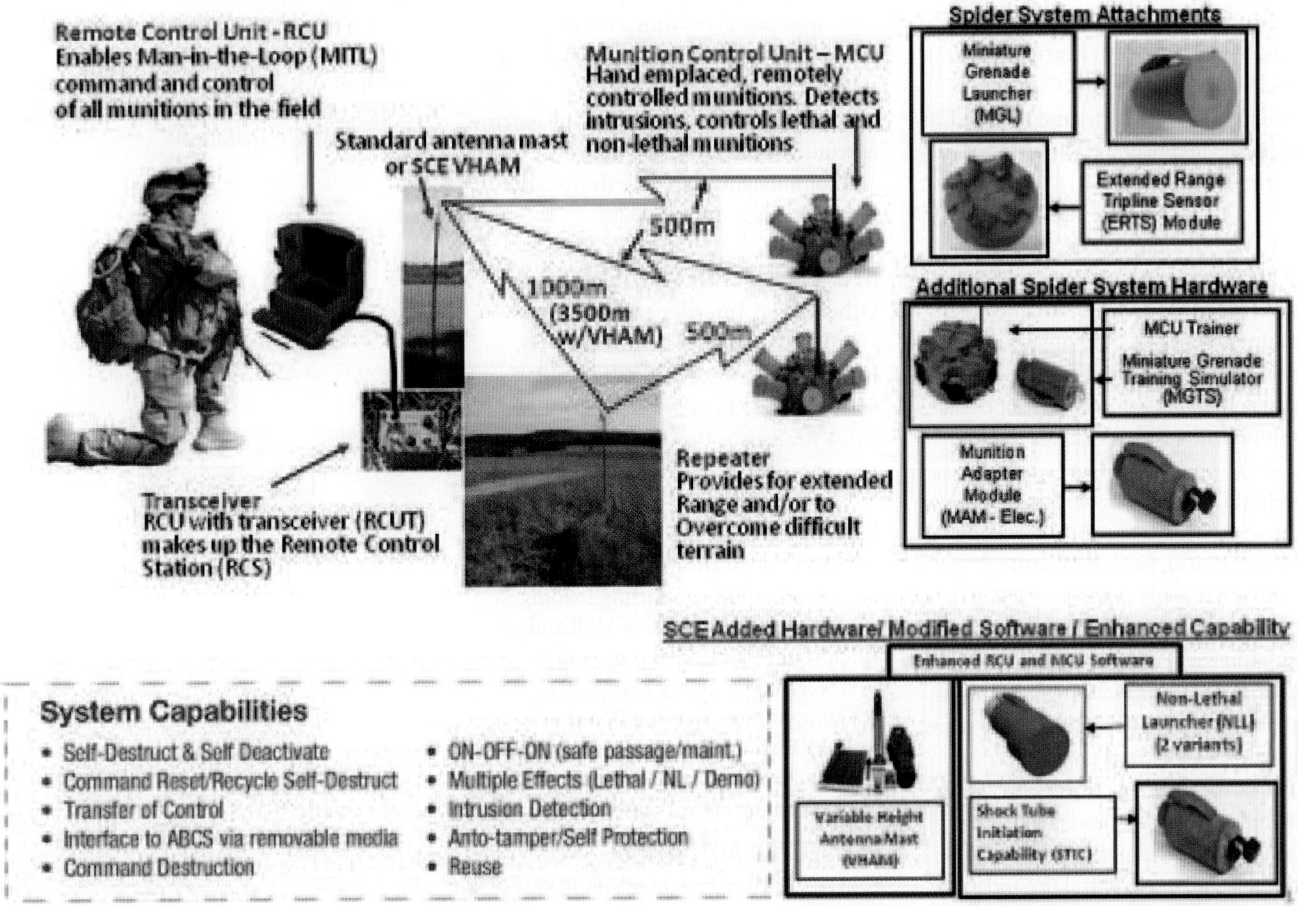


**FOREIGN MILITARY SALES**
None

**CONTRACTORS**

**Prime:**

Textron Defense Systems (Wilmington, MA)

Alliant Techsystems (Plymouth, MN)

**Subcontractors:**

Alliant Techsystems (Rocket Center, WV)

BAE Systems/Holston (Kingsport, TN)

American Ordnance (Milan, TN)

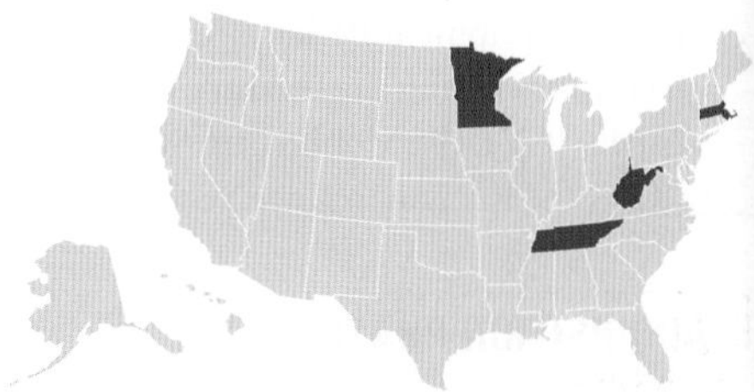

# Stryker Family of Vehicles

**INVESTMENT COMPONENT**

Modernization

Recapitalization

Maintenance

## MISSION

Enables the Army to immediately respond to urgent operational requirements anywhere in the world using rapidly deployable, agile, and strategically responsive support vehicles.

## DESCRIPTION

As the primary combat and combat support platform of the Stryker Brigade Combat Team (SBCT), the Stryker Family of Vehicles fulfills an immediate requirement for a strategically deployable (C-17/C-5) brigade capable of rapid movement anywhere on the globe in a combat-ready configuration. The Stryker Family of Vehicles is built on a common chassis, each with a different Mission Equipment Package. There are 10 variants, including the Infantry Carrier Vehicle (ICV), the Mobile Gun System (MGS), the Reconnaissance Vehicle (RV), Mortar Carrier, Commanders Vehicle, Fire Support Vehicle (FSV), Engineer Squad Vehicle, Medical Evacuation Vehicle (MEV), Anti-tank Guided Missile (ATGM) Vehicle, and the Nuclear Biological Chemical Reconnaissance Vehicle (NBCRV).

The ICV (excluding the MEV, ATGM, FSV, and RV) is armed with a Remote Weapon Station supporting an M2 .50 caliber machine gun or MK19 automatic grenade launcher, the M6 grenade launcher, and a thermal weapons sight. Stryker supports communication suites that integrate the Single Channel Ground and Air Radio System (SINCGARS) radio family; Enhanced Position Location Reporting System (EPLRS); Force XXI Battle Command Brigade and Below (FBCB2) or Blue Force Tracker (BFT); Global Positioning System (GPS); high-frequency (HF) and multiband very-high and ultra-high frequency (VHF/UHF) radio systems. Stryker provides 360-degree protection against armor-piercing threats. Stryker is powered by a 350-hp diesel engine, runs on eight wheels that possess a run-flat capability, and has a central tire-inflation system. It also incorporates a vehicle-height management system.

The Stryker program leverages non-developmental items with common subsystems and components to allow rapid acquisition and fielding. Stryker integrates government furnished materiel subsystems as required and stresses performance and commonality to reduce the logistics footprint and minimize costs.

## SYSTEM INTERDEPENDENCIES

**Other Major Interdependencies**

DAGR, DVE, EPLRS, FH MUX, FS3, KNIGHT, LRAS3, MCS, MFCS, RWS, SHADOWFIRE, SPITFIRE, STORM, VIS VIC, Sensor Processing Group, Sensor Suite

## PROGRAM STATUS

- **3FY11:** Acquisition Decision Memorandum supporting fielding of the Stryker Double-V Hull and approving continued production is received following March 2011 Configuration Steering Board
- **4QFY11:** Continuing Combat Vehicle Portfolio Review to determine strategy to enable future network integration

## PROJECTED ACTIVITIES

- **2QFY12:** Stryker NBCRV Full-Rate Production Decision
- **3QFY12:** SBCT 8 completes Stryker fielding
- **2QFY13:** SBCT 8 reaches Initial Operational Capability
- **3QFY13:** SBCT 9 completes Stryker fielding
- **1QFY14:** SBCT 9 reaches Initial Operational Capability

**ACQUISITION PHASE**

Technology Development | Engineering and Manufacturing Development | Production and Deployment | Operations and Support

## Stryker Family of Vehicles

**FOREIGN MILITARY SALES**
None

**CONTRACTORS**
General Dynamics Land Systems (Sterling Heights, MI)
**Manufacturing/Assembly:**
General Dynamics Land Systems-Canada (London, Ontario, Canada)
Joint Systems Manufacturing Center (JSMC) (Lima, OH)
General Dynamics Assembly Operations (Anniston, AL)
**Engineering:**
General Dynamics (Sterling Heights, MI)
**Kits:**
Verhoff Machine (Continental, OH)
**Manifold/Alternator:**
North American Controls (Shelby Twp, MI)
**Sensors/CCA:**
Raytheon (El Segundo, CA)
**Fire System Assembly:**
Kidde Dual Spectrum (Goleta, CA)

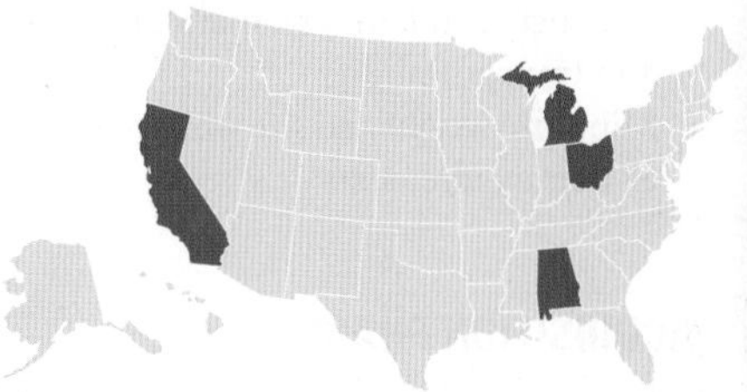

# Tactical Electric Power (TEP)

**INVESTMENT COMPONENT**

Modernization

Recapitalization

Maintenance

## MISSION

Provides standardized tactical electric power to the Department of Defense in support of national security.

## DESCRIPTION

The Tactical Electric Power (TEP) program consists of small (2-3 kilowatt [kW]), medium (5-60kW), and large (100-840kW) electrical power generating systems, trailer-mounted power units and power plants, and electrical distribution equipment that provide standardized power management solutions to all Department of Defense agencies and numerous Allied nations. The Project Manager Mobile Electric Power's systems:

- Maximize fuel efficiency
- Increase reliability (750 hours mean time between failures), maintainability, and transportability
- Minimize weight and size while meeting all user requirements
- Operate at rated loads in all military environments
- Reduce infrared signature and noise (less than 70 decibels at seven meters)
- Are survivable in chemical, biological, and nuclear environments
- Meet power generation and conditioning standards in accordance with military standards (MIL-STD 1332)

TEP systems provide essential power for Brigade Combat Team command posts, command, control, communications, computers, intelligence, surveillance, and reconnaissance (C4ISR) systems, air defense, aviation, field artillery, force provider, and combat support and service support systems. The military-ruggedized commercial components use alternative and renewable energy sources. The TEP has a variety of generator set sizes: 2kW Military Tactical Generator (MTG), 3kW Tactical Quiet Generator (TQG), 5kW TQG, 10kW TQG, 15kW TQG, 30kW TQG, 60kW TQG, 100kW TQG, 200kW TQG, and 840kW Deployable Power Generation and Distribution System (DPGDS); of these, the 2kW MTG and 3kW TQG are man-portable.

The newest systems are the Advanced Medium Mobile Power Sources (AMMPS), which will replace the Tactical Quiet Generators (TQG): 5kW AMMPS, 10kW AMMPS, 15kW AMMPS, 30kW AMMPS, and 60kW AMMPS.

## SYSTEM INTERDEPENDENCIES

None

## PROGRAM STATUS

- **FY11:** Continued Production and Fielding of 2kW MTG, 3kW TQG, 5kW TQG, 10kW TQG, 15kW TQG, 30kW TQG, 60kW TQG, 100kW TQG, 200kW TQG, and 840kW DPGDS
- **2QFY11:** Large Advanced Mobile Power Sources (LAMPS) Milestone B Approved, enter Engineering and Manufacturing Development (EMD)
- **4QFY11:** AMMPS Type Classification Standard (TC-Std), Full Materiel Release (FMR), and Full-Rate Production (FRP) Approved

## PROJECTED ACTIVITIES

- **1QFY12-2QFY12:** 3kW TQG Re-procurement
- **3QFY12:** Large Advanced Mobile Power Sources (LAMPS) Contract Award for Engineering and Manufacturing Development (EMD)
- **3QFY12-2QFY13:** Power Distribution Illumination System Electrical (PDISE) Re-procurement
- **FY12-FY14:** Continue Production and Fielding of Advanced Medium Mobile Power Sources (AMMPs), 3kW TQG, 100kW TQG, and Power Distribution Illumination System Electrical (PDISE)

**ACQUISITION PHASE**

Technology Development | Engineering and Manufacturing Development | Production and Deployment | Operations and Support

## Tactical Electric Power (TEP)

**FOREIGN MILITARY SALES**
Tactical Quiet Generators (TQGs) have been purchased by 38 countries

**CONTRACTORS**
**3kW, 5kW, 10kW, 15kW, 100kW, and 200kW TQG:**
DRS Fermont (Bridgeport, CT)
**30kW, 60kW TQG:**
L-3 Westwood (Tulsa, OK)
**2kW MTG:**
Dewey Electronics (Oakland, NJ)
**Deployable Power Generation and Distribution System (DPGDS):**
DRS Fermont (Bridgeport, CT)
**Power Distribution Illumination System Electrical (PDISE):**
Fidelity Technologies Corp. (Reading, PA)
**Advanced Medium Mobile Power Sources (AMMPS) 5-60kW:**
Cummins Power Generation (Minneapolis, MN)

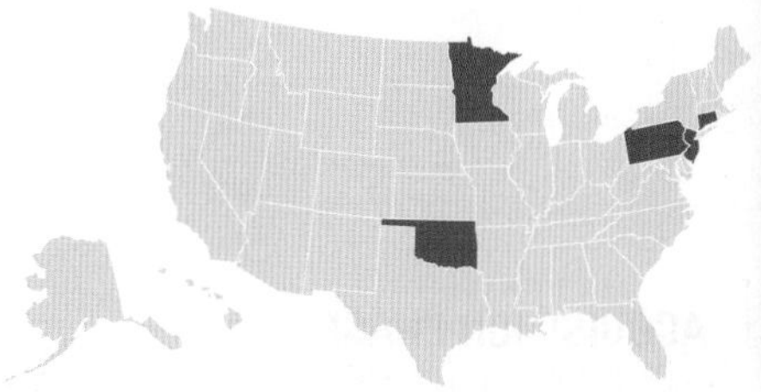

# Tactical Mission Command (TMC)/Maneuver Control System (MCS)

**INVESTMENT COMPONENT**

- **Modernization**
- Recapitalization
- Maintenance

## MISSION

Provide the core collaborative computing environment and common services infrastructure of Army Mission Command and the Mission Command Collapse Migration Strategy. Direct acquisition management, development, implementation, deployment, fielding and training in support of the worldwide deployment of Army Mission Command.

## DESCRIPTION

Tactical Mission Command (TMC) is a suite of products that provides Army and Joint community commanders and their staffs a human-centered collaborative capability with integrated Voice over Internet Protocol (VoIP), a user-defined common operational picture (COP), and real-time situational awareness. TMC provides Army Battle Command System (ABCS) interoperability to support staff functions. In addition, TMC funding provides a tactical SharePoint portal and aids in data management and enterprise services that include email, Active Directory, security, data backup, and failover capabilities. Products include:

- **Command Post of the Future (CPOF):** CPOF is the Army's primary Mission Command system that allows commanders and their staffs the ability to enhance operational effectiveness by enabling broad human collaboration.
- **Command Workstation:** A central piece of Mission Command Collapse strategy that seeks to consolidate MC systems, the Command Workstation will leverage CPOF's ongoing migration to a Third Generation Architecture (3G), which will enable full-spectrum operations, global scalability, and seamless transition between connected and disconnected operations.
- **Command Web:** A key element of the Battle Command Collapse strategy for a consolidated, thin client environment, it gives the non-provisioned users a Web-based COP viewer and data management capability.
- **Personal Assistant that Learns (PAL):** The Defense Advanced Research Projects Agency (DARPA) Personalized Assistant that Learns (PAL) technology enables units to automate staff procedures and tasks.

## SYSTEM INTERDEPENDENCIES

**Other Major Interdependencies**

AMDWS, AMPS, DCGS-A, GCCS, IMETS, JTCW/C2PC, NCES, TAIS, TBMCS, WIN-T

## PROGRAM STATUS

- **1QFY09:** Fielding decision (CPOF QR1)
- **3QFY10:** Operational demonstration of CPOF software with Personalized Assistant that Learns technology
- **1QFY11:** Quarterly release of CPOF software version BC10.0.1

## PROJECTED ACTIVITIES

- **1QFY12:** Beta release of BC Web in Operation Enduring Freedom
- **1QFY12:** Completion of Phase 2 of Personalized Assistant that Learns
- **2QFY12:** Quarterly release of software
- **4QFY12:** Development complete for Phase 3 of CPOF 3rd Generation (3G) architecture

**ACQUISITION PHASE**

- Technology Development
- **Engineering and Manufacturing Development**
- **Production and Deployment**
- Operations and Support

## Tactical Mission Command (TMC)/ Maneuver Control System (MCS)

**FOREIGN MILITARY SALES**
None

**CONTRACTORS**
General Dynamics (Taunton, MA; Scottsdale, AZ)
Sensor Technologies (Red Bank, NJ)
Lockheed Martin (Tinton Falls, NJ)
CACI (Chantilly, VA)

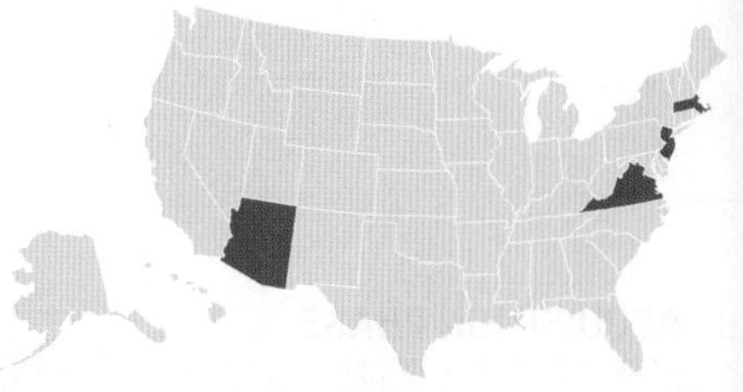

# Tank Ammunition

INVESTMENT COMPONENT

Modernization

Recapitalization

Maintenance

## MISSION

Provides overwhelming lethality overmatch in tank ammunition.

## DESCRIPTION

The current 120mm family of tactical tank ammunition consists of fourth-generation kinetic energy, multipurpose, and canister ammunition. Kinetic energy ammunition lethality is optimized by firing a maximum-weight sub-caliber projectile at the greatest velocity possible, defeating advanced threat armor. The M829A3 kinetic energy cartridge provides armor-defeat capability. Multipurpose ammunition uses a high-explosive warhead to provide blast, armor penetration, and fragmentation effects. The shotgun shell-like M1028 canister cartridge provides the Abrams tank with effective, rapid, lethal fire against massed assaulting infantry, and it is also used in training. The 120mm family has dedicated training cartridges in production: M865, with its reduced range, simulates tactical trajectory to 2,500 meters; and M1002, which simulates the M830A1 size, weight, and nose switch.

To support the Stryker force, the 105mm Mobile Gun System uses M1040 canister cartridges. The M1040 canister cartridge provides rapid, lethal fire against massed assaulting infantry at close range, and it is also used in training. The M467A1 training cartridge is a ballistic match to the M393A3 tactical round, and both completed production in FY10.

## SYSTEM INTERDEPENDENCIES

**Other Major Interdependencies**

The Abrams Main Battle Tank fires 120mm ammunition; the Stryker Mobile Gun System fires 105mm ammunition

## PROGRAM STATUS

- **FY10:** M829A3, M830, M830A1, M1002, M908, M1028, M1040, M393A3, and M467A1 are fielded

## PROJECTED ACTIVITIES

- **FY11:** M865, M1002, and M1040 are in production
- **FY14:** M829E4 MS-C

ACQUISITION PHASE

Technology Development | Engineering and Manufacturing Development | Production and Deployment | Operations and Support

## Tank Ammunition

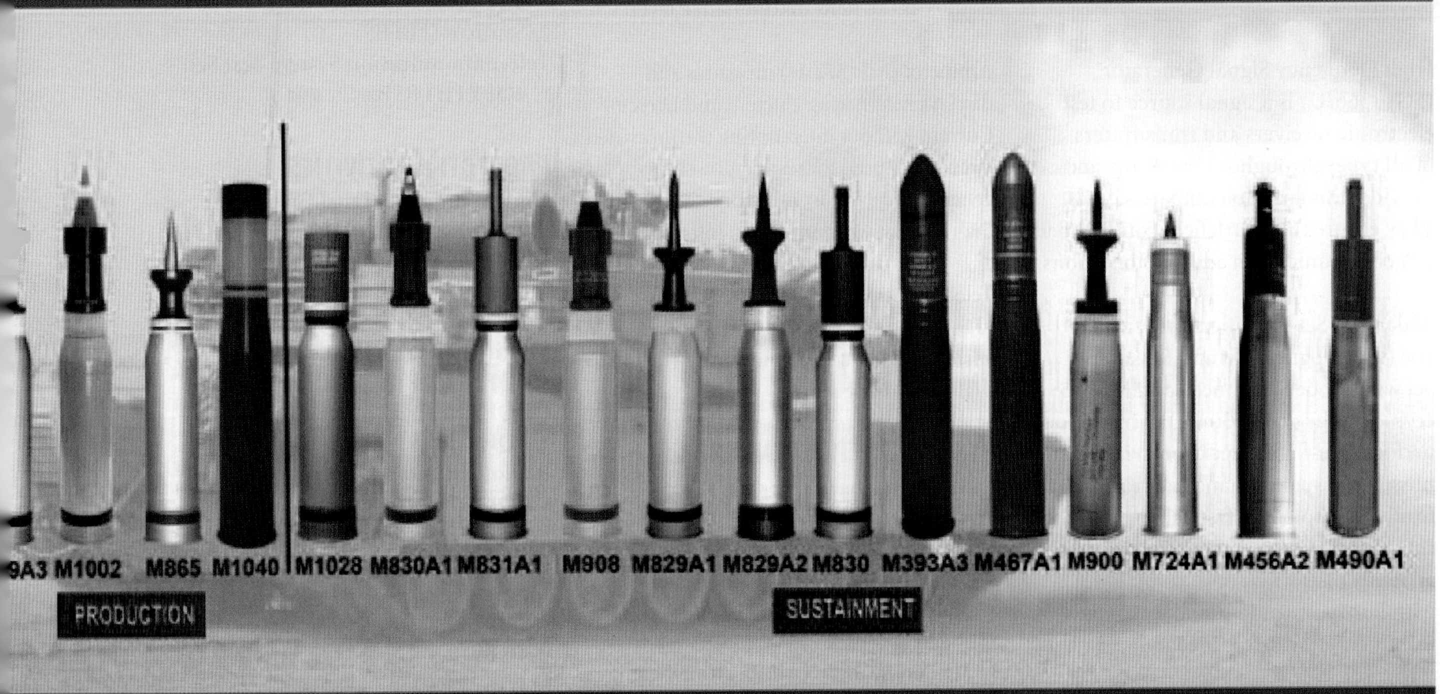


**FOREIGN MILITARY SALES**

**M831A1 and M865:**
Iraq

**KE-WA1:**
Kuwait

**CONTRACTORS**

**M1002 and M865:**
Alliant Techsystems (Plymouth, MN)

**M1002, M865, and KEW:**
General Dynamics Ordnance and Tactical Systems (St. Petersburg, FL)

**M1040:**
L-3 Communications (Lancaster, PA)

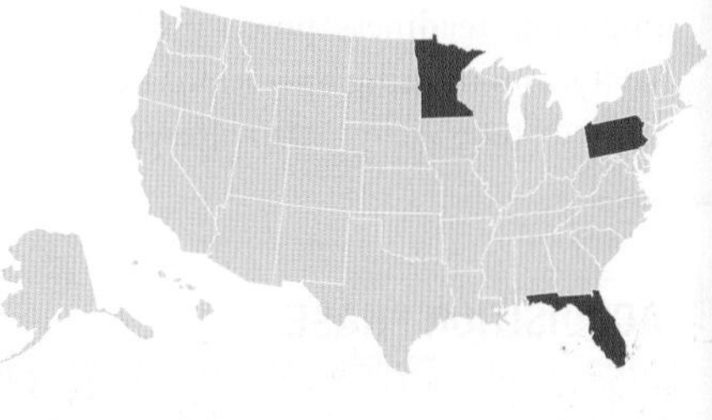

# Test Equipment Modernization (TEMOD)

**INVESTMENT COMPONENT**

Modernization

Recapitalization

Maintenance

## MISSION

Improves readiness of Army weapon systems; minimizes test, measurement, and diagnostic equipment proliferation and obsolescence; and reduces operations/support costs.

## DESCRIPTION

The Test Equipment Modernization (TEMOD) program replaces obsolete General Purpose Electronic Test Equipment (GPETE) with new state-of-the-art equipment. This new equipment reduces proliferation of test equipment, modernizes the Army's current existing inventory, and is essential to the continued support of systems and weapon systems. Acquisitions are commercial items that have significant impact on readiness, power projection, safety, and training operations of the United States Army, Army Reserve, and National Guard. The TEMOD program has procured 38 products replacing over 334+ models.

High Frequency Signal Generator (SG- 1366/U) is a signal source to test electronic receivers and transmitters of all types throughout the Army and provide standards to compare signals. They ensure that battlefield commanders can communicate in adverse conditions.

Radar Test Set Identification Friend or Foe (IFF) Upgrade Kit and Radar Test Set with Mode S enhanced and Mode 5 cryptography (TS-4530A/UPM) is used to perform pre-flight checks on aviation and missile transponders and interrogators to alleviate potential fratricide concerns. It is also required to ensure all Army platforms are in compliance with European and Federal Aviation Administration airspace mandates.

Multimeter (AN/GSM-437) enables quick, reliable troubleshooting, which positively affects operational availability.

Radio Test Set (AN/PRM-36) will be used to quickly and effectively diagnose the SINCGARS, ARC-186, ARC-201, GRC-245, PRC-148, PRC-150, and PSC-5 Radios at the field maintenance level.

Ammeter (ME-572/U) measures and displays Alternating Current and Direct Current without interrupting the measured circuit. It is used for testing power generators cables, installation wiring, and high current weapon system interfaces.

Telecommunication System Test Set (TS-4544/U) measures and displays various bit-data information as related to digital transmission.

## SYSTEM INTERDEPENDENCIES

None

## PROGRAM STATUS

**High Frequency Signal Generator:**
- **2QFY11:** Low-Rate Initial Production (LRIP)
- **3QFY11:** Product Verification Testing (PVT)

**IFF Radar Test Set Mode S (Enhanced) Mode 5:**
- **4QFY11:** PVT

**Multimeter:**
- **4QFY11:** Contract Award

**Radio Test Set:**
- **4QFY11:** Contract Award

**Ammeter :**
- **4QFY11:** Issue Letter Request For Bid Samples (LRFBS)

**Telecommunication System Test Set:**
- **4QFY11:** LRFBS

## PROJECTED ACTIVITIES

**High Frequency Signal Generator:**
- **1QFY12:** FRP

**IFF Radar Test Set Mode S (Enhanced) Mode 5:**
- **1QFY12:** FRP

**Multimeter:**
- **1QFY12:** LRIP
- **3QFY12:** PVT
- **1QFY13:** FRP

**Radio Test Set:**
- **1QFY12:** LRIP
- **3QFY12:** PVT
- **1QFY13:** FRP

**Ammeter:**
- **3QFY12:** Contract Award
- **4QFY12:** LRIP
- **1QFY13:** PVT
- **4QFY13:** FRP

**Telecommunication System Test Set:**
- **4QFY12:** Contract Award
- **1QFY13:** LRIP
- **3QFY13:** PVT
- **1QFY14:** FRP

**ACQUISITION PHASE**

Technology Development | Engineering and Manufacturing Development | Production and Deployment | Operations and Support

Signal Generator SG-1366/U

Radar Test Set TS-4530A/UPM

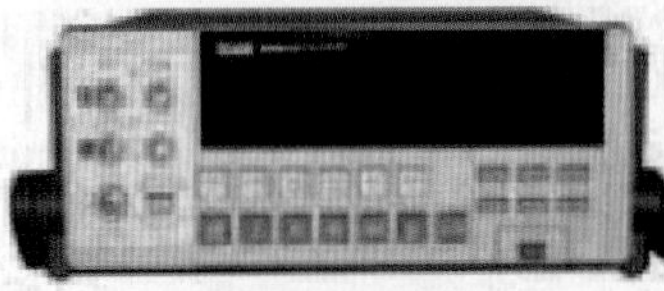

Multimeter AN/GSM-437

Radio Test Set AN/PRM-36

Ammeter ME-572/U

Telecommunication System Test Set

## Test Equipment Modernization (TEMOD)

**FOREIGN MILITARY SALES**

**IFF Radar Test Set Mode S (Enhanced) Mode 5:**
Azerbaijan, Greece, Hungary, Kuwait, Netherlands, Norway, Portugal, Saudi Arabia, Singapore, United Kingdom

**CONTRACTORS**

**High Frequency Signal Generator:**
Agilent Technologies (Englewood, CO)
**IFF Radar Test Set Mode S (Enhanced) Mode 5:**
Tel-Instrument Electronics Corp. (Carlstadt, NJ)
**Multimeter:**
To be determined
**Radio Test Set:**
To be determined
**Ammeter:**
To be determined
**Telecommunication System Test Set:**
To be determined

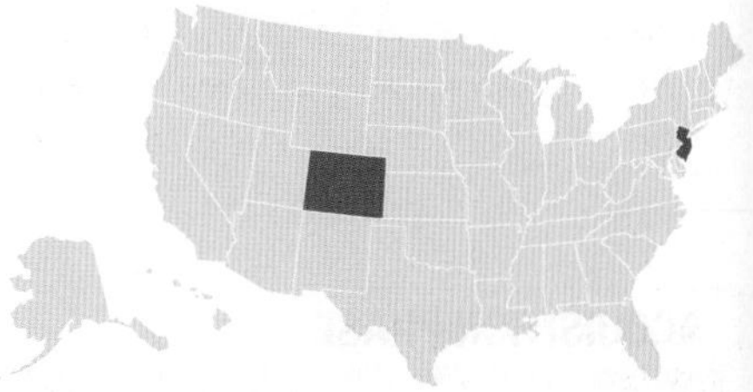

# Transportation Coordinators' Automated Information for Movement System II (TC-AIMS II)

INVESTMENT COMPONENT

- **Modernization**
- Recapitalization
- Maintenance

## MISSION

Facilitates movement, management, and control of personnel, equipment, and supplies from a home station to a theater of operations and back, and provides in-theater support for onward movement, sustainment planning requirements, and source in-transit visibility data.

## DESCRIPTION

The Transportation Coordinators' Automated Information for Movement System II (TC-AIMS II) is a service migration system. Characteristics include: source feeder system to Joint Force Requirements Generation II, Joint Planning and Execution System, Global Transportation Network, and Services' command and control systems; common user interface to facilitate multiservice user training and operations; commercial off-the-shelf hardware/software architecture; net-centric implementation with breakaway client-server and/or stand alone/workgroup configurations; and incremental, block upgrade developmental strategy.

## SYSTEM INTERDEPENDENCIES

None

## PROGRAM STATUS

- **1QFY11:** Completed TOPS implementation in Iraq and Kuwait
- **2QFY11:** Released TC-AIMS II v6.1.1
- **2QFY11:** JUONS approved to provide in-transit visibility and automate capability to manage surface and air transportation services
- **4QFY11:** Will reach FOC

## PROJECTED ACTIVITIES

- **4QFY12:** Complete TC-AIMS II version 7 (Wilton); provide Vista/Windows 7 compatibility, data checks/validations; publish CMP to SIPRNET
- **4QFY12:** Complete AMR Phase II fielding
- **3QFY13:** Complete TC-AIMS II version 8; integrate with SLPC, migrate reference data

ACQUISITION PHASE

Technology Development | Engineering and Manufacturing Development | Production and Deployment | **Operations and Support**

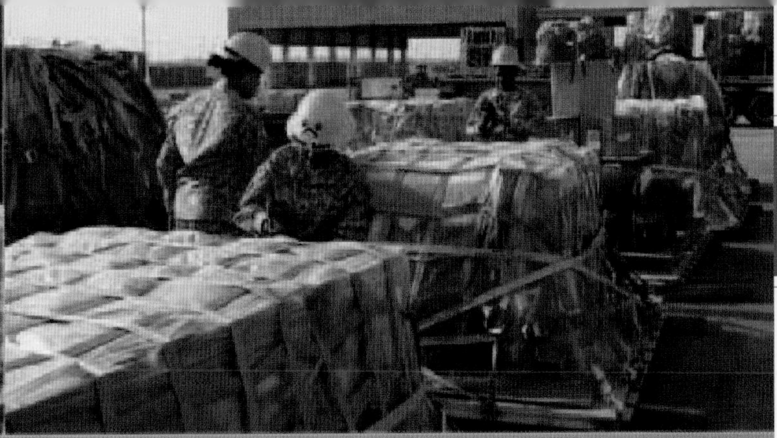

## Transportation Coordinators' Automated Information for Movement System II (TC-AIMS II)

**FOREIGN MILITARY SALES**
None

**CONTRACTORS**

**Systems Integration:**
Engineering Research and Development Command (Vicksburg, MS)
Future Research Corp. (Huntsville, AL)
Apptricity Corp. (Dallas, TX)

**Program and Fielding/Training support:**
L-3 Services, an MPRI Company (Alexandria, VA)

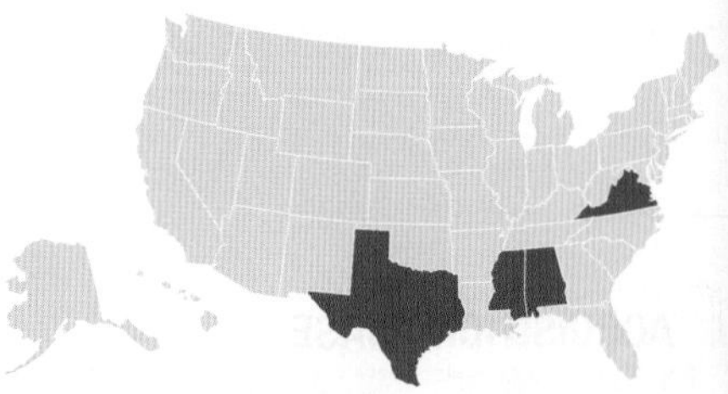

# Tube-Launched, Optically-Tracked, Wire-Guided (TOW) Missiles

**INVESTMENT COMPONENT**

Modernization

Recapitalization

Maintenance

## MISSION

Provides long-range, heavy anti-tank and precision assault fire capabilities to Army and Marine forces.

## DESCRIPTION

The Close Combat Missile System-Heavy (CCMS-H) Tube-Launched, Optically-Tracked, Wire-Guided (TOW) is a heavy anti-tank/precision assault weapon system, consisting of a launcher and a missile. The missile is six inches in diameter (encased, 8.6 inches) and 49 inches long. The gunner defines the aim point by maintaining the sight cross hairs on the target. The launcher automatically steers the missile along the line-of-sight toward the aim point via a pair of control wires or a one-way radio frequency (RF) link, which links the launcher and missile.

TOW missiles are employed on the High Mobility Multipurpose Wheeled Vehicle (HMMWV)-mounted Improved Target Acquisition System (ITAS), HMMWV-mounted M220A4 launcher (TOW 2), Stryker Anti-Tank Guided Missile (ATGM) Vehicles, and Bradley Fighting Vehicles (A2/A2ODS/A2OIF/A3) within the Infantry, Stryker, and Heavy Brigade Combat Teams, respectively. TOW missiles are also employed on the Marine HMMWV-mounted ITAS, HMMWV-mounted M220A4 launcher (TOW 2), LAV-ATGM Vehicle, and AH1W Cobra attack helicopter. TOW is also employed by allied nations on a variety of ground and airborne platforms.

The TOW 2B Aero is the most modern and capable missile in the TOW family, with an extended maximum range to 4,500 meters. The TOW 2B Aero has an advanced counteractive protection system capability and defeats all current and projected threat armor systems. The TOW 2B Aero flies over the target (offset above the gunner's aim point) and uses a laser profilometer and magnetic sensor to detect and fire two downward-directed, explosively formed penetrator warheads into the target. The TOW 2B Aero's missile weight is 49.8 pounds (encased, 65 pounds).

The TOW Bunker Buster is optimized for performance against urban structures, earthen bunkers, field fortifications, and light-skinned armor threats. The missile impact is at the aim point. It has a 6.25 pound, 6-inch diameter high-explosive, bulk-charge warhead, and its missile weighs 45.2 pounds. The TOW BB has an impact sensor (crush switch) located in the main-charge and gives a pyrotechnic detonation delay to enhance warhead effectiveness. The PBXN-109 explosive is housed in a thick casing for maximum performance. The TOW BB can produce a 21- to 24-inch diameter hole in an 8-inch thick, double reinforced concrete wall at a range of 65 to 3,750 meters.

## SYSTEM INTERDEPENDENCIES

**Other Major Interdependencies**

M1121/1167 HMMWV, Stryker ATGM

## PROGRAM STATUS

- **Current:** TOW 2B Aero RF and BB RF in production

## PROJECTED ACTIVITIES

- **FY12-FY16:** TOW Multiyear Contract

**ACQUISITION PHASE**

Technology Development | Engineering and Manufacturing Development | Production and Deployment | Operations and Support

## Tube-Launched, Optically-Tracked, Wire-Guided (TOW) Missiles

**FOREIGN MILITARY SALES**

The TOW weapon system has been sold to more than 43 allied nations over the life of the system.

**CONTRACTORS**

**TOW 2B Aero and TOW BB**

**Prime:**
Raytheon Missile Systems (Tucson, AZ)

**Control Actuator, Shutter Actuator:**
Moog Inc. (Salt Lake City, UT)

**Warheads:**
Aerojet General (Socorro, NM)

**Gyroscope:**
BAE Systems (Cheshire, CT)

**Sensor (TOW 2B only):**
Thales (Basingstoke, United Kingdom)

**Launch Motor:**
ATK (Radford, VA)

**Flight Motor:**
ATK (Rocket Center, WV)

**Machined/Fabricated Parts:**
Klune (Spanish Fork, UT)

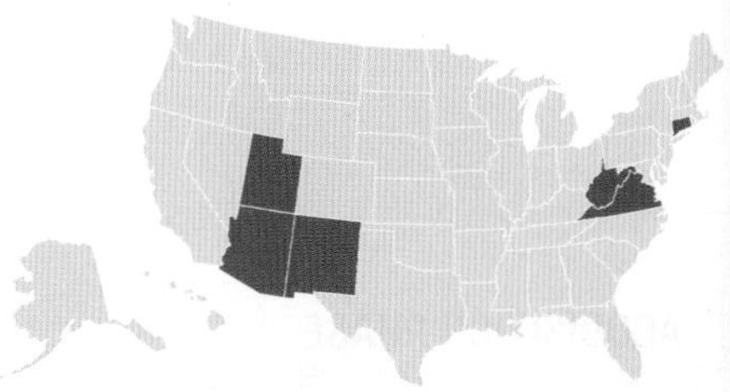

# Unit Water Pod System (Camel II)

## INVESTMENT COMPONENT

- **Modernization**
- Recapitalization
- Maintenance

## MISSION

Receives, stores, and dispenses potable water to units at all echelons throughout the battlefield.

## DESCRIPTION

The Unit Water Pod System (Camel II) is the U.S. Army's primary water distribution system. Camel II replaces the M107, M149, and M1112 series water trailers. It consists of an 800-900 gallon capacity baffled water tank with integrated freeze protection and all hoses and fittings necessary to dispense water by gravity flow. The acquisition strategy consists of two increments: Increment 1 is the basic system with freeze protection; Increment 2 will provide modular component(s) to give the Camel II water chilling, pumping, circulation, and onboard power generation as add-on capabilities.

The Camel II is mounted on an M1095 Trailer, allowing for better transportability on and off the road by utilizing the Family of Medium Tactical Vehicle Trucks. It holds a minimum of 800 gallons of water and provides a one-day supply of potable water for drinking and other purposes. If the unit has another source of drinking water, such as bottled water, then the Camel II can provide two days of potable water for other purposes. It is operational from -25 to 120 degrees Fahrenheit. The system also contains six filling positions for filling canteens and five-gallon water cans.

## SYSTEM INTERDEPENDENCIES

**Other Major Interdependencies**
M1095 Medium Tactical Vehicle Trailer

## PROJECTED ACTIVITIES

- **FY11:** Contract Awarded
- **FY12:** Deliver test units
- **FY12:** Conduct government testing
- **FY13:** Full Materiel Release; type classification standard
- **FY13:** First unit equipped

## ACQUISITION PHASE

Technology Development | Engineering and Manufacturing Development | **Production and Deployment** | Operations and Support

## Unit Water Pod System (Camel II)

**FOREIGN MILITARY SALES**
None

**CONTRACTORS**
Choctaw Defense Manufacturing Contractors (CDMC) (OK)

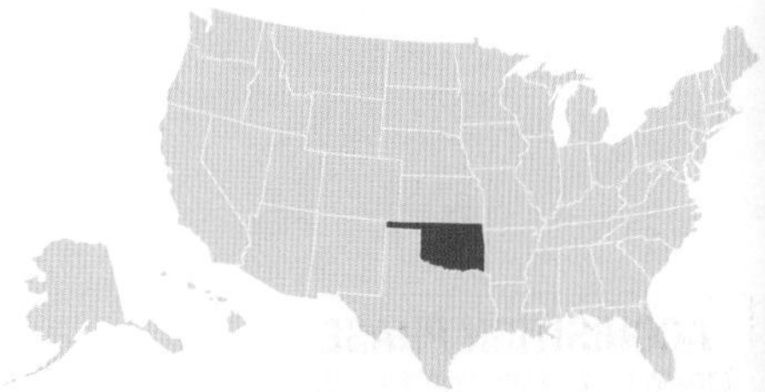

# Warfighter Information Network-Tactical (WIN-T) Increment 1

INVESTMENT COMPONENT

Modernization

Recapitalization

Maintenance

## MISSION

Provides the Warfighter seamless, assured, mobile communications, along with advanced network management tools.

## DESCRIPTION

Warfighter Information Network-Tactical (WIN-T) Increment 1 is the Army's current and future tactical network, representing a generational leap forward in allowing widely dispersed, highly maneuverable units to communicate. Increment 1 is a converged tactical communications network providing voice, data, and video capability to connect the battalion-level Warfighter, allowing greater flexibility of troop movement and is scalable to meet the mission commander's requirements. It is divided into two sub-increments defined as Increment 1a, "extended networking at-the-halt," and Increment 1b, "enhanced networking-at-the-halt." Increment 1 is a rapidly deployable, early entry system housed in a Lightweight Multipurpose Shelter (LMS) and mounted on an Expanded Capacity High Mobility Multipurpose Wheeled Vehicle for roll-on/roll-off mobility.

Increment 1a upgrades the former Joint Network Node satellite capability to access the Ka-band defense Wideband Global Satellite, reducing the reliance on commercial Ku-band satellites.

WIN-T Increment 1b introduces the Net Centric Waveform, a dynamic wave form that optimizes bandwidth and satellite utilization. It also introduces a colorless core security architecture, which meets Global Information Grid Information Assurance security compliance requirements and incorporates industry standards for network operations and intrusion detection.

WIN-T Increment 1 is a Joint compatible communications package that allows the Warfighter to use advanced networking capabilities, interface to legacy systems, retain interoperability with Current Force systems, and keep in step with future increments of WIN-T

## SYSTEM INTERDEPENDENCIES

**In this Publication**

Warfighter Information Network-Tactical (WIN-T) Increment 2, Warfighter Information Network-Tactical (WIN-T) Increment 3

**Other Major Interdependencies**

ACUS Mod, Army Battle Command System, C2OTM, GPS, C2OTM, Teleport, SMART-T, TOCS

## PROGRAM STATUS

- **2QFY11:** Operational Test and Data Evaluation Report (BLRIP)
- **3QFY11:** Acquisition Decision Memorandum (ADM) on 21 May 2011 to waive a requirement for a Full-Rate Production (FRP) Decision
- **3QFY11:** Approval for Type Classification

## PROJECTED ACTIVITIES

- **2QFY12:** Increment 1a completed Fieldings
- **2QFY12:** Increment 1b Operational Test

ACQUISITION PHASE

Technology Development | Engineering and Manufacturing Development | Production and Deployment | Operations and Support

Joint Network Node (JNN)

Tactical Hub

Satellite Terminal Trailer (STT)

Battalion Command Post Node

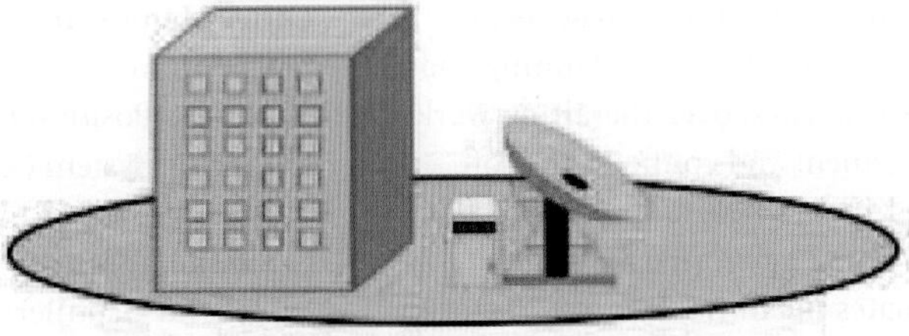
Fixed Regional Hub Node (FRHN)

## Warfighter Information Network-Tactical (WIN-T) Increment 1

**FOREIGN MILITARY SALES**
None

**CONTRACTORS**

**Modem/Integration:**
General Dynamics C4 Systems Inc. (Taunton, MA)

**Transportable Terminals:**
General Dynamics SATCOM Technologies (Duluth, GA)

**PM Support:**
Engineering Solutions and Products (Eatontown, NJ)
SRC (Shrewsbury, NJ)

# Warfighter Information Network-Tactical (WIN-T) Increment 2

**INVESTMENT COMPONENT**

- **Modernization**
- Recapitalization
- Maintenance

## MISSION

Provides "initial networking on-the-move" as a converged tactical communications and transport layer network leveraging proven commercial and government technology, enabling Joint land forces to engage enemy forces deeper and more effectively, while incurring fewer losses.

## DESCRIPTION

Warfighter Information Network-Tactical (WIN-T) Increment 2 accelerates delivery of a self-forming, self-healing mobile network infrastructure via commercial off-the-shelf and government off-the-shelf technologies. Increment 2 leverages an early release of the objective Highband Networking Waveform running on the Highband Networking Radio to provide high throughput line-of-sight communications and leverages an early release of the objective Net Centric Waveform on a ruggedized R-MPM-1000 modem for on-the-move (OTM) satellite communications enabling greater situational awareness and command and control. Multiple configuration items tailor capability from division down to company. It provides an accelerated delivery of network operations capability that allows management, prioritization, and protection of information while reducing organizational and operational support.

Increment 2 network operations include automated planning, on-the-move node planning, automated link planning for currently fielded systems, initial automated spectrum management, initial quality of service planning and monitoring, and over-the-air network management and configuration of WIN-T radios. Additionally, Increment 2 network operations automates the initial Internet Protocol planning and routing configurations.

Fielding is planned to 54 Brigade Combat Teams and 10 Divisions by 2018.

## SYSTEM INTERDEPENDENCIES

**In this Publication**

Bradley Fighting Vehicle Systems Upgrade, Distributed Common Ground System-Army (DCGS-A), Integrated Air and Missile Defense (IAMD), Joint Tactical Radio System Ground Mobile Radios (JTRS GMR), Joint Tactical Radio System Handheld, Manpack, Small Form Fit (JTRS HMS), Mine Resistant Ambush Protected Vehicles (MRAP), Single Channel Ground and Airborne Radio System (SINCGARS), Stryker Family of Vehicles, Warfighter Information Network-Tactical (WIN-T) Increment 1, Warfighter Information Network-Tactical (WIN-T) Increment 3

**Other Major Interdependencies**

Battle Command Servers (BCS), Enhanced Position Location and Reporting System (EPLRS), Light Tactical Vehicle (LTV), Tactical NW Operations Security Center (TNOSC), Wideband Gapfiller

## PROGRAM STATUS

- **1QFY11:** Low-Rate Initial Production (LRIP) Lots 1B and 2 Contract Award
- **2QFY11-3QFY11:** Production Qualification Test (Contractor)
- **3QFY11:** Logistics demonstration
- **4QFY11:** Product qualification test (Government)

## PROJECTED ACTIVITIES

- **2QFY12:** Cold Region Test; New Equipment Training (NET)
- **3QFY12:** Force Development Test
- **3QFY12:** Initial Operational Test
- **4QFY12:** Full-Rate Production Decision Review
- **4QFY12:** First Unit Equipped
- **3QFY13:** Initial Operational Capability

**ACQUISITION PHASE**

- Technology Development
- Engineering and Manufacturing Development
- **Production and Deployment**
- Operations and Support

## Warfighter Information Network-Tactical (WIN-T) Increment 2

**FOREIGN MILITARY SALES**
None

**CONTRACTORS**
**WIN-T System:**
**Prime:**
General Dynamics (Taunton, MA)
**Subcomponent:**
Lockheed Martin (Gaithersburg, MD)
**Subcontractors:**
Harris Corp. (Melbourne, FL)
L-3 Communications (San Diego, CA)
General Dynamics (Richardson, TX)

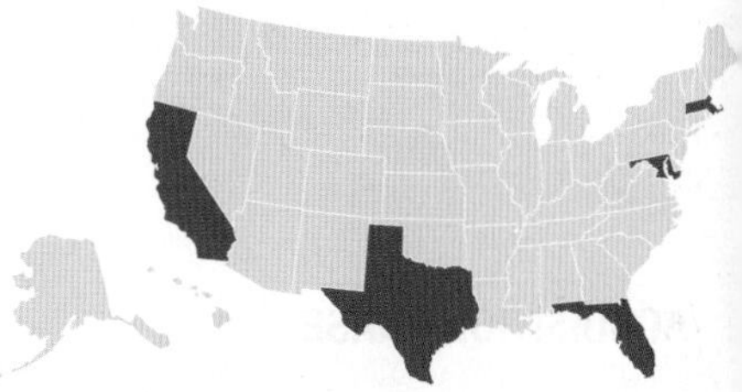

# Warfighter Information Network-Tactical (WIN-T) Increment 3

**INVESTMENT COMPONENT**

- **Modernization**
- Recapitalization
- Maintenance

## MISSION

Provides "full networking on-the-move" as a mobile, multitiered, tactical communications/transport layer network, enabling Joint land forces to engage enemy forces effectively.

## DESCRIPTION

The Warfighter Information Network-Tactical (WIN-T) Increment 3 enables the full-objective mobile, tactical network distribution of command, control, communications, computers, intelligence, surveillance, and reconnaissance information via voice, data, and real-time video. Building on previous increments, Increment 3 provides more robust connectivity and greater network access via military specification radios, higher bandwidth satellite communications (SATCOM) and line-of-sight (LOS) waveforms, an aerial tier (LOS airborne relay), and integrated network operations. It manages, prioritizes, and protects information through network operations (network management, quality of service, and information assurance) while reducing organizational and operational support. WIN-T Increment 3 ensures communications interoperability with Joint, Allied, Coalition, Current Force, and commercial voice and data networks. Using communications payloads mounted on Unmanned Aerial Systems, Increment 3 introduces an air tier to increase network reliability and robustness with automatic routing between LOS and SATCOM. This extends connectivity and provides increased Warfighter mobility, providing constant mobile communications.

## SYSTEM INTERDEPENDENCIES

**In this Publication**

Bradley Fighting Vehicle Systems Upgrade, Integrated Air and Missile Defense (IAMD), Joint Tactical Radio System Ground Mobile Radios (JTRS GMR), Joint Tactical Radio System Handheld, Manpack, Small Form Fit (JTRS HMS), Distributed Common Ground System-Army (DCGS-A), Stryker Family of Vehicles, Warfighter Information Network-Tactical (WIN-T) Increment 1, Warfighter Information Network-Tactical (WIN-T) Increment 2

**Other Major Interdependencies**

Assistant Secretary of the Army for Acquisition, Logistics, and Technology System-of-Systems (ASA(ALT) SOS), BCT Modernization, Enhanced Position Location and Reporting System (EPLRS), Light Tactical Vehicle (LTV), PEO Integration, PM Unmanned Aircraft System (UAS), Tactical NW Operations and Security Center (TNOSC), Wideband Gapfiller

## PROGRAM STATUS

- **1QFY11:** Revised Acquisition Program Baseline (APB)

## PROJECTED ACTIVITIES

- **3QFY12:** Transmission subsystem critical design review
- **4QFY13:** Full critical design review
- **2QFY14-3QFY14:** Transmission subsystem developmental test/limited user test

**ACQUISITION PHASE**

- Technology Development
- **Engineering and Manufacturing Development**
- Production and Deployment
- Operations and Support

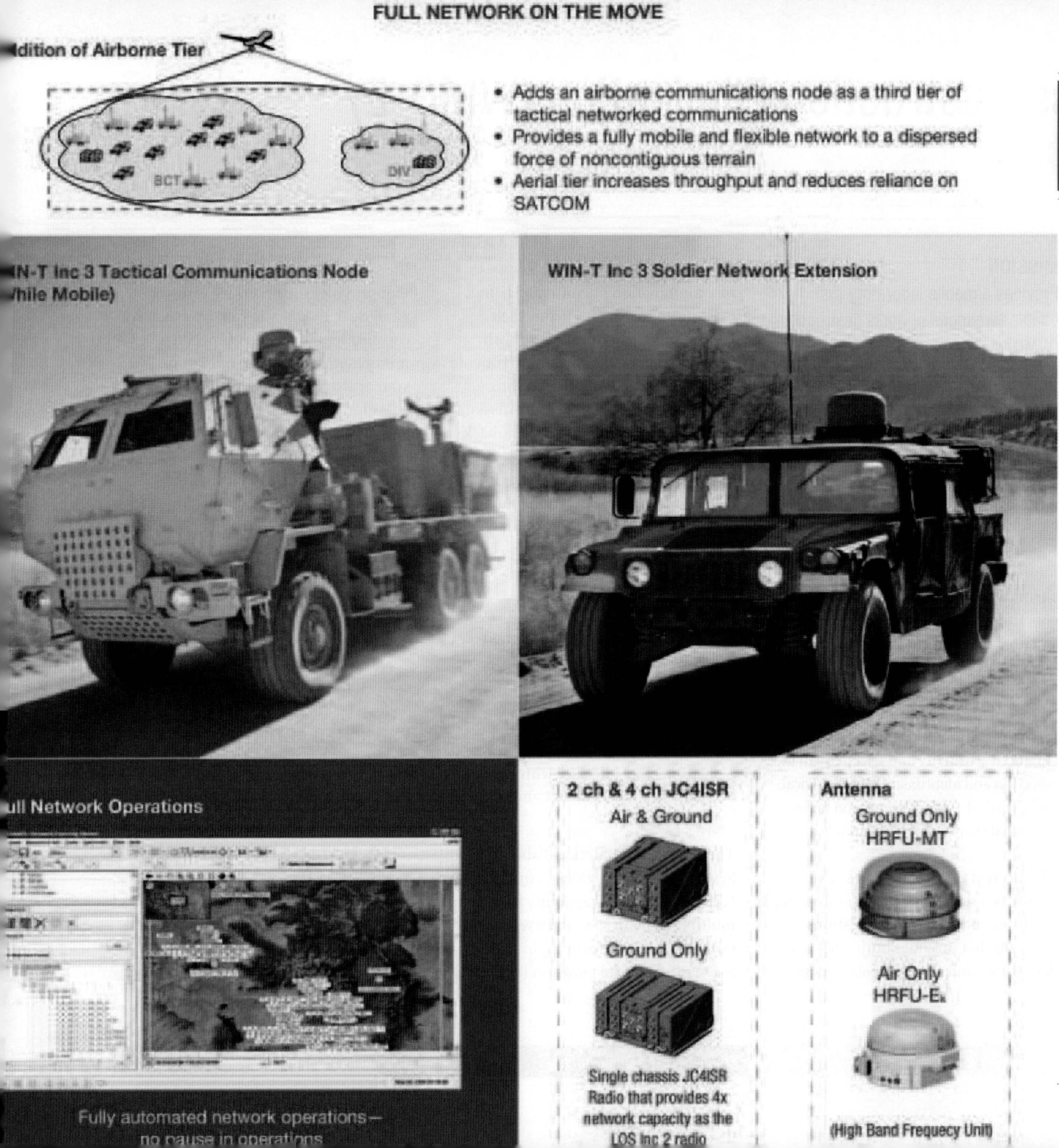
FULL NETWORK ON THE MOVE
dition of Airborne Tier
BCT
DIV
• Adds an airborne communications node as a third tier of tactical networked communications
• Provides a fully mobile and flexible network to a dispersed force of noncontiguous terrain
• Aerial tier increases throughput and reduces reliance on SATCOM
IN-T Inc 3 Tactical Communications Node
hile Mobile)
WIN-T Inc 3 Soldier Network Extension
ull Network Operations
Fully automated network operations—
no pause in operations
2 ch & 4 ch JC4ISR
Air & Ground
Ground Only
Single chassis JC4ISR Radio that provides 4x network capacity as the LOS Inc 2 radio
Antenna
Ground Only
HRFU-MT
Air Only
HRFU-E
(High Band Frequecy Unit)

## Warfighter Information Network-Tactical (WIN-T) Increment 3

**FOREIGN MILITARY SALES**

None

**CONTRACTORS**

**Prime:**

General Dynamics (Taunton, MA; Sunrise, FL)

**Subcomponent:**

Lockheed Martin (Gaithersburg, MD)

**Subcontractors:**

Harris Corp. (Melbourne, FL)

BAE Systems (Wayne, NJ)

L-3 Communications (San Diego, CA)

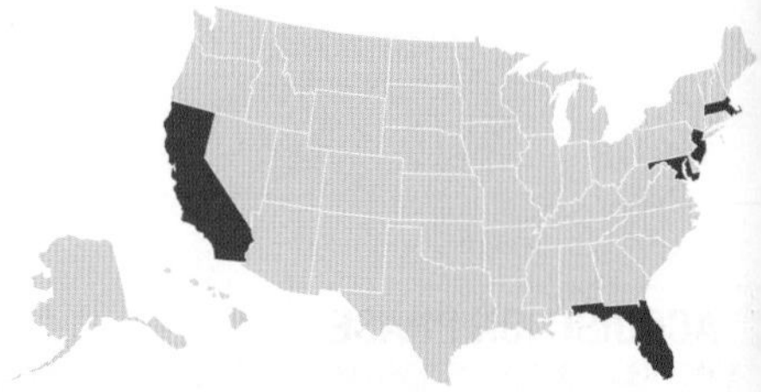

# Weapons of Mass Destruction Elimination (WMD-E)

**INVESTMENT COMPONENT**

Modernization

Recapitalization

Maintenance

## MISSION

Provides a mobile laboratory that enables weapons of mass destruction (WMD) civil support teams to perform on-site analysis of contaminants in support of first responders.

## DESCRIPTION

Analytical Laboratory System (ALS) Increment 1 is a mobile analytical laboratory that provides the civil support team (CST) capabilities for detecting and identifying chemical, biological, or radiological contamination. ALS Increment 1 is a system enhancement program to replace the current Mobile ALS and interim Dismounted Analytical Platform.

It provides advanced technologies with enhanced sensitivity and selectivity in the detection and identification of biological and chemical warfare agents and toxic industrial chemicals and materials.

The Unified Command Suite (UCS) vehicle is a self-contained, stand-alone, C-130 air-mobile communications platform that provides both voice and data communications capabilities to CST commanders. The UCS consists of a combination of commercial and existing government off-the-shelf communications equipment (both secure and non-secure data) to provide the full range of communications necessary to support the CST mission. It is the primary means of reach-back communications for the ALS and acts as a command-and-control hub to deliver a common operational picture for planning and fulfilling an incident response. It provides:

- Digital voice and data over satellite network
- Secure Internet Protocol Router Network (SIPRNET) and Non-Secure (NIPRNET)
- Radio remote and intercom with cross-banding
- Over-the-horizon communication interoperable interface with state emergency management and other military units

The Common Analytical Laboratory System (CALS) provides a common CBRNE analytical capability across multiple domain spaces. Developed in both a mobile platform (light) as well as a semi-fixed site platform (heavy), the CALS has a modular design that provides the necessary array of analytical, diagnostic, and investigative capabilities tailored for a specified mission or contingency operation. The system also provides voice and data communications to enhance assessment of and response to WMD events.

## SYSTEM INTERDEPENDENCIES

**Other Major Interdependencies**

Unified Command Suite (UCS)

## PROGRAM STATUS

- **UCS:** Modernization of radio distribution system, news gathering capability, server/IT systems capability, and ultra-high frequency repeater capability as part of Change III LCM.

## PROJECTED ACTIVITIES

- **ALS-Environmental Toxin Analytics Upgrade UCS**: Modernization of communication on-the-move system, radio crossbanding system, and secondary reachback system as part of Change IV
- **ALS-Environmental Toxin Analytics Upgrade UCS**: Engineering development on platform modernization

**ACQUISITION PHASE**

Technology Development | Engineering and Manufacturing Development | Production and Deployment | Operations and Support

# ALS
## ANALYTICAL LABORATORY SYSTEM

# UCS
## UNIFIED COMMAND SUITE

**Weapons of Mass Destruction Elimination (WMD-E)**

**FOREIGN MILITARY SALES**
None

**CONTRACTORS**
**ALS Vehicle:**
Wolf Coach Inc., an L-3 Communications Company (Auburn, MA)
**ALS Integrator:**
EAI Corporation/SAIC (Abingdon, MD)
**UCS Vehicle:**
Wolf Coach Inc., an L-3 Communications Company (Auburn, MA)
**UCS Communications System Integrator:**
Naval Air Warfare Center Aircraft Division (Patuxent River, MD)

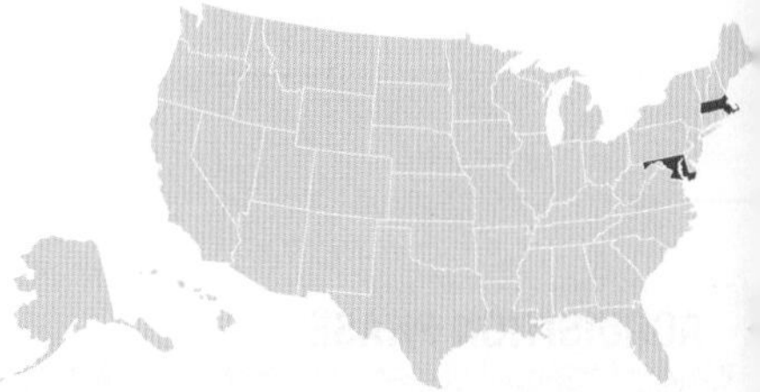

# XM806 .50 Caliber Machine Gun

INVESTMENT COMPONENT

Modernization

Recapitalization

Maintenance

## MISSION

Provides vehicle and weapon squads with a lightweight .50 caliber weapon system that is easily dismounted.

## DESCRIPTION

The XM806 .50 Caliber Machine Gun weighs approximately one-half of a similarly configured M2 and reduces the recoil by at least 60 percent. This lighter weight permits easy dismount and ground transportability. The lower recoil reduces strain on vehicle mounts and permits the use of an optic for greater lethality through increased first-burst accuracy and control.

The XM806 can fire all of the .50 caliber service ammunition in the current inventory and is capable of defeating personnel and lightly armored targets out to 2,000 meters. It is designed to augment the M2 .50 Caliber Machine Gun, but it can also be used to replace the M2 in select operational locations. Safety is improved through a manual safety and a quick change barrel that eliminates the requirement for the operator to adjust headspace and timing.

The weapon is ideal for light infantry and Special Operations Forces, as well as for vehicles demanding more lethality but lighter weight.

## SYSTEM INTERDEPENDENCIES

**Other Major Interdependencies**

None

## PROGRAM STATUS

- **3QFY11:** Completed Development Test Phase 1
- **4QFY11:** Development Test Phase 2 initiated

## PROJECTED ACTIVITIES

- **1QFY12:** Start Limited User Test
- **2QFY12:** Milestone C—Low-Rate Initial Production

ACQUISITION PHASE

Technology Development | Engineering and Manufacturing Development | Production and Deployment | Operations and Support

## XM806 .50 Caliber Machine Gun

**FOREIGN MILITARY SALES**
None

**CONTRACTORS**
General Dynamics Armament and Technical Products (Williston, VT)

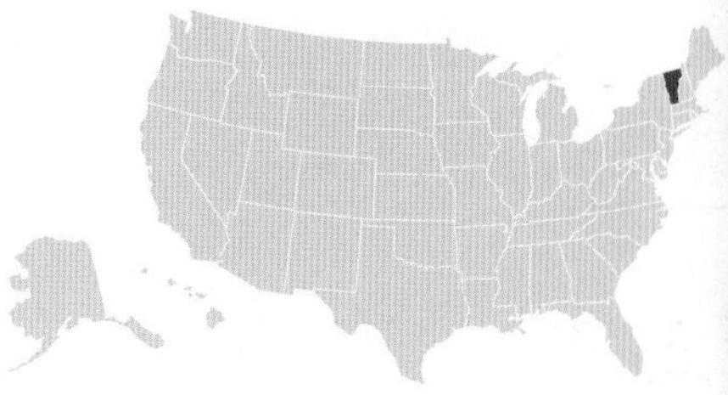

# Science and Technology

The Army Science and Technology (S&T) strategy supports the Army's goals to restore balance between current and future demands by providing new technologies to enhance and modernize systems in the Current Force and to enable new capabilities in the Future Force. This strategy is enabled through a portfolio of investments, each providing different results in distinct timeframes.

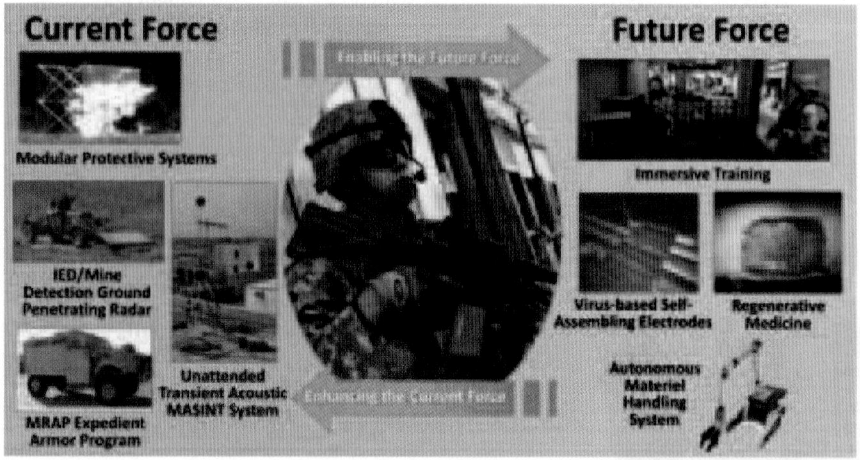


**Figure 1:** Army S&T Strategy—Develop and mature technology to enable the Future Force while seeking to enhance the Current Force

These S&T investments include: far-term, funding basic research for discovery and understanding of phenomena; mid-term, funding applied research laboratory concept demonstrations; near-term, funding advanced technology development demonstrations in relevant environments outside the laboratory; manufacturing technology processes; and technology maturation, which addresses technologies that will expedite technology transition to programs of record. The technology demonstrations prove technology concepts and their military utility to inform the combat developments process and provide the acquisition community with evidence of technologies' readiness to satisfy system requirements. This portfolio supports overseas contingency operations in three ways: 1) Soldiers benefit today from technologies that emerged from our past investments; 2) we exploit transition opportunities by accelerating mature technologies derived from ongoing S&T efforts; and 3) we leverage the expertise of our scientists and engineers to develop solutions to unforeseen problems encountered during current operations, such as armor applied to Mine Resistant Ambush Protected (MRAP) combat vehicles for enhanced protection from Rocket Propelled Grenades. The entire S&T program is adaptable and responsive to the Army Modernization Strategy.

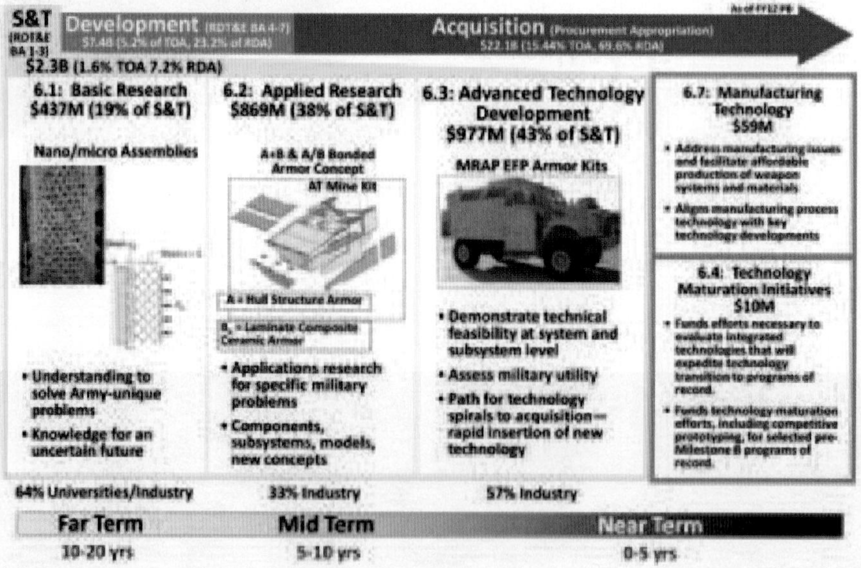


**Figure 2:** The S&T portfolio consists of five types of investments

# FORCE PROTECTION

## Advanced Aircraft Survivability

The Advanced Aircraft Survivability effort develops and demonstrates an integrated, multispectral (ultraviolet, infrared, acoustic), distributed aperture aircraft survivability solution to simultaneously detect, identify, and cue integrated countermeasures against current operational and emerging Hostile Fire and Man Portable Air Defense (MANPAD) technology threats. Elements of this program include: improved missile and small arms fire detection sensors; lightweight laser countermeasure for MANPAD missiles and integrated visual laser dazzling of small arms threats; lightweight beam directors; and closed-loop threat identification techniques.

## Threat Detection and Neutralization for Route Clearance

This effort demonstrates and matures threat/mine detection and neutralization capabilities to address a broader spectrum of in-road threats for route clearance vehicles. This will also integrate improvised explosive device/mine detection and neutralization technologies, communications, and electronic warfare equipment to provide an effective system concept of operations for route clearance. In addition, this will also provide multiple sensor technologies for effective standoff detection of deeply buried targets in primary and secondary roads and surface targets located on roadsides. The benefits to the Soldier include higher speed operations and rates of advance, as well as enhanced mobility and survivability of U.S. forces while clearing and maintaining travel routes in urban and rural areas.

## Defense Against Rockets, Artillery, and Mortars (RAM) Technologies

Technology efforts in defense against RAM mature and demonstrate critical technologies to provide the mobile capability to defeat threats at extended ranges and across a 360-degree hemisphere. Technologies of missile and gun-launched interceptors to protect against RAM threats include the following subsystems developments: technical fire control node to process the decision logic for intercept; tracking and fire control radar to provide a precise location of the threat; launch systems; a guided missile-based interceptor with a high-explosive warhead; a miniature hit-to-kill missile-based interceptor; and a guided 50mm course-corrected projectile and gun.

**Figure 3:** Defense against RAM

# INTELLIGENCE, SURVEILLANCE, RECONNAISSANCE

## Advanced Common Sensor Payload

The Advanced Common Sensor Payload will provide day/night wide-area persistent imaging and enhanced reconnaissance, surveillance, and target acquisition capabilities for insertion into the common sensor payload (CSP). This CSP has a high-definition sensor and a dual-color, third-generation, forward-looking radar. This system will include "Step-Stare" software that provides persistent imaging scan modes to improve resolution and tiered data processing that adds onboard modules for enhanced data exploitation and compression to allow operation over extended-range and multipurpose data links. The payoff for the unmanned aircraft system will be a payload that provides persistent wide-area activity monitoring and enhanced capabilities to include target search at ID resolution, reduced operator workloads, and improved data exploitation.

## Integrated Radio-frequency Operations Network (IRON) Symphony

IRON Symphony will define and develop a next-generation Army Electronic Warfare (EW) networking capability, based on an integrated and distributed EW framework, to enable the coordinated detection, geo-location, reporting, and engagement of multiple diverse threat waveforms. Most current EW systems are designed to mitigate a single threat waveform. Multiple threats force the development of multiple systems, resulting in a rapid escalation of interoperability and spectral de-confliction issues. The robust proliferation and simultaneous use of modern communication threats, as well as the complexity of the threat signals themselves, have created an environment where the use of individualized solutions is no longer feasible.

## Flexible Display Initiative

The flexible display initiative develops flexible display technologies for affordable, lightweight, rugged, low-power, and reduced-volume displays in conjunction with the development of human factors parameters for systems utilizing flexible displays. Flexible displays have reduced weight and are inherently rugged with ultra-low power electro-optic technologies as compared to traditional liquid-crystal, glass-based displays. The development of displays on flexible substrates will enable novel applications that cannot be achieved by glass-based technologies (e.g., wearable and conformal for Soldier applications, conformal for vehicle and cockpit applications, and compact display that can be rolled out for multiuser applications).

**Figure 4:** Flexible display technology for Soldiers and vehicles

# COMMAND, CONTROL, COMMUNICATIONS, AND COMPUTERS

## Collaborative Battlespace Reasoning and Awareness (COBRA)

The COBRA initiative develops and demonstrates multiplatform, cross-community applications and software services that support the integration and synchronization of intelligence and operations functions through the design, development, and implementation of information interoperability, and through collaborative management and decision-support technologies. This technology also develops software techniques that will improve mission execution success by providing software to more tightly coupled operations and intelligence and to better facilitate collaboration. Research and development will be focused on mapping intelligence and geospatial information requirements to military tasks. This effort will make possible faster and higher-quality decision cycles and increased battle command unification through collaboration and real-time sharing, exploitation, and analysis to support the operational mission, tasks, and desired effects.

## Multi-Access Cellular Extension (MACE)

The MACE effort is investigating adapting and connecting commercial-off-the-shelf (COTS) smartphone and cellular base station technology to a military network such as the Warfighter Information Network-Tactical (WIN-T) or the Joint Tactical Radio System. MACE inserts smartphone technologies into the tactical environment, applies appropriate security measures, and integrates them into military network operations' management capabilities. It will allow Soldiers to take full advantage of the mixed WiFi/cellular capabilities of the smartphone while maintaining interoperability with the military network. MACE technology will include a WiFi mesh networking application to allow groups of Soldiers with smartphones to automatically form into a local network when they are not able to connect to a cellular base station or WiFi hot spot on the military network, and then reconnect to the larger network when they come back within range. This will allow dismounted Soldiers to remain connected with each other when they lose connectivity with the tactical networks. MACE also seeks to improve Soldier position/location understanding by augmenting the GPS in COTS smartphones with radio frequency ranging to better adapt to GPS-challenged environments.

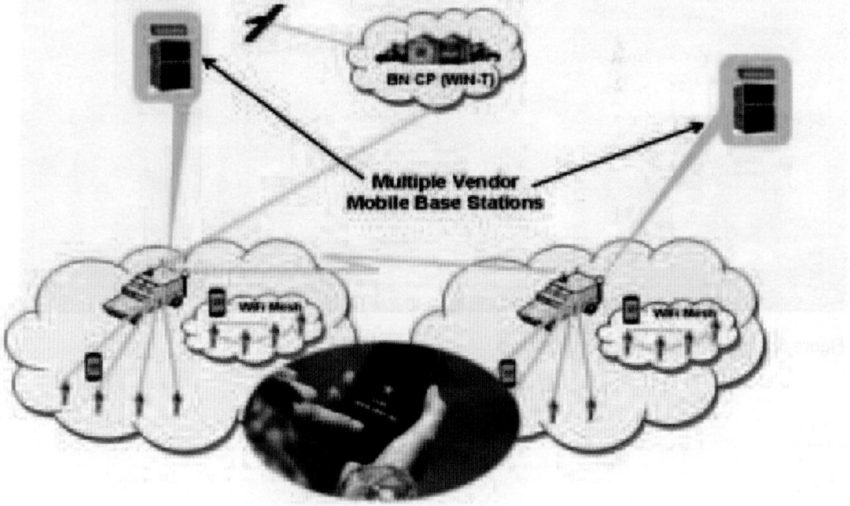


**Figure 5:** MACE

## LETHALITY

### Small Organic Precision Munitions

This effort demonstrates critical technologies for a 5-7lb Soldier-carried, guided, non-line-of-sight munition. The critical technologies demonstrated will improve target acquisition, increase lethality against soft targets, provide a secure data-link, and increase battery life. This technology will provide forward operating bases with improved situational awareness, lethality, and survivability against combatants on ridgelines or overhangs, snipers in close urban terrain, and insurgents placing improvised explosive devices, while reducing collateral damage/fratricide.

**Figure 6:** Small organic precision munitions

### Medium Caliber Weapon and Ammunition

This effort demonstrates a more accurate medium caliber weapon and ammunition for extended range engagements, as well as design and demonstration of a simple, low-cost remote armament system. This effort provides an accurate medium caliber weapon system for stationary and fire on-the-move. It provides an airburst munition with integrated fuzing, warhead, and safe-and-arm for improved effects against personnel (behind walls and in the open) at extended ranges. The technology provides ground-up remote weapon system design and demonstration with accurate aiming, improved stabilization, fast slew rates, target handoff, and hunter/killer-capable lethal and non-lethal ammunition. For extended ranges, technology products will provide improved accuracy, eliminating small elevation errors, which create large miss distances.

### Next-Generation Kinetic Energy Cartridge

This effort demonstrates a 120mm next-generation direct-fire advanced kinetic energy round capable of defeating current and future threat targets without a depleted uranium (DU) penetrator. This effort provides novel penetrator designs with new materials for the most difficult threat targets, and provides methodology to demonstrate the contribution of velocity design and materials to maintain current lethality with DU. Additionally, this technology provides penetration and lethality data and models of novel penetrator performance against advanced full-scale armor threat targets from ordnance velocity through hypervelocity impact, and also a potential replacement for DU at ordnance velocity.

# MEDICAL

## Advanced Transition Training Strategies for Post-Deployment: ArmySMART

This research documents the significant impact of combat on Soldier behavioral health and adjustment. It also focuses on developing and validating advanced unit-level training to reduce combat-related psychological problems. The in-depth training program, Army Stress Management and Resilience Training (ArmySMART), is designed to provide a systematic and effective behavioral health intervention for high-combat units. The training package incorporates an occupational health model specifically developed for Soldiers that leverages Soldier strengths, unit cohesion, leadership skills, and individual cognitive skill building. Additionally, this research included problems such as post-traumatic stress disorder symptoms, relationship problems, anger problems, and risk-taking behavior during the post-deployment resetting phase. Adjunct training is also being developed to target the management of intrusive deployment-related thoughts. Each training product is being tested using a randomized controlled trial to ensure training efficacy.

## Detection and Treatment of Traumatic Brain Injury (TBI)

This technology is testing a candidate drug to treat TBI to determine its safety and effectiveness in 200 human subjects that have suffered TBI. It is estimated that 15 to 25 percent of all injuries in recent conflicts are to the head. TBI survivors often have physical and cognitive impairment, memory loss, and mood and personality disorders. There are currently no drugs to treat or reduce brain-related injuries.

**Figure 7:** Detection and treatment of TBI

## Alternative Dengue Fever Vaccine Strategy

The objective of this effort is to develop a single vaccine that is effective against the four major types of dengue. This strategy should demonstrate human safety and provide initial data on the body's immune response. The current live-attenuated dengue virus vaccine in advanced development is suboptimal for rapid deployment since it uses three doses at 0, 3, and 12 months. A vaccine fitting this dosing schedule will meet the U.S. military Capability Development Document (CDD) threshold. Ideally, the time to protection could be achieved more rapidly (within 3 months per CDD). Successful completion will produce a vaccine strategy that will lead to a more rapid and complete protection from dengue infection.

## Candidate Multivalent Vaccine Against HIV-1

The goal is to develop a Food and Drug Administration-licensed, globally effective, human immunodeficiency virus (HIV-1) vaccine to prevent HIV-1 infection in U.S. and allied Warfighters through the use of a multicomponent vaccine platform. The current program is focused on studying a range of vaccine candidates in an effort to identify and elicit the immune responses needed to protect humans from HIV and acquired immunodeficiency syndrome. These vaccine strategies are aimed at global protection, which could be tested in a broad spectrum of genetically diverse HIV epidemics worldwide. The current strategy is based on an attenuated viral vector, Modified Vaccinia Ankara, as the delivery vehicle of candidate vaccines into the human body. The objective is to demonstrate that these vaccines are safe for human subjects and capable of inducing an immune response that protects against HIV-1. Initial Phase 1 clinical trials conducted in CONUS and OCONUS sites showed that these vaccines are safe and immunogenic. Researchers are also working on a next-generation vaccine aimed to expand the breadth of protective immune responses by using mosaic HIV inserts in a prime-boost strategy in delivery vectors derived from different species.

## Damage Control Resuscitation

This pursues the best combination and optimal use of alternatives to whole blood (e.g., plasma, red blood cells, blood-clotting agents) to prevent bleeding and maintain oxygen delivery and nutrients to tissue. These products will likely enhance survival of casualties after severe blood loss, which is the leading cause of death to injured Warfighters. Recent data from the battlefield suggests that blood-clotting disorders and immune system activation, which damage normal cellular metabolic processes, commonly occur in severely injured patients. Therefore, a priority is to maintain blood-clotting capability and oxygen and nutrient delivery to tissues by using the best resuscitation products that can be administered at far-forward locations.

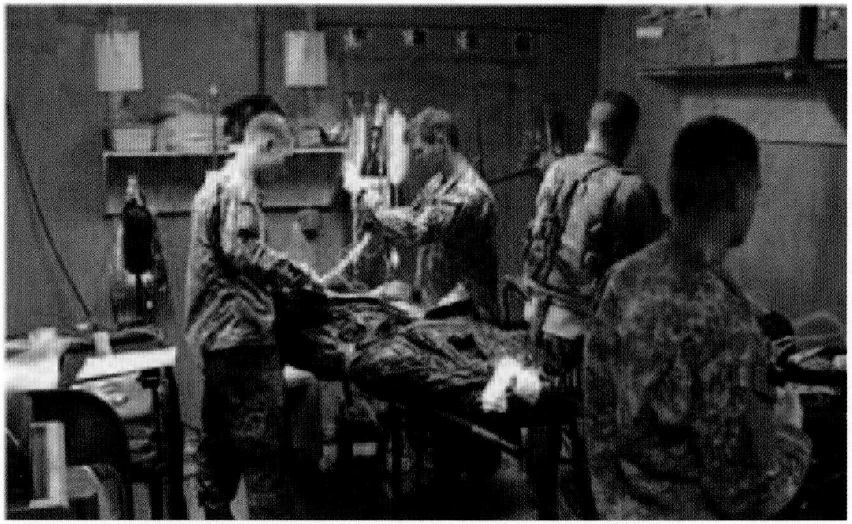

**Figure 8:** Damage control resuscitation

## UNMANNED SYSTEMS

### Safe Operations of Unmanned Systems for Reconnaissance in Complex Environments

This effort develops, integrates, and demonstrates robust robotic technologies required for Future Modular Force unmanned systems. This technology will advance the state-of-the-art in perception and control technologies to permit unmanned systems to autonomously conduct missions in populated, dynamic urban environments while adapting to changing conditions; develop initial tactical/mission behavior technologies to enable a group of heterogeneous unmanned systems to maneuver in collaboration with mounted and dismounted forces; optimize Soldier operation of unmanned systems; and provide improved situational awareness for enhanced survivability. Modeling and simulation will be used to develop, test, and evaluate the unmanned systems technologies (e.g., tactical behaviors and perception algorithms). Test bed platforms will be integrated with the software and associated hardware developed under this program, as well as appropriate mission modules, to support Warfighter experiments in a militarily significant environment.

**Figure 9:** Safe operation of unmanned systems for reconnaissance in complex environments

## SOLDIER SYSTEMS

### Soldier Planning Interfaces and Networked Electronics

This initiative develops a government-owned, Soldier-borne electronic equipment architecture that incorporates a National Security Agency-approved wireless personal area network subsystem. The Soldier Planning Interfaces and Networked Electronics (SPINE) reduces the Soldier-borne footprint and electronics system weight by 30 percent through the loss of wires and connectors. The wireless network will be powered by a conformal battery currently under development that increases power by 50 percent for a 24-hour period. This technology utilizes emerging software services to enable Soldier connectivity and data exchange to current and future tactical radio networks and battle command systems. Throughout this effort, capability demonstrations are conducted at the Command, Control, Communications, Computers, Intelligence, Surveillance, and Reconnaissance On-The-Move test bed at Ft. Dix, NJ, to monitor progress.

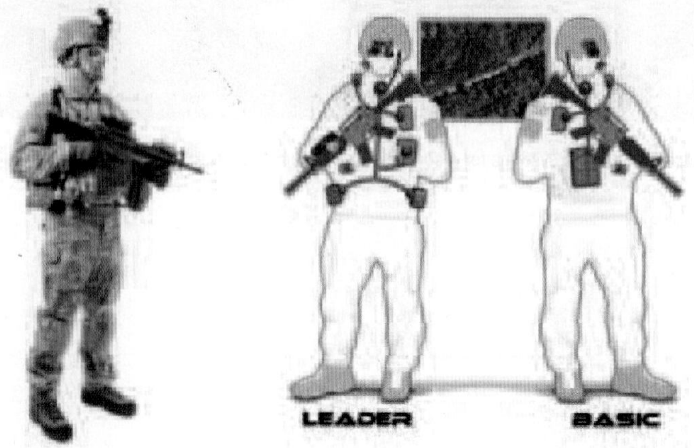


**Figure 10:** SPINE

### Helmet Electronics and Display System-Upgradeable Protection (HEADS-UP)

The purpose of HEADS-UP is to design and demonstrate a headgear system for mounted and dismounted Soldiers, which can provide tailored protection and capabilities for a variety of missions. This effort provides a head, face, and neck protection system incorporating modular, upgradeable protection to include traumatic brain injury; integrated sensor inputs; and optimized display hardware and software. Products include tailorable ballistic/blast protection; MOS-common mounting platform for sensors; tailorable Chemical, Biological, Radiological, and Nuclear protection (snap-on); and increased Soldier visual and audio data representation. Benefits to the Soldier include reduced weight for equivalent protection, small increased weight for significantly increased capabilities, and increased situational awareness in all environmental and obscurant conditions without sacrificing mobility and agility.

### Reducing Soldier and Small Combat Unit Load

The objective of this effort is to understand and employ a holistic approach to solve the Soldier and Small Combat Unit physical and cognitive load problem. This effort provides representative physical and cognitive load baselines—the art/science of the possible for load reductions when considered in a holistic manner. This effort will also deliver advanced mission-planning tools to enable individual and/or unit-level tradeoffs, which have the potential to make a difference in Soldier load. Benefits to the Soldier include improved Small Unit mobility and endurance, as well as improved Small Unit cognitive performance, resulting in enhanced mission performance.

## AVIATION

### Advanced Rotary Wing Vehicle Technology

This effort develops and demonstrates transformational vertical lift technology-enabled capabilities for the next generation of joint rotorcraft, addressing operational capability gaps for aviation along with reduced cost of ownership. This effort will result in a flying Technology Demonstrator that provides enhanced operational efficiencies, such as reduced fuel burn rates, more responsive (faster) operating speeds, extended unrefueled range (longer reach), and increased high/hot time-on-target. It will provide enhanced platform survivability with reduced signatures and increased ballistic protection. Benefits to the Soldier include increased range and on-station time to deliver troops, weapons, and sensors on target, and increased Soldier survivability.

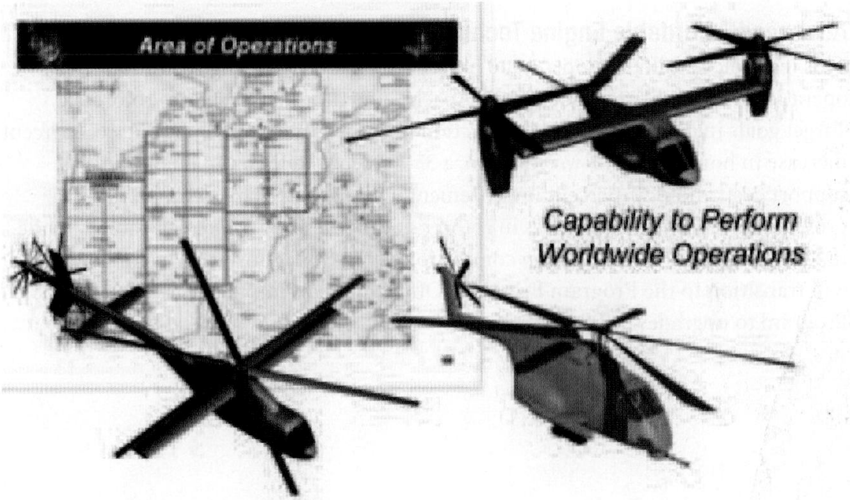


**Figure 11:** Advanced rotary wing vehicle technology

## LOGISTICS

### Advanced Affordable Engine Technology

This technology will develop a 3,000 horsepower gas turbine engine for improved operational capability for Blackhawk, Apache, and other Future Force rotorcraft. Target goals include a 25-percent reduction in specific fuel consumption, a 65-percent increase in horsepower-to-weight ratio, a 35-percent reduction in operation and support cost, and a 20-percent improvement in design life. This demonstration provides for significant increases in rotorcraft range and/or payload capability while reducing logistical burden. Upon completion of the S&T effort, this technology will transition to the Program Executive Office Aviation Improved Turbine Engine Program to upgrade the Blackhawk fleet.

### Transformational Vehicle Management System

The objective of the Transformational Vehicle Management System is to allow Soldiers to conduct safe aviation missions in high task-loaded environments and in urban/complex terrain conditions by exploiting Full Authority Control Systems and active control technologies in legacy upgrades and new platform configuration. This effort will result in handling quality requirements and integrated control system concepts for legacy upgrades, multirole, and heavy-lift. It will provide simulation and control methods and tools for evolving manned and unmanned aerial vehicle (UAV) rotorcraft configurations, as well as Guidance-Navigation-Control technologies for Autonomous Flight Operations in urban and/or teaming environments. Potential benefits include reduced pilot workload and improved mission task performance for all-weather multimission operations; reduced development costs and design-cycle time; and technologies for UAV rotorcraft urban operations and teaming.

**Figure 12:** Advanced affordable engine technology

# BASIC RESEARCH

**Figure 13:** Basic research investments

Basic research investments are a critical hedge in acquiring new knowledge in areas that hold great promise in advancing new and technically challenging Army capabilities and concepts to enable revolutionary advances and paradigm-shifting future operational capabilities. Areas of emerging interest and focus in basic research are autonomous systems, biotechnology, immersive technology, materials modeling, nanotechnology, network science, neuroscience, and quantum effects. Investment in basic research within the Army provides insurance against an uncertain future and guards against technological surprise. And if we are successful, these investments will make it possible to conduct ever more complex military operations, with greater speed and precision, to devastate any adversary on any battlefield. The following is a brief summary of the areas of investment, the synergy among them, and some of the capabilities they may provide.

## Autonomous Systems—Extending the operational effectiveness of Soldiers through robotic systems

A major military objective is to totally frustrate and defeat our adversaries across a wide spectrum of conflicts while dramatically increasing the survivability of our Soldiers by keeping them out of harm's way. Autonomous systems of extraordinary capability can fulfill this objective; however, they must be completely safe and secure while operating in highly complex operational environments. Achieving such levels of capability will require significant investments in highly sophisticated sense, response, and processing systems approaching that of biological systems; major advances in artificial intelligence; the development of intelligent agents approaching human performance levels; and advances in machine learning, swarming, and actuation and control.

## Biotechnology—Leveraging four billion years of evolution

The increasing importance and demands for wide-area persistent surveillance create significant challenges for sensor systems, real-time processing of vast amounts of data, the real-time interpretation of information for decision making, and power and energy requirements to support such demanding systems. Through four billion years of evolution, biological systems have engineered solutions to some of these challenges. We seek to leverage research in these areas for improving the performance of our Soldiers. Major investments in this area through reverse engineering will lead to totally new sensing systems, new ways for the rapid processing of data into information, the development of novel sense and response systems, and biologically inspired power and energy solutions.

## Immersive Technology—The path to virtual reality training

The evolving threat environment continues to put increasing demands on the diversity and effectiveness of Soldier skills. To meet these demands, superior training tools and methods are needed. Virtual worlds can provide this capability; however, we are currently at primitive stages in their realization. With advances in computational processing and steady progress in understanding the brain's "software" comes the possibility of creating highly realistic virtual training environments inhabited by humanlike avatars. Such environments will provide a paradigm shift in the way we provide training, while achieving low-cost, safe, low-environmental impact, highly variable simulation environments for the future training of our Soldiers.

### Materials Modeling—Atomic to the continuum research

Materials modeling research develops fundamental scientific principles across scales—from the atomic to the continuum—and develops underpinning, cross-cutting, and transferrable physics-based modeling capabilities. Research focuses on two-way multiscale modeling for predicting performance and designing materials; investigating analytical and theoretical analyses to effectively define the interface physics across length scales; advancing experimental capabilities for verification and validation of multiscale physics; and modeling and strategies for the synthesis of high-loading rate-tolerant materials. The intent is to provide the Army with next-generation multifunctional materials for ballistic and electronic applications, lightweight vehicle and facility protection, and energy storage and electronic devices, and to provide new materials to address the extreme challenges associated with understanding and modeling materials subject to Army operational environments. This research supports the development of computational tools, software, and new methods for material characterization to make the process of discovery and development of advanced materials faster, less expensive, and more predictable.

### Nanotechnology—Dramatically changing our ability to manufacture new material by design

The last century was dominated by advances in the physical sciences through the discovery of the atom, its structure, and the laws that govern its behavior. This century will be dominated by the complex world of biology and nanoscience whose mysteries will be unraveled by our understanding of systems of atoms and molecules. Nanotechnology is the manipulation of matter on a near-atomic scale to produce new structures, materials, and devices. Nanotechnology research makes it possible to explore the emerging biotech field and dramatically change our capability in creating new materials by design. This technology has the ability to transform many industries in discovering and creating new materials with properties that will revolutionize military technology and make Soldiers less vulnerable to the enemy and to environmental threats. Research in nanoscale technologies is growing rapidly worldwide. By 2015, the National Science Foundation estimates that nanotechnology will have a one trillion dollar impact on the global economy and employ two million workers, one million of whom may be in the United States.

### Network Science—Managing complex military operations with greater speed and precision

Networks tie together the following: highly distributed sensor systems for reconnaissance and surveillance, information for decision making, Soldiers, and the execution of fast distributed precision fires. Better-functioning networks are essential to advancing our ability to conduct complex military operations with greater speed and precision. However, our state of knowledge of these networks is relatively primitive and, as such, significantly impairs our ability to fully realize the potential that networks can provide on current and future battlefields. A new multidisciplinary approach is being implemented that combines communications, information, and the social/human component of networks, and that changes the way we address the challenges associated with optimizing the use of networks. Advances in network science will allow us to predict and optimize network performance before we build them through the creation of wholly new design tools.

### Neuroscience—Understanding how the human brain works

Fundamental to the conduct of military operations is superior Soldier performance. Understanding how the human brain works, i.e., determining the brain's "software," is key to developing these capabilities. When embedded in a wide range of military platforms, this "software" will provide superior training methods and human system interfaces that will be tuned to an individual's characteristics, thereby resulting in superior Soldier performance. Research in this area will also dramatically advance our ability to prevent and treat those suffering from various types of battlefield brain injury.

### Quantum Effects—Leap ahead in super computing

Increasing demands for information to support rapid and effective decision making on the battlefield require advanced sensor systems to collect relevant data, as well as the means for processing it into actionable forms. Major advancements in processing power are required to cope with the demand to process ever-larger amounts of data. Investments in this area will achieve super computers that will dwarf the capabilities of the most powerful computers today, making them look like pocket calculators. The development of such computational systems will enable the embedding of high-performance computing in all military platforms, including the Soldier's uniform.

## SUMMARY

Army research investments are targeted in areas that are fundamental to realizing superior land warfighting capabilities and discovering new knowledge from research in areas highly relevant to the Army mission. These areas include research in network science to better understand, predict performance, and design future networks; neuroscience to better understand how the brain works so that we might improve human-machine interfaces and Soldier performance; new materials science to better protect our Soldiers and equipment; immersive virtual systems to improve our training capability; and biotechnology and nanotechnology autonomous systems. In addition, continued research is conducted in human dimension efforts relating to health and wellness, leader training, cultural awareness, and individual and unit readiness.

Army S&T has made significant progress establishing persistent night surveillance of large areas for real-time situational awareness and forensic backtracking of suspect vehicles and personnel. We've advanced the computational understanding of the battlefield through the development of practical, intelligent, and operationally relevant software tools aiding analysis and interpretation of battlefield intelligence. We are key participants in an advanced Automotive Battery Initiative with over $2 billion committed to dual-use battery manufacturing through the Department of Energy. We have developed and deployed several lightweight power sources to reduce the demand for delivering fuel or batteries, such as the Rucksack Enhanced Portable Power System, a lightweight, portable power system capable of recharging batteries and/or acting as a continuous power source. Through the Fuel Efficiency Demonstrator, we demonstrated multiple energy-reduction technologies and techniques to achieve a 70-percent overall improvement in fuel economy over the High Mobility Multipurpose Wheeled Vehicle through power train efficiencies, lightweight materials, reducing friction losses, and encouraging efficient driver behavior. In the past year, we conducted 12 independent readiness reviews to assess technology maturity of systems transitioning through acquisition milestones. The Army Science Board (ASB) completed two studies on increasing tactical mission effectiveness. In "Strengthening Sustainability and Resiliency of a Future Force," the ASB concluded that changes in shelters, barriers, power, and aerial resupply could provide increased survivability at combat outposts and patrol bases, reduce fuel demand, reduce the number of ground convoys, and result in fewer casualties and greater mission effectiveness. In "Tactical Non-Cooperative Biometric Systems," the ASB recommended that non-cooperative biometrics be integrated into the current cooperative biometrics base programs and be further integrated into intelligence, surveillance, and reconnaissance systems for improved mission effectiveness.

In the coming years, the Army's S&T community will continue pursuing basic and applied research and technology development in the five S&T portfolio areas: Soldier; ground; air; command, control, and communications; and basic research.

# Appendices

# Glossary of Terms

## Acquisition Categories (ACAT)

ACAT I programs are Milestone Decision Authority Programs (MDAPs) or programs designated ACAT I by the Milestone Decision Authority (MDA).

Dollar value: estimated by the Under Secretary of Defense (Acquisition and Technology) (USD [A&T]) to require an eventual total expenditure for research, development, test and evaluation (RDT&E) of more than $365 million in fiscal year (FY) 2000 constant dollars or, for procurement, of more than $2.190 billion in FY 2000 constant dollars. ACAT I programs have two subcategories:

1. **ACAT ID**, for which the MDA is USD (A&T). The "D" refers to the Defense Acquisition Board (DAB), which advises the USD (A&T) at major decision points.
2. **ACAT IC**, for which the MDA is the DoD Component Head or, if delegated, the DoD Component Acquisition Executive (CAE). The "C" refers to Component. The USD (A&T) designates programs as ACAT ID or ACAT IC.

**ACAT IA** programs are MAISs (Major Automated Information System Acquisition Programs), or programs designated by the Assistant Secretary of Defense for Command, Control, Communications, and Intelligence (ASD [C3I]) to be ACAT IA.

Estimated to exceed: $32 million in FY 2000 constant dollars for all expenditures, for all increments, regardless of the appropriation or fund source, directly related to the AIS definition, design, development, and deployment, and incurred in any single fiscal year; or $126 million in FY 2000 constant dollars for all expenditures, for all increments, regardless of the appropriation or fund source, directly related to the AIS definition, design, development, and deployment, and incurred from the beginning of the Materiel Solution Analysis Phase through deployment at all sites; or $378 million in FY 2000 constant dollars for all expenditures, for all increments, regardless of the appropriation or fund source, directly related to the AIS definition, design, development, deployment, operations and maintenance, and incurred from the beginning of the Materiel Solution Analysis Phase through sustainment for the estimated useful life of the system.

**ACAT IA** programs have two subcategories:

1. **ACAT IAM**, for which the MDA is the Chief Information Officer (CIO) of the DoD, the ASD (C3I). The "M" refers to Major Automated Information System Review Council (MAISRC). (Change 4, 5000.2-R)
2. **ACAT IAC**, for which the DoD CIO has delegated milestone decision authority to the CAE or Component CIO. The "C" refers to Component.

**ACAT II** programs are defined as those acquisition programs that do not meet the criteria for an ACAT I program, but do meet the criteria for a major system, or are programs designated ACAT II by the MDA. The dollar value is estimated to require total expenditure for RDT&E of more than $140 million in FY 2000 constant dollars, or for procurement of more than $660 million in FY 2000 constant dollars.

**ACAT III** programs are defined as those acquisition programs that do not meet the criteria for an ACAT I, an ACAT IA, or an ACAT II. The MDA is designated by the CAE and shall be at the lowest appropriate level. This category includes less-than-major AISs. The dollar values are under the threshold for ACAT II.

## Acquisition Phase

All the tasks and activities needed to bring a program to the next major milestone occur during an acquisition phase. Phases provide a logical means of progressively translating broadly stated mission needs into well-defined system-specific requirements and ultimately into operationally effective, suitable, and survivable systems. The acquisition phases for the systems described in this handbook are defined below:

### Technology Development Phase

The purpose of this phase is to reduce technology risk, determine and mature the appropriate set of technologies to be integrated into a full system, and to demonstrate critical technology elements on prototypes. Technology Development is a continuous technology discovery and development process reflecting close collaboration between the Science and Technology (S&T) community, the user, and the system developer. It is an iterative process designed to assess the viability of technologies while simultaneously refining user requirements. Entrance into this phase depends on the completion of the Analysis of Alternatives (A0A), a proposed materiel solution, and full funding for planned Technology Development Phase activity.

**Engineering and Manufacturing Development (EMD) Phase**
The purpose of the EMD phase is to develop a system or an increment of capability; complete full system integration (technology risk reduction occurs during Technology Development); develop an affordable and executable manufacturing process; ensure operational supportability with particular attention to minimizing the logistics footprint; implement human systems integration (HSI); design for producibility; ensure affordability; protect critical program information by implementing appropriate techniques such as anti-tamper; and demonstrate system integration, interoperability, safety, and utility. The Capability Development Document, Acquisition Strategy, Systems Engineering Plan, and Test and Evaluation Master Plan (TEMP) shall guide this effort. Entrance into this phase depends on technology maturity (including software), approved requirements, and full funding. Unless some other factor is overriding in its impact, the maturity of the technology shall determine the path to be followed.

**Production and Deployment Phase**
The purpose of the Production and Deployment phase is to achieve an operational capability that satisfies mission needs. Operational test and evaluation shall determine the effectiveness and suitability of the system. The MDA shall make the decision to commit DoD to production at Milestone C and shall document the decision in an Acquisition Decision Memorandum. Milestone C authorizes entry into low rate initial production (for MDAPs and major systems), into production or procurement (for non-major systems that do not require LRIP) or into limited deployment in support of operational testing for MAIS programs or software-intensive systems with no production components. Entrance into this phase depends on the following criteria: acceptable performance in developmental test and evaluation and operational assessment (OSD OT&E oversight programs); mature software capability; no significant manufacturing risks; manufacturing processes under control (if Milestone C is full-rate production); an approved Initial Capabilities Document (ICD) (if Milestone C is program initiation); an approved Capability Production Document (CPD); a refined integrated architecture; acceptable interoperability; acceptable operational supportability; and demonstration that the system is affordable throughout the life cycle, fully funded, and properly phased for rapid acquisition. The CPD reflects the operational requirements, informed by EMD results, and details the performance expected of the production system. If Milestone C approves LRIP, a subsequent review and decision shall authorize full-rate production.

**Operations and Support Phase**
The purpose of the Operations and Support phase is to execute a support program that meets materiel readiness and operational support performance requirements, and sustains the system in the most cost-effective manner over its total life cycle. Planning for this phase shall begin prior to program initiation and shall be documented in the Life-Cycle Sustainment Plan (LLSP). Operations and Support phase has two major efforts: life-cycle sustainment and disposal. Entrance into the Operations and Support Phase depends on meeting the following criteria: an approved CPD; an approved LCSP; and a successful Full-Rate Production (FRP) Decision.

## Acquisition Program
A directed, funded effort designed to provide a new, improved or continuing weapons system or AIS capability in response to a validated operational need. Acquisition programs are divided into different categories that are established to facilitate decentralized decision-making, and execution and compliance with statutory requirements.

## Advanced Concept Technology Demonstrations (ACTDs)
ACTDs are a means of demonstrating the use of emerging or mature technology to address critical military needs. ACTDs themselves are not acquisition programs, although they are designed to provide a residual, usable capability upon completion. If the user determines that additional units are needed beyond the residual capability and that these units can be funded, the additional buys shall constitute an acquisition program with an acquisition category generally commensurate with the dollar value and risk of the additional buy.

## Automated Information System (AIS)
A combination of computer hardware and software, data, or telecommunications, that performs functions such as collecting, processing, transmitting, and displaying information. Excluded are computer resources, both hardware and software, that are physically part of, dedicated to, or essential in real-time to the mission performance of weapon systems.

### Commercial and Non-Developmental Items

Market research and analysis shall be conducted to determine the availability and suitability of existing commercial and non-developmental items prior to the commencement of a development effort, during the development effort, and prior to the preparation of any product description. For ACAT I and IA programs, while few commercial items meet requirements at a system level, numerous commercial components, processes, and practices have application to DoD systems.

### Demilitarization and Disposal

At the end of its useful life, a system must be demilitarized and disposed of. During demilitarization and disposal, the program manager shall ensure materiel determined to require demilitarization is controlled and shall ensure disposal is carried out in a way that minimizes DoD's liability due to environmental, safety, security, and health issues.

### Developmental Test and Evaluation (DT&E)

DT&E shall identify potential operational and technological capabilities and limitations of the alternative concepts and design options being pursued; support the identification and description of design technical risks; and provide data and analysis in support of the decision to certify the system ready for operational test and evaluation.

### Full Materiel Release

The process that ensures all Army materiel is safe, operationally suitable, and is supportable before release of issue to users. The PM determines necessary activities to certify materiel release readiness. This decision should be accomplished prior to full-rate production.

### Joint Program Management

Any acquisition system, subsystem, component or technology program that involves a strategy that includes funding by more than one DoD component during any phase of a system's life cycle shall be defined as a joint program. Joint programs shall be consolidated and collocated at the location of the lead component's program office, to the maximum extent practicable.

### Live Fire Test and Evaluation (LFT&E)

LFT&E must be conducted on a covered system, major munition program, missile program, or product improvement to a covered system, major munition program, or missile program before it can proceed beyond low-rate initial production. A covered system is any vehicle, weapon platform, or conventional weapon system that includes features designed to provide some degree of protection to users in combat and that is an ACAT I or II program. Depending upon its intended use, a commercial or non-developmental item may be a covered system, or a part of a covered system. Systems requiring LFT&E may not proceed beyond low-rate initial production until realistic survivability or lethality testing is completed and the report required by statute is submitted to the prescribed congressional committees.

### Low-Rate Initial Production (LRIP)

The objective of this activity is to produce the minimum quantity necessary to provide production-configured or representative articles for operational tests; establish an initial production base for the system; and permit an orderly increase in the production rate for the system, sufficient to lead to full-rate production upon successful completion of operational testing. LRIP quantity may not exceed 10 percent of the total production quantity without an approved waiver by the Acquisition Executive and documented in the Acquisition Decision Memorandum.

### Major Automated Information System (MAIS) Acquisition Program

An AIS acquisition program that is (1) designated by ASD (C3I) as a MAIS, or (2) estimated to require program costs in any single year in excess of $32 million in FY 2000 constant dollars, total program costs in excess of $126 million in FY 2000 constant dollars, or total life cycle costs in excess of $378 million in FY 2000 constant dollars. MAISs do not include highly sensitive classified programs.

### Major Defense Acquisition Program (MDAP)

An acquisition program that is not a highly sensitive classified program (as determined by the Secretary of Defense) and that is: (1) designated by the USD (A&T) as an MDAP, or (2) estimated by the USD (A&T) to require an eventual total expenditure for research, development, test and evaluation of more than $365 million in FY 2000 constant dollars or, for procurement, of more than $2.190 billion in FY 2000 constant dollars.

### Major Milestone
A major milestone is the decision point that separates the phases of an acquisition program. MDAP milestones include, for example, the decisions to authorize entry into the engineering and manufacturing development phase or full rate production. MAIS milestones may include, for example, the decision to begin program definition and risk reduction.

### Major Systems
Dollar value: estimated by the DoD Component Head to require an eventual total expenditure for RDT&E of more than $140 million in FY 2000 constant dollars, or for procurement of more than $660 million in FY 2000 constant dollars. (Lowest category for major system designation is ACAT II.)

### Materiel Solution Analysis Phase
The purpose of this phase is to assess potential materiel solutions and to satisfy the phase-specific entrance criteria for the next program milestone designated by the MDA. Entrance into this phase depends upon an approved ICD resulting from the analysis of current mission performance and an analysis of potential concepts across the DoD components, international systems from allies, and cooperative opportunities.

### Milestone Decision Authority (MDA)
The individual designated in accordance with criteria established by the USD (AT&L), or by the ASD (C3I) for AIS acquisition programs, to approve entry of an acquisition program into the next phase.

### Modifications
Any modification that is of sufficient cost and complexity that it could itself qualify as an ACAT I or ACAT IA program shall be considered for management purposes as a separate acquisition effort. Modifications that do not cross the ACAT I or IA threshold shall be considered part of the program being modified, unless the program is no longer in production. In that case, the modification shall be considered a separate acquisition effort.

### Operational Support
The objectives of this activity are the execution of a support program that meets the threshold values of all support performance requirements and sustainment of them in the most life cycle cost effective manner. A follow-on operational testing program that assesses performance and quality, compatibility, and interoperability, and identifies deficiencies shall be conducted, as appropriate. This activity shall also include the execution of operational support plans, to include the transition from contractor to organic support, if appropriate.

### Operational Test and Evaluation (OT&E)
OT&E shall be structured to determine the operational effectiveness and suitability of a system under realistic conditions (e.g., combat) and to determine if the operational performance requirements have been satisfied. The following procedures are mandatory: threat or threat representative forces, targets, and threat countermeasures, validated in coordination with Defense Intelligence Agency (DIA), shall be used; typical users shall operate and maintain the system or item under conditions simulating combat stress and peacetime conditions; the independent operational test activities shall use production or production representative articles for the dedicated phase of OT&E that supports the full-rate production decision, or for ACAT IA or other acquisition programs, the deployment decision; and the use of modeling and simulation shall be considered during test planning.

For additional information on acquisition terms, or terms not defined, please refer to AR 70-1, Army Acquisition Policy, available on the Internet at http://www.army.mil/usapa/epubs/pdf/r70_1.pdf; or DA PAM 70-3, Army Acquisition Procedures, available on the Internet at http://www.dtic.mil/whs/directives/corres/pdf/500002p.pdf.

# Systems by Contractors

**A/S Hydrenna**
Countermine

**AAI Corp.**
MQ-1C Gray Eagle Unmanned Aircraft System (UAS)
RQ-7B Shadow Tactical Unmanned Aircraft System (TUAS)

**AAR Mobility Systems**
Mobile Maintenance Equipment Systems (MMES)

**Aardvark Technical**
Improvised Explosive Device (IEDD)

**Aberdeen Test Center**
Paladin/Field Artillery Ammunition Supply Vehicle (FAASV)

**Acambis plc**
Chemical Biological Medical Systems (CBMS)-Prophylaxis

**Accenture**
General Fund Enterprise Business Systems (GFEBS)
Global Command and Control System-Army (GCCS-A)

**Acme Electric**
Javelin

**Action Manufacturing**
2.75 Inch Rocket Systems (Hydra-70)

**ADSI**
High Mobility Engineer Excavator (HMEE) I and III

**AEPCO**
Advanced Threat Infrared Countermeasure/Common Missile Warning System (ATIRCM/CMWS)
Longbow Apache (AH-64D) (LBA)

**Aerial Machine and Tool Corp.**
Air Warrior (AW)

**Aerojet**
Guided Multiple Launch Rocket System (GMLRS) DPICM/Unitary/Alternative Warhead (Tactical Rockets)
Javelin
Joint Air-to-Ground Missile (JAGM)
PATRIOT Advanced Capability-Three (PAC-3)

**Aerojet General**
Tube-Launched, Optically-Tracked, Wire-Guided (TOW) Missiles

**Aerovironmnent Inc.**
RQ-11B Raven Small Unmanned Aircraft System (SUAS)

**Agilent Technologies Inc.**
Calibration Sets Equipment (CALSETS)
Test Equipment Modernization (TEMOD)

**Airborne Systems North America**
Joint Precision Airdrop System (JPADS)

**All American Racers Inc.**
RQ-11B Raven Small Unmanned Aircraft System (SUAS)

**Alliant Techsystems**
2.75 Inch Rocket Systems (Hydra-70)
Future Tank Main Gun Ammunition (FTMGA)
HELLFIRE Family of Missiles
Individual Semi-Automatic Airburst System (ISAAS)-XM25
Joint Air-to-Ground Missile (JAGM)
Medium Caliber Ammunition (MCA)
Precision Guidance Kit (PGK)
Tank Ammunition
Small Arms-Crew Served Weapons
Small Caliber Ammunition
Spider

**Allison Transmission**
Abrams Tank Upgrade
Family of Medium Tactical Vehicles (FMTV)
Heavy Expanded Mobility Tactical Truck (HEMTT)/HEMTT Extended Service Program (ESP)
Palletized Load System (PLS) and PLS Extended Service Program (ESP)

**ALS**
Weapons of Mass Destruction Elimination (WMD-E)

**AM General (AMG)**
High Mobility Multipurpose Wheeled Vehicle (HMMWV) Recapitalization (RECAP) Program
Improved Ribbon Bridge (IRB)

**American Eurocopter**
Light Utility Helicopter (LUH)/UH-72A Lakota

**American Ordnance**
Artillery Ammunition
Spider

**American Science & Engineering Inc.**
Non-Intrusive Inspection Systems (NIIS)

**AMT**
Mortar Systems

**AMTEC Corp.**
Medium Caliber Ammunition (MCA)

**Anniston Army Depot**
Abrams Tank Upgrade

**ANP Technologies**
Joint Chemical, Biological, Radiological Agent Water Monitor (JCBRAWM)

**Apptricity Corp.**
Transportation Coordinators' Automated Information for Movement System II (TC-AIMS II)

**ArgonST Radix**
Guardrail Common Sensor (GR/CS)

**Armaments R&D Center**
Paladin/Field Artillery Ammunition Supply Vehicle (FAASV)

**ATK**
Joint Air-to-Ground Missile (JAGM)
Tube-Launched, Optically-Tracked, Wire-Guided (TOW) Missiles

**Atlantic Inertial Units**
Excalibur (M982)

**Avenge**
Enhanced Medium Altitude Reconnaissance and Surveillance System (EMARSS)

**Aviation and Missile Solutions LLC**
Longbow Apache (AH-64D) (LBA)

**Avnet**
Joint Air-to-Ground Missile (JAGM)

**Avon Protection Systems**
Joint Service General Purpose Mask (JSGPM) M-50/M-51

**AVT**
Aviation Combined Arms Tactical Trainer (AVCATT)

**Azimuth Inc.**
Distributed Common Ground System-Army (DCGS-A)

**BAE Systems**
Advanced Threat Infrared Countermeasure/Common Missile Warning System (ATIRCM/CMWS)
Air Warrior (AW)
Airborne Reconnaissance Low (ARL)
Bradley Fighting Vehicle Systems Upgrade
Enhanced Medium Altitude Reconnaissance and Surveillance System (EMARSS)
Heavy Loader
High Mobility Artillery Rocket System (HIMARS)
High Mobility Engineer Excavator (HMEE) I and III
Joint Effects Targeting System (JETS) Target Location Designation System (TLDS)
Joint Tactical Ground Station (JTAGS)
Joint Tactical Radio System Airborne and Maritime/Fixed Station (JTRS AMF)
Joint Tactical Radio System Ground Mobile Radios (JTRS GMR)
Joint Tactical Radio System Handheld, Manpack, Small Form Fit (JTRS HMS)
Joint Tactical Radio System Multifunctional Information Distribution System (MIDS)
Lightweight 155mm Howitzer System (LW155)
Mine Protection Vehicle Family (MPVF)
Multiple Launch Rocket System (MLRS) M270A1
Night Vision Thermal Systems-Thermal Weapon Sight (TWS)
Paladin/Field Artillery Ammunition Supply Vehicle (FAASV)
Tube-Launched, Optically-Tracked, Wire-Guided (TOW) Missiles
Warfighter Information Network-Tactical (WIN-T) Increment 3

**BAE Systems (Holston Army Ammunition Plant)**
Spider

**BAE Systems Land & Armaments, Ground Systems Division**
Mine Resistant Ambush Protected Vehicles (MRAP)

**BAE-TVS**
Mine Resistant Ambush Protected Vehicles (MRAP)

**Battelle Biomedical Research Center**
Chemical Biological Medical Systems-Therapeutics

**Battelle Memorial Institute**
Chemical Biological Medical Systems-Therapeutics

**Beacon Industries**
High Mobility Artillery Rocket System (HIMARS)

**Bell Helicopter Textron**
Advanced Threat Infrared Countermeasure/Common Missile Warning System (ATIRCM/CMWS)
Kiowa Warrior

**Berg Companies Inc.**
Force Provider (FP)

**Binary Group**
General Fund Enterprise Business Systems (GFEBS)

**Boeing**
CH-47F Chinook
Enhanced Medium Altitude Reconnaissance and Surveillance System (EMARSS)
Joint Air-to-Ground Missile (JAGM)
Joint Tactical Radio System Ground Mobile Radios (JTRS GMR)
Joint Tactical Radio System, Network Enterprise Domain (JTRS NED)
Longbow Apache (AH-64D) (LBA)
PATRIOT Advanced Capability-Three (PAC-3)

**Booz Allen Hamilton**
Distributed Common Ground System-Army (DCGS-A)
Enhanced Medium Altitude Reconnaissance and Surveillance System (EMARSS)
Global Command and Control System-Army (GCCS-A)
Joint Land Component Constructive Training Capability (JLCCTC)
Medical Communications for Combat Casualty Care (MC4)
Secure Mobile Anti-Jam Reliable Tactical Terminal (SMART-T)

**Breeze**
High Mobility Artillery Rocket System (HIMARS)

**Bren-Tronics**
RQ-11B Raven Small Unmanned Aircraft System (SUAS)

**CACI**
Advanced Field Artillery Tactical Data System (AFATDS)
Airborne Reconnaissance Low (ARL)
Army Key Management System (AKMS)
Battle Command Sustainment Support System (BCS3)
Biometric Enabling Capability (BEC)
Combat Service Support Communications (CSS Comms)
Common Hardware Systems (CHS)
Distributed Common Ground System-Army (DCGS-A)
Enhanced Medium Altitude Reconnaissance and Surveillance System (EMARSS)
Force XXI Battle Command Brigade and Below (FBCB2)
Joint Battle Command-Platform (JBC-P)
Joint Personnel Identification Version 2 (JPIv2)
Nuclear Biological Chemical Reconnaissance Vehicle (NBCRV)-Stryker Sensor Suites
Tactical Mission Command (TMC)/Maneuver Control System (MCS)

**Cangene Corp.**
Chemical Biological Medical Systems (CBMS)-Prophylaxis

**Capgemini (IV & V)**
Global Combat Support System-Army (GCSS-Army)

**Carleton Technologies Inc.**
Air Warrior (AW)

**CAS Inc.**
Enhanced Medium Altitude Reconnaissance and Surveillance System (EMARSS)
Sentinel

**Case New Holland**
High Mobility Engineer Excavator (HMEE) I and III

**Casteel Manufacturing**
Line Haul Tractor

**Caterpillar**
Family of Medium Tactical Vehicles (FMTV)
Heavy Expanded Mobility Tactical Truck (HEMTT)/HEMTT Extended Service Program (ESP)

**Caterpillar C-15**
Palletized Load System (PLS) and PLS Extended Service Program (ESP)

**Caterpillar Defense and Federal Products**
Heavy Loader

**CEP Inc.**
Air Warrior (AW)

**Ceradyne Inc.**
Interceptor Body Armor

**CGI Federal**
Meteorological Measuring Set-Profiler (MMS-P)/Computer Meteorological Data-Profiler (CMD-P)

**Charleston Marine Containers**
Force Provider (FP)

**Choctaw Defense Manufacturing Contractors (CDMC)**
Unit Water Pod System (Camel II)

**Cloudera**
Distributed Common Ground System-Army (DCGS-A)

**CMC Electronics**
Joint Air-to-Ground Missile (JAGM)

**CMI**
RQ-7B Shadow Tactical Unmanned Aircraft System (TUAS)

**Colt's Manufacturing Co.**
Small Arms-Crew Served Weapons
Small Arms-Individual Weapons

**Communications Security Logistics Activity**
Cryptographic Systems

**Computer Sciences Corp. (CSC)**
Advanced Field Artillery Tactical Data System (AFATDS)
Advanced Threat Infrared Countermeasure/Common Missile Warning System (ATIRCM/CMWS)
Defense Enterprise Wideband SATCOM Systems (DEWSS)
Installation Protection Program (IPP)
Medical Simulation Training Center (MSTC)

**Comtech Mobile Datacom Corporation (CMDC)**
Movement Tracking System (MTS)

**CONCO**
2.75 Inch Rocket Systems (Hydra-70)

**Critical Solutions International Inc.**
Mine Protection Vehicle Family (MPVF)

**CSS**
Army Key Management System (AKMS)

**CTT**
RQ-7B Shadow Tactical Unmanned Aircraft System (TUAS)

**CUBIC Defense Systems**
Instrumentable-Multiple Integrated Laser Engagement System (I-MILES)

**Cummins Power Generation**
Tactical Electric Power (TEP)

**Curtiss-Wright**
Bradley Fighting Vehicle Systems Upgrade

**Daimler Trucks North America LLC-Freightliner Division**
Line Haul Tractor

**David H. Pollock Consultants**
Advanced Threat Infrared Countermeasure/Common Missile Warning System (ATIRCM/CMWS)

**Dedicated Computing**
Close Combat Tactical Trainer (CCTT)

**Dell Computer Corp.**
Battle Command Sustainment Support System (BCS3)
Distributed Common Ground System-Army (DCGS-A)

**Detroit Diesel**
Line Haul Tractor
Palletized Load System (PLS) and PLS Extended Service Program (ESP)

**Dewey Electronics**
Tactical Electric Power (TEP)

**DHS Systems**
Harbormaster Command and Control Center (HCCC)

**Digital Reasoning**
Distributed Common Ground System-Army (DCGS-A)

**DISA Satellite Transmission Services-Global NETCOM**
Combat Service Support Communications (CSS Comms)

**DMD**
Integrated Air and Missile Defense (IAMD)

**Draper Laboratories**
Joint Precision Airdrop System (JPADS)

**DRS-ES**
Improved Environmental Control Units (IECU)

**DRS Fermont**
Tactical Electric Power (TEP)

**DRS Mobile Environmental**
Close Combat Tactical Trainer (CCTT)

**DRS Optronics Inc.**
Kiowa Warrior
Night Vision Thermal Systems-Thermal Weapon Sight (TWS)

**DRS Sustainment Systems Inc.**
Armored Knight
Modular Fuel System (MFS)

**DRS Tactical Systems**
Armored Knight

**DRS Technologies**
Bradley Fighting Vehicle Systems Upgrade
Force XXI Battle Command Brigade and Below (FBCB2)
Javelin
Joint Battle Command-Platform (JBC-P)
Joint Service Transportable Small Scale Decontaminating Apparatus (JSTSS DA) M26
Movement Tracking System (MTS)

**DRS Fermont**
Tactical Electronic Power (TEP)

**DRS-TEM**
Integrated Family of Test Equipment (IFTE)

**DSE Inc. (Balimoy Manufacturing Company Inc.)**
Medium Caliber Ammunition (MCA)

**DynCorp**
Longbow Apache (AH-64D) (LBA)

**Dynetics Inc.**
Calibration Sets Equipment (CALSETS)

**DynPort Vaccine**
Chemical Biological Medical Systems (CBMS)-Prophylaxis

**E&TS Ktrs**
Joint Land Attack Cruise Missile Defense Elevated Netted Sensor System (JLENS)

**EAI Corporation/SAIC**
Weapons of Mass Destruction Elimination (WMD-E)

**EADS**
Joint Tactical Radio System Multifunctional Information Distribution System (MIDS)

**EADS North America**
Light Utility Helicopter (LUH)/UH-72A Lakota

**Eaton Aeroquip**
High Mobility Artillery Rocket System (HIMARS)

**Eaton-Vickers**
High Mobility Artillery Rocket System (HIMARS)

**ECC International**
Javelin

**E.D. Etnyre and Co.**
Modular Fuel System (MFS)

**EFW**
High Mobility Artillery Rocket System (HIMARS)

**EG&G Technical Services Inc.**
Force Protection Systems

**Elbit Systems of America**
Bradley Fighting Vehicle Systems Upgrade
Kiowa Warrior
Mortar Systems

**Electronic Consulting Services Inc.**
Close Combat Tactical Trainer (CCTT)

**Emergent BioSolutions (Bioport)**
Chemical Biological Medical Systems (CBMS)-Prophylaxis

**Engineering Research and Development Command**
Transportation Coordinators' Automated Information for Movement System II (TC-AIMS II)

**Engineering Solutions and Products (ESP)**
Common Hardware Systems (CHS)
Force XXI Battle Command Brigade and Below (FBCB2)
Global Command and Control System-Army (GCCS-A)
Movement Tracking System (MTS)
Warfighter Information Network-Tactical (WIN-T) Increment 1

**EPS Corp.**
Secure Mobile Anti-Jam Reliable Tactical Terminal (SMART-T)
Single Channel Ground and Airborne Radio System (SINCGARS)

**Esri**
Distributed Common Ground System-Army (DCGS-A)

**EuroMIDS**
Joint Tactical Radio System Multifunctional Information Distribution System (MIDS)

**Fabrique National Manufacturing LLC**
Small Arms-Crew Served Weapons

**FASCAN International**
Countermine

**FBM Babcock Marine**
Improved Ribbon Bridge (IRB)

**Fidelity Technologies Corp.**
Tactical Electric Power (TEP)

**Fluke Corp.**
Calibration Sets Equipment (CALSETS)

**Force Protection Industries Inc.**
Mine Protection Vehicle Family (MPVF)
Mine Resistant Ambush Protected Vehicles (MRAP)

**Future Research Corp.**
Transportation Coordinators' Automated Information for Movement System II (TC-AIMS II)

**General Atomics, Aeronautical Systems Inc.**
MQ-1C Gray Eagle Unmanned Aircraft System (UAS)

**General Dynamics**
Advanced Field Artillery Tactical Data System (AFATDS)
2.75 Inch Rocket Systems (Hydra-70)
Common Hardware Systems (CHS)
Counter-Rocket, Artillery, Mortar (C-RAM) /Indirect Fire Protection Capability (IFPC)
Distributed Common Ground System-Army (DCGS-A)
Forward Area Air Defense Command and Control (FAAD C2)
Joint Air-to-Ground Missile (JAGM)
Joint Tactical Radio System Handheld, Manpack, Small Form Fit (JTRS HMS)
Medical Communications for Combat Casualty Care (MC4)
Nett Warrior (NW)
Prophet
RQ-7B Shadow Tactical Unmanned Aircraft System (TUAS)
Small Caliber Ammunition
Stryker Family of Vehicles
Tactical Mission Command (TMC)/ Maneuver Control System (MCS)
Warfighter Information Network-Tactical (WIN-T) Increment 2
Warfighter Information Network-Tactical (WIN-T) Increment 3

**General Dynamics Armament and Technical Products (CD-ATP)**
Joint Air-to-Ground Missile (JAGM)
Joint Biological Point Detection System (JBPDS)
Small Arms-Crew Served Weapons
XM806 .50 Caliber Machine Gun

**General Dynamics Armament and Technical Products Manufacturing Facility**
Small Arms-Crew Served Weapons

**General Dynamics Assembly Operations**
Stryker Family of Vehicles

**General Dynamics C4 Systems**
Air Warrior (AW)
Command Post Systems and Integration (CPS&I) Standardized Integrated Command Post Systems (SICPS)
Harbormaster Command and Control Center (HCCC)
Joint Battle Command-Platform (JBC-P)
Joint Tactical Radio System Airborne and Maritime/Fixed Station (JTRS AMF)
Mortar Systems
Warfighter Information Network-Tactical (WIN-T) Increment 1

**General Dynamics Communications Systems**
Cryptographic Systems

**General Dynamics European Land Systems-Germany (GDELS-G)**
Improved Ribbon Bridge (IRB)

**General Dynamics (GD IT)**
Global Command and Control System-Army (GCCS-A)

**General Dynamics Land Systems**
Abrams Tank Upgrade
Nuclear Biological Chemical Reconnaissance Vehicle (NBCRV)-Stryker Sensor Suites
Stryker Family of Vehicles

**General Dynamics Land Systems-Canada**
Mine Resistant Ambush Protected Vehicles (MRAP)
Stryker Family of Vehicles

**General Dynamics Ordnance and Tactical Systems**
2.75 Inch Rocket Systems (Hydra-70)
Artillery Ammunition
Excalibur (M982)
Javelin
Joint Air-to-Ground Missile (JAGM)
Medium Caliber Ammunition (MCA)
Tank Ammunition
Small Caliber Ammunition

**General Dynamics SATCOM Technologies**
Warfighter Information Network-Tactical (WIN-T) Increment 1

**General Electric**
Black Hawk/UH/HH-60

**General Transmissions Products**
High Mobility Multipurpose Wheeled Vehicle (HMMWV) Recapitalization (RECAP) Program

**Gentex Corp.**
Air Warrior (AW)

**Georgia Tech Applied Research Corp.**
Advanced Threat Infrared Countermeasure/Common Missile Warning System (ATIRCM/CMWS)

**GEP**
High Mobility Multipurpose Wheeled Vehicle (HMMWV) Recapitalization (RECAP) Program

**Gibson and Barnes**
Air Warrior (AW)

**Global Defense Engineering**
Force Provider (FP)

**Goodrich**
CH-47F Chinook

**Group Home Foundation Inc.**
Joint Chem/Bio Coverall for Combat Vehicle Crewman (JC3)

**Gulfstream**
Fixed Wing

**GTSI**
Global Command and Control System-Army (GCCS-A)

**H&K Gmbh**
Individual Semi-Automatic Airburst System (ISAAS)-XM25

**Hamilton Sundstrand**
Black Hawk/UH/HH-60

**Harris Corp.**
Cryptographic Systems
Defense Enterprise Wideband SATCOM Systems (DEWSS)
High Mobility Artillery Rocket System (HIMARS)
Multiple Launch Rocket System (MLRS) M270A1
Warfighter Information Network-Tactical (WIN-T) Increment 2
Warfighter Information Network-Tactical (WIN-T) Increment 3

**Hawker Beechcraft Corporation**
Enhanced Medium Altitude Reconnaissance and Surveillance System (EMARSS)
Fixed Wing

**Heckler and Koch Defense Inc.**
Small Arms-Individual Weapons

**Helicopter Support Inc.**
Light Utility Helicopter (LUH)/UH-72A Lakota

**Honeywell**
Abrams Tank Upgrade
Armored Knight
CH-47F Chinook
Guided Multiple Launch Rocket System (GMLRS) DPICM/Unitary/Alternative Warhead (Tactical Rockets)
Kiowa Warrior
Longbow Apache (AH-64D) (LBA)

**Howmet Castings**
Lightweight 155mm Howitzer System (LW155)

**Hunter Manufacturing**
Force Provider (FP)

**IBM**
Battle Command Sustainment Support System (BCS3)
Distributed Learning System (DLS)

**ICx Technologies**
Chemical, Biological, Radiological, Nuclear Dismounted Reconnaissance Sets, Kits, and Outfits (CBRN DR SKO)

**Idaho Technologies**
Chemical Biological Medical Systems-Diagnostics

**iLuMinA Solutions**
General Fund Enterprise Business Systems (GFEBS)

**Independent Pipe Products**
Javelin

**Indigo System Corp.**
RQ-11B Raven Small Unmanned Aircraft System (SUAS)

**Indra**
Joint Tactical Radio System Multifunctional Information Distribution System (MIDS)

**Intelligent Decisions**
Close Combat Tactical Trainer (CCTT)

**Intercoastal Electronics**
Improved Target Acquisition System (ITAS)

**Intuitive Research and Technology**
Medium Extended Air Defense System (MEADS)
PATRIOT Advanced Capability-Three (PAC-3)

**ITT**
Defense Enterprise Wideband SATCOM Systems (DEWSS)
Helmet Mounted Night Vision Devices (HMNVD)
Joint Tactical Radio System, Network Enterprise Domain (JTRS NED)
Single Channel Ground and Airborne Radio System (SINCGARS)

**ITT Geospatial Systems**
Helmet Mounted Night Vision Devices (HMNVD)

**JANUS Research**
Secure Mobile Anti-Jam Reliable Tactical Terminal (SMART-T)

**Javelin Joint Venture**
Javelin

**JB Management**
Enhanced Q-36

**JCB Inc.**
High Mobility Engineer Excavator (HMEE) I and III

**JLG Industries Inc.**
All Terrain Lifter Army System (ATLAS)

**Johns Hopkins University Applied Physics Laboratory**
Defense Enterprise Wideband SATCOM Systems (DEWSS)

**Joint Systems Manufacturing Center (JSMC)**
Stryker Family of Vehicles

**Juniper Networks**
Combat Service Support Communications (CSS Comms)

**Kaegan Corporation**
Close Combat Tactical Trainer (CCTT)

**Kalmar Rough Terrain Center (KRTC) LLC**
Rough Terrain Container Handler (RTCH)

**Kaydon**
High Mobility Artillery Rocket System (HIMARS)

**KDH Defense Systems**
Interceptor Body Armor

**Kforce Government Solutions (KGS)**
Medical Simulation Training Center (MSTC)

**Kidde Dual Spectrum**
Stryker Family of Vehicles

**King Aerospace**
Fixed Wing

**Kipper Tool Company**
Mobile Maintenance Equipment Systems (MMES)

**Klune**
Tube-Launched, Optically-Tracked, Wire-Guided (TOW) Missiles

**Knight's Armament Co.**
Clip-on Sniper Night Sight (SNS)

**Kongsberg Defense and Aerospace**
Common Remotely Operated Weapon Station (CROWS)

**Kratos**
Joint-Automatic Identification Technology (J-AIT)

**L-3**
Advanced Field Artillery Tactical Data (AFATDS)

**L-3 Communications Corp.**
Aviation Combined Arms Tactical Trainer (AVCATT)
Bradley Fighting Vehicle Systems Upgrade
Cryptographic Systems
Distributed Common Ground System-Army (DCGS-A)
Excalibur (M982)
Guardrail Common Sensor (GR/CS)
HELLFIRE Family of Missiles
Medical Communications for Combat Casualty Care (MC4)
MQ-1C Gray Eagle Unmanned Aircraft System (UAS)
RQ-7B Shadow Tactical Unmanned Aircraft System (TUAS)
RQ-11B Raven Small Unmanned Aircraft System (SUAS)
Secure Mobile Anti-Jam Reliable Tactical Terminal (SMART-T)
Tank Ammunition
Warfighter Information Network-Tactical (WIN-T) Increment 2
Warfighter Information Network-Tactical (WIN-T) Increment 3

**L-3 Communications Brashear**
Individual Semi-Automatic Airburst System (ISAAS)-XM25

**L-3 Communications-East**
Force Protection Systems

**L-3 Communications Electro-Optic Systems**
Helmet Mounted Night Vision Devices (HMNVD)

**L-3 Communications Space & Navigation**
High Mobility Artillery Rocket System (HIMARS)
Multiple Launch Rocket System (MLRS) M270A1

**L-3 Communications-West**
Enhanced Medium Altitude Reconnaissance and Surveillance System (EMARSS)

**L-3 CyTerra Corp.**
Countermine

**L-3 Global Communications Solutions Inc.**
Combat Service Support Communications (CSS Comms)

**L-3 Insight**
Helmet Mounted Night Vision Devices (HMNVD)

**L-3 Interstate Electronics Corp.**
Precision Guidance Kit (PGK)

**L-3 Services, an MPRI company**
Transportation Coordinators' Automated Information for Movement System II (TC-AIMS II)

**L-3 Vertex**
Fixed Wing

**L-3 Westwood**
Tactical Electric Power (TEP)

**Letterkenny Army Depot**
Force Provider (FP)
High Mobility Multipurpose Wheeled Vehicle (HMMWV) Recapitalization (RECAP) Program
Improvised Explosive Device (IEDD)

**Lex Products Corp.**
Force Provider (FP)

**Lincoln Labs**
Secure Mobile Anti-Jam Reliable Tactical Terminal (SMART-T)

**Linquest Corp.**
Secure Mobile Anti-Jam Reliable Tactical Terminal (SMART-T)

**Litton Advanced Systems**
Airborne Reconnaissance Low (ARL)

**LMI Consulting**
Battle Command Sustainment Support System (BCS3)
Global Combat Support System-Army (GCSS-Army)

**Lockheed Martin**
Airborne Reconnaissance Low (ARL)
Close Combat Tactical Trainer (CCTT)
Distributed Common Ground System-Army (DCGS-A)
Distributed Learning System (DLS)
Enhanced Medium Altitude Reconnaissance and Surveillance System (EMARSS)
Enhanced Q-36
Global Command and Control System-Army (GCCS-A)
Guardrail Common Sensor (GR/CS)
Guided Multiple Launch Rocket System (GMLRS) DPICM/Unitary/Alternative Warhead (Tactical Rockets)
HELLFIRE Family of Missiles
High Mobility Artillery Rocket System (HIMARS)
Instrumentable-Multiple Integrated Laser Engagement System (I-MILES)
Javelin
Joint Air-to-Ground Missile (JAGM)
Joint Tactical Radio System Airborne and Maritime/Fixed Station (JTRS AMF)
Joint Tactical Radio System, Network Enterprise Domain (JTRS NED)
Longbow Apache (AH-64D) (LBA)
Medium Extended Air Defense System (MEADS)
Multiple Launch Rocket System (MLRS) M270A1
PATRIOT Advanced Capability-Three (PAC-3)
Tactical Mission Command (TMC)/ Maneuver Control System (MCS)
Warfighter Information Network-Tactical (WIN-T) Increment 2
Warfighter Information Network-Tactical (WIN-T) Increment 3

**Lockheed Martin Global Training and Logistics**
Joint Land Component Constructive Training Capability (JLCCTC)

**Lockheed Martin Gyrocam Systems LLC**
Countermine

**Lockheed Martin Missiles and Fire Control**
Guided Multiple Launch Rocket System (GMLRS) DPICM/Unitary/Alternative Warhead (Tactical Rockets)
PATRIOT Advanced Capability-Three (PAC-3)

**Longbow LLC**
Longbow Apache (AH-64D) (LBA)

**LTI DataComm Inc.**
Combat Service Support Communications (CSS Comms)

**M-7 Aerospace**
Fixed Wing

**MacAulay-Brown Inc.**
Advanced Threat Infrared Countermeasure/Common Missile Warning System (ATIRCM/CMWS)

**Mainstream Engineering**
Improved Environmental Control Units (IECU)

**Mandus Group**
Mobile Maintenance Equipment Systems (MMES)

**MaTech**
Mortar Systems

**ManTech**
Force XXI Battle Command Brigade and Below (FBCB2)

**ManTech Sensor Technologies Inc.**
Army Key Management System (AKMS)
Meteorological Measuring Set-Profiler (MMS-P)/Computer Meteorological Data-Profiler (CMD-P)

**Marsh Industrial**
Force Provider (FP)

**Marvin Engineering**
Joint Air-to-Ground Missile (JAGM)

**McAlester Army Ammunition Plant**
Artillery Ammunition

**MCT Industries Inc.**
Mobile Maintenance Equipment Systems (MMES)

**Medical Education Technologies**
Medical Simulation Training Center (MSTC)

**Michelin**
Heavy Expanded Mobility Tactical Truck (HEMTT)/HEMTT Extended Service Program (ESP)
Palletized Load System (PLS) and PLS Extended Service Program (ESP)

**MEADS, Intl.**
Medium Extended Air Defense System (MEADS)

**Med-Eng Systems Inc.**
Air Warrior (AW)

**Meggitt Training**
Close Combat Tactical Trainer (CCTT)

**Meridian Medical Technologies**
Chemical Biological Medical Systems-Therapeutics

**Meritor**
Family of Medium Tactical Vehicles (FMTV)
Line Haul Tractor

**Mil-Mar Century Inc.**
Load Handling System Compatible Water Tank Rack (Hippo)

**MITRE**
Distributed Common Ground System-Army (DCGS-A)
Enhanced Medium Altitude Reconnaissance and Surveillance System (EMARSS)
Joint Battle Command-Platform (JBC-P)

**Moog Inc.**
HELLFIRE Family of Missiles
Joint Air-to-Ground Missile (JAGM)
Tube-Launched, Optically-Tracked, Wire-Guided (TOW) Missiles

**Mountain High Equipment and Supply Co.**
Air Warrior (AW)

**MPRI, an L-3 Company**
Distributed Learning System (DLS)
Global Combat Support System-Army (GCSS-Army)

**N-Link Corp**
Distributed Learning System (DLS)

**Naval Air Warfare Center Aircraft Division**
Weapons of Mass Destruction Elimination (WMD-E)

**Navistar Defense**
Mine Resistant Ambush Protected Vehicles (MRAP)

**NetApp**
Distributed Common Ground System-Army (DCGS-A)

**NextPoint Group**
Joint-Automatic Identification Technology (J-AIT)

**NITEK**
Countermine

**North American Controls**
Stryker Family of Vehicles

**Northrop Grumman**
Air/Missile Defense Planning and Control System (AMDPCS)
Biometric Enabling Capability (BEC)
Command Post Systems and Integration (CPS&I) Standardized Integrated Command Post Systems (SICPS)
Common Hardware Systems (CHS)
Counter-Rocket, Artillery, Mortar (C-RAM) /Indirect Fire Protection Capability (IFPC)
Defense Enterprise Wideband SATCOM Systems (DEWSS)
Distributed Common Ground System-Army (DCGS-A)
Force XXI Battle Command Brigade and Below (FBCB2)
Guardrail Common Sensor (GR/CS)
Harbormaster Command and Control Center (HCCC)
Integrated Air and Missile Defense (IAMD)
Integrated Family of Test Equipment (IFTE)
Joint Land Attack Cruise Missile Defense Elevated Netted Sensor System (JLENS)
Joint Tactical Radio System Airborne and Maritime/Fixed Station (JTRS AMF)
Joint Tactical Radio System Ground Mobile Radios (JTRS GMR)
Longbow Apache (AH-64D) (LBA)
Movement Tracking System (MTS)

**Northrop Grumman Guidance and Electronics, Laser Systems**
Joint Effects Targeting System (JETS) Target Location Designation System (TLDS)
Lightweight Laser Designator/Rangefinder (LLDR) AN/PED-1

**Northrop Grumman Information Systems**
Global Combat Support System-Army (GCSS-Army)
Joint Warning and Reporting Network (JWARN)

**Northrop Grumman Electronic Systems**
Joint Tactical Ground Station (JTAGS)

**Northrop Grumman Mission Systems**
Joint Effects Model (JEM)

**Northrop Grumman Space and Mission Systems Corp.**
Forward Area Air Defense Command and Control (FAAD C2)

**Olin Corp.**
Small Caliber Ammunition

**OshKosh Corp.**
Dry Support Bridge (DSB)
Family of Medium Tactical Vehicles (FMTV)
Heavy Expanded Mobility Tactical Truck (HEMTT)/HEMTT Extended Service Program (ESP)
Improved Ribbon Bridge (IRB)
Mine Resistant Ambush Protected Vehicles (MRAP)
Palletized Load System (PLS) and PLS Extended Service Program (ESP)

**Osiris Therapeutics**
Chemical Biological Medical Systems-Therapeutics

**OverWatch Systems**
Distributed Common Ground System-Army (DCGS-A)

**Oxygen Generating Systems International**
Air Warrior (AW)

**Pearson Engineering**
Improvised Explosive Device (IEDD)

**Pennsylvania State University**
Meteorological Measuring Set-Profiler (MMS-P)/Computer Meteorological Data-Profiler (CMD-P)

**Perkin Elmer**
Joint Air-to-Ground Missile (JAGM)

**Pine Bluff Arsenal**
M106 Screening Obscuration Device (SOD)-Visual Restricted Terrain (Vr)

**PKMM**
Forward Area Air Defense Command and Control (FAAD C2)

**Potomac Fusion**
Distributed Common Ground System-Army (DCGS-A)

**Precision CastParts Corp.**
Lightweight 155mm Howitzer System (LW155)

**Protective Products**
Interceptor Body Armor

**Prototype Integration Facility**
Force XXI Battle Command Brigade and Below (FBCB2)

**R&D Technologies**
High Mobility Artillery Rocket System (HIMARS)

**Rapiscan Systems**
Non-Intrusive Inspection Systems (NIIS)

**Raytheon**
Advanced Field Artillery Tactical Data System (AFATDS)
Armored Knight
Battle Command Sustainment Support System (BCS3)
Bradley Fighting Vehicle Systems Upgrade
Distributed Common Ground System-Army (DCGS-A)
Excalibur (M982)
Helmet Mounted Night Vision Devices (HMNVD)
Improved Target Acquisition System (ITAS)
Integrated Air and Missile Defense (IAMD)
Javelin
Joint Air-to-Ground Missile (JAGM)
Joint Land Attack Cruise Missile Defense Elevated Netted Sensor System (JLENS)
Joint Tactical Radio System Airborne and Maritime/Fixed Station (JTRS AMF)
Nett Warrior (NW)
Night Vision Thermal Systems-Thermal Weapon Sight (TWS)
PATRIOT Advanced Capability-Three (PAC-3)
RQ-7B Shadow Tactical Unmanned Aircraft System (TUAS)
Secure Mobile Anti-Jam Reliable Tactical Terminal (SMART-T)
Stryker Family of Vehicles

**Raytheon Missile Systems**
Counter-Rocket, Artillery, Mortar (C-RAM) /Indirect Fire Protection Capability (IFPC)
Javelin
Tube-Launched, Optically-Tracked, Wire-Guided (TOW) Missiles

**Raytheon Solipsys**
Joint Land Attack Cruise Missile Defense Elevated Netted Sensor System (JLENS)

**Raytheon Technical Services**
Air Warrior (AW)
Improvised Explosive Device (IEDD)

**ReadyOne Industries**
Joint Chem/Bio Coverall for Combat Vehicle Crewman (JC3)

**Real Time Labs**
High Mobility Artillery Rocket System (HIMARS)

**Red River Army Depot**
High Mobility Multipurpose Wheeled Vehicle (HMMWV) Recapitalization (RECAP) Program

**Redhat**
Distributed Common Ground System-Army (DCGS-A)

**Ringtail Design**
Distributed Common Ground System-Army (DCGS-A)

**Rock Island Arsenal**
Mobile Maintenance Equipment Systems (MMES)

**Rockwell Collins**
Advanced Threat Infrared Countermeasure/Common Missile Warning System (ATIRCM/CMWS)
Black Hawk/UH/HH-60
CH-47F Chinook
Close Combat Tactical Trainer (CCTT)
Enhanced Medium Altitude Reconnaissance and Surveillance System (EMARSS)
Joint Tactical Radio System Ground Mobile Radios (JTRS GMR)
Joint Tactical Radio System Handheld, Manpack, Small Form Fit (JTRS HMS)
Joint Tactical Radio System Multifunctional Information Distribution System (MIDS)
Joint Tactical Radio System, Network Enterprise Domain (JTRS NED)
NAVSTAR Global Positioning System (GPS)
Nett Warrior (NW)
RQ-7B Shadow Tactical Unmanned Aircraft System (TUAS)

**Rolls Royce Corp.**
Kiowa Warrior

**Rosetta Stone**
Distributed Learning System (DLS)

**SCI Technology Inc.**
Command Post Systems and Integration (CPS&I) Standardized Integrated Command Post Systems (SICPS)
Harbormaster Command and Control Center (HCCC)

**Science and Engineering Services Inc. (SESI)**
Air Warrior (AW)
Joint Biological Standoff Detection System (JBSDS)

**Science Applications International Corporation (SAIC)**
Advanced Threat Infrared Countermeasure/Common Missile Warning System (ATIRCM/CMWS)
Army Key Management System (AKMS)
Aviation Combined Arms Tactical Trainer (AVCATT)
Enhanced Medium Altitude Reconnaissance and Surveillance System (EMARSS)
Installation Protection Program (IPP)
Joint Tactical Radio System Handheld, Manpack, Small Form Fit (JTRS HMS)
Non-Intrusive Inspection Systems (NIIS)
Weapons of Mass Destruction Elimination (WMD-E)

**Secure Communication Systems Inc.**
Air Warrior (AW)

**Segovia Global IP Services**
Combat Service Support Communications (CSS Comms)

**Selex**
Joint Tactical Radio System Multifunctional Information Distribution System (MIDS)

**Sensor Technologies**
Common Hardware Systems (CHS)
Enhanced Medium Altitude Reconnaissance and Surveillance System (EMARSS)
Tactical Mission Command (TMC)/ Maneuver Control System (MCS)

**SETA**
Joint Land Attack Cruise Missile Defense Elevated Netted Sensor System (JLENS)

**Sierra Nevada Corp.**
Airborne Reconnaissance Low (ARL)
Army Key Management System (AKMS)

**Sigmatech Inc.**
Command Post Systems and Integration (CPS&I) Standardized Integrated Command Post Systems (SICPS)
Harbormaster Command and Control Center (HCCC)

**Sikorsky**
Black Hawk/UH/HH-60

**Skillsoft Corp.**
Distributed Learning System (DLS)

**Smiths Detection Inc.**
Chemical Biological Protective Shelter (CBPS) M8E1
Longbow Apache (AH-64D) (LBA)
Joint Chemical Agent Detector (JCAD) M4E1
Meteorological Measuring Set-Profiler (MMS-P)/Computer Meteorological Data-Profiler (CMD-P)

**Smiths Industries**
High Mobility Artillery Rocket System (HIMARS)

**Snap-On Industrial**
Mobile Maintenance Equipment Systems (MMES)

**SNC Technologies**
Small Caliber Ammunition

**Software Engineering Center-Belvoir (SEC-B)**
Combat Service Support Communications (CSS Comms)

**Software Engineering Directorate (SED), AMRDEC**
Joint Battle Command-Platform (JBC-P)

**Southwest Research Institute**
Chemical Biological Medical Systems-Therapeutics

**SPAWAR Pacific**
Harbormaster Command and Control Center (HCCC)

**Spectrum Microwave**
Secure Mobile Anti-Jam Reliable Tactical Terminal (SMART-T)

**Sprint Communications**
Distributed Learning System (DLS)

**SRA**
Joint Tactical Radio System, Network Enterprise Domain (JTRS NED)

**SRC**
Warfighter Information Network-Tactical (WIN-T) Increment 1

**SRCTec**
Lightweight Counter Mortar Radar (LCMR)

**Sypris**
Army Key Management System (AKMS)

**Syracuse Research Corporation**
Lightweight Counter Mortar Radar (LCMR)

**Systems, Studies, and Simulation**
Guided Multiple Launch Rocket System (GMLRS) DPICM/Unitary/Alternative Warhead (Tactical Rockets)

**Systems Technologies (Systek) Inc.**
Combat Service Support Communications (CSS Comms)
Global Command and Control System-Army (GCCS-A)

**Tank-Automotive and Armaments Command (TACOM)**
Paladin/Field Artillery Ammunition Supply Vehicle (FAASV)

**Tapestry Solutions Inc.**
Battle Command Sustainment Support System (BCS3)
Joint Land Component Constructive Training Capability (JLCCTC)

**Taylor-Wharton**
Air Warrior (AW)

**TCOM**
Joint Land Attack Cruise Missile Defense Elevated Netted Sensor System (JLENS)

**Tecom**
RQ-7B Shadow Tactical Unmanned Aircraft System (TUAS)

**Teledyne**
Secure Mobile Anti-Jam Reliable Tactical Terminal (SMART-T)

**Telephonics Corp.**
Air Warrior (AW)

**Telos Corp.**
Combat Service Support Communications (CSS Comms)

**Tel-Instrument Electronics Corp.**
Test Equipment Modernization (TEMOD)

**Textron Marine and Land Systems**
Armored Knight

**Textron Defense Systems**
Spider

**Thales**
Joint Tactical Radio System Handheld, Manpack, Small Form Fit (JTRS HMS)
Joint Tactical Radio System Multifunctional Information Distribution System (MIDS)
Tube-Launched, Optically-Tracked, Wire-Guided (TOW) Missiles

**Thales Raytheon Systems**
Sentinel

**The Research Associates**
Biometric Enabling Capability (BEC)
Joint Personnel Identification Version 2 (JPIv2)

**TJM Electronic**
Joint Air-to-Ground Missile (JAGM)

**Tobyhanna Army Depot**
Combat Service Support Communications (CSS Comms)
Command Post Systems and Integration (CPS&I) Standardized Integrated Command Post Systems (SICPS)
Forward Area Air Defense Command and Control (FAAD C2)
Harbormaster Command and Control Center (HCCC)
Lightweight Counter Mortar Radar (LCMR)

**Transtector**
Secure Mobile Anti-Jam Reliable Tactical Terminal (SMART-T)

**Triumph Structures**
Lightweight 155mm Howitzer System (LW155)

**Tri-Tech USA Inc.**
Force Provider (FP)

**Tucson Embedded Systems**
Distributed Common Ground System-Army (DCGS-A)

**US Divers**
Air Warrior (AW)

**U.S. Ordnance**
Small Arms-Crew Served Weapons

**Ultra Inc.**
Air/Missile Defense Planning and Control System (AMDPCS)

**UNICOR**
Single Channel Ground and Airborne Radio System (SINCGARS)

**Unisys Corporation**
Joint-Automatic Identification Technology (J-AIT)

**URS Corp.**
Chemical Demilitarization

**U.S. Army Information Systems Engineering Center (USAISEC)**
Combat Service Support Communications (CSS Comms)

**USFalcon**
Single Channel Ground and Airborne Radio System (SINCGARS)

**Verhoff Machine**
Stryker Family of Vehicles

**Vertigo Inc.**
Force Provider (FP)

**Vertu Corp.**
Small Arms-Individual Weapons

**ViaSat Inc.**
Cryptographic Systems
Force XXI Battle Command Brigade and Below (FBCB2)
Joint Tactical Radio System Multifunctional Information Distribution System (MIDS)

**VIATECH**
Advanced Field Artillery Tactical Data System (AFATDS)

**Vision Technology Miltope Corp.**
Integrated Family of Test Equipment (IFTE)

**Vmware**
Distributed Common Ground System-Army (DCGS-A)

**Waterlivet Arsenal**
Lightweight 155mm Howitzer System (LW155)
Mortar Systems

**WESCAM**
Airborne Reconnaissance Low (ARL)

**Westwind Technologies Inc.**
Air Warrior (AW)

**Williams Fairey Engineering Ltd.**
Dry Support Bridge (DSB)

**Wolf Coach Inc., an L-3 Communications Company**
Weapons of Mass Destruction Elimination (WMD-E)

**XMCO**
Dry Support Bridge (DSB)
Heavy Loader
High Mobility Engineer Excavator (HMEE) I and III

**Yuma Proving Ground**
Lightweight Counter Mortar Radar (LCMR)
Paladin/Field Artillery Ammunition Supply Vehicle (FAASV)

**ZETA**
Guardrail Common Sensor (GR/CS)

# Contractors by State

**Alabama**
AEPCO
Anniston Army Depot
Aviation and Missile Solutions LLC
BAE Systems
Boeing
CAS Inc.
CEP Inc.
CMI
Computer Sciences Corp. (CSC)
DHS Systems
DMD
DRS-TEM
Dynetics Inc.
E&TS Ktrs
EADS North America
Future Research Corp.
General Dynamics Assembly Operations
General Dynamics Ordnance and Tactical Systems
Helicopter Support Inc.
Intuitive Research and Technology
Javelin Joint Venture
Lockheed Martin
MEADS, Intl.
Northrop Grumman
Prototype Integration Facility
R&D Electronics
Raytheon
Science Applications International Corporation (SAIC)
SCI Technology Inc.
Science and Engineering Services Inc. (SESI)
SETA
Sigmatech Inc.
Software Engineering Directorate (SED), AMRDEC
Systems, Studies, and Simulation
Taylor-Wharton
URS Corp.
Vision Technology Miltope Corp.
Westwind Technologies Inc.

**Arizona**
Acme Electric
Alliant Techsystems
Avnet
BAE Systems
Boeing
Communications Security Logistics Activity
DISA Satellite Transmission Services-Global NETCOM
General Dynamics
General Dynamics C4 Systems
Honeywell
Intercoastal Electronics
L-3 Communications
L-3 Communications Electro-Optic Systems
Lockheed Martin
Raytheon
Raytheon Missile Systems
TJM Electronic
Tucson Embedded Systems
U.S. Army Information Systems Engineering Command (USAISEC)
Yuma Proving Ground

**Arkansas**
Aerojet
AMTEC Corp.
General Dynamics Ordnance and Tactical Systems
Lockheed Martin
Pine Bluff Arsenal
URS Corp.

**California**
Aardvark Technical
Aerovironment Inc.
Agilent Technologies Inc.
All American Racers Inc.
ArgonST Radix
ATK
BAE Systems
Boeing
Ceradyne Inc.
Cloudera
CTT
CUBIC Defense Systems
Esri
General Atomics, Aeronautical Systems Inc.
General Dynamics Ordnance and Tactical Systems
Gentex Corp.
Gibson and Barnes
IBM
Indigo System Corp.
Kidde Dual Spectrum
Kratos
L-3 Communications Corp.
L-3 Interstate Electronics Corp.
Lockheed Martin
Marvin Engineering
NetApp
Northrop Grumman
Northrop Grumman Mission Systems
Northrop Grumman Space and Mission Systems Corp.
Rapiscan Systems
Raytheon
Science Applications International Corporation (SAIC)
Secure Communication Systems Inc.
SPAWAR Pacific
Tapestry Solutions Inc.
Tecom
Thales Raytheon Systems
Triumph Structures
US Divers
Vertigo Inc.
ViaSat Inc.
Vmware

**Colorado**
Agilent Technologies
ITT
Linquest
Lockheed Martin
Northrop Grumman Electronic Systems

**Connecticut**
BAE Systems
Colt's Manufacturing Co.
DRS Fermont
Goodrich
Hamilton Sundstrand
Helicopter Support Inc.
Lex Products Corp.
Sikorsky

**Delaware**
ANP Technologies

**Florida**
AVT
Booz Allen Hamilton
Computer Sciences Corp. (CSC)

DRS
DRS Optronics Inc.
DRS Tactical Systems
DRS Technologies
DSE Inc. (Balimoy Manufacturing Company Inc.)
ECC International
General Dynamics
General Dynamics Ordnance and Tactical Systems (GD-OTS)
Harris Corp.
Honeywell
Kaegan Corporation
Knight's Armament Co.
L-3 CyTerra Corp.
Lockheed Martin
Lockheed Martin Global Training and Logistics
Lockheed Martin Gyrocam Systems LLC
Longbow LLC
Mainstream Engineering
MEADS, Intl.
Medical Education Technologies
Northrop Grumman
Northrop Grumman Guidance and Electronics, Laser Systems
Northrop Grumman Information Systems
Protective Products
Raytheon
Real Time Labs
Science Applications International Corporation (SAIC)
Smiths Industries
Sypris
Thales Raytheon Systems

**Georgia**
CSS
EPS Corp.
General Dynamics SATCOM Technologies
Georgia Tech Applied Research Corp.
Gulstream
JCB Inc.
Kipper Tool Company
Meggitt Training

**Idaho**
Transtector

**Illinois**
Boeing
Caterpillar
Caterpillar C-15
Caterpillar Defense and Federal Products
E.D. Etnyre and Co.
General Dynamics Ordnance and Tactical Systems
L-3 Communications
Mandus Group
Navistar Defense
Northrop Grumman
Olin Corp.
Rock Island Arsenal
Snap-on Industrial

**Indiana**
Allison Transmission
AM General
General Transmissions Products
ITT
Raytheon
Raytheon Technical Services
Rolls Royce Corp.

**Iowa**
American Ordnance
Rockwell Collins

**Kansas**
Detroit Diesel
Hawker Beech Corporation

**Kentucky**
CONCO
DRS ES
DRS Technologies

**Louisiana**
Textron Marine and Land Systems

**Maine**
General Dynamics Armament and Technical Products
General Dynamics Armament and Technical Products Manufacturing Facility
Group Home Foundation Inc.

**Maryland**
AAI Corp.
Aberdeen Test Center
BAE Systems
Binary Group
Booz Allen Hamilton
Comtech Mobile Datacom Corporation (CMDC)
DynPort Vaccine
EAI Corporation/SAIC
FASCAN International
Global Defense Engineering
IBM
iLuMinA Solutions
JANUS Research
Johns Hopkins University Applied Physics Laboratory
Litton Advanced Systems
Lockheed Martin
MaTech
Meridian Medical Technologies
Naval Air Warfare Center Aircraft Division
Northrop Grumman
Osiris Therapeutics
Raytheon
Raytheon Solipsys
Science and Engineering Services Inc. (SESI)
Sierra Nevada Corp.
Smiths Detection Inc.
TCOM
Textron Systems
Thales

**Massachusetts**
Acambis plc
American Science & Engineering Inc.
BAE Systems
Curtiss-Wright
Draper Laboratories
General Dynamics
General Dynamics C-4 Systems Inc.
General Dynamics Communication Systems
General Electric
L-3 CyTerra Corp.
Lincoln Labs
Lockheed Martin Missiles and Fire Control
Raytheon
Spectrum Microwave
Textron Defense Systems
Wolf Coach Inc., an L-3 Communications Company

**Michigan**
AAR Mobility Systems
AM General (AMG)
Avon Protection Systems
Detroit Diesel
Eaton Aeroquip
Emergent BioSolutions (Bioport)
General Dynamics
General Dynamics Land Systems
Howmet Castings
Kaydon
L-3 Communications Corp.
Marsh Industrial
Meritor
North American Controls
Tank-Automotive and Armaments Command (TACOM)
XMCO

**Minnesota**
Alliant Techsystems
Cummins Power Generation

**Mississippi**
American Eurocopter
BAE Systems
Eaton-Vickers
Engineering Research and Development Command
L-3 Vertex
Thales Raytheon Systems

**Missouri**
Alliant Techsystems
Boeing
DRS Sustainment Systems Inc.

**Nebraska**
General Dynamics Armament and Technical Products (GD-ATP)

**Nevada**
PKMM
Sierra Nevada Corp.
U.S. Ordnance

**New Hampshire**
BAE Systems
L-3 Communications Electro-Optic Systems
L-3 Insight
Skillsoft Inc.

**New Jersey**
Airborne Systems North American
AMT
Armaments R&D Center
BAE Systems
Booz Allen Hamilton
Breeze
CACI
Computer Sciences Corp. (CSC)
David H. Pollock Consultants
Dewey Electronics
DRS
Engineering Solutions and Products (ESP)
EPS Corp.
ITT
L-3 Communications
L-3 Communications-East
L-3 Communications Space & Navigation
Lockheed Martin
Mantech Sensor Technologies Inc.
MITRE
Northrop Grumman
Sensor Technologies
Smiths Industries
SRC
Systems Technologies (Systek) Inc.
Tel-Instrument Electronics Corp.

**New Mexico**
Aerojet General
EG&G Technical Services Inc.
Honeywell
Lockheed Martin Missiles and Fire Control
MCT Industries Inc.

**New York**
ADSI
Bren-Tronics
Capgemini (IV &V)
Carleton Technologies Inc.
L-3 Global Communications Services Inc.
Lockheed Martin
MEADS, Intl.
Med-Eng Systems Inc.
Moog Inc.
Northrop Grumman
Oxygen Generating Systems International
SRCTec
Syracuse Research Corporation (SRC)
Telephonics Corp.
The Research Associates
Waterlivet Arsenal

**North Carolina**
Daimler Trucks North America LLC-Freightliner Division
General Dynamics Armament and Technical Products (GD-ATP)
TCOM
USFalcon

**Ohio**
BAE
Battelle Biomedical Research Center
Battelle Memorial Institute
CMC Electronics
DRS Mobile Environmental
GEP
Hunter Manufacturing
Joint Systems Manufacturing Center (JSMC)
MacAulay-Brown Inc.
Mil-Mar Century Inc.
Perkin Elmer
Verhoff Machine

**Oklahoma**
CGI Federal
Choctaw Defense Manufacturing Contractors (CDMC)
L-3 Communications
L-3 Westwood
McAlester Army Ammunition Plant
VIATECH

**Oregon**
Daimler Trucks North America LLC-Freightliner Division
Mountain High Equipment and Supply Co.
Precision CastParts Corp.
URS Corp.

**Pennsylvania**
Action Manufacturing
BAE Systems
BAE Systems Land & Armament, Ground Systems Division

Boeing
Fidelity Technologies Corp.
General Dynamics Ordnance and Tactical Systems-Scranton Operations
ICx Technologies
JLG Industries Inc.
KDH Defense Systems
Kongsberg Defense and Aerospace
L-3 Communications
L-3 Communications Brashear
Letterkenny Army Depot
Pennsylvania State University
Tobyhanna Army Depot

**South Carolina**
Caterpillar
Charleston Marine Containers
DSE Inc. (Balimoy Manufacturing Company Inc.)
Fabrique National Manufacturing LLC
Force Protection Industries Inc.
Michelin

**Tennessee**
American Ordnance
BAE System-Holston Army Ammunition Plant
Digital Reasoning
Teledyne

**Texas**
American Eurocopter
Apptricity Corp.
BAE Systems
BAE-TVS
Beacon Industries
Bell Helicopter Textron
Boeing
Casteel Manufacturing
Critical Solutions International Inc.
Dell Computer Corp.
DRS Optronics
DRS Technologies
DynCorp
EFW
Elbit Systems of America
General Dynamics
Helicopter Support Inc.
Independent Pipe Products
L-3 Communications
L-3 Communications Electro-Optic Systems
Lockheed Martin
M-7 Aerospace
MANTECH
Kalmar Rough Terrain Center (KRTC) LLC
King Aerospace
OshKosh Corp.
OverWatch Systems
Potomac Fusion
Raytheon
ReadyOne Industries
Red River Army Depot
Ringtail Design
Southwest Research Institute
Thales Raytheon Systems
Ultra Inc.

**Utah**
Idaho Technologies
Klune
L-3 Communications
Moog Inc.
Rockwell Collins
URS Corp.

**Vermont**
General Dynamics
General Dynamics Armament and Technical Products
Tri-Tech USA Inc.

**Virginia**
Accenture
Aerial Machine and Tool Corp.
Aerojet
Alliant Techsystems
ATK
BAE Systems
Booz Allen Hamilton
CACI
Computer Sciences Corp. (CSC)
EADS North America
Electronic Consulting Services Inc.
General Dynamics
General Dynamics (GDIT)
GTSI
Heckler and Koch Defense Inc.
IBM
Intelligent Decisions
ITT
ITT Geospatial Systems
JB Management
Juniper Networks
Kforce Government Solutions (KGS)
L-3 Communications
L-3 Services, an MPRI company
LMI Consulting
Lockheed Martin
LTI DataComm Inc.
MPRI, an L-3 Company
NextPoint Group
NITEK
Northrop Grumman Information Systems
Raytheon
Rockwell Collins
Rosetta Stone
Science Applications International Corp. (SAIC)
Segovia Global IP Services
Software Engineering Center-Belvoir (SEC-B)
Sprint Communications
SRA
Tapestry Solutions Inc.
Telos Corp.
Unisys Corporation
Vertu Corp.
ZETA

**Washington**
Berg Companies Inc.
Fluke Corp.
N-Link Corp.

**Washington, DC**
UNICOR

**West Virginia**
Alliant Techsystems
ATK
Azimuth Inc.

**Wisconsin**
AMTEC Corp.
Case New Holland
Dedicated Computing
OshKosh Corp.

## INTERNATIONAL CONTRACTORS

**Canada**
Cangene Corp.
General Dynamics Land Systems-Canada
General Dynamics Ordnance and Tactical Systems
SNC Technologies
WESCAM

**Denmark**
A/S Hydrenna

**France**
EuroMIDS
Thales

**Germany**
EADS
General Dynamics European Land Systems-Germany (GDELS-G)
H&K Gmbh

**Italy**
Selex

**Spain**
Indra

**United Kingdom**
Atlantic Inertial Units
BAE Systems
FBM Babcock Marine
Pearson Engineering
Thales
Williams Fairey Engineering Ltd.

# Points of Contact

**2.75 Inch Rocket Systems (Hydra-70)**
JAMS Project Office
SFAE-MSLS-JAMS
5250 Martin Road
Redstone Arsenal, AL 35898-8000

**Abrams Tank Upgrade**
HBCT
SFAE-GCS-CS-A
6501 E. 11 Mile Rd.
Warren, MI 48397-5000

**Advanced Field Artillery Tactical Data System (AFATDS)**
Product Director, Fire Support Command and Control
SFAE-C3T-MC-FSC2
6007 Combat Drive
5th Floor
APG, MD 21005

**Advanced Threat Infrared Countermeasure/Common Missile Warning System (ATIRCM/CMWS)**
Advanced Threat Infrared Countermeasure Quick Reaction Capability (ATIRCM QRC)
SFAE-IEW-ASE
6726 Odyssey Drive
Huntsville, AL 35806

**Air Warrior**
PM Air Warrior
SFAE-SDR-AW
6726 Odyssey Drive NW
Huntsville, AL 35806

**All Terrain Lifter Army System (ATLAS)**
Product Manager, Combat Engineer/MHE
SFAE-CSS-FP-C
6501 E. 11 Mile Rd.
Mail Stop 401
Warren, MI 48397-5000

**Air/Missile Defense Planning and Control System (AMDPCS)**
Counter-Rocket, Artillery, Mortar (C-RAM) Program Directorate
SFAE-C3T-CR
121 Research Boulevard
Madison, AL 35758

**Airborne Reconnaissance Low (ARL)**
PM Airborne Reconnaissance and Exploitation Systems (ARES)
SFAE-IEWS-ACS
Building 6006, Room B1-125
Combat Drive
Aberdeen Proving Ground, MD 21005

**Armored Knight**
Product Manager, Combat Engineer/MHE
SFAE-CSS-FP-C
6501 E. 11 Mile Rd.
Mail Stop 401
Warren, MI 48397-5000

**Army Key Management System (AKMS)**
Project Director, Communications Security (PD COMSEC)
SFAE-C3T-COMSEC
6007 Combat Drive, 5th Floor
Aberdeen Proving Grounds, MD 21005

**Artillery Ammunition**
PM Combat Ammunition Systems
SFAE-AMO-CAS
Picatinny Arsenal, NJ 07806

**Aviation Combined Arms Tactical Trainer (AVCATT)**
Project Manager Combined Arms Tactical Trainers
SFAE-STRI-PMCATT
12350 Research Parkway
Orlando, FL 32826-3276

**Battle Command Sustainment Support System (BCS3)**
PM Battle Command Sustainment Support System (BCS3)
SFAE-C3T-BC-BCS3
6007 Combat Drive
5th Floor
APG, MD 20115

**Biometric Enabling Capability (BEC)**
Project Manager PM DoD Biometrics
SFAE-PS-BI
Building 1445
Ft. Belvoir, VA 22060-5526

**Black Hawk/UH/HH-60**
Utility Helicopters Project Office (UHPO)
SFAE-AV-UH
Bldg 5308
Redstone Arsenal, AL 35898

**Bradley Fighting Vehicle Systems Upgrade**
Program Manager, Heavy Brigade Combat Team
SFAE-GCS-CS-A
6501 E. 11 Mile Rd.
Warren, MI 48397-5000

**Calibration Sets Equipment (CALSETS)**
Test, Measurement, and Diagnostic Equipment Product Director
SFAE-CSS-JC-TM
Building 3651
Redstone Arsenal, AL 35898

**CH-47F Chinook**
SFAE-AV-CH-ICH
Building 5678
Redstone Arsenal, AL 35898

**Chemical Biological Medical Systems-Diagnostics**
JPM CBMS
1564 Freedman Dr
Ft. Detrick, MD 21702

**Chemical Biological Medical Systems (CBMS)-Prophylaxis**
JPM CBMS
1564 Freedman Dr
Ft Detrick, MD 21702

**Chemical Biological Medical Systems-Therapeutics**
JPM CBMS
1564 Freedman Dr
Ft Detrick, MD 21702

**Chemical Biological Protective Shelter (CBPS) M8E1**
Joint Project Manager Protection
JPM P
Suite 301
50 Tech Parkway
Stafford, VA 22556

**Chemical, Biological, Radiological, Nuclear Dismounted Reconnaissance Sets, Kits, and Outfits (CBRN DR SKO)**
Joint Project Manager Contamination Avoidance
SFAE-CBD-NBC-R
Building E4465
5183 Blackhawk Road
Aberdeen Proving Ground, MD 21010-5425

**Chemical Demilitarization**
Chemical Materials Agency
AMSCM-D
5183 Blackhawk Road
APG-EA, MD 21010-5424

**Clip-on Sniper Night Sight (SNS)**
PM Soldier Sensors and Lasers
SFAE-SDR-SW
10170 Beach Road
Building 325
Ft. Belvoir, VA 22060

**Close Combat Tactical Trainer (CCTT)**
Project Manager Combined Arms Tactical Trainers
SFAE-STRI-PMCATT
12350 Research Parkway
Orlando, FL 32826-3276

**Combat Service Support Communications (CSS Comms)**
PM Defense Communications and Army Transmission Systems
SFAE-PS-TS-DWT
6700 Springfield Center Dr.
Suite E
Springfield, VA 22150

**Command Post Systems and Integration (CPS&I) Standardized Integrated Command Post Systems (SICPS)**
Product Manager Command Post Systems & Integration (PdM CPS&I)
SFAE-C3T-WIN-CPSI
Redstone Arsenal, AL 35898

**Common Hardware Systems (CHS)**
Product Director Common Hardware Systems (PD-CHS)
SFAE-C3T-MC-CHS
Building 6007
Aberdeen Proving Ground, MD 21005

**Common Remotely Operated Weapon Station (CROWS)**
Project Manager Soldier Weapons
SFAE-SDR-SW
Building 151
Picatinny Arsenal, NJ 07806

**Countermine**
PM Countermine & EOD
SFAE-AMO-CCS
10205 Burbeck Road
Suite 100
Ft Belvoir, VA 22060-5811

**Counter-Rocket, Artillery, Mortar (C-RAM)/Indirect Fire Protection Capability (IFPC)**
C-RAM Program Directorate
SFAE-C3T-CR
121 Research Boulevard
Madison, AL 35758

**Cryptographic Systems**
PD Cryptographic Systems
SFAE-CCC-COM
6007 Combat Drive
F5-148
APG, MD 21005

**Defense Enterprise Wideband SATCOM System (DEWSS)**
PM Defense Communications and Army Transmission Systems
Building 1456
Ft. Belvoir, VA 22060

**Distributed Common Ground System-Army (DCGS-A)**
PM Distributed Common Ground System-Army (DCGS-A)
SFAE-IEW-DCG
Building 6006
C5ISR Complex
Aberdeen Proving Ground, MD 21005-0001

**Distributed Learning System (DLS)**
PD DLS
SFAE-PS-DL
11846 Rock Landing Dr.
Suite B
Newport News, VA 23606

**Dry Support Bridge (DSB)**
PM Bridging Systems
SFAE-CSS-FP-H
6501 East 11 Mile Rd.
Mail Stop 401
Warren, MI 43897-5000

**Enhanced Medium Altitude Reconnaissance and Surveillance System (EMARSS)**
PdM Medium Altitude Reconnaissance and Surveillance Systems (MARSS)
SFAE-IEWS-ACS
Building 6006, Room B1-125
Combat Drive
Aberdeen Proving Ground, MD 21005

**Enhanced Q-36**
PM Radars
SAFM-IEW&S
Aberdeen, MD 21010

**Excalibur (M982)**
PM Excalibur
SFAE-AMO-CAS-EX
Building 172
Buffington Road
Picatinny Arsenal, NJ 07806-5000

**Family of Medium Tactical Vehicles (FMTV)**
Product Manager-Medium Tactical Vehicles
SFAE-CSS
6501 E. 11 Mile Rd.
Warren, MI 43897-5000

**Fixed Wing**
DA Systems Coordinator-Fixed Wing ASA (ALT) Aviation, Intelligence & Electronic Warfare
SAAL-SAI
2511 S. Jefferson Davis Highway
Room 10023
Arlington, VA 22202

**Force Protection Systems**
Joint Project Manager Guardian
SFAE-CBD-GN-F
5109 Leesburg Pike
Falls Church, VA 22041

**Force Provider (FP)**
PM Force Sustainment Systems
SFAE-CSS-FP-F
Kansas Street
Natick, MA 01760-5057

**Force XXI Battle Command Brigade and Below (FBCB2)**
PM FBCB2
SFAE-C3T-FBC
6007 Combat Drive
4th Floor
Aberdeen Proving Ground, MD 21005-1846

**Forward Area Air Defense Command and Control (FAAD C2)**
C-RAM Program Directorate
SFAE-C3T-CR
121 Research Boulevard
Madison, AL 35758

**Future Tank Main Gun Ammunition (FTMGA)**
PM Maneuver Ammunition Systems
SFAE-AMO-MAS
Picatinny Arsenal, NJ 07806

**General Fund Enterprise Business Systems (GFEBS)**
SFAE-PS-GF
5911 Kingstowne Village Parkway
Suite 600
Alexandria, VA 22315

**Global Combat Support System-Army (GCSS-Army)**
Product Manager GCSS-Army
SFAE-PS-GC
3811 Corporate Rd
Suite C
Petersburg, VA 23805

**Global Command and Control System-Army (GCCS-A)**
Product Manager, Strategic Mission Command
SFAE-C3T-MC-SMC
Building 6007
Aberdeen Proving Ground
Aberdeen, MD 21005

**Ground Combat Vehicle (GCV)**
PM GCV
SFAE-GCS-GV
5500 Enterprise Dr.
Warren, MI 48043

**Guardrail Common Sensor (GR/CS)**
PM Airborne Reconnaissance and Exploitation Systems (ARES)
SFAE-IEWS-ACS
Building 6006
Combat Drive
Aberdeen Proving Ground, MD 21005

**Guided Multiple Launch Rocket System (GMLRS) DPICM/Unitary/Alternative Warhead (Tactical Rockets)**
Precision Fires Rocket and Missile Systems
SFAE-MSLS-PF
Building 5250 Martin Road
Redstone Arsenal, AL 35898

**Harbormaster Command and Control Center (HCCC)**
Product Manager Command Post Systems & Integration (PdM CPS&I)
SFAE-C3T-WIN-CPSI
Redstone Arsenal, AL 34898

**Heavy Expanded Mobility Tactical Truck (HEMTT)/HEMTT Extended Service Program (ESP)**
PM Heavy Tactical Vehicles
SFAE-CSS-TV-H
6501 E. 11 Mile Rd.
Mail Stop 429
Warren, MI 48397-5000

**Heavy Loader**
PM for Combat Engineer Materiel Handling Equipment
SFAE-CSS-FP-C
6501 E. 11 Mile Rd.
Warren, MI 48397-5000

**HELLFIRE Family of Missiles**
JAMS Project Office
SFAE-MSLS-JAMS
5250 Martin Road
Redstone Arsenal, AL 35898

**Helmet Mounted Night Vision Devices (HMNVD)**
PM Soldier Sensors and Lasers
SFAE-SDR-SSL
10170 Beach Rd.
Building 325
Ft. Belvoir, VA 22060

**High Mobility Artillery Rocket System (HIMARS)**
Precision Fires Rocket and Missile Systems Project Office
SFAE-MSL-PF-FAL
Building 5250
Redstone Arsenal, AL 35898

**High Mobility Engineer Excavator (HMEE) I and III**
Product Manager Combat Engineer/MHE
SFAE-CSS-FP-C
6501 E. 11 Mile Rd
Warren, MI 48397-5000

**High Mobility Multipurpose Wheeled Vehicle (HMMWV) Recapitalization (RECAP) Program**
Product Manager Light Tactical Vehicles
SFAE-CSS-TV-L
6501 11 Mile Road MS 245
Warren, MI 43897

**Improved Environmental Control Units (IECU)**
Project Manager Mobile Electric Power
SFAE-C3T-MEP-OPM
5850 Delafield Rd
Bldg 324
Ft. Belvoir, VA 22060-5809

**Improved Ribbon Bridge (IRB)**
PM Bridging Systems
SFAE-CSS-FP-H
6501 E. 11 Mile Rd.
Mail Stop 401
Warren, MI 43897-5000

**Improved Target Acquisition System (ITAS)**
PM Close Combat Weapon Systems Project Office
SFAE-MSL-CWS-J
Redstone Arsenal, AL 35898

**Improvised Explosive Device (IEDD)**
PdM IED Defeat/Protect Force
SFAE-AMO-CCS
Picatinny Arsenal, NJ 07806-5000

**Individual Semi-Automatic Airburst System (ISAAS)-XM25**
PEO Soldier Weapons
SFAE-SDR-SW
PEO Soldier
Picatinny Arsenal, NJ 07806

**Installation Protection Program (IPP)**
Joint Project Manager Guardian
SFAE-CBD-Guardian
5109 Leesburg Pike
Falls Church, VA 22041

**Instrumentable-Multiple Integrated Laser Engagement System (I-MILES)**
Project Manager Training Devices
SFAE-STRI-PMTRADE
12350 Research Parkway
Orlando, FL 32826

**Integrated Air and Missile Defense (IAMD)**
PEO Missiles and Space
SFAE-MSLS-IAMD
Program Executive Office Missiles and Space Integrated Air and Missile Defense Project Office
Building 5250
Redstone Arsenal, AL 35898-8000

**Integrated Family of Test Equipment (IFTE)**
Test, Measurement, and Diagnostic Equipment Product Director
SFAE-CSS-JC-TM
Building 3651
Redstone Arsenal, AL 35898

**Interceptor Body Armor**
Product Manager Soldier Protective Equipment
SFAE-SDR-SPE
10170 Beach Rd.
Building 328T
Ft. Belvoir, VA 22060

**Javelin**
PM Close Combat Weapon Systems Project Office
SFAE-MSL-CWS-J
Redstone Arsenal, AL 35898

**Joint Air-to-Ground Missile (JAGM)**
Joint Air to Ground Missile Product Office
SFAE-MSL-JAMS-M
5250 Martin Rd.
Redstone Arsenal, AL 35898

**Joint-Automatic Identification Technology (J-AIT)**
Product Manager, Joint-Automatic Identification Technology (PM-JAIT)
SFAE-PS-AI
200 Stovall Street
Alexandria, VA 22332

**Joint Battle Command-Platform (JBC-P)**
PM Force XXI Battle Command Brigade and Below
SFAE-C3T-FBC
6007 Combat Drive
4th Floor
Aberdeen Proving Ground, MD 21005-1846

**Joint Biological Point Detection System (JBPDS)**
Joint Project Manager Biological Defense
SFAE-CBD-BD-BDS
5183 Blackhawk Road
Aberdeen Proving Ground, MD 21010-5425

**Joint Biological Standoff Detection System (JBSDS)**
Joint Project Manager Biological Defense
SFAE-CBD-BD-BDS
5183 Blackhawk Rd (Bldg E3549)
Edgewood Area-Aberdeen Proving Ground, MD 21010-5424

**Joint Biological Tactical Detection System (JBTDS)**
Joint Project Manager Biological Defense
SFAE-CBD-BD-PD-FoS
5183 Blackhawk Rd (Bldg E3549)
Aberdeen Proving Grounds, MD 21010-5424

**Joint Chem/Bio Coverall for Combat Vehicle Crewman (JC3)**
Joint Project Manager Protection
Suite 301
50 Tech Parkway
Stafford, VA 22556

**Joint Chemical Agent Detector (JCAD) M4E1**
Joint Project Manager Contamination Avoidance
SFAE-CBD-NBC-D
Building E4465
5183 Blackhawk Rd
Edgewood Area-Aberdeen Proving Ground, MD 21010-5424

**Joint Chemical, Biological, Radiological Agent Water Monitor (JCBRAWM)**
Joint Project Manager Contamination Avoidance
SFAE-CBD-NBC-D
Building E4465
5183 Blackhawk Road
Aberdeen Proving Ground, MD 21010

**Joint Effects Model (JEM)**
Joint Project Manager Information System
4301 Pacific Highway
San Diego, CA 92110

**Joint Effects Targeting System (JETS) Target Location Designation System (TLDS)**
Project Manager Soldier Sensors and Lasers
SFAE-SDR-SSL
10170 Beach Rd.
Building 325
Ft. Belvoir, VA 22060

**Joint Land Attack Cruise Missile Defense Elevated Netted Sensor System (JLENS)**
PEO Missiles and Space
SFAE-MSLS-CMDS-JLN
P.O. Box 1500
Huntsville, AL 35807

**Joint Land Component Constructive Training Capability (JLCCTC)**
Project Manager Constructive Simulation
STRI-SFAE-PMCONSIM
12350 Research Parkway
Orlando, FL 32826

**Joint Light Tactical Vehicle (JLTV)**
PM Joint Light Tactical Vehicle (JLTV)
SFAE-CSS-JC-JL
43087 Lake Street, NE
Building 301/2rd Floor/Mail Stop 640
Harrison Twp, MI 48045-4941

**Joint Personnel Identification Version 2 (JPIv2)**
PM DoD Biometrics
SFAE-PS-BI
Building 1445
Ft. Belvoir, VA 22060-5526

**Joint Precision Airdrop System (JPADS)**
PM Force Sustainment Systems
SFAE-CSS-FP-F
Kansas St.
Natick, MA 01760-5057

**Joint Service General Purpose Mask (JSGPM) M-50/M-51**
Joint Project Manager Protection
JPM P
Suite 301
50 Tech Parkway
Stafford, VA 22556

**Joint Service Transportable Small Scale Decontaminating Apparatus (JSTSS DA) M26**
Joint Project Manager Protection
JPM P
Suite 301
50 Tech Parkway
Stafford, VA 22556

**Joint Tactical Ground Station (JTAGS)**
Lower Tier Project Office
SFAE-MSLS-LT
5250 Martin Road
Redstone Arsenal, AL 35898-8000

**Joint Tactical Radio System Airborne and Maritime/Fixed Station (JTRS AMF)**
Joint Program Executive Office (JPEO)
Joint Tactical Radio System (JTRS)
33000 Nixie Way
Building 50, Suite 339
San Diego, CA 92147-5110

**Joint Tactical Radio System Ground Mobile Radios (JTRS GMR)**
Joint Program Executive Office (JPEO)
Joint Tactical Radio System (JTRS)
33000 Nixie Way
Building 50, Suite 339
San Diego, CA 92147-5110

**Joint Tactical Radio System Handheld, Manpack, Small Form Fit (JTRS HMS)**
Joint Program Executive Office (JPEO)
Joint Tactical Radio System (JTRS)
33000 Nixie Way
Building 50, Suite 339
San Diego, CA 92147-5110

**Joint Tactical Radio System Multifunctional Information Distribution System (MIDS)**
Joint Program Executive Office (JPEO)
Joint Tactical Radio System (JTRS)
33000 Nixie Way
Building 50, Suite 339
San Diego, CA 92147-5110

**Joint Tactical Radio System, Network Enterprise Domain (JTRS NED)**
Joint Program Executive Office (JPEO)
Joint Tactical Radio System (JTRS)
33000 Nixie Way
Building 50, Suite 339
San Diego, CA 92147-5110

**Joint Warning and Reporting Network (JWARN)**
Joint Project Manager Information System
JPM IS
4301 Pacific Hwy.
San Diego, CA 92110

**Kiowa Warrior**
COL Robert Grigsby
SFAE-AV-ASH-KW
5681 Wood Rd.
Redstone Arsenal, AL 35898

**Light Utility Helicopter (LUH)/UH-72A Lakota**
LUH PM
PEO AVN-UH-LUH
Light Utility Helicopter (LUH)/UH-72A Lakota, LUH PM
Huntsville, AL 35898-5000

**Lightweight 155mm Howitzer System (LW155)**
JPMO Towed Artillery Systems
SFAE-AMO-TAS
Building 151
Picatinny Arsenal, NJ 07806

**Lightweight Counter Mortar Radar (LCMR)**
LTC Robert Thomas, PM RADAR
SFAE-IEW&S
ACC-APG HQ ACC-APG
6001 Combat Drive,
Aberdeen Proving Ground
Aberdeen, MD 21005-1846

**Lightweight Laser Designator/ Rangefinder (LLDR) AN/PED-1**
PM Soldier Sensors and Lasers
Soldier
10170 Beach Road
Building 325
Ft. Belvoir, VA 22060

**Line Haul Tractor**
PM Heavy Tactical Vehicles
SFAE-CSS-TV-H
Mail Stop 429
6501 E. 11 Mile Rd.
Warren, MI 48397-5000

**Load Handling System Compatible Water Tank Rack (Hippo)**
PM Petroleum and Water Systems
SFAE-CSS-FP-P
6501 E. 11 Mile Rd.
Mail Stop 111
Warren, MI 43897

**Longbow Apache (AH-64D) (LBA)**
PM Apache
SFAE-AV
Building 5681
Redstone Arsenal, AL 35898

**M106 Screening Obscuration Device (SOD)-Visual Restricted Terrain (Vr)**
Joint Project Manager Contamination Avoidance
SFAE-CBD-NBC-R
Building E4465
5183 Blackhawk Road
Edgewood Area-Aberdeen Proving Grounds, MD 21010-5425

**Medical Communications for Combat Casualty Care (MC4)**
PM Medical Communications for Combat Casualty Care (MC4)
524 Palacky St.
Ft. Detrick, MD 21702

**Medical Simulation Training Center (MSTC)**
Project Manager Combined Arms Tactical Trainers
SFAE-STRI-PMCATT
12350 Research Parkway
Orlando, FL 32826-3276

**Medium Caliber Ammunition (MCA)**
PM Maneuver Ammunition Systems
SFAE-AMO-MAS
Picatinny Arsenal, NJ 07806

**Medium Extended Air Defense System (MEADS)**
Project Manager, Lower Tier Project Office
SFAE-MSLS-LT-MEADS
PEO Missiles and Space
5250 Martin Road
Redstone Arsenal, AL 35898-8000

**Meteorological Measuring Set-Profiler (MMS-P)/Computer Meteorological Data-Profiler (CMD-P)**
Product Manager Joint Cooperative Target Identification-Ground (JCTI-G)
SFAE-IEWS-NS-JCTI-G
Building 4504
Springfield Street
Aberdeen Proving Ground, MD 21005

**Mine Protection Vehicle Family (MPVF)**
Product Manager Assured Mobility Systems
SFAE-CSS-MRA
6501 E. 11 Mile Rd.
Warren, MI 43897-5000

**Mine Resistant Ambush Protected Vehicles (MRAP)**
JPO MRAP
SFAE-CSS-MR
6501 E. 11 Mile Rd
Warren, MI 48397

**Mobile Maintenance Equipment Systems (MMES)**
PM-SKOT
SFAE-CSS-JC-SK
Building 302, 2nd Floor
29661 George Avenue
Harrison Twp, MI 48045-4941

**Modular Fuel System (MFS)**
PM Petroleum and Water Systems
SFAE-CSS-FP-P
6501 E. 11 Mile Rd.
Mail Stop 111
Warren, MI 48397

**Mortar Systems**
PM Combat Ammunition Systems
SFAE-AMO-CAS-MS
Picatinny Arsenal, NJ 07806

**Movement Tracking System (MTS)**
PM Force XXI Battle Command Brigade and Below (FBCB2), PD MTS
SFAE-PS-C3T-FBC-MTS
800 Lee Ave.
Building 5100
Ft. Lee, VA 23801

**MQ-1C Gray Eagle Unmanned Aircraft System (UAS)**
Project Manager Unmanned Aircraft Systems (UAS)
SFAE-AV-UAS
5300 Martin Road
Redstone Arsenal, AL 35898-5000

**Multiple Launch Rocket System (MLRS) M270A1**
Precision Fires Rocket and Missile Systems Project Office
SFAE-MSL-PF-FAL
Building 5250
Redstone Arsenal, AL 35898

**NAVSTAR Global Positioning System (GPS)**
Product Director Positioning, Navigation and Timing (PD PNT)
SFAE-IEW&S-NS-PNT
6006 Combat Drive
B2101
Aberdeen Proving Ground, MD 21005

**Nett Warrior (NW)**
Project Manager Soldier Warrior
SFAE-SDR-SWAR
10125 Kingman Rd
Building 317
Ft. Belvoir, VA 22060

**Night Vision Thermal Systems-Thermal Weapon Sight (TWS)**
PM Soldier Sensors and Lasers
PEO Soldier
10170 Beach Road
Building 325
Ft. Belvoir, VA 22060

**Non-Intrusive Inspection Systems (NIIS)**
Joint Project Manager Guardian
SFAE-CBD-GN
5109 Leesburg Pike
Falls Church, VA 22041

**Nuclear Biological Chemical Reconnaissance Vehicle (NBCRV)-Stryker Sensor Suites**
Joint Project Manager Contamination Avoidance
SFAE-CBD-NBC-R
Building E4465
5183 Blackhawk Road
Aberdeen Proving Ground, MD 21010-5425

**One Semi-Automated Force (OneSAF)**
Project Manager Constructive Simulation
SFAE-STRI-PMCONSIM
12350 Research Pkwy.
Orlando, FL 32826

**Paladin/Field Artillery Ammunition Supply Vehicle (FAASV)**
HBCT
SFAE-GCS-HBCT
6501 E. 11 Mile Rd.
Warren, MI 48397

**Palletized Load System (PLS) and PLS Extended Service Program (ESP)**
PM Heavy Tactical Vehicles
SFAE-CSS-TV-H
6501 E. 11 Mile Rd.
Mail Stop 429
Warren, MI, 48397-5000

**PATRIOT Advanced Capability-Three (PAC-3)**
Project Manager, Lower Tier Project Office
SFAE-MSLS-LT
Program Executive Office, Missiles and Space
Bldg. 5250, Martin Road
Redstone Arsenal, AL 35898-8000

**Precision Guidance Kit (PGK)**
PM Combat Ammunition Systems
SFAE-AMO-CAS
Picatinny Arsenal, NJ 07806

**Prophet**
PM PROPHET
SFAE-IEW EWP
Building 4504
Aberdeen Proving Ground, MD 21005

**Rough Terrain Container Handler (RTCH)**
Product Manager Combat Engineer/MHE
SFAE-CSS-FP-C
6501 E. 11 Mile Rd.
Mail Stop 401
Warren, MI 48397-5000

**RQ-11B Raven Small Unmanned Aircraft System (SUAS)**
Product Manager Small Unmanned Aircraft Systems (SUAS), Project Manager Unmanned Aircraft Systems (UAS)
SFAE-AV-UAS-SU
5300 Martin Road
Redstone Arsenal, AL 35898-5000

**RQ-7B Shadow Tactical Unmanned Aircraft System (TUAS)**
Project Manager Unmanned Aircraft Systems (UAS)
SFAE-AV-UAS
5300 Martin Road
Redstone Arsenal, AL 35898-5000

**Secure Mobile Anti-Jam Reliable Tactical Terminal (SMART-T)**
PM WIN-T
SFAE-WIN-SAT
6010 Frankford Street
Aberdeen Proving Ground, MD 21005

**Sentinel**
PEO Space and Missile Defense
SFAE-MSLS
Redstone Arsenal, AL 35898

**Single Channel Ground and Airborne Radio System (SINCGARS)**
PEO C3T Product Director TRCS
Aberdeen Proving Ground, MD 21005

**Small Arms-Crew Served Weapons**
PM Soldier Weapons
SFAE-SDR-SW
PEO Soldier
Picatinny Arsenal, NJ 07806

**Small Arms-Individual Weapons**
PM Soldier Weapons
SFAE-SDR-SW
PEO Soldier
Picatinny Arsenal, NJ 07806

**Small Caliber Ammunition**
PM Maneuver Ammunition Systems
SFAE-AMO-MAS
Picatinny Arsenal, NJ 07806

**Spider**
PM Close Combat Systems
SFAE-AMO-CCS
Picatinny Arsenal, NJ 07806

**Stryker Family of Vehicles**
Project Manager-Stryker Brigade Combat Team
SFAE-GCS-BCT MS 325
6501 E. 11 Mile Rd.
Warren, MI 48397

**Tactical Electric Power (TEP)**
Project Manager Mobile Electric Power
SFAE-C3T-MEP-OPM
5850 Delafield Road Bldg 324
Ft. Belvoir, VA 22060-5809

**Tactical Mission Command (TMC)/ Maneuver Control System (MCS)**
Project Manager Mission Command
SFAE-C3T-MC-TMC
Bldg 6007, Floor 5
Aberdeen Proving Ground
Aberdeen, MD 21001

**Tank Ammunition**
PM Maneuver Ammunition Systems
SFAE-AMO-MAS
Picatinny Arsenal, NJ 07806

**Test Equipment Modernization (TEMOD)**
Product Director, Test, Measurement, and Diagnostic Equipment
SFAE-CSS-JC-TM
Building 3651
Redstone Arsenal, AL 35898

**Transportation Coordinators' Automated Information for Movement System II (TC-AIMS II)**
Product Manager, Transportation Information Systems
SFAE-PS-TC
200 Stovall Street
Suite 9S23
Alexandria, VA 22332-2700

**Tube-Launched, Optically-Tracked, Wire-Guided (TOW) Missiles**
PM Close Combat Weapon Systems Project Office
SFAE-MSL-CWS-T
PM Close Combat Weapon Systems Project Office
Redstone Arsenal, AL 35898

**Unit Water Pod System (Camel II)**
PM Petroleum and Water Systems
SFAE-CSS-FP-P
6501 E. 11 Mile Road
Mail Stop 111
Warren, MI 43897

**Warfighter Information Network-Tactical (WIN-T) Increment 1**
PdM WIN-T Inc 1
SFAE-C3T-WIN-T Inc 1
6010 Frankford St.
Aberdeen Proving Ground, MD 21005-1848

**Warfighter Information Network-Tactical (WIN-T) Increment 2**
PdM WIN-T Inc 2/3
SFAE-C3T-WIN-T Inc 2/3
6010 Frankford St.
Aberdeen Proving Ground, MD 21005-1848

**Warfighter Information Network-Tactical (WIN-T) Increment 3**
PdM WIN-T Inc 2/3
SFAE-C3T-WIN-T Inc 2/3
6010 Frankford St.
Aberdeen Proving Ground, MD 21005-1848

**Weapons of Mass Destruction Elimination (WMD-E)**
Joint Project Manager Guardian
SFAE-CBD-GN
5109 Leesburg Pike
Falls Church, VA 22041

**XM806 .50 Caliber Machine Gun**
PM Soldier Weapons
SFAE-SDR-SW
PEO Soldier
Picatinny Arsenal, NJ 07806

Prepared by:
ASA(ALT)
Strategic Communications &
Business Transformation SAAL-ZG

Zachary Taylor Building
2530 Crystal Drive
Arlington, VA 22020